MICROCOMPUTERS
FOR
MANAGERS

BAY ARINZE

Department of Management
Drexel University

Wadsworth Publishing Company
A Division of Wadsworth, Inc.
Belmont, California

To my father, who generously gives wisdom without finding fault

Computer Science Editor: Kathy Shields
Development Editor: Alan Venable
Editorial Assistant: Tamara Huggins
Production Editor: Stacey Sawyer, Sawyer & Williams
Print Buyer: Randy Hurst
Permissions Editor: Peggy Meehan
Designer: John Edeen
Copy Editor: Rene Lynch
Technical Illustrator: Graphic World, Inc.
Cover: Stuart Paterson
Signing Representative: Amy Whitaker
Compositor: Graphic World, Inc.
Printer: R. R. Donnelley

International Thomson Publishing
The trademark ITP is used under license

1 2 3 4 5 6 7 8 9 10—98 97 96 95 94

Library of Congress Cataloging-in-Publication Data
Arinze, Bay.
   Microcomputers for managers / Bay Arinze.
      p.   cm.
   Includes bibliographical references and index.
   ISBN 0-534-19398-6
   1. Management Information systems—Study and teaching.
   2. Business—Data processing.   3. Microcomputer workstations.
   4. Local area networks (Computer networks)   5. Business enterprises—United States—Case studies.   I. Title.
   HD30.213.A75   1994
   004′.024658—dc20   93-30972
                                                                      CIP

ISBN 0-534-19398-6

THE WADSWORTH

MIS

SERIES

The Wadsworth Series in Management Information Systems

Applying Expert System Technology to Business, Patrick Lyons

Business Systems Analysis and Design, William S. Davis

Database Systems: Design, Implementation, and Management, Peter Rob and Carlos Coronel

Intelligent Systems for Business: Expert Systems with Neural Networks, Fatemeh Zahedi

Microcomputers for Managers, Bay Arinze

Multimedia Presentation Technology, Fred T. Hofstetter

Networks in Action: Business Choices and Telecommunications Decisions, Peter G. W. Keen and J. Michael Cummins

The New Software Engineering, Sue Conger

Forthcoming Titles

Development of Quality Multimedia, Donald Carpenter

Information Technology in a Global Business Environment: Readings and Cases, P. Candace Deans and Jaak Jurison

Information Technology in Action, Peter G. W. Keen

Human Resources for Information Managers, Pamela K. D'Huyvetter

Local Area Networks with Novell, H. Rene Baca, Christopher M. Zager, and Margaret A. Zinky

Management Handbook of Multimedia, Antone F. Alber

Managing Quality Information Systems, Fatemeh Zahedi

MIS Classics, Peter G. W. Keen and Lynda Keen

CONTENTS IN BRIEF

PREFACE

1. Background

The 1980s saw the introduction and explosive growth of microcomputer use in organizations. In the 1990s, microcomputers have become widely used in varied business and manufacturing settings, with more than 50 million systems currently installed in U.S. businesses. As microcomputers become the dominant computing platform, large numbers of them are being interconnected in both local and remote (or wide-area) networks and now serve an expanding number of functions. Current microcomputer-based networks present a complex array of options for information systems deployment and use. Consequently, there is a growing need for systems managers who are familiar with new microcomputer and data communications technologies that are central components of networked systems. Also, functional-area managers (for example, in Accounting and Marketing) frequently require more than the basic "computer literacy" skills that were sufficient in the less complex business and computing environments of the 1980s.

2. Target Courses

Microcomputers for Managers represents the first of a new generation of texts designed to support the learning requirements of microcomputer technology and applications *beyond* the traditional courses covering the introduction to MIS and data processing. It builds on these and other computer literacy courses by supplying the knowledge of microcomputers that managers require, as well as covering related technologies and the effective deployment and management of microcomputers. This text may be used by both undergraduate and graduate MIS majors in such courses as Managing Microcomputers and Microcomputers for Managers, which are rapidly becoming a part of modern MIS curricula. It is also suitable as an elective for non-MIS majors. This latter set of students may have had the computer literacy course but require more detailed knowledge of today's computing technology, system architectures, and software choices, particularly for the purpose of end-user system development.

3. Textbook Objectives

Microcomputers for Managers combines discussion and comparative analyses of the major computing technology choices faced by today's managers, with real-world examples of the deployment and use of these technologies in organizations. The varied computing platforms, system architectures (for example, client/server), and software alternatives have brought about the need for this course, which will aid the manager in making better choices among complex technological options. The objectives of the textbook are as follows:

- *To address the important computing issues currently faced by managers*: In particular, the transition from large, centralized mainframe installations to networks of microcomputers, currently affecting an estimated 80% of MIS departments, is clearly described. The different transition paths and their implications for firms are a major focus of the text.
- *To illustrate productive uses of contemporary microcomputer technologies and applications*: Many real-world, primarily microcomputer-based solutions to a broad spectrum of business problems and reports of their effectiveness are presented to communicate their risks and opportunities to managers of microcomputer resources.
- *To enable the manager to make more effective information technology choices*: Present and future computing technologies are examined, together with comparative analyses, to enable managers to make better-informed choices of hardware platforms, operating systems, applications software, and data communications devices.
- *To show how current system development approaches integrate, and are affected by, new computing technologies*: New approaches to system development have accompanied technology advances. One in particular, Joint Application Development, has been enabled by the technology itself. These methods are compared and discussed.
- *To describe how current technology trends are likely to affect future technologies and required skills*: The transition to networks of mainly microcomputers to support mission-critical applications implies new skills for both developers and users in response to new computing platforms and tools. These requirements and underlying technology trends are examined in detail.

4. Learning Objectives

After using this book in a one-semester course, the student will be better able to:

- Understand the central features of current and future computing technologies and the tradeoffs between them.
- Identify and select information system components to satisfy mission-critical system requirements for the cooperative processing systems of the 1990s and beyond.
- Analyze user information requirements and design information systems using methodologies that incorporate advanced computer technologies.

5. Textbook Structure and Organization

Microcomputers for Managers is divided into six parts:

Part I: Introduction to Microcomputers

Part I introduces the student to contemporary hardware platforms, information systems, and applications. Chapter 1 describes different computer types, the microprocessor, and the growing importance of the microcomputer to organizations. It traces the transition from centralized mainframes to today's enterprise and client/ server computing models that make extensive use of microcomputers. Chapter 2 includes three cases that demonstrate uses of microcomputers in small, single sites.

Part II: Microcomputer Hardware Module

Part II focuses on current and major hardware platforms and computing devices. This is not a mere "technology listing"; instead, it is a series of comparative analyses of strengths, weaknesses, and applications in actual use. Chapter 3 examines in detail "PC-compatible" and other major microcomputer platforms. Their complementary roles to mainframes and workstations are also discussed. Chapter 4 discusses data input and output devices and the importance of existing standards. Finally, Chapter 5 compares available data storage devices, including optical disks and other hardware options, emphasizing their importance and use for new applications and data types.

Part III: Microcomputer Software Module

Part III covers the major categories of software. In Chapter 6, the discussion encompasses important operating system platforms and the impact of graphical user interfaces and multimedia on computer usage. Utilities, compilers, and such "productivity tools" as spreadsheets are also covered. Chapter 7 continues by examining the current and imminent database management software for supporting transaction processing on networked systems and the rapidly growing area of document imaging. Chapter 8 describes software applications used at all organizational levels for both managerial and end-user support.

Part IV: Microcomputer-Based Information Systems

The importance of connectivity and data communications technologies is the focus of Part IV. Chapter 9 centers on connectivity within the organization using local area networks (LANs) and other data communications architectures. A comparative analysis of LAN choices is presented as a tool to improve the student's effectiveness in LAN design and deployment. Chapter 10 examines connectivity across remote locations such as cities and countries, and among heterogeneous computing resources. LAN management issues and vendors are also described, together with now-popular cooperative processing architectures (for instance, client/server computing). These latter issues are presented in the context of making appropriate choices in information systems downsizing. Chapter 11 reinforces the preceding two chapters with four cases that illustrate the use of large multi-site cooperative processing information systems and describe insights gained in their design and use.

Part V: Building Microcomputer-Based Information Systems

The systems development life cycle (SDLC) is the subject of this knowledge module, with insights offered on the development emphases associated with microcomputer-based systems. Chapter 12 describes structured systems analysis and design methods, and the roles of CASE tools, Joint Application Development (JAD), and Rapid Application Development (RAD) in contemporary systems development. Connectivity issues as they relate to systems development are also examined. Chapter 13 scrutinizes the "back-end" development and implementation activities of the SDLC and outlines approaches to purchasing and leasing computer equipment. Issues relating to system security and integrity in cooperative processing systems are also discussed, as are common system implementation strategies.

Part VI: Human Aspects

Part VI discusses the necessary personnel skills for cooperative processing systems and previews advances in computing technology. Chapter 14 sketches the interpersonal skills and new specialist skills required of systems personnel and examines legal and ethical issues affecting information system design and use. The subject of improving ergonomics concludes the chapter, with an appraisal of importance and costs. Chapter 15 anticipates imminent computing technologies and their potential uses based on current technological and organizational trends. Their growth in power and sophistication, together with advances in data communications, are placed in context as key aspects of future information systems.

6. Textbook Features

Microcomputers for Managers incorporates features that make it an effective learning tool. Each chapter contains the following components:

Introduction

An introduction section identifies the central ideas of the chapter and offers important background material.

Learning Objectives

A set of key concepts and methods describing the chapter's major contribution follows the chapter introduction and represents a learning framework for the student.

Minicases

Chapters 1–10 begin with a minicase that highlights an aspect of microcomputer implementation and use in an organization.

Body of the Chapter

Each chapter is logically organized into sections and subsections, with presented concepts reinforced by many real-world examples. Comparative analyses of computing technology and methodologies play a key role in communicating effective approaches to selecting and deploying contemporary information systems.

Art and Photographs

The textbook includes many well-prepared line art drawings and photographs illustrating key concepts, methods, and technologies.

Chapter Summary

The chapter summary reviews the major ideas presented in the chapter.

Review Questions

Review questions are designed to test the students' grasp of key concepts presented in the chapter.

Exercises

These are more detailed questions that test the students' abilities to formulate system solutions based on the technologies and methodologies presented.

Suggested Readings and References

This section lists sources of additional information to enable the interested student to explore further material on the topics in each chapter.

Acknowledgments

Writing a book of this kind can be a challenging and often lonely task. I am profoundly grateful for the help and encouragement that I have received from old and new friends alike on this project.

First many thanks to the following reviewers, who offered many helpful comments and suggestions:

David Bird
University of Missouri-St. Louis

J. Stephanie Collins
Northeastern University

Barry Floyd
California Polytechnic State University

George C. Fowler
Texas A&M University, College of Business

C. Brian Honess
University of South Carolina

Leonard M. Jessup
California State University, San Marcos

Kenneth Marr
Hofstra University

R. Waldo Roth
Taylor University

Joseph Sass
University of Toledo

I would also like to especially thank my editor, Kathy Shields, who made working on this book a pleasurable experience; Stacey Sawyer of Sawyer and Williams, for making difficult tasks seem easy again and again; and to everyone at Wadsworth involved in this project.

Thanks also to Murugan Anandarajan, whose tireless efforts made my deadlines achievable; and Donna Weaver, whose class testing resulted in valuable student feedback. I also appreciate the valuable help I received from Max Maw; from Oscar Gutierrez of The University of Massachusetts at Boston (my fellow LSE alumni); and from Rebecca Abney and Steve Parnell.

Throughout this project, my colleagues at Drexel hung in there for me and offered excellent insights and direction. They are Milton Silver, Chair of the Management Department, and Magid Igbaria, Snehamay Banerjee, Thomas Wieckowski, and Seung-Lae Kim. I hope to do the same for you real soon. My *Microcomputers for Managers* classes were also quite helpful and responsive to early drafts of the text.

I would also like to thank Frank Ruggirello and Peter Keen for challenging me to begin and complete this project. You were both right. It could be done.

Finally, I appreciate the vast amounts of encouragement given to me by my brothers and sister: Onuora Amobi, Emmanuel Arinze, and Cathy Gorzalski; and of my wonderful mother, Rose Ugbode. I'm really returning, however briefly, to "non-project" life.

CONTENTS

APPENDIX A: COMPUTER GENERATIONS AND PROGRESSION   **467**

Early Computers
Transistors and the Second Generation
The Integrated Circuit and the Third Generation
Microprocessors and the Fourth Generation
Entering the Fifth Generation

APPENDIX B: LARGE AND MEDIUM-SIZED COMPUTERS   **470**

Mainframes, Minicomputers, and Supercomputers

GLOSSARY   **474**

INDEX   **485**

THE MICROCOMPUTER REVOLUTION

INTRODUCTION

Fabricated on a slice of silicon no bigger than your thumbnail, the **microprocessor** is the heart of the microcomputer, the machine that has radically transformed the society in which we live. The microcomputer began a new phase of the computer revolution, in which both individuals and organizations obtained new and powerful forms of computing resources. Microcomputer-centered information systems, consisting of both stand-alone and networked microcomputers, now support most organizational information processing requirements. They offer firms end-user computing opportunities, lower-cost processing, and increased flexibility in building information systems. Harnessing this new power and potential has proven to be a complex and challenging task. For managers responsible for any part of the firm's information system strategy, understanding microcomputer hardware, software, and methodological alternatives has become a top priority. We begin by discussing the features of the microcomputer and the opportunities it presents to organizations.

Learning Objectives

After reading this chapter, you will be able to:

- Describe the main features and components of the microcomputer
- Describe the opportunities microcomputers offer to different types of firms
- Identify the components of a firm's computer-based information system
- Propose one or more of the four major classes of computers for a firm's processing needs
- Identify central issues involved in the transition from mainframes to microcomputer-based information systems
- Understand how future microcomputer technologies will affect both the developers and users of information systems

---

CASE 1.1

UNION ELECTRIC CO.: DOWNSIZING ON SUN WORKSTATIONS AND IBM MICROCOMPUTERS

Union Electric (UE) operates the Callaway County, St. Louis, nuclear plant. Its engineers constantly analyze the nuclear plant's fuel assembly with computationally hungry simulations. These were originally performed on an IBM 3090 mainframe using FORTRAN programs. The simulations were expensive to run on the mainframe, at about $39,000 per MIP (million instructions per second). Moreover, demand for mainframe computing capacity was increasing by about 33% yearly.

UE invested $170,000 to purchase 16 microcomputers and two powerful workstations in order to divert some of the mainframe processing to these less-expensive processing platforms. The microcomputers and workstations were connected in a local area network (LAN), and the software was converted from the mainframes to run on the workstations. UE engineers now run their simulations on the workstations and simulate plant conditions there instead of on the mainframe.

One benefit of using microcomputers and workstations was to reduce the time required for the engineers' simulations to minutes instead of the 16 hours required by the mainframe. By taking advantage of less-expensive workstation processing, UE saved $105,000 in mainframe upgrade costs and another $100,000 per year in lower plant maintenance and operating costs.

Adapted from Mark Schlack, ``Unix on the LAN Eases Mainframe Load'' *Datamation*, February 15, 1992, pp. 58–60.

1.1 TECHNOLOGICAL REVOLUTION IN THE 80s—THE MICROCOMPUTER

The 1980s saw the beginning of a revolution in computing that promises to accelerate right through the year 2000 and beyond. This revolution, led by the development of the microprocessor chip, has affected industry and society at large: Both the service and manufacturing sectors of industry have been transformed by the microcomputer and other microprocessor-based devices; in fact, the use of microcomputers has affected practically all areas of society, ranging from recreational activities to new work patterns and business practices.

The **microprocessor** (see Figure 1.1) is a miniaturized central processing unit that is the focal point of the microcomputer. It contains many thousands, or even millions, of individual circuits and transistors packed into an area as small as a quarter of an inch across. Microcomputers consist of a microprocessor(s) and interconnected devices within a system unit. Increases in microcomputer capabilities, along with continually declining prices, have enabled them to spearhead a radical change in the structure and function of information systems in organizations.

The microcomputer was initially used as a tool for increasing personal productivity through the use of software for word processing, database management, and spreadsheet calculations among others. These software packages initially enabled the nontechnical user to create and use small applications. As microcomputer capabilities increased, they began to take on regular transaction processing functions. Later, they were connected in networks to enable the sharing of information and devices such as printers and disks, enabling users to make better use of expensive hardware resources and to work more effectively in collaborative work groups.

The widespread use of microcomputers has been a major factor leading to today's information society—a society in which the majority of workers are involved in the collection, processing, and dissemination of information. Figure 1.2 illustrates the growth of information workers since 1900 to become the largest category of workers in today's economy. Information has subsequently gained greater recognition as an important organizational resource, with the firms that succeed being those who make the most effective use of their information resources.

Features of the Microcomputer

The microcomputer stands out among all computer categories. Its features and capabilities have brought about extensive changes in the work practices of practically every industry. Understanding these features is a prerequisite to grasping the implications for today's firms. Following are four of its major features:

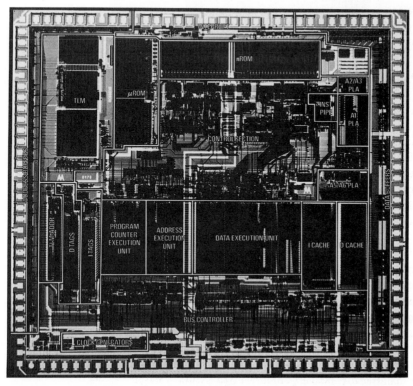

FIGURE 1.1   Motorola's 32-bit 68030 microprocessor, used in several Apple Macintosh microcomputers

FIGURE 1.1 *(continued)* Intel's 32-bit 80386 microprocessor, used in
entry-level IBM-compatible microcomputers

1. ***Smaller size.*** Before the microcomputer, computing was performed on minicomputers, mainframes, and supercomputers. The latter two types, in particular,
   required large rooms, air conditioning, raised floors, and special wiring. Miniaturization of electronic circuits led directly to the smaller sizes of today's microcomputers. Solid-state integrated circuitry enabled the computer's main functions to be
   incorporated on circuit boards measuring several inches across. Moreover,
   microcomputers have few of the special environmental requirements of the larger
   machines.
2. ***Improved price and performance.*** The microcomputer is a great improvement in
   price and performance over mainframes and minicomputers. Miniaturization enabled
   the fabrication of cheap microchips containing millions of circuits. This signaled the
   end to the *economy-of-scale* argument, which held that larger mainframes reduced
   the cost of processing per instruction. Current large-scale integration of circuits is
   seen in such microprocessors as Intel's Pentium chip, with over 3 million circuits.
   Microcomputers with such microprocessors provide much greater computing power
   per dollar than larger mainframe computers (Figure 1.3).
3. ***Improved user interfaces.*** Users of larger systems historically had to work with
   rudimentary user interfaces, which exhibited little user-friendliness. In fact, the term

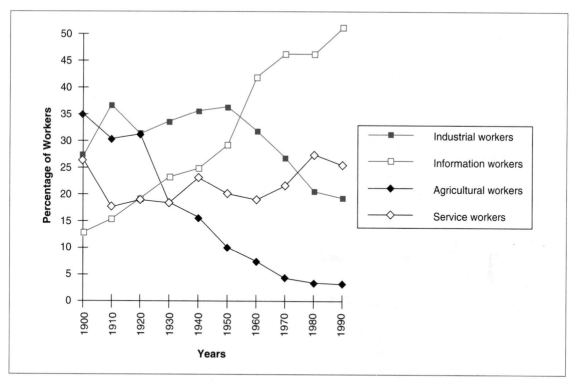

FIGURE 1.2   Proportion of workers in various industries

user-friendly has its origins in the microcomputer age, in which users expect intuitive and easy-to-use interfaces. Single-user microcomputer systems have evolved with more sophisticated and powerful *graphical user interfaces*, or *GUIs* (see Figure 1.4). A GUI is a system/user interface that uses *icons* (pictorial images) to represent files, folders, and other objects. It also uses *pointing* (and selection) *methods* and devices to control operations and *graphical imagery* to represent events and relationships— for example, dragging a file to the "trash" to delete it.

4. ***Microcomputer industry standards.*** Large systems such as mainframes are largely **proprietary**. This means that they are usually based on internal company designs and standards and not on common or widely embraced architectures. Hence, applications created for specific mainframe and minicomputer environments are usually incompatible in others. Areas of incompatibility include *hardware architecture, peripheral usage,* and *software programs.* Conversely, in the microcomputer industry, open standards have emerged, most notably, the IBM-compatible. This refers to the largest segment of the microcomputer market, containing microcomputers manufactured not only by IBM but also by other system vendors. These machines are based on the Intel 80x86 (or compatible) microprocessor line.

These four factors characterize the development and expansion of the microcomputer industry. The introduction of the computer signaled a permanent change in the way firms

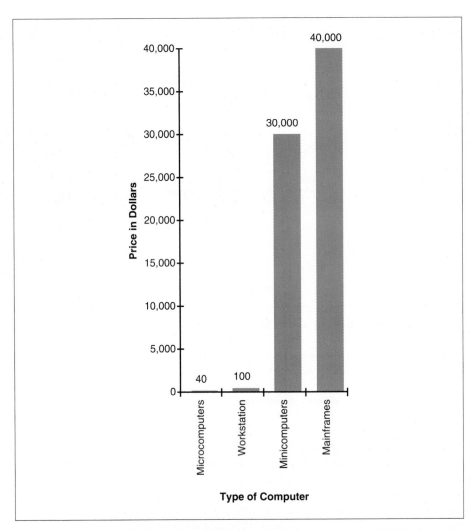

FIGURE 1.3   Price per MIP (millions of instructions per second) for various
computers. MIP ratings are a common benchmark for all
classes of computers.

operated, but the microcomputer-based part of the computer revolution is having its own
significant effects on business practices. Several of these are now discussed.

Impact and Effects of the Microcomputer on Business

The microcomputer revolution has widely affected both business and manufacturing
strategies and practices. It is significant to present-day managers for several reasons. The
first is the microcomputer's **affordability**. Low prices and high performance mean that

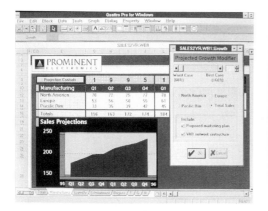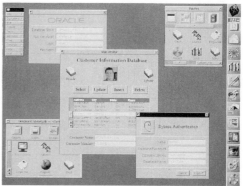

FIGURE 1.4   (*Left*) Micro-based GUI: Borland's Quattro Pro/Windows; (*right*) NEXTStep operating environment

for the first time, the computer is affordable to a larger number of individuals and organizational departments. In one generation, the computer moved from being a "big-ticket" item classification and major capital investment to being a machine that could be purchased from discretionary departmental funds and by the individual. One particular travel company, for example, recently spent $1 million to purchase and integrate into a network 120 high-end IBM microcomputers and three servers to meet the needs of its travel agents servicing customer inquiries and reservations. This sum would barely be sufficient to purchase a large-scale minicomputer or mainframe.

Another impact of the microcomputer is **wider accessibility** to all work groups. Direct users of mainframes and minicomputers consisted almost entirely of information systems professionals. This was due in part to the low level of the computer/user interfaces to which interaction was restricted. These interfaces typically comprised complex, technical languages. As newer productivity packages and sophisticated graphical interfaces made computer/user interaction much easier, the number of potential computer users dramatically increased. In addition, the reduced size and less rigorous environmental requirements facilitated the concept of one computer per desktop, rather than one per room!

The microcomputer revolution brought in its wake the development of a new generation of **user-oriented software**. Powerful operating system environments, improved software for system development, and programs that increased office productivity have marked this revolution and served to expand the microcomputer's accessibility to the user. These new software tools have also fueled the growth of **end-user computing (EUC)**. EUC involves user-led development and direct use of computer information systems, in contrast to systems development by information systems (IS) professionals. The new tools enabled the rapid creation of software by end users in functional areas such as sales, accounting, and production. Using spreadsheets, fourth-generation languages (4GLs), database management systems (DBMSs), and other specialized packages, end users now routinely satisfy their own information requirements. See Figure 1.5.

FIGURE 1.5 Microcomputer users in education, science, and construction

Microcomputers have also helped to extend **distributed processing** within organizations. The expanding use of microcomputers was followed by the desire to interconnect them across *networks*. These networks were important from the organizational viewpoint to distribute different processing functions within the organization and allow information sharing. In addition, expensive devices such as laser printers could be shared and mainframe data accessed through networks, all benefits obtained in the travel company discussed above.

The trend toward more powerful and sophisticated yet cheaper microcomputer systems led to the widespread acquisition and deployment of microcomputers in organizations. In the United States alone, there is an installed base of over 60 million microcomputers in the workplace—roughly one for every two workers. Furthermore, as computer literacy increases, there is a trend toward greater user involvement in both information systems planning and systems development.

At the organizational level, microcomputers have increased the flexibility and complexity of firms' operations. Networking advances have combined with new and powerful hardware and software to make the *networked organization* the computing model of the 1990s, with microcomputers as a major enabling technology for these networks. What are the implications for the manager? A major one is greater participation by managers in information systems development and use in organizations.

Also, opportunities have opened up for the manager to apply current and impending information technologies to a larger variety of organizational tasks.

1.2 COMPUTER HARDWARE
AND SOFTWARE

Computer **software**, or sets of program instructions, are executed on computer hardware to fulfill user information processing requirements. There are parallels between people performing procedures and hardware executing software instructions. In fact, much of the early impetus for deploying computers, such as in the U.S. Census of 1950, involved the use of computers to perform repetitive tasks previously performed by humans. In the census human counters were replaced by counting devices called *tabulators*, used to read numbers encoded on *punchcards*, which were in turn replaced by computers. Computer **hardware** refers to the computer itself. **Peripherals**, on the other hand, refer to all devices connected to and controlled by the computer (for example, keyboards, monitors, and modems).

Of Mainframes and Micros:
Computer Classifications

Computers can be grouped into four major classes: *microcomputers, workstations, minicomputers*, and *large-scale computers* (see Table 1.1).

1. ***Microcomputers.*** Microcomputers, also called *personal computers* (or *PCs*), fit on or just under the desktop. They are mostly, but not exclusively, inexpensive single-user machines, priced between $800 and $5,000, including the computer system, a monitor and keyboard, documentation, and software. Also included are attached devices such as a mouse. Unlike larger machines, microcomputers do not require stringent environmental controls (for example, dust, temperature, and humidity regulation) and can be used directly in the workplace. Microcomputer hardware is examined in Chapter 3.

2. ***Workstations.*** Workstations are also desktop machines with minimal environmental requirements. They are single-user, high-performance computers with powerful graphics and computational capabilities and are priced in the $4,000 to $10,000 range. Workstations are characterized by *RISC* (or *reduced instruction set chip*) architectures (see Chapter 3). Compared to *CISC* (*complex instruction set chip*) architectures used in most microcomputers, RISC yields improvements in overall execution time mainly by using a smaller set of microprocessor instructions. Workstations are special-purpose machines used for scientific, engineering, and graphical applications and as network servers.

3. ***Minicomputers.*** Minicomputers such as IBM's AS400 are larger than micro-computers and workstations and support multiple applications and users concurrently. They require some support personnel but rarely the strict environmental regulation needed by larger machines. The two groups of minicomputers are small-scale and medium-scale minicomputers. The former cost between $10,000

TABLE 1.1 Different types of computers and their features

	Microcomputer	Workstation	Minicomputer	Mainframe	Supercomputer
Cost	$800–$5,000	$4000–$10,000	$10,000–$1 million	More than $1 million	$2 million–$20 million
Size	Desktop or portable	Desktop	Room-sized	Large, special-purpose room	Large, special-purpose room
Environmental regulation	Minimal	Minimal	Some regulation	Dust, temperature, and humidity	Dust, temperature, and humidity
Main usage mode	Single user	Single user	Multiuser	Multiuser	Multiuser
Number of users	1 to 16	1 to 16	1 to 128	Hundreds of users	Several users
Features	CISC architecture, command line interface, graphical user interface	RISC architecture, GUI	Powerful I/O capabilities	Powerful I/O capabilities	Array processing
Users	Personal and network applications	CAD/CAM; graphics, network server	On-line transaction processing	On-line transaction processing	Computationally intensive tasks (weather forecasting, aircraft design)

[handwritten margin note: more less than mainframe used for crunching]

and $100,000 and support up to 16 users, while the latter (which include superminis) can top $1 million but support 17 to 128 users. The capabilities of the current generation of top-end microcomputers currently overlap those of minicomputers, with cheaper *supermicros* often exceeding minicomputer performance.

4. ***Large-scale computers.*** These include both mainframes and supercomputers. *Mainframes* are large computers costing from $1 million upward, which are housed in facilities requiring environmental regulation (for example, temperature, humidity, and dust) and operations personnel. Mainframes such as IBM's 9121 allow hundreds of users to run multiple tasks concurrently, by accessing the system through "dumb" terminals (a keyboard/screen combination that lacks a processor) or microcomputers. Their powerful processing capabilities are complemented by massive data storage and retrieval capabilities. *Supercomputers* cost between $2 million and $20 million and offer the most powerful computer processing capabilities currently available. Their use of *array processing* (processing strings of data rather than single data elements) boosts their performance significantly. Their vast computing power makes them suitable for computationally intensive work, such as weather forecasting, movie special effects, nuclear research,

and aircraft design. The simulation of phenomena on supercomputers usually saves the time and expense of building expensive small-scale models. The CRAY-XMP is an example of a supercomputer used worldwide for many of the preceding applications.

Computer Peripherals

Computer peripherals include *input devices,* such as keyboards and scanners, for entering data into the computer for processing and *output devices*, such as video display units and printers. Also included are *input/output* or *I/O* devices, for example, modems and fax machines. *Storage devices*, used to store and retrieve data, are a fourth category of peripheral that includes magnetic tapes and disks. Peripherals may be connected to the microprocessor using expansion cards that fit into special expansion slots in the microcomputer. In other cases, communications ports (for example, printer ports) connected to the system bus—a data-carrying pathway within the computer—provide the interface between peripheral devices and the computer. Peripherals are examined in Chapters 4 and 5.

Computer Software

Computer software includes the programs that run on computer hardware to fulfill the user's processing requirements. Software varies in sophistication, cost, and functionality and may be developed internally or externally to the firm. When developed internally, it is written by either end users or professional programmers. End-user versus MIS software development issues are discussed in detail in Chapters 6 and 13. The cost of developing and/or acquiring software varies markedly between mainframe and microcomputer environments.

A major type of software is *operating systems*, which include MS-DOS (Microsoft disk operating system), used on IBM-compatible microcomputers. An operating system (OS) controls the low-level hardware operations of the computer and insulates the end user from direct contact with hardware. OSs are featured in Chapter 6. *Utility programs* accompany operating systems and perform such housekeeping tasks as formatting disks, listing and copying files, and data compression.

Programming languages, another software category, are rarely used as an end in themselves but as a means of developing other software to fulfill specific requirements. They range from low-level assembly languages to high-level third- and fourth-generation languages, such as COBOL and FOCUS, respectively. The level of a language relates to its closeness to human syntax, with higher-level languages being closer to English. *Productivity packages* refer to programs like the Lotus 1-2-3 spreadsheet package, developed for the mass market. They are developed and sold as a solution for the generic needs of a large market. Their capabilities and configurability provide a rapid microcomputer software development alternative.

Custom-designed software includes programs developed to fulfill specific user requirements, using a programming language, a productivity package, or a specialized software product. Additionally, custom-designed software can be developed by either end users or system development professionals. *Specialized software* is software written for specific problem types. An example is IFPS (interactive financial planning system),

TABLE 1.2   A comparison of software for PCs and mainframes

Features	IBM-Compatible Microcomputers	IBM Mainframes
Installed base	100 Million	25,000
Software packages available	25,000	1,000
Software prices*		
Operating systems	$50–$1,600	$30,000–$200,000
Major applications (e.g., DBMSs)	$99–$1,000	$50,000–$300,000
Other applications (e.g., communications software, language compilers)	$5–$500	$50–$150,000

Sources: 1992 Datapro Workgroup Computing Series Reports on System Software; International Data Corporation.
*Most microcomputer software is purchased outright, whereas mainframe software is leased on a yearly basis.

used for financial modeling. Another is SPSS-PC (statistical package for the social sciences), a statistical analysis package on the PC.

Microcomputer use is characterized by *lower costs of software development* coupled with a *larger base of potential users* than, say, mainframes (see Table 1.2). A much wider range of software is available for microcomputers, with many more software development firms than there are in mainframe markets. Over 25,000 software titles currently exist for IBM-compatible microcomputers, with packaged solutions available for most business functions (see Figure 1.6).

1.3   STRUCTURE AND USE OF INFORMATION SYSTEMS IN ORGANIZATIONS

Every organization possesses and uses information systems to process transactions, communicate internally and externally, and support its users' information needs. Information systems may vary in both sophistication and degree of automation. However, we are concerned primarily with computerized information systems, which employ computer hardware and software as integral parts. This is the sense in which we use the term *information system*.

Information systems (ISs) consist of more than hardware and software; they also include people, procedures, and data. Figure 1.7 graphically illustrates the five parts of an information system: It shows **data** being manipulated by **software** running on **hardware** on one hand and by **procedures** carried out by **people** on the other. The arrows illustrate the potential for automating procedures in software and the subsequent support or replacement of personnel in many roles. While it is tempting to view all

FIGURE 1.6   Varied software packages and computer accessories on display at an Egghead
software store

procedures as candidates for automation, this is not always feasible. The reasons include
the *qualitative*, *intuitive*, and *subjective* aspects of many organizational tasks. Also, the
human touch is required for many service functions. Nevertheless, computers will play
a greater role in organizational activity, particularly in areas where artificial
intelligence–based systems (see Chapter 7) can be successfully applied.

Information System Users and Developers

Information systems (ISs) exist solely to serve their users, which makes it vital for their
design and technical sophistication to meet user needs very closely. IS users and
developers are active participants in system development and use. The two roles, while
distinct, may be fulfilled by the same person. There are different user categories, each
with differing roles, functions, and, frequently, expectations from the information
system, as shown in Table 1.3.

These categories include the **end user**, who makes direct operational use of the
system for daily tasks. This category includes clerks, accountants, lawyers, and so on.
The **user manager** has authority over the system's direct end users and responsibility

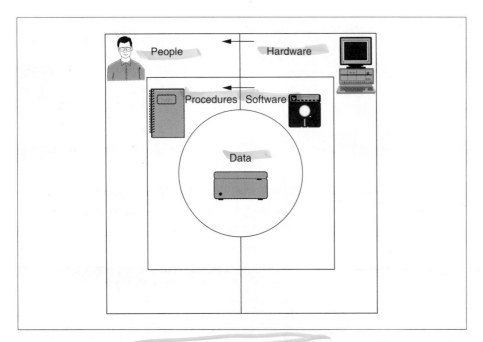

FIGURE 1.7   Five components of an information system

for the system's performance in their departments. **Senior managers** are responsible for the development of organizational and information systems plans, policies, and priorities within the overall firm and therefore set the direction for information systems development within the organization.

Just as there are various categories of end users, there are also different IS personnel involved in designing, developing, and maintaining the system. Again, many of these roles overlap in practice, with multiple roles potentially served by a single person. The categories include the **systems analyst**, who analyzes information requirements and creates a design specification for the information system. **Programmers** design, code, and test the software programs of the information system, with the quality of their work depending on the quality of the analyst's specification.

Operations personnel ensure that computer hardware and software are operated correctly. Another function is the **database administrator (DBA)**, who translates user data requirements into working databases and maintains created databases. Finally, the **network administrator**, a communications specialist, designs, develops, and maintains the firm's data communications resources. These roles are more fully discussed in Chapters 10, 13, and 14.

Procedures for People

Another part of an information system comprises the procedures performed by people. We have already seen that many operations and maintenance procedures are now performed by software. Our discussion here encompasses procedures involved in using the computer system to perform sales, marketing, design, and other business tasks.

TABLE 1.3   Participants in IS development and use

	Type	Responsibilities
Information system users	End user	Makes direct use of the firm's IS to carry out the firm's operational activity, for instance, retailing, manufacturing
	User manager	Supervises end users in the performance of their duties
	Senior manager	Originates directions and priorities for IS deployment in the firm
IS development and maintenance personnel	Systems analyst	Determines IS requirements for specific projects
	Programmer	Produces programs to support the IS requirements
	Database administrator	Analyzes users' data requirements and develops a database to support them
	Network administrator	Analyzes users' data communications requirements and designs networks to support them

Different types of procedures are *normal* operating procedures, *error-handling* procedures, and *recovery* procedures. We can also distinguish between procedures performed by users and by systems personnel.

Normal procedures occur in operational use of the information system and include entering data, loading programs, and printing invoices and reports. **Error-handling procedures** are performed in the event of an information system failure (that is, failure caused by hardware, software, or other system components). For the user, this may mean resorting to a manual system or to an alternative computer-based backup system. Finally, **recovery procedures** restore the system to normal operation after a failure. They range from restarting the computer to rekeying transactions from the period of system failure. These procedures are discussed in Chapters 13 and 14.

Data and Information

Data and information make up the fifth component of an information system. **Data** consists of a raw collection of facts, such as transaction, customer, and product details, which enter the information system for processing. For example, at an auto spare parts retailer a new customer provides relevant data, such as the name, address, telephone number, ordered items, and method of payment to the sales clerk when ordering. All this data is stored in the organizational database. If, some time later, a manager wanted to find out the number of automobile spare parts that had been sold over the previous week, broken down by auto type, this manager could request information from the information system.

Information is processed data that is useful or meaningful to a specific individual(s). Transforming data into information involves operations such as sorting, calculating, summarizing, and refining the data. Significantly, information is widely viewed as a resource in the same way as people, capital, and equipment. Two important issues are

how the data is stored and the **human procedures** that ensure that high-quality information is provided by the IS.

Improvements in storage methods and devices also affect the usability of the stored data. Storage devices commonly include tape- and disk-based media. A study of price and performance data for disk storage shows performance improvements by a factor of about 10:1 over the past ten years, with greater amounts of data being stored on smaller devices, which are accessible at faster speeds. A new generation of storage devices—optical disks—feature larger-capacity storage to support new forms of input such as scanning and new data types (for example, digitized images and sound). Furthermore, utilities like *data compression software* provide new efficiencies and opportunities for data/information storage and use. These are discussed in Chapter 7.

Increasingly, competitive advantage among firms is being decided by the accuracy and timeliness of data obtained from internal and external sources, how this data is processed to yield information, and effective presentation of the processed information to its recipients. For example, valuable information for a product manager would include reports on both the firm's and competitors' product performance. Also included would be the implications and analyses of this information in the form of trends, opportunities, and threats. Information systems centered on competitive advantage are discussed in Chapter 8, in the form of decision support and executive information systems.

1.4   Transition to Microcomputer-Based Information Systems

The first generation of mainframe computers in the commercial environment was used for applications with the most obvious benefits from automation (see Appendix A for a chronology of computer developments). These included *payroll*, *accounting*, *inventory control*, and *order processing* applications. Here, the mode of computing was usually batch processing on *single centralized mainframes*, not direct or on-line processing through connected terminals. Since early operating systems could not handle multiple programs running together, each new batch of jobs (programs) would periodically be set up, input, and then run sequentially. With the advent of minicomputers, a common strategy was to use a number of independent mainframes and minicomputers in different departments (for example, manufacturing, accounting, and marketing). Each computer processed applications and maintained files exclusively for the department or area in which it was located, as shown in Figure 1.8. This is known as *decentralized processing*.

Decentralized and Centralized Processing

As **decentralized computing** became widely used during the 1960s, several problems were evident to the users and developers of such systems. These included:

- **Data redundancy.** The example in Figure 1.10 (p. 20) illustrates minicomputers in three departments—production, marketing and accounting. Both marketing and accounting departments store information on salespeople. Marketing uses this information to allocate sales territories and register transactions, whereas ac-

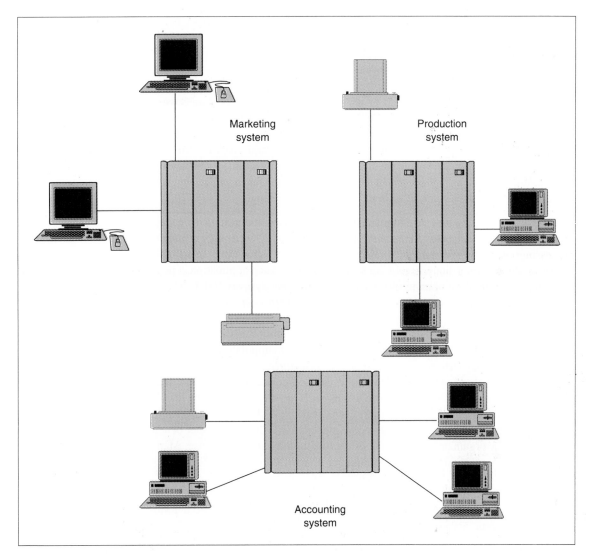

FIGURE 1.8   A decentralized computing system

counting uses it for payroll processing. Likewise, marketing and production departments store similar information on items produced and sold—for marketing and manufacturing purposes. Storing the same information in two or more places simultaneously is known as *data redundancy,* which incurs greater storage costs. In the case of manual filing, extra folders, paper, and cabinets, and so on are required, whereas for computer-based systems, additional disk space is needed.

- *Data inconsistency.* As data redundancy increases, so does the risk of inconsistency of the data held in isolated files. In the marketing-accounting example, consider the case of the worker who resigns or retires. Conceivably the employee's record might be purged in the marketing department while left unchanged in accounting. This might eventually result in paychecks being sent to a nonemployee!

■ *Limited uses of data.* A further problem with decentralized processing becomes evident when attempts are made to process applications requiring data from different departments. In preparing budgets, for example, detailed data concerning departmental expenditures is required. In decentralized settings, this data is stored in different locations and often in incompatible formats, which makes it difficult to collect and integrate the data and to resolve inconsistencies in data sets.

■ *Limited access to data.* In decentralized settings, data and programs for different functional areas or departments are situated in different locations. Even when related departments must work closely together, accessing data (for example, reports) from other functional areas can be difficult and time-consuming.

In the late 1960s, the first mainframe operating systems with multitasking capabilities appeared. **Multitasking OSs** manage the concurrent (that is, seemingly simultaneous) processing of multiple computer jobs by successively allocating small slices of processor time, or timeslices, to running applications until each application is processed to completion. The development of *database management systems (DBMSs)* followed in the 1970s, enabling simultaneous access to files by a firm's computer users, as shown in Figure 1.9. The user applications access a *database* (that is, an integrated collection of data), which is managed by the DBMS. The DBMS minimizes data redundancy and inconsistency and allows multiple users to access and manipulate data in the central repository. This approach began a new cycle of *centralized processing*.

Centralized processing with a DBMS also enabled concurrent access to files from more than one functional area in the firm's database. One file could then be read by two or more applications running concurrently (see Chapter 6). Also, data redundancy, with its attendant problems of cost and data inconsistency, was reduced. Another benefit was the potential for organizationwide uses of data using the central database. Many new applications were developed in this computing era, including *forecasting*, *budgeting*, and *reporting* systems.

The growth of larger computing installations was justified by what was referred to as *Grosh's Law*, which stated that doubling the cost of (or investment in) a computing facility would result in squaring the computing power. This *economy-of-scale* argument, often used in manufacturing environments, assumed net savings in personnel and facilities by avoiding the duplication associated with multiple computer centers.

Economy-of-scale was rendered irrelevant by microprocessors. Large-scale integration using microchips led to the development of powerful microcomputers at a fraction of the cost of larger machines. Over a few years, it became possible for a network of computers to provide greater aggregate computing power than a mainframe at a much lower cost. Additionally, advances in data communications helped to further the concept of **distributed processing**, to handle problems inherent in the centralized computing model.

Computer Networks and Distributed Processing

A **distributed processing** system comprises components of a computer system in different locations, with interconnections accomplished through *data communications*. While centralization reduced data redundancy, problems still remained. One such

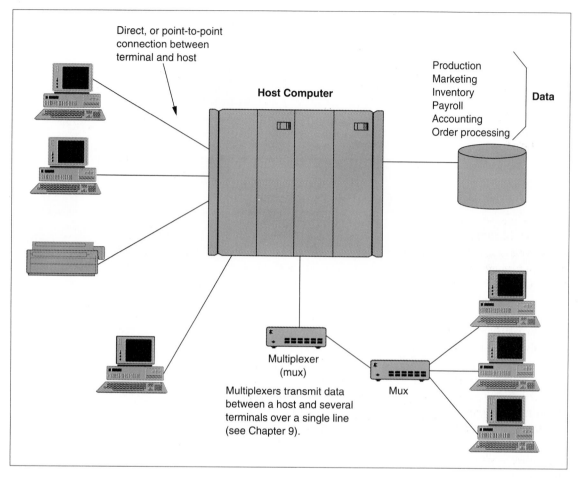

Direct, or point-to-point
connection between
terminal and host

Host Computer

Production
Marketing
Inventory   **Data**
Payroll
Accounting
Order processing

Multiplexer
(mux)

Mux

Multiplexers transmit data
between a host and several
terminals over a single line
(see Chapter 9).

FIGURE 1.9   A centralized computing system

problem was the *vulnerability* of such systems to failure. The failure of a single computer meant the cessation of activity in nearly every functional area until it was repaired. A system failure was an expensive proposition, involving not just the cost of diagnosing and repairing the information system but that of lost business as well.

Second, the cost of centralized installations was prohibitive to all but the larger firms. While minicomputers made cheaper processing power available to a wider range of customers, it was the microprocessor that ensured computer deployment among the widest base of users—computer and noncomputer professionals alike.

On-line computing, or the connection of terminals to the mainframe for direct data and program input, was widespread by the 1970s. This signaled a change from processing programs in batches (batch processing) to direct user interaction through terminals. Some consequences of centralized systems included uneven response times and request servicing, due to the use of a single processor. With distributed processing, processing tasks could be spread out among different locations on the network, depending on their spare capacity (see Figure 1.10)

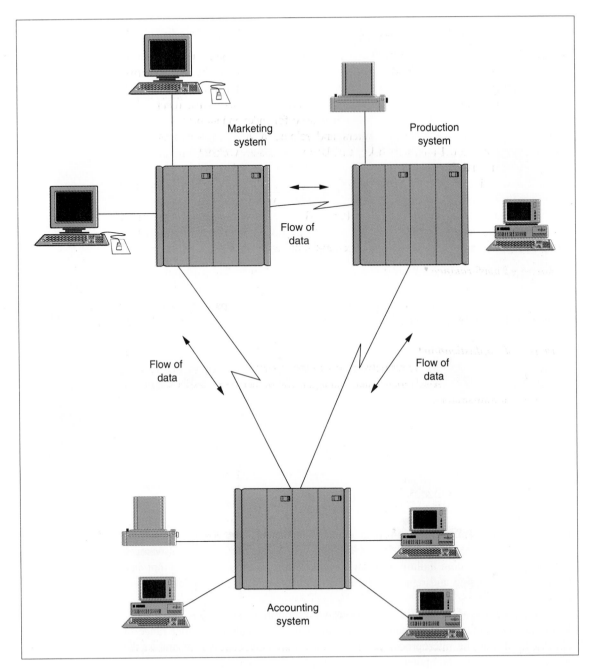

FIGURE 1.10   A distributed computing system

Microcomputer-Centered Information Systems

As we move through the 1990s, the transition to the **microcomputer-centered information system** is well under way. This model views networks of (primarily) microcomputers as the most effective form of information systems organization. End users make use of microcomputers on their desktops in both *stand-alone* and *networked* modes (see Figure 1.11). The microcomputer is used for independent processing tasks while still connected to other computers and related devices in networks. Other computers in such local area networks (LANs) may include workstations, minicomputers, or even mainframe computers. Related devices may also include data communications equipment, such as modems, bridges, and network cabling (Chapters 9 and 10); or input/output devices, such as printers and fax machines.

Many organizations, such as United Parcel Service, have successfully migrated from mainframe-centered information systems to microcomputer-based systems (see Chapter 2). Here are some of the influences and motivations for these changes:

- *Improved performance* of microcomputer and communications hardware against a background of declining costs. More significantly, these technologies have proved adequate for supporting transaction processing. The past few years have also seen growth in networking hardware, which is the glue for such networks.
- *Increased sophistication* of critical classes of microcomputer software has also facilitated this transition. Better network operating systems (NOSs) and networking capabilities of new applications make management of networks much easier for network administrators.

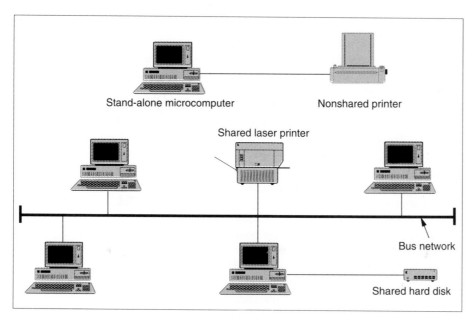

FIGURE 1.11   Stand-alone and networked microcomputers

- *More computer-literate users* of organizational systems also generate pressure for organizations to move to networked systems. The old text-driven interfaces of mainframe terminals, once standard fare in these firms, have been replaced by the GUIs being adopted by many microcomputer users. In addition, the need for internal and external data resources makes the provision of networking capabilities necessary to many firms.

- The growth of *end-user applications* provides even more impetus for microcomputer-based information systems. Also, basic communications functions such as E-mail allow electronic transmission of data previously handled by internal and external mailing services. Additionally, the growth of computer-based work groups, involving group scheduling, document creation, and other activities, provide motivation for networks.

- Much has been written about the growth of *end-user system development*, particularly as a response to the MIS backlog—the many applications awaiting development by the typical MIS department. As user-developed applications have increased, networks have proved important in enabling full use of these applications, many of which require data external to the microcomputer. Ironically, incorporating microcomputers into organizational information system networks has helped MIS departments to regain some control over scattered companywide microcomputers.

This vision of microcomputer-centered information systems does not exclude the mainframe as an important organizational computing resource. Rather, as described in the next section, larger-scale systems can play some roles within these new distributed systems. Two important forms of organizing distributed processing capabilities within the firm are *client/server processing* and *enterprise computing*.

Client/Server Computing

Early microcomputer networks were created to enable users to share such expensive devices as laser printers and hard disks. Another use was to facilitate communication between system users and from users to external computer systems. Small networks comprise several interconnected microcomputers and peripherals, often with a powerful microcomputer functioning as a file or database server, which stores both user files and user applications, as shown in Figure 1.12.

Changes to this form of network organization originated from the need to perform tasks requiring more processing power than individual microcomputers could provide. File servers in networks worked inefficiently, generating high volumes of traffic as they sent large files and applications to the requesting terminal for processing. The appearance of sophisticated, state-of-the-art NOSs has helped to bring about a new paradigm for distributed computing, namely, client/server computing.

Client/server computing uses a network of **clients** (microcomputers) and **servers** (any computers), in which clients' requests are processed at the server and only the results are returned to the client. Servers in the network are high-performance computers that are optimized for the specific function requested. *Database servers* are the most visible type, with complex, resource-hungry database queries performed on the server and query results returned to the requesting client. Other types of servers

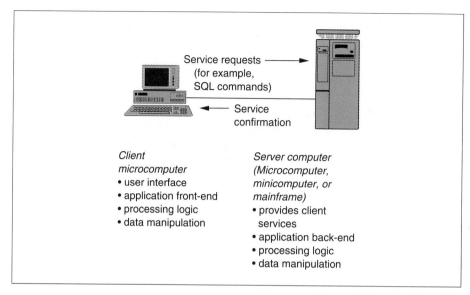

Service requests
(for example,
SQL commands)

Service
confirmation

*Client
microcomputer*
• user interface
• application front-end
• processing logic
• data manipulation

*Server computer
(Microcomputer,
minicomputer, or
mainframe)*
• provides client
  services
• application back-end
• processing logic
• data manipulation

FIGURE 1.12   Client/server computing. SQL (structured query language) is
the leading database query language, especially for interplat-
form querying.

include *processing servers*, for computationally intensive tasks, *communications servers* for communication tasks, and, as mentioned earlier, *file servers*. The client is often referred to as the *front-end*; the server is also known as the *back-end*. The efficiencies produced by the client/server model result from performing specialized tasks on subsystems best suited to the job, and equally important, avoiding communications overhead.

For example, the Harvard Community Health Plan in Boston has implemented a client/server information system using Macintosh microcomputers as clients and several VAX minicomputers and workstations as servers. The system enables doctors to enter patient data directly into databases from their desks and allows patients to access preventive health care information, even from their homes. This client/server system has reduced the paper traffic in the firm, enabled better tracking of patient history and tests, and provided more accurate billing information.

Enterprise Computing

Enterprise computing is another popular computing model. It links local area networks (LANs) and corporate computer resources together in an **enterprise network**. The main difference between this and the client/server model is in the use of mainly mainframe servers in the enterprise network vs. workstations or microcomputers. This model is therefore important for firms with mainframe resources *and* LANs as a means of ensuring enterprisewide connectivity. It takes "LAN islands" within the organization, ties them together, and supplies a centrally managed data repository. Client/server and enterprise models are discussed in Chapters 10 and 11.

1.5 KEY ISSUES OF THE _____ MICROCOMPUTER REVOLUTION _____

With over 100 million home and office microcomputers in use in the United States today, there are several important issues for firms making the transition to microcomputer-centered information systems. They are directing many questions to manufacturers and vendors of systems. Such questions include whether microcomputers will fulfill the role of complementary or replacement technology for larger-scale systems in organizations, whether compatibility and interoperability problems will increase or decrease over time, and whether microcomputer-centered systems will offer the same reliability as larger systems. Other issues include downsizing information systems, the future impact of multimedia, and new skills for information systems professionals in the middle to late 1990s. (See Box 1.1.)

Complementary or Replacement Technology?

The transition to microcomputer-based information systems described in this book does *not* project wholesale abandonment of mainframes or minicomputers in the organization in the short or medium term. Mainframes will still be around in the year 2000. However, there are two important caveats:

- Many small- and medium-sized firms can (and do) use solely microcomputer-based technology for all aspects of their information processing. This number will grow as the technology improves.
- The role of the larger computers in some organizations will change from providing raw processing power to users to serving as massive data repositories for clients.

The rate of replacement of the new technologies with the old is also important, to make maximum use of the new technologies while limiting their exposure to costly failures.

Compatibility and Interoperability

Compatibility is the ability to combine hardware and software from different manufacturers, that is, to be able to run a software program unchanged on two different but compatible computers. The largest category of microcomputers is *IBM-compatibles*, microcomputers manufactured by IBM and other firms that run programs developed for Microsoft's disk operating system or MS-DOS. Compatibility may be established at the operating system, application program, or hardware level. It is becoming less hardware related and more software related all the time (that is, provided by OSs and NOSs) and is important to firms in new organizations attempting to interconnect heterogeneous resources.

Interoperability, on the other hand, refers to the ability of two devices or systems to work together, with each understanding the other's language. For example, two incompatible computers, such as a microcomputer and a connected mainframe, may be made interoperable through software. This software translates requests from the microcomputer into requests understandable by the larger machine. Compatibility and

A PERSPECTIVE FROM A "MICROCOMPUTER REVOLUTIONARY"

DEC's Alpha, HP's PA-RISC, Mips's R4000, IBM's Power PC, and Intel's Pentium are high-powered microcomputing rockets, but what corporate MIS department is going to rely on them? No one is going to jeopardize a multi-million dollar application to save a few bucks on hardware—unless the microcomputer OS that runs on it has the security, multiprocessor capabilities, sophisticated system management and crash protection that mainframe OSs like MVS and VMS offer.

Today's micro users choose from five operating systems: DOS, Apple's System 7, Unix, Windows NT, and Netware. The first two are a joke—no security, no multi-user capability, no crash protection, and no sophisticated features like multithreading or symmetric multiprocessing (SMP). Until recently, Unix and Netware fared little better. Neither had multithreading or SMP. Neither was secure. All you needed to break into Netware's trapdoor, designed to let in forgetful system managers, was physical access to the server. So it is no surprise that most traditional MIS managers viewed the hype about workstation chips as Macbeth viewed life, "a tale told by an idiot, full of sound and fury, signifying nothing."

The truth is that operating systems, not silly things such as I/Os, processors or DASDs, are the real difference between mainframes and microcomputers. The VAX 9000 mainframe uniprocessors are no faster than today's $10,000 workstation—the reason why DEC is touting Alpha, which replaces the 9000, as a workstation chip. VMS (the VAX OS), not the VAX, is what keeps DEC going.

Without its OS, the AS400 is a joke, slower than many PCs. No one even thinks of running UNIX on one.

This situation cannot last. Micro OSs will catch up to mainframe systems for three fundamental reasons. First, the prize for the winner of the current OS design contest is billions of dollars, ensuring that no resource will be spared. Second, desktop and work group users are demanding OS features formerly restricted to the data center. Finally, people are going to realize that those trusted mainframe OSs aren't up to their press clippings.

Successful OSs are extremely valuable merchandise. A VAX 9000 mainframe is really a $100,000 computer with a $1.1 million operating system. VMS and OS/400, which turn rather ordinary midrange computers into respectable machines, are literally worth billions of dollars to DEC and IBM. The bad news for mainframers is that the microcomputer OSs of the 1990s won't be merely as good as mainframe OSs, they will be far better. Taligent's Pink (Apple and IBM) and Windows NT (Microsoft) will have features that MVS will never have, like object-oriented file systems, cross-platform portability, and microkernels. What's more, they will run on multiprocessing RISC boxes, which cost a fraction of what today's mainframes cost yet are far faster.

Adapted from "Reality Check," *Robert Ziff/Micro Revolutionary, Corporate Computing,* August 1992, 33–34.

interoperability are key concerns to developers of enterprisewide and localized networks and are covered in Chapters 3 and 10.

Security and Reliability

In networked information systems, control and reliability are concerns to end users and information systems personnel. With mainframes and minicomputers, OSs have historically provided a high degree of *system security* and *reliability*. A source of concern to IS managers is whether microcomputer-based systems, particularly those that exclude larger computers, can provide the same level of security available on larger machines.

New microcomputer-based multitasking operating systems, for example, AT&T's *UNIX*, Microsoft's *NT*, and Novell's *Netware* NOS, now have many of the security and integrity features once found only on larger machines. Also, data organization methods, including *RAID (redundant arrays of inexpensive disks)*—discussed in Chapter 5—and fault-tolerant microcomputers are contributing to improved user confidence in such systems. These technologies and associated security/reliability issues are discussed in Chapters 7 and 10, respectively.

Downsizing Organizations

The term *downsizing* is often applied to the transition from centralized mainframe systems to less expensive networks. This transition promises economic benefits from savings in hardware costs, maintenance contracts, facilities costs, and large, centralized mainframe support staffs. Aside from the cost motivation, it has the effect of shifting applications development to individual departments. Additionally, downsizing to client/server models provides a more flexible information system infrastructure to the organization. The resistance often shown to downsizing by MIS departments is partly a response to this dispersion of information, processing, and maintenance responsibilities. Economic and other arguments for downsizing are discussed in

FIGURE 1.13 A manager using a microcomputer for data analysis. Micro-computers help managers in downsized firms to manage greater areas of activity.

Chapters 13 and 14, which describe the systems development life cycle for microcomputer-based information systems.

Media Convergence and Multimedia

Multimedia represents technologies that integrate text, graphics, video, animation, and sound on the desktop. It has spread in use in the 1990s, with the backing of companies as diverse as Microsoft, Apple, and Tandy. Sales of multimedia-ready microcomputers and software reached the $1.9 billion mark in 1993. Multimedia promises newer and more sophisticated software and applications than any previously used. It is examined in detail in Chapter 8.

The New Information Systems Professional

The role of the information systems professional is being transformed by the transition to microcomputer-based information systems. The focus is shifting from mainframe-based skills to microcomputer and data communications skills for the MIS professional. Current training in mainframe/minicomputer-based hardware, OSs (VM, MVS, TSO, CICS) and software (COBOL, JCL) is still pragmatic, given the large amounts of development work still performed using these tools and the huge COBOL inventories that still exist. A reported 60–80% of all IS effort is devoted to maintenance of old systems, further underlying some continuing need for these skills. Nevertheless, the pace of networked system adoption will greatly escalate in the near term, with important subjects including *microcomputer hardware* and *operating systems*, *data communications technology, managing end-user development*, and *distributed information systems*. New career opportunities and paths for the systems professional are discussed in Chapter 15.

CHAPTER SUMMARY

The microcomputer has led a revolution in computing, and its effects have been felt in almost all types of organization. Microcomputers offer many challenges and opportunities to contemporary managers, and they feature not only lower costs and smaller sizes but also sophisticated user interfaces, powerful price/performance ratios, and widely embraced computing standards. As the use of microcomputers has spread in organizations, they have become the largest category of computers in use, greater even than mainframe or minicomputer segments of the market.

Information systems comprise not only hardware and software but also people, procedures, and data. As more powerful microcomputers are introduced, information system configurations are undergoing a transition from mainframe- and minicomputer-based systems to networks of interconnected (mainly micro) computers. This transition, its benefits, and the approaches to effectively managing it are crucial to all managers with responsibility for, or involvement with, the organization's information system.

Key issues of the microcomputer revolution and the transition to microcomputer-based systems include how microcomputers are interconnected to other computers, and associated compatibility and interoperability concerns. Additionally, as these new systems begin to support transaction processing, security and reliability issues have grown in significance. Other important issues are the role of the microcomputer in downsizing organizations and the integration of multimedia on the desktop.

As the technology continues to accelerate even further, many new roles are emerging for the new information systems professional. These include network and database administration and consultative roles to the end user. The microcomputer will continue to significantly impact the roles and functions of both end users and system professionals in coming years in practically every business area and industry.

REVIEW QUESTIONS

1. Describe four ways in which a microcomputer differs from a mainframe computer.
2. What is an IBM-compatible microcomputer?
3. Which type of computer represents the largest category of computers in use?
4. What is the difference between the microcomputer and its peripherals?
5. Describe the main differences among the major categories of computers.
6. What are the five major components of an information system?
7. List two types of information that have considerable value to a marketing manager.
8. What was the major limitation of early isolated mainframes?
9. Discuss three limitations each of decentralized and centralized computing.
10. What major development led to the invalidation of economy-of-scale in computing?
11. Describe four major benefits of microcomputer-based information systems.
12. What are two reasons why "rumors of the mainframe's death are greatly exaggerated"?
13. What are three important subject areas for the new information systems professional?

EXERCISES

1. How would you describe the benefits of computerization using microcomputers to the owner of a medium-sized retailer of men's clothing who is still processing all transactions manually?
2. How would computerization of the retailer's operations today differ from what it would have been fifteen years ago? Of the five information system components, which would have cost significantly more?
3. What are four major constraints a firm might face in making the transition from a mainframe-based information system to one based on microcomputers? How might these be effectively dealt with?
4. Describe the implications to organizations of the ability of individual departments to purchase microcomputers independently of the MIS department.
5. What are circumstances in which microcomputer hardware and software incompatibilities can pose major problems in the functioning of two departments (for example, production and marketing)?

6. Discuss possible reasons why MIS professionals may resist the development of microcomputer-based information systems and what might be done to overcome this resistance.

SUGGESTED READINGS

Beer, J., & Freifel, K. Multimedia Special Report: Super Tutorials, *PC World,* May 1991, 192–194.

Burger, R. M., & Holtong, W. C. Reshaping the Microchip, *Byte Magazine,* February 1992, 137–150.

Datapro Workgroup Computing Series, Volumes 1–3. New York: McGraw Hill, 1992.

Halfhill, T. R. Intel Launches Rocket in a Socket, *Byte Magazine,* May 1993, 92–108.

Hayes, F., & Baran, N. A Guide to GUIs, *Byte Magazine,* July 1989, 250–257.

Keen P.G.W. *Shaping the Future: Business Design Through Information Technology.* Boston: Harvard Business School Press, 1991.

Keyes J. *Infotrends: The Competitive Use of Information.* New York: McGraw-Hill, 1993.

Morris, M. D. RISC vs CISC, *PC Today,* May 1991, 35–39.

Stamper, D. A. *Business Data Communications* (3rd Edition). Redwood City, CA: Benjamin Cummings, 1992.

CHAPTER 2

BUSINESS APPLICATIONS INVOLVING MICROCOMPUTERS

INTRODUCTION

Microcomputers are in widespread use in organizations, and they process a large variety of applications in diverse functional areas. As noted in Chapter 1, the capabilities of newer machines enable them to fulfill a broad range of functions in the organization, some of which are examined here through case studies. These cases are real-world examples of microcomputer use that demonstrate the costs and benefits of their deployment, their implementation process, and how they are integrated with other types of computers. The three cases discussed in this chapter focus on networked microcomputers used in single (or a small number of) locations, whereas Chapter 12 examines larger systems spread out over several locations.

Case 2.1 involves the use of microcomputers at a grocery retailer to speed sales, improve sales tracking, manage inventory, and run productivity software—for example, spreadsheets and word processors. Case 2.2 moves to the insurance industry, where an insurance firm deployed a large network of microcomputers to manage claims. In particular, its use of the network for document imaging created efficiencies in its operation. Case 2.3, is taken from the banking industry, where microcomputers were used to relieve the pressure on a bank's mainframe computer by offloading reporting and budgeting functions to a microcomputer-based network.

Learning Objectives

After reading this chapter, you will be able to:

- Understand some of the practical issues involved in implementing networked systems in small- to medium-sized businesses

- Identify benefits offered to these businesses by microcomputer-centered systems
- Better visualize how actual applications in major functional areas can be supported by microcomputer-based technologies
- Describe how microcomputers and larger computers can be used cooperatively to support an organization's transaction processing

---

CASE 2.1

AUTOMATING SALES AND INVENTORY MANAGEMENT AT B & R STORES, INC.

Robert Tracy, Director of Information Systems for B & R Stores, Inc., a Lincoln, Nebraska, company that operates seven grocery stores, agrees that efficiency is a major computer benefit. "Computers help customer service through faster checkout and increased productivity," Tracy says. "These benefits help to keep prices low because they cut costs—costs that would be passed down to the customer."

The 30-year-old company, which employs about 900 people, started using computers in 1985 and updated them in 1988. Personal computers in each store are connected to System 36 and AS/400 minicomputers found in B & R's main office, Tracy explains. Each store also has stand-alone PCs and in-store LANs.

Tracy says computers help B & R Stores in many ways, both in the outlet stores and at the main office. The computers are used in the stores' video departments to keep track of the movie inventory and of customer accounts when customers check movies in and out. "In the past, we entered all the information manually in a record book," Tracy says. "Now the computer keeps track of who has the movies and when they are due back. All the clerk needs to do to check out a movie is to get the customer's identification number, find the movie, run the movie's code across a bar-code scanner, and punch a couple of buttons."

The stores also use PCs in the back room, Tracy says, when they receive inventory shipments. Each back-room PC is hooked by modem to the IBM System 36 minicomputer at the main office. As trucks unload food shipments at the stores, the receivers key in the delivered items' UPC numbers and the quantity of each item that was delivered. This process saves money too because the employees can search the screen, find the order, and know if the store is being charged the correct amount. They can make sure that any quantity deduction a wholesaler promised is received. The system is shown in Figure 2.1.

Personal computers are just as important at the main office, Tracy says, where they are used for spreadsheets and word processing. Some store managers also use personal computers for scheduling and accessing hourly productivity and sales information. "Most of our systems are on-line," Tracy says, "so all of the information we get is 100 percent current. Because of our access to current information, there just isn't any comparison between life without computers and the automated way we run the stores now."

Adapted from Lori Beckmann, "Computers at Work," *PC Today*, March, 1991, pp. 67–72.

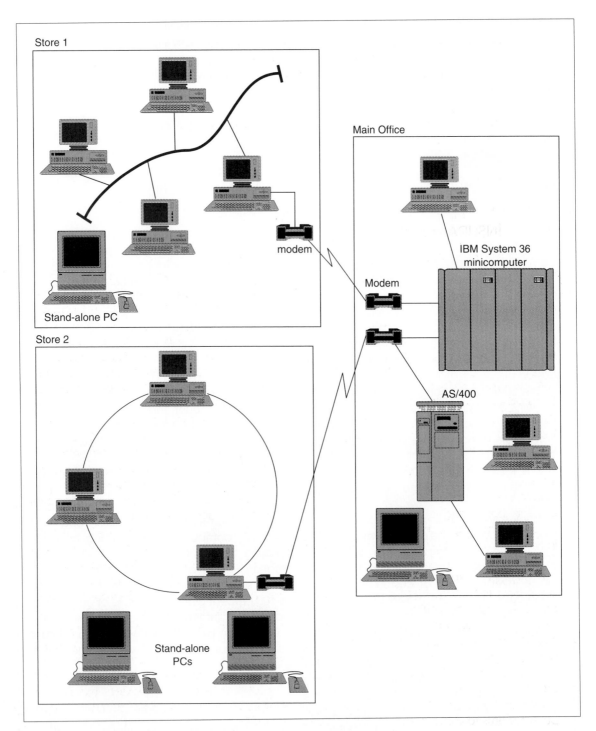

Store 1

Stand-alone PC

modem

Main Office

Modem

IBM System 36 minicomputer

AS/400

Store 2

Stand-alone PCs

FIGURE 2.1   The computer configuration at B & R Stores, Inc.

Questions for Discussion

1. Microcomputers have been widely applied in the retailing industry. In what ways do you think B & R's use of microcomputers has made it more competitive?
2. How has B & R's network helped to improve inventory management, as compared to the manual inventory management process?
3. What do you think is the importance to managers of having the microcomputers linked to the minicomputers in the main office? If these central computers did not exist, what would the consequences be?

CASE 2.2

COMPLETE HEALTH: USING LAN-BASED IMAGING IN THE INSURANCE INDUSTRY

As business giant Ross Perot proved with Electronic Data Systems Corp., the insurance industry is a prime consumer of network technology due to the sheer amount of information being handled and the need to disseminate that information throughout the organization. Complete Health, Inc. of Birmingham, Alabama, is continuing that tradition. The company has implemented imaging technology across its corporate local area network (LAN), which has virtually eliminated the internal use of paper. It has also provided users across the organization with access to data and improved the efficiency of its services.

Complete Health's successful accrual of benefits from using LAN-based technology, including imaging, won it honorable mention in Network World's User Excellence Awards in 1992. Founded in 1986, Complete Health quickly began experiencing ''good growth,'' according to William Featheringill, president and chief executive officer of the company. Today, the company covers more than 300,000 people in the Southeast. But along with that growth came the insurance industry's bête noire: Complete Health began drowning in paper. The health care provider's avowed policy is to invest in computer systems to improve service, and several years ago, the company began looking

for a technological solution. It needed to integrate all of its departments, track claims, enter data, and quickly redistribute information. After doing some research, Complete Health discovered that no off-the-shelf system could meet its needs. The company contacted a local firm, Macess Corp., to develop a total network solution that would include imaging capabilities, and it came up with a product called I-MAX. ''We basically gave Macess the functional requirements from a business operations point of view,'' Featheringill says. ''We told them what we wanted to do, and they took it from there.''

Today, the company operates a very large LAN: about 350 80386-based personal computer users operating under Microsoft Corp. Windows are tied together in a Novell, Inc. NetWare network. The main server is from NetFRAME Systems, Inc. ''We used to have a lot of problems with network stability until we put (the NetFRAME Server) in,'' says Featheringill. The network is, in turn, connected via gateways to the company's IBM Application System/400 minicomputers, which house claims processing systems. Information is scanned into the system on the LAN, where it is indexed and filed in electronic folders. Images of claims—over 400 MB

(continued)

COMPLETE HEALTH: USING LAN-BASED IMAGING IN THE INSURANCE INDUSTRY

are processed overnight. The extracted data is passed on to the host. Customer representatives have access to all the data in the folders, including claims, enrollment forms, logged telephone calls, and correspondence. "Our data entry rate has doubled since the system was implemented in 1991," Featheringill reports. Complete Health currently scans over 8,000 claims—more than 17,000 discrete images—every workday.

"We don't like to think of it as an imaging system," Featheringill says. "The interesting things are those that go far beyond imaging. We measure work flow. We handle customer service calls, archive computer reports—all of these are things that imaging allows us to do." Storing the images electronically has improved the company's service in several respects. For one thing, accountability has improved. "A big problem used to be that things would get lost," Featheringill says. Things would be forwarded from one department to another and just languish about. We used to make a lot of copies whenever we forwarded anything because claims would get lost (between offices). And that's the stuff of lawsuits."

With imaging, redundant claims copies are eliminated and 50,000 pages of reports are stored on optical disk. "A lot of reports are generated that people don't really read," Featheringill says. Even when the reports are briefly glanced over, most people don't want the entire report, only a few pages. "For those exceptions, they can always send the file to a printer. That one little thing saves us $12,000 to $13,000 a month." See Figure 2.2 for a look at Complete Health's information system.

Complete Health recognized that image access time is a problem on networks that support imaging systems. What most people are using is WORM (write-once, read-many optical disk) drives with a jukebox, Featheringill says, and although that's fine for one or two users, it's awkward for an insurance company. "When you get into a situation where you have 300 people trying to get into one jukebox with six heads and six seconds to change disks, you get a heck of a response-time problem." The I-MAX solution is perhaps unique: Complete Health has 150 optical storage devices on-line at once. They're off-the-shelf CD-ROM players. "We press our own platters," Featheringill explains. The company puts one in dead storage and the other on-line. "The system is designed to take the platters off-line after they get old, but the storage is so inexpensive, we just add another drive," he says. "Basically, all our data (since the system went up) is on-line and available."

Adapted from Jerry Lazar, "Alterings Its Image," *NETWORK WORLD*, November 23, 1992, p. 43.

Questions for Discussion

1. Imaging applications represent one of the fastest-growing areas, particularly in the insurance and legal industries. What are the competitive advantages imaging has brought to Complete Health, Inc.? In particular, how has it improved internal efficiencies and customer service?

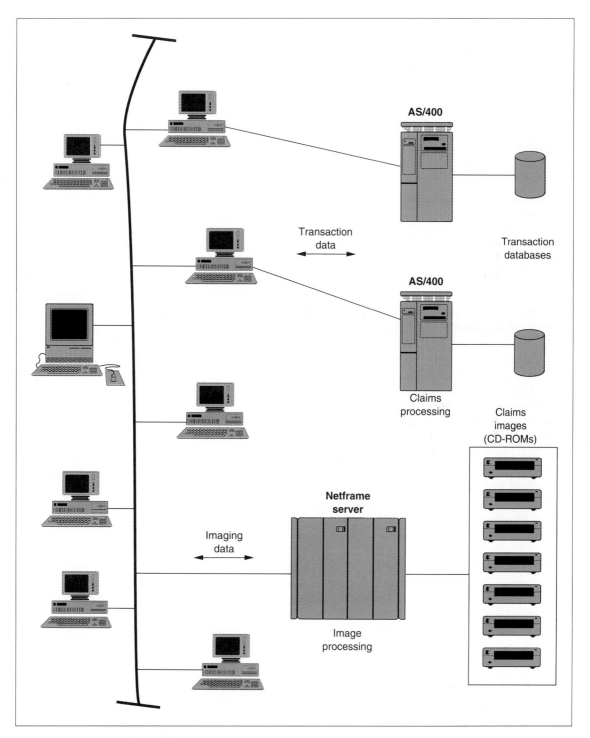

FIGURE 2.2   Complete Health's LAN-based imaging system

2. Macess Corp. was contracted to develop a total network solution. What are the benefits of having a single solution provider, instead of separate microcomputer, networking, and imaging providers—even at a lower (component) price?
3. Why do you think two sets of CD-ROMs are created by Complete Health, Inc.? What, if any, would the risks be of maintaining only one set of disks?

CASE 2.3

BANK OF THE WEST: DOWNSIZING TO LANS

Modern banking has relied mainly on mainframe computers in developing electronic services, such as automated teller machines, electronic funds transfers, and foreign exchange trading. The reason for this is the high volume of transactions involved; the need to centralize customer data and use powerful database management software; and issues of telecommunications, management, security, and guaranteeing availability. Powerful mainframe computers can combine all these functions efficiently. Personal computers and local area networks are increasingly used to distribute functions and ``front-end'' processing, such as error-checking and message formatting. Many new applications, for budgeting, electronic mail, word processing, financial analysis, and management reporting, are built on LANs. However, the mainframe remains the core of most banks' information systems and telecommunications.

Bank of the West is headquartered in California. It expanded rapidly in the late 1980s and early 1990s, acquiring another bank. It controlled costs tightly and kept its information systems staff lean. Expansion increased the need for new systems and the mainframe computer was increasingly over-loaded in handling the additional processing plus that of the acquired bank. Bank of the West decided to use LANs to remove reliance on the mainframe. It already had several in place for departmental computing and communica-

tions. The other bank also had some in use, but these were incompatible with Bank of the West's LANs.

The most immediate need was in the controller's department, which was a heavy user of the mainframe system for budgeting, accounting, regulatory reporting, and management reporting. This required the department to integrate data from the mainframe into reports that go to a variety of people inside and outside the bank, a process that was time consuming, clumsy, and expensive. Staff downloaded data onto their stand-alone personal computers and collected other data from many sources. They use the PC to organize the information and produce reports. Several people might manipulate the data before it was finalized in a report; errors were frequent; floppy disks were passed around as were hard copy reports; the same numbers were entered and reentered in different systems. Information used in the central mainframe systems then had to be ``massaged'' into the format these required. It could take up to two days to schedule mainframe processing plus another day to get the outputs.

This is hardly a satisfactory way to manage in the 1990s. Bank of the West brought in a systems integrator, PC Edge, to create a LAN-based solution initially for twelve users. The service would build on PC software already in use, including Lotus 1-2-3. The first

(continued).

CASE 2.3 *(continued)*

BANK OF THE WEST: DOWNSIZING TO LANS

problem PC Edge encountered was cabling: Bank of the West's wiring conduits were filled to capacity and new cables could not be added. PC Edge recommended re-placing the existing ARCNET cables with twisted-pair Ethernet products to ensure adequate capacity. The bank decided to standardize on 10Base-T, a standard that extends, but is compatible with, Ethernet. The electrical contractor installed this in a few days. Adding new PC hardware and software took around the same amount of time. The PCs selected were 386-based, operating at 25 megahertz, with 1 MB of memory. The file server had 600 MB of disk storage. This adds up to a fast and powerful capability at low cost.

It is also a simple system. Several of the workstations have an IRMA board that lets the PC emulate a terminal so that they can communicate directly with the mainframe, but the controller's department's data now resides on the file server. Lotus 1-2-3 is the standard software for budgeting, analysis, and reporting. The LAN users also handle investment tracking, asset and liability management, and treasury operations. Branches submit their budget data on floppy disks, and this data is stored on the file server. Only

when all inputting and relevant analysis, verification, and approval are complete is the data up loaded to the mainframe general ledger system for regular budget variance reporting. Figure 2.3 shows Bank of the West's information system.

Turnaround time for developing and finalizing the budget has been halved, and the resulting figures are far more accurate and consistent. The strain on the mainframe has been greatly reduced; Bank of the West has not had to add capacity. It has outsourced many mainframe applications, such as payroll. It continues to add LANs across the bank, with 10Base-T its standard. There are now many software packages available for banking applications at low cost. The LAN file server ensures that these share a common data-base and can also share such devices as high-speed color laser printers. In the future, Bank of the West expects to create an internetwork for the departmental LANs, though there is no LAN-to-LAN link at present.

Adapted from P. Keen & M. Cummins, *Networks in Action.* Belmont, CA: Wadsworth, 1994.

Questions for Discussion

1. What are the major reasons that Bank of the West chose to distribute computing functions to microcomputer-based networks instead of investing in additional mainframe capacity?
2. In your view, why was the first attempt to use microcomputers at Bank of the West unsuccessful? What made the difference the second time?
3. What functions have been made more efficient at Bank of the West through the introduction of the microcomputer network? How exactly have these functions been improved?

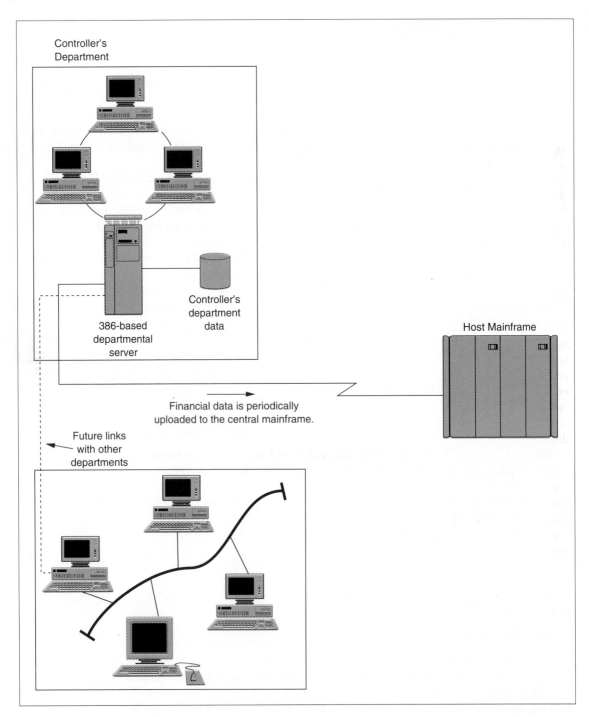

FIGURE 2.3   Bank of the West's LAN

MICROCOMPUTER PROCESSORS AND SYSTEMS

INTRODUCTION

Computers have had an impact on today's society in ways unlike any other technology. Microcomputers make up the largest category of computers. Their central feature is the *microchip,* a semiconducting, typically silicon-based device used to process data. At the heart of the microcomputer is a microchip called a *microprocessor.* This electronic device supplies the computational and control capabilities of the microcomputer and executes up to several million instructions per second in processing programs. Other microchips are used for data storage, supporting video displays, and other functions.

Microchips embody **very large scale integration (VLSI),** involving the fabrication of millions of individual circuits on thumbnail-sized microchip surfaces. Powerful desktop microcomputers that incorporate VLSI have more raw processing power than some five-year-old mainframes. This chapter introduces the features of microcomputers and workstations, discusses the central elements of microcomputer-centered information systems, and examines the major microprocessor platforms.

Learning Objectives

After reading this chapter, you will be able to:

- Describe the architecture of a microcomputer
- Select appropriate combinations of microprocessors and memory/peripheral subsystems
- Apply the knowledge of major microprocessor platforms to evaluate each platform's suitability in different contexts
- Identify which type of computer is most suitable for diverse problem types
- Match user requirements to appropriate microcomputer systems

CASE 3.1

MIDLAND MUTUAL LIFE INSURANCE CO.: TAILORING TECHNOLOGY TO THE BUSINESS

The mid-1980s introduced banking deregulation, allowing banks to offer services formerly the exclusive preserve of insurance companies. In addition, competition among insurance companies themselves greatly increased. Midland Mutual Life Insurance Co. initially faced these challenges with a computing infrastructure consisting of a mainframe, minicomputers, and terminals. However, multiple operating systems and programming languages ended up increasing computing costs.

In 1985, Midland chose to drastically reorganize both its organizational and computing infrastructures. The mainframe and minicomputers were eliminated and replaced with Compaq microcomputer servers and desktop units. Applications for each of the firm's groups were transferred to Compaq SystemPro servers attached to desktop units through an Ethernet Local Area Network (LAN). For example, mainframe-based McCormack & Dodge accounting software was replaced by microcomputer-based accounting programs from Macola. The replacement network comprised 23 servers and 325 desktop units.

Benefits reported from LAN ``rightsizing'' include a reduction to 8 hours of tasks that once took 2–3 days to do on the mainframe. In addition, the different units have become more decentralized and flexible in their operations. The employee base has been reduced from 360 to 204, while revenue has doubled and record profits have occurred. Also, the time taken to bring out a new insurance product is now 45 days vs. 1–5 years previously. Finally, in the 5000-square-foot computer room, StairMasters have replaced the mainframe, because the space has been converted into an employee health club.

Adapted from Timothy Haight; ``Rightsizing: Tailoring the Technology to the Business,'' *Network Computing,* February, 1993, pp. 87–94.

3.1 COMPONENTS OF A MICROCOMPUTER

The microcomputer best illustrates the use of microchip-based technology in the computer industry. This technology has enabled reductions in size and increases in density of the circuits and transistors that perform the computer's functions. While the major elements of the microcomputer are microchip based, other components are also important. These include *system buses,* or pathways for data transmission between different devices, *ports* for data input and output to external devices, the microcomputer's *power supply,* and other circuitry. The microcomputer also requires *peripheral devices,* such as the keyboard, the video display unit, and various types of storage devices, such as floppy and fixed disk drives. These devices all operate under the computer's control, for inputting programs and data for processing, storing the results of processing, and outputting these results to the user in appropriate formats, for example, on printouts. We begin by discussing the **microchip.**

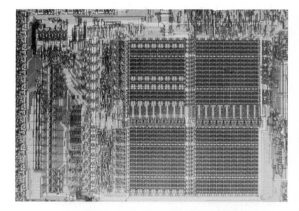

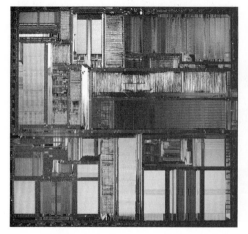

FIGURE 3.1   Microprocessors like Intel's 80386 (*bottom left*), 80486 (*top left*), and Pentium (*right*) have provided almost tenfold increases in processing power every four years at the same or lower prices.

The Development of the Microchip

Microchips, also dubbed "industrial rice" by the Japanese, are the basic building blocks of the microcomputer (Figure 3.1). They are miniaturized semiconductor-based (for example, silicon) circuitry used to process and store data *electronically,* that is, using no moving parts to transmit electrical signals. Earlier *transistors* shown in Figure 3.2 were the first solid-state computer devices created from semiconductors. They could represent discrete electrical states and be switched between these states using electrical pulses.

Microchips such as microprocessor, memory, and logic chips, are also solid-state semiconductor-based devices, featuring thousands of miniaturized transistors. The term **semiconductor** is applied to the *wafers* of silicon (or other material) used in chip fabrication. It is derived from its partial resistance to electrical current. By overlaying conducting metals on the silicon, electronic circuitry is created for use in storing and processing data.

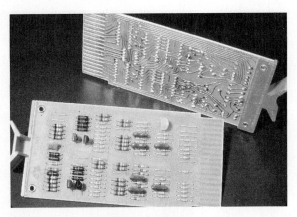

FIGURE 3.2   Transistors on a PDP-8 computer module (circa 1965)

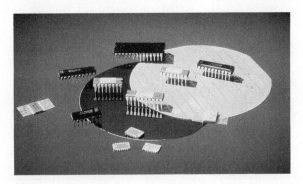

FIGURE 3.3   INMOS microchips in dual inline package (DIP) form

Based on a photograph or "map" of the required on-chip circuitry, the circuitry is produced by "doping" or mixing the silicon semiconductor with various substances. Junctions of positively and negatively charged doped surfaces give the microchip its ability to conduct electricity, and the layout of these junctions determines the microchip's design. The completed chip is then checked for defects and enclosed in a ceramic or plastic carrier for protection. The carrier possesses extruding pins that pass signals between the processor and motherboard. The entire package is called a **dual inline package,** or **DIP,** shown in Figure 3.3. It derives this name from the two lines of pins used to connect the chip to the board. The DIP is subsequently inserted in the appropriate location on the microcomputer's main circuit board or **motherboard.**

Different types of microchips include *microprocessors, memory* and *graphics chips,* and *math coprocessors.* These microchips are discussed next.

Structure of the Microprocessor

The **microprocessor** or "computer-on-a-chip" is the central part of the microcomputer. It is truly a complex and powerful device, with a size that contrasts starkly with its

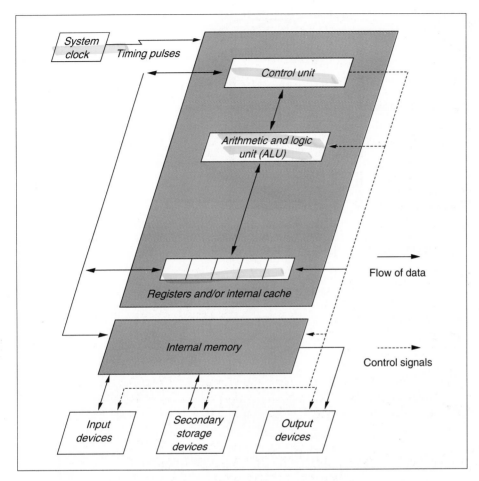

FIGURE 3.4   Structure of a microprocessor

capabilities. In fact, the microprocessor is a collection of integrated components that work together to synchronize computer operations and process user-entered instructions. **Instructions** are codes that specify operations to be performed on data. The components of the microprocessor are illustrated in Figure 3.4 and include *the control unit, the arithmetic and logic unit (or ALU), a clock,* and *internal registers.*

The **control unit** directs and synchronizes the operations of the ALU and other microcomputer components. Instructions to be executed must be in the microprocessor's native machine code (see *instruction set*), which is decoded and executed by the control unit and ALU, respectively. To enable high-speed data transfers between these two components, they are connected by a fast *CPU bus,* and each instruction is processed using a *fetch-decode-execute-store* cycle (see Figures 3.5 and 3.6) as follows:

1. *Fetch.* The control unit fetches the next instruction to be executed from the computer's primary memory. This instruction consists of an *operation code,* or

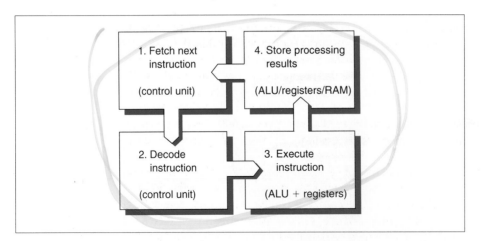

FIGURE 3.5 The fetch-decode-execute-store processing cycle

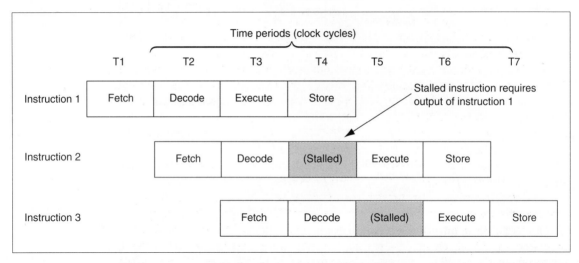

FIGURE 3.6 In microprocessor pipelining, the processing cycle for a second instruction begins before that of its predecessor ends, increasing processing efficiency.

opcode, and an *operand.* The opcode might be for an addition operation, while the operand is the number to be added to a previously fetched number.

2. ***Decode.*** The opcode is interpreted by the control unit, with appropriate electronic signals sent to the ALU or other hardware to initiate execution.

3. ***Execute.*** The instruction is executed by the ALU or other hardware component.

4. ***Store.*** Processing results are written back to primary memory.

The **arithmetic and logic unit (ALU)** performs the arithmetic and logic operations of the computer required by software programs. Based on the instructions decoded by the control unit, the ALU performs electronic switching of its components to execute arithmetic and logic operations. Examples of *arithmetic operations* include addition, subtraction, division, and multiplication, while *logic operations* include <, >, and = comparisons of data items.

Microprocessors synchronize instruction execution to pulses emitted by a **clock,** also called a **system clock.** This device within the microprocessor directly affects its speed of instruction execution. It is a quartz crystal oscillator that emits an evenly spaced number of pulses, which are used as timing cycles for synchronizing the execution of CPU instructions. Each machine code instruction is executed in a specified number of clock cycles ranging from one to four. The frequency of clock cycles is measured in **megahertz (Mhz),** or millions of cycles per second. Thus, a computer running at 20 Mhz has a processor clock emitting 20 million timing pulses every second.

Generally, the same processor can be clocked at different speeds in different systems. For example, Intel 80486 microprocessors can be clocked at 25 Mhz, 33 Mhz, 50 Mhz, and 66 Mhz. Slower microprocessors are less expensive than their faster counterparts and have lower reliability as a trade-off. Therefore, each microprocessor must be rated by its manufacturer for the speed at which the **value added reseller** or **VAR** (the firm selling the assembled microprocessor) wishes to operate the system.

Internal registers are temporary, special-purpose storage locations within the microprocessor. The actual number used varies, depending on the microprocessor's features. Some reside in the control unit while others are located within the ALU. They are used to temporarily hold both instructions and executable data.

Operations performed in registers occur much faster than data storage and retrieval from the computer's main memory. This is because data transfers occur on the chip, rather than between chips, as happens with memory access. This speed differential has led to the use of on-chip RAM caches, discussed later on in this section.

Three important additional features of the microprocessor are *the word size, the microprocessor instruction set,* and *buses.*

The microprocessor's **word size** refers to the size of its *data registers* and provides an indication of the amount of data that may be processed within the microprocessor at one time. Larger word sizes mean that data may be transferred in and out of the processor for execution in larger units. In the Intel 80386DX chip, for example, the 32-bit word size (1 bit being a binary digit—0 or 1) means that data are held and processed in 32-bit chunks in registers. While many parameters determine a microcomputer's overall performance, a machine with 32-bit word size will process data roughly twice as fast as one with a 16-bit word size, given appropriate 16- and 32-bit data pathways or buses, respectively. Microprocessors have come a long way since the Intel 4004, an early microchip with a 4-bit word size. Successive microprocessors have had 8, 16, and, currently, 32-bit word sizes, a common size on minicomputers and mainframes.*

Microprocessors represent data internally in binary form, that is, in the form of 0s and 1s. Different sequences of 0s and 1s are used to represent different instructions, data, and characters (text and numbers). Microprocessors execute instructions that are unique to that processor's physical design or architecture, collectively referred to as its **instruction set.** Therefore, a chip such as the Intel 80486DX has one instruction set, while Motorola's 68040 processor has an entirely different instruction set.

In processor families like Intel's 80x86 and Motorola's 680x0 (x is an integer, that is, 1, 2, 3, 4, and so on), successive generations of processors are usually

---

* There are indications that future microprocessors from Intel and others will use 64-bit word sizes for even greater processing power.

downward-compatible. This means that newer chips offer supersets of instruction sets of earlier chips, enabling instructions for earlier chips to run unmodified on newer processors and easing the upgrade process for users of older machines.

Buses are used to transmit *data, control signals,* and *instructions* between different locations in the microprocessor, and externally, to memory and other devices. A bus is simply a set of wires along which electronic signals are passed. These signals are in binary form, that is, 0s and 1s, with the number of wires determining how many discrete signals can be passed at one time. This is known as the *bus*

BOX 3.1

TRAVEL BY BUS FOR SPEED: ISA, EISA, MCA, AND LOCAL BUS

The original IBM-XT used an 8-bit data bus to transfer data between the processor and peripheral devices. With data transfer rates of up to 0.5 Mb per second (MBps), this bus was able to handle the maximum data demands of the 8086. With the introduction of the 80286-based AT, the XT bus was replaced by the 16-bit **industry standard architecture (ISA)** or **AT bus,** which was a better match to a 16-bit word size and faster processing speeds. The ISA bus has a transmission rate of up to 5 MBps.

As 386- and 486-based machines appeared, the ISA bus became a bottleneck between faster processors (often running at 25 Mhz upward) and faster peripherals (for example, monitor displays and some hard disks), which could accept data faster than the ISA bus could provide it. This began to result in only marginal system improvements from major upgrades in processors and peripherals.

Micro channel architecture (MCA) and **extended industry standard architecture (EISA)** buses were developed to relieve these bottlenecks in 386- and 486-based machines. They are 32-bit buses and permit faster transfer rates of up to 40 Mbps (MCA) and 33 Mbps (EISA). EISA was developed by a consortium of nine members, led by Compaq Computers,

while MCA is a proprietary IBM design. EISA has become more widely adopted than MCA, owing to its backward compatibility with ISA and ISA expansion cards. One downside, however, is that EISA-based machines can cost up to $600 more than equivalent ISA microcomputers.

While ISA, EISA, and MCA were being used, computer memory was treated as a special case, and connected directly to the processor by a local bus. This local bus transferred data between the processor and memory at the speed of the processor and not the "external" data bus (for example, ISA, EISA, and MCA). **Local bus architecture** was introduced in 1992, as a means of extending this fast data transfer to peripherals also. The two major local bus designs, **VL-BUS** (created by VESA, the Video Electronics Standards Association), and **PCI** (created by Intel Corporation) can achieve transfer rates of over 120 Mbps, depending on processor speed. With most new microcomputer models sporting a "local bus" design, and a 64-bit VL-BUS expected in the near future, the bottleneck between peripherals and the processor has been all but eliminated. Local bus designs cost almost half that of EISA designs (about $300) and have already overtaken EISA in use.

width. Three buses within the microcomputer are the *data bus, control bus,* and *address bus.*

The **data bus** is the pathway along which data are transferred between the processor and the computer's internal memory and peripherals. The first part of the data bus is the **local bus,** which is used to transfer data between the processor and high-speed devices. Though historically used for fast data transfers between the processor and internal memory, the local bus has been extended to other devices, such as display and disk controllers.

The **system bus** is the traditional extension of the local bus to peripherals. Data travel on it between the microprocessor and peripherals, with wider highways permitting faster data transfers and better computer performance. For example, the 16-bit **industry standard architecture (ISA)** system bus used in AT-compatibles (microcomputers based on Intel's 80286 microprocessor) transfers data to the processor 16 bits at a time.

Lately, much attention has been paid in the microcomputer industry to the relative merits of two 32-bit system buses, **micro channel architecture (MCA)** and **extended industry standard architecture (EISA)**—see Box 3.1. Both 32-bit buses are used on 386- and 486-based microcomputers and transfer twice as much data as 286-based machines during a single fetch or store operation. Another bus architecture is NUBUS, used in Macintosh microcomputers. The 32-bit data buses now as wide as those of many mainframes (for example, IBM 9121 mainframes), although certain mainframes and supercomputers employ 64- or even 128-bit system buses.

System and local buses are laid in parallel with control and address buses. The *control bus* is used by the processor to send control and synchronization signals to memory and system peripherals, while the *address bus* is used to transmit the (binary) address of the requested data to memory or peripheral subsystems, for example, disks, to enable their access.

Reduced Instruction Set Computing (RISC) versus Complex Instruction Set Computing (CISC)

Microcomputers and workstations use two computer architectures dubbed **CISC** and **RISC.** While CISC microprocessors predate the RISC variety, RISC processors typically process instructions faster and are widely used for computing- and graphics-intensive tasks. RISC workstations are often used for computer-aided design (CAD), computer-aided engineering (CAE), and for artificial intelligence (AI) applications. CISC machines, on the other hand, are more general-purpose machines and are directed at a broad mix of business applications.

The key difference between CISC- and RISC-based computers lie in the nature of their microcode. *Microcode* is the computer's lowest, most primitive level of instructions, which direct electronic operations on the processor chip itself. A processor's microcode is embedded in ROM on the microprocessor. On receiving a software instruction, a search is made for the appropriate microcoded instructions to satisfy the instruction. CISC microprocessors use a relatively large number of microcoded instructions, numbering between 150 and 300. RISC processors usually have 70 to 80 instructions, resulting in a shorter retrieval time for microcode than with

CISC processors. RISC designers observed that many of the CISC microcoded instructions were rarely used, and they removed them from RISC instruction sets. These were then substituted with groups of simpler microcoded instructions.

Streamlining RISC instruction sets provided initial efficiencies in their design. Extra benefits of RISC microprocessors are provided through the use of *optimizing compilers,* which prestore groups of frequently used instruction groups in an on-chip cache for faster performance.

Other features traditionally associated with RISC include *instruction pipelining,* or processing instructions in an assembly-line fashion, as shown in Figure 3.6. In this example, the first instruction in a sequence is decoded as the second is being fetched. In the next clock cycle, the second instruction is decoded while the first is being executed and the third is fetched. In the third stage, the first instruction is output, the second is executed, and the third decoded, and so on. This enables a processor to produce one result every clock cycle. The exception to this sequence is when an instruction requires the output of a preceding one. The dependent instruction then stalls until the prior one is completed. Pipelining, multiple math units, and an on-chip cache qualify RISC chips as *superscalar,* or able to execute more than one instruction per clock cycle.

While RISC processors have historically been more powerful than CISC processors, the latter have begun to take on RISC-like features, such as pipelining, on-chip caches, and on-chip coprocessors. In fact, top-end CISC microprocessors, such as Intel's Pentium and Motorola's 68040 processors, differ little from RISC processors in performance. As they continue to borrow techniques from each other, a convergence is occurring, with both providing equally powerful support for new applications.

Memory Chips and Organization

The registers within the microprocessor are used to hold small amounts of data and instructions being processed by the control unit and ALU. However, other types of storage are required by the microcomputer. Some are transient or temporary, to hold current processing tasks, while others are used to permanently store data. Semiconductor development also provided **memory chips,** on which large amounts of data are stored in miniaturized transistors and circuits. Successive generations of memory chips continue to improve upon their predecessors in storage densities and cost per unit of stored data.

Figure 3.7 illustrates data storage on a memory chip. These chips contain grids or arrays of miniaturized transistors and capacitors, which may be either OFF, signifying no charge (a value of 0); or ON, or charged (a value of 1). Individual cells are addressed using a column and row addressing system. Two electrically conducting lines link the cells both vertically and horizontally. To read the state of a cell, both the column and row lines are used.

Since memory locations are accessed instantaneously through the intersecting address lines, any memory location may be accessed in the same amount of time. This form of data access is called *random access* and it characterizes most memory chips discussed in this section. In contrast, the term *direct access* is applied to secondary storage, for example, hard disks, where record access time is near-uniform for all locations. As shown in Figure 3.8, each address line may be referenced by a binary number. This gives each storage location a unique memory address, which is derived by combining the two column and row line addresses.

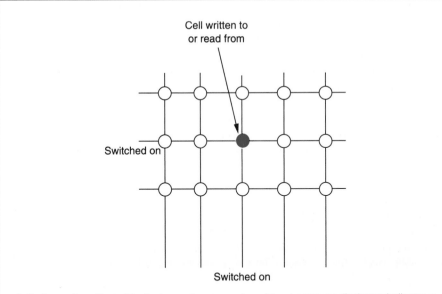

Cell written to
or read from

Switched on

Switched on

A discharge from the cell indicates a charge or value of 1, whereas no discharge indicates a value of 0. Cells may be written to by charging them using intersecting lines, giving them a value of 1, or discharging them—giving them a value of 0.

FIGURE 3.7   Organization of random access memory

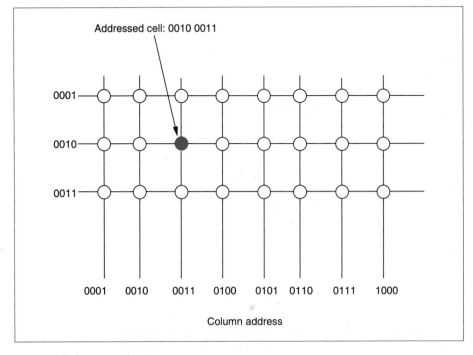

Addressed cell: 0010 0011

0001

0010

0011

0001   0010   0011   0100   0101   0110   0111   1000

Column address

FIGURE 3.8   Addressing random access memory

The smallest unit of data stored in semiconductor memory is a bit, and common capacities of memory chips range from 256 Kilobits to 16 Megabits (1 Kilobit = 1024 bits; 1 Megabit = 1024^2 bits). As the density of components in microprocessors has increased, the same phenomenon has occurred with memory chips, with capacities doubling every three or four years, even while the cost per bit of storage has fallen sharply.

The amount of memory each microprocessor can access depends on its addressing capability, determined by the width of the microprocessor's address bus. For example, a hypothetical computer with an 8-bit address bus can address memory locations in the range 00000000 to 11111111, given that each line carries a 0 or 1 electronic signal. This produces 2^8 or 256 distinct storage locations, each capable of storing one byte of data. XT-class and AT-class microcomputers have address buses 20 bits and 24 bits wide each and can address a maximum of 1 Megabyte (2^{20} locations) and 16 Megabytes (2^{24} locations) of data respectively.

For 386DX, 486, and the successor to the 486, Pentium-based machines, with 32-bit address buses, their addressing capability is 2^{32} distinct storage locations, or 4 Gigabytes (1 Gigabyte = 1024 Megabytes) of data. The exception among 386-class machines are those based on the 80386SX chip, which uses a 24-bit address bus (see Section 3.3).

The two major types of internal memory, *read-only memory (ROM)* and *random-access memory (RAM)* each allow random access storage and retrieval of data but differ with respect to the permanence of data stored.

Read-Only Memory

Read-only memory, or **ROM,** is semiconductor memory that is *nonvolatile.* This means that it retains stored data even when the computer is switched off (that is, in the absence of electrical current). ROM-based instructions are permanently written to the chip during manufacture and this permanence lends itself to certain applications. They are used most extensively for storing the programs needed when the computer is switched on or "booted." The program code includes start-up instructions and the *basic input-output system* (known as the *BIOS*), which forms an interface between the user's programs and microcomputer devices. Programs stored in ROM are called *firmware* (as opposed to software and hardware). When the computer is booted, a signal is generated that causes the processor to set its instruction register to the first firmware instruction, the location of the start-up instructions and BIOS.

Several variants of ROM have been developed. *Programmable ROM (PROM),* for example, allows data to be written to the chip after manufacture, following which, it behaves like ROM, or is permanent in nature. *Erasable programmable ROM (EPROM)* is another ROM variant that can be erased repeatedly using ultraviolet light and reprogrammed. Between rewrites, it has the properties of ROM. Finally, *electrically erasable programmable ROM (EEPROM)* is ROM that can be electrically erased by applying a higher voltage than is used for normal memory read/writes. Following a subsequent rewrite, it assumes ROM's properties. EPROM and EEPROM are used when firmware must be changed frequently, such as in hardware systems under development.

Random Access Memory

Random access memory or **RAM** is used to temporarily store programs and data being processed. This form of memory is volatile, meaning that it loses the charge (signifying data values) stored in its cells when electrical current is removed. It is used to temporarily store data or programs while they are executed by the microprocessor. Data in RAM is located by the processor using the address bus, and fetched over the data bus. The four major types of RAM are *Dynamic RAM (DRAM), Static RAM (SRAM), Video RAM (VRAM),* and *Flash RAM.*

Dynamic RAM (DRAM). **DRAM** is used for the bulk of immediate access storage requirements on microcomputers and requires constant electrical refreshing to maintain stored charges in its cells. Otherwise, the charge would slowly leak, and the data would be lost. Data can only be accessed between refresh cycles, making DRAM slower than other memory types that have no need for refreshing.

The amount of a microcomputer's DRAM is one of its central features and a major determinant of its capabilities. Large amounts of DRAM enable more program instructions and data to be stored in primary memory, enabling quick access by the processor. Insufficient DRAM forces the remainder of the programs and data to be stored on slower secondary storage devices (for example, fixed disks), where they are accessed in a piecemeal fashion (see the discussion of virtual memory in Section 6.2).

IBM-compatibles use a memory architecture based on operating system and processor characteristics (see Box 3.2), comprising *conventional, high, expanded,* and *extended memory.*

DRAM is linked to the processor by the **CPU (or local) bus,** which provides faster data transfers than the standard data bus. One reason for the higher speed of the CPU bus is that the processor and the DRAM are more closely matched speedwise than the CPU and external devices, for example, floppy and fixed disks. While DRAM access times and processor instruction cycles are in the order of *nanoseconds* (billionths of a second), the fastest fixed disks have access times in *milliseconds* (thousandths of a second), and typically do not require a high-speed data pathway.

DRAM chips range in capacity from 32 and 64 Kilobits in early chips to 1, 4, 8, and 16 Megabit capacities of current chips. Access times have also fallen from 150 nanoseconds (ns) to about 60 ns in an effort to keep up with the demands of faster processors. Nevertheless, even the fastest DRAM chips have failed to keep pace (Table 3.1), as processing speeds have climbed from 0.5 **millions of instructions per second** or **MIPS** (XT-class machines), through 2 MIPS (AT-class machines), to 100 MIPs and beyond in Pentium-based microcomputers.

For example, consider a microcomputer with a 1 MIP rating, for example, an 8088-based XT operating at 10 Mhz. Suppose it requires on average one data operation (fetch or store) every instruction cycle. Such a microcomputer would be satisfied by a memory subsystem with a memory access time of 180ns. The 180ns access time would mean that roughly 5.56 million data items could be accessed every second—greater than the 1 million required (5.56 million* 180 ns = 1 second). We might also consider another, more powerful 80386DX, 33 Mhz microcomputer, operating at approximately 12 MIPs. Given the same assumption of 1 memory access per instruction, 12 million memory accesses (fetch or store operations) are required every second. However, using

BOX 3.2

USING MEMORY ON IBM-COMPATIBLES: CONVENTIONAL, HIGH, EXPANDED, AND EXTENDED MEMORY

On IBM-compatibles, the amount of memory available to run the user's programs is determined by the amount of physical memory available, the operating system, and the processor. 80386-based machines for example, can address up to 4 Gb of memory, but were once limited by MS-DOS to 1 Mb. MS-DOS allocates available memory into the following components:

- Conventional memory, which ranges from 0 to 640 K and is used primarily for user programs.
- High memory, which ranges from 640 K to 1 Mb, which is used to map ROMs, video, keyboards, and disk buffers.

Older MS-DOS versions could not run programs above 640 K in size or run several programs in memory concurrently (switching rapidly between each one). Now, however, MS-DOS and other programs enable these microcomputers to use memory above the artificial 1 Mb limit, officially designated as expanded or extended memory.

Extended memory is the better memory model, and it involves using the memory directly above the 1 Mb limit (Figure 3.9). Most programs cannot directly use this memory without a major rewrite to enable them to address it. Extended memory managers, however, from Microsoft (HIMEM.SYS) and Quarterdeck (Desqview 386), among others, can be used to enable programs to run unmodified in extended memory to the limits supported by the processor (for example, 4 Gb on true 386s and above).

Expanded memory is a less preferred method for using additional memory. Expanded memory managers use a 64 K "page frame" in high memory to access memory outside DOS's 1 Mb limit. Program chunks of 16 K are swapped into this page frame as needed, managed by the expanded memory manager. This makes expanded memory slower than extended. This form of memory initially had to be purchased on special add-in expansion boards conforming to the Lotus/Intel/Microsoft expanded memory specification (LIM EMS) version 3.2 or 4.0. Today, expanded memory can be emulated in extended memory using a special program, such as Microsoft's EMM386 program or Quarterdeck's Desqview 386.

100 ns DRAM chips would provide only 10 million possible memory accesses each second, 2 million short of the processor's requirements.

To prevent instructions from being executed without the data they require, "wait states" are inserted by the processor. A wait state involves skipping one clock cycle and this occurs repeatedly until the data arrives in the processor. To prevent excessive wait states from degrading the microcomputer's overall performance, fast SRAM is used as a buffer, or more accurately, a **cache**, to hold frequently accessed data. (See Box 3.3.)

Static RAM (SRAM). **SRAM** is a form of RAM that stores data using sets of two-state electronic devices called *flip-flops*. Unlike DRAM, SRAM does not require constant electrical refreshing to maintain its contents. Once data is stored in SRAM, it remains there until overwritten. Turning off electrical current entirely also results in a loss of SRAM's contents. The processor does not have to wait for access opportunities

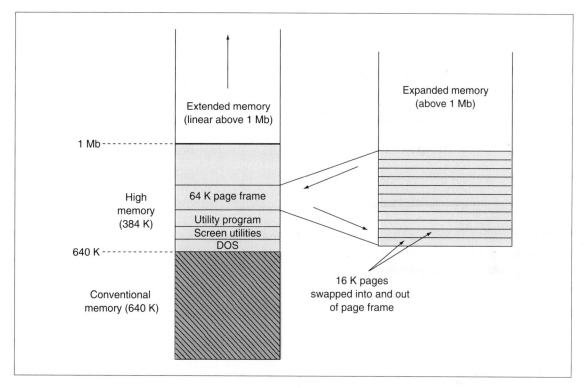

FIGURE 3.9   Expanded and extended memory on IBM-compatible microcomputers

TABLE 3.1   Matching processor speeds to speed of memory access

Processor Speed (MIPs)	Minimum Memory Access Time Required to Avoid Wait States*
1	1,000 ns
5	200 ns
10	100 ns†
20	50 ns†
40	25 ns†

*assuming one read/write operation per machine instruction
†memory caching recommended

between refresh cycles as with DRAM. Due to this architecture, memory access is usually faster for SRAM than for DRAM—in the 20–35 ns range. SRAM is characterized by lower densities and more complex circuitry than DRAM and is considerably more expensive than DRAM. It is used primarily for RAM caching (see Box 3.3), as a buffer between the CPU and DRAM, to reduce the number of wait states.

BOX 3.3

MEMORY AND DISK CACHING

It is tempting, but misleading, to view the microprocessor as the only determinant of the system's performance. Bottlenecks between the CPU and RAM and between RAM and disks can hamstring the performance of a system with a fast processor, such as a 486-based machine. The speed disparities between these devices have led to the use of **caches,** buffer areas used to compensate for these speed differences. Caching works by reading more data than required from a storage device (for example, disk) and storing it in a reserved area on a faster device (for example, DRAM). Subsequent requests for data are made first to the DRAM cache before the slower device, saving time if the data are found. Hit rates (that is, the percentage of times required data are found in the cache) are typically above 90 percent.

RAM caches, which buffer the processor and DRAM, are incorporated into the 486 and the newer Pentium processor (it is 8 K on the 486 and 16 K on the Pentium.) If the data is found in cache, up to 80 ns of access time is saved. RAM caches also use separate SRAM chips, with faster access

times than DRAM. They are suitable for CPU-intensive work, where instructions and data must be fed rapidly to the processor for processing.

Disk caches, on the other hand, can be software- or hardware-based. They buffer slow disks and DRAM and prefetch data in close proximity to the fetched data item. **Software caching programs** use an area of the microcomputer's DRAM for caching, while **hardware caching controllers** on expansion cards have their own RAM (often SRAM for speed). Improvements due to caching are significant between disk and DRAM, with a cache hit making the difference between 80ns access time (DRAM) and 11 ms access time (on a fast hard disk).

Even with local and EISA buses, caching is necessary for practically all microcomputer systems, to compensate for the imbalances between microcomputer subsystems. *MSDOS* and *Windows* incorporate disk caching programs, as do utility programs, such as *PC Tools* and *PC-Kwik.* Though firms make much of their proprietary caching algorithms, comparative performances are generally similar.

Video RAM (VRAM). **VRAM** is used to store monitor-bound display images. It is faster than DRAM due to its ability to support read operations (for screen refresh) and write operations (for storing new images) *simultaneously.* This *dual-ported* capability gives VRAM its high speed but results in a higher price tag.

Flash RAM. **Flash RAM** is a new type of RAM used primarily in notebook microcomputers. It is sold in the form of solid-state memory cards. Flash RAM is nonvolatile memory that is comparable to EEPROMs and EPROMs in handheld and laptop microcomputers (see Chapter 5) and offers significant speed benefits compared to hard disks.

In early microcomputers, memory chips were hardwired or soldered to the main system board. In present-day systems, however, **single inline memory modules** or **SIMMs** enable even end users to easily upgrade the microcomputer's memory capabilities. A SIMM consists of several memory chips mounted on a small board that is inserted into specially constructed slots on the system's motherboard, as shown in Figure 3.10.

Peripheral Devices

Peripheral devices are devices connected to, and controlled by, the processor. They represent a means of communication with the world outside the processor. They are either internal peripherals within the microcomputer's casing, or external, self-contained units connected to the motherboard. Examples include floppy, fixed, and optical disks; printers; monitors; and keyboards. They fall into input, output, or storage categories. Some devices, such as modems (devices used to transmit data between computers over telephone lines), perform both input and output functions, while mass storage devices such as disks and tapes are used for input, output, and storage purposes. Peripherals are connected to the microprocessor through the data bus, along which data are transferred to and from the CPU and memory subsystems. The speed of data transfer along the data bus, as indicated, is affected by whether ISA, EISA or local buses are used. **Expansion slots** enable peripherals to be connected to the system bus using an expansion card, as shown in Figure 3.10, while specialized ports (for example, for the keyboard, monitor, or printer) are an alternative method for connecting peripherals.

Data from peripheral devices are transferred into RAM to be accessed by the microprocessor. In contrast to the electronic nature of instruction execution by the processor and of memory access, most peripheral devices are *electromechanical* in

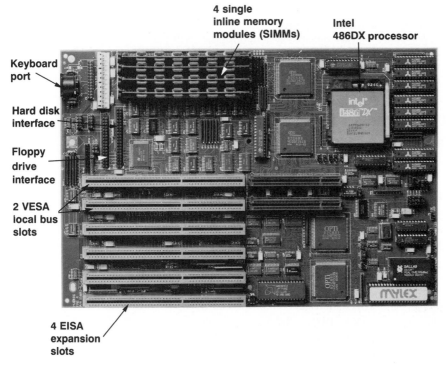

FIGURE 3.10   The layout of a typical microcomputer motherboard, showing
             memory chips installed in Single Inline Memory Modules
             (SIMMs).

nature (with moving parts) and thus process data much slower. These speed imbalances lead to bottlenecks, with fast CPU and memory waiting for slower printers, keyboards, and disks, and so on. Overcoming these bottlenecks involves the use of various RAM buffers and caches. Peripheral devices are discussed more fully in Chapter 4.

Computer Facilities

Unlike minicomputers and mainframes, which are usually housed in isolated locations within the firm, microcomputers are integrated into both the workplace and the home. As discussed earlier in Chapter 1, the environmental regulation required for larger machines is unnecessary for most microcomputers. In fact, the alternative term *desktop computer* suggests the common location of the microcomputer, namely, on the desktop.

While microcomputer facility requirements are modest compared to those of larger computers, they are essential for successful implementation. The primary concern in integrating microcomputer hardware into the workplace relates to *ergonomics,* an area covering user health and comfort during use of the system. Other concerns include effective and efficient organization of computer work groups, in particular, wiring and other physical issues involved in using local area networks (LANs).

Physical security of hardware is an additional concern for end-user managers. Important issues include securing smaller and more portable microcomputer-based computers and peripherals, the need for preventive and nonpreventive maintenance, and a greater risk of unauthorized access to physically dispersed system components. Additionally, microcomputer systems must be electrically protected from "spikes," surges, brownouts, and blackouts. Knowledgeable system designers will pay attention to these concerns. These issues are covered in more detail under system implementation in Chapters 12 and 13.

3.2   MICROCOMPUTER AND WORKSTATION ARCHITECTURES AND FEATURES

In the preceding section, various components of the microcomputer were discussed. This section continues the discussion by examining how these components are assembled to form a working hardware subsystem. In addition, benchmarks are discussed as a means of comparing the performance of different computer systems.

Detailed Microcomputer Architecture

Assembling microcomputers and workstations and bringing these systems to the market is usually done by *value added retailers (VARs).* The microcomputer is most often sold as a *system unit,* containing the processor, supporting chips, and devices. Also part of this package are peripherals such as the keyboard and monitor, as shown in Figure 3.11. Occasionally, as with the Apple Macintosh Classic II, the IBM PS/1, and the SPARCStation ELC workstation, the system unit is integrated with the monitor. With *laptop* and *notebook* computers (see Figure 3.12), all three primary components, that is, the system unit, monitor, keyboard, and sometimes a mouse are integrated.

FIGURE 3.11   The ALR, IBM, and Compaq systems are shown here representing the standard user package—system unit, monitor, and keyboard.

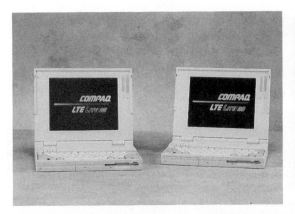

FIGURE 3.12 Portable units, such as the system on the left, have been eclipsed by smaller notebook microcomputers (on the right) with even greater capabilities.

The most important component of the microcomputer is the **system board** (also called the **motherboard**), on which the processor, memory chips, support chips, and buses reside. (See Figure 3.13). Many of these chips and circuits are hardwired or soldered onto the system board. However, many newer machines utilize easy-to-remove *surface mounted chips,* which make chip replacement easier.

The motherboard also plays host to other devices. The **math coprocessor,** or **floating-point unit (FPU),** is a logic chip designed to efficiently execute complex mathematical operations. These operations include floating-point (decimal) additions, power and square root functions, and interest calculations. Microprocessors perform operations like addition and subtraction easily enough, but more complex operations may be delegated to the coprocessor.

Applications that benefit most from math coprocessors include spreadsheets and statistical packages, which require floating-point computations, and CPU-intensive graphic and font-generation tasks. Math coprocessors produce performance gains ranging from a few percent to over 400 percent with computation-intensive applications. Microprocessors such as Intel's Pentium and Motorola's 68040 chips have integrated the coprocessor within the microprocessor to yield even better system performance.

Another important device is a **graphics coprocessor,** which performs functions analogous to those of the math coprocessor. It is used for the computations required for generating fonts and graphics. Functions such as line and curve generation, object fills, and resizing fonts benefit from use of a specialized graphics coprocessor. These functions are present in such applications as presentation and desktop publishing packages and drawing programs. Graphics cards, which fit into expansion slots, provide graphics processors on expansion boards, together with additional video RAM for premium graphics performance.

The **microcomputer system bus** is also found on the system board, and it serves to connect the processor to expansion slots and I/O ports. Typical expansion cards feature LAN interfaces, additional memory, hard disks, and even processors. *Processor cards,* for example, contain a microprocessor and represent a convenient way to upgrade the system's CPU.

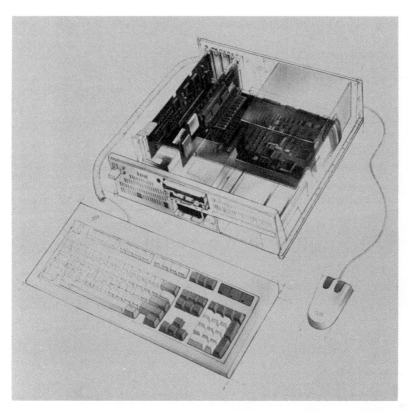

FIGURE 3.13 A microcomputer system board, showing how it is situated within the system unit and connected to internal and external peripherals.

Floppy, fixed, optical, and tape drives may be integrated within the system unit. While controller electronics for these devices are frequently incorporated on the system board, expansion slots enable the addition of disk controller cards for expanding the existing configuration (see Chapter 4).

The microcomputer's **power supply** is usually housed in the system unit and provides power to the system board, keyboard, and devices within the system unit (for example, fixed and floppy disk drives). Frequently, the monitor draws power from the system unit's power supply.

Finally, standardized **input/output (I/O) interfaces** are provided on the system board, to enable connection to a wide range of input and output devices (see Figure 3.14). Serial and parallel ports, for example, facilitate the connection of the microcomputer to printers, external disks, and computer networks. Other ports provide interfaces for pointing devices (for example, mice and light pens), the keyboard, numeric keypads and microphones, and so on.

From the preceding discussion, it is evident that microcomputers may be configured in a variety of ways. There are many possible combinations of microprocessors, coprocessors, and buses; DRAM and secondary storage; ports; and power supplies.

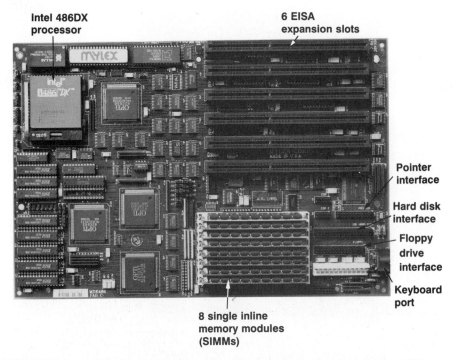

Intel 486DX processor

6 EISA expansion slots

Pointer interface

Hard disk interface

Floppy drive interface

Keyboard port

8 single inline memory modules (SIMMs)

FIGURE 3.14   Another system board, with interfaces for the mouse, disk drives, keyboard, and expansion slots *(Continued)*

Some manufacturers, for example, Advanced Logic Research (ALR) and Radius provide processors and memory in easily replaceable modules or expansion cards, which may be inserted in expansion slots, as shown in Figure 3.15. While this makes it easier to upgrade obsolete or defective components, selecting an appropriate microcomputer still requires careful planning. Some approaches to microcomputer selection, together with cases and examples, are described in Section 3.5.

Parallel Processing

Using less expensive additional microprocessors in parallel architectures is becoming a more attractive proposition than doubling a single chip's performance. **Parallel processing** offers a considerable increase in system performance for a modest additional investment. It involves the use of multiple processors within a computer, and though well established in the mainframe realm, parallel processing is relatively new to microcomputers and offers the greatest promise of supercomputer-type performance on the desktop.

Parallel processing uses multiple processors to execute different parts of a single program. This architecture excludes microcomputers with independent CPUs in a single casing (that is, separate processors, DRAM, and buses), each serving a single user. Systems using *timesharing*—processing several programs concurrently—are also excluded. Third, *auxiliary processors,* such as graphics and math

FIGURE 3.15   Microcomputers can be upgraded using expansion cards with newer processors, some of which are shown above.

coprocessors that coexist with the main processor, are not true examples of parallel processing.

The development of parallel processing architectures has accelerated because of the physical limits of microprocessor miniaturization. These limits include the difficulty of constructing circuits of increasingly smaller sizes and heat dissipation problems involved in running processors at ever faster clock speeds.

The two major parallel architectures are shared-memory and distributed-memory systems, as shown in Figure 3.16. In the *shared-memory system,* processors share a common memory (DRAM) and use various methods to prevent contention for access to memory. The fact that user programs can run without modification on such systems using an appropriate operating system such as SCO Unix has been a major reason for this architecture's popularity. In a *distributed-memory system,* processors possess independent memory areas and communicate via messages. The difficulty of

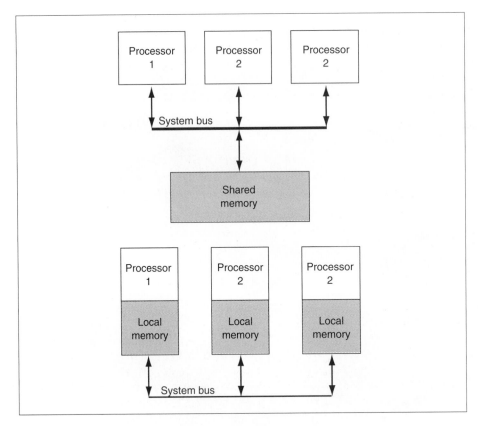

FIGURE 3.16   Shared and distributed memory parallel architectures

interconnections and the overhead this communication adds to processing are two drawbacks of this type of parallel architecture.

Benchmarking Microcomputers

As microcomputers become more powerful through the use of RISC and parallel processing, an important subject for both original equipment manufacturers (OEMs) and VARs is that of **benchmarks.** A benchmark is simply a measure of component or system performance and is more meaningful in the context of historical or contemporary systems. Benchmarks are also important to VARs, who purchase system components, and to retail consumers buying complete systems. A benchmark or performance measure differs from a *feature,* which is a characteristic of the system or component (for example, 4 Mb of RAM).

A common microprocessor benchmark discussed earlier is **MIPS** (**m**illions of **i**nstructions **p**er **s**econd). It indicates how many machine code instructions can be executed by the microprocessor in one second. It can often be a misleading or inaccurate figure because different machine code instructions require different numbers of clock cycles (1–4 typically) for execution. Using an unrealistic mix of mostly one-clock cycle instructions may give a false representation of the processor's comparative performance against other processors benchmarked using a different mix of instructions. Additionally, the MIPs rating gives an idea of processor and not system performance. Complete benchmarks for a microcomputer system will include tests for CPU, I/O, graphics, and overall system performance.

Several relatively neutral benchmarks exist for measuring microcomputer performance. Two of these are the *Whetstones* and *Dhrystones* benchmarks, which measure numerical and nonnumerical CPU performance. Other tests focus on system I/O capabilities. Also, many microcomputer publications (for example, *Byte Magazine, InfoWorld, MacWorld*) utilize custom benchmark tests for measuring CPU, I/O, and overall system performance. Many involve the use of commercially available software, such as word processing, database, and spreadsheet packages, to measure the performance of realistic tasks.*

3.3 PROCESSOR PLATFORMS FOR MICROCOMPUTERS

Earlier in this chapter, we discussed the various components and special features of microcomputers and workstations. It is equally important to be aware of the specific microcomputer and workstation platforms that dominate the present desktop environment, as well as representative standards. Whereas over 400 VARs and OEMs supply more than 50 million microcomputers used in the U.S. workplace, only a small number of microprocessor platforms is utilized. *IBM-compatible* microcomputers represent by far the majority of these, with $50 billion worth of machines sold in the United States in 1991—over 80 percent of all hardware bought. Apple *Macintosh* computers have achieved a smaller market share, at about 12 percent. *Workstations,* another fast-growing market segment, generated over $4 billion of sales in 1991. These three major markets and the main features that characterize them are discussed next.

80x86-Based Microcomputers

Microcomputers based on Intel's 80x86 (and compatible) microprocessors ushered the microcomputer into the U.S. workplace. Responding to the challenge posed by Apple's microcomputers, IBM rapidly developed a microcomputer to counter Apple's penetration of the corporate market. This crash project resulted in the *IBM Personal Computer* (or *IBM PC*), launched in 1981. The IBM-PC was based on Intel Corporation's **8088** microprocessor. A then-young software company, Microsoft, was awarded the contract for the machine's OS. This OS was acquired from a third firm and became **Microsoft disk operating system** or **MS-DOS.** In addition, it was packaged with a **BASIC interpreter.** The **IBM PC,** as it was called, and later the **IBM XT,** ran at 4.77 Mhz and was rated at 0.33 MIPs. The 8088 chip was followed by the 8086, with a wider 16-bit data bus (see Table 3.2). However, the 8086 retained the 8088's 16-bit

---

* Intel's iComp benchmark, which measures total system performance, is used in Table 3.3.

TABLE 3.2   Intel processors and technical features

Processor Name	Year Introduced	Data Bus (bits)	Address Bus (bits)	Data Word Length (bits)	Typical Clock Speeds (Mhz)	Addressing Capability
8086	1974	8	20	16	4.77	1 megabyte
8088	1978	8	20	16	4.77	1 megabyte
80286	1982	16	24	16	12, 16	16 megabytes
80386SX	1988	16	24	32	16, 20, 25	16 megabytes
80386DX (& 8038SL)	1985	32	32	32	16, 20, 25, 33, 40	4 gigabytes
80486SX	1991	32	32	32	20	4 gigabytes
80486DX (& 80486SL)	1989	32	32	32	25, 33, 50	4 gigabytes
80486DX2	1992	32	32	32	50, 66	4 gigabytes
Pentium	1993	64	32	32	60, 66	4 gigabytes

internal data bus and word size. They both addressed one megabyte of DRAM and were used with the 8087 math coprocessor.

An evolutionary step in IBM's microcomputer strategy came in 1984 with the launch of the **IBM AT.** This later became a major standard in the PC industry. The IBM AT was based on Intel's 80286 (the 286) microprocessor, which again had a 16-bit data bus and word size. Unlike the 20-bit address buses of the 8088 and 8086, however, the AT had a 24-bit address bus, enabling it to address up to 16 Megabytes of RAM. Additionally, the 286 was a more powerful processor, delivering 1.2 MIPs at 8 Mhz and able to use an optional math coprocessor, the 80287. The other important development in the AT era was the emergence of clone manufacturers, who produced microcomputers based on the AT architecture.

Prominent clone manufacturers included companies like Compaq, AST, and Dell. Fierce competition succeeded in reducing IBM's market share first to 27 percent by 1985, and then to 12 percent in 1993. In 1986, Intel introduced the **80386DX** (the 386DX) microprocessor. Incorporating 275,000 transistors, the 386DX was initially rated at 6 MIPs (operating at 16 Mhz), and introduced the possibility of powerful LAN servers and even multiuser processing, as shown in Table 3.3, using microcomputers based on the new processors. Other features of the 386DX microprocessor include a 32-bit word length, address bus, and CPU bus. This enables 4-byte data transfers through the data bus, 32-bit internal processing, and an immense addressing capability of 4 Gigabytes. Faster clock speeds have stretched the 386DX's capabilities to above 11 MIPs. The external data bus for most 386DXs remains the 16-bit **ISA** bus.

The trend toward increasingly powerful processors seemingly reversed in 1988, with the introduction of Intel's **80386SX.** This was an 80386DX internally, except for a 24-bit address bus, similar to the 286. This enabled the 386SX chip to be used with the 286's

TABLE 3.3   Intel processors—capabilities and uses

Processor Name	Clock Speed (Mhz)	MIPS	Intel's iComp Index*	Organizational Uses
80286	12 16	2.66	—	Entry-level desktop computing, cheap network node, portable computing
80386SX	20 25	2.50 4.20	32 39	Entry-level desktop computing, cheap network node
80386DX (and 80386SLC)	25 33	8.50 11.40	49 (SLC: 41) 68	Desktop computing, small network server (SLC version is used in notebooks)
AM386†	40	13.80	—	Advanced desktop computing, small-medium network server
80486SX	20 25 33	16.50 20.00 27.00	78 100 136	
80486DX (and 80486SLC)	25 33 50	20.0 27.00 40.70	122 166 249	Medium-large network server, computation-intensive tasks (SLC version used in notebooks)
80486DX2	50 66	34.00 45.00	231 297	Medium-large network server, computation-intensive tasks
Pentium	66	114.00	520	Large network server, computation-intensive tasks

*Intel's iComp Index is based on a weighted average of integer, floating point, graphics, and video benchmarks.
†Advanced micro devices (AMD) 32-bit 386-equivalent processor

address and data buses (that is, in AT boxes), and substituted for the 80286, resulting in less expensive 386-based microcomputers and peripherals. It limited addressing to 16 Megabytes (see Table 3.2) but required less complex support circuitry and provided slower processing than true 386DX-based machines. As software has grown larger and more sophisticated, the 386DX, clocked at 33 Mhz and above (with optional 80387 math coprocessor), is now viewed by many as the minimum entry-level machine for current applications.

IBM introduced the proprietary *micro channel architecture (MCA)* system bus on their PS/2 line of microcomputers in 1987, followed by the now more popular 32-bit *EISA* bus architecture from a consortium led by Compaq. Due to backward compatibility with the ISA bus (unlike MCA), the EISA standard has rapidly gained more adherents than MCA (see Box 3.1).

Intel's **80486DX** microprocessor, introduced in 1989, advanced personal computing another notch. Possessing several RISC features such as pipelining, on-chip cache, and math coprocessor, plus a high transistor count of 1.2 million transistors, the i486DX provided processing power on a par with many workstations. Delivering 20 MIPs in the 25 Mhz version, the i486DX created greater opportunities for microcomputer use in transaction processing, network configurations, multimedia, and multiuser applications. Tables 3.2 and 3.3 illustrate the vast jump in processing power represented by the 32-bit 386, 486, and Pentium processors.

The early 1990s saw the first challenge to Intel's dominance of the PC-compatible market. New 386- and 486-compatible processor chips developed by *Advanced Microcomputer Devices Inc. (AMD)* and *Cyrix* have made inroads into the Intel/MS-DOS–based microcomputer marketplace. One Intel response was the **486SX,** an 80486DX with a disabled math coprocessor, directed at a lower price point than the full-fledged i486DX chip. Subsequently, Intel's "clock-doubled" 486DX2 processors were introduced. They are essentially 25 Mhz and 33 MHz versions of the 486DX processors running at doubled speeds internally (50 Mhz and 66 Mhz), while communicating with the rest of the system at the slower speeds.

Intel chose the copyrightable "Pentium" name instead of noncopyrightable 80586 for their successor to the 80486 microprocessor. Released in 1993, the Pentium rivals the processing power of workstations but is backward-compatible with the 80486. There are 60 and 66 Mhz versions, with the 66 Mhz version generating 114 MIPs. The intent is for Pentium-based machines to support new, powerful OSs and to serve in traditional workstation roles, for example, as servers for large LANs or as CAD/CAM workstations.

The first *portable computer* accepted in the business environment was introduced by Compaq in 1982. Since then, portable computing has come a long way. Smaller *laptops* (Figure 3.17) were introduced by IBM and other manufacturers in the mid to late 1980s. These were battery or mains-powered, with monochrome displays. Newer

FIGURE 3.17   A fully configured laptop computer such as this one possesses significant computing power but could be heavy (often weighing more than 8 pounds).

systems include *notebook computers* (Figure 3.18), measuring roughly 8″ by 11″. Some of these feature color displays and new microprocessors such as the power-conserving 386SLC and 486SLC. These processors use 3.3 volts versus the 5 volts used by other microprocessors and have power-conserving and sleep modes. Lastly, recent *slate computers* (see Chapter 4) feature pen-based user interaction.

In an unprecedented move, *IBM* and *Apple* have teamed up to plan for the next generation of microcomputers, based on Intel's 80x86 and Motorola's 680x0 processor lines. A rival consortium, called the *Advanced Computing Environment (ACE),* including Microsoft and other key players, plans to use both the Intel processors and MIPS R3000 and R4000 RISC processors for future systems. Whichever strategy prevails, future microcomputer platforms will offer new opportunities for developing more powerful and flexible distributed systems. The Intel 80x86/MS-DOS platform seems set to continue market domination in the near future. Newer OSs and more powerful chips from both Intel and its competitors will enable the transition to the microcomputer-centered information systems discussed in Chapter 1.

Motorola 680x0-Based Microcomputers

Motorola has traditionally represented a powerful source of competition to Intel's dominance of the microprocessor marketplace. Using the Motorola 680x0 microprocessors line, firms such as Apple have sought to provide alternatives to PC-compatible microcomputers for corporate, educational, and personal markets. Apple's first computer was the *Apple II,* which used the 8-bit 6502 processor, but it was the *Apple Macintosh,* introduced in 1984, that established Apple's current microcomputer strategy. The original Apple Macintosh was based on Motorola's 68000 processor, which had 68,000 transistors and ran at 8 Mhz. It also had a 32-bit chip word length, and 16-bit and 24-bit data and address buses, respectively.

Later advances from Motorola led to the *68020,* then *68030,* and most recently, the *68040* microprocessors (see Table 3.4). All these processors are full 32-bit chips, with 32-bit CPU, data, and address buses. The *Mac Classic II*, the entry-level Macintosh,

FIGURE 3.18   Current notebook computers use smaller components (for example, disks) to fit in an 8″ x 11″ format; they usually weigh less than 7 pounds.

TABLE 3.4 **Some Apple microcomputers and their specifications**

Features	Classic II	Color Classic	LC II	LC III	IIvi	IIvx
Processor	68030	68030	68030	68030	68030	68030
Processor speed	16 Mhz	16 Mhz	16 Mhz	25 Mhz	16 Mhz	32 Mhz
Memory	2–10 Mb	2–10 Mb	2–10 Mb	4–36 Mb	4–20 Mb	4–68 Mb
Configuration	Integrated	Integrated/color	Modular	Modular	Modular	Modular
Operating systems	Mac OS	Mac OS	Mac OS, A/UX	Mac OS, A/UX	Mac OS, A/UX	Mac OS, A/UX
I/O devices included	SCSI, audio, mouse, AppleTalk	SCSI, audio, mouse, AppleTalk	SCSI, audio, mouse, AppleTalk	SCSI, audio, mouse, AppleTalk	SCSI, CD-ROM audio, mouse, AppleTalk	SCSI, CD-ROM audio, mouse, AppleTalk

Features	Centris 610	Centris 650	Quadra 800	Quadra 950	Powerbook 165c	Powerbook 180
Processor	68040	68040	68040	68040	68030	68030
Processor speed	20 Mhz	25 Mhz	33 Mhz	33 Mhz	33 Mhz	33 Mhz
Memory	4–68 Mb	4–132 Mb	4–20 Mb	4–68 Mb	4–14 Mb	4–14 Mb
Configuration	Modular	Modular	Modular	Tower	Notebook	Notebook
Operating systems	Mac OS	Mac OS	Mac OS, A/UX	Mac OS, A/UX	Mac OS, A/UX	Mac OS, A/UX
I/O devices included	SCSI, audio, mouse, AppleTalk	SCSI, audio, mouse, AppleTalk	SCSI, audio, mouse, Ethernet	SCSI, audio, mouse, Ethernet	SCSI, audio, color mouse, Ethernet	SCSI, audio, FPU mouse, Ethernet

uses the more powerful 68030 processor, and runs at roughly 6 MIPs (Figure 3.19). The *Color Classic, Macintosh II, IIsi, IIci, LCIII, Powerbook portables,* and *IIfx* models also use the 68030, each running at different clock speeds (also see Table 3.4). The 68030 is therefore the de facto entry-level Macintosh processor.

Motorola's 68040 processor is a contemporary of Intel's 486DX chip and is used to power Apple's top-end machines, the *Quadra 800* and *Quadra 950*. The 68040 possesses an on-chip cache, memory management functions, and math coprocessor capabilities, similar to the i486DX. Operating at over 20 MIPs, Apple's Quadras possess enough power to serve as hosts of multiuser systems, as database and file servers, and for computationally intensive scientific and engineering tasks. Excluding the Classic II,

FIGURE 3.19   The Macintosh Classic II and the Color Classic, with their integrated system unit and monitor, are the entry-level Macintoshes.

Color Classic, and Powerbook systems, the current line of Macintosh systems comes in the same two-piece system unit/monitor configuration that is featured in IBM-compatible systems. See Figure 3.20.

NeXT microcomputers were launched in 1988 by NeXT Microcomputer Inc., headed by an Apple Computer co-founder, Steven Jobs. In 1993, the microcomputer arm of the business was sold to Canon Inc. NeXT microcomputers are based on Motorola's 680x0 processors and the first model used a 25 Mhz version of the 68030 chip. A later model, the NeXT station, as shown in Figure 3.21, uses a fast 68040 chip. This enables it to post performance ratings at par with some workstations. Similar to Macintosh microcomputers, NeXT systems are known for their graphical user interface. They also use the Unix operating system, discussed in Chapter 5.

Workstations

High-end Macintoshes, NeXTstations, and 486- and Pentium-based microcomputers have for the first time brought microcomputers into direct competition with workstations. The traditional dividing line between the capabilities of both classes of computers has become blurred in the 1990s, as new and more powerful generations of processors have emerged on both sides. While microcomputers based on the 680x0 and 80x86 processors are *CISC* machines, with top-end models incorporating features such as pipelining and caching, workstations have almost all been developed using *RISC* technology.

Apollo dominated the early workstation market, but their product line was later acquired by Hewlett-Packard. By 1990, Sun Microsystems, Hewlett-Packard, and Digital Equipment Corporation were the major players in the workstation market, with Sun being the market leader selling the **SPARCStation** line (as shown in Figure 3.22) (32.4 percent of the market in 1990). Like other workstations, the SPARCStation uses the Unix operating system, plus the Open Look GUI operating system shell (see Chapter

FIGURE 3.20   More powerful desktop Macintosh units come in both the separate system unit and the tower configurations common to PC-compatibles. The Powerbook note-book computer (*bottom left*) also features the top-end 68040 processor.

6). The SPARCStation IPC, for example, uses a 25 Mhz Sparc chip with a custom system bus called the S-bus. Sun has been successful in establishing a workstation standard, as evidenced by a later generation of Sparc-compatible machines from *Solbourne, Opus, CompuAdd,* and others.

Workstations such as the SPARCStation are typically used for CPU-intensive and graphics-based tasks, such as real-time modeling of solids, CAD, CAM, and artificial intelligence applications. They have superior graphics capabilities, in addi-tion to sheer number-crunching ability. As CISC processors catch up with RISCs, workstation manufacturers have responded by directing their sales efforts not only to scientific and engineering areas but also to mainstream business customers. New GUIs and DOS-compatibility have complemented developments in architecture. To the degree that workstations remain successful in making a transition to the business environment while retaining an edge in engineering/scientific markets, they will continue to experience the rapid growth rates incurred in past years (for example 21.5 percent in 1990).

FIGURE 3.21   NeXTStations made a memorable entrance into the microcomputer market with their striking, all-black design and
acclaimed graphical user interface.

FIGURE 3.22   Sun's SparcStations are the most widely used workstations, featuring powerful
RISC processors and high-end graphics capabilities.

3.4 CHANGING CAPABILITIES AND _____ ROLES OF SMALLER COMPUTERS _____

Large-scale computers, particularly minicomputers and mainframes, represent very large capital investments. They require large facilities, environmental regulation, and maintenance by skilled personnel. Their cost usually places them beyond the reach of many small companies. However, the technological advances resulting in advanced microcomputers now enable microcomputer-based information systems to perform many functions previously reserved for large-scale systems. Features like memory caching, direct memory access (DMA) by devices independent of the CPU, parallel processing, and floating-point coprocessors, once found only on mainframes, are now commonplace on microcomputers.

A New Role for Microcomputers

Distributed processing and _client/server processing_ models have enabled micro-computer-based subsystems to be linked together in powerful networks. These networks have enough collective processing power to satisfy the processing requirements of increasingly larger companies. Nevertheless, these advancements do not sound an automatic death knell for the mainframe. In many instances, they will continue to be used and tied into networks of heterogeneous computers (including microcomputers, minicomputers, and workstations). It means though, that mainframes are no longer an automatic part of information systems in medium- to large-sized firms. Instead, their functions may be partly or entirely replaced by networks of microprocessor-based machines.

At the Turner construction company, for example, a centralized mainframe and 24 regional minicomputers were used to satisfy information requirements of 2,800 employees working on construction projects all over the country. Delays in response time and waiting lines for terminals were only two problems with the overloaded mainframe. To improve system flexibility and user access to data, Turner began an eight-year transformation to move from a mainframe-minicomputer architecture to a 100 percent microcomputer solution. Now, the larger machines have been dis-carded and 2,000 networked IBM-compatibles and microcomputer-based servers are used to provide improved service and the benefits of distributed processing to users. Turner also estimates that their hardware maintenance costs have been reduced by 50 percent.

Integration with Microcomputers

In other cases, firms own mainframes that have not yet been fully depreciated. For them, _downsizing_ to solely microcomputer-based networks may not be the best option. Some applications may also require more processing power than smaller systems can provide. In these circumstances, many firms have integrated their mainframes and minicomputers in networks with smaller computers. The role of the larger machine is then usually changed from supplying processing power for multiple users to providing storage for vast amounts of data, that is, as database servers.

The Illinois Department of Commerce, for example, recently moved its application development to microcomputers while retaining its mainframes for the purpose of running mission-critical applications. This move reduced the costs of application development by 67 percent and saw the $0.5 million investment in LAN technology paid for in fourteen months. Often, integration of multiple platforms is made possible by the introduction of cross-platform software tools, such as the OS/2 COBOL compilers that enabled the developers to code mainframe-intended applications in this case.

3.5 MATCHING REQUIREMENTS TO ALTERNATIVES—KEY DECISION CRITERIA

There are many choices available to the microcomputer purchaser today. Alternative microcomputer solutions to user requirements may number in the tens, or even hundreds. However, while many systems might fulfill user requirements, some may be more *cost effective, efficient,* or *relevant* than others. Consequently, we must understand how microcomputer systems can be tailored to fit user requirements and what the relevant decision criteria are for their selection. System selection is what it implies, namely, the selection of a set of complementary parts, including hardware, software, people, procedures, and data. Moreover, selecting any individual component, for example, hardware, cannot be done independently of others. As we focus on hardware selection in this chapter, our initial discussion must include the conditions or constraints under which hardware selection is made.

Constraint-Driven Hardware Selection

Hardware selection is almost always constraint driven. The first major constraint is *software.* Software is of first importance as it embodies the functions and processes desired by the user. If it neither exists nor can be developed on a particular hardware platform, the hardware's capabilities are irrelevant. Identification of the most appropriate software to fulfill requirements must therefore precede hardware selection. Following software identification, appropriate hardware may then be selected. Three types of software, namely *operating systems, programming languages,* and *applications,* are discussed in Chapter 5.

Interestingly enough, *hardware* constraints may also affect the acquisition of hardware in certain circumstances. For example, an organization with a large installed base of IBM-compatibles would need to justify purchasing different machines, for example, Macintoshes, to perform functions within the capabilities of the existing machines. Relevant issues include compatibility or interoperability between old and new hardware resources, simpler maintenance arrangements from fewer suppliers, and familiarity of in-house technicians or users with specific hardware.

A third area of constraints is *financial.* Hardware is seldom evaluated solely on its capabilities. Its cost is also important, particularly when finances are limited. Financial constraints will eliminate some systems from consideration regardless of their capabilities, and affordable systems will differ in their cost effectiveness.

PC Compatibility

Microcomputers based on the Intel 80x86/MS-DOS platform are the largest category of hardware, with over 80 percent of the microcomputer market. The term *PC-compatible* denotes microcomputers that conform to this standard. PC compatibility is important because of *software availability, price,* and *standards.* Market dominance by this hardware platform has resulted in the largest selection of software for any platform. Additionally, fierce competition by hundreds of OEMs and VARs has made this platform the least expensive for the hardware capabilities acquired. Many of the hardware and software standards in the microprocessor industry are also closely associated with this platform.

The ability to purchase hardware with the largest available software base, the best price and performance, and the majority of popular standards is important in the minds of microcomputer purchasers. These factors have led suppliers of other hardware platforms to incorporate PC compatibility into their systems. This is accomplished by *software* or *hardware emulation.* **Software emulation** uses software that mimics the 80x86's functions to higher layers of operating system software and programs. Calls for 80x86 functions are intercepted by this software and translated into appropriate instructions for the native processor, to provide the desired functions. Using this additional layer, PC-based software may therefore be processed, but the two-stage process is inefficient, limiting powerful processors to only a fraction of their true power when operating in nonnative mode. Apple Macintoshes, for example, can process DOS-based software through software emulation, using software such as Insignia Solutions' *Soft-PC*—an Intel 80x86/MS-DOS software emulator (Figure 3.23).

Hardware emulation, on the other hand, involves the use of an actual Intel 80x86 or compatible processor within the non-PC machine. This is usually done using an add-in board, which is inserted into an available expansion slot. This processor is then used to execute the required DOS-based programs directly. Several manufacturers produce add-in processor cards to supply PC compatibility for Apple Macintosh and other microcomputers.

Vendor Selection

Vendor selection affects the implementation and maintenance of a microcomputer-based information system. Microcomputer vendors provide varying levels of service and support, so it is important for the hardware buyer to be well informed about both the system manufacturer and retailer from whom the system is purchased. Some important vendor characteristics are

- How long the vendor has been in business, and the vendor's financial stability. There have been many examples of bankrupted manufacturers resulting in impossible-to-enforce support and guarantees. Prospective buyers must be convinced of the vendor's long-term viability.
- Guarantees and service agreements. Most vendors offer 30-day money-back (minus shipping costs) guarantees. The standard one-year parts and labor warranty is routinely extended by many vendors to 15 and even 24 months. Other vendors offer on-site repair of malfunctioning microcomputers, overnight delivery of replacement parts, and toll-free technical support.

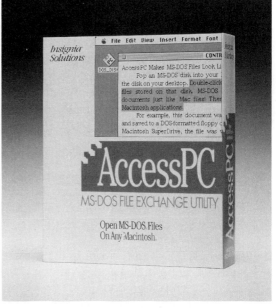

FIGURE 3.23   **Insignia's Soft-PC programs provide Macintosh microcomputers with the ability to run MS-DOS and Windows programs through software emulation and to read MS-DOS-formatted files.**

- The quality of systems. Methods of verification include reading product reviews in trade magazines, and where possible, obtaining recommendations from product users. Furthermore, agreement can often be reached with vendors to supply a system or systems for testing by a firm planning multiple purchases of the product.

Processor Selection

Following requirements analysis of the type discussed in Chapter 12, the system user decides on the appropriate level of processing power needed to satisfy existing and future requirements. A primary determinant of processing power is the microcomputer's processor, as discussed earlier. When purchasing a PC-compatible (or processor card for hardware emulation), the major decision is the choice of the processor. Table 3.3 provides a description of organizational uses of the Intel family of processors. Processors developed prior to the 386 are generally regarded as outdated and underpowered for current applications. The 286 processor is used today only in some laptops. Systems (and microprocessors) can be divided into three groups: entry-level, mid-level, and high-end systems.

1. ***Entry-level systems.*** For noncomputationally intensive work (for example, word processing), the ability to handle GUIs such as Windows, and multimedia capability, requires a minimum of a 386DX-based machine operating at 33 Mhz or above. In the Motorola lineup, the 68030 (at 16 Mhz) has become the entry-level processor.
2. ***Medium-capability systems.*** When user requirements include more resource-hungry applications, additional processor power is required. Examples of such applications include extensive use of GUIs and newer operating systems such as OS/2. Also,

---

BOX 3.4

BUYING DURING A SHAKEOUT: SMART TIPS FOR SAVVY SHOPPERS

1. Check the Better Business Bureau in the vendor's city as well as the state Consumer Affairs Department to determine if complaints have been filed against the company.
2. Ask colleagues and business associates if they've done business with the company.
3. Get written confirmation from the vendor about pricing, warranty, and return policy.
4. Verify availability of merchandise and ship dates.
5. Don't pay cash. Use a credit card.
6. When your equipment arrives, make sure the configuration and components are what you ordered.

7. If the equipment is defective, keep a written diary of its problems and the steps you've taken to correct them (including phone calls to the vendor and return ship dates).
8. Before you return defective equipment, get a return merchandise authorization from the vendor.
9. Sign a service contract with a third-party service provider.

Excerpted from "Buying During a Shakeout: Smart Tips for Savvy Shoppers," Jeff Bertolucci, *PC World*, June 1993, page 56.

applications like graphics, CAD, and spreadsheets may need more processing power than entry-level systems can provide. Medium-capability processors include Intel's 486DX (at 33 Mhz and above), and Motorola's 68030, running at 25 Mhz and faster.

3. ***High-end systems.*** For applications requiring the most power, even the medium-range processors are insufficient. Examples of such applications include complex CAD tasks, engineering and scientific simulations, and file and database server capabilities. These capabilities are best satisfied by 486-based microcomputers (with graphics coprocessors) running at 50 MHz and above, Pentium-based systems, 68040 systems, or workstations (for example, Sun SparcStations).

The selected hardware should fulfill both existing and expected requirements. Methods for estimating future hardware requirements are discussed in Chapter 12. As mentioned earlier, system performance is not solely dependent on hardware, but the prospective purchaser of a microcomputer-based system must also consider different subsystem options (for example, memory, storage, and peripherals) when configuring their overall system.

Subsystem Configuration

Further decisions must be made regarding the configuration of the microcomputer's subsystems. These include the type and amount of system memory and the choice of system buses. The first concern is to ensure that the memory subsystem is an appropriate match for the processor, as we saw earlier. For higher-end systems, it may be necessary to purchase faster DRAM chips (at about 70ns) and SRAM caches of up to 512 Kb, to complement on-chip caches. Otherwise, overall system throughput will be degraded by a mismatch of the processor and memory subsystem. Even for entry-level and medium-capability systems using 80–100 ns DRAM, modest caches (64 K and up) provide significant boosts in overall performance.

With the advent of 8- and 16-Megabit SIMMS, it is possible to configure 32-bit systems with 32, 64, or even 128 Mb of RAM. Memory requirements are determined by the software applications used with the system. Entry-level systems require 2–4 Mb of RAM, to effectively run new GUIs and basic applications such as word processing. Medium-capability systems, on the other hand, are usually fitted with 4–8 Mb of DRAM to cope with larger applications, datasets, and multitasking requirements. High-end systems often come equipped with 8–32 Mb of DRAM, to handle database and file server tasks requiring buffers and large programs; multiuser environments, in which the microcomputer is host to a network of dumb terminals; CAD/CAM; and modeling, all of which require considerable memory. Memory management for PC-compatible computers under MS-DOS is discussed in Chapter 5.

For PC-compatibles, the choice of the system bus is also important. From 386-based machines upward, the ISA bus is standard and provides a 16-bit path for data transfers between the processor and peripherals. On 386-, 486-, and Pentium-based systems, the EISA, MCA, and local bus alternatives provide a wider 32-bit pathway for even faster data transfers. The wider data pathway and higher speeds of new bus architectures are especially important for database servers that are required to provide high throughput.

Peripherals are the final part of the system configuration requiring discussion. They include keyboards, video display units, printers, and secondary storage and must be carefully studied to complete the final system configuration. These peripherals are discussed in the following chapters.

Networking Considerations

Microcomputers are either nodes in a network or servers whose processing capabilities are generally superior to those of stand-alone systems. As we move toward microcomputer-based networks, microcomputers must increasingly be network ready, necessitating additional hardware, such as cabling, expansion cards for LAN nodes, and LAN software. Also, network managers can purchase *diskless nodes,* in which no secondary storage is provided on the node. This helps to enforce security and integrity and lowers system maintenance costs. Networking hardware considerations are discussed in Chapter 8.

CHAPTER SUMMARY

Microprocessors represent the heart of today's microcomputers and workstations. They are fabricated using semiconductors (typically silicon), on which millions of circuits may be etched. The microprocessor chip is a complex solid-state device containing a control unit, an arithmetic and logic unit (ALU), and registers, which operate together to process program instructions.

Memory chips are also semiconductor based. They store programs and data being processed using random access memory (RAM). They also store start-up commands for the microcomputer, using read-only memory (ROM). Other important features of the microcomputer are buses, which carry data, addressing information, and control signals between the microcomputer's components; disk and RAM caches, for speeding up throughput within the microcomputer; and the word size, speed, and power of the microprocessor.

Two microprocessor architectures are complex instruction set computing (CISC) and reduced instruction set computing (RISC) architectures, the latter of which is used primarily in workstations. Other features, such as virtual memory and parallel processing, enable multiple users' requirements to be satisfied cost effectively. As a system buyer compares systems with various features, the dangers of misleading performance benchmarks must also be understood.

The predominant microcomputer platform is the IBM-compatible class of micro-computers, based on Intel's 80x86 processors. Others, like the Apple Macintosh and the Canon's NeXTstation, are built around Motorola's 680x0 processor family. Worksta-tions such as Sun's SPARCStation utilize their own proprietary designs.

As microcomputer capabilities have increased, so have the capabilities of larger computers, that is, minicomputers, mainframes, and supercomputers. However, microcomputers have become the major processing resource used to satisfy transaction processing needs in many contexts. They may also be interconnected to existing larger machines in networks.

In selecting a microcomputer system, hardware, software, financial, and other constraints limit available alternatives. Microcomputers are evaluated based on the processor's features (for example, speed, instruction set, power), the system's cost and features (for example, buses and peripherals), networking considerations, and vendor characteristics. By systematically evaluating potential systems based on these criteria, system buyers may select systems with a high degree of confidence that the system will match their requirements.

REVIEW QUESTIONS

1. What is a dual inline package (DIP)?
2. List two functions of the control unit within the microprocessor.
3. Which two classes of operations does the ALU perform?
4. What processor component determines the speed of the processor's operations?
5. What is a microprocessor's word size, and how does 32-bit processing differ from 16-bit?
6. What is the significance of "downward compatibility" among microprocessor families?
7. Why does the CPU bus operate at a faster speed than the external system bus?
8. Why are memory chips described as being "random access" in nature?
9. List three types of RAM.
10. For 386DX and 486 processors with 32-bit address buses, what are their addressing limits?
11. What is the main use of ROM?
12. List five microcomputer peripherals.
13. Describe three applications that will benefit from a math coprocessor.
14. What is the main difference between CISC and RISC processors?
15. What is the purpose of virtual memory and how is it used?
16. What are Whetstones and Dhrystones?
17. How does the 386SX processor differ from the 386DX processor?
18. Which processor family is used in the Apple Macintosh line of micro-computers?

EXERCISES

1. Suppose you have decided to purchase a microcomputer to automate your record-keeping in your small business. What would be the disadvantages of a 386SX-based machine? Would you recommend purchasing a Pentium-based micro-computer? Why or why not?
2. Describe the functions of a cache. Compare critically the functions and operation of disk and RAM caches. Which type is more suited to disk-intensive applications?
3. What are the three types of constraints that limit the choices of hardware? How might any of these limit the choices of a retailer who seeks to upgrade from an IBM-AT microcomputer?

4. Discuss how entry-level microcomputers have evolved over the past ten years. What are the major changes that have occurred in system performance and features?

5. Suppose you are considering the purchase of a 386 microcomputer that operates at 12 million instructions per second (MIPs). Assuming every two instructions require one memory access on average, and RAM access time is 80 nanoseconds (ns), how many wait states occur during processing? If the system's RAM is upgraded to 60 ns, how many wait states now occur? Would you recommend the use of a RAM cache?

6. What are EISA and MCA? How do they improve the performance of microcomputers based on ISA? What advantages does EISA have over MCA?

Suggested Readings

Carpenter, S. "The NeXTstation: A High-Performance Graphical Workstation with a PC Price Tag." *Byte Magazine,* June 1991, pp. 297–299.

Depke, D. A., and Brandt, R. "PCs: What the Future Holds." *BusinessWeek,* August 12, 1991, pp. 58–64.

Hsu, J. "Inside the CPU." *PC Today,* January 1992, pp. 55–58.

Intel. *A Report on Understanding Personal Performance Measurement.* 1992.

Marshall, T. "Fast Transit." *Byte Magazine,* October 1992, pp. 122–136.

Microbytes Section. "80486, 68040 Open New Season of CPU Power." *Byte Magazine,* June 1989, pp. 13–14.

Morris, M. D. "RISC vs. CISC." *PC Today,* May 1991, pp. 35–39.

Myslewski, R. "Shopping for the Right Mac." *MacUser,* March 1992, pp. 128–156.

Resnick, R., and Taylor, G. "What's Happening with NeXt?" *PC Today,* September 1991, pp. 33–36.

Ryan, B. "Built for Speed." *Byte Magazine,* February 1992, pp. 122–135.

Supplement to *PC Week,* November 11, 1991, Vol. 8, No. 45.

Vaughn-Nichols, S. J. "What to Stash in a Cache." *Byte Magazine,* March 1992, pp. 175–181.

Whang, M., and Kua, J. "Join the EISA Revolution." *Byte Magazine,* May 1990, pp. 241–247.

Yager, T. "Five New SPARC-based Workstations Compete with Sun." *Byte Magazine,* July 1991, pp. 210–214.

CHAPTER 4

INPUT AND OUTPUT DEVICES

INTRODUCTION

Microcomputer architectures were described in Chapter 3. However, computers are useless without a means of communication with their users. Microcomputer **peripherals** are hardware devices, connected to and controlled by the microprocessor, which enable user/computer interaction. There are many types of *input* and *output* peripherals designed to satisfy different user requirements. These devices are discussed in this chapter, and storage devices are featured in Chapter 5. Also discussed is how peripheral devices are matched to user requirements and to specific processor platforms.

Learning Objectives

After reading this chapter, you will be able to:

- Describe how input and output devices are used in microcomputer systems
- Propose the use of keyboard and nonkeyboard-based input devices in different contexts
- Select the most cost-effective display options for a user's applications
- Understand available printer technologies and select from among them in single-user and workgroup settings

---

K-MART'S CLIENT SERVER SYSTEM: TECHNOLOGICAL RENOVATION AT A RETAIL GIANT

Ninety percent of the population of the United States lives within five miles of a K-Mart Store. In the mid-1980s however, powerful competitors like Wal-Mart emerged to challenge the retail giant with new stores. K-Mart was forced to respond in 1990 by improving its store format and overhauling its archaic information systems architecture. This architecture was based on an IBM Series 1 minicomputer.

K-Mart's new UNIX-based client/server architecture includes a multiprocessor server in each store connected by a token ring LAN to Intel-compatible microcomputers. The applications were ported to the UNIX-based Informix fourth-generation language (4GL) and relational DBMS. Fifty thousand scanners were also installed between 1987 and 1990 as part of a point-of-sale automation system. Hand-held computers are used to transmit scanned data from the retail floor to the Informix database on the store's server. Data from the store servers is then routinely transmitted via satellite to headquarters, where it is used for reports and inventory replenishment. The old minicomputer was replaced by a Teradata system, which uses 300 486-based processors.

The new information systems architecture allows K-Mart buyers to access up-to-date data on merchandise availability. Also, employees have up-to-the-minute data about prices, inventory, and expected product shipments, all without having to leave the retail floor. The new client/server architecturehas provided K-Mart with a powerful weapon to compete more effectively with its competitors.

Adapted from Alice LaPlante, ''K-Mart's Client/Server Special,'' *DBMS*, December, 1992, pp. 55–58.

4.1   AN OVERVIEW OF INPUT DEVICES _____

An information system transforms input data into relevant information outputs for its users. In a computer-based system specifically, inputs must be in computer-readable form. These inputs are collected through input devices and may or may not be human-readable.

Data entry using the **keyboard** is the most widely used input method. The keyboard's use is continually supplemented by other forms of input, including *mice, pens, scanners, bar-code readers, touch screens, cameras,* and *voice recognition hardware*. These devices enable **direct-entry** data input.

Input may not always be keyboard based or by direct entry but can involve data transferal from secondary storage media such as magnetic tape or disks. Data input from these devices is known as **secondary data entry** of previously stored data. The three means of input, keyboard-based, direct-entry, and secondary data entry, are illustrated in Table 4.1.

The evolution of data communications has also introduced data transfer devices that are classified as both input and output (I/O) devices. They include *facsimile* (or *fax*) *machines* and *modulator-demodulators*—otherwise called *modems*. These devices

TABLE 4.1   Methods of data entry

Input Methods	Examples
Keyboard Input (Dumb or intelligent terminals)	84-key keyboard 101-key enhanced keyboard Kinesis keyboard
Direct entry	Mice Light-pens Styli Scanners (bitmaps, MICR, OCR) Bar-code readers Touch screens Cameras Voice recognition systems
Secondary data entry	Floppy/fixed disks Magnetic tape

perform data transfers over telephone lines, and while they are technically I/O devices, a detailed discussion is reserved for Chapters 9 and 10, which focus on data communications.

In Chapter 3, we learned that the speed of instruction execution by the processor is measured in millions of instructions per second (MIPs). Also, several million memory accesses can be made to RAM each second. However, input devices operate at much slower speeds. For example, a fast typist may type at a rate of 60 words per minute, or approximately five characters a second. Similar rates are also typical for other direct-entry devices. Even in the case of data entry from secondary storage media, a fixed disk may provide only about 100 disk accesses every second while operating at peak performance. The result of this speed disparity between the processor/memory subsystem and the input/output (I/O) subsystem is that the former is not used efficiently. In effect, the processor may be idle for most of the time, waiting for data from slow input devices or waiting to transmit data to slow output devices.

This problem is handled using various types of buffers. *Buffers* are temporary data storage locations used to compensate for the speed differences between devices. Some buffers, like the front-end processor (or FEP) discussed in Appendix B, collect data from slow channels (devices) and transmit aggregated data along a fast channel to the processor. Memory caches buffer the fast CPU and slower DRAM by precollecting data for future use. Others, like printer buffers, free the CPU to process other tasks. Their use is widespread among the input and output devices we will be discussing.

Keyboard Input

The **keyboard** is a standard component of a computer system, along with the system unit, monitor, and secondary storage devices. The basis for its layout is the typewriter,

FIGURE 4.1   Variations of the standard 101-key keyboard (on the left) include the ergonomic Kenesis keyboard, designed to reduce stress on the typist's wrists and fingers.

plus some additional keys. The majority of microcomputer users use the keyboard as their primary input device. Although a variety of keyboard designs have been developed, the *QWERTY* layout is the most widely used (shown in Figure 4.1). Interestingly, the QWERTY layout was introduced to accommodate fast touch typists using mechanical typewriters, who often jammed frequently used adjacent keys on earlier keyboard designs. One of the increasingly popular variations of the traditional QWERTY format, the ergonomic Kinesis keyboard, is shown in Figure 4.1, right.

Microcomputer keyboards are connected to a special interface device on the system motherboard, called the *keyboard port*. When a key on the keyboard is depressed, it completes an electrical circuit which in turn generates and transmits a unique binary code to the system unit. The code may be an *ASCII* (American Standard Code for Information Interchange) code, or a less frequently used code on microcomputers, *EBCDIC* (Extended Binary Coded Decimal Interchange Code). Keys may be pressed singly or in combination to generate different ASCII or EBCDIC codes. There are five different groups of keys.

1. *Alphanumeric keys.* These represent alphabetic (A, . . , Z, a, . . , z), numeric (0, . . , 9), and special (for example, @, #, $, &, !) characters. Some of these characters cannot be generated by depressing just one key but only in combination with *special-purpose keys* (see below).
2. *Function keys.* Function keys (for example, F1 to F12) are used by software applications for specific tasks, therefore their use is dependent on the application. A common convention is to use the F1 key to activate the application's *Help* function.
3. *The numeric keypad.* The numeric keypad was introduced into the microcomputer's configuration with the advent of the IBM PC. The numeric keypad is distinct from the main alphanumeric and function keys and it therefore allows dedicated and rapid data entry. Independent numeric keypads attached to the microcomputer's serial port may also be used with laptop and notebook computers.
4. *Cursor control keys.* The blinking cursor represents the position on the screen where data entered through the keyboard will be displayed. It is commonly represented as

TABLE 4.2   Table of keyboard characters

Key Groups	Subgroups	Functions
Alphanumeric keys	Upper-case (A . . . Z) Lower-case (a . . . z) Special characters (@, &, #, !)	Document/file creation
Function keys	F1 to F12	Used within applications to activate specific functions
Numeric keys	0 . . . 9	Used to enter numeric data
Cursor control keys	→, ←, ↑, ↓	Used to select program menu options or to move the cursor
Special-purpose keys	Enter/Return	Enter a line of input
	Shift	To type upper-case characters
	Control	To produce special codes in conjunction with other keys
	Alternate	
	Numeric Lock	To get the numeric keypad in numeric values
	Tab	Used for indentation purposes in various programs
	Delete/Backspace	To erase typed characters

a *flashing rectangle* or *underscore.* There are usually four cursor keys on the keyboard, recognized by four arrows at right angles to each other. They are used to move the cursor in four directions—up, down, left, and right.

5. **Special-purpose keys.** These are keys used for a variety of purposes. *Shift, Alternate, Control,* and *Caps Lock* keys are used in combination with other keys for upper-case character generation and to produce new key codes. *Tab* and *Delete* keys are used for spacing and delete operations. Table 4.2 describes key functions in greater detail.

Mouse-Driven Input

The **mouse** (Figure 4.2a) is the second most common input device for microcomputers. It is a pointing and selection device that is connected to the system's motherboard, usually through a serial port. It was invented by Doug Englebart at Xerox Corporation's Palo Alto Research Center (PARC) as a complementary input device for keyboard-shy executives. However, it has become a standard device for working with GUIs used on contemporary microcomputers and workstations. Mice are also used for drawing and painting functions in CAD and other applications.

The mouse is a small handheld device with one to three buttons on its top, containing a small ball partly exposed on the underside of the mouse. Moving the mouse along a flat surface rotates the ball, which in turn, moves *motion sensors* surrounding the ball. Signals representing motion in the horizontal and vertical planes are transmitted to the computer, which moves an on-screen pointer in the direction of the original motion.

(a)

(b)

FIGURE 4.2   Mice, shown in the two top photos, are a standard form of pointing device for data input. The bottom photos show trackballs, which take the place of mice in desktop, but particularly notebook, microcomputers.

When the desired point on the screen is reached, a button is depressed once or twice, to select a menu option, activate an icon, or reposition the cursor.

Some mice are equipped with small rollers instead of a ball, to detect motion. Other cordless mice use infrared transmission to the mouse port, eliminating the need for a direct cable between the mouse and mouse port. Because of the required motion, using a mouse requires a modest amount of desktop space. In many instances, such as cluttered desktops and on airplanes, space is limited. Partially in response to this problem, the **trackball** was developed. The trackball (Figure 4.2b) resembles a stationary, upside-down mouse, with a protruding ball and buttons on its top. As the user rotates the ball in its socket, this motion is detected and the pointer moves across the screen. The trackball's buttons are used to activate a selected option.

Pen-Based Computing

Keyboards enjoy widespread use and are packaged with most microcomputers. However, users have often sought other input alternatives to supplement and even

FIGURE 4.3   A slate computer allows data entry using a pen-shaped stylus.
This unit can also be attached to a keyboard and used as a
standard notebook microcomputer, as shown at left.

replace keyboard input. One such replacement for keyboard input is pen-based input.
Light pens have been used for some years with microcomputers and workstations,
particularly for applications involving menu or field selection, and for drawing. A light
pen emits a narrow beam of light that is detected by special sensors surrounding the
screen. The sensors establish the exact position of the beam of light, and software
interprets these coordinates and forwards them in the proper format to the appropriate
application.

Another form of pen-based computing uses the **stylus.** This device has a magnetized
tip and is used primarily with *slate computers* (Figure 4.3). In slate computers, a
magnetic field is created just below the surface of the microcomputer's screen. The
magnetized stylus tip breaks the magnetic field when it touches or comes close to the
screen, indicating its relative position to the underlying hardware and software. Patterns
(for example, characters and lines) traced by the user are then generated by the computer
and duplicated on the screen. Use of *handwriting recognition software* (see below) and
the appropriate operating system permit the understanding of written commands and
gestures. For example, tapping on a menu option activates it. Popular pen-based systems
utilize GUIs, running on Microsoft Windows or other operating environments (see
Chapter 6). Leading vendors of pen-based operating environments include *Go Corp.,*
with its **Pen Point** operating system, and *Microsoft,* with the **Pen Windows** operating
environment.

Dow Chemicals, the pharmaceutical giant, was an early adopter of pen-based
computing. Prior to using pen computing, sales representatives sent doctors' drug
sample requests by mail, after which the requests were entered at a terminal by a
clerk. Now the sales reps enter sample requests and the doctors' digitized signatures
directly into GridPad slate computers using pen-based data entry and transmit these

data via modem to the mainframe host. Drug samples are now shipped immediately instead of in a week and access to the mainframe provides the sales representatives with inventory status and order-tracking information. Furthermore, the Gridpads allow the representatives to upload their expense reports to the mainframe for faster reimbursement.

Reach Out and Touch: The Touch Screen

A form of input similar to the stylus is the touch screen (Figure 4.4). With this technology, practically any pointing device, including the finger, may be used to point to and activate a desired area (for example, a menu option) on the screen. All touch screens have two primary elements: the *touch-sensitive membrane* (and associated hardware), which overlays the monitor screen, and *controller driver software,* which controls the hardware and generates screen coordinates for application software.

Firms such as Microtouch produce touch screens for use in locations as diverse as the trading floor of the stock exchange, museums, hospitals, and interactive presentations. These applications present an easy and entertaining way for users to access a system's database. One drawback of touch screens, however, is that keeping the arm constantly outstretched can be tiring; another is the fingerprint smudges constantly made on the screen.

Scanners

The use of **scanners** is now widespread as a means of capturing graphics, photographs, and text. The images are primarily captured from documents, but solid objects can also be scanned. Scanners are connected to the computer via special interface cards that fit into expansion slots. They can capture both *black-and-white* and *multicolor* graphics and text. A scanner operates by using a lamp to illuminate the input document. Dark areas of the page (lines and text, and so on) absorb light while lighter areas reflect it. Reflected light is sampled by a *charge-coupled device* (CCD) and the scanned information is passed to the controller card.

The information passed to the controller is a **bitmap** of the scanned page, resulting from dividing the page into a grid of dots. The *resolution* of this bitmap is the detail of the scanned image and is measured in *dots per inch* or *dpi.* Common scanning resolutions are 300 dpi and 400 dpi, although high-end scanners have resolutions of up to 600 dpi and beyond.

There are four major types of scanners:

- **Handheld scanners.** These are slightly larger than mice (Figure 4.5) and are manually guided by the user over the document or object being scanned. They contain both the light source and CCD and are the least expensive and most popular type of scanner.
- **Flatbed scanners.** These scanners resemble a small photocopier, with the CCD and light source attached to a mobile rack under the unit's clear glass top. In operation, the CCD moves in controlled intervals down the length of the page, which is placed face down on the glass. They are easier to use than handheld units and permit the scanning of books or nonstandard documents.

FIGURE 4.4   Touch screens are popular choices for simple, consumer-oriented computer interfaces found in information kiosks and other applications.

- **Overhead scanners.** These look like overhead projectors, with the light source and sampling device overlooking the document, which faces upward.
- **Sheetfed scanners.** This last category of scanners is characterized by a static CCD, but has a feeder that moves the document over the light source and CCD.

The scanned image is stored as a file by *scanning software,* which is often included with the scanner. The stored file may later be input and used by desktop publishing

FIGURE 4.5   Handheld scanners provide a convenient means of inputting graphics and text to microcomputers.

software or drawing and painting programs. Scanners interpret and store scanned images in three formats—halftones, grayscale, and color. In *halftone* images, large dots represent darker areas of the image, while smaller dots approximate lighter areas, as in newspaper photographs. *Grayscale* images have a specific hue of gray assigned to a dot. Each dot may have 2-8 levels of gray, depending on how many bits are used to store information. Two bits signify 4 gray levels (00 to 11), while eight bits represent 256 gray levels. Owing to the number of bits stored and the page resolution, grayscale images consume large amounts of memory.

Color scans also require considerable memory, with 16 bits per pixel used for 65,536-color photographic quality scans. Colored filters or lamps from three primary colors (for example, red, green, and blue) are used to produce a three-channel mix used to generate all colors.

Figure 4.6 shows some different applications for scanners.

Optical Character Recognition (OCR)

The *Datapro Report* indicates that 20 to 30 percent of all scanners sold in 1991 were routinely packaged with **optical character recognition (OCR)** software. OCR involves the use of specialized software to read text contained in scanned images. Scanning is thus an integral component of OCR. OCR is a method for rapidly inputting text from documents without keying them in, and can reduce the costs of manual data entry. An OCR program matches scanned characters from the bitmapped page with a library of text images and produces ASCII characters as output, as shown in Figure 4.7. Thus, while a scanned page of text is merely a bitmapped image, OCR produces a page of ASCII text that may be imported into word processors.

The best OCR hardware/software combinations are about 99 percent accurate for single, typewritten fonts, but faxed text may result in 50 to 80 percent accuracy. At 80 percent accuracy, for example, scanning a 10-page document (400 words/page) would result in an unacceptably high 800 errors. Current OCR software packages incorporate both spelling and grammar checkers to improve the accuracy of text recognition.

Another OCR device used to grade examinations and input questionnaire surveys is the **optical mark reader (OMR).** Employing predefined, standard formats for response sheets, the OMR subjects these sheets to a light source. Selected (shaded-in) answers absorb light, letting less light through than nonselected answers. Measuring light intensities behind or in front of the response sheet enables the OMR to recognize user choices. Using this information and an exam key, an OMR can rapidly record an examination or questionnaire response answer sheet.

Handwriting Recognition

The trend in user interfaces is clearly toward human-oriented forms of interaction. User interfaces based on **handwriting recognition** and voice-based interaction are currently available on microcomputers. Slate microcomputers, in particular, embody *pen-based computing,* in which user input takes place through handwriting. The user's handwriting, created using a stylus on a slate microcomputer, is initially captured as an image bitmap. The handwritten characters are then matched against a library of characters to complete their interpretation as ASCII characters.

AI-based *neural networks* typify current recognition software. These networks are loosely modeled on the brain's physical structure and operation and can be "trained" to correctly match and identify handwritten characters from samples of previously stored patterns (see Figure 4.8). By propagating image features (that is, the handwritten characters) through the network, a trained network matches these characters with the most probable ASCII characters, with accuracy rates often exceeding 95 percent (see Chapter 8 for a fuller discussion of neural networks).

Magnetic Ink Character Recognition (MICR)

In **magnetic ink character recognition (MICR),** magnetized ink is used to print characters and numbers on input documents. An example of this is bank checks, which have data preprinted with magnetic ink on the bottom of the check. This data includes the bank identification code, customer account number, and check number (Figure 4.9). In processing the check, a specialized MICR device passes the document under a magnetic field. By detecting the magnetic pattern, the data is read and input to the computer for processing. Additional data such as the dollar amount of the transaction is encoded during processing.

Camera-Based Input

A more recent form of input is the **digital camera,** which resembles a compact camera but does not use film. Instead, it uses a RAM chip to store digitized images. Logitech's Fotoman, for example (shown in Figure 4.10a), captures and stores black and white

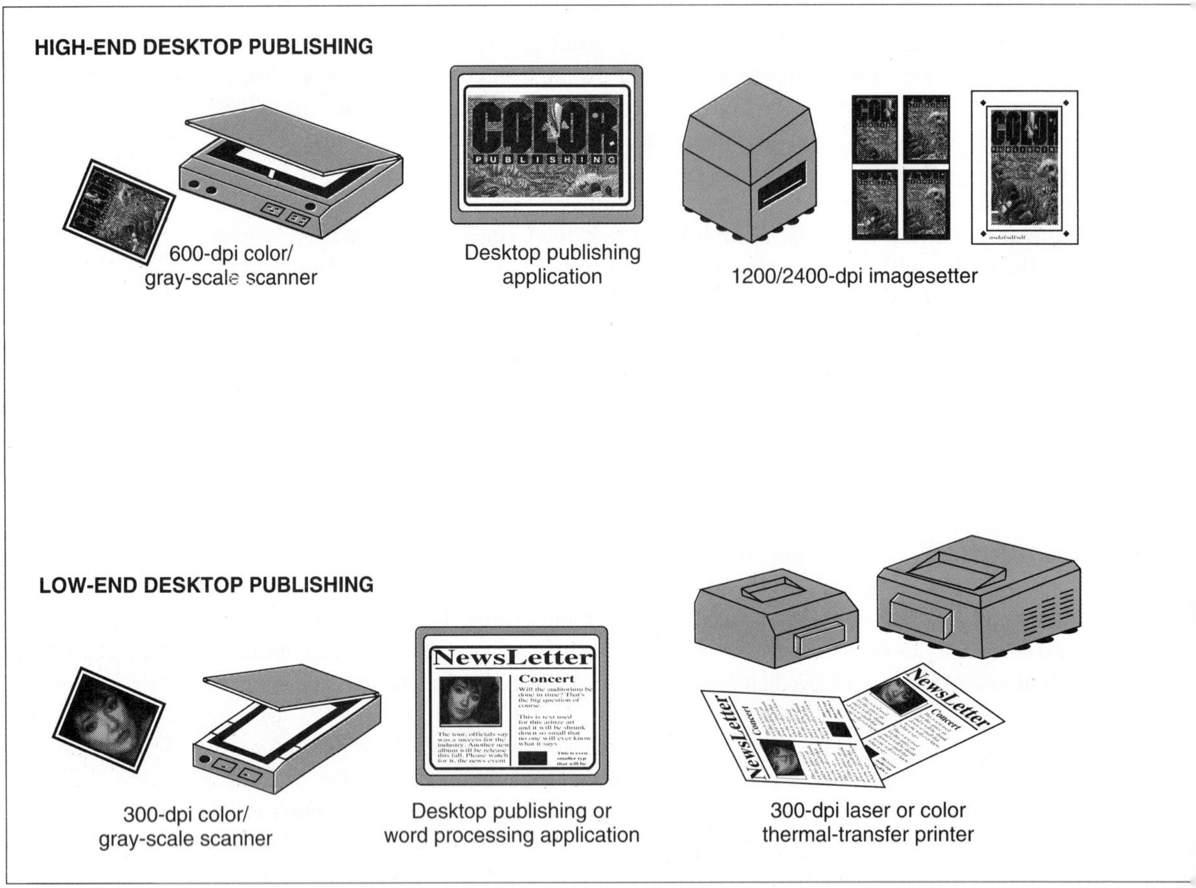

HIGH-END DESKTOP PUBLISHING

600-dpi color/
gray-scale scanner

Desktop publishing
application

1200/2400-dpi imagesetter

LOW-END DESKTOP PUBLISHING

300-dpi color/
gray-scale scanner

Desktop publishing or
word processing application

300-dpi laser or color
thermal-transfer printer

FIGURE 4.6   Different scanners for different applications. Desktop publishing, OCR, and word
processing require different scanning capabilities.

images with up to 256 shades of gray. Images stored in RAM can be downloaded onto
the microcomputer through a serial port and imported into design and desktop
publishing applications in several accepted graphic formats. In these applications,
images may be deleted and modified as the user pleases (see Figure 4.10b). Digital
cameras produce digitized images, similar to scanners, but are used to capture
three-dimensional images (for example, of buildings and people), which cannot be
scanned in a single step by scanners.

Bar-Code Readers

A familiar device in many supermarket and manufacturing environments is the **bar-code
reader.** Bar-code readers (Figure 4.11) are used to input data encoded as *bar codes* in
the form of a *Universal Product Code,* or *UPC.* In supermarkets, for example, grocery

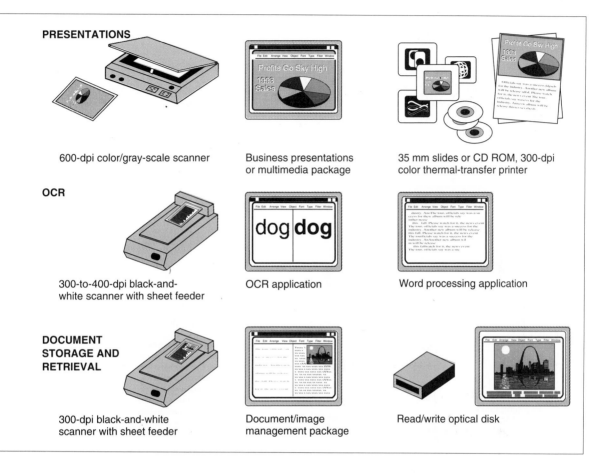

PRESENTATIONS

600-dpi color/gray-scale scanner

Business presentations or multimedia package

35 mm slides or CD ROM, 300-dpi color thermal-transfer printer

OCR

300-to-400-dpi black-and-white scanner with sheet feeder

OCR application

Word processing application

DOCUMENT STORAGE AND RETRIEVAL

300-dpi black-and-white scanner with sheet feeder

Document/image management package

Read/write optical disk

items have bar codes signifying the product type, manufacturer's identification number, and product number. Scanning the code involves directing a low-intensity laser beam or light-emitting diode over the bar code. Dark strips absorb more light than the intervening gaps, and light reflected off strips and gaps is captured. This data is translated into electronic signals for the computer and interpreted as numeric codes.

Handheld and desktop readers are the two major types of bar-code readers. *Handheld readers* are self-contained and small enough to be held in the user's hand, with the light source and detection apparatus residing in the unit. This unit communicates with the computer through an attached cable, or by radio transmission. Private mail carriers like Federal Express and UPS use cordless wands for scanning bar codes on packages in transit to provide up-to-date information about the location of the package. *Desktop readers* are built into supermarket checkout counters and have both the light source and sensors built into the counters. To read the bar code, the packaged product is passed over the whole desktop assembly. See Figure 4.12 for examples of handheld readers.

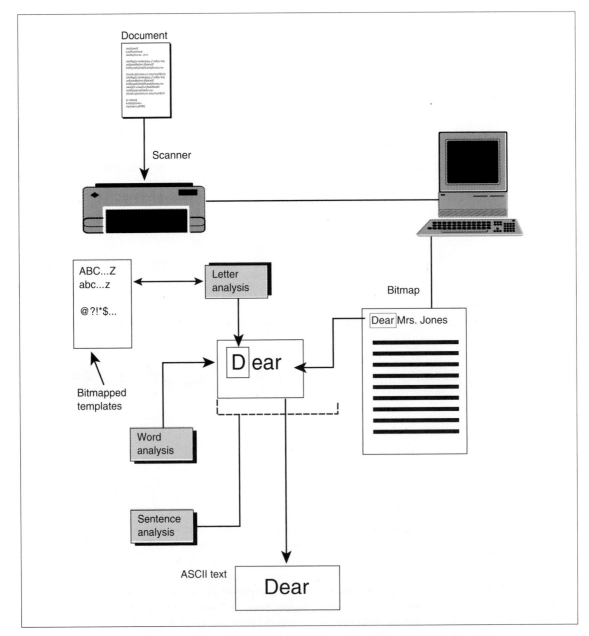

FIGURE 4.7 The optical character recognition (OCR) process translates a bitmapped image into ASCII text using specialized software.

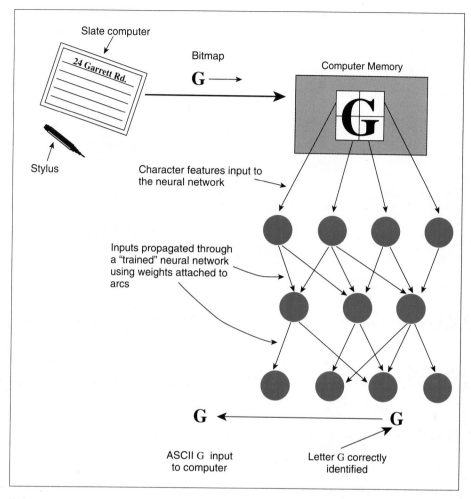

Slate computer

Bitmap

G ⟶

Computer Memory

24 Garrett Rd.

Stylus

Character features input to
the neural network

Inputs propagated through
a "trained" neural network
using weights attached to
arcs

G ⟵   G

ASCII G input
to computer

Letter G correctly
identified

FIGURE 4.8   Using neural networks for handwriting recognition

Touch Tone Input

Many firms use **touch tone** input for consumer interaction with computer applications over telephone lines. Uses include the provision of automated product ordering and other services to the firm's customers. Using a touch tone telephone (Figure 4.13), the customer may check on the status of his or her bank account. Entering a secret code enables the user to access the account balances, and even pay bills, by selecting from a menu of spoken options. The touch tone telephone input pad produces twelve distinct tones (0–9, #, and * keys), which are used to select from a menu of services offered by firms, and to input credit card numbers, dates, and other data. For relatively simple consumer-oriented transactions, it is an effective way to automate consumer interaction with transaction processing systems. Touch tone input, however, is generally unsuitable for large-volume transactions.

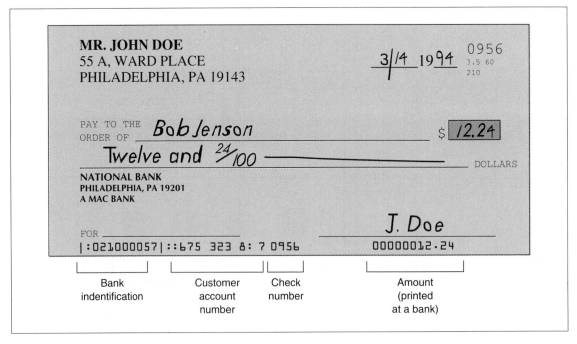

MR. JOHN DOE
55 A, WARD PLACE
PHILADELPHIA, PA 19143

3/14 19 94   0956
3.5 60
210

PAY TO THE
ORDER OF _____ *Bob Jenson* _____ $ 12.24

_____ *Twelve and* 24/100 _____ DOLLARS

NATIONAL BANK
PHILADELPHIA, PA 19201
A MAC BANK

FOR _____   *J. Doe*

|:021000057|::675 323 8: 7 0956   00000012.24

Bank
indentification

Customer
account
number

Check
number

Amount
(printed
at a bank)

FIGURE 4.9   Use of MICR for check processing

FIGURE 4.10   (a) Logitech's digital camera stores images in RAM; these
bitmapped images can later be downloaded to a computer.

(continued)

Voice Recognition

Like handwriting recognition, voice recognition reflects the trend toward more natural user interfaces. **Voice recognition** capabilities enable input of spoken words to the computer and their subsequent translation into text or ASCII symbols. This mode of interaction is significant because of (1) the potential for many new, noncomputer–literate users who will be able to comfortably interact with computers and (2) the increased efficiency of task performance where either the hands or eyes (or both) are engaged, such as typing from source data entry sheets, or using a mouse in computer-aided design (CAD).

In the area of voice recognition, there are two related functions: voice-to-text conversion and natural language translation of the text to its underlying meaning. *Voice-to-text conversion software* is more common and is available in packages such as *Dragon Software's* **Dragon Dictate** (Figure 4.14). It enables the capture or sampling

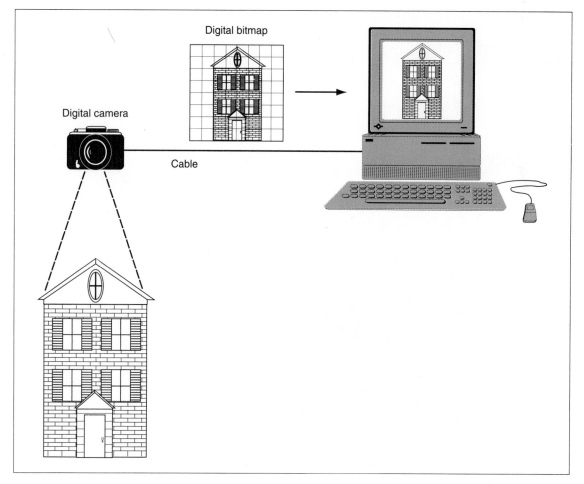

FIGURE 4.10 *(continued)*   (b) Use of a digital camera for data capture

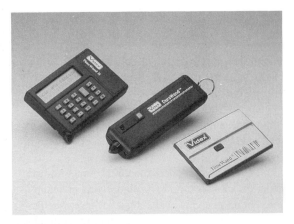

FIGURE 4.11 Handheld scanners for scanning bar codes

FIGURE 4.12 Handheld readers represent a convenient tool for scanning and transmitting bar codes.

FIGURE 4.13 Touch-tone telephones, such as those shown here, are an effective means of automating many customer services—for example, ordering and account querying.

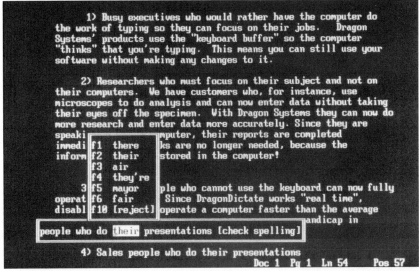

FIGURE 4.14   The use and accuracy of voice recognition as a means of data input is increasing and can be an important tool for both handicapped and nonhandicapped information workers.

of voice input through a microphone. This analog signal is converted into digital form, using a *digital signal processor* (or *DSP*), and compared with a library of digitized words. The closest match forms the basis for selection, and the chosen word is then written to the screen, as shown in Figure 4.15. The matching process may be further enhanced using grammatical and spelling checks.

Small-vocabulary voice-to-text conversion systems recognize several hundred words and are used mainly to activate commands in software packages. Conversely, *large-vocabulary* systems recognize up to 30,000 words. The latter are more expensive and are used for wide-ranging dictation purposes. Also, some systems are *speaker dependent* and require adaptation to the speech patterns of the intended user. *Speaker-independent* voice conversion systems are less accurate but can recognize speech from different users. Dragon Dictate's voice-driven typewriter, for example,

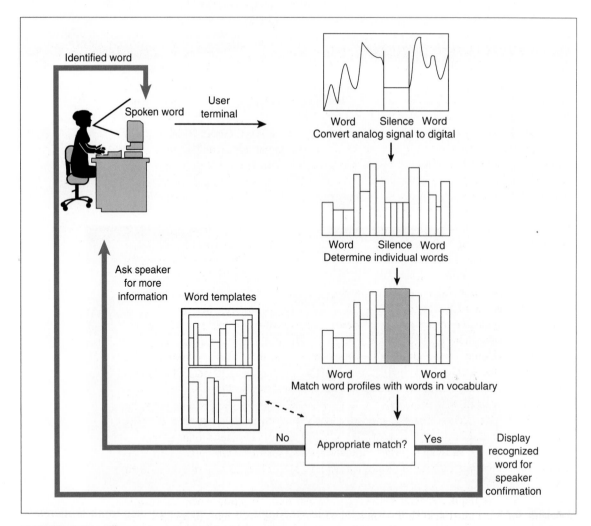

FIGURE 4.15   The voice recognition process

offers up to 98 percent accuracy in recognizing and translating speech. Potential problems with such systems include differentiating between similar-sounding words and eliminating background noise, for example, from office environments.

Natural language understanding is understanding and acting on underlying meaning in vocalized commands. It is used for database querying or menu selection, as described above. Such *command and control systems* are distinct from speech-to-text systems and offer even greater opportunities for user-computer interaction than are available with current systems.

Selecting Input Devices

Selecting appropriate input devices is an important task for the user of a microcomputer system. Using inappropriate input devices may result in *data errors* and *higher input costs*. For example, if OCR is used on a faxed document, a large number of errors might result from the low image resolution, and subsequent correction might result in greater costs than simple keyboard-based data entry. Likewise, replacing automated teller machines (ATMs) with human tellers would be cost prohibitive. **Input controls** have also grown in significance as microcomputer-based systems undergo use for transaction processing. The axiom *"garbage-in, garbage-out"* (or *GIGO*) is as valid today in current computing architectures as it was for mainframe-based information systems. Input controls are discussed in greater detail in Chapter 13.

As discussed previously, *keyboards* and *mice* are included with most microcomputer systems and are suitable for the majority of users' daily interactions with microcomputer systems. Important keyboard features include layout, feedback (soft, or responsive), and, increasingly, ergonomic aspects. *Mice* require more desktop space than trackballs, which are more appropriate when space is restricted. Both are almost a necessity in GUI environments, for menu selection, and to ease computer usage difficulties for nontypists.

Pen-based computing using styli and *slate computers* is appropriate for drawing applications, inputting signatures, and situations where a keyboard would be unwieldy. This includes package delivery where the user is mobile and a notebook or portable computer would be cumbersome. As handwriting recognition software improves, the potential for more general use of the technology is increasing. In comparison, *light pens* have been used in such design applications as CAD/CAM, where the pen is a more natural drawing device than a mouse or keyboard. The cost of specialized hardware and software is a constraint on wider adoption of these input methods and devices.

For large amounts of good-quality printed input data, that is, tens or hundreds of printed pages, the *scanner* is an increasingly popular alternative to keyboard-based data entry. *OCR software* achieves rates of over 99 percent accuracy in translating good-quality printed text, especially when used with spell checkers and grammar checkers. For capturing images, the scanner is the most cost-effective method. Camera-based input is closely related to the scanner, as both devices produce digitized images. Scanners are most appropriate for hardcopy scans, while *cameras* are most often used to capture details of three-dimensional objects. See Table 4.3 for criteria for input device selection.

Touch screens require special hardware to detect item selection when a screen is touched. Software must also be written to handle the unique demands of touch screen interfaces. The application must fit the display mode demanded by touch screens—

TABLE 4.3 Criteria for input device selection

Input Method	Cost	Type of Input	Packaging	Pluses	Minuses	Major Applications
Keyboard	$50–100	Keypress	Standard with microcomputer	Familiar to most users	Skill required for fast data entry, repetitive motion injuries	Universally used
Mouse	$20–80	Gestures	Standard	Good for GUIs	Requires free desk space	Most GUI applications
Trackball	$20–80	Gestures	Optional	Good for GUIs	Requires manual dexterity	Most GUI applications
Scanner	$100–500	Documents, 3-D objects	Optional	Exact images are input	Requires resetting for hues, colors, etc.	Input of text and images
Digital camera	$150–250	3-D objects	Optional	1-step capture of images of 3-D objects, screening, portability	Relatively high cost	Same uses as film-based cameras
Touch screens	Built-in ($100+)	Touch	Optional	Allows simple user interface	Screen smudges, user arm strain	Multimedia, GUI-based presentations
Light pen	$40 upward	Gestures	Optional	Natural input method	Expensive additional hardware	CAD, CAM
Stylus	$40 upward	Gestures	Standard on slate computer	Natural input method	Evolving handwriting recognition	GUIs, handwritten output
Voice recognition	$130–500	Spoken word	Optional expansion card and software	Natural input method	Background noise, accuracy can be low	Voice-to-text conversion
OCR	$0 (bundled)–200	Bitmapped text	Software	Can input large amounts of text quickly	Accuracy can be low	Image-to-text conversion
MICR	Up to several $1000s	Magnetized text	Stand-alone	Very accurate for special fonts	Specialized emphasis and applications	Input of bank check codes
Touch tone input	Cost of telephone	Sound frequencies	Stand-alone	Universally available	Has only 12 frequencies input range	Automated customer order management system

graphic, presentation-oriented interaction (as found in the stock exchange or museums)—otherwise touch screens will be unsuitable as an input medium. Their disadvantages include the necessity for users to constantly keep their arms upraised and permanently smudged screens. Finally, *touch tone telephones* are useful in situations involving remote users interacting with the computer system over telephone lines.

MICR and *bar-code readers* are also specialized devices, suitable only if the system's inputs can be obtained in an appropriate form, that is, in magnetized ink fonts or bar codes. Compared to keyboard-based input, they are very accurate and operate at high speeds. Given the proper conditions, they are both effective and efficient data input methods.

Regarding the newer, more natural forms of input, pen-based computing (with handwriting recognition), and voice recognition (with natural language understanding) appear to offer the most opportunities to computer novices, who do not have to learn typing but can enter data naturally by writing. *Voice-based word processing* is a reality in systems such as *Dragon Dictate,* and will be affordable for most users in a few years. Voice-based interaction is particularly useful for the disabled, but it will be used by most users in the long term, bringing what was once the stuff of science fiction to everyday microcomputer use.

4.2   OUTPUT DEVICES: DISPLAY UNITS _____

Input devices enable the user to enter program instructions and data for processing. **Output devices** are also needed to communicate processing results to the user. Without guidance in the form of on-screen prompts, for example, the user will not know when to enter data, or what and how much data to enter. Interestingly, the earliest forms of data output were not display units but *teletypes,* which printed computer outputs on paper. These were followed by IBM's *Selectric typewriter,* which was connected to computers for similar output of processing results. The development of **display units** represented a major advance in output devices, allowing the user to view computer outputs on screens while retaining the option to print them. The display unit was also used to echo or display user input from the keyboard and other devices onto the screen.

Several technologies are used to produce computer display units. The most widespread is the *cathode ray tube* or *CRT.* Others include *liquid crystal displays (LCDs), electroluminescent displays (ELDs),* and *gas plasma displays (GPDs),* used mostly in notebook computers.

Cathode Ray Tubes (CRTs)

CRTs are the most popular form of microcomputer display; most television sets are also based on CRT technology. A CRT consists of a *vacuum tube,* which is narrow at one end and flares out to form a *screen* at the other. The narrow end contains an *electron gun assembly,* consisting of a cathode, a heating element, a deflection yoke, and a focus control device, as shown in Figure 4.16. At the other end, the screen is coated on the inside with phosphor, which glows when struck by electrons from the electron gun assembly. Images are not generated by the electron beam in an ad-hoc manner. Instead, the generated beam sweeps the screen in a regular pattern called a *raster,* from left to

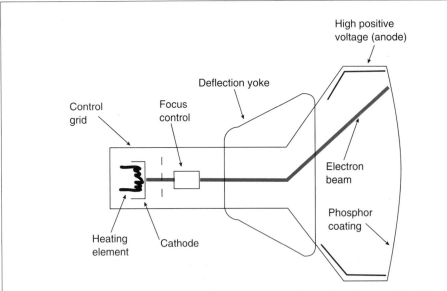

High positive
voltage (anode)

Deflection yoke

Control
grid

Focus
control

Electron
beam

Phosphor
coating

Heating
element

Cathode

The inner screen is flanked by an anode that generates a positive voltage. In operation, the cathode is heated, generating a beam of high-speed electrons. The electrons are attracted to the screen by the positive voltage of the anode and strike the phosphor coating on the inner screen, making the the phosphor glow. The electron beam is directed to specific points on the screen (that is, the desired image) by the use of the deflection yoke and the focus control unit

FIGURE 4.16   Schematic of a cathode ray tube (CRT)

right and top to bottom, as in Figure 4.17. Only phosphors which are a part of the desired image are struck by the electron beam.

As the glow of struck phosphors fades quickly, the electron beam must repeatedly scan the screen surface to maintain created images. The number of scans or sweeps made by the electron beam every second is known as the **refresh rate.** A refresh rate of 70 Hz, for example, means that the screen is refreshed or redrawn 70 times every second. Rates below this produce *screen flicker,* a shimmering effect caused by the glow of the illuminated phosphor almost dissipating before it is refreshed. This effect is noticeable by the user and causes eye fatigue.

With a monochrome monitor, only one electron beam is used to produce screen images. A black-and-white monitor, for example, uses white phosphors and produces white images on a black background. Likewise, green phosphors produce green text and other images on a black background. The screen is divided into a grid of picture elements or **pixels,** which dictate the amount of detail the monitor is capable of producing. So, the more pixels that are individually addressable by the electron gun in a given area, the greater detail the monitor can produce. This detail, or the maximum number of pixels a monitor can display, is referred to as the *screen resolution.* A resolution of 640×200, for example, means that the CRT can display 640 dots horizontally and 200 vertically, or a total of 128,000 pixels.

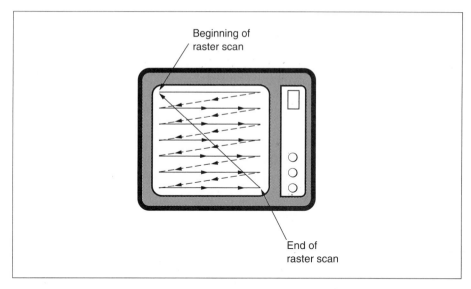

Beginning of
raster scan

End of
raster scan

FIGURE 4.17   Raster pattern of a cathode ray tube (CRT)

Color Display Units

In color monitors, a single color phosphor cannot produce multiple colors. A special case is the grayscale CRT, which utilizes a white phosphor capable of achieving multiple gray scale levels. For example, *NEC's Multisync GS* monitor produces 64 gray scales (Multisync monitors can vary their frequencies to match those of different video cards). **Color CRTs** generally utilize *triads,* or groups of three phosphors of different colors. These three primary colors are typically *red, green,* and *blue*—thus color monitors are often described as RGB monitors. A group of three phosphor triads make up a color pixel, with different electron beam intensities used to generate a whole spectrum of colors. The three electron guns in the assembly are arranged in a pattern called a "delta" configuration (Figure 4.18). The three electron beams pass through a metal grille called a *shadow mask,* which sits directly in front of the screen and prevents the beams from falling on the wrong phosphors.

Features of Display Units

A monitor's resolution determines the amount of detail that can be produced by the monitor, but an equally important property of a color monitor is its **dot pitch,** which refers to the distance between phosphor triads. Triads that are closer together produce finer, better quality images, while wider-spaced triads produce blurrier images. Monitor dot pitches range from 0.26 mm to 0.48 mm, with 0.28 mm being common.

An important feature related to screen refresh is **screen interlacing** (see Figure 4.19). With *interlaced screens* (as with television sets), even and odd lines are alternately scanned in every pass. Therefore a line of pixels is scanned only in alternate refreshes, and long-glowing phosphors are used to avoid flicker. With *noninterlaced screens,* all lines are scanned in every pass, requiring faster scans and better equipment. Interlacing

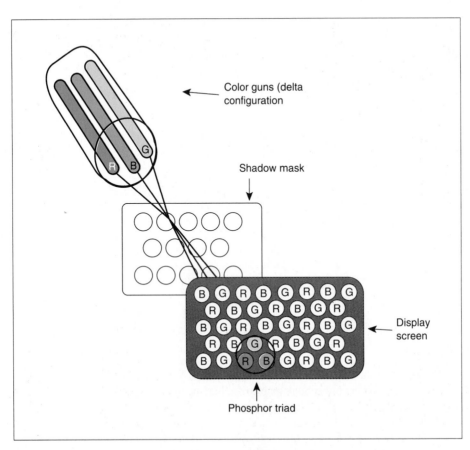

FIGURE 4.18 Using an electron gun to target a phosphor triad

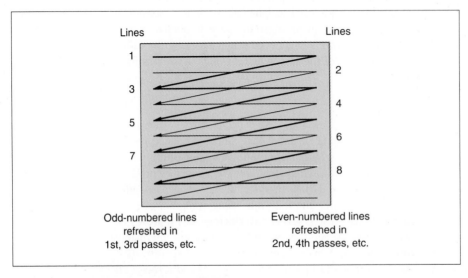

FIGURE 4.19 Interlacing on a CRT

allows less expensive monitors to be used for high-resolution graphics, but the eye must approximate adjacent lines to avoid noticing absent lines. Screen flicker results if the lines are some distance apart, as the phosphor's glow may diminish significantly between refreshes. The use of long-glowing phosphors can create a "ghosting" effect when the cursor and other objects are moved around on the screen. Only the highest monitor resolutions are suitable for interlacing, and noninterlaced screens are always preferable, other features remaining constant.

The display circuitry that generates and transmits video signals to the CRT is an important microcomputer component. It is located on the main system board of the microcomputer, or alternatively supplied by a *graphics expansion card*. The graphics card determines the usable resolution of the monitor and the number of colors that may be produced. Every generated image is stored in DRAM on the graphics card before it is sent to the CRT. The *color depth* of a graphics card refers to the number of possible colors that a pixel may display; examples include 4-bit, 8-bit, 16-bit, and 32-bit color. An 8-bit color graphics card can support 256 different colors (2^8 colors), while a 16-bit graphics card may support up to 65,536 distinct colors. The major consequence of supporting a large number of colors is a greater memory (DRAM) requirement, as more memory is needed to represent more colors (see Table 4.4).

The main characteristics of graphics cards are (a) the resolution they support, (b) the refresh rate they provide, (c) interlacing versus noninterlacing modes, and (d) their color depth. There are three major types of cards.

1. **Dumb frame buffers.** These have no graphics processor and store image data only in their memory. They are the cheapest type of graphics card.

TABLE 4.4 Monitor colors, resolution, and required memory

Number of Colors	Bits per Pixel	Monitor Resolution	Number of Pixels	Minimum Memory Required (K)
2	1	640×200	128,000	15.63
8	3	800×600	480,000	175.78
8	3	1024×768	786,432	288.00
16	4	800×600	480,000	234.38
16	4	1024×768	786,432	384.00
256	8	800×600	480,000	468.75
256	8	1024×768	786,432	768.00
64,536	16	800×600	480,000	937.50
64,536	16	1024×768	786,432	1,536.00
16,777,216	24	800×600	480,000	1,406.25
16,777,216	24	1024×768	786,432	2,304.00

2. *Graphics accelerator cards.* These cards perform a limited number of shape-generation tasks (for example, line and circle drawing tasks) to speed up the generation of graphics.

3. *Graphics coprocessor cards.* This is the most powerful type of card, possessing full-function microprocessors that perform the calculations necessary to generate whole screen images. They thereby relieve the CPU of this task and speed up graphics displays. Graphics coprocessor cards are the most expensive type of graphics card and are used primarily for high-end applications such as CAD and desktop publishing.

The speed of a monitor's display is affected not just by the type of video card used but also by the type of random access memory it uses to store screen images. Most graphics cards utilize ordinary DRAM for storing screen images, but high-end graphics cards use faster VRAM (see Chapter 3), which carries a higher price tag.

Another important consideration for the graphics card is the available *device drivers* for the user's intended applications. Device drivers are software programs that translate display outputs from the user's application to commands for the graphics card to generate the required screen image. If a correct device driver does not exist, results may range from no display at all to a resolution well short of the graphics card's (and monitor's) capabilities. For IBM-compatibles, commands to load the device drivers into RAM are placed in the **config.sys** file, which is run on start-up.

IBM-Compatible Graphics Standards

For IBM-compatible machines, several graphics standards are available. Many have been developed by IBM, and they relate both to screen resolution and to the number of colors supported. Table 4.5 lists these standards chronologically. The **color graphics adaptor (CGA)** standard was the first graphics standard offered by IBM on IBM-PCs.

TABLE 4.5 Display standards for IBM-compatible microcomputers

Display Standard	Resolution	Number of Colors
Color graphics adapter (CGA)	640×200	2
	320×200	4
Extended graphics adapter (EGA)	640×350	16 from a palette of 64
Video graphics array (VGA)	640×480	256 from a palette of 256,000
Super VGA (SVGA)	800×600	256 from a palette of 256,000
Extended graphics array (XGA) and SVGA	1024×768	256 from a palette of 256,000 or 65,536 from a palette of 16 million
SVGA	1280×1024	256 from a palette of 256,000 or 65,536 from a palette of 16 million

Its two- and four-color modes were very grainy. IBM's **enhanced graphics adapter** **(EGA),** with 640×350 resolution, was used mainly on IBM AT-class machines and upward. It offered 16 simultaneous colors from a palette of 64. The **video graphics array** (or **VGA**) is today's most popular standard, and it is used on a majority of machines. It increased the resolution offered by EGA by almost a half, to 640×480 or 307,200 pixels, with 256 colors (from a palette of 256,000). The *Video Electronics Standard Organization* (*VESA,* for short) later introduced a graphics standard called **Super VGA,** which exceeded VGA's resolution, at 800×600 (or 480,000 pixels), with 256 colors similarly available from 256,000. Furthermore both SVGA and IBM's **extended graphics array** **(XGA)** standard support very high resolution—1024×768 pixels, using 256 colors (or 640×480 with 65,536 colors). Another recent SVGA screen resolution is 1280×1024.

As display resolutions and available colors have increased, screen displays have become a bottleneck in microcomputer systems. For example, the amount of data required to refresh a 1280×1024 resolution, 24-bit per pixel 72 times every second, is 4 Mbps, enough to strain the ISA system bus. Fast machines may therefore appear sluggish due to this video bottleneck. Local-bus- and EISA-based systems have helped to support faster data pathways and faster redraws, sometimes increasing the display speed by several times. These systems, however, must use appropriate graphics cards that can handle the increased data volumes.

Flat-Panel Alternatives: LCDs, ELDs, and GPDs

CRTs represent the earliest type of microcomputer display and are the predominant display device for desktop microcomputers. However, they are unsuited for notebook microcomputers, which must be easy to transport. Since CRTs would make such systems too bulky, *flat-panel* displays were developed for these machines. Examples of these displays are *liquid crystal displays (LCDs), electroluminescent displays (ELDs),* and *gas plasma displays (GPDs),* none of which use the electron gun approach.

Flat-panel displays use a set of current-carrying intersecting wires to turn a pixel on or off, rather than a CRT-style electron gun. With LCDs, liquid crystals are placed between two glass panels behind which a light source is fixed. These crystals are arranged at either a 90° angle *(twisted LCDs)* or a 270° angle *(supertwisted LCDs),* both of which allow light through the glass panels. (Thus, a blank LCD screen is lighted, rather than dark.) When a voltage is applied to an on-screen location, the liquid crystals that are normally at an angle "untwist," preventing light from passing through the glass panels. Images are formed by dark areas, that is, areas where light is prevented from escaping. Twisted LCDs provide poorer contrast and display quality than supertwisted LCDs, and in dim lighting, they are even more difficult to read. Supertwisted LCDs are now the popular choice, with *backlighting* from within the display unit often added to further improve the displayed image.

Passive-matrix LCDs, which use intersecting electrodes to control a pixel, differ from *active-matrix LCDs* (see Figure 4.20), which use individual transistors at each pixel to turn them on or off, and a 90° twist. The advantage of active-matrix LCDs, however, is quicker images, resulting from more precise control over each pixel, using individual transistors. This speeds up screen refresh and reduces "ghosting," where an image leaves a trail as it moves across the screen. Active-matrix screens cost correspondingly

FIGURE 4.20   Active-matrix LCDs on notebook computers provide sharper and more responsive on-screen images than those of the passive-matrix variety.

more than passive-matrix technology. Newer LCDs display color images through the use of three closely grouped red, green, and blue or RGB subpixels to mix different colors at each pixel location in the same way as color CRTs. The market trend is toward active-matrix LCDs, which accounted for over 40 percent of flat-panel shipments in 1992.

LCDs are the most popular flat-panel display, but other alternatives also exist. **Electroluminescent displays** or **ELDs** use a thin film containing manganese, sandwiched between two layers containing intersecting wires or electrodes. When a voltage is directed at a specific point, the manganese becomes phosphorescent, emanating a green-yellow light. Therefore, an ELD screen displays green text or images on a black background, in contrast to LCDs. The monochrome ELD display is better than the LCD's but is more expensive.

Gas plasma displays, or **GPDs,** operate in a similar manner to ELDs but use an inert gas, instead of a liquid film. When a voltage is applied, the gas produces an orange glow, creating orange images on a black background. GPDs are monochrome only, consume more power than LCDs, and cost more.

Macintosh and Other Display Standards

The proprietary display standards of the Macintosh differ from those of PC-compatibles. For the 9-inch monochrome displays used in the Macintosh Classic II and SE, screen resolution is 512×342 pixels, and the video electronics are integrated on the system board. Other systems like the Macintosh II, IIsi, and IIci use Apple's video card, which provides a resolution of 640×480 pixels and 256 colors (8-bit color depth). Apple, a leader in desktop publishing, also offers a 24-bit graphics card with a 1152×872-pixel resolution, as do several third-party vendors. These vendors also produce graphics cards with even higher resolutions.

Other microcomputers and workstations generally have their own proprietary graphics standards and video cards. These include machines such as the NeXTstation, which uses a nonstandard 1120×832 display resolution. In such cases, it is more difficult to obtain monitors from third-party vendors, as is common with IBM-compatibles.

Choosing a Display Unit

Purchasers should consider several factors in selecting a monitor, such as *cost of the display system; system, monitor, and video card features; application type;* and *future needs.* Three levels of display needs may be defined as follows:

- **Low-level requirements.** These are displays for low-level systems discussed in Chapter 3. These displays are usually packaged with the overall system but may (with the exception of Macintosh Classic II, the Color Classic, and IBM PS/1 computers) be upgraded by the user. VGA's 640×480 resolution is the entry-level display for IBM-compatible machines and provides adequate displays for most DOS-based programs. Such displays can be adequately driven from the system board (using DRAM), or a dumb frame buffer. Macintosh Classic II users are limited to the 512×342 monochrome resolution, while basic color needs can be satisfied by the 640×480 resolution of the LC II.
- **Mid-range requirements.** These requirements are typical for users working in GUI environments, such as Windows. Such users also make use of presentation packages, desktop publishing, drawing programs, and so on, which stretch a system's display capabilities. A *multiscan monitor* (one with a variable scanning range) is recommended as part of the upgrade path for the display system. This capability permits it to be used with higher frequency graphics cards in future upgrades. For DOS-based systems, extended VGA (EVGA), at 1024×768 resolution (with interlacing) is appropriate, but super VGA (800×600) is also acceptable, both with at least a graphics accelerator. Apple Macintosh users will be best served by replacing the standard Macintosh monitor with a higher-resolution monitor.
- **High-end requirements.** For demanding applications, sophisticated display capabilities are needed to avoid the bottlenecks that occur when the graphics subsystem cannot keep pace with the microprocessor; and to drive the many colors and high resolution that accompany high-end display solutions. These applications include desktop publishing, 3D wireframe and solids modeling, and powerful painting/drawing programs. *Multiscan, noninterlaced monitors* are appropriate for these requirements.
- *PC-compatible users* will find extended graphics array (XGA) or higher-resolution capabilities suitable, used with a full graphics coprocessor or local bus (see Chapter 3). *Macintosh users* also have many high-resolution alternatives (for example, Apple's 1152×870 color display), and benefit from an accelerator card to speed up the generation of graphics. *Portrait* and *landscape* monitors, displaying one and two full pages respectively (and common in desktop publishing), are further options for either the PC-compatible or Macintosh user, in monochrome or color.

The dot pitch for all selected systems should be 0.26 mm or 0.28 mm (with a maximum of 0.31 mm on entry-level systems) to reduce eyestrain. Additionally, scan rates above 70 Hz reduce flicker and the eyestrain it causes.

For notebook computers, active-matrix LCDs are the most popular choice. ELDs and GPDs offer excellent displays, but the greatest color advances have been in LCDs, with

TABLE 4.6 A monitor selection guide

Display Type	Resolution(s)	Applications
High-resolution monochrome monitors, for example, "paper white" monitors	1280×1024	Desktop publishing (DTP), GUI applications
VGA	640×480	Entry- and mid-level, DOS, Windows
Super VGA	800×600	
XGA, SVGA	1024×768	GUI applications, CAD, DTP
	1280×1024	
LCDs, ELDs, GPDs	640×480	Entry and mid-level applications
	800×600	Reduced emissions, used in notebooks

few ELD and GPD color units available so far. Finally, users must make certain that the appropriate programs (drivers) to drive the graphics card and monitor are available for their applications. See Table 4.6 for help in selection.

4.3 OUTPUT DEVICES: PRINTERS, AUDIO OUTPUT, AND MICROFILM

Forms of output other than display units are required for a wide range of uses. Paper output *(hardcopy)* is preferred to on-screen output *(softcopy),* when the user wants to use the output in a different location. Hardcopy is also often required as a user-readable record of a transaction. In addition to printers, the more specialized audio output and microfilm output are discussed.

Printers

While microcomputers are usually sold as complete systems, with installed disk drives and display units, other peripherals are typically sold separately. **Printers** are the peripheral most likely to be purchased after the display unit. We saw in Chapter 3 that most microcomputers possess serial and parallel ports through which printer output is transmitted. Using a printer allows the output of text and graphics to paper. Four major classes of printers used with microcomputers are *dot matrix, ink jet, thermal transfer,* and *laser printers.* As important are the concepts of *fonts* and the *page control languages* used to describe a page's contents to printers.

Dot Matrix Printers

Dot matrix printers are the most popular printers. They produce output through the use of a print head consisting of a matrix of *pins* or *wires* (see Figure 4.21). The pins required

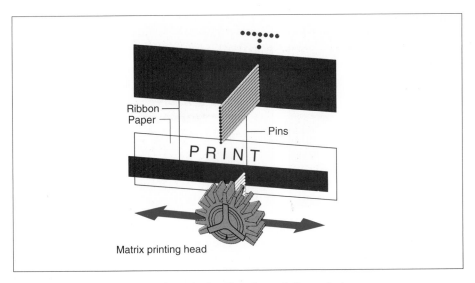

FIGURE 4.21   A dot matrix printing head used for printing

to form the desired character are extruded from the print head, and impact against a ribbon on paper to produce printed characters. They are the cheapest category of printers for microcomputers, ranging in cost from $100 to $900, depending on their capabilities. Dot matrix printers are character-based printers, meaning that they receive and print output a character at a time, unlike laser printers, which require a complete page's description before the page is printed.

Dot matrix printers are versatile in that their matrix of pins enables graphics and different fonts (families of character shapes) in various font sizes to be generated. With a dot matrix printer, many fonts may be mixed in the same document, and graphics may be interspersed with text. Also, effects like superscript, subscript, and italics are easily achieved. Dot matrix printers are impact printers, relying on an impact of the pins on the printer ribbon to create the desired character on the page.

There are two major classes of dot matrix printers: **9-pin** and **24-pin** printers. Nine-pin printers have a print head consisting of a 9×9 matrix, or 81 pins in total. Conversely, 24-pin dot matrix printers have print heads 24 pins across and either 18 or 36 pins vertically (giving totals of 432 and 864 pins, respectively). High-end dot matrix printers thus achieve resolutions as high as 360 dpi (dots per inch), which is nominally higher than the 300 dpi of standard laser printers. However, this figure can be misleading, as the dots created by the pins usually overlap.

Dot matrix printers generally print in three modes: draft mode, near-letter-quality (NLQ) mode, and, for the best printers, letter-quality (LQ) mode. *Draft mode* is achieved by a single pass of the print head and is suitable for internal documents, customer bills and receipts, and preliminary copies of formal correspondence. *Near-letter-quality (NLQ) mode* is achieved using two passes of the print head. In the second pass, the same line is printed at a slight offset to the first line, making the characters fuller, better formed, and usable for external correspondence. The penalty paid for this improved print quality, however, is the time required to perform two passes over each line. *Letter-*

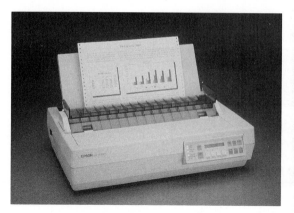 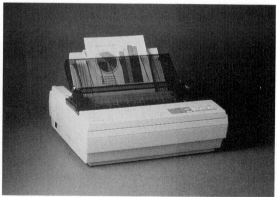

FIGURE 4.22   Printing in color is now commonplace on dot-matrix printers using a combination of color strips in the printer ribbon. They are an inexpensive source of color output.

quality (LQ) printing requires more time and two to three passes of the print head, but the resulting print rivals that of laser printers and can be used for almost any high-quality external correspondence. This quality is mostly available on 24-pin printers.

Firms such as Epson, Inc. have introduced *color dot matrix printers,* as shown in Figure 4.22. They are relatively expensive printers that use a single ribbon with red, yellow, green, and black strips. These different strips are mixed to provide other colors as needed. Printing speeds of dot matrix printers range from 18 to 800 characters per second (cps), with the highest rates available in draft mode.

Ink Jet Printers

Ink jet printers are closest in operation to dot matrix printers. They use a moving print head, containing a set of nozzles that fire small droplets of ink onto the paper (Figure 4.23). Each nozzle contains a tiny crystal at its tip. Electricity applied to this crystal makes it expand and then contract, forcing out a small droplet of ink at high speed onto the paper to create characters and images. There is no impact between the print head and the paper, making ink jet printers quieter than dot matrix printers, but they are as versatile in printing multiple fonts, superscript, subscript, and so on. With printing resolutions of up to 300 dpi (180 dpi typically) and speeds of up to 120 cps, ink jet printers match the print quality of many laser printers. As they also have fewer moving parts than both dot matrix and laser printers, ink jet printers are among the easiest printers to maintain.

Ink jet printers print in draft and letter-quality modes, similar to dot matrix printers, and color versions are now common. These use primary subtractive colors (cyan, yellow, magenta), and black inks to mix a variety of colors, and they can be purchased for about $600.

Thermal Printers

Thermal printers are a common choice for high-quality printed color output. The print head on thermal printers comprises pins that may be electrically heated. Unlike

FIGURE 4.23   An ink-jet printer is a popular choice as a personal printer due to its low cost, high resolution, and ease of maintenance.

FIGURE 4.24   Thermal printers once required specially coated paper for printing but now produce high-quality output on standard paper.

dot matrix and ink jet printers, the print head stretches across the width of the sheet. During printing, heat from the activated pins in the print head matrix melts wax impregnated in the ribbon's ink to form characters or images on the paper (Figure 4.24). Thermal printers are usually slower than either laser or ink jet printers, with one page per minute being a common printing speed. Top-end printers can achieve print resolutions of up to 300 dpi; and color, through the use of multiple ribbons (for example, cyan, magenta, and yellow plus black), making them the printer of choice for graphics presentations. Using a new technique called *dye diffusion,* in which the inks are turned to gas and mixed just before they hit the paper, newer thermal printers can produce near-photographic-quality outputs on specially coated thermal paper. Prices start at about $500 and $1,500 for single- and multiple-color thermal printers, respectively.

Laser Printers

Laser printers have made the greatest inroads into the printer market previously dominated by dot matrix printers. Laser printers were initially expensive and used almost exclusively by work groups, not individuals; however, prices have dropped steadily over the years, so that the personal laser printer is now a reality. For example, the *Okidata OL400,* which first broke the $1,000 barrier, now costs about half that amount. Unlike dot matrix, ink jet, and thermal printers, laser printers are page printers, meaning that complete information on a page's contents must be received prior to the page being output. They also produce the best output available, with standard resolutions of 300 dpi and high-end resolution reaching 800 dpi.

Laser printers (Figure 4.25) have increased in popularity with the spread of microcomputers. Unlike dot matrix printers, the printing mechanism of the laser printer does not involve impact against an inked ribbon but rather, revolves around the use of a light source, typically a low-intensity laser or *light-emitting diode (LED).*

Recently, new technologies have been developed for laser printers. These include *ion deposition* and *magnetography* (the use of magnetic particles), rather than the static charge created by the laser or LED. Both of these technologies result in high-speed printers suitable for use in high-volume settings. Since the printed page on a laser printer is divided into a grid at such high resolution, different fonts, effects (for example, superscript), and shapes are easily created. Laser printers produce printed output at rates ranging from four and sixteen pages per minute (ppm) to 200 ppm, common rates in mainframe environments serving many users. They are primarily

FIGURE 4.25   Laser printer operation

Once the page image is received by the laser printer, it is processed by a raster image processor. The page is then sent to the image device, which uses a laser beam (or LED) to "write" the dots of the required page on a rotating, positively charged *drum.* The images are written by discharging the points on the drum that correspond to the desired image. As the drum passes by the *toner,* which contains positively charged dry ink particles, the particles are attracted to the discharged parts of the drum and repelled from the other (nonimage) parts, which remain positively charged. The sheet of paper is passed between the toner and a negatively charged device called a *corona,* which pulls the ink particles onto the paper. As the sheet exits between two rollers, the ink is fused to the paper by heat or pressure.

used for formal correspondence, desktop publishing (DTP), and CAD/CAM applications.

Plotters

A **plotter** is a specialized device for producing hardcopy output. Plotters are used to create drawings such as maps and complex engineering designs. The printing mechanism for plotters is different from other classes of printers in that a computer-controlled pen or other writing device is used to create the desired image. The two major classes of plotters are pen plotters and electrostatic plotters. **Pen plotters** use a pen that is moved by printer control to draw lines or curves on paper. The paper may be static, with a pen capable of movement along both x and y coordinates, as in a *flatbed plotter*. In the *drum plotter* (Figure 4.26), the plotter pulls the paper under the pen and requires only lateral pen movement. The desired image is sent from the computer to the printer and used by the pen controller to direct the pen in creating the desired image. Pen plotters are the cheapest and most widely used type of plotter. A single pen is typically used, but many plotters use several colored pens to produce multicolor designs.

FIGURE 4.26   Drum plotters, such as the one above, are especially suited to printing complex designs and detailed maps on oversized paper.

BOX 4.1

UNDERSTANDING FONTS

A knowledge of fonts is essential for obtaining quality printed output. A **font** is a set of characters in a typeface, such as Times Roman or Courier, and in a set size, such as 10-point or 12-point. There are three types of fonts: **resident fonts,** built into the printer at the factory; **cartridge fonts,** located on a logic card that fits into a specialized printer slot; and **soft fonts,** which are downloaded to the printer from the microcomputer before printing.

Resident fonts are usually limited in number; *cartridge-based fonts* are usually many, but cannot be changed by the user. As both font types are contained on ROM chips, printer output is produced rapidly. Cartridge fonts are sold by manufacturers like Bitstream to expand a printer's capabilities. *Soft fonts* are generated by the microcomputer prior to its downloading to printer RAM. It is a slow process but can be performed just once daily, as the fonts remain in printer RAM until the printer is switched off. Sufficient memory is required by laser printers to store both the downloaded fonts and the contents of each printed page.

Soft fonts do not usually come in any one-point size, but as outline fonts. **Outline fonts** are descriptions (or calculations) that enable different font sizes to be created from one typeface (for example, Times Roman). **PCL 4** and **PCL 5** from *Hewlett-Packard* and **Postscript** by *Adobe Software* are the two leading page description languages (PDLs) used to produce outline fonts and print them on paper. PCL is the most widely used PDL and is used primarily on HP's laser printers. Postscript is licensed by Adobe to various printer manufacturers and is used on a wide range of printers. A newer PDL, *Truetype,* is being promoted by Microsoft and Apple, and is used in Windows™.

Printer buyers must ensure that adequate RAM exists to download soft fonts, and should be aware of the speed differences between resident and soft fonts. Postscript printers are an important print standard and are favored for high-quality printing. Additionally, the buyer must ensure that **printer drivers,** which interface between the printer and the user application, are available to support the application.

Electrostatic plotters use a raster of the printed surface (that is, they produce a bitmap of the whole surface). They are drum-based plotters but use a whole row of small styli, which sits across the paper being fed, rather than a single pen. Supplied vectors are converted to a bitmap, which is created using the styli. Electrostatic plotters are expensive, but they provide shading effects, high resolution (up to 400 dpi), and other features unavailable on pen plotters.

The performance of both types of plotters is enhanced in the same way as laser printers, by using a microprocessor within the plotter itself to take on much of the image-processing load involved. Features such as buffers, ASCII (or character)-generation capabilities, and off-line printing has increased the sophistication of plotters. A new type of plotter, the *direct imaging plotter,* based on a thermal print head and special paper or film, offers the potential for inexpensive, high-resolution plotting.

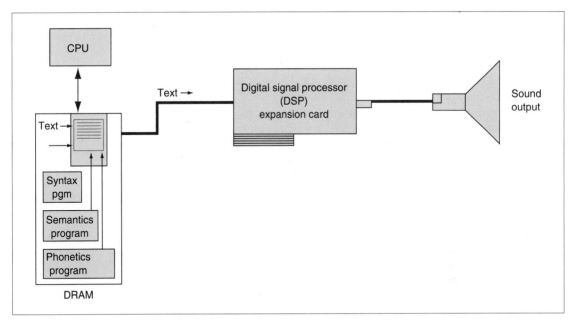

FIGURE 4.27   Text-to-speech processing

Using Audio Output

A popular vision of user-computer interaction, as evidenced in the *Star Trek* series and the computer, *HAL,* in *2001,* is voice-driven interaction. The two complementary parts of voice or audio-based interaction are voice recognition (discussed in the section on input devices) and **audio output,** from the computer to the human user. Audio output is also referred to as **speech synthesis,** involving audible and comprehensible computer-based speech generation. It is roughly the reverse of voice recognition, with text-based output from an application delivered to the user through a speaker by means of a digital signal processor (DSP), speech chips, or even mainstream microprocessors. Similar to voice recognition, varying levels of intelligence may be offered, as shown in Figure 4.27. These include the use of dictionaries, rules of syntax, semantics, phonetics, and so on, which generally improve the quality and meaningfulness of the uttered output. Audio output is useful for vision-impaired individuals, especially if accompanied by voice recognition. Such systems are also becoming more affordable.

Computer Output on Microfiche/Microfilm (COM)

Maintaining paper-based historical records is expensive and space consuming. Information systems are producing greater amounts of paper output as the number and types of printing options have grown. **Computer output on microfiche/microfilm (COM) systems** help to reduce the size of computer outputs, by storing them on compact and cheaper media, namely microfiche and microfilm. **Microfiche** consists of small sheets of film, on which rows of pages of output are stored. With COM, output may be recorded either on microfiche or on rolls of **microfilm.**

Using COM involves transferring the image from the computer to a specialized COM machine, which in turn records the image on microfiche or microfilm and is used to magnify and display the film for later viewing by the user. COM systems are widely used for archival systems, where the stored information changes very slowly. COM systems can output information at rates exceeding 500 lines of text per second, and stored images are reduced by factors of up to 100. They are popular in libraries, for maintaining book catalogs, and in banks, for disseminating records of customer accounts. One disadvantage of COM is the expensive, special-purpose machines required (which often exceed $100,000). Additionally, newer imaging technologies, many based on optical media (discussed in Chapter 5), provide a cheaper and more effective archival option.

Selecting Output Devices

Similar to the selection of input devices, the user must consider the purchase and maintenance costs, speed, print quality, generated noise, and future uses of the output device. The two major types of output devices are printers and plotters. Only very specialized applications, such as map-drawing, complex CAD/CAM and architectural designs, and applications that need oversize paper, require plotters. Options such as color and text may be added as required. With printers, the choices are between dot matrix, ink jet, laser, and thermal printers.

- **Dot matrix printers,** ranging in cost from $100 to $900, are the cheapest printers to purchase and operate. 24-pin dot matrix printers produce both draft- and correspondence-quality output and cheap color graphics. Some dot matrix printers can also produce *postscript-quality output* using Adobe™ printer drivers. Furthermore, they are the only choice for multipart forms—multiple sheets with carbon paper or other interleaving material. This is because of their impact on the paper. Purchase considerations also include *the number of available fonts* and *printer memory,* which determines how much output data can be transferred into the printer buffer, and how fast the user is released to go on to other tasks. As print rates are relatively slow, dot matrix printers are less suitable for high-volume printing needs. Dot matrix printers are among the cheapest to maintain, but they are the noisiest of those considered.
- **Ink jet printers** range from $300 to $2,000 and up. They compete with dot matrix and laser printers and produce resolutions of up to 300 dpi. While ink jet output is often comparable with laser printing, the sharper resolution of lasers gives the latter an edge for formal correspondence. Also, ink jet printers cannot produce multipart forms as no impact is involved in the printing process. This also makes them very quiet to use, and they are less expensive to maintain than laser printers.
- **Laser printers** are the printer of choice for many users as their prices continue spiraling downward. Low-end $600 laser printers now fall into the dot matrix price range. With resolutions of 300 dpi and up, they are suited to *draft* and *high-quality correspondence* and *graphics.* With Postscript or PCL 5 page description languages, their capabilities are enhanced even further. Disadvantages include costs of

maintenance and their inability to print on oversized sheets. Laser printers operating at four to eight pages per minute (ppm) are suitable for the average user. Large networks, on the other hand, will benefit from $5,000 to $20,000 laser printers capable of sixteen to twenty-two ppm to satisfy the printing demands of multiple users. Other considerations include the amount of RAM in the printer, the type of processor, available fonts, and printer interfaces.

- **Thermal printers** posed difficulties to early users due to their need for special thermal paper. While some newer thermal printers use standard paper, the greatest use of thermal printers has been at the high end, where high-resolution color output is required. These printers are priced in the $500 to $10,000 range. Thermal printers have the same limitations as ink jet and laser printers, for example, with oversize sheets and multipart forms. However, they are the top choice for those applications requiring almost photo-realistic color separation.

Other output devices include *audio output,* which is suited to automated systems and vision-impaired computer users. Specialized software and hardware are usually required, but new multimedia-ready systems, for example, already have audio capabilities built in. Audio is clearly an important future output medium for the vision impaired and for applications that are not eyes- free, for example, computer-assisted repair, voice mail, voice-annotated applications, and multimedia-based training (see Chapter 8). Computer output on microfiche/microfilm is still widely in use, but many potential users are considering more effective alternative technologies, such as optical storage (see Chapter 8). See Table 4.7 for aid in selecting output devices.

TABLE 4.7   Table for output device selection (for CRTs, see Table 4.6)

Device Category	Device Type	Price Range	Description
Printers	Dot matrix	$100–$1,000	Draft and near-letter-quality (NLQ) for individual use; multipart forms
	Ink jet	$300–$1,500	Draft and letter-quality (LQ) for individual use
	Personal laser	$600–$3,000	High-quality printing for individual and small group use
	Network laser	$5,000–$20,000	High-quality printing for small and large group use
	Thermal	$5,000–$10,000	Photographic-quality color printing
Audio output	DSP/speaker	$300 upward	Specialized applications
COM	Microfilm/ microfiche	$1,000 upward	High-density output medium, superceded by optical media
Plotters	Flat-bed drum	$500 upward	Computer-aided design

CHAPTER SUMMARY _____

To enable the microcomputer to process the user's programs, they are entered into the microcomputer using input devices. Processing results and system outputs during interaction are also conveyed to the user through output devices. Technological advances have increased the number and sophistication of input and output devices to include more options than at any time previously.

Keyboards and mice remain the most common input devices, with mice being used with GUIs like Windows and the Macintosh OS. Pen-based computing, particularly using styli on slate computers, is growing in popularity as a more natural user interface, allowing handwriting recognition and freehand drawings. Scanners are a key component of document imaging, which can speed up data entry and lower its costs. They often include optical character recognition software that extracts text from scanned pages. Other specialized input devices include magnetic ink character recognition, used to input data on bank checks and bar-code inputs. Touch tone inputs are made through telephones, and a further natural input medium is voice recognition.

The oldest and most widely used display technology is the cathode ray tube (CRT). Many CRT displays exist in the PC-compatible world, ranging from the chunky CGA to the very high-resolution XGA displays and beyond. Other display standards also exist for Macintosh microcomputers and for workstations, such as the Sun SPARCStation. The greatest promise lies in flat-panel displays, commonly used on notebook microcomputers. Once monochrome only, color options are now available and increasingly affordable on notebooks. Liquid crystal displays (LCDs) dominate the market, but electroluminescent and gas plasma displays (ELDs and GPDs) represent newer flat-panel alternatives.

Other output devices include printers. Dot matrix printers are the cheapest and most widely used type, with 9-pin and 24-pin choices offering the user a wide range of print quality. Their share of the market is being steadily reduced, however, by the inroads made by ink jet, laser, and thermal printers, which, at steadily falling prices, produce faster, higher-resolution, and better quality print than dot matrix printers. Plotters, on the other hand, are used for specialized map-drawing or design functions. Synthesized audio output represents a cutting-edge and user-friendly output method that is also advancing in quality. Finally, microfilm/microfiche, a traditional mainstay of banks and libraries, will be replaced eventually with optical storage.

Selecting appropriate input and output (I/O) devices must take into account the features and cost of the devices and an understanding of the user's requirements. Other issues, such as compatibility and industry standards, will affect the selection of both I/O devices and those for office automation tasks.

REVIEW QUESTIONS _____

1. What is a buffer? Give an example of its use in outputting data to a printer.
2. What set of keys on the keyboard is used for specific tasks (for example, Help information) by individual programs?
3. In what situation(s) is a trackball preferred to a mouse?

4. What are the main differences between a light pen and a stylus?
5. What are the disadvantages of the touch screen as an input device?
6. Why does a scanned page of text require much more storage than a typed page?
7. For a grayscale scanner with eight gray levels, how many bits are needed to represent a pixel?
8. What are suitable applications for small- and large-vocabulary voice recognition systems?
9. What are phosphors, and how are they used to generate CRT images?
10. Describe how interlaced and noninterlaced screens differ. Which are superior?
11. How does video RAM differ from DRAM and how is it used?
12. In poor viewing conditions, would you recommend twisted or supertwisted LCDs? Why?
13. Is a larger dot pitch better or worse for a monitor's user?
14. How does a dot matrix printer produce near-letter-quality output?
15. What type of printer fires droplets of ink onto paper to produce printed output?
16. Do you regard laser printers as personal or group printers? Why or why not?
17. For what type of output is a dot matrix printer more suitable than a laser or ink jet printer?

EXERCISES

1. What type of microcomputer would you recommend for your delivery personnel who deliver corporate mailings within the city for your private mail delivery service? Which method of input would have the most benefits and why?
2. What types of data input tasks would benefit the most from scanning? What features would you advise a manager about to purchase OCR software to look for? Why are these features important?
3. How much storage would be required to store a scanned or digitized page (7" by 10" effective page size), using a high-resolution, 400 dpi scanner? How much storage would be required if a data compression rate of 15:1 was achieved through software?
4. What is the minimum amount of video RAM required to support a super VGA (SVGA) display capable of generating 256 colors? Would you recommend a graphics coprocessor card for a mix of primarily word processing and database tasks? Why or why not?
5. An architectural firm is seeking to purchase several microcomputers to automate their drafting tasks. What factors must they consider in making their decision? What combination of monitor and graphics card would you recommend to support their needs?
6. An organization is seeking to purchase several printers to support various printing needs, which include printing sales invoices, internal company newsletters, documents for personal use, letters to stockholders, and color brochures. Which printers would you recommend for each of these needs? Which of these printers would be best for supporting a group of users on a network?

SUGGESTED READINGS _____

Caudill, M. "Kinder, Gentler Computing." *Byte Magazine,* April 1992, pp. 135–150.

Fraser, B., and Yi, P. "Capturing Color: 24-bit Scanners." *MacUser,* December 1991, pp. 153–166.

Huttig, J. W., Jr. "Font Wars: Consumers Win the Battle between Adobe and Apple." *PC World,* August 1992, pp. 25–27.

Johnson, L. B. "Choices at Your Fingertips." *PC Today,* January 1992, pp. 24–31.

Mann, S. "Unlocking the Secrets of Laser Printer Fonts." *PC Today,* May 1990, pp. 88–97.

Marshall, P. "Full-Page Scanners." *PC World,* April 1992, pp. 188–196.

Martin, G., et al. "Sign Here, Please." *Byte Magazine,* July 1990, pp. 243–252.

Nelson, N. D. "Hot Colors." *Byte Magazine,* October 1991, pp. 177–182.

Smith, R. "Fonts Made Easy." *PC World,* June 1990, pp. 158–164.

SECONDARY STORAGE DEVICES

INTRODUCTION

Random access memory (RAM) is used to temporarily store programs and data being processed. However, users also require devices to store processing results and their programs and files on a more permanent basis. This form of storage must be nonvolatile, or able to retain its contents in the absence of electrical current, unlike RAM. There are several types of secondary storage devices, and they differ in regard to cost and storage capacities. This chapter examines secondary storage options available to the user, ranging from sequential access storage devices (SASDs) to direct access storage devices (DASDs). Also, methods for improving the efficiency of data storage and retrieval and matching user requirements to appropriate storage devices are discussed.

Learning Objectives

After reading this chapter, you will be able to:

- Describe how microcomputers store data on secondary storage devices
- Propose sequential and direct access devices for diverse information requirements
- Propose appropriate methods for improving the efficiency of secondary storage devices
- Recommend newer storage devices such as optical disks when appropriate to handle bitmapped, sound, and other data types

CASE 5.1

NEW YORK DEPARTMENT OF CIVIL SERVICE: A CLIENT/SERVER SOLUTION FOR AN EMPLOYEE HEALTH CARE CRISIS

In 1989, the New York Department of Civil Service faced a massive $320 million deficit in its health insurance budget. An archaic and inefficient information system was producing an information system that was rapidly bringing the organization to its knees. It took two months to add new employees to the system, fraudulent claims were common, and many employees were "lost" in the system and unable to claim benefits. Hospitals also had no way to verify coverage.

The mainframe-based COBOL system with flat-file databases was replaced by a client/server network comprising 4,000 point-of-service terminals at care providers and 1,100 microcomputers. This Ethernet-based network connects doctor's offices, hospitals, pharmacies, state personnel departments, and insurance companies. A client/server program called *Benefits*, by *Peoplesoft*, was installed on new microcomputers and on an IBM mainframe host. Information entered on microcomputers is uploaded to the DB2 database on the IBM mainframe, which contains the latest employee records. Users can also query this database using a wide range of report formats. Each employee was also issued a plastic card with a magnetic strip that could be read by a health care provider, showing the employee's status.

Total development costs of the new system came to about $3 million, but the system has paid for itself. Almost $1 million is saved annually by eliminating the biannual reissue of plastic cards. The cost of printing and distributing reports, which can be accessed locally has also been eliminated. Finally, fraudulent claims were virtually eliminated. Best of all, the new client/server system has helped to turn the department's deficit into a surplus.

Adapted from Alice LaPlante, "New York State Agency Turns Cost Crisis into Profit," *Infoworld*, February 22, 1993, p. 63.

5.1   THE NEED FOR SECONDARY STORAGE

User requirements for ever larger amounts of storage have increased over the years. More storage capacity makes for larger applications and data bases, which in turn stimulate demand for even greater storage capabilities. Additionally, GUIs and applications like multimedia create more demand for storage. The market for secondary storage devices has exceeded the $5 billion mark and continues to grow rapidly. Similar to keyboards, secondary storage devices are incorporated into most microcomputers, and their sales closely mirror those of microcomputers. They also feature increasing storage densities, newer media and storage techniques, and lower costs.

Why Is Secondary Storage Important?

In Chapter 3, the roles of RAM, in storing programs and data, and of ROM, in storing the microcomputer's fixed start-up instructions, were discussed. While ROM cannot be overwritten, programs and data can repeatedly be rewritten to RAM during processing. For example, as you create a document using a word processing package, the application software is stored in memory with the document being created. After the document is created, it is saved to secondary storage, because turning off the computer would result in the loss of RAM contents (that is, the document). As a permanent form of storage, secondary storage devices are used to store:

- *Historical data.* These include past transactions, for example, sales transactions, inventory reorders, and so on, or other processing outputs, such as word processing documents, updated databases, and spreadsheets.
- *Transaction data.* In running a payroll processing program, for example, secondary storage might be used to store data describing the hours worked by each employee. These data would later be read into RAM and processed while calculating the payroll.
- *Applications, utilities, and operating systems.* These software types are usually stored in secondary storage, from where they are loaded into memory and processed. Applications include word processing, accounting, and database programs. On the other hand, utilities are used for disk and file management tasks, and so on. OSs are also disk based, to allow updates by their creators. If they were ROM-based, the user would have to open up the computer, remove the ROM chips, and insert the new ones, a cumbersome process.

Secondary storage may also function as

- *Virtual memory.* This is described in Chapter 6, where secondary storage acts as extra RAM, in instances where the application's memory requirements exceed available RAM.
- *Backup storage for data.* Secondary storage devices are often vulnerable to theft, device failure, and accidental or intentional damage. Other secondary storage devices are used to create backups of existing data to reduce the exposure to risk.

Secondary storage is therefore an important part of microcomputer systems, enabling the user to store *processing results, programs,* and *entered inputs* in computer-readable formats. To make an informed selection of the appropriate type and quantity of secondary storage, the user must understand the capabilities of secondary storage devices and the configuration and usage options for secondary storage hardware and software.

Characteristics of Secondary Storage

In Chapter 3, processor and memory chips were understood to be solid-state electronic devices, that is, they contain no moving parts, performing all their functions through electronic switching. **Secondary storage devices** are *electromechanical* in nature, with electrical as well as moving mechanical parts. This makes them much slower than processor and memory chips and creates a bottleneck in data transfers between RAM and secondary storage. Many hardware and software innovations in secondary storage have therefore been aimed at overcoming this bottleneck, for example, disk caching, discussed in Chapter 3. Secondary storage also costs less per byte than RAM, as seen in the storage pyramid of Figure 5.1, which illustrates increasing costs and faster data access in moving from slow secondary storage to faster RAM and registers.

As the user works on the microcomputer and creates documents, spreadsheets, and so on, the need often arises to backtrack and erase or modify prior data entries. This results in storage locations in RAM being overwritten to reflect needed changes. In the same way that data can be rewritten several times on RAM, the majority of secondary storage devices are also write-many or *rewritable* devices, enabling previously stored data to be deleted or modified as necessary.

An additional aspect of secondary storage devices is that the media on which data are stored are not in human-readable form but in computer- (or storage device)-readable form. While output formats (such as hardcopy and screen display) are oriented toward the human user, secondary storage is optimized toward device access and compatibility. The actual representation of data on these devices is described next.

5.2   How Are Data Represented?

Data are physically represented on secondary storage devices in ways that vary according to which media (for example, magnetic or optical) are used. Additionally, users may manipulate fields, records, and files during processing, and not just text within files. This file hierarchy aids understanding of how data are grouped, organized, and, ultimately, stored.

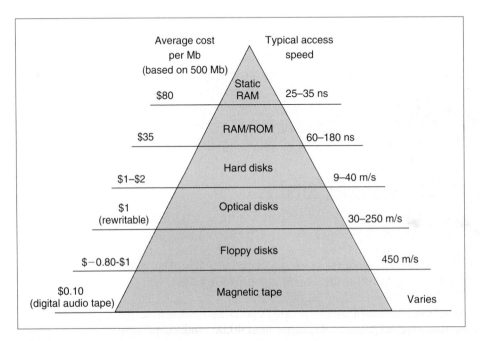

FIGURE 5.1   Pyramid of storage costs and access times

Data Representation on Storage Devices

In creating documents, spreadsheets, and so on, users employ symbols such as A, . . , Z and 0, . . , 9. Such symbols are not directly represented within the computer. ***Binary representation*** is particularly suited to computers, which rapidly switch miniaturized devices (for example, transistors) between two states: off signifying 0 and on signifying 1. On secondary storage devices, data are also represented in binary form. On magnetic disks, for example, bits are encoded by magnetizing the coating on the disk surface. Some laser disk drives store data differently, with bits created by using a small laser to burn microscopic holes in the disk's surface (to signify 1s).

ASCII and *EBCDIC* (see Chapter 4) are two coding systems used to encode data stored on disks. ASCII is prevalent on microcomputers, whereas EBCDIC is used on mainframes and minicomputers. The ASCII version used on most secondary storage devices is 8-bit ASCII. It is capable of representing 256 characters (2^8) and differs from 8-bit EBCDIC. Microsoft's recent introduction of 16-bit modified ASCII enables representation of 2^{16}, or 65,536 characters. It is an important requirement for programs written for users of Asian languages like Japanese Kanji (Figure 5.2).

File Hierarchy—Fields, Records, and Files

Characters are the smallest meaningful units of data, but other higher-level structures are important to understanding secondary storage. For example, consider an inventory file maintained on a microcomputer system. Stored inventory details include the name and serial number of the inventory item, its description, and stock level. These attributes are called **fields.** All the fields of a particular inventory item are also called a **record** (in this case, an inventory item record), and the set of records for all items in inventory is called the inventory **file.** See Figure 5.3 for an example.

FIGURE 5.2   The Japanese version of the Macintosh operating system uses the Kanji script, which includes more than 40,000 individual symbols.

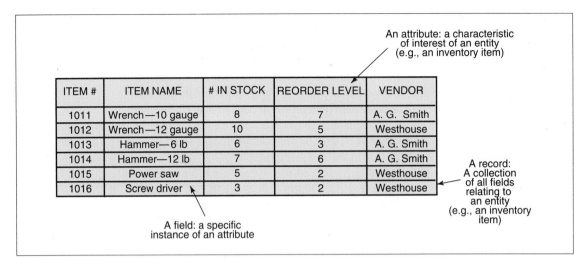

FIGURE 5.3   An inventory file and records

The inventory file is called a *data file,* as it stores an item's attributes. Other file types, such as *text, program, image,* and *sound files,* are discussed in Chapter 7. Data files are organized based on the fact that when used, only a part of the data file, such as a record, is normally required. Their records must have a **key field,** whose value is unique for each record, to enable identification of, and access to, any single record in the file. Furthermore, records may be organized *serially* (that is, one following the other, randomly); or *sequentially,* where records are stored in ascending or descending order of their keys, as shown in Figure 5.4.

Records may be stored and accessed on secondary storage devices using *sequential, indexed,* or *direct access methods.* The selected access method depends on the physical structure of the secondary storage devices. Also, an access method may simply reflect the application for which it is being used. Secondary storage alternatives are discussed below, with the discussion on data access methods reserved until Chapter 7.

5.3   SEQUENTIAL ACCESS STORAGE DEVICES (SASDS)

An important category of secondary storage devices is sequential access storage devices (SASDs), which includes magnetic tapes and magnetic cartridges. *Magnetic tape* is common in mainframe and minicomputer environments, while *magnetic cartridges* are more popular in microcomputer systems. Each consists of a long strip of mylar tape that is 0.5 or 0.25 inches wide and coated on one side with iron oxide. The 0.5-inch tape used on large tape reels is prevalent in mainframe environments, while the smaller 0.25-inch tapes in *quarter-inch cartridges (QICs)* are used mostly in microcomputer systems. Other magnetic cartridge technologies, such as *8mm tape* and *digital audio tape* are important alternatives.

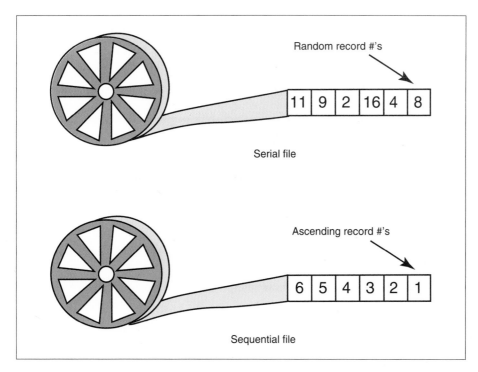

FIGURE 5.4   Serial and sequential files on magnetic tape

In the hierarchy of storage devices shown in Figure 5.1, SASDs are at the bottom of the storage pyramid. They are the least costly secondary storage medium but also the slowest, with regard to the speed of storage and retrieval. The major reason is the sequential nature of reading and writing operations, as the physical medium prevents direct access to a record without reading all records physically preceding it. Access time varies according to the physical location of the record on tape, with records at the start of the tape accessed quicker than those at the end.

Data is stored on, and retrieved from, magnetic tape media using a *tape drive.* Data in binary form is written to tape using the drive's *read/write head* to create magnetic patterns in the tape's iron oxide coating. Subsequently, data is read by detecting the same patterns on the tape as it passes under the drive head. A motor within the tape drive rotates the tape reel to position the required data at the desired position for reading, as shown in Figure 5.5.

Magnetic Tape

Magnetic tape, also called *reel-to-reel tape,* is in widespread use in mainframe installations. It consists of a single reel of tape 0.5 inches wide. The length of tape on a reel is typically 2,400 feet, and the use of differing *recording densities* (1,600–6,250 bpi) makes it possible to store between 35 Mb and 100 Mb of data on a single tape. In storing data on tape, records are usually grouped into *blocks.* A block is treated as a single unit during read or write operations, and transfers to and from RAM take place

FIGURE 5.5   A tape drive enables data storage on magnetic cartridges for hard disk backup and archival purposes.

in blocks. As the block factor (the number of records per block) grows, more records can be written on the same length of tape. However, the block size cannot be made unduly large, as RAM buffers have capacity limitations. **Streamer tapes,** which are used to "dump" the contents of hard disks, do not need to stop and restart and consequently have much smaller spaces between blocks, leaving more space available on them for data storage.

Magnetic Cartridges

Magnetic tapes require large and costly tape drives. **Magnetic cartridges** are tape-based secondary storage devices used mainly in microcomputer-based systems. The most popular type of magnetic cartridges use a 0.25-inch-wide (¼-inch-wide) tape, which fits in the enclosed unit, somewhat like an audio cassette. Also like an audio tape, both the takeup reel and the tape reel are contained within the cassette. Tape drives may be full-height or half-height, and either internal or external to the system unit.

In addition to *quarter-inch cartridges (QICs), 8 mm tape,* and *digital audio tape (DAT),* there are two available alternatives. **QICs** are the prevalent form of magnetic cartridges. Their storage capabilities range from 40 Mb to 1.35 Gb of data, with data transfer rates of up to 600 Kbps. They are also mostly full-height devices. **8 mm magnetic cartridges** are the premium form of microcomputer tape storage. As the name implies, the tape medium is 8 mm wide, with storage capacities of up to 5 Gb per cartridge and transfer rates of up to 500 Kbps. Both half- and full-height devices are available. Finally, **DAT cartridges,** which have the narrowest width of tape, 4 mm, are identical to cassette tapes. They store 1.3 Gb and 2 Gb on 60-meter and 90-meter cartridges, respectively, with slower data transfer rates in the region of 180 Kbps.

In general, magnetic cartridges require a *tape drive controller card,* which fits into an expansion slot in the microcomputer. This card contains the logic circuitry used to control tape operations and the DRAM buffers required to hold incoming or outgoing data. Some tape drives require proprietary controller cards; others use industry-standard controller cards to control the tape drives, as described in the next section. Additionally, various third-party software programs may be used to automate and control tape operations. Important features of these software packages include

- Support for multiple cartridge formats
- Security features, such as passwords
- Unattended operations, such as tape backup
- Support for network use

Magnetic tape cartridges, controllers, and software are available for the major microcomputer platforms. As the capabilities of magnetic cartridge subsystems improve, their uses have naturally expanded from single-user to multiuser microcomputer configurations. We examine below the different ways in which magnetic tapes and cartridges are used.

Uses and Limitations of SASDs

Early uses of magnetic tape with mainframes consisted of *key-to-tape* data entry. Here, the user keyed in source data onto the tape, after which the data would be read into the computer's memory and processed. The tape might be on-line—implying a communication link between the tape drive and the computer, or off-line, in which case, the tape was later loaded onto an on-line drive and read into memory (see Figure 5.6).

For most users, magnetic cartridges are used for backup and archival purposes. **Tape backups** are copies of programs or files that are stored for the short term on magnetic cartridges to enable recovery from system failures resulting in data loss. Following such failures, data is restored from the cartridge to the fixed disk. **Archival tapes** are longer term in nature. They usually serve a reference function, or as a means to store data no longer being used but which must remain available for legal or other reasons. Hence, tape backups are made more frequently than archival tapes, that is, weekly, daily, or even several times a day.

Backing up data is an integral part of transaction processing on all computers used in business functions. For example, the company whose customer database is damaged following a hard disk failure and does not possess any backup storage will face major difficulties. Current balances owed, existing orders, and management reports will remain unavailable until the data are restored. As all hard disks will eventually fail, backups are not just prudent but indispensible, even for the single user. The spread of networks has prompted the development of *LAN backup software.* This software is used to produce backups to satisfy networking requirements such as involuntary backup of user's hard disks on the network, unattended backup of data base and file servers, and security features. LAN backup is discussed more fully in Chapter 10.

Disadvantages of SASDs include the fact that tapes fail with repeated readings since they are in constant contact with the read/write head. Others include relatively slow data access times and an inability to provide direct access to individual records, which can be significant even if magnetic tape is used only for backup purposes. For example, not

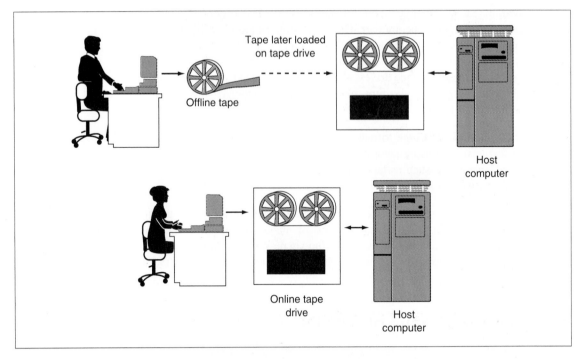

FIGURE 5.6   Online and offline tape drives

all files may be needed after a system failure. Selective restoration of files would take more time using tape than if a hard disk was used for backup. In fact, many firms use both magnetic and optical disks for backup for just this reason.

5.4 DIRECT ACCESS
STORAGE DEVICES (DASDs)

SASDs satisfy only a limited number of secondary storage requirements. In particular, their inability to support direct access makes them unsuitable for many applications. For example, a prospective air traveler might have an unacceptably long wait for seat availability if magnetic tape were used. Likewise, storage and retrieval of word processing, spreadsheet, or other files from tape would suffer from unacceptable performance degradation. Direct access means that a record can be accessed from a storage device without having to read all the records that physically precede it. Hence, the twentieth record in sequence can be retrieved without the need to access all the preceding nineteen, as is necessary with SASDs. To use a direct access method, the technology must support random access to individual storage locations. **Direct access storage devices (DASDs)** possess this feature.

DASDs include *magnetic disks (floppy and fixed), optical disks,* and *flash RAM.* Relevant features include their cost, access time, capacities, and portability.

FIGURE 5.7   High density (1.44 Mb) and double density (720 Kb) 3.5-inch
floppy disks

Floppy Disks

Floppy disk drives are the most widespread type of DASD and are an integral
component of most microcomputers. The **floppy disk** (or **diskette**) is a flexible mylar
disk that is coated with a layer of iron oxide and surrounded by a protective plastic
jacket. Historically, 8-inch disks were common, but current disks are of the 5.25-inch,
or more likely, the 3.5-inch variety, as shown in Figure 5.7. A *floppy disk drive* is used

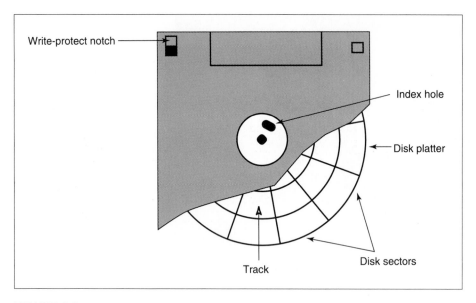

FIGURE 5.8

to write to, and read from, floppy disks. Data are written to the disk using a read/write head assembly, which magnetizes the iron oxide particles on the disk surface in patterns signifying 0s or 1s.

An *index hole* is a cavity in the hub of the floppy disk, as shown in Figure 5.8. It conveys information about the disk's position as it rotates. The disk surface is divided into sectors and into concentric rings, called *tracks*, as shown in Figure 5.8. Neither is visible to the naked eye but is created when the disk is formatted by the microcomputer operating system (the OS). Different OSs format identical disks differently, creating varying numbers of sectors and tracks for their own use. These diverse formats are also rarely compatible. The first sector (sector 0) is always set to the floppy disk's index hole and the first track, but since the creation of sectors is operating system and microcomputer dependent, they are called soft sectoring schemes. This is in contrast to a previous sectoring scheme, hard sectoring, in which a set of concentric holes defined disk sectors.

Figure 5.9 shows how data is written to, and read from, the floppy disk. Each disk has an exposed area, called a head window, which allows the read/write head to read and write to the disk. On the 5.25-inch disk, the head window keeps the disk surface permanently exposed. However, on the 3.5-inch disk, a spring-loaded shutter covers the window and is drawn aside to expose the disk surface only on insertion into the drive. In the disk drive, the disk hub (Figure 5.9) is used to rotate the disk at 300 revolutions per minute. The drive head actually touches the disk surface as it creates magnetic bit patterns on the disk surface (writing and formatting), or detects existing patterns (reading). *Data access time,* about 450 milliseconds for floppy disks, is a sum of the three components listed below.

1. **Seek time.** This is the time taken for the disk head to move over the desired track. This is about 8–10 ms for hard disks and 50–200 ms for floppy disks

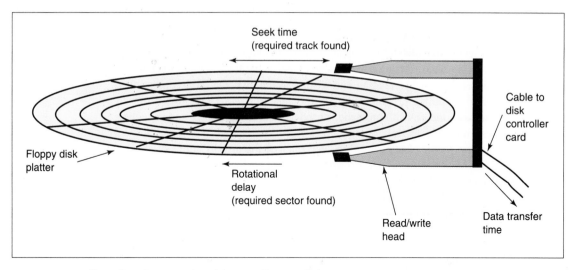

Seek time
(required track found)

Cable to
disk
controller
card

Floppy disk
platter

Rotational
delay
(required sector found)

Read/write
head

Data transfer
time

FIGURE 5.9   Reading from and writing to floppy disks

TABLE 5.1   Floppy disk sizes, features, and capacities

Disk Size (Inches)	Tracks	Sectors/Track*	Capacity
3.5	80	9	720 k
3.5	80	18	1.44 Mb
3.5	80	36	2.88 Mb
5.25	40	9	360 k
5.25	80	17	1.2 Mb
Floptical 3.5	1250+	varies	20 Mb–50 Mb

Floppy disk storage capacity is determined by the number of sectors and tracks, and the data stored on each track. For example, the 5.25-inch floppy disks used on 386-based microcomputers feature 17 512-byte sectors and 80 tracks of data on each side. As each sector holds 512 K of data, the total capacity of the disk is (17 sections(512 bytes/sector)*80 tracks*2 sides], or 1.2 Mb of data. 3.5-inch disks are organized differently on PC-compatibles, with 80 tracks and 9 512 K sectors for single-density disks (720 K capacity).

2. ***Rotational delay (or latency).*** This is the time taken by the required sector to come under the read/write head. This ranges from 5–10 ms for hard disks to 60–100 ms for floppies

3. ***Transfer time.*** This is the time taken by the drive circuitry to read data sectors and transfer them into memory. Hard disk transfer rates range from 500 Kb to over 3 Mb per second while floppy rates are in the 30 K to 500 K per second range.

Floppy disk storage capacity ranges from 360 K on 5.25-inch disks to 2.88 K on very high-density disks. On laser-based floptical disks, capacities exceed 20 Mb per disk. See Table 5.1.

Before a floppy disk is used, it must be *formatted* by the disk drive. Formatting maps out the sectors and tracks on the disk by writing a *sector header* at the start of all sectors on every track. Sectors are also tested during formatting, with bad sectors identified as such to avoid storing data in them. This header contains the track and sector number and is used as a reference when reading and writing to the disk. On IBM-compatibles, running a FORMAT utility program formats the disk for MS-DOS files. Prior to formatting hard disks, the FDISK command is used to reserve a disk partition or section for storing files under MS-DOS.

The *file allocation table (FAT)* is used to keep track of the disk locations of all files on floppy and hard disks, while a *root directory* stores file attributes such as name, size, and creation date. As files are constantly stored, updated, and deleted, the FAT is constantly updated by MS-DOS. Interestingly, many FORMAT programs do not delete stored files, only their entries in the FAT and root directory, enabling them to be recovered by disk management utilities, such as Central Point's *PC Tools*™. Low-level formatting programs, however, erase both the files and their entries in the FAT and root directories (see Section 5.5).

Often, the user seeks to prevent the contents of a floppy disk from being modified. A *write-protect notch* on the floppy disk (see Figure 5.8) prevents the drive from writing data to a floppy disk, while allowing its contents to be read. On 3.5-inch disks, write-protection involves shifting a tab to expose a hole in the disk, which is detected by the drive. On 5.25-inch floppy disks, the notch must be covered by a small tape strip, which usually accompanies purchased floppy disk packs.

Floppy disks are a portable form of secondary storage, with the 3.5-inch disk able to fit into a shirt pocket. Recent trends have included an increase in floppy disk capacities, to 2.88 Mb on 3.5-inch disks, through the use of new magnetic coatings, such as *barium ferrite*. Other technologies put 20 Mb or more of data on floppy disks, using special encoding schemes and multiple data recording layers. **Floptical disks** (shown in Figure 5.10), for example, which use a combination of optical and magnetic data recording, are also 3.5 inches in size and support data storage capabilities of over 20 Mb per disk. Users should be aware that floppy disks suffer from wear and tear as the drive head repeatedly touches on their surfaces. This eventually results in a loss of data.

Hard Disks

Floppy disks are a transportable form of secondary storage but have shortcomings, which include slow data access times (relative to the CPU/memory subsystem and to hard disks) and limited data capacity. Magnetic **hard disks** represent a form of secondary storage with faster access times (9–27 ms) and larger capacities (40 Mb–2 Gb). They are mostly fixed within the microcomputer, although some are transportable. Hard disks are similar in structure to floppy disks but have multiple disks or *platters,* rather than a single one (Figure 5.11). These platters are metal, in contrast to mylar floppy disks. A read/write head is assigned to every disk surface, enabling access to data on different tracks. The head assembly moves the read/write heads together, so that they are always positioned on the same track on different disk surfaces.

The disk platters are attached to a central spindle, which rotates them at 3,600–7,200 revolutions per minute, more than twelve times faster than a floppy disk. Unlike

FIGURE 5.10   Floptical disks use a combination of magnetic storage and optical guidance to store between 20 and 50 Mb of data on a single disk.

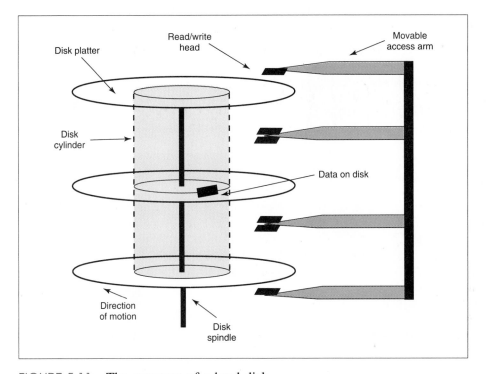

FIGURE 5.11   The structure of a hard disk

the floppy disk drive, the drive heads do not touch the disk surface. Rather, they use a *flying head* design, in which they float 14–20 millionths of an inch over the disk surface. In comparison, a particle of dust may be 300 millionths of an inch in size, the major reason for sealed disk units. In addition, disk drives come in an assembly with a built-in shock absorber, to absorb sudden impact during use. As the disk platters rotate, a *stepper motor* positions the drive heads over the track to read or write desired data.

Platters in a hard disk unit range in number from two to six. Instead of writing on disk surfaces in sequential order, the disk controller guides the read/write head to store files first on all track 1s, then track 2s, all the way to the last track. This reduces seek time for the read/write head and the corresponding data access time. On a hard disk, these concentric tracks are called *cylinders* (see Figure 5.11), with cylinder 1 comprising all track 1s on every disk surface.

Hard disks may be purchased in different sizes, such as 2.5-, 3.5-, and 5.25-inch hard disks. They may be half-height or full-height devices, as shown in Figure 5.12. Smaller drives, that is, 2.5- and 3.5-inch drives, are generally used in notebook computers in a half-height format. Hard disks may also be *internal,* fitted into the microcomputer system, or *external* to the microcomputer. A *removable hard disk* is a further type of hard disk that fits into an internal or external docking bay and can be removed and transported. A fourth variation is the *hardcard,* a hard disk mounted on an expansion card. Both the disk controller and the hard disk reside on this same card, saving a half- or full-height docking bay in the microcomputer.

The **hard disk controller** is a logic card that sits in one of the microcomputer's expansion slots. It serves as an interface between the system's processor and the hard disk by translating data requests from the processor to the hard disk. It also transfers data between DRAM and disk. Two methods for storing data on the disk are *modified*

FIGURE 5.12   Hard disks in 5.25-inch and 3.5-inch form factors. Storage capacities for individual hard disks now exceed 2 Gb.

frequency modulation (MFM) encoding, which uses 17 sectors on each track, and *run length limited (RLL)* encoding, which places 26 sectors on each track for higher capacities. The different disk controllers (see also Table 5.2) include the following:

- **ST 506 or XT/AT drive controllers.** These are serial controllers used primarily for disk drives under 40 Mb. They utilize MFM encoding to perform serial data transfers up to 510 K/bytes per second (Kbps) but are almost never used in newer systems.
- **ST-506 RLL controllers.** These controllers use RLL encoding and higher-quality disks to create 50 percent more sectors per track than the XT/AT controller. They support capacities of up to 200 Mb, with serial data transfer rates of 750 Kbps.
- **Intelligent drive electronics (IDE) controllers.** IDE controllers are a popular choice for high-capacity disk drives of 100 Mb and beyond. They place 100+ sectors on individual tracks, compared to MFM's 17 sectors, and they transfer data at up to 2 Mbps.
- **Small computer system interface (SCSI) and SCSI-2 controllers.** These are currently the most popular hard disk controllers. The SCSI (pronounced *scuzzy*) interface uses parallel data transfers for faster rates. SCSI and SCSI-2 controllers feature transfer rates of 2 Mbps and 5 Mbps, respectively. Also, up to seven devices (hard disks, printers, and so on) may be connected in a daisy chain, using only one SCSI expansion card and slot. Macintosh microcomputers have historically used SCSI drive controllers.
- **Enhanced small device interface (ESDI) controllers.** ESDI controllers are an extension of the ST506 controller, but incorporate buffering and intelligence on the drive. ESDI controllers support disks of up to 765 Mb and serial data transfer rates of 2.5 Mbps.

ST506-based controllers utilize a *stepper motor* to position the disk heads over the required tracks. Older, inexpensive stepper-based mechanisms provided no feedback to the disk head and were limited in precision. Newer **voice-coil actuators** provide

TABLE 5.2   Table of hard disk controllers

Controller Name	Machine Used	Data Transfers	Transfer Rates*	Disk Capacities Supported
ST 506	XTs/ATs	Serial	510 Kbps	up to 40 Mb
ST 506 RLL	AT/386	Serial	750 Kbps	up to 200 Mb
IDE	386 and above	Parallel	2 Mbps	100 Mb+
SCSI	386 and above	Parallel	2 Mbps	100 Mb+
SCSI II	386 and above	Parallel	5 Mbps	100 Mb+
ESDI	386 and above	Serial	2.5 Mbps	up to 765 Mb

*kilobytes and megabytes per second

feedback to the disk head and increased accuracy and are now widely used with all controllers to increase reading precision to levels required for higher disk recording densities.

Another innovation is to replace *variable-density recording,* in which data is written at a constant rate on both inner and outer disk tracks, with *constant-density recording,* where data is stored at the same density on all tracks. This increases the number of sectors on outer tracks, to make more effective use of the disk surfaces and raising overall disk capacities. Other advances include efforts to replace metal platters with *glass platters,* which support even higher recording densities.

Hard disks are necessary forms of secondary storage for today's microcomputer users. Their storage capacities continue to increase even while storage costs decrease. The 10 Mb hard disk, which cost over $1,000 in 1981, has been replaced by the 100 Mb drive, costing under $200 today. Furthermore, the storage requirements for programs and files used in newer operating environments such as OS/2, Windows™, and UNIX are typically very large. As users move from DOS-based software to software written for these environments, greater capacity disk drives are needed. The advent of digital imaging and multimedia also provide stimulus for increased capacities, a trend that will continue well into the future.

Optical and Magneto-Optical Storage Devices

Optical disks are recent additions to secondary storage devices. They are based on laser technology and provide immense secondary storage capabilities at a low cost per stored byte. Access times for optical storage media are nearer those of hard disks than floppies, but they compete with both these media and with magnetic cartridges. Storage capacities on optical disks range from 128 Mb to 5 Gb on a single side. Optical disks are usually made of glass or plastic, covered by a thin metallic layer. Data is stored on this layer and the whole disk is sealed in an airtight plastic casing to prevent oxidation of the metal layer (see Figure 5.13).

The three types of optical disks are *compact disk read-only memory (CD-ROM),* *write once read many (WORM),* and *rewritable optical disks.* Each of these requires a unique type of drive, but *multifunction drives* can read both WORM and rewritable optical disks. CD-ROM and WORM disks were the earliest optical storage media available, and neither was rewritable. They were therefore used primarily for archival purposes and software distribution. Rewritable disks, introduced in 1989, allowed the use of optical disks in a greater variety of functions.

- *CD-ROMs.* CD-ROMs are based on the same technology as audio compact disks. Unlike the concentric tracks of magnetic media, a CD-ROM stores data on one long spiraling track, which, if straightened out, would stretch for over three miles! A close-up view of the surface of the disk would reveal *pits* at various points on the CD-ROM track. These pits are burned into the surface of the disk by a laser beam during a mastering process prior to mass distribution. While a pit represents a 1, a flat surface represents a 0, enabling binary data representation. The data is encoded in sectors of 2,048 bytes, for a total capacity of 635 Mb per CD-ROM. Since 82 Mb is used for redundant *error-correction data,* effective disk capacity is about 553 Mb. A CD-ROM drive may read from, but not write to, the disk. It reads from the disk by focusing a low-intensity laser on the disk

FIGURE 5.13   Rewritable optical disks currently store 128 Mb or 256 Mb of
data on 3.5-inch disks or 1 Gb and more on 5¼-inch disks.

surface and detecting the reflected beam. Flat surfaces reflect the beam (interpreted
as 0) while pits scatter it (interpreted as 1). The signals are then passed to the
controller card within the microcomputer. Additionally, the 4.7-inch CD-ROMs
may be either internal or external units.

- **WORMs.** WORMs are broadly similar to CD-ROMs, with one major difference.
  They can be written to once by the user, unlike CD-ROMs, but thereafter, their
  contents are permanent. They use two laser beams, one for writing to the disk surface

and another low-intensity laser for reading from the disk. The components of an optical system with read and write lasers is shown in Figure 5.14. WORMs span all sizes, including 3.5 inch, 5.25 inch, 8 inch and even 12 inch drives and may be internal or external to the microcomputer. Larger disks hold greater data amounts, reaching 5 Gb on 14 inch disks.

- **_Rewritable disks._** Rewritable disks hold the most promise for optical technology. They are usually magneto-optical and utilize both magnetic and optical storage mechanisms. They can be rewritten up to one million times, unlike both CD-ROMs and WORMs and similar to magnetic media. The rewritable disk's recording layer consists of a magnetic alloy. A laser beam is used to heat the disk surface to its Curie point (150° C), after which it is magnetized. Based on the polarity of magnetization, the disk surface becomes more or less reflective when subjected to a low-intensity laser beam. The reflectivity at different points is interpreted as a 0 or 1 by the reading mechanism, and the data is conveyed to controller. Rewritable disks transfer data at up to 625 Kbps, but access times lag behind faster hard disks, at about 30 ms.

The cost of optical disk drives remains high, at about five times that of a 200 Mb hard disk. However, the cost of each disk may be as low as $50 for rewritable disks, making optical disks cheaper (per byte) as more disks are used. CD-ROMs are the most

FIGURE 5.14   Optical disk drives range from small, single-disk units (foreground) to larger optical "jukeboxes" (background), which
hold multiple drives and even more disks that are inserted
and removed under machine control.

limited optical storage medium, and coupled with high mastering costs and slow access times (typically 100 ms and over), are restricted to publishing and mass distribution purposes. WORM devices, too, are limited owing to the permanent nature of written data and costly disks and drives. However, they lack the high mastering costs of CD-ROMs. They are used for archival purposes or for normal storage, with updated files taking up new space on the disk.

Rewritable disks are the most exciting and useful optical disk technology, accounting for over 80 percent of the market. They feature the fastest access times—reaching 30 ms—which are comparable to slow hard drives. Some firms have begun to use these drives as replacements for magnetic cartridges for data backup, due to their random access capabilities and data transfer speeds. Also, optical jukeboxes allow automatic loading of multiple optical disks to create aggregate mass storage capacities in the terabyte (a trillion bytes) range.

PCMCIA Memory Cards

PCMCIA memory cards are credit-card-sized memory cards that conform to the **Personal Computer Memory Card International Association** format. They are 1.8 inches long and reach a maximum of 12.5 mm high (PCMCIA Type 3). These memory cards are primarily used in palmtops and portable microcomputers as fast secondary permanent storage.

One category of PCMCIA cards are solid-state cards containing memory microchips, that is, DRAM, EPROM, EEPROM, or Flash RAM. DRAM-based memory cards contain batteries, which supply electrical current. With EPROM and EEPROM, however, memory contents may be altered by using electricity or ultraviolet radiation to selectively modify data on the memory card and rewrite the chip's contents. With Flash RAM, data can be stored and erased cost effectively, providing roughly 100-fold speed gains over hard disks but costing up to ten times more.

Vendors such as Conner Peripherals also manufacture miniature hard disks in the PCMCIA Type 3 format in capacities exceeding 30 Mb (Figure 5.15). Weighing only

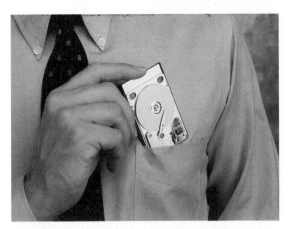

FIGURE 5.15   PCMCIA hard disks are credit-card size for use in noteɒook microcomputers.

2.5 ounces, the 32 Mb version can be inserted into and removed from machines with compatible slots.

5.5   IMPROVING THE EFFICIENCY _____ OF STORAGE DEVICES _____

Hard disks are the predominant mass storage medium in use. Most single-user microcomputer systems purchased today are likely to include a hard disk with a minimum capacity of 80 Mb, with larger capacities required for network servers. As disk capacities have increased, software programs have been written to make more efficient use of hard disks, including *disk optimizers, disk caching programs,* and *data compression utilities.* They offer improved efficiency in the use of magnetic storage and are important tools for the microcomputer user.

Disk Optimizers

Two examples of disk optimizers are Central Point's *PC Tools* and Symantec's *Norton Utilities.* They contain suites of programs that tune the hard disk for improved performance. They may be run occasionally by the user to perform these functions:

- **Disk defragmentation.** In typical disk usage, files become fragmented all over the disk surface over time. Earlier, we saw that disks were organized into cylinders, cylinders consisted of tracks, and tracks contained a number of 512-byte sectors. In storing files, MS-DOS divides the data into clusters, each consisting of four sectors. In Figure 5.16, we see an example of fragmentation. On a new disk, File 1 is initially

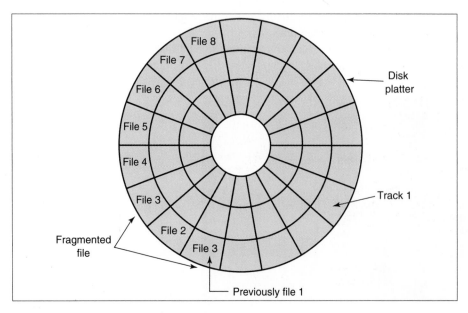

FIGURE 5.16   Disk defragmentation

written and occupies one cluster. File 2 is then written to the disk and occupies the next cluster. File 1 is then deleted, and the user stores File 3, which is two clusters long, on the disk. It occupies the first cluster used previously by File 1 and an additional cluster after File 2 and is thereby fragmented. Subsequent modification, updating, and rewriting of files increases fragmentation. This slows down disk access, as the read/write head has to go to far-flung locations to retrieve (and store) segments of the same file. A *disk defragmentation program* rearranges all files sequentially, from the beginning of the disk, using the free parts of the disk as temporary swap storage during the rearrangement. Performance gains of up to 20 percent may result from the use of such software.

- *Low-level disk formatting.* Over time, hard disks experience a gradual *alignment drift* of the read/write heads (as in Figure 5.17). Since the sector headers (which precede each sector) remain static from the initial low-level format, the time may come when the sector head can no longer be found, rendering the data in the sector inaccessible. Performing a low-level format rewrites all the data, sector headers and all. As this is done using the existing alignment, alignment drift up to that point is eliminated. Microcomputer packages (for example, Gibson Research's *Spinrite*) may be used to perform regular nondestructive low-level formatting, which leaves all the data on the hard disk intact.

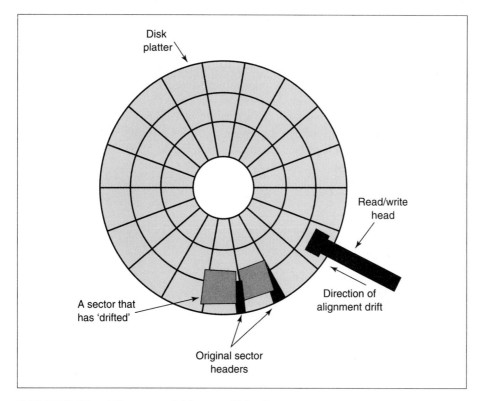

FIGURE 5.17   Alignment drift on a disk platter

Improving Disk Access through Disk Caching

Another function offered by disk utilities is disk caching (see Chapter 3), directed at easing the bottleneck between memory and secondary storage subsystems. While memory accesses take between 60 and 120 ns, the fastest hard disk accesses are made in about 9 ms, or nearly 100,000 times slower than DRAM access. Many disk utility programs (for example, Central Point's *PC Tools,* Symantec's *Norton Utilities*) and memory management programs (for example, Quarterdeck's *QEMM*) provide disk caching support. They use caching algorithms to achieve hit rates (locating data in cache) of 95 percent and above, easing much of the CPU/secondary storage bottleneck.

Data and Image Compression

Technological advances supply larger amounts of secondary storage at lower costs, but the need for secondary storage continues to grow almost exponentially. This arises from new applications such as *image processing* using scanners, and so on, *multimedia,* 24- and 32-bit *color applications* (for example, CAD/CAM and DTP), *larger applications,* and *full-motion video* on the desktop. For example, consider the 24-bit color image that is scanned at 300 dpi from a 8.5 × 11-inch page. Assuming a 7-inch × 10-inch effective page surface, the data requirements are (7 * 10) square inches * (300 * 300) dots/square inch * 24 bits/dot or almost 18 Megabytes. Also, the requirements of an OS like Windows NT are about 12 Mb.

Data compression produces efficiencies in data storage by enabling the user to store more data on the same amount of physical secondary storage. Both *general-purpose compression* and *image compression* software have been developed. In each case, savings result from the creation of additional symbols in a dictionary to substitute for longer and repeated substrings of text or numbers. In compressing a file, the compression program substitutes these repeated strings with shorter codes and stores the new compressed file. In decompressing the file, the reverse process takes place using a dictionary of abbreviated symbols. Compression and decompression take place instantly and are therefore called *on-the-fly compression and decompression* (see Figure 5.18). Both text and image compression can produce data reductions of up to 20:1, reducing the 18 Mb file to 921 K.

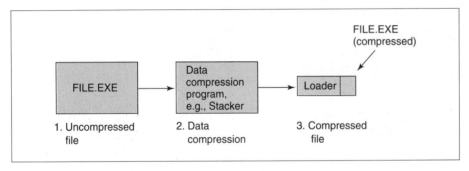

FIGURE 5.18 On-the-fly data compression

Data compression can be used on all types of files, but different file types and compression algorithms result in different compression ratios. In particular, already compressed files will respond poorly to additional compression, in some cases even growing larger. An additional benefit of data compression results from having less data to transfer to storage, leading to improved data access times overall.

Data compression can be performed by either hardware or software. *Hardware compression,* using an expansion card with the compression logic encoded on-chip, is faster but more expensive. *Software compression* is performed by the microcomputer's processor but is still in real-time on powerful microcomputers. Compression can also be used on all forms of secondary storage, ranging from magnetic to optical media.

Popular general-purpose compression packages include Stac Electronics' *Stacker* (Figure 5.19) and PKWare's shareware product, *PKZIP,* which reduce files between 25 percent and 95 percent. The greatest gains come from image bitmaps, while the least come from operating system files (for example, .SYS and .EXE files on IBM-compatibles). Overall, these programs double storage capacity for the average user. The two major standards for image compression are the *joint photographics experts group (JPEG)* algorithm for still images and the *motion picture experts group (MPEG)* algorithm for full-motion video. Each of these produces reductions ranging from 12:1 to 25:1. With image compression algorithms, it is important for the user to know if the algorithm is lossless or complete in every detail when compressed or "lossy," meaning that some detail is lost in compression.

Data compression is not without its problems. Some of these include the software's requirements for 25–45 K of RAM, reducing the space available for programs. Some LAN NOSs, for example, Novell's Netware, do not tolerate disk compression programs other than theirs. Incompatibilities have also been reported with utilities. These include disk defragmentation, disk caching, and memory management programs and could result in disk corruption. Furthermore, attempting to boot a crashed, compressed disk from a floppy is difficult or impossible as the OS may not understand the compressed file formats. Using special compressor-compatible boot disks is necessary.

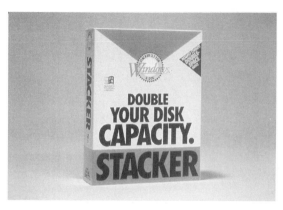

FIGURE 5.19   Stacker: A popular data compression package

Redundant Arrays of Inexpensive Disks (RAID)

Two continual concerns managers of LANs have are to provide sufficiently large fast-access secondary storage to network users and to reduce the risk of lost data if a hard drive fails. RAID is a new hardware/software combination proposed as a solution to these concerns. It consists of high-capacity, high-performance hard disk drive arrays with built-in fault tolerance. There are six RAID methods or levels for storing data, ranging from *RAID level 0* to *RAID level 5*. (Figure 5.20 shows four major RAID levels.)

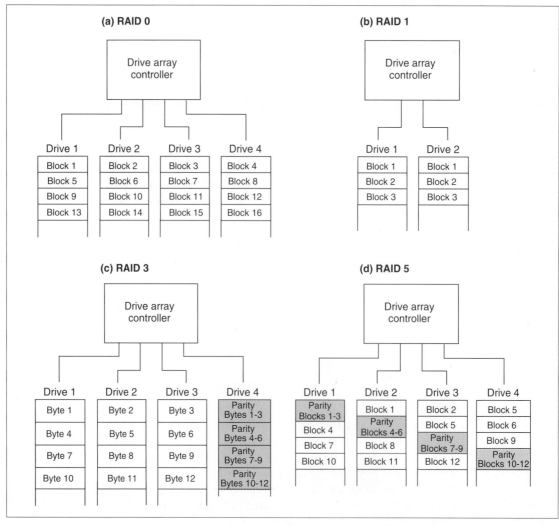

FIGURE 5.20   Four RAID levels

- ***Raid level 0.*** This method breaks files into blocks, which are stored sequentially on different disks. This method is also called *data striping*. Several users can access different blocks simultaneously, and one user can read data from multiple drives simultaneously, making for fast data access. However, the failure of one drive causes an entire disk subsystem failure, as fragments of many files are stored on every drive.
- ***Raid level 1.*** Here, the entire disk's contents are duplicated on a second disk, in a process called *disk mirroring*. Access is restricted to a single user, and simultaneous reads and writes are made to each drive. The risk of failure is much reduced, but the cost of secondary storage is doubled.
- ***Raid level 2.*** This method performs data striping using individual bits and is seldom used.
- ***Raid level 3.*** This RAID level also involves data striping. It writes bytes in sequential order across several hard disks, with the last hard disk in the sequence containing a parity byte (see Figure 5.20c). The parity byte is used to safeguard against failure by ensuring that the totals of all stored bits are either even (even parity) or odd (odd parity). For example, if similarly positioned bits in disks 1, 2, and 3 are 1, 0, and 1, respectively, under an odd parity scheme, a 1 would be stored in the fourth drive to produce an odd total, that is, $1 + 0 + 1 +$(parity bit, 1) to add up to 3. Using the parity scheme, the contents of a failed disk can be regenerated.
- ***Raid level 4.*** This is similar to level 3, with the major difference being that blocks are written sequentially on disks, rather than single bytes.
- ***Raid level 5.*** This final RAID level also makes use of data striping. It writes blocks of data sequentially across several hard disks and spreads the parity block across all the hard disks, as shown in Figure 5.20d. Multiple users can access disk storage simultaneously, as long as their data and parity blocks do not overlap. For example, blocks 4 and 9 may be written to and their parity blocks updated simultaneously.

RAID levels 3 and 5 are the most widely used methods. However, some disk controllers also support RAID level 1, or the interactive duplication of a hard disk's contents. RAID level 3 facilitates faster disk access for the single user. It allows only one user's accesses at one time because two updates cannot be made to the parity disk simultaneously. Conversely, level 5 suits multiple users accessing smaller files, as parity bits are spread out between all hard drives. RAID is used in high-end file and data base servers as a means of increasing storage efficiency and of providing larger storage capabilities.

Disk Duplexing

The disk mirroring method used in RAID level 1 and other RAID methods provides a significant amount of protection from catastrophic disk failure. However, if a single disk controller card, cable, or power supply is used, a failure of any one of these components will bring down a server, despite the use of RAID. Disk duplexing provides redundant components in the form of duplicate disk controllers, power supplies, cables, and buses. If any of these fail, the redundant component takes over without any interruption to the network. Disk duplexing is supported by server vendors such as Netframe, Parallan, and Compaq. Several NOSs, especially Novell's Netware SFT and Netware Version 4 support disk duplexing.

5.6   SELECTING SECONDARY STORAGE DEVICES

When purchasing a microcomputer system, decisions must be made regarding the choice of secondary storage devices. If the purchase involves a multiuser system with several microcomputers serving different roles, then the decision can be even more complex. As we saw in Figure 5.1, all storage devices can be arranged in ascending order of cost and capabilities. Specifically, secondary storage devices may also be organized into a hierarchy, as in Figure 5.1, with devices like floppy disks at the bottom of the hierarchy and hard disks at the top. The basic objective can be narrowed down to configuring a system with adequate amounts of each type of storage, while making the trade-off between cost and capabilities. This section explores the decisions you are likely to make for both single-user and multiuser contexts. See Table 5.3 for help in selecting secondary storage devices.

Secondary Storage Issues and Requirements in Single- and Multiuser Environments

For the user purchasing a single machine for personal use, an initial consideration is the number and the type of slower secondary storage devices to be included in the system.

TABLE 5.3   Selecting secondary storage devices

	Capacity	Drive Cost	Media Cost/Mb	Portability	Uses
Floppy disks	720k–2.88 Mb	$40–$100	$1	High	Individual use, limited bit-mapped files
Floptical disks	20–50 Mb	$300	$1.50	High	Individual use, several bit-mapped files
Hard disks	up to 2 Gb	$200–$2,000	$1–$3	For portable types only	Individual/group use. All types of files, hot backups
Flash RAM	1–4 Mb	$50	$3	High	Individual use, limited bit-mapped files
CD-ROM	550 Mb	$250	3¢	High	All file types, encyclopaedic and other reference material
WORM	1–5 Gb	$2,500	30¢	High	All file types, archival and reference material
Rewritable disks	128Mb–2 Gb	$1,000–$4,000	10¢–25¢	High	All file types, individual or group use, database, backup
Magnetic cartridges	up to 5 Gb	$250–$2,000	4¢–9¢	High	All file types, individual or group use, backups, batch processing

Floppy drives are typically the first devices to be considered. Users of IBM-compatible microcomputers have several size/capacity standards available, each with different advantages. These standards are primarily 3.5-inch drives, then 5.25-inch drives, and to a much lesser extent, 2.5-inch drives. Although the 3.5-inch drive is now standard, IBM-compatibles are often purchased with two drives, to handle both the older standards and the new. The newer 2.88 Mb 3.5-inch drive, marketed by Sony and others, has received a boost through its adoption by IBM on its PS/2s but is unlikely to become a standard, as it will probably be overtaken by higher-density floppy drives.

Macintosh and most workstation users face simpler choices in drive selection, as their standard is the 3.5-inch drive. Most Macintoshes also have one floppy drive, rather than two. While it makes copying from across floppy disks more difficult, this is not a serious drawback to everyday use.

Practically all microcomputer users will require a form of faster secondary storage. A majority of purchasers opt for hard (magnetic) disks. Currently, the cost of optical disk drives is still too high for all but a few single users, though this situation is expected to change. The key question is: "How much hard disk capacity is enough?" The answer, of course, depends on the number and types of applications to be used. For users in a DOS-based environment with an average set of applications (for example, word processor, spreadsheet, created files, data manager, and utilities), 100 Mb is about the minimum, although 170 Mb would be preferred. As it is certain that user needs will grow, data compression utilities are a wise investment, keeping the risks in mind. For users in a *GUI environment,* where applications (and operating system programs) tend to be larger, 170 Mb would be the minimum hard disk capacity, though 200 Mb and upward is more appropriate. The user with specialized needs, such as a large number of graphical applications, would benefit from even greater hard disk capacities.

Both IBM-compatible and other microcomputer users will have data backup needs. Optical disks provide a means of backing up, but tape drives are currently cheaper and more standardized. They are almost indispensable in transaction processing environments where a single microcomputer is being used to support business activities. IDE controllers are standard for this level of user requirements, but SCSI drive controllers may be purchased, especially if future drive expansion is desired.

Larger budgets and the need for random access may result in optical media being selected for backup purposes. For all devices, data compression utilities greatly reduce the amount of storage required often up to 50 percent. Even using data compression, backup using floppy disks is now only practical in the case of the low-capacity hard disks (40 Mb or less). For larger databases, magnetic tape or optical disks are recommended to avoid constantly inserting disks. Consider the case of the 200 Mb hard disk, where 1.44 Mb floppy disks are used for backup and 50 percent of the disk is in use. With a data compression factor of 2:1, the number of disks used is 100 Mb / (1.44 * 2), or 35 disks, clearly unacceptable in time and effort. (However, incremental, daily backups of modified files would be only a fraction of this.)

For microcomputers designated as file or database servers in multiuser environments, secondary storage requirements are greater than those of single users. First, such machines are better served by either local bus, EISA, or MCA buses, and not the slower ISA bus, to cope with high data throughput. Second, the selected drive controller should be at the top end of the range, typically ESDI or SCSI 2. Third, disk capacities are much greater than for single-user configurations, ranging from 200 Mb upward. The user often finds it desirable to break up this capacity over two or more drives, to ensure against the risk of drive failure and to enable backup methods such as RAID. Again, depending on the budget, users may select optical media for backup, or even as the major means of secondary storage.

These larger systems will also benefit from having both 3.5-inch and 5.25-inch floppy drives, and a case (probably of the tower design) with enough drive bays to allow the installation of further hard drives if required. With such large systems, the need for disk utilities for backup, defragmentation, caching, and disk maintenance are as important as in single-user systems. In the future, floptical disks offering 20 Mb and above may see wider use as replacements for current floppy disks. Also optical disks, with their capabilities and portability, are already a viable replacement for magnetic (hard) drives in some instances. Their use will increase in the future, as will that of flash RAM. Access times for flash RAM are comparable to DRAM, and not hard disks. Many view them as the eventual replacement for all types of secondary storage—when densities have increased and costs decreased sufficiently.

CHAPTER SUMMARY

Secondary storage devices are commonplace and almost indispensable in today's desktop microcomputers and workstations. They provide permanent storage of programs and data and are therefore nonvolatile storage devices. The prices of secondary storage devices have mirrored those of the processor subsystem, with larger storage capacities developed and sold at continually lower prices. Data is represented on secondary storage devices in binary form, that is, in sequences of 0s and 1s, and various types of files stored include program, data, image, sound, and text files.

Sequential access storage devices (SASDs) represent data by creating magnetic patterns on a long strip of mylar tape. The SASD used in microcomputer systems is the magnetic cartridge. It is the most limited type of secondary storage device, requiring all preceding records to be read prior to accessing any individual record. The three types of magnetic cartridge are quarter-inch cartridge (QIC), 8 mm cartridge, and digital audio tape (DAT). Their primary use is in maintaining backup copies of direct access storage devices (DASDs), such as hard disks.

DASDs offer direct access to individual records stored on the disk, that is, in roughly the same amount of time. The earliest and most common DASD for microcomputers was the floppy or flexible disk. Its tracks contain encoded data magnetized by a read/write head that moves in and out over the plastic disk's surface as it rotates. Fixed disks have several metal disks and many read/write heads (one for each surface). They offer the fastest available data access times and are featured on the majority of purchased systems, ranging in capacity form 40 Mb to 2 Gb and above. Optical disks use a laser assembly, rather than a magnetized read/write head, to encode information on their surfaces. CD-ROMs and WORMs do not allow the rewriting of optical disks, but newer rewritable optical disks do, making them directly competitive with both hard disks and magnetic tape. Newer technologies include Flash RAM and Holographic Storage.

Almost as important as DASDs are methods for improving their efficiency during use. These methods include optimizing the disk through low-level reformatting and defragmentation, disk caching, and using data compression software to increase the disk's effective capacity. In addition, RAID provides both heightened data security and speed of access, particularly for hard disk subsystems within LAN servers.

The major advances in DASD technologies have unfortunately not kept up with developments in microcomputer processor/memory subsystems. As such input/output (I/O) bottlenecks characterize most medium- to high-end systems, caches, 32-bit I/O buses (for example, the EISA bus), and bus mastering are increasingly important features on microcomputer systems, as indicated in Chapter 3.

Secondary storage devices must be carefully matched to the user's requirements. Microcomputer features, device controller cards, device type and features, prices, and available disk utilities must be evaluated by the buyer of the storage subsystem to arrive at a suitable selection. As newer and more sophisticated applications are developed, they make increasingly greater demands on the storage subsystem. Advances in storage technologies must still be complemented by knowledge and informed selection of storage devices in specific situations.

REVIEW QUESTIONS

1. Why are secondary storage devices necessary for microcomputers?
2. Name three types of data that are stored on secondary storage devices.
3. Why is it impractical to use DRAM for secondary storage in microcomputers?
4. How is data stored on magnetic cartridges? How does it differ from storage on optical disks?
5. Are DASDs or RAM responsible for the data transfer bottleneck between the two?
6. What is 8-bit ASCII and what is it used for?
7. What is the purpose of parity bits? Differentiate between even and odd parity. How are parity bits used on magnetic tape?
8. What are the most common physical dimensions for floppy disks, and how is data organized on them?
9. What are two advantages of removable hard disks?
10. Describe and compare three kinds of optical disks? Which is the most versatile?
11. What are the causes and effects of disk fragmentation, and how is a disk defragmented?
12. What is the difference between hardware and software disk compression?
13. What are major motivating factors behind the use of RAID methods?
14. Why are operating systems disk-based and not ROM-based?

EXERCISES

1. What is the difference between electronic storage (for example, using DRAM) and electromechanical storage (on disks)? What are two major consequences of this difference?
2. Assuming a disk cache has a 90 percent hit rate (that is, 90 times out of 100, the requested records are found in the cache), disk access time is 28 ns, and RAM access

time is 80 ns, how much time is saved retrieving 20 records from disk using the cache?

(1 ms = 1/1000 s; 1 ns = 1/1,000,000,000 s)

3. A university is considering storing student records on magnetic cartridges, to give employees in student records access to them over the departmental network. These employees make queries throughout the day to deal with student questions and administrative tasks. Is this the best form of secondary storage for this situation? Why or why not? If not, what storage devices would you recommend?

4. A small brokerage firm is considering backup options for its central database, which resides in its LAN file server. The planned backup schedule calls for disk backups to be made on Wednesdays, Fridays, and Sundays. Is this schedule an appropriate one? If not, propose a better schedule.

5. Critically compare CD-ROMs, WORMs, and rewritable optical disks. Which are the least versatile? Which are the most versatile? Which are most appropriate for archiving purposes; distributing software; student use for projects and papers; hard disk backup; hard disk replacement; distribution of existing U.S. patents?

SUGGESTED READINGS

Alford, R. C. "Life above 1 Gigabyte: DAT vs. 8-mm vs. QIC." *Byte Magazine,* April 1992, p. 197.

Harvey, D. A. "Downsizing Media: 3 1/2-inch MO Drives Arrive." *Byte Magazine,* May 1992, pp. 240–250.

Hsu, J. "The Latest in Data Storage." *PC Today,* September 1992, pp. 34–38.

Huttig, J. A., Jr. "Get Ready for RAID." *PC Today,* May 1992, pp. 48–50.

"New LAN Backup Tools." *Byte Magazine,* April 1992, pp. 192–208.

MICROCOMPUTER SOFTWARE

INTRODUCTION

Software comprises instructions written in a programming language that direct computer hardware to carry out electronic processing of data. The software used with a computer defines the set of available commands for interacting with the computer system, the interface presented to the user, and the functions performed by the computer. This chapter introduces the subject of software, and in particular, microcomputer software. It examines the major software categories, ranging from operating systems to user applications. It also describes how software is developed or acquired and three widely used microcomputer programs: word processing, spreadsheet, and database programs. The selection of appropriate combinations of hardware and software in different contexts is also discussed.

Learning Objectives

After reading this chapter, you will be able to:

- Describe the different categories of microcomputer software
- Recognize situations that call for end-user or IS software development
- Make an informed selection of an operating system for a microcomputer
- Identify the usefulness of productivity tools—word processing, spreadsheet, and database programs in different problem contexts
- Make software selections under hardware, operating system, and other constraints

---

INTEC AND COMPANY: SIMPLIFYING CATALOG AND LIST PUBLISHING WITH VENTURA DATABASE PUBLISHER

INTEC is an Indianapolis-based marketing and buying cooperative for 33 independent computer supply firms in the United States and Canada. This four-employee firm produces a 100-page catalog for its member companies, who use their buying power to negotiate volume discounts from computer product manufacturers. The software runs on IBM-compatibles and comprises Ventura Publisher 4.1 for Windows™, Microsoft Excel 3.0, and Microsoft Windows™ 3.1. Items and their prices are stored in Excel, whose capabilities enable discounts and other computations to be easily performed. Periodically, the Excel data is imported into Ventura Publisher, where it is combined with scanned-in company logos and formatted.

The near-complete catalog is then sent to a service bureau for production.

The benefits of the microcomputer-based system include hundreds of hours saved by not having to rekey and proofread the Excel data into Ventura Publisher. This data is automatically formatted in Ventura Publisher, saving more time. Windows™ Dynamic Data Exchange (DDE) capability also allows changes in Excel files to be automatically reflected in Ventura Publishing files. Prepress costs are also reduced by Ventura Publisher's advanced desktop publishing features.

Adapted from J.W. Huttig, Jr., "Computers at Work: Untrivial Pursuit," *PC Today*, March, 1993, pp. 50–52.

6.1 UNDERSTANDING THE ROLE OF SOFTWARE

Microcomputers process and store data in binary form, as described in Chapter 3. The binary data represent either program instructions to be executed by the processor or data that is used by these programs. Most computer users do not interact with the computer at the level of binary numbers. Instead, they use *operating systems* to manage the microcomputer's hardware and operation; *programming languages* to create programs that fulfill their processing requirements; and *applications,* created by software firms. In fact, the trend of software has always been toward high-level or English-like user interfaces, rather than low-level machine code. Since computers process data in binary form, translating programs are used to transform higher-level languages to the computer's native machine code. Programs developed for this purpose include *interpreters and compilers* and are discussed in Section 6.2.

Operating Systems Software

To insulate the user from complex hardware details, operating systems and operating environments are used. An **operating system** is a set of programs that

- Manages the operation of the computer hardware
- Ensures that user programs are executed correctly
- Hides the system's complexity from the user or user programs

Conversely, *operating environments* are mostly mouse-driven, GUI-based software which make it easier to work with the operating system. They also offer added features in the form of data exchange between programs and file and memory management functions. Figure 6.1 shows the computer's operating system and operating environment as the first two layers immediately surrounding the hardware.

Applications Software

The top three levels of software are programming languages, applications, and utilities. *Programming languages* are used to develop all software running on computers. They include low-level languages like assembler language and high-level English-like languages such as COBOL. *Productivity tools* include data base management systems (DBMSs) and spreadsheet and word processing programs (or packages), which enable the user to automate a wide range of common office tasks, such as filing, typing, and performing calculations and analyses.

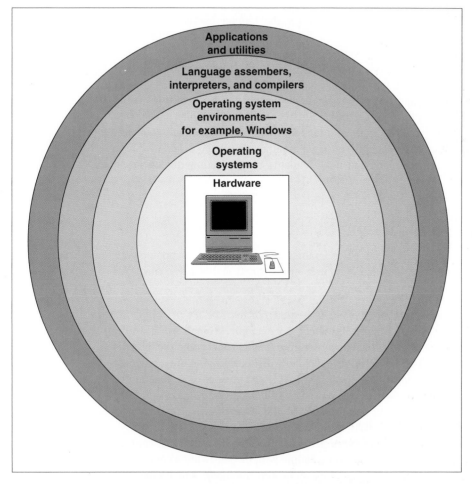

FIGURE 6.1   The operating system and other software layers

Applications are programs created either by the user or the computer professional, using programming languages or productivity tools. They directly support the user's daily business activities and include software such as accounts receivable or inventory control applications. Finally, *utility programs* perform diverse housekeeping tasks. For example, *operating system utilities* perform mostly file and disk management functions, while *general utilities* fulfill user needs ranging from antivirus to screensaver functions. The discussion of software begins with operating systems and environments.

6.2 OPERATING SYSTEMS AND ENVIRONMENTS

Operating systems were introduced in the 1960s on third-generation mainframe computers. Many operating system functions had earlier been performed by a *computer operator,* who mounted and unmounted tape drives and initiated the execution of programs through a console, among other duties. The speed of computer operations (even the slower electromechanical devices) relative to human actions created a processing bottleneck, as the computer waited for the human operator to initiate processing sequences. This ultimately led to the incorporation of these capabilities into *system software,* that is, the operating system and utility programs.

Newer, more powerful processors soon made it cost effective to service multiple user requests concurrently on a single machine. The term **concurrent** does not mean simultaneous. Instead, it means that the processor rapidly alternates between processing multiple tasks, which appear to be processed simultaneously. More complex and sophisticated operating systems were required, with the required *multitasking, multiuser,* and *multiprocessor* features. These capabilities have traditionally been associated with mainframes and minicomputers, but are now available in microcomputer operating systems.

Functions of an Operating System

The operating system (OS) is a set of programs that manage the computer's resources more efficiently and insulate the user from direct hardware contact. Its functions are

1. *To perform the complex series of operations required to start up or 'boot' the computer.* On MS-DOS-based microcomputers, for example, a small subset of the operating system is stored in ROM. This program is run as soon as the computer is switched on. First, it checks the floppy and hard disk drives for the remaining operating system components, loads them into RAM, and presents a command line interface to the user. In addition, it executes batch initialization files created by the user to customize the operating environment to the user's needs (for example, CONFIG.SYS and AUTOEXEC.BAT files).

2. *To insulate the user and user-developed program from direct hardware contact.* The operating system relieves the user from dealing with the hardware's complexity, for example, transmitting data along buses, allocating memory, and issuing and handling interrupts (a task's request for service). It provides program code and user

commands that hide this detail and ensures that devices are operated in a uniform and appropriate manner. Software developers who directly access hardware for speed gains in their programs risk software incompatibility with newer OS versions.

3. ***To provide a command interface for the user and user programs.*** In mainframe computing systems, this command interface is called the *job control language* or *JCL.* The mainframe's JCL enables the computer operator to program sequences of operations for the computer to follow, such as loading tapes and providing a processing log. OS commands on microcomputers perform a similar function, allowing the user to read from and write to files and to format, copy, and read disks, among other functions. User programs may make similar use of OS commands.

4. ***To manage the processing of programs efficiently.*** The OS also ensures that programs run correctly by allocating areas of RAM for the programs and their data, video displays and drivers, and input or output buffers. The memory map supplied by the OS indicates to the processor where input data are stored, the data paths and protocols, and where to store output data.

5. ***To provide advanced processing features.*** These include multiuser, multitasking, and multiprocessor capabilities, and virtual memory. Some microcomputer OSs, like their mainframe counterparts, provide *multiuser capabilities,* such as UNIX. Figure 6.2 shows how a single-processor microcomputer can serve multiple users using timesharing, that is, allocating timeslices (usually thousandths of a second) to each user's tasks in sequence. To the user, the computer's response appears instantaneous due to the high speed of the computer relative to the user. The operating system rotates tasks in and out of memory as required, and allocates timeslices to each task.

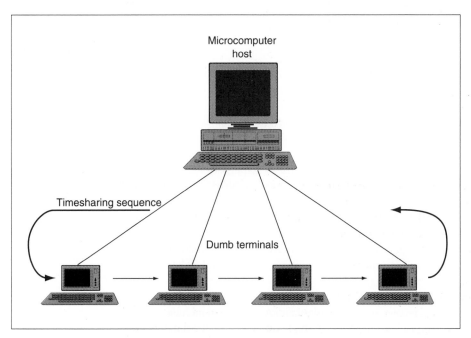

FIGURE 6.2   Multiuser microprocessor configuration based on a microcomputer host and dumb terminals

---

MULTITASKING, TASK SWITCHING, MULTIPROCESSING, AND VIRTUAL MEMORY

Multitasking refers to an operating system's ability to support multiple processing jobs run by one or more users. It is similar to a multiuser capability in that timeslices are allocated to each task in turn, with foreground tasks usually receiving larger time-slices than background tasks. A less powerful variation of multitasking is **task switching.** This feature suspends active tasks until they return to the foreground, while executing only one current active program. Windows' OS has both capabilities.

Some operating systems (for example, UNIX and Windows NT) can supervise multiple processors. **Multiprocessing** introduces several problems, including the division of labor between processors, simultaneous access to identical memory locations, and interaction among processors. Nevertheless, parallel processing is becoming more widespread, as seen in Compaq's SystemPro.

Operating systems such as Windows and the Macintosh OS support virtual memory. **Virtual memory** provides user applications with more memory than installed RAM and is often used to support the memory requirements of multiple users and multitasking. OSs provide virtual memory using DASDs and a technique called memory paging. Programs are divided into segments called pages, of which only a subset is in memory at any one time. The remainder are stored on a restricted portion of a disk. A request for a page residing on the disk generates a page fault, causing the OS to load a copy of the required page from DASD and to move a page in RAM (often the most recently used page) to disk. The disk area plus the computer's RAM are together known as virtual memory, with page swapping performed under operating system control. See Figure 6.3.

Using timesharing, high-end microcomputers can satisfy the processing needs of several users. Another operating system feature, *virtual memory,* enables the user to combine both hard disk and RAM as primary memory.

6. *To manage input and output devices effectively.* The OS supervises input and output to and from the computer to peripherals through the computer's ports. It specifies how devices such as keyboards, scanners, and printers are used, for example, where their buffers (keyboard buffers, for example) are located in RAM, how data are routed to the computer's ports, and protocols for coding and transmitting the data.

7. *To manage filing operations on secondary storage devices.* Operating systems maintain a *file allocation table (FAT),* for keeping track of stored files. In addition, they maintain RAM *buffers* for data flowing to and from secondary storage devices. Users may also use provided commands to create, modify, and delete files and directories.

8. *To handle error conditions.* Finally, the OS must be able to detect errors in processing and take corrective action to handle them. Actions may include providing messages to the user, for example, "File not Found" messages, or closing down tasks that are not running properly.

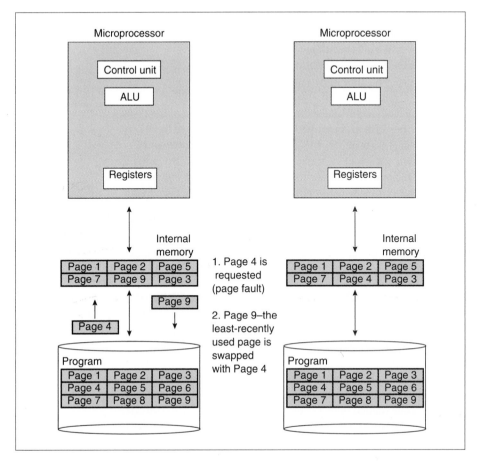

Microprocessor

Control unit

ALU

Registers

Internal memory

| Page 1 | Page 2 | Page 5 |
| Page 7 | Page 9 | Page 3 |

Page 9

Page 4

Program

Page 1	Page 2	Page 3
Page 4	Page 5	Page 6
Page 7	Page 8	Page 9

1. Page 4 is requested (page fault)

2. Page 9–the least-recently used page is swapped with Page 4

Microprocessor

Control unit

ALU

Registers

Internal memory

| Page 1 | Page 2 | Page 5 |
| Page 7 | Page 4 | Page 3 |

Program

Page 1	Page 2	Page 3
Page 4	Page 5	Page 6
Page 7	Page 8	Page 9

FIGURE 6.3   Use of virtual memory and paging

Structure of an Operating System

Microcomputer OSs comprise a *supervisor program, utility programs,* and *language translators.* The **supervisor,** sometimes called a monitor or executive, represents a small part of the overall operating system. It is the first program to be loaded during booting, and it remains resident in RAM thereafter, in contrast to utilities, which are loaded as required from secondary storage. The supervisor contains commonly used commands, which in the case of MS-DOS, include DIR (to list files) and CHDIR (to change directories), among others. It controls the entire operating system and calls up the other utility programs as they are required.

Utility programs serve many disk and file management functions, together with other general functions. The disk- and file-related utilities are used for

- Formatting disks
- Creating, deleting, and selecting directories and subdirectories
- Listing files in directories

- Creating, copying, naming, and deleting files
- Displaying and printing file contents
- Launching or initiating processing of executable files
- Switching between peripheral devices for input/output routing
- Displaying and modifying date and time functions

These and other functions are included in major microcomputer OSs. Most also allow the user to create batch files that perform programmed sequences of the above functions. User interaction with some OSs (for example, MS-DOS) is through a *command line interface* or *CLI* (Figure 6.4 *top*). Other OSs, such as Apple's System 7, use a *GUI,* where commands are selected by using the mouse to "point and shoot" at either icons or menu items (Figure 6.4 *bottom*). *Operating environments* or *shells,* discussed later, also provide GUI features to CLI-based operating systems.

Language translators complete the trio of programs that are closely associated with operating systems. They transform programs written in high-level languages into directly executable machine language or code (see Section 6.4 for a discussion of levels and generations of languages). There are three categories of language translators:

1. *Assemblers.* Assemblers convert assembly language into executable machine code. Assembly language consists of three- or four-letter codes that represent machine code instructions (for example, ADC for add and SBC for subtract) and is regarded as low-level, or close to the machine's native language. It is used mostly by trained professional programmers.
2. *Compilers.* Compilers work in a similar way as assemblers but are used for third- and fourth-generation languages. They transform the whole program (known as *source code*) into machine code (called *object code*), which can be executed directly by the processor without further need of the compiler. One widely used compiler is Micro Focus's COBOL compiler (Figure 6.5).
3. *Interpreters.* Interpreters execute third- and fourth-generation language programs one statement at a time. They translate each line of source code to machine code and execute it before proceeding to the next, making them slower in execution than either assemblers or compilers. Each time a statement is executed, it must be interpreted, so statements in a loop, for example, run slowly compared to a compiled program where the interpretation is done only once. Interpreters also require greater memory, as the interpreter and program must be in RAM together. BASIC is one of the most popular interpreted languages.

MS-DOS

The **Microsoft disk operating system (MS-DOS)** is the most widely used microcomputer operating system. MS-DOS (or just DOS) was developed by Microsoft Corporation in 1981 for the IBM PC, and over 50 million copies have since been sold. It also represents the software program that began Microsoft's rise to become the world's largest independent software vendor. Over 25,000 different programs are commercially available for DOS, and the total sales of DOS programs exceed 100 million. A modified version of MS-DOS sold specifically for IBM's Intel-based microcomputers is known as **PC-DOS.**

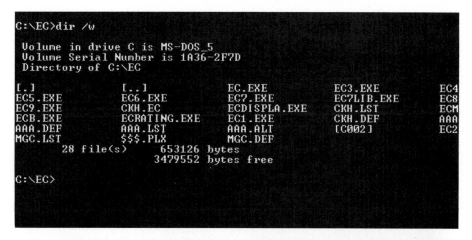

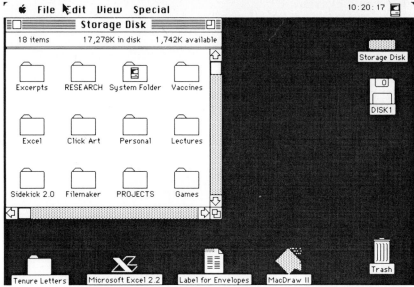

FIGURE 6.4   Two types of user interface: (*top*) command-line interface (MS-DOS); (*bottom*) graphical user interface (Macintosh OS).

   MS-DOS was developed as a *single-user, single-tasking* operating system, for use on Intel 80x86-based, IBM-compatible microcomputers. It has evolved through many versions since MS-DOS 1.0 in 1981. The latest MS-DOS (Figure 6.6) provides memory and disk management capabilities, task-switching capabilities, an interface for application programs, and utilities, for example, for data compression. It supports 3.5-inch and 5.25-inch floppy and hard disks in different data formats, ranging from 360 K to 2.88 Mb (for newer 3.5-inch floppy disks). MS-DOS supports both *interactive* use (from the command line), a *menu-driven shell,* and the use of *batch* files. Filenames are restricted to eight characters with a three-character suffix and are stored in directories and subdirectories (directories within directories) and tracked using the *FAT.*

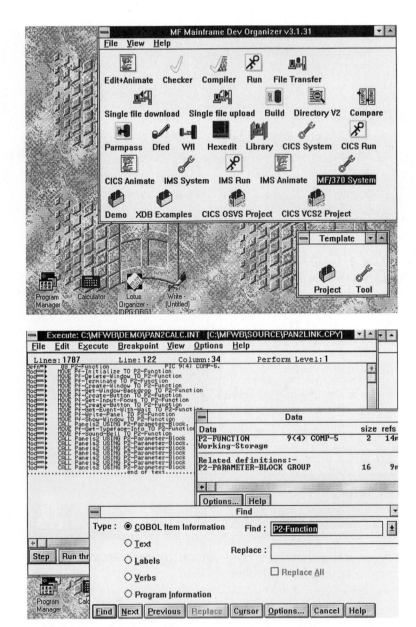

FIGURE 6.5   PC-based Micro Focus COBOL running under Windows
(*continued*)

MS-DOS has two parts: the permanent kernel (or supervisor), which is loaded into RAM on booting, and utilities, which are loaded from the hard (or floppy disk) as needed. Examples of the 50+ commands supported by MS-DOS are FORMAT commands, for formatting disks; CHDIR, for changing directories; DIR, for listing files in a directory; and TYPE, for displaying the contents of a file. Additionally, the TIME function displays the time, while the PRINT command directs a file's contents to the

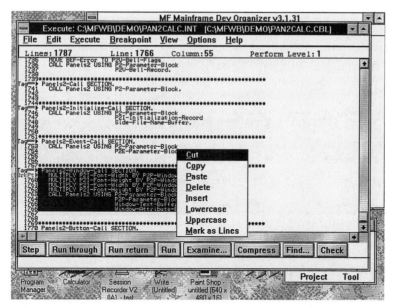

FIGURE 6.5 *(continued)*   Micro Focus COBOL screen program running
under Windows

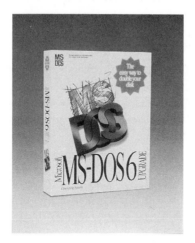

FIGURE 6.6   Microsoft's MS-DOS version 6 adds data compression, memory management, and virus checking to its regular functions.

printer. Any command used on the DOS command line can be included in a batch file,
which is characterized by a .BAT suffix and referred to as a *BAT* file. BAT files enable
sequences of tasks to be run by the user and are used in configuring application
environments for the user (for example, activating menu options, setting system options,
printing jobs, and so on).

A growing partnership now exists between MS-DOS and the Windows environment (see environments ahead), where Windows™ adds additional capabilities and a
GUI to MS-DOS.

DR-DOS

A recent competitor to Microsoft's MS-DOS is Novell's operating system, **DR-DOS.** DR-DOS was developed to run programs written for MS-DOS and is marketed as a substitute OS, offering improved performance. While keeping DR-DOS compatible with MS-DOS, Novell added new features, including larger amounts of RAM reserved for programs, an improved file editor, and a high-performance caching utility. DR-DOS also incorporates improved task switching and password protection for files, directories, and hard disks. Security features such as disk and directory password protection are also integrated into DR-DOS.

Windows NT

Windows NT is widely regarded as the most significant recent advance in operating systems (see Figure 6.7). More than DOS or Windows, its features have brought reliable client/server computing to the desktop. It is aimed primarily at IS departments and intended as an industrial-strength OS for mission-critical applications. Using NT, these applications can run securely and reliably on high-performance servers and attached clients.

Unlike MS-DOS and Windows, NT is designed to run on multiple hardware platforms, not solely Intel-based machines. DEC's Alpha and MIPS's R4000 microprocessors are two RISC platforms capable of running NT. Some key NT features are as follows:

- Symettric multiprocessing, specifically the ability to make simultaneous use of 2, 4, 8, or 16 microprocessors, not just a single one
- Built-in networking, to allow client/server interaction using several communication methods or protocols
- The ability to run MS-DOS, Windows 3.1, and OS/2 1.3 programs
- Advanced security features to control file and application sharing
- Support of RAID for increased storage reliability

 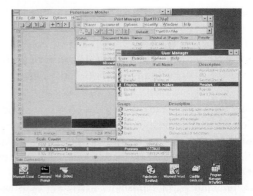

FIGURE 6.7　Windows NT screens have the same "look and feel" as Windows, but it has much greater functionality for supporting mission-critical applications.

There are two versions of Windows NT: the Standard version for clients and the Advanced Server version. Both products possess full networking capabilities, but the latter has additional services for security, external links to mainframes, and LAN management. For managers, NT's major benefit is in supplying the ability to build microprocessor-based distributed networks. In these networks, multiple-processor workstations or microcomputers can act as servers, replacing larger mainframes. The new servers include machines from Trident, Compaq, Sequent, NCR, DEC, and others.

Ultimately, NT represents a major OS for supporting affordable, yet secure and reliable micro-based transaction processing for most types and sizes of organization.

OS/2

MS-DOS was developed when microcomputers were used as single-tasking and single-user machines. As microcomputers adopted full 32-bit architectures and greatly increased in power, the limitations of MS-DOS became apparent. Newer Intel microprocessors, capable of driving several concurrent applications, were hampered by MS-DOS. For example, even if 4–8 Mb of RAM were installed in 386- and 486-based machines, MS-DOS would still "see" only 640 K of usable memory without memory expanders. IBM and Microsoft began a collaboration in 1987 to develop **Operating System/2 (OS/2)** as the operating system to succeed MS-DOS. However, IBM soon took over OS/2's development when Microsoft's interest waned following the success of Windows (see below).

OS/2 is a single-user OS but supports true multitasking, in contrast to MS-DOS's (and DR-DOS's) task switching. It was developed primarily for 386-based machines and upward, and has greater RAM and secondary storage requirements than DOS. OS/2 features a GUI, the Presentation Manager, which resembles the Macintosh System 7, with windows, icons, pull-down menus, and mouse-driven user interaction.

OS/2 is also a 32-bit operating system, taking full advantage of Intel's 32-bit chips. It supports more than 50 concurrent tasks and eliminates DOS's 8-bit file naming conventions using its *high performance filing system (HPFS)*, which supports 32-character filenames. Applications written for OS/2 are not subject to the memory workarounds of DOS-based programs (for example, extended memory) but can be as large as available memory. OS/2 supports virtual memory, using available hard disk capacity, and runs programs written for DOS and Windows. It provides better security and error-handling capabilities than DOS.

Dynamic data exchange (DDE) is an additional feature of OS/2 that establishes links between programs. This allows, for example, updated numbers in a spreadsheet to be automatically reflected in a word processing document that draws on data in the spreadsheet.

UNIX

MS-DOS and OS/2 feature task-switching and multitasking capabilities, respectively, but are single-user operating systems and incapable of serving several users concurrently, as mainframes do. The UNIX operating system has received attention in the microcomputer industry, particularly because of its multiuser capabilities. It is a *multiuser, multitasking* OS, which is dominant in the workstation arena. It was developed by AT&T in 1969 in assembly language, and its *kernel* (or core component) was rewritten in the C language in 1973. Subsequently, AT&T licensed UNIX to both universities and various firms. Since it was written in C, the UNIX kernel was *portable,* meaning that other firms could easily transfer it to different platforms. Such firms needed only to code a relatively small, machine-specific part of the OS.

As it was licensed widely, many variants of the UNIX operating system were developed for all types of computers, ranging from PCs and workstations to large mainframes. Some of the more well-known UNIX versions include the Berkeley Software Distribution or **BSD;** the Santa Cruz Operation's **SCO UNIX** for Intel 80x86-based machines; and **AIX,** IBM's version of UNIX for its RS6000 workstations.

Apart from its multiuser and multitasking capabilities, SCO UNIX has the added advantage of being able to run both MS-DOS and OS/2 as "clients," meaning that programs written for these operating systems can be run without modification. Other features include *piping,* which is designating the output of one file as an input of another, and security features, such as the designation of a *superuser* (or system administrator) who controls access to files and programs by other users. A large number of UNIX utilities allow the user to create programs for a wide variety of tasks and link them through piping. UNIX is also thought to be particularly suited to many of the new forms of distributed processing, including client/server systems. See Table 6.1 for a comparison of operating systems.

TABLE 6.1   Microcomputer operating systems and environments

	MS-DOS	Windows 3.1	OS/2	Unix	NeXT Step	Macintosh	Windows NT
Company	Microsoft	Microsoft	IBM	AT&T/SCO (many versions)	NeXT	Apple	Microsoft
Type	Single-user	Single-user	Multi-user	Multi-user	Single-user	Single-user	Multi-user
Hardware	Intel 80x86	Intel 80x86	Intel 80x86	Intel 80x86 Motorola 680x0 others	680x0	680x0	Intel 80x86, MIPS 4000, Alpha
Software available	More than 25,000 programs	More than 25,000 programs	Several '00	Several '000	Several '00	Many '000	More than 25,000
Interface	Command-line interface (CLI)	Graphic user interface (GUI)	GUI	CLI or GUI	GUI	GUI	GUI
Task switching	Yes	Yes	Yes	Yes	Yes	Yes	Yes
Multitasking	No	Yes	Yes	Yes	Yes	No	Yes
Virtual memory	No	Yes	Yes	Yes	Yes	Yes	Yes
Multi-processing	No	No	No	Yes	No	No	Yes

Increased sales of high-end 386 and 486 microcomputers, coupled with the need for network operating systems, has stimulated growth of the microcomputer UNIX market. This market is expected to top $7 billion in 1995, from $1.4 billion in 1990. Current concerns include the many varieties of UNIX, and its somewhat complex and arcane commands, which make it difficult to learn. There are as many as 200 versions of UNIX in the commercial marketplace, creating a fragmented market. Often, software written for one version of UNIX will not run directly on another version, unlike the software written for MS-DOS and OS/2 operating systems. Seeing this as a major barrier to the acceptance of UNIX, the two main UNIX developers, the *Open Software Foundation (OSF)* and (AT&T's) *Unix International,* plan to make their two main UNIX variants, *OSF/1-* and *System V Release 4 (SVR4)*-compatible.

Similar to MS-DOS, GUIs have been developed for UNIX operating systems. Two primary GUIs are **Motif,** developed by the OSF, and **Open Look,** developed jointly by AT&T and Sun Microsystems, shown in Figure 6.8. They have similar features to other GUIs, such as the Macintosh GUI and OS/2's Presentation Manager, and have helped to make UNIX more accessible to business users.

The Macintosh Operating System

Apple Macintosh and Quadra microcomputers use a proprietary operating system developed by Apple Computer. The Macintosh OS (currently system version 7) is not independently marketed for microcomputers from diverse vendors, like MS-DOS, but instead, is used solely on Apple's microcomputers and included with every Apple Macintosh purchase. It began as a GUI-based OS and not as a command-driven OS with a GUI shell added on, as in the MS-DOS/Windows combination (see Figure 6.9). Its interface is therefore one of the most mature and refined. In fact, unlike DOS/Windows usage, where the user may exit Windows and enter commands at the DOS prompt, System 7 is primarily icon and menu based.

FIGURE 6.8   Sun Sparcstation running UNIX and using the Open Look GUI

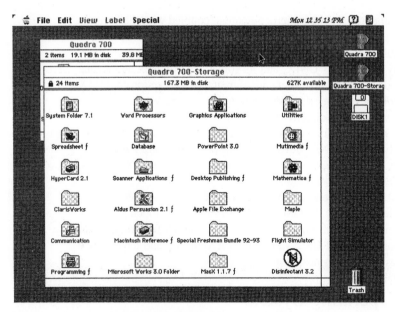

FIGURE 6.9   Apple's System 7 operating system is one of the most mature and robust GUIs available on the desktop.

System 7 is markedly different from earlier OS versions. While it is still a *single-user* operating system, it multitasks up to 31 tasks concurrently and supports *virtual memory* and *DDE.* It also features built-in networking support in the form of *AppleTalk,* for low-speed data transmission, and high-speed *Ethernet* networking. An OS utility, *Apple File Exchange,* also enables Macintosh microcomputers to read disks formatted by IBM-compatibles.

In System 7, files are opened by pointing to them using the mouse and pressing the mouse button twice. To delete files, the user points to their icons, presses the mouse button to highlight them, and then drags them to a *trash icon.* Other icons represent floppy and hard disks. Files are stored in *folders,* which are the equivalent of directories in MS-DOS, and can be searched for, printed, opened, or listed (filenames) in different formats. Thousands of applications run on System 7, covering a wide range of business software, desktop publishing (DTP) applications, and language compilers. Also, all software has the same "look and feel" (that is, a common user interface), providing an easier learning curve for new users.

Operating Environments

An important category of OS software is **operating environments** or **shells.** Operating environments provide added capabilities to MS-DOS, UNIX, and so on through:

- *A GUI.* This uses the now-familiar set of windows, icons, and menu- and mouse-driven interaction methods. The GUI provides an alternative means to access the operating system's command set and the ability to cut and paste data between applications in different windows.

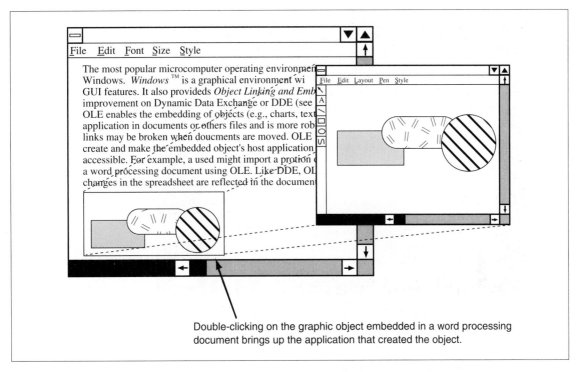

Double-clicking on the graphic object embedded in a word processing document brings up the application that created the object.

FIGURE 6.10   Object linking and embedding

- **Task-switching or multitasking capabilities.** This allows multiple programs to be active and/or run simultaneously.
- **Simultaneous display of, and switching between, concurrently executing programs.** These programs may be inactive in the background, or active, running in the foreground.
- **Improved memory and hard disk management capabilities.** In addition, there are extra utilities, such as disk compression.

The most popular microcomputer operating environment is *Microsoft (MS) Windows.* Windows is a graphical environment with a full range of GUI features. It also provides *object linking and embedding (OLE),* an improvement on dynamic data exchange or DDE (see OS/2). OLE enables the embedding of objects (for example, charts, text) from one application in documents or other files and is more robust than DDE, whose links may be broken when documents are moved. OLE's links are easier to create and make the embedded object's host application automatically accessible. For example, a user might import a portion of a spreadsheet into a word processing document using OLE. Like DDE, OLE would ensure that changes in the spreadsheet are reflected in the document. However, to change the spreadsheet from within the document the user would normally exit the program, open and modify the spreadsheet, and return to the word processor. With OLE links, clicking on the embedded spreadsheet calls up the spreadsheet application automatically and allows changes to be made directly. See Figure 6.10. Windows also improves DOS's memory management, supplying a 32-bit memory model, virtual memory, a disk cache, and user-controlled timeslices for concurrent programs.

Quarterdeck Office Systems' *Desqview X* (Figure 6.11) and *Software Carousel* are shells that provide multitasking and task switching, respectively. Desqview X is a GUI, whereas Software Carousel uses a command line interface. Desqview can also run other graphic-based programs (including Windows) in windows. Like Windows, it allows the user to modify the timeslices allocated to different tasks and to cut and paste between applications in different windows.

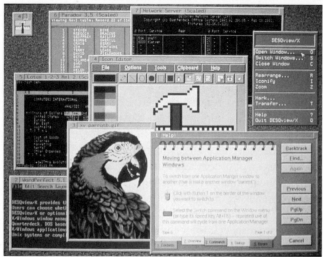

FIGURE 6.11   The sophisticated Desqview X operating environment enables the user to run multiple MS-DOS, Windows, and UNIX programs concurrently on the user's or remote microcomputers.

Other operating environments include *Presentation Manager*, the GUI tightly integrated with IBM's OS/2. It offers much the same capabilities and windowing environment as MS Windows. However, the underlying operating system is much more sophisticated than DOS, being a full-fledged 32-bit operating system. In the UNIX world, as mentioned earlier, the two major operating environments are *Open Look* (AT&T and Sun) and *Motif* (Open Software Foundation). *NeXTStep* (NeXT Computer) is another alternative OS platform on NeXT and, recently, Intel-based microcomputers. These environments provide windowing capabilities and help to mask the complexity of the UNIX OS.

6.3 A UTILITY PROGRAM
FOR EVERY NEED

Utility programs, or simply, **utilities,** serve many purposes. Several utilities are included with operating systems for listing, displaying, storing, and printing files, and so on. However, other utilities with more sophisticated capabilities are sold by many software vendors. These include programs that perform tasks like system diagnostics, checking disks for viruses, and managing both RAM and hard disks more efficiently.

Terminate-and-Stay-Resident Programs (TSRs)

Many DOS-based utilities are **terminate-and-stay-resident (or TSR)** utilities. They are also called *memory-resident* programs due to their ability to remain in memory even after they have been exited from. TSRs must be installed or initially loaded into memory. They are subsequently activated by a special combination of keystrokes, for example, CTRL-F2. This combination keystroke is also known as a *hot-key* combination and it launches the TSR while suspending the current application.

Inactive TSRs continually watch incoming keystrokes in the microcomputer's interrupt-vector table for the specific combination that makes them active. Often, conflicts result from incompatible TSRs, that is, TSRs that use the same hot-keys. As TSRs take up valuable memory, many are able to load themselves automatically into extended/expanded memory on IBM-compatibles, or be loaded by a TSR management program. Other TSRs can be stored "virtually" on the hard disk. An example of a TSR is Borland's *Sidekick,* which provides such functions as a notebook, a calendar, and communications functions. See Figure 6.12.

Memory Management Software

Memory management software can manage TSRs as well as perform other functions. This software category includes programs like Quarterdeck's *QEMM386* and Qualitas' *BlueMax*. Their main function is to make as much memory available to programs and data as possible, while limiting conflicts between them. Most memory managers are used for IBM-compatibles, to overcome the limitations of MS-DOS. QEMM386, for example, makes more conventional memory available by moving TSRs to high RAM between 640 K and 1 Mb and by providing both expanded and extended memory to applications requiring them. As a result, programs that cannot run due to a lack of

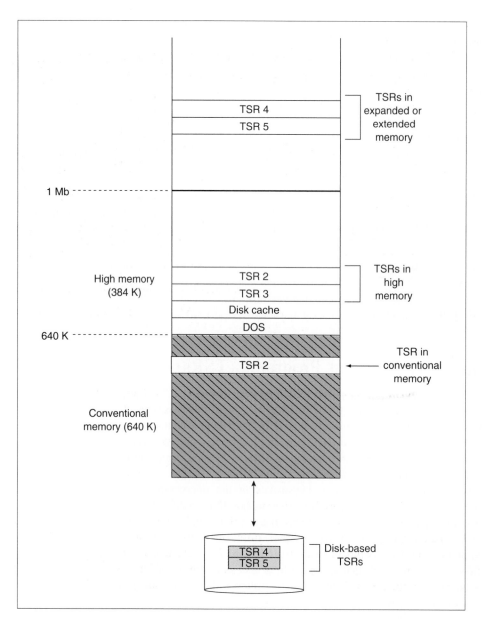

FIGURE 6.12   Terminate-and-stay-resident utilities (TSRs) on IBM-
compatible microcomputers

available memory become usable following reclamation of the base 640 K of memory. Memory management software also enables the user to view current memory utilization through memory maps and suggests ways of reorganizing programs and data. Memory management is more straightforward in Macintoshes, which have a flat 32-bit memory model. These utilities are shown in Figure 6.13.

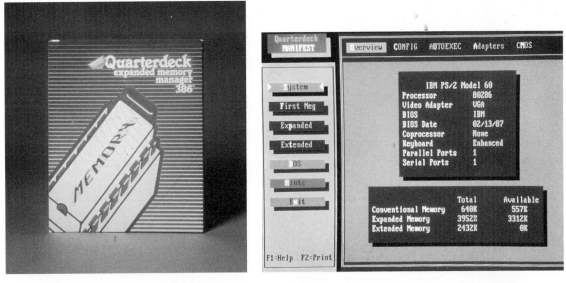

FIGURE 6.13   Memory managers, such as Quarterdeck's EMM386, attempt to maximize the amount of RAM available to user programs.

Disk Utilities

Disk utilities complement memory managers but are designed to manage the hard disk more effectively. Examples include Symantec's *Norton Utilities* and Central Point's *PC Tools.* They provide most of the disk optimization features discussed in Chapter 5, such as defragmentation, low-level reformatting, and resetting the disk's interleave factor. However, many other utilities are also provided for a variety of disk management functions. One of the more important is the *undelete utility,* which enables the recovery of files accidentally deleted.

Disk utilities also detect and correct logical and physical disk errors, often by marking bad sectors and transferring their data elsewhere on disk. Additionally, they provide *file viewers,* which enable the viewing of files stored in different formats, without launching their parent applications. Next are *disk caches,* which may be created to speed disk access; the ability to sort files in a directory; and the ability to prune and graft subdirectories under MS-DOS. Some of these utilities are shown in Figure 6.14.

Anti-Virus Software

Computer viruses are a category of programs most users could do without. They are created with the purpose of adversely affecting the operations of as many computers as possible. Viruses are a worldwide phenomenon, with hundreds of viruses originating in places as diverse as South Africa and Pakistan. They have now spread to practically every country using computers. Viruses propagate by copying themselves from disks to memory and vice versa, enabling the "infection" of hundreds of user disks from one source. They also have the ability to avoid identification by standard file

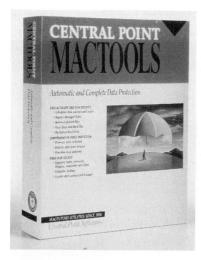
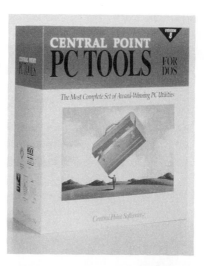
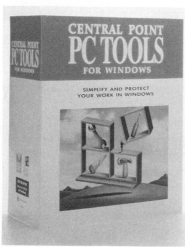
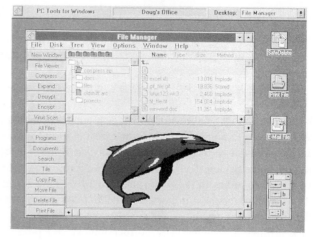

FIGURE 6.14 Disk management utilities such as PC Tools are often available for multiple platforms—for example, Windows, MS-DOS, and Macintosh.

management functions, for example, in file listings. The actions of viruses include the following:

- Sudden reformatting of the user's hard disk—erasing all stored data
- Overwriting data on the file allocation table, making the hard disk unreadable
- Overwriting disk directories or random parts of the hard disk, thus destroying existing data
- Adding themselves to files, to facilitate unknowing propagation to other user's disks
- Producing strange screen effects, such as falling characters
- Displaying messages, like the Cookie Monster program's, "I want a cookie"

Examples of viruses include the Jerusalem virus and its descendants (Jerusalem B, Fu Manchu, Frere Jacques, and so on); the Pakistani Brain; the Stoned Virus, and its notorious descendant, Michelangelo. The "who's who" of viruses also includes programs with names like Yankee Doodle, Frodo, Azusa, and Disk Killer.

There are four major categories of computer viruses. The first is the *simple virus,* which is propagated by infected disks. Another type is the *worm,* which copies itself across computer networks to infect interconnected computers. The most famous case involved Robert Morris, a student at Cornell University, whose introduction of a worm into the Internet network in 1987 brought the network to its knees. The third type of virus is the *bomb,* which is primed to wreak its havoc on a certain date. Examples include the Joshi virus (January 5th), the Jerusalem B virus (every Friday 13th), and again, Michelangelo (March 6th).

A further type is the *Trojan horse,* which masks as a legal program, often as a utility, application, or game. However, when run, it destroys data on disks like the other viruses. A distinction is also made between boot sector and file viruses. The former hide in the disk's boot sector while the latter attach themselves to normal files to avoid detection.

To handle the very real and destructive problems of computer viruses, a new category of **anti-viral software** has emerged almost overnight. Examples are Central Point's *Anti-Virus,* Symantec's *Norton Antivirus,* and Microcom's *Virex-PC,* among others. Their functions include issuing warnings about attempts to format the hard disk, scanning hard and floppy disks for viruses, and removing detected viruses. Other functions include warnings of virus attacks on files and the examination of launched applications (for example, MS-DOS .exe and .com files) for viruses. The latter involves studying *checksums,* the permanent error-correction codes contained in every file.

Anti-virus programs can be set up as TSRs, to maintain constant protection over a computer's disks. Automatic scanning options also enable scanning of the hard disk whenever the microcomputer is booted or shut down. In addition, most of these programs can scan floppy disks on their insertion into the computer. Unfortunately, the problem of computer viruses is likely to remain for the foreseeable future, as hundreds of new and more destructive viruses are created yearly. As anti-virus programs add new viral signatures to keep up, it is necessary to update them every few months, an additional expense for the microcomputer user. See Table 6.2 for the important features of this software.

Other Utilities

Many other classes of utility programs exist. They include *personal information managers* or *PIMs,* which organize information in a free-form, unstructured manner. Programs like Micro Logic's *Infoselect* store, retrieve, and display related information in many different ways to provide more flexibility than traditional DBMSs. Related utilities include *desktop organizers,* such as Borland's *Sidekick* (shown in Figure 6.15). These programs manage appointments, provide a calculator and notepad, and also provide auto-dialing capabilities, among other functions. Many utilities have, however, been incorporated into operating systems and environments, such as Windows and OS/2.

TABLE 6.2   Important features of anti-virus software

Features	Description
1. Range of files scanned for viruses	Types include a. Executable files b. Data files c. Hidden files Number of viruses detected is 600–1,500
2. Memory areas scanned for viruses	Memory areas are a. 640 K conventional memory b. High memory c. Extended memory
3. Secondary storage devices scanned for viruses	Range of devices a. Hard disks b. Floppy disks Areas of hard disk a. File allocation table b. Boot sector c. Partition table
4. Network support	Stand-alone or network anti-virus support
5. Amount of RAM required for memory-resident mode	Varies from 4 K to 40 K
6. Functions	Scope of actions include a. Logging suspect activity b. Virus detection c. Virus removal d. Blocking viruses from becoming memory resident e. Automatic scanning of inserted floppy disks
7. Anti-virus versions available	Platforms available include a. MS-DOS b. MS-DOS/Windows c. Macintosh
8. Vendor policies	Vendor policies include a. Several free upgrades b. Downloading of program upgrades via modem and bulletin boards c. Price for upgrades
9. Average cost of packages	Under $100

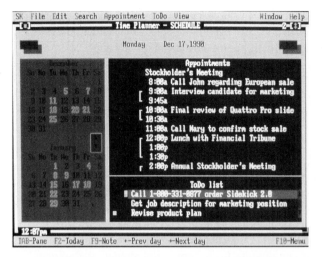

FIGURE 6.15   Borland's Sidekick utility is a multifunction desktop orga-
nizer with notepads, appointment scheduling, calculator, and
other useful functions.

6.4   SOFTWARE DEVELOPMENT OPTIONS _____

The outer layer of software includes **user applications** and utilities. *Sales order
processing, accounts receivable, general ledger, inventory management,* and *marketing
analysis* applications, for example, directly support the user's business functions. Each
major business area is characterized by many competing packages, particularly on the
IBM-compatible hardware platform. In addition, a large variety of software also exists
in niche markets, such as *solids modeling, CAD/CAM,* and *digital signal processing.*
Specialized software packages, for example, SPSS (for statistical analysis) and IFPS (for
financial modeling) are also available to support analytical and reporting requirements.
Software that supports the user's activities may either be (1) purchased off-the-shelf,
(2) created by the user, or (3) coded by internal or external professional programmers.

To Acquire or to Build?

Off-the-shelf software is prepackaged software intended for a general market and is the
first source of software for most users' business functions. Microcomputer users have a
large variety of products to choose from, with thousands of prepackaged applications
available. This software may be obtained from a variety of sources, including *mail order
houses, computer/software retail outlets,* or as part of the *VAR's (value added retailer's)*
package.

    User-developed software, on the other hand, is usually created with so-called
"productivity" packages, such as spreadsheets and database packages. They are less
sophisticated than prepackaged software, but well suited to personalized, less complex
functions. For example, a spreadsheet may be used to create an application for analyzing
the profitability of sales strategies. A user may also employ a database package to
develop a client database. More skilled users, however, may choose to develop their
software using third- or fourth-generation languages.

Software may also be developed by in-house or external systems development personnel. *IS-developed software* has historically been more commonplace with larger systems development, for example, on mainframes, but the relatively high costs of custom software developed by systems professionals makes this practice less frequent on microcomputer systems, where such costs can easily exceed those of the hardware.

Advantages of buying off-the-shelf software therefore include its *low cost* compared to developing it internally or externally. Prewritten software is more likely to have greater investments (time, money, and skill) in its design, coding, and testing, and thus it is apt to be of *higher quality* than the results of internal efforts. Such software can also be *implemented quicker* than software developed in-house. Of course, off-the-shelf software must fit the users' needs at least very closely, if not exactly, for it to be usable. It is in this area of *greater relevance* that custom-written software may be a significantly better choice than prepackaged software. Additionally, source code is usually not included with prepackaged software, making it more difficult to validate its accuracy or modify it. In custom development, the source code is available.

Third- and Fourth-Generation Languages

All software programs are written in one of several programming languages, including operating systems, language compilers, utilities, and business applications. There are different types of languages at various levels, depending on how near they are to natural language or to machine code. Every programming language also has a *syntax,* which defines the rules for using the language constructs and must be adhered to by the program to ensure correct program execution. Incorrect syntax is detected by translating programs, such as *assemblers, compilers* and *interpreters* (see Section 6.2). The choice of a programming language is dependent on available hardware, the operating system, and user requirements. The question of who uses various types of programming languages is also relevant, and is discussed below.

Assembly language is rarely used for developing business applications, even by programmers. Rather, it is mostly used for specialized systems programming, or in cases where speed or compactness of code is critical. Professional programmers typically use third- and fourth-generation languages, which may be either compiled or interpreted. **Third-generation languages** (3GLs) such as FORTRAN, COBOL, PL/1, and C are procedural languages, requiring fairly strict usage conventions. They are English-like in nature and are available on most computer platforms. Consequently, they are fairly portable between different environments, although some conversions require considerable effort.

Fourth-generation languages (4GLs), on the other hand, are examples of nonprocedural languages, with looser coding conventions. They are much more English-like, and are usually specific to certain hardware platforms. For this reason, they are not as portable, that is, transferable between environments as 3GLs. In addition, they generally consume more resources (CPU and I/O) than 3GLs, and are typically interpreted, instead of compiled, degrading their performance even further. 4GLs have often been regarded as prototyping rather than production languages. However, this view has changed with the development of newer, more powerful, and often compiled,

4GLs. Some of these languages even produce 3GL source code as an output, which can then be compiled. Examples of 4GLs include

1. *Spreadsheet macros.* All major spreadsheet packages (for example, Lotus 1-2-3 and Microsoft's Excel, and Borland's Quattro Pro) have macro languages. "Macro" means that one instruction represents many instructions, indicating their high-level nature. For example, a single Excel macro instruction can present a prompt, collect an input from the user, perform limited input checking, and insert this value in a cell on the spreadsheet. This makes it easy for users to build relatively sophisticated applications using macros. Macros can also be directly programmed by the user or automatically learned by the package, by recording a sequence of user actions.

2. *DBMS languages.* Similar to spreadsheet macros, data base languages accompany DBMSs. These languages are used for file creation, manipulation (for example, searching, sorting, and deleting), and data retrieval. Applications with preprogrammed functions can therefore be built using DBMS languages. These high-level languages facilitate complex reports and queries and accompany such packages as dBase IV, Foxpro, Paradox, and Rbase. INTELLECT is another package that provides natural language querying abilities to the user. *Structured query language (SQL)* is a popular language that is being adopted as the standard language for making queries across different platforms.

3. *Application generators.* These software programs are typically more comprehensive than other 4GLs. They possess great functionality, allowing the user to generate an entire application, including input, processing, output, and storage components. A command in an application generator can be equated to a set of commands, or a module in a 3GL, and in fact, several application generators produce 3GL code. Examples of application generators available on microcomputer platforms include TELON, NATURAL, and FOCUS.

4. *Report generators.* This last category of 4GLs comprises specialized programs that are designed to access databases and present the data in a variety of ways. "Canned" report formats are usually available for the user, but users may modify these or even create their own. Examples of report generators include RPG III, EASYTRIEVE PLUS, and DATATRIEVE. See Table 6.3 for a comparison of 4GLs.

Most system development by system professionals takes place with 3GLs or 4GLs, in contrast to the productivity packages and query languages used by end users. In some cases, *end-user development* or *EUD* may not be the best approach to system development. Instead, the task may better suit development by system professionals. This occurs in cases where the scope of the system is too large for EUD, development requires detailed technical knowledge, or the application is mission critical and requires the highest-quality development approach.

Object-Oriented Languages

A new programming approach developed to improve the efficiency of traditional programming techniques is object-oriented programming (OOP). Traditional programming languages have usually treated procedures and the data they use separately, with programmers coding entire new programs even when they closely resemble past programs. **Object-oriented programming languages (OOPLAs)** are part of a new

TABLE 6.3   A comparison of four types of 4GLs

	Application Types	Typical Functions	Program Execution	Examples
Spreadsheet macros	Financial-based modeling	Statistical and financial calculations, modeling, graphing	Mostly interpreted, but compilation options, e.g., baler for Lotus 1-2-3	Excel, Lotus 1-2-3, Quattro Pro macros
DBMS languages	Database applications	Data retrieval, manipulation, and querying	Compiled or interpreted	xBase language variants, SQL, INTELLECT
Application generators	Wide-ranging applications	Multiple functions to create entire applications	Interpreted (prototype) or compiled (final system)	TELON, FOCUS, NATURAL
Report generators	Generation of reports	Database access and data presentation	Mainly compiled	RPG III, DATATRIEVE EASYTRIEVE PLUS

approach that stresses reusability of created programs. In these languages, users define *objects,* or entities, which are created by packaging together procedures and data. For example, in a GUI, a window might be defined as an object, possessing a header bar and horizontal and vertical scroll bars (Figure 6.16). Objects also possess *methods,* which are actions available to them, or ways in which they can be used. For example, the previous window can be displayed on-screen, and expanded or reduced in size. Also, the programmer need not know all the internal details of the object, only its function.

Another key characteristic of objects is *inheritance,* or their ability to acquire the attributes of other objects. For example, a window for displaying customer information automatically inherits the properties of its ancestor, a basic window. A third feature is *dynamic binding,* in which the object's functions are determined at run time, based on existing conditions and parameters. OOPLAs supply the constructs required by programmers to create easily reusable objects. Examples are the C++ compilers of Microsoft and Borland (shown in Figure 6.17), which contain object-oriented extensions to the C programming language. Micro Focus's COBOL also possesses similar language extensions. Conversely, languages like Smalltalk 80 are completely object oriented in nature, only allowing the creation of object-oriented programs, in contrast to the C++ and COBOL compilers.

6.5   USING PRODUCTIVITY TOOLS _____

Many information workers use productivity tools daily, as a major part of their activities. **Productivity tools** are programs enabling the user to perform a wide variety of office tasks such as filing, calculations and analyses, word processing, and communications

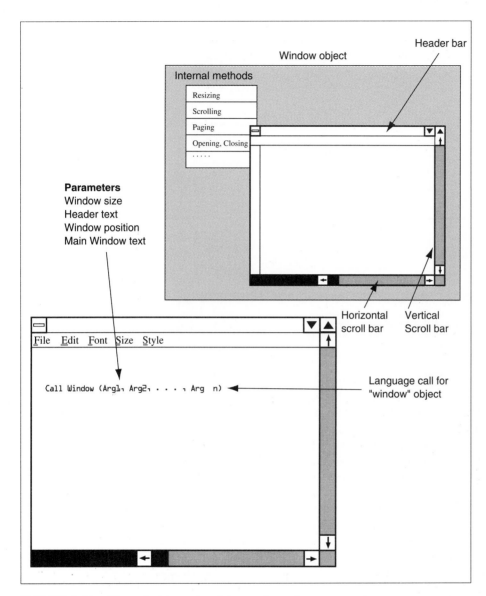

FIGURE 6.16   Use of objects in object-oriented programming

effectively and efficiently. They even enable the user to create programs using language constructs to automate these tasks. Productivity tools are the largest segment of the microcomputer market, and they have done the most to aid the spread of microcomputers. The three major classes of productivity tools are word processing, database management, and spreadsheet software.

Word processing software is the second most widely used software type (after OSs) on microcomputers. A word processing program enables the user to create and manipulate text and graphics electronically on the computer. These document files may

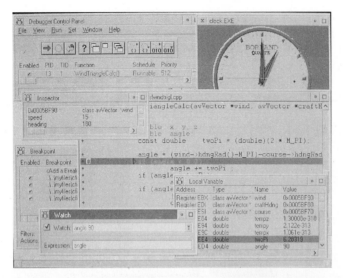

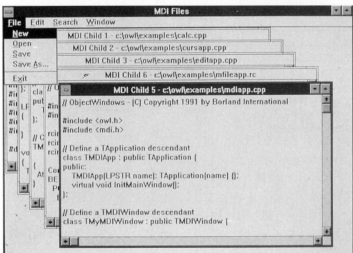

FIGURE 6.17 C++ compilers provide a powerful and integrated coding, compilation, and debugging environment for programmers.

be reedited, displayed on-screen, printed on paper, or transmitted electronically to other users. The earliest word processors were text based, but these have been succeeded by GUI-based programs. Increasingly, word processors feature *spelling checkers, grammar checkers, graphics manipulation, user macros,* and many other sophisticated functions.

The user's need to store and manage records of customer information, transactions, inventory, and other business-related information may be satisfied by **database management software.** These programs enable the user to create, manipulate, and retrieve information effectively and efficiently from a database stored on secondary storage devices. Two major types of database management products are *flat-file data managers* and *relational data base management systems (RDBMSs),* which are discussed in Chapter 7.

The availability of **electronic spreadsheets** like VisiCalc and Lotus 1-2-3 stimulated many initial microcomputer purchases. Spreadsheets are based on the common metaphor of ledgers. They provide a grid of cells into which numbers, names, or formulas are entered. Numbers are added, multiplied, sorted, and otherwise related to each other using formulas, to carry out a wide range of financial calculations and analyses. The software provides a movable window into the entire sheet, which in the case of Microsoft's Excel, is 256 columns by 16,384 rows. If a completely full spreadsheet were printed out, it would be over 20 floors high! Apart from the very sophisticated financial models that can be built using spreadsheet software, prepackaged user programs can be created using macros (see Section 6.4). Spreadsheets can also produce high-quality 2-D and 3-D graphs and charts for display and presentation purposes.

6.6 MATCHING SOFTWARE, _____ HARDWARE, AND REQUIREMENTS _____

Software selection ranges in difficulty from timing a software upgrade to choosing a new operating system or major new application. An information system's design should be *application* or *software driven,* as it is software that provides the functionality to satisfy the user's requirements. Hardware simply provides a vehicle on which to run the software, although it does define many performance issues. Hardware-driven system design can result in a lack of appropriate software for the hardware platform, but conversely hardware constraints can also affect the software selection decision.

Software Selection under Hardware and Operating System Constraints

In some instances, software decisions must be made under *hardware and/or operating system constraints.* For example, a firm may be standardized on IBM-compatible microcomputers. This affects the consideration of new software. The costs of software for another platform will minimally include the cost of new hardware (or a reliable software emulator) in addition to the software itself. If the new computer must be networked, there are additional costs for hardware and software to connect it and to translate data between the different formats. Newer printers, for example, which print from both Macintosh and IBM-compatible machines, are still considerably more expensive than dedicated printers.

Hardware may impose a limiting factor on software if it is not powerful enough to run either the new software or its operating system or environment. For example, 80286-based microcomputers cannot effectively run Windows or OS/2. Using an OS/2-based application would not be feasible on the 80286-based platform without a very significant hardware upgrade, which would minimally include the processor. Furthermore, even if the selected software runs on existing hardware, for example, IBM-compatibles, it may require a different operating system, say, OS/2 versus MS-DOS. To use the software, two things are required: (1) the purchase and installation of the new operating system, and (2) compatibility between the new and old operating system, if the old application base is to be maintained. In the case of OS/2 (versus MS-DOS), only one-way compatibility (running DOS applications on OS/2) exists.

For IBM-compatibles specifically, the user can consider evolutionary modifications to the operating system. For example, operating environments like Windows and Desqview provide additional features to MS-DOS (for example, multitasking and cut-and-paste functions) while retaining compatibility with it. OS/2 also offers a compatibility box for DOS applications.

On microcomputer platforms, cross-compatibility with mainframe platforms can also be vital. Take Hewitt Associates, an information systems consulting firm, as an example. This firm chose the microcomputer-based Micro Focus COBOL compiler to generate new applications as part of a downsizing effort. This decision was governed largely by the ability of the Micro Focus compiler to generate object code that was executable on their IBM mainframes where COBOL was still prevalent for application development. Development work could then take place on the less expensive platforms and later be ported to the mainframe.

Software-Led Hardware Selection

Greenfield sites, that is, totally new applications, allow one of the few opportunities for pure software-driven hardware selection. Another opportunity is the freedom to move to an entirely new hardware platform. In reality, it is natural for considerations external to the firm to affect software selection. For example, the best software program may have been developed for a hardware platform that is more expensive (per unit of computing power) than another available platform. It may also be less popular, or have dimmer prospects of survival. In these cases, it may be prudent to select less capable software on the more promising hardware platform.

Resolving Incompatibility

Incompatibility occurs when the selected software is unable to work with the existing hardware or software. For example, new word processing software may be unable to read certain graphics or spreadsheet files, TSRs may conflict when loaded into memory together, and software may require a newer version of the existing operating system to run properly. More serious problems occur when purchased hardware is not compatible with the current hardware base.

Several solutions exist to handle incompatibility. Most programs have the ability to *import* (or read) data in a large variety of file formats. Where this is lacking, the first package may have the ability to *export* (output) data in the required format to the new program. *Cut-and-paste* abilities in operating environments, or the use of the lowest common denominator, ASCII, as an intermediate (text) format may resolve other incompatibilities. File exchange utilities also enable microcomputers to read data from disks formatted for other computers. For example, Macintosh microcomputers using the 3.5-inch Superdrive can read MS-DOS-formatted 3.5-inch diskettes using the *Apple File Exchange* utility. Many hardware solutions also exist to interconnect diverse microcomputers on networks.

Software Portability

Resolving incompatibilities is an important issue, but often, the user must migrate to another hardware platform, for several reasons. One reason may be that the user's hardware vendor has gone out of business. Another may be the price/performance advantage of another hardware platform. A further one might be an upgrade to a more powerful processor in the same family (for example, from 80286 to 80486DX). **Software portability** refers to the ease of porting or transferring existing applications to the new hardware platform so that they run correctly.

Moving within the same processor family offers the fewest problems, as newer processors are usually kept binary compatible with earlier processors. This means that they run a superset of the earlier chip's machine language instruction set, making them upwardly compatible. Moving applications to a different microcomputer/processor combination is more difficult, in general. If the applications are available in the new environment, these difficulties are less. For example, moving from Microsoft Word or Excel on the Macintosh to their counterparts on PC-compatibles offers minimal difficulties, while another transition between two different accounting packages on Macintosh and IBM platforms without transition aids can be very costly.

CHAPTER SUMMARY _____

Software is as important as hardware in supplying the features and capabilities of an information system. The term *software* describes the programming language instructions that direct hardware components to electronically process data. At a basic level, microcomputers process machine code instructions, strings of binary data that signify instructions or the data they process. Programs written in any other programming language must be converted to machine language prior to execution by the processor.

Operating system software manages the hardware resources of the microcomputer efficiently, and shields the user from complex hardware details. Applications software, on the other hand, comprises programs that support the user's business activities. The potential choices of both operating system and application software have greatly increased over the past few years, providing more opportunities but also posing more challenges to the software buyer.

Operating systems and operating environments are the two types of operating system software. Popular microcomputer OSs include Microsoft's MS-DOS, Apple's Macintosh OS, and UNIX. Multiuser, multitasking, virtual memory management, and multiprocessor features are now available for microcomputer platforms. Utility programs complement the OS's core supervisor program and provide much of its functionality. Newer OSs have graphical user interfaces (GUIs), but older ones (for example, DOS) can acquire both a GUI and added features through an operating environment or shell such as Windows. Examples of other shells include Open Look and Motif, which are used with UNIX.

In software development, programs may be custom written by end users or systems personnel, or purchased as off-the-shelf packages. Systems personnel are most likely to use 3GL, 4GL, and object-oriented languages for coding. Conversely, end users use mostly higher-level tools to develop custom software. These include specialized packages like IFPS and SPSS, productivity packages like Lotus 1-2-3, and microcomputer database management systems like dBase. Utility programs are used by all classes of system users to perform a diverse range of functions, from memory management to virus protection.

Software is the major determinant of the information system's functionality. Nevertheless, software selection must often be made under both hardware and operating system constraints. Given these constraints, and existing financial ones, the appropriateness of specific software is based on the program's features and on their fit to the user's requirements. Other concerns, such as portability and compatibility, also feature prominently, especially in environments containing a heterogeneous mix of resources.

REVIEW QUESTIONS _____

1. Name the software program that insulates the user from hardware details.
2. What is the difference between an operating system and an operating environment?
3. Name two operating environments and the operating systems they are associated with.
4. What is the function of a translation program? Give examples.
5. Differentiate between a programming language and an application.
6. What is the difference between multitasking and task switching?
7. How does virtual memory work? In what circumstances would you use virtual memory?
8. List five operating system utility programs and describe their functions.
9. How does a compiler differ from an interpreter? In which circumstances would you use each one?
10. How does object linking and embedding (OLE) improve the use of productivity tools?
11. Briefly discuss four risks of end-user development (EUD).
12. What category of fourth-generation languages is most appropriate for database applications?
13. What are two features of object-oriented programming?
14. What is a terminate-and-stay-resident program? What programs manage multiple TSRs?

EXERCISES _____

1. What are the advantages of purchasing off-the-shelf software over custom development by the end user? In what circumstances would you employ custom development?
2. What are the advertised benefits of object-oriented programming languages? In what way can they offer increased productivity to the programmer?
3. Why is the problem of computer viruses such a serious and constant threat? What three virus-prevention strategies would you recommend to microcomputer users?
4. The user manager for a small sales firm has become attracted to the newer operating system software on the IBM platform. Currently, during the processing of sales over

the telephone, the salespeople (who use a DOS-based sales package) have to refer to a manual with product descriptions. Even though this information is now accessible through another DOS-based program, their DOS version does not allow both applications to be open simultaneously. Are there any operating system software solutions? If so, what are they? Which would you recommend?

5. A marketing manager has just commissioned a programmer to create a program that produces and displays sales forecasts for the three sales regions of the firm, using historical data and different scenarios. The programmer has chosen to use COBOL as the development tool for this project. Do you support this choice of a programming language? Why or why not? If not, which language would you recommend?

SUGGESTED READINGS

Fox, J. "All About Memory-Resident Software." *PC Today,* July 1990, pp. 28–31.

Fox, J. "The Once and Future UNIX." *PC Today,* December 1991, pp. 49–52.

Goldsborough, R. "PC Tools 7.0: A Power-Packed Collection of Utility Programs." *PC Today,* August 1991, pp. 50–51.

Hayes, F., and Baran, N. "A Guide to GUIs." *Byte Magazine,* July 1989, pp. 250–257.

Mann, S. W. "Making the Most of 1Mb of Memory." *PC Today,* May 1991, pp. 59–64.

Miastkowski, S. "Digital Research Creates a Better DOS." *Byte Magazine,* November 1991, p. 68.

Semich, J. W. "NT: Is it Ready for Critical Apps?" *Datamation,* May 15, 1993, pp. 29–33.

Spanbauer, S. "DOS vs. DOS." *PC World,* July 1991, pp. 215–218.

Udell, J. "The All-in-One DOS." *Byte Magazine,* July 1991, pp. 36–40.

Udell, J. "OS/2 2.0: A Pilgrim's Journey." *Byte Magazine,* December 1991, pp. 46–47.

Udell, J. "Windows™ 3.1 Is Ready to Roll." *Byte Magazine,* April 1992, p. 34.

MICROCOMPUTER DATA MANAGEMENT

INTRODUCTION

Paper filing cabinets were, and still are, a part of many work environments, reflecting the firm's need to store and retrieve data about its customers, products, personnel, and other business-related subjects. The secondary storage devices discussed in Chapter 5 enable the storage and retrieval of this data in electronic form much faster and more efficiently than paper filing systems.

The ways in which data is organized from the user's perspective, and how it is stored and accessed most efficiently through software, greatly differ. The user perspective focuses on the business environment, while software methods are geared to making most efficient use of secondary storage devices. Both views are important in data storage and retrieval, and data management software is used to reconcile them. *Database management systems (DBMSs)* are the most popular type of data management software. A DBMS manages a firm's electronic database and allows the user to conveniently store, access, and manipulate data stored in it. It also ensures that the data is efficiently stored on physical devices. Both the logical (or user) view and the physical (or device) view are described in this chapter, as is the role of the DBMS. Document imaging, a newer storage alternative for nonrecord-based data, is also discussed.

Learning Objectives

After reading this chapter, you will be able to:

- Identify appropriate data access methods for different storage devices
- Distinguish between situations requiring flat-file managers and those requiring DBMSs
- Create logical or user data models for different business applications, for example, order processing, accounting, and inventory management
- Understand the special requirements for multiuser and distributed DBMSs

MANAGING DATA WITH AN ENTERPRISE COMPUTING SYSTEM AT ROADWAY EXPRESS

In the package delivery business, reputations and repeat business depend on the carrier's capability to deliver the right parcel to the right place at the right time. Roadway Express was one of the first trucking companies to recognize just how hungry its customers were for up-to-the-second data. Customers desired this data to better manage inventories, plan for production, allocate warehouse personnel, and to market their products. However, access to package information was a problem, even for Roadway's employees. The company's information system was out-of-date, comprising three 15-year old Sperry 9090 mainframes. Telecommunications were also problematic, with 600 locations out in the field using teletypes. Customer enquiries could be laboriously satisfied only over 24 hours.

Roadway chose to replace its entire system with a distributed client/server architecture using SQL database technology. The goal of the system was to provide both employees at Roadway's remote field offices and customers real-time access to sales, delivery, and freight information. AT&T serves and interconnected microcomputers were installed at each site and all the servers were connected to the central IBM mainframes in Akron. Now, when a Roadway truck is loaded, its attached bar code is scanned and transmitted by radio to the Informix database on the local server. This data is then uploaded to headquarters via an SNA network. An EDI (Electronic Data Interchange) message is then transmitted to the Roadway customer indicating the shipment's arrival time. About 12,000 or 15% of Roadway's customers have EDI links.

Customers and Roadway employees can also access Roadway's central databases using a Touch-Tone telephone. By dialing a toll-free number, customers can dial into AT&T Conversant communication servers that are linked to the DB2 databases on the mainframes. This access method results in 209,000 calls per month, indicating its popularity among customers.

Adapted from Alice LaPlante, "Roadway Finds Electronic Highway Paved with Gold," *Infoworld*, March 8, 1993, p. 54.

- Make simple structured query language (SQL) queries to access relational databases
- Select the most appropriate document imaging technology for different business situations

7.1 DATABASE ORGANIZATION _____

Every firm selling goods and services needs to store and retrieve data about its goods and services, its customers, and the transactions involving these customers. This data includes the types of goods or services being sold and the quantity available. Customers, too, have names, addresses, telephone numbers, and credit limits, among other attributes. Likewise, transactions are made on a certain date, by a specific salesperson, and involve specific quantities of various products. Storing this information requires different *files,* such as customer files, product files, and files recording transactions.

The different files usually overlap, as in the above example. Customer information is typically included in the transaction record, as are descriptions of purchased goods. Data redundancy and inconsistency, risks of separate filing systems, are greatly minimized by using *databases,* integrated collections of data that are managed by *database management systems (DBMSs).* DBMSs manage both high-level user views and a low-level device-specific view of the data to allow the user to easily access and manipulate it. We begin with a recap of the physical devices and access methods used by the DBMS to store and retrieve data.

Storage Devices and File Design Techniques

Data is physically stored on secondary storage devices. The two basic types of secondary storage device are sequential access storage devices *(SASDs)* and direct access storage devices *(DASDS).* SASDs are more limited in nature, requiring (n–1) record accesses to reach the nth record (see Chapter 5). They are mainly used for backup purposes, with most other uses left to DASDs. DASDs enable rapid access to every piece of stored data and use more powerful *data access methods.*

Files stored on secondary storage devices include *program files,* containing the user's instructions to the computer for performing specific functions (see Chapter 6); *image files,* which are digitized bit-patterns that are either drawn or scanned into the computer; *sound files,* which capture aural input; and *text files,* which are created by word processors. All these files require little organization. They are simply stored, retrieved, and used as a whole.

Data files, on the other hand, comprise similar records, which are themselves composed of related fields. Various alphanumeric characters are used to create fields, with the record *key* being the field(s) in the record that uniquely identifies the record. *Logical records* consist of fields from one or more entities, although most will usually be from one (see the discussion of foreign keys in the next section). Conversely, a *physical record* is the data that is fetched in one disk access and comprises one or more logical records. On SASDs, records are stored in blocks (see Chapter 5), each containing several logical records separated by interblock gaps.

Data Access Methods

The **data access method** used with a secondary storage device directly affects the amount of time needed to retrieve a record from the device. For example, in a paper filing system containing customer data, the records are not generally stored in the sequence in which new customers are made but instead in ascending order of customer number (or name). This allows direct access to a customer record in seconds as opposed to minutes, or even hours if the records were ordered randomly. Another familiar example of organizing data is seen in card catalogs in libraries, which are organized by book author and title. Electronically stored files on secondary storage devices also require data access methods that ensure access to data in an efficient and consistent form. They must be efficient, for rapid access, and also consistent, to ensure that the correct data is retrieved.

Several data access methods may be used with secondary storage devices. These methods vary in efficiency and complexity and are suited to different types of applications. The choice of such methods may also be constrained by the storage device. SASDs offer the most constraints with regard to data access methods, because of the inability to physically reach a record without accessing its predecessors. They are limited to using the **sequential access method** for data access. The data itself may be *serially organized,* that is, stored in the order of creation, or *sequentially organized,* in ascending order of a record characteristic, for example, customer number. Figure 7.1 shows serially stored records on a SASD.

The **sequential access method (SAM)** requires each record to possess a *key,* which naturally occurs in the record or is assigned to it by the data management software. With SAM, records are stored on a SASD such as magnetic tape or cartridge in ascending (or descending) order of the key. Sequential organization of the data is preferred to serial organization and has been historically used for *master file updating.* Consider, for example, a SASD-based master file containing inventory records arranged in ascending order of item number, as in Figure 7.2a. Transactions (for example, purchases, returns) occurring through the day are stored in random (key) order on a second SASD. To update the master file, the transaction file is initially sorted, to place it in the same order as the master file. It is then used to update the master file to create a new updated master file (Figure 7.2b). Use of a serial file, that is, an unsorted transaction file, would be problematic, as the master file tape reel would have to be moved back and forth very inefficiently.

Master file updating using SASDs, as shown in Figure 7.2, is of limited use today. When it is used, access to records is not direct and may be time consuming. This makes SASDs impractical for ad hoc queries that must be answered quickly. Queries that require data from multiple files are also difficult to satisfy. Additionally, this form of batch processing leaves files out of date, as they are updated only periodically. Master file updating has largely been replaced by DASDs and improved access methods, which deal with these concerns. Payroll processing, whereby all records are updated, represents one of the few remaining examples of master file updating using SASDs.

Data is stored on DASDs using two main approaches: **indexed file organization** and the **direct access method** (or **DAM**). The idea behind these methods is to access a record

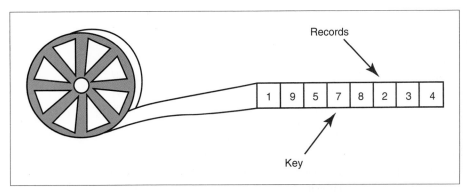

FIGURE 7.1   Serially stored records on a SASD

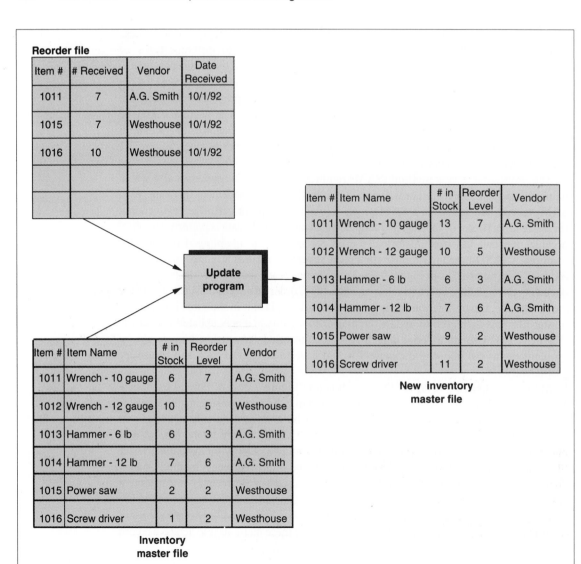

Reorder file

Item #	# Received	Vendor	Date Received
1011	7	A.G. Smith	10/1/92
1015	7	Westhouse	10/1/92
1016	10	Westhouse	10/1/92

Update program

Item #	Item Name	# in Stock	Reorder Level	Vendor
1011	Wrench - 10 gauge	13	7	A.G. Smith
1012	Wrench - 12 gauge	10	5	Westhouse
1013	Hammer - 6 lb	6	3	A.G. Smith
1014	Hammer - 12 lb	7	6	A.G. Smith
1015	Power saw	9	2	Westhouse
1016	Screw driver	11	2	Westhouse

New inventory master file

Item #	Item Name	# in Stock	Reorder Level	Vendor
1011	Wrench - 10 gauge	6	7	A.G. Smith
1012	Wrench - 12 gauge	10	5	Westhouse
1013	Hammer - 6 lb	6	3	A.G. Smith
1014	Hammer - 12 lb	7	6	A.G. Smith
1015	Power saw	2	2	Westhouse
1016	Screw driver	1	2	Westhouse

Inventory master file

FIGURE 7.2 Master file updated by transaction file

without reading all its predecessors, as is necessary under SAM. Under the *indexed sequential access method (ISAM)*—one indexing method—records may be arranged sequentially or serially. It uses a higher-level index, similar to a "table of contents" for the file. Each file is divided into blocks, pointed to by records in the index. An index record contains two fields: the highest key in a particular block and the physical location of that record on the DASD (see Figure 7.3).

To access a record for which the key is known, the index is searched first, instead of the file itself, as shown in Figure 7.4. This dramatically shortens the time taken to reach a specified record.

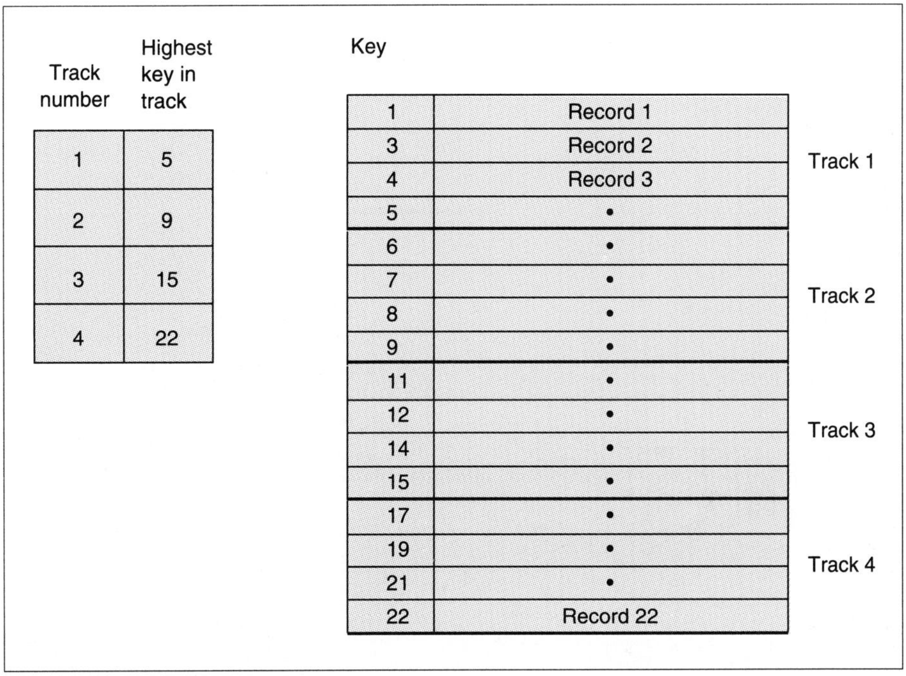

Track number	Highest key in track		Key		
			1	Record 1	
			3	Record 2	Track 1
1	5		4	Record 3	
			5	•	
2	9		6	•	
			7	•	Track 2
3	15		8	•	
			9	•	
4	22		11	•	
			12	•	
			14	•	Track 3
			15	•	
			17	•	
			19	•	
			21	•	Track 4
			22	Record 22	

FIGURE 7.3 **ISAM** data organization

DAM differs from ISAM, but they share the same objective of more efficient data access from DASDs. DAM uses a *hashing algorithm* to transform the record's key value into a unique physical storage address on the DASD (see Figure 7.5). The hashing algorithm is used to generate this address before storing and retrieving the record, and it must be:

1. Repeatable, to guarantee that stored data can be retrieved
2. Efficient, in allocating the minimum space necessary on the DASD for the file
3. Simple, to avoid processing overhead for complex algorithms
4. Sophisticated enough to minimize collisions that occur when different keys generate the same physical address

Many different hashing algorithms are used to store records under DAM. They include:

1. Dividing the key by the prime number closest to the total number of expected records, with the remainder of the division being the physical address
2. "Folding" the key upon itself to generate the address
3. Squaring the key

The division-by-a-prime method is illustrated in Figure 7.6.

Collisions occur when the hashing algorithm generates the same physical address from two different keys. Because collisions are undesirable, better algorithms minimize them. If a collision occurs, the second record is stored in an *overflow area*, and

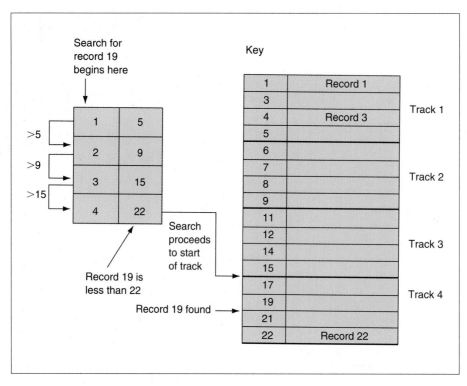

FIGURE 7.4   **ISAM operation.**
When an index record is found with a higher key value than the search key, the sought record will be in the block pointed to by the index record. Using this address, the block is searched sequentially until the desired record is found. In the example above, the record for customer 19 is requested from the customer file. Each block (in this case, a track) holds four records and has an entry in the index. In retrieving the customer's record (where the key = 19), the index is searched until the key entry 22 is reached, indicating that the desired record is in the indexed track. The track is then searched sequentially, with success coming in the second read operation. Instead of the nineteen read operations required by SAM, only six reads are needed to retrieve the desired record under ISAM.

a *pointer* (or address) of this record is attached to the first (see Figure 7.6). In seeking to retrieve the second record, the hashing algorithm generates the first address and the first record is accessed. After comparing keys (and finding a mismatch), the pointer is used to access and retrieve the desired record. Efficient hashing algorithms provide the fastest possible access on DASDs, making hashing suitable for critical real-time applications.

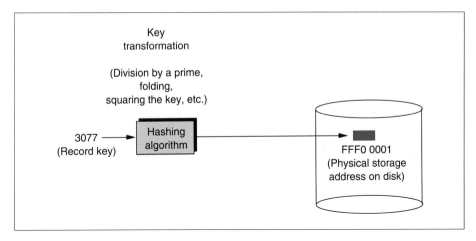

FIGURE 7.5   Using the direct access method (DAM) for data access

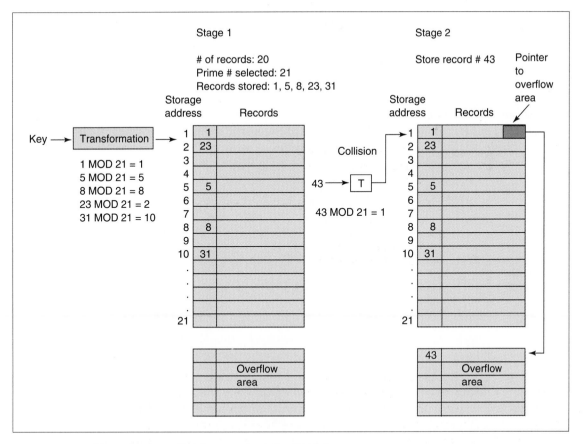

FIGURE 7.6   Use of prime-division method for DAM

Data Structures

ISAM and DAM provide rapid data storage and retrieval for DASDs, but their dependence on the record key limits their usefulness when another search field must be used. For example, in the student file shown in Figure 7.7, a user might require a list of all students with a particular major, such as marketing. However, the student file is stored in ascending order on its key, the student ID, under ISAM. This represents the file's *physical ordering*.

To retrieve records using nonkey fields, either a new physical ordering or a different *logical ordering* of the file based on the nonkey field is required. A new physical ordering of the file would involve duplicating the file on the disk, ordered by the new field. However, this is inefficient and would introduce redundancy and possible inconsistency. It would also be impractical to create the desired number of files for every field to be used as a search field.

Two **data structures** are used to create new logical orderings for files: *inverted lists* and *multilists* (or *linked lists*). Each accomplishes the new orderings in different ways. An *inverted list* is a separate index file, similar to ISAM's index, which indexes every record in the original file based on the nonkey field desired. In the student file example, the inverted list file would have two fields, one containing the nonkey field (major) and the other the physical address of the corresponding record (see Figure 7.8). Thereafter, a query to list all marketing students would be answered by going to the inverted list, locating the record with marketing as the nonkey field and all subsequent physical record addresses the record contains.

Multilists are another data structure used to create a logical ordering of records. A multilist uses pointers to create chains of records with the same value in the desired nonkey field. For example, one chain would link the MIS students, while another would link marketing students, and so on. A head list provides a means to start the chain at the first record for each value of the nonkey field. So, as in Figure 7.9, record number

	Student ID	Student Name	Address	Major
Records → ordered by student ID	0975	James Harper	77, Endicott Avenue, Carpsville, NY 10101	MIS
	0977	Ann Brown	81, Steady Drive, Corona, PA 19103	MKTG
	1001	John King	401, Dalmation Place, Pekah, MO 29303	ACCTG
	1005	Susan Penn	30, Albert Road, Gilgal, PA 19103	ACCTG
	1010	Ed Thomson	25, Harper Ferry, Cooper Hill, NY 10132	MIS
	1012	Wyn Cary	44, Cloudy Drive, Manyunk, PA 19103	MKTG
	1015	Sam Chung	31, Metarie Road, Nice Town, PA 19104	ACCTG

FIGURE 7.7   An example student file

Physical storage address	Student ID	Student name	Address	Major
11000	0975	James Harper	77, Endicott Avenue, Carpsville, NY 10101	MIS
11001	0977	Ann Brown	81, Steady Drive, Corona, PA 19103	MKTG
11002	1001	John King	401, Dalmation Place, Pekah, MO 29303	ACCTG
11003	1005	Susan Penn	30, Albert Road, Gilgal, PA 19103	ACCTG
11004	1010	Ed Thomson	25, Harper Ferry, Cooper Hill, NY 10132	MIS
11005	1012	Wyn Cary	44, Cloudy Drive, Manyunk, PA 19103	MKTG
11006	1015	Sam Chung	31, Metarie Road, Nice Town, PA 19104	ACCTG

Inverted list

ACCTG	11002	11003	11006
MIS	11000	11004	
MKTG	11001	11005	

FIGURE 7.8   Using inverted lists on the student file

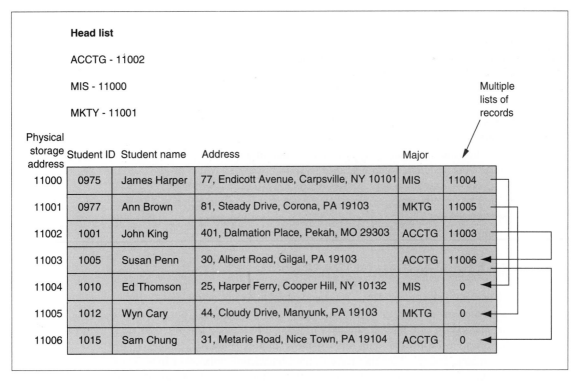

Head list

ACCTG - 11002

MIS - 11000

MKTY - 11001

Multiple lists of records

Physical storage address	Student ID	Student name	Address	Major	
11000	0975	James Harper	77, Endicott Avenue, Carpsville, NY 10101	MIS	11004
11001	0977	Ann Brown	81, Steady Drive, Corona, PA 19103	MKTG	11005
11002	1001	John King	401, Dalmation Place, Pekah, MO 29303	ACCTG	11003
11003	1005	Susan Penn	30, Albert Road, Gilgal, PA 19103	ACCTG	11006
11004	1010	Ed Thomson	25, Harper Ferry, Cooper Hill, NY 10132	MIS	0
11005	1012	Wyn Cary	44, Cloudy Drive, Manyunk, PA 19103	MKTG	0
11006	1015	Sam Chung	31, Metarie Road, Nice Town, PA 19104	ACCTG	0

FIGURE 7.9   Using multilists on the student file

1001 (John King) would be the first record in the accounting chain, Susan Penn, the second, and so on. The final record in the chain has its pointer set to 0. Another chain can be created to order records according to the student's minor. Note that the *order* of the chain can be on any desired field.

Advantages of inverted lists and multilists are that you can add a record to the end of the file and just update the pointers, and you can delete a record simply by changing a few pointers. Inverted lists and multilists allow many queries to be quickly satisfied. They are created invisibly by the data management software, but setting up indexes in such DBMSs as dBase requires understanding of their use. In particular, the user should be aware that a storage performance overhead results from many indexes.

Files and Databases

Our discussion up to this point has involved the concept of files, for storing data relating to various entities of interest to the organization. However, the simple file concept is insufficient for the information needs of today's firms. Frequently, the user must use several files concurrently, making relationships between files necessary. Different files may also contain similar information. In the master file updating activity shown in Figure 7.2, for example, the transaction list would be repeatedly used to update not just inventory but the salesperson file (performance) and the customer file (for example, change of address), a lengthy and complex process. Other types of redundancy are common in such filing systems, with fields like `customer-name` repeated in accounts receivable and customer files, and `supplier-name` stored in both supplier and inventory reorders files.

Databases are designed to address these problems of inflexibility, inconsistency, and unnecessary duplication of data. Hansen and Hansen (1992, p. 33) define a database as "a collection of interrelated, shared, and controlled data." A database may also be defined as a set of related files. Figure 7.10 illustrates the difference between separate files and a relational database that minimizes redundancy. Note that redundancy in a database is greatly minimized but not totally eliminated, because of the need for index files and for intersection files that link others. The shared part of the database definition reflects the fact that multiple users may have data stored in the database. For example, the sales department requires customer and sales information, while production is interested in inventory data and manufacturing schedules. To manage the different views of data expected by various database users and the complexity of interrelating different files, a complex software program called a *DBMS* is typically used. Its functions and those of its simpler sibling, *flat-file managers,* are discussed next.

Flat-File Managers and DBMSs

Some users have relatively modest data storage and retrieval requirements. For example, they might require an on-line inventory of equipment for a small business or a computer-maintained list of a limited number of clients. For them, a **flat-file manager** may be the most cost-effective data management option. Flat-file managers are programs that maintain single files that have limited interaction with other files. They are generally about half the cost of full-fledged DBMSs but satisfy simple storage and retrieval needs using such methods as query-by-forms (QBF) and query-by-example

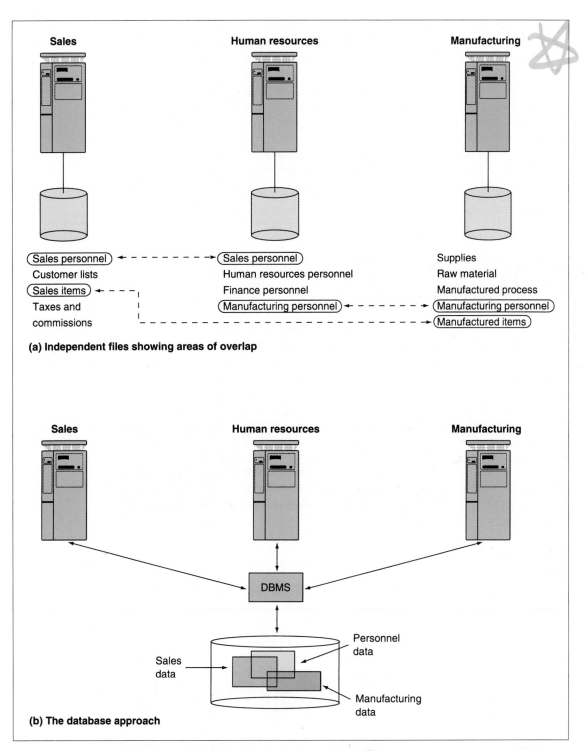

FIGURE 7.10 Independent files versus the database approach

(QBE). Their drawbacks include difficulty in making joint use of files to satisfy data requests and associated problems of data redundancy and loss of data integrity.

Integrity is violated if, for example, two records of an individual in a firm show two different ranks, for example, "salesperson" in the file used by marketing and "senior salesperson" in the personnel department's file. This may result from holding marketing and personnel files with considerable overlap, that is, data on salespeople.

For most microcomputer users, a DBMS is a superior alternative to flat-file managers at an affordable cost. Many microcomputer DBMSs are available for prices comparable with word processing and spreadsheet packages. A DBMS is a software program that manages a computer-based database and has a number of key functions:

- To provide links between different files that are used together
- To allow the storage, updating, and retrieval of data in the database
- To ensure that data integrity, data security, and control constraints are applied to data
- To supply coordination mechanisms for multiuser database access
- To support data reliability through backup and recovery features

The DBMS provides an intervening level of software between database users (and applications) and the data stored on secondary storage devices. The system's data is described to the DBMS using a *data definition language (DDL)*, while users' requests for data access, storage, and manipulation are made in a *data manipulation language (DML)*. Figure 7.11 shows various levels or views of data and the role of the DBMS. It shows the DBMS supporting several potential user data models (or *subschemas*) in the database, helped by its own global view of the stored data (or *schema*), plus details of the physical storage devices and access methods. Each subschema represents one or more users or applications in an organization who require different sets of data to fulfill their individual tasks.

These different views are used by the DBMS to provide *data independence*—an important DBMS feature that signifies that user data models are resistant to changes in the database's physical structure. This is convenient for system developers, who may then change storage devices and data access methods without having to modify subschemas.

The Database Development Life Cycle

The **database development life cycle (DDLC)** refers to the process of developing an organization's database system. It is a part of the overall systems development life cycle, which is discussed in Chapters 12 and 13. The DDLC is often advanced as a means of providing a *data-oriented* rather than a *process-oriented* approach to developing information systems. The reason is that data structures developed using the former approach will be more resistant to change than those developed under the latter. This is because they are predicated upon the underlying entities in the user's business environment and not on processes that frequently change.

There are three major steps in database development:

1. **In database requirements analysis,** user data requirements are determined. Interviews, study of business documents, questionnaires, and process observation are

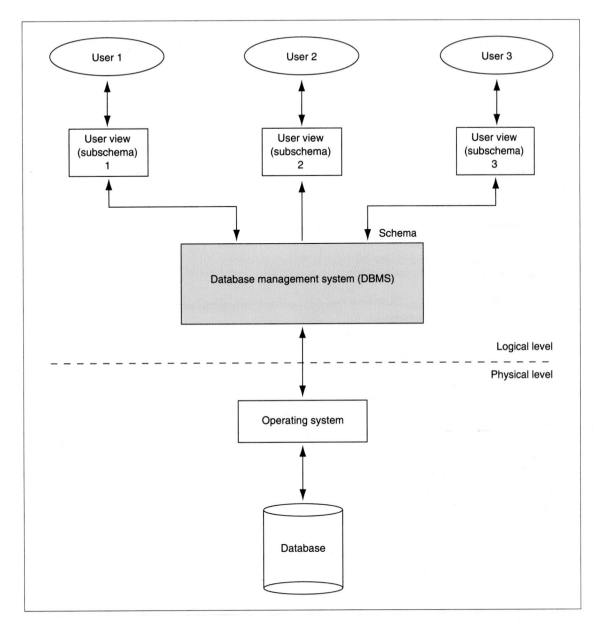

FIGURE 7.11   Overall view of a database system

all used to define the database contents and its intended uses. A data dictionary is also developed, to catalog the data elements in the database.

2. **Logical database design,** to create the database schema and all subschemas. These logical views of the data are developed using such methods as *object-oriented modeling.*

3. **Implementation,** which is divided into two stages: the conversion of the logical

database design into a suitable implementation model, for example, the *relational* model, and defining of secondary storage devices, data access methods, and required data structures and population of the database.

7.2 LOGICAL AND IMPLEMENTATION _____ DATABASE MODELS _____

Every firm is engaged in activities involving entities or objects it deals with, trades in, sells, or manages. Objects are things or concepts that the user is interested in modeling. Examples are the firm's customers, its suppliers, and the goods and services the firm produces. To develop a database, these objects must be identified and the characteristics of interest (referred to as attributes) determined. For example, a CUSTOMER object has attributes of interest to the firm that include the customer's account number, name, address, and telephone number. For another object, such as the ORDER(s) sold by the firm, relevant attributes include order number, date, purchase order number, pricing code, and so on. (Figure 7.12)

The process of detailing objects (and their attributes) of interest to the organization is called **object-oriented data modeling.** This process is *logical* in nature as it is not concerned with the physical characteristics of secondary storage devices and low-level data structures, such as ISAM and inverted lists. Instead, it provides a means to describe the underlying objects in the user's business environment, their attributes, and the relationships between these objects. **Implementation models,** on the other hand, which include the hierarchical, network, and relational models, bridge the logical and physical levels and have been used for many years. In the following section, we discuss logical and implementation modeling in greater detail.

Logical Database Approaches— Object-Oriented Data Models

The object-oriented data modeling approach centers around objects that possess attributes. Again, consider the CUSTOMER object shown in Figure 7.12. Its attributes are the characteristics of the firm's customers that are of interest to the organization. For example, we are not interested in a customer's height, though we might be if we sold suits! Data relating to *specific* customers, for example, "489801, Peter Jones, 34 Drummond Drive, Philadelphia, PA 44545, (215) 555-1212" are called *instances* of the object. A **key** is an attribute or attributes of an object whose value(s) is/are unique for each record, allowing an instance of an object to be individually retrieved from a database. For example, a Social Security number, being unique, may be used as an identifier. For our purposes, we have used a customer number that is generated by the system as the object's key.

Objects are related to other objects through *relationships.* In this case, customers place orders with the firm. We introduce this new object, ORDER, in Figure 7.13. The relationship between entities is shown using a line joining the two object rectangles, accompanied by the name of the relationship. The relationship shown is *places,* that is, "the customer *places* orders." It is also important to know the number of objects allowed

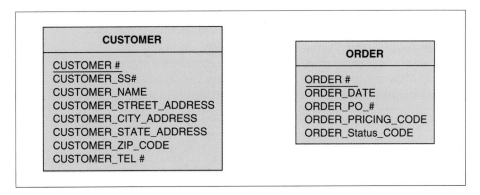

FIGURE 7.12   **CUSTOMER and ORDER objects and attributes**

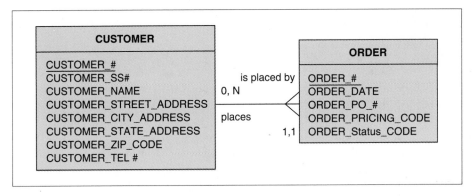

FIGURE 7.13   **CUSTOMER and ORDER entities and relationship**

to participate in relationships between objects, as this affects the use of the datasets. For example, do we allow customer records to exist if they have no orders? How many orders can a customer make? Can two customers make a joint order? These aspects of the relationships between objects are defined through cardinalities. A relationship's *cardinality* provides information about the number of object instances allowed in the relationship. We are concerned with two types of cardinality: minimum and maximum.

Minimum cardinality answers the question: "How many instances of an entity *must* the first entity be related to?" In the relationship between CUSTOMER and ORDER, this number is 0 if we allow customer records to exist regardless of whether they have current orders. With *maximum cardinality,* the question: "How many instances of an entity *can* the first entity be related to?" is answered. In the CUSTOMER–ORDER relationship, the answer is many, represented as N, as a customer may have several orders pending. So the cardinalities in the CUSTOMER–ORDER relationship are 0:N (minimum and maximum). In the opposite direction, the relationship is read "*is placed by,*" signifying that an order is placed by a customer. The minimum and maximum cardinalities are 1:1, signifying that an order must be made by a customer and that we do not allow multiple customers to make the same order. Figure 7.13 shows these cardinalities.

Figure 7.14a shows a more fully developed object-oriented model that incorporates additional objects in the form of product items and invoices. It illustrates the *relationships* between objects and their cardinalities, plus object attributes and identifiers. Figure 7.14a illustrates the concept of an *intersection entity* (ORDER-LINE), an object used to replace two M:N (many-to-many) relationships between objects with two 1:N relationships. The intersection entity, ORDER-LINE, is created because it is not possible to identify a specific order in the ORDERS object through a single ITEM

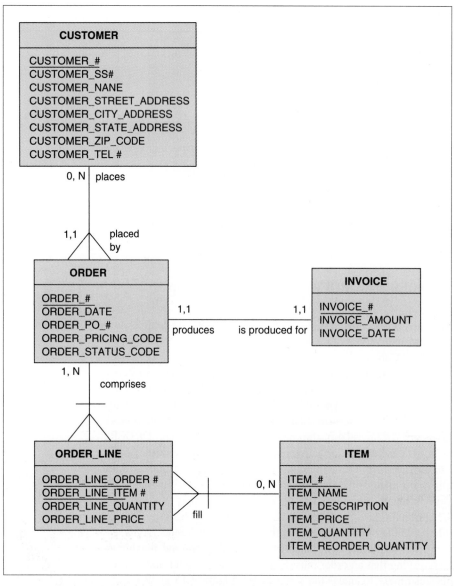

FIGURE 7.14   (a) Object-oriented data model   *(continued)*

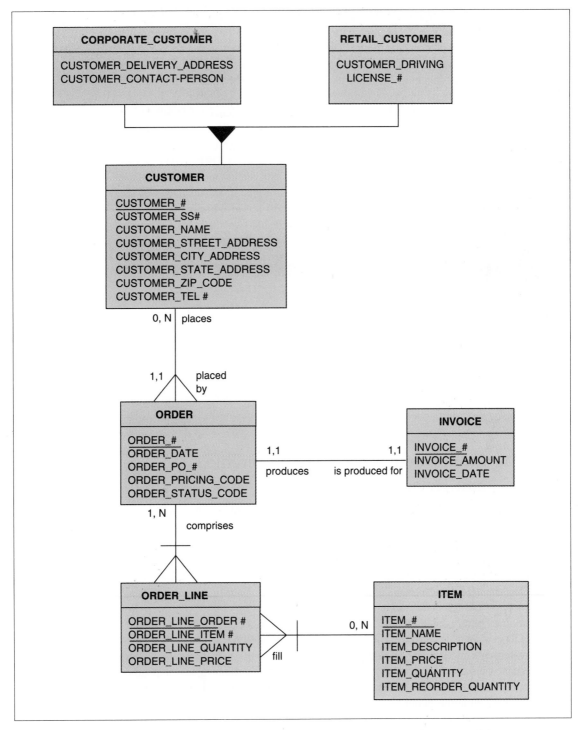

FIGURE 7.14 *(continued)* (b) Object-oriented data model with specialized entities

number; there may be several orders an item is related to, and vice versa. ORDER-LINE intersects ORDERS and ITEMS, contains identifiers from both objects, and serves to match single instances of orders to items. The perpendicular bar on the relationships between the intersection entity and the objects it intersects signifies an *identifier dependency,* or a dependence on them for its own identifier. The intersection entity's identifier is a composite of the two identifiers from the intersected objects.

In addition, the cardinality, <1>, on the relationship between CUSTOMER and ORDER, illustrates an *existence dependency,* indicating that one object depends on the other for its existence. Usually, ORDERS cannot exist without the customers who make them, creating a dependence on the CUSTOMER entity. Finally, CORPORATE_CUS-TOMER is shown as a new object in Figure 7.14b, derived from the *object class* CUSTOMER. An object derived from an object class inherits all the attributes of the object class, but in addition, it may have separate attributes. It is also known as an *object specialization.* For example, CORPORATE_CUSTOMER has two attributes, Delivery_ Address and Contact_Person, in addition to those it inherits from the CUSTOMER object class.

Logical database design can therefore be viewed as a multistage process in which:

1. Objects and object classes are defined.
2. Object attributes and identifiers are described.
3. The key relationships between objects are determined, together with their cardinalities.
4. Intersection entities, object specializations, and existence and identifier dependencies are determined.

The logical design may then be transformed into an implementation design using a selected implementation model, as discussed below.

Database Implementation Using Hierarchical, Network, and Relational Models

Object-oriented data models, as shown in Figures 7.16a and 7.16b, are the main output of data requirements analysis, and they are subsequently translated into one of several **database implementations,** such as the hierarchical, network, and relational models. The first two were the earliest used to develop databases, particularly in mainframe environments. Since the introduction of the relational model in 1970 by Codd, it has become the most popular model, and on microcomputer platforms, practically all DBMSs support the relational model.

An important part of database implementation is the construction of a *data dictionary (DD).* A DD is a central repository for data definitions and describes the data elements of the created data model. The DD defines the data elements used, their lengths and types, aliases, objects in which they are used, constraints on their values, and other important information. A DD is beneficial for documentation purposes, regardless of the database implementation model chosen. Figure 7.15 illustrates a common DD format that relates to the object-oriented model of Figure 7.14b.

The **hierarchical model** is based on one-to-many (or hierarchical) relationships between different objects. Records are arranged in a hierarchical fashion, with *parent*

Field Name:	Customer number		
Aliases:	Account number, master account number		
Description:	A unique number that identifies an individual customer of the firm. The first digit indicates whether the customer is a corporate or noncorporate customer.		
Format:	9-999999		
Type:	Numeric		
Width:	7 digits		
Value and Meaning:	Digits	Valid Ranges	Meaning
	1	1-2	A 1 denotes a corporate customer A 2 denotes a private individual
	2-7	000000-111111	Unique customer number assigned by the firm.
Where Used:	Customer statement Customer billing Cancelled check report Shipping note Customer analysis report		
Source and Maintenance:	A customer is assigned by the new account creation program when a customer orders merchandise for the first time. It is updated when a customer requests accounts to be closed.		
Storage:	Customer master file (key) Orders file (foreign key)		

FIGURE 7.15   Printout of a data dictionary page

records capable of having one or more *child records*. For example, the CUSTOMER-ORDER relationship shown earlier would translate to a hierarchical model shown in Figure 7.16, with a customer record being the parent record and the order record being the child. Each customer record is linked to several orders, but each order is linked to only one parent customer record. Links are established through fields attached to each record called *pointers*. The hierarchical model is typically optimized for certain queries but inefficient for others. In Figure 7.16, for example, the query: "What orders did customer 1017 make?" is easily answered by locating the parent record with CUSTOMER #1017 and examining the child record (ORDER). However, the query: "How many customers made orders on July 5th?" is more problematic. Answering it involves accessing all parent records and their children and consumes considerable computing resources.

The **network model** is more powerful than the hierarchical model as it represents many-to-many (M:N) relationships. In fact, the hierarchical model is simply a subtype of the network model. For example, consider again the ORDER-ITEM relationship shown in Figures 7.13 and 7.14. It has multiple cardinalities in both directions, calling for an intersection entity. This relationship may be directly represented using the network model. Here, a parent record may have several child records, but a child may also have many parents. Thus, the fact that items may be found in different orders and orders have multiple items is captured in the network model, as in Figure 7.17. Pointers are again used to capture links between different records. The network model is more complex than the hierarchical, and the pointers are correspondingly more difficult to maintain.

Most microcomputer DBMSs are based on the **relational database model,** which is our major focus in the following pages. This model organizes data into two-dimensional tables called relations (see Figure 7.18), consisting of rows or *tuples*

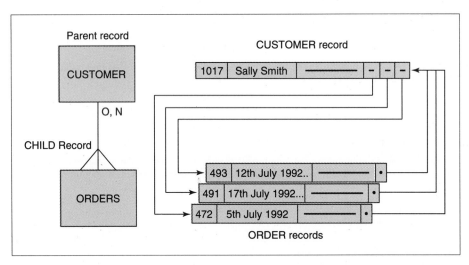

FIGURE 7.16   Hierarchical database model for the CUSTOMER-ORDER relation

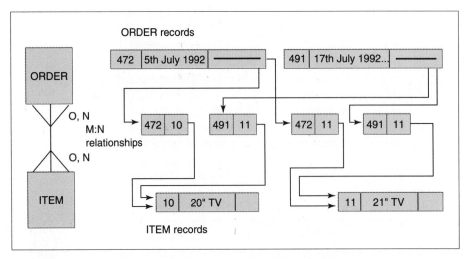

FIGURE 7.17   Network database model for the ORDER-ITEM relations

of data. Each tuple represents an instance of an object and comprises the object's attributes. The order of the attributes is immaterial, as is the order of the tuples. The set of allowable values for an attribute is known as the *domain of the relation,* and the number of the attributes in a relation is called the *degree of the relation.*

The attribute(s) that uniquely identifies a tuple is called a **key** (similar to an object's key). A tuple may have more than one potential key, each of which is called a *candidate key.* The key selected for use in the DBMS is called the primary key. If the primary key has only one attribute, it is a *singular key;* otherwise, it is a *composite key.* Finally, a nonkey attribute(s) in a relation, which is a primary key in another relation, is called a *foreign key* in the first relation and enables cross-referencing between relations.

When using the relational model, the modeler's task is to convert the object-oriented model to relations. Figure 7.19 illustrates how the model of Figure 7.14 is transformed into the relational model. Primarily, object attributes may be converted in a relatively straightforward fashion into relations, for example, CUSTOMER and ORDER. The more difficult task is that of representing the relationships between objects. Remember, however, that using intersection entities, the object-oriented model eliminates M:N (many to many) relationships. The remaining 1:N relationships are represented in the relational model by replicating the key of the object (relation) on the "1" side of the relationship as a foreign key in the object on the "N" side. For example, the customer number is incorporated in the order record. This enables us to identify a specific

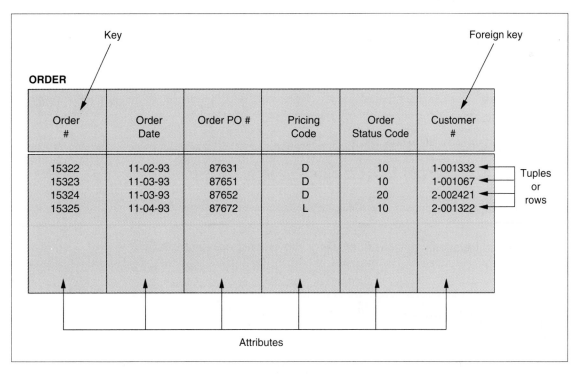

FIGURE 7.18   A portion of the relation ORDER

Customer Table

Customer #	Customer SS #	Customer Name	Street Address	City Address	Zip Code	Telephone #	Moody #	Contract Person	License #

Order Table

Order #	Order Date	Order PO #	Pricing Code	Order Status Code	Customer #

Invoice Table

Invoice #	Invoice Amount	Invoice Date	Order #

Order Line Table

Order Line Order #	Order Line Item #	Order Line Quantity	Order Line Price

Item Table

Item #	Item Name	Item Description	Item Cost	Item Quantity	Item Reorder Level

FIGURE 7.19   Relational database model for the order processing example

customer from an order record, in contrast to the many orders that could be pointed to by a customer.

The final part of converting the object-oriented model into the relational implementation model uses a process called *normalization,* a multistage process that involves:

- Moving repeating groups of attributes to new relations (1st normal form or 1NF)

- Moving to new relations all nonkey fields not fully dependent on the whole key and the parts of the key on which they are fully dependent (2NF)
- Removing nonkey fields that are dependent on other nonkey fields (3NF)

Other normal forms include fourth normal form (4NF), Boyce-Codd (BCNF), and domain-key normal form (DKNF). However, 3NF is acceptable for most relational database implementations. A detailed treatment of normalization is found in database texts.

Using a data manipulation language or DML, the user can manipulate the data in the relational database in several ways. For example, tuples (records) in a relation may be inserted, deleted, updated, displayed, or printed. Other relational operations are used to extract answers to the user's queries. They include the *projection* operation, which creates a new relation based on a subset of the first relation's columns; the *select* operation, which returns a new relation with a subset of the relation's rows; and the *join* operation, which creates one new relation from two that have a common attribute. These operations are illustrated in the next section.

7.3   MICROCOMPUTER DATABASE _____
MANAGEMENT SYSTEMS (DBMSS) _____

Firms have come a long way from paper filing systems to today's electronic databases. **Database management systems (DBMSs)** are the key piece of software that has brought about this change. The DBMS manages data stored in the database. It allows new data to be stored, permits access to existing data, maintains controls on data integrity, and prevents unauthorized access to data. The first DBMSs were developed for mainframes and minicomputers, but the past few years have seen the creation of microcomputer DBMSs with many of the capabilities of mainframe-based packages. The ability of DBMSs to interact with each other has also risen in importance with the advent of client-server technology, as described in Chapters 9 and 10.

Functions of a DBMS

Both large and small DBMSs provide the same general features, although they vary in sophistication. They include the ability to create and manipulate new files and records using DBMS commands. For example, a relational DBMS should allow the user to set up an inventory database with ORDER and ITEM relations by defining the fields and field types, as in Figure 7.20. Subsequently, it should allow the user to populate the files by entering new records, or by importing or reading the data from another application, for example, a word processed document or spreadsheet.

Another DBMS feature is *minimizing redundancy* among data elements, to ensure consistency within the various data elements in the database. The fields shown in Figure 7.20 are stored just once. In a paper filing system (or flat-file), the supplier name would have to be stored with every inventory item to be able to initiate a back order for the items. The ability of the DBMS to link and use files together removes this inefficiency. DBMSs also support *data independence*, relieving the user of the need to know exactly how the data (for example, supplier records) in the database is physically stored.

```
CREATE SCHEMA
    AUTHORIZATION JOHN RICHARDS
CREATE TABLE ORDER TABLE
    ORDER _ #              NUMERIC (6)        NOT NULL UNIQUE
    ORDER_DATE            CHARACTER (8)
    ORDER_PO#             NUMERIC (6)
    PRICING_CODE         NUMERIC (4)
    ORDER_STATUS_CODE    NUMERIC (3)
    CUSTOMER_#           NUMERIC (6)        NOT NULL
CREATE TABLE ITEM TABLE
    ITEM_#               NUMERIC (6)        NOT NULL UNIQUE
    ITEM_NAME            CHARACTER (12)
    ITEM_DESCRIPTION     CHARACTER (30)
    ITEM_COST            NUMERIC (7)
    ITEM_QUANTITY        NUMERIC (6)
    ITEM_REORDER_LEVEL   NUMERIC (4)
```

FIGURE 7.20   **Creation of ORDER and ITEM tables using SQL.**
These SQL instructions create ORDER and ITEM tables comprising six fields each. ORDER_# and ITEM_# are the key fields for each relation and are not allowed to take on null values. In addition, CUSTOMER_# is a foreign key in the ORDER table. Authorization privileges are also given to John Richards.

DBMSs also support *user queries* using a DML. The **structured query language (SQL)**—pronounced *sequel*—developed by IBM is the leading relational DML and is used in products such as Borland's dBase IV. To find out which inventory items are below their reorder levels, for example, the user might issue a SQL query:

SELECT ITEM_#, ITEM_NAME

FROM INVENTORY

WHERE ITEM_QUANTITY ≤ ITEM_REORDER_LEVEL

The above query uses the INVENTORY relation and returns the item numbers and names for inventory items that must be reordered. Other SQL commands may be used to extract data in other ways (see Figure 7.21).

DBMSs must also provide *security features* to protect records and files from unauthorized access or modification. Files may be protected by using *passwords* to deny access completely to certain users, to provide read-only access, or to allow unlimited access. For example, the supplier file may have read-only access restrictions placed on certain users using passwords to prevent possible fraud, for example, rerouted payments.

1. **Query:** List all data on orders made on 9-11-92.

   SELECT *
   FROM ORDER
   WHERE DATE = '09-11-92'

The symbol * denotes that all fields in the ORDERS table should be listed.

2. **Query:** List order numbers of all orders made by Fred Oppenheimer.

   SELECT ORDER_#
   FROM ORDER, CUSTOMER
   WHERE CUSTOMER.CUSTOMER_# = ORDER.CUSTOMER_#
   AND CUSTOMER_NAME = 'Fred Oppenheimer'

This is a matching or JOIN operation between two tables with a common field.

3. **Query:** Which products to be reordered cost over $50?

   SELECT ITEM_NAME
   FROM ITEM
   WHERE ITEM_QUANTITY ≤ ITEM_REORDER_LEVEL
   AND ITEM_COST > 50

This is a PROJECTION operation that retrieves one field from a subset of a relation's tuples.

FIGURE 7.21   Example SQL queries using ORDER and ITEM tables

Finally, DBMSs allow the user to create interactive programs that manipulate data in the database in support of the user's business applications. For example, programs can be developed using the command languages of DBMs such as dBase or Paradox to present a set of packaged procedures through menus to the user. Each menu option would activate a group of DBMS commands that create, access, or print data from the database, or even perform analyses using this data.

Single-User and Multiuser DBMSs

The first microcomputer DBMS was dBASE II, developed in 1981 by Wayne Ratliff. It revolutionized data management on microcomputers by providing sophisticated data management capabilities for the first time. Since its initial introduction, over four million copies of dBASE have been sold. dBASE II was a **single-user DBMS,** implying that only one user could make use of the database at any one time. Single-user microcomputer DBMSs are prevalent today, but many now provide multiuser capabilities. The majority of personal data management products today are *flat-file managers,* such as Alpha Software's *Alpha Four,* Borland's *Reflex* and *RapidFile,* and Symantec's *Q&A.*

Multiuser DBMSs are more sophisticated than the personal data managers and allow concurrent database access by up to 64 users. If the inventory database described above were implemented using a multiuser DBMS, two users on different terminals would be able to access multiple supplier records at the same time. However, problems arise in a multiuser context. The first is *data integrity.* For example, imagine a situation where two users retrieve an inventory record (50 items, say), withdraw 40

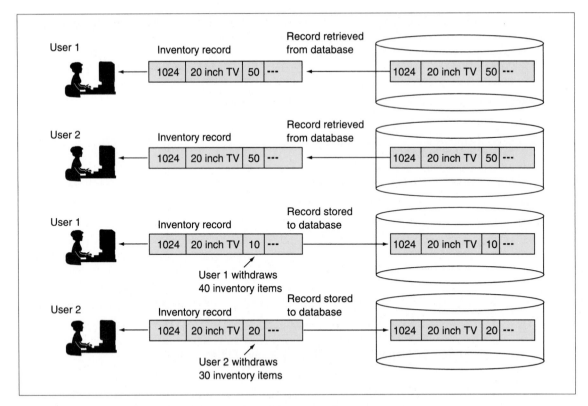

FIGURE 7.22   Problems of unrestricted multiuser database access

and 30 items each, and end up with 20 items (see Figure 7.22). Such problems are handled using *file locks* and *record locks,* to restrict access to records in use. These locks are an important part of multiuser DBMSs.

Another problem multiuser DBMSs must handle is "deadly embrace" or *deadlock,* which occurs when two processes require resources (for example, records) held by the other. The result is that they wait and wait . . . and wait—forever, if the ability to detect and break deadlock were not incorporated into multiuser DBMSs. Two types of multiuser DBMSs are those developed on microcomputer platforms (for example, dBase, Foxbase and Paradox), and those ported from mainframe environments (for example, ORACLE). The latter help to ensure compatibility in heterogeneous environments but are often more difficult to learn and use. Table 7.1 compares the capabilities of various DBMS and flat-file products.

Database Servers and Distributed DBMSs

As computer networks have become more widespread, the need for **database servers** has increased. In particular, requests for data from a central database in a multiuser setting usually result in the DBMS sending over whole files to be processed at the user's terminal, creating heavy network traffic. For example, a request for suppliers in a certain

TABLE 7.1   Major differences between microcomputer DBMSs and flat-file managers

	Multiuser DBMS e.g., dBASE, Sybase	Flat-File Managers e.g., Q&A, PC-File
RAM requirements	Usually Large (> 1Mb)	Small (>512K)
Hard disk requirements	5 Mb upward	1 Mb upward
Multiplatform availability	Often multiple platforms (micros, minis, and mainframes)	Usually limited to microcomputers
Architecture	Fully relational capabilities	Flat-file or semirelational capabilities
Server functionality	Fully functional database server capabilities	Mostly unavailable; exceptions include Alpha 4
Programmability	Extensive programmability; often compiled	Limited programmability; mostly macros and keystroke recording provided
Query method	DBMS languages, SQL, QBF, QBE	Usually QBF or QBE; Q&A has a natural language query capability
Multiuser features	Concurrent multiuser access to multiple files using record locking	Mostly unavailable; Alpha 4 supports multiuser access over networks
Use of SQL	Extensive SQL query capabilities	Absent, or provided through software links to SQL servers
On-line transaction processing	System stays up during backups, recovery, and tuning; supports roll-forward operations Maintain transaction logs	Mostly absent

city may result in the whole SUPPLIERS relation being sent to the user's terminal and the request processed there. Database servers process queries at the server, greatly reducing communications overhead and returning only the query results to the requesting terminal.

Distributed databases are finding their way onto microcomputer platforms as well. A distributed database's components are spread out over multiple locations. In this case, the DBMS is required to provide location transparency, relieving the user of the need to know where files are physically located. Both distributed databases and database servers are tightly integrated with data communications and are discussed in more detail in Chapters 9 and 10. See Figure 7.23.

7.4   SELECTING MICROCOMPUTER DBMSS _____

Selecting a database management product follows the same procedure as selection of any other software type. Its costs are evaluated against the product's capabilities, and

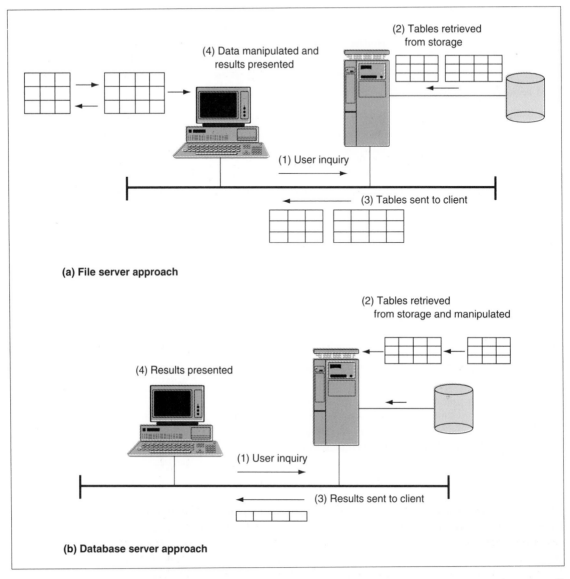

FIGURE 7.23   Operation of a file server and a database server   *(continued)*

additional concerns such as compatibility with the existing platform are considered. In selecting flat-file managers or relational DBMSs, many products are available, some of which have been ported down from mainframe products. Others, like dBase, were developed from scratch on microcomputers. Three important questions for the decision maker are as follows:

- Will a flat-file manager be sufficient, or is a relational DBMS required?

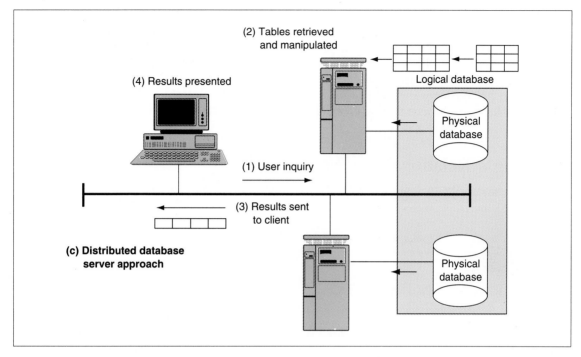

(2) Tables retrieved
and manipulated

(4) Results presented

Logical database

Physical
database

(1) User inquiry

(3) Results sent
to client

**(c) Distributed database
server approach**

Physical
database

FIGURE 7.23 *(continued)*

- If a relational DBMS is required, what are the factors to consider in making this selection?
- What additional features are required for multiuser DBMSs?

Flat-File Managers versus DBMSs

Flat-file managers are generally less expensive than microcomputer RDBMSs but have fewer capabilities. Although newer flat-file managers such as *Alpha Font* and *Q&A,* now relate multiple files, they are not yet comparable to their RDBMS counterparts in flexibility of data manipulation and programability. This makes sophisticated stand-alone applications the province of tools such as *dBASE, Foxbase,* or *Paradox.*

Flat-file managers are excellent tools for simple file storage and retrieval and report extraction even though they do not support the same range of ad hoc queries as full-featured RDBMSs. The latter are more costly than flat-file managers, but their costs are comparable to those of spreadsheet and word processing programs. They are thereby more cost effective, making them the recommended choice for more sophisticated user needs.

Multiuser DBMS Considerations

There are two types of **multiuser DBMSs.** The first type is used in settings characterized by a host, which could be a Pentium-based machine or workstation with attached dumb terminals. The second is used in LAN-based systems, with a server and intelligent terminals. In the first example, the host computer might use an operating system like SCO UNIX to provide multiuser access to the database. Examples of such products are Foxbase and dBase. On a LAN-based system, a more sophisticated (and expensive) LAN version of the DBMS is usually required to interface with the NOS. For example, the Foxbase LAN version was developed for use with Novell Netware—the leading NOS. LANs are more common than host/terminal configurations and are discussed in greater detail in Chapters 9 and 10.

Selecting a Relational Database

Two broad classes of microcomputer RDBMSs are mainframe-based products (for example, DB2) and native, more popular microcomputer-based products, such as dBase,

---

INDUSTRIAL-STRENGTH MICROCOMPUTER RDBMSs DRIVE DOWNSIZING

For most IS managers, traditional microcomputer DBMSs such as dBASE and Paradox do not offer enough features or power to replace the complex and heavy database processing on mainframes. Full support for SQL, distributed databases, and performance in transactions per second provided by these micro-based programs do not match up to programs like DB2 (IBM's mainframe RDBMS) running on IBM 9000 mainframes.

Fortunately, a new breed of RDBMSs that offer promise for supporting mainframe-level transaction processing using UNIX workstations and microcomputers is emerging. These include programs such as Sybase Inc.'s *SQL Server for Netware*, Oracle Corp.'s *Oracle 7*, Cincom's *Supra*, and Gupta Technologies *SQLBase*. Many of these RDBMSs obtain much of their performance gains over traditional micro DBMSs by running on the Novell Netware NOS, as attached Netware Loadable Modules (NLMs); or on UNIX (some also have mainframe versions—for example, *Oracle 7* and *Supra*). They benefit from the speed of the fully 32-bit microcomputer NOSs, with Gupta's SQLBase generating over 100 trans

actions per second on 50 Mhz 486 machines (some mainframe systems also generate TPSs in this range). Using multiple Pentium processors in servers, combining multiple servers on a LAN, and using workstations gives IS managers the ability to support several hundred TPSs on these comparatively less-expensive platforms.

Although the prices for these RDBMSs can be high (up to $30,000 for unlimited users), they are much less expensive than the hundreds of thousands of dollars mainframe DBMSs cost. They offer firms a path to fully downsize their systems or to partially offload database processing from mainframes. General Electric for example, is in the process of moving from a centralized mainframe MIS shop to a three-tiered IS infrastructure. The middle tier of UNIX-based workstation servers will use the Sybase RDBMS to supply hundreds of PC and Macintosh users with data extracted from corporate mainframe databases. This will reduce the demand for expensive mainframe cycles and provide more responsive query responses to users.

Paradox, Foxpro, and RBASE. An important criterion for the potential purchaser is the *operating system* for the RDBMS. Some combinations are unavailable, for example, Paradox on the Macintosh. Also, some RDBMSs may not be usable in the user's graphical environments, for example, Windows or OS/2.

With DBMS *hardware requirements* (for example, the minimum hard disk and RAM requirements), it is important to know if their use is feasible on existing platforms and to know their upgrade implications. The *DBMS's performance* is also a central consideration. Foxbase, for example, uses a proprietary indexing scheme to produce some of the best performance (for example, searches, sorts, response to queries) available on microcomputers.

Users may also examine the underlying structure of the database, for example, ISAM, DAM, and inverted lists, to better predict DBMS performance and flexibility. *Database features* like maximum sizes of fields, records, and files are also important, to eliminate DBMSs that cannot satisfy the requirements of the database design. *File compatibility,* too, can be critical, for importing and exporting files from other software. The more sophisticated DBMSs can import data from many word processor, text, spreadsheet, and even graphic file formats. The user should research the user *interface* before purchase, especially if the user is technically unsophisticated. Power users may be comfortable with command-line interfaces, but inexperienced users will prefer menu-driven interaction and *query-by-example* query methods.

The *programmability* of the DBMS should be considered if the user desires to build stand-alone applications using the DBMS's DML. Tools such as menu generators, screen builders, and macro recorders, which record sequences of user actions in the DML, are available in several DBMSs. A related issue is whether the RDBMS incorporates SQL. SQL is now the national (ANSI) standard for querying databases, in configurations ranging from LANs to enterprise networks. RDBMS that lack SQL are unlikely to receive consideration for serious database use.

As microcomputer databases (see Figure 7.24) begin to undergo use for transaction processing, *security* and *reliability functions* have become top issues for DBMSs. Many now provide features previously found only on mainframe products, such as transaction logs, rollback of uncompleted transactions, and audit trails for database recovery after failure. Also, encryption and password protection are now common on RDBMSs, particularly those in use on multiuser systems.

Microcomputer RDBMSs should be evaluated for their ability to work in a Windows environment, as it represents a major user interface in the 1990s. They should also have large memo fields for incorporating free-form text to records and be able to handle data in multiple formats, for example, PICT and TIFF graphic file formats, sound files, and scanned images. In addition, no package is given serious consideration if it cannot create compiled run-time program modules that can be run in a stand-alone mode by the end user.

Vendor-related considerations are important to the DBMS purchaser, including the vendor's financial history, money-back guarantees, toll-free support, replacement and upgrade policies, and so on. Lastly, the cost of the DBMS will be assessed against the background of the capabilities discussed above. Generally, single-user versions of the software cost significantly less than LAN versions, but site licenses are available for sites with many users. These all factor into the overall price equation.

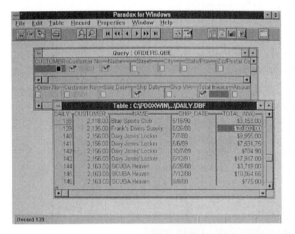
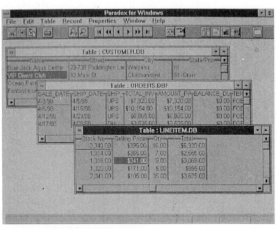
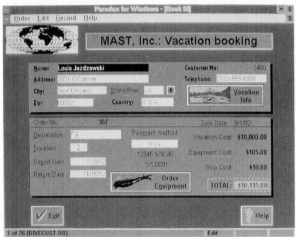

FIGURE 7.24   Borland's Paradox DBMS, showing query-by-example (*top*)
and a user-developed application (*bottom*).

7.5   DOCUMENT IMAGE PROCESSING

Another form of data management used for competitive advantage by organizations is
document image processing (DIP). Consider these facts:

- Over 90 billion paper documents are produced yearly.
- 300–400 billion photocopies are made each year.
- The number of active files in corporations doubles every 3.5 years.
- The cost of floorspace has increased by 300 percent in the last decade.

Against a background of spiraling costs and greater emphasis on environmental
conservation, DIP has been developed as a means of reducing the costs and space
requirements of document storage and management. A DIP system captures and
manages document images on secondary storage devices, from where they can later be

retrieved. Hard copy can be dispensed with and replaced by the DIP system's rapid access to the electronically stored documents, reducing paper costs.

A document stored in a DIP system differs from one created using a word processing package. The word processed file is a text file, interspersed with control codes that denote formatting commands. Conversely, the document image comprises bitmapped pages input using a scanner at 300 dpi (dots per inch) for text images, or up to 800 dpi for high-quality photographs. While a page of text takes up about 2 Kb of disk space, a scanned page of text requires up to 1.5 Mb (uncompressed) or about 80 Kb (compressed) (refer to Chapter 3 for data compression details). Only recently have storage devices become large enough to support the data requirements of DIP.

Hardware and Software Requirements for Document Imaging

Document imaging is still in its relative infancy in U.S. corporations. The desktop imaging process consists of several steps:

1. The input document is captured using a scanner and stored on a secondary storage device.
2. The stored document is then labeled and indexed, through the document imaging software.
3. The document is then destroyed.
4. Requests for the document image may be made by the user through the software.
5. The retrieved document can be displayed on a monitor or printed on a laser printer.

Several firms have written specialized software to support document imaging on a variety of platforms, including microcomputers. They include *Total Recall* by Orion and TAB Products' *File Tracker.* Functions supported by these packages include labeling, indexing, storage, and tracking. File activity reports are also provided, as are security features. The hardware requirements for document imaging are considerable. For stand-alone systems, a scanner, a laser printer, and a fast 80486- or 68030-based microcomputer are minimum requirements (see Figure 7.25). Most document imaging is centered around optical disks due to their large capacities. For volatile data (most business applications), rewritable optical disks are used, but for static or sensitive data, CD-ROMs or WORMS are more appropriate.

Many firms implementing document imaging require considerably more than the minimum configuration shown in Figure 7.25. As more than half of all corporate microcomputers are now networked, LAN configurations are more likely settings for DIP. Figure 7.26 shows how DIP is used on a computer network. Scanners on the network capture documents, which are then stored on a central server. Requests for stored documents may be made from terminals anywhere on the network and displayed on these terminals, or printed on laser printers attached to the network. With larger networks, for example, enterprisewide networks, *optical "jukeboxes"* may be used to provide gigabytes or even terabytes (1 terabyte = 1,024 gigabytes) of data for document image storage.

OCR is a further capability often included in DIP systems, enabling the conversion of captured images into text (see Chapter 4, Section 4.1). This may be basic text

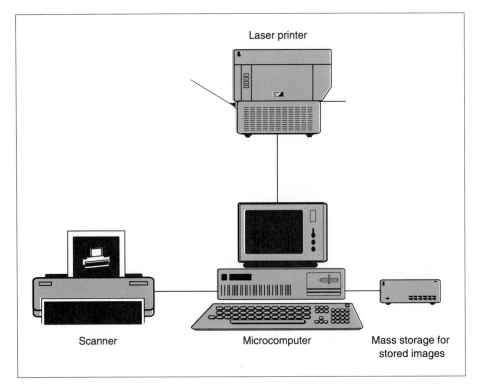

Laser printer

Scanner   Microcomputer   Mass storage for
stored images

FIGURE 7.25   Minimum configuration for document image processing (DIP)

conversion or more sophisticated conversion, which retains the formatting within the document and preserves the placement of graphics within the text. OCR has been embraced by firms seeking to obtain both the benefits of DIP and lower costs of data entry.

Using Document Imaging

Suitable applications for DIP are documents like receipts, formal correspondence, resumes, and other free-form documents. Data files, such as inventory and supplier records, are better suited to formal databases managed by a DBMS. The important question relates to the benefits of DIP. A major benefit is the capture of *exact* document bitmaps, which reduces problems and disputes resulting from incorrect manual data entry. The scanner produces an exact representation of the original document, which may be printed out on a laser printer if required; an example is American Express charge slips. Additionally, the cost of storage on optical disks is lower than that of the equivalent paper files. Third, the stored document images may be rapidly accessed using filenames, keywords, and other means. This eliminates costly manual searches of paper filing cabinets and storage rooms and the cost of recreating lost documents.

Some of the problems with DIP include the lack of imaging standards (although *CCITT 3 and 4* standards are now being widely accepted). The major problem, however,

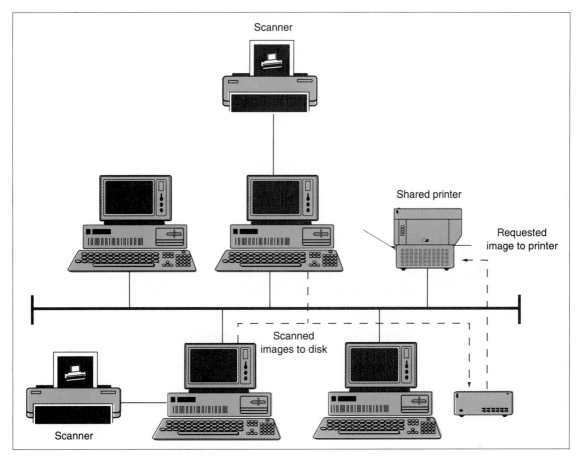

FIGURE 7.26   Networked document image processing (DIP) configuration

occurs on networks, where document traffic over the network can be many times greater than normal text-based traffic, creating network bottlenecks. This problem is alleviated somewhat by data compression, but it will be ultimately resolved by faster networks, such as FDDI, discussed in Chapter 10.

An example of an early adopter of DIP is Pacific Bell Directory, publisher of a Yellow Pages directory. An extreme records management problem was characterized by customer representatives who often spent hours searching for documents on microfilm instead of interacting with customers. Most customer claims could not be handled in one call due to the time required to locate records, leading to a claims backlog of 60 days and losses from settling claims due to misplaced records. A 50-node imaging system was installed to handle nearly two million documents, which included customer contracts and advertising copy. This led to much smoother operations, faster resolution of claims, and the backlog of claims over 30 days old falling from over 4,000 to fewer than 400. At Pacific Bell Directory, DIP is clearly seen as an innovative technology that has proven to be efficient and effective in improving work flow management.

Chapter Summary

Every firm needs to store and retrieve data on its services, customers, operations, and environment to support activities at all transaction and managerial levels. Storage devices are complemented by data management software that enables easy data management and access to stored data. Different types of files include text, data, image, and sound files.

For data files, the major data access methods include the sequential access method, used primarily by SASDs, and the indexed and direct access methods, used exclusively by DASDs. ISAM enables rapid access to any record in a sequentially ordered file through the use of indexes, while DAM makes use of a hashing algorithm to provide direct access to records. Data structures such as inverted files and multilists also enable data in a file to be logically reordered and accessed using nonkey fields.

Flat-file managers are simple and easy-to-use software programs originally aimed at managing single files. More recent flat-file managers can interrelate files, but they lack the sophisticated features of database management systems (DBMSs) in indexing, linking, and querying groups of interrelated files (databases). DBMSs are recommended for most file and database management activities in organizations for these and other features such as data integrity, security, and use of querying tools such as SQL.

Logical database design approaches aid the database developer in specifying the logical data model for a particular firm. The object-oriented approach defines the objects of interest to the user, their attributes, and relationships using specific constructs and rules. The object-oriented model for the firm is then transformed into an implementation model. The major implementation models include the hierarchical, network, and relational models. The relational model, which dominates microcomputer DBMSs, is based on interrelated tables, or relations containing data.

Microcomputer-based relational DBMSs are either single- or multiuser systems. Like other DBMSs, their functions include managing files efficiently, minimizing data redundancy, providing data reliability and integrity, enabling database creation, and allowing user access to data through query languages and other means. Special DBMS versions also exist for use as database servers and for distributed databases.

Whole documents do not have the same format as data (or records) but instead can be digitized and stored as bitmaps. Document imaging has sprung up almost overnight as a means of managing not data but images. It involves scanning documents onto secondary storage as bitmaps, and in most cases, dispensing of the original source document. Document access and retrieval by the user makes use of keywords and filenames stored with the file, and documents can either be displayed on-screen or printed out on laser printers. DIP takes advantage of scanners and large storage capacities of optical disks and can result in storage cost savings, faster document access, and fewer lost documents.

Review Questions

1. What are the differences between the direct access and sequential access methods?
2. What is the key element that enables direct access to files under ISAM?

3. Can DAM be used in concert with magnetic cartridges? Why or why not?
4. Which data structure requires separate index files—inverted files or chained lists?
5. List three objectives of a DBMS.
6. What is the difference between a data manipulation language (DML) and a data description language (DDL)?
7. What occurs during the implementation stage of the database development life cycle?
8. Define the minimum cardinality of a relationship between two objects.
9. What is the major disadvantage of the hierarchical database implementation model?
10. What is another term for the number of attributes in a relation?
11. Which relational database operation creates a new relation from two relations with a common attribute?
12. What is the meaning of data independence, and what is its importance?
13. List two applications for which you believe flat-file managers would be suitable.
14. What are the minimum hardware requirements you would specify for a document image processing system?
15. Describe the difference between a query language and a DML.

EXERCISES _____

1. Describe and compare ISAM and DAM. Which of these access methods would you recommend if you required direct access for queries but also needed to use the file sequentially, for report generation?
2. A retailer of men's suits seeks to automate both the sales and inventory activities using microcomputers. Presently, the manager is deciding whether to use a flat-file manager or a microcomputer DBMS product to keep track of an extensive product line and about 10,000 sales per year to about 300 customers. In the future, she wants to obtain detailed reports regarding customers and sales, that is, tracking of sales after shipment for trend analysis. Do you recommend a flat-file manager or a DBMS? Explain.
3. Write a set of SQL commands that use the EMPLOYEE relation to find all the managers in the marketing department who earn more than $100,000 per year. Attributes in the relation include employee name, number, address, salary, functional area, and date hired.

SUGGESTED READINGS _____

Datapro Reports on Computers, Volume 3. New York: McGraw-Hill, 1991.

Codd, E. F. *The Relational Model for Database Management, Version 2.* Reading, MA: Addison-Wesley, 1990.

Date, C. J. *An Introduction to Database Systems: Volume 1.* Reading, MA: Addison-Wesley, 1990.

Hansen, G. W., and Hansen, J. V. *Database Management and Design.* Englewood Cliffs, NJ: Prentice-Hall, 1992.

Litwin, P. "*Personal Data Managers.*" *PC World,* July 1992, pp. 230–240.

CHAPTER 8

MICROCOMPUTER APPLICATIONS IN THE ORGANIZATION

INTRODUCTION

Information is now generated in greater volumes and in more forms than ever
before. Firms use different types of software to process data in textual, graphic,
and even audio formats to satisfy information needs at various organizational levels.
Increasingly, the most effective managers and firms are those who make the best
use of available information to monitor and control the firm's activities and to plan
for the future. Management information systems (MISs) are designed to satisfy
the information needs of managers and include reporting systems and structured
decision systems. Other categories of systems are decision support systems (DSSs),
executive information systems (EISs), and expert systems (ESs), which are useful in
many managerial decision-making contexts.

Other, mainly microcomputer-based applications support multimedia, computer-
based work groups, and office information systems. These provide the technological
infrastructure for modern transaction processing and managerial information systems. Consequently, they are also discussed in this chapter.

Learning Objectives

After reading this chapter, you will be able to:

- Identify information requirements of managers at various organizational
  levels
- Determine appropriate types of support systems (for example, MIS, DSS, EIS,
  and ES) for aiding managerial decisions
- Identify specific organizational applications that would benefit from the use of
  artificial intelligence technologies, particularly expert systems
- Propose advanced computer applications, for example, multimedia, group-
  oriented software, and office information systems to satisfy organizational
  requirements

USING INFORMATION KIOSKS FOR CUSTOMER SERVICE

Jon Webb is browsing in suburban San Diego's Parkway Plaza Mall when an unfamiliar contraption catches his eye. "Touch my screen," implores the video monitor in the seven-foot structure wedged between a T-shirt cart and a lottery ticket booth. Intrigued, the bearded 34-year-old places his index finger on the glass. Suddenly, California Governor Pete Wilson appears and talks about the many services Info/California, this audio-video computer, offers: job listings, information on HIV testing, an electronic application for a fishing license, and more. Webb selects data on area beaches. "Cool," he says as he tears off a printout.

Now that nearly everyone is comfortable with automatic teller machines, many businesses and government agencies figure Americans are ready to retrieve information and order products via computer kiosks such as the one Webb used. Housed in wood-and-plastic cabinets and equipped with touch screens and simple menus, they are popping up everywhere—in supermarkets, auto showrooms, malls, and schools. About 59,400 such kiosks are in use in the United States today, says market researcher Inteco Corp. But by 1996, Inteco says there will be 2 million, making them more common than gasoline pumps.

That forecast is based on a new breed of multimedia machines. Unlike the electronickiosks that have been gathering dust in airports for a decade, these machines have colorful graphics and sound and allow consumers to conduct transactions. From the 15 Info/California kiosks around San Diego and Sacramento, for example, you can order a copy of your birth certificate.

Businesses are also adopting kiosks. Four music stores in California have installed Note Stations, kiosks that sell sheet music. A customer uses a touch screen to scan more than 1,000 titles. When one is selected, the score is displayed and the computer plays a few bars. For $3.95, the music lover can have the score printed in any key. Music Writer Inc. in Los Gatos, Calif., says it plans to install its kiosks in 1,800 stores.

In Toronto, for example, Allstate Insurance Co. is selling policies at kiosks in Sears and Food City stores. Some folks, no doubt, will miss the human touch of the counter person who gives you a sample of the salami-or even an insurance salesman. But for a nation pressed for time, kiosks could prove irresistible. Says mallgoer Webb: "They're convenient for people who don't want to run all over the place." Instead, you may just be running down to the corner kiosk.

Adapted from Evan I. Schwartz, with Paul M. Eng, S. Lynne Walker, and Alice Cuneo, "The Kiosks Are Coming, the Kiosks Are Coming." *BusinessWeek* (BW), Vol. 3271, p. 122.

8.1 MANAGEMENT INFORMATION SYSTEMS

Over the years, computers have become extremely effective "factories" for generating large and varied amounts of data. Managers are, in fact, currently faced with the possibility of "drowning in a sea of data." *Management information systems (MISs)* are created to use this data more effectively and to assist managers in planning and controlling the activities of their firms. MIS departments view information as an organizational resource and have created information systems for assisting top-, middle-, and operational-level managers. We begin by examining the hierarchy of organizational information systems and their value to the firm, followed by a discussion of managerial information needs and the information systems used to satisfy them.

Types of Managerial Activities

The activities at different organizational levels and the information systems required to support them are illustrated in Figure 8.1. At the base of the pyramid are the daily transaction-level activities, performed by clerical, sales, blue collar manufacturing, and secretarial staff, among others. Various **transaction processing systems (TPSs)** satisfy these operational information processing requirements, which include selling, manufacturing, and other financial/accounting functions within the firm (see the sales processing system example in Figure 8.2). Our current focus is on the levels of management above the transaction processing level: *operational control, tactical planning,* and *strategic planning* levels.

The top level of management performs **strategic planning.** Managers at this level determine the mission and long-term direction for the firm. Targeting new product areas

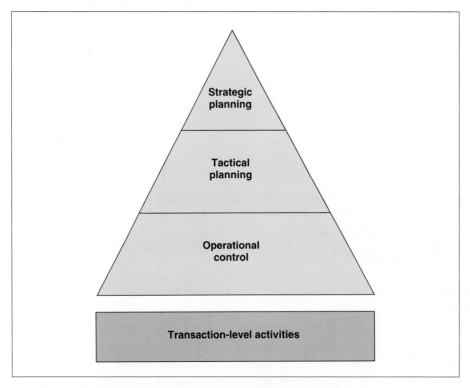

FIGURE 8.1   Hierarchy of organizational activities

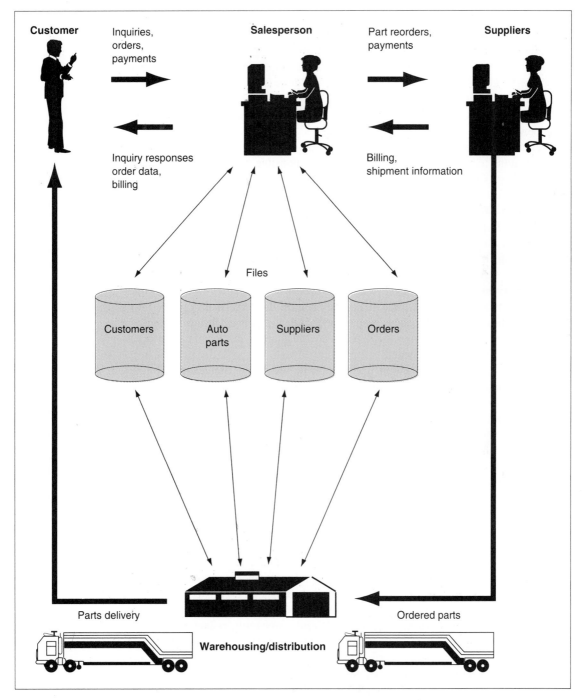

FIGURE 8.2   Data and materials flow in a sales order processing system

and businesses the firm should be involved with are examples of strategic planning activities, as is the formulation of broad strategies to achieve long-term goals of the firm. Examples of the senior executives at this level of the organization include CEOs, presidents, and major functional vice presidents, for example, in production, marketing, accounting, and research and development. In a car dealership, these executives might decide that, in addition to selling car parts, selected outlets should offer service and maintenance of cars. In addition, they would decide on the speed of the transition to these new services.

Tactical planning is performed by middle managers. They do not control the activities at the transaction level directly but are responsible for producing short-term plans and targets for the departments under their control and ensuring that these plans are met. Tactical managers translate the objectives and strategies of upper management into concrete schedules and plans to be carried out at the transaction level under the control of operational managers. Examples of these middle-level managers are *plant managers, marketing managers, warehouse managers,* and *personnel directors.* In our car dealership, area managers responsible for different outlets would create a detailed plan for their transition to full-service outlets.

The **operational control** level features lower-level managers whose primary responsibilities are the firm's transactions. They control the performance of the firm's primary business activities, such as sales, production, and payroll. In our example, a branch manager sees that car sales and services are of suitable quality and that sufficient inventory is available when needed.

In practice, one manager might serve at more than one organizational level, particularly in small organizations. Furthermore, the flattening of organizations is serving both to thin middle managerial levels and to increase the span of control exercised by managers in an effort to reduce costs. As we shall see, information systems play an essential part of this downsizing process by providing improved monitoring and control to the manager. Although the TPS was the earliest information system developed in firms, much attention is now being paid to higher-level information systems that improve the effectiveness of managers.

Structure of Managerial Decisions

An important characteristic of decisions is their **structuredness.** Decisions may be defined as more or less structured, based on their inherent certainty. In *structured decisions,* the decision process, available data, possible outcomes, and solution methods are well known, with little uncertainty. Decisions to restock an exhausted inventory or to prepare a delivery schedule are good examples, possessing clear-cut, quantifiable procedures. In fact, another term for structured is *programmable,* reflecting the ability to write computer programs to perform the function automatically.

Unstructured decisions are more intractable. Their decision process is often experimental and intuitive, data is of poor quality and incomplete, and the range of possible outcomes (and solution methods) is not fully known. This form of decision making takes place under uncertainty. Decisions to hire a new CEO or to introduce a new, revolutionary product are examples of unstructured decisions. See Figure 8.3 for a continuum of such decisions.

Unstructured decisions	Semi-structured decisions	Structured decisions
• Hiring a manager • Research and development • Selecting an advertising slogan	• Product marketing • Portfolio management • Facilities location	• Accounts receivable • Order processing • Payroll processing

FIGURE 8.3   Structured, semistructured, and unstructured decisions

Managerial Information Requirements

The information requirements of managers at various levels are important in determining appropriate forms of information systems. Operational managers, middle managers, and senior executives have very different information requirements due to differences in their focus. Thus, they are involved in differing types of decision-making activities.

For junior managers supervising transaction activities (see Figure 8.4a), decisions tend to be well structured and well defined and to utilize quantitative data. The approval of a credit limit for a new corporate customer, for example, will utilize a clearly defined sequence of steps. Also, poor sales performance by a particular store would result in a sequence of supervisory actions, such as retraining or using new local advertising. The forecasting horizon is usually short, focusing, say, on deliveries for a few weeks. Also, the level of detail will be high, relating to specific items, for example, auto parts sold to specific customers. Current data is required for operational control, for example, details of present transactions and inventory levels, and the scope of decisions is narrow, with data coming from such internal sources as customer and inventory files.

Middle managers make less structured decisions than those of their junior counterparts. In formulating the firm's short-to-medium-term plans and schedule, managers depend more on creativity and intuition. They often require complex analyses beyond the factual reports used by operational managers. They forecast further into the future, require more aggregated data, and use historical data for analyses. The scope of required information is wider, to match their managerial span of control, and more external data is likely to be used. The area manager deciding on new equipment for servicing autos might collect historical usage data for the new equipment and create a model to predict how it would enhance production in that work environment; brand managers might collect data on brand and competitor sales to support pricing and advertising decisions; and so on. See Figure 8.4b.

Strategic managers who formulate the firm's long-term strategy make mostly unstructured decisions, using intuition and qualitative data. The decisions are the longest-term in nature and have the widest scope (see Figure 8.4c). They require mainly highly aggregated data (for example, across departments, plants, and divisions) to understand trends, patterns, and the industry's direction. Much of this competitive data is external and broad in scope. The decision by the spare parts retailer to offer service and maintenance at selected outlets would require data on competitors in the auto repair

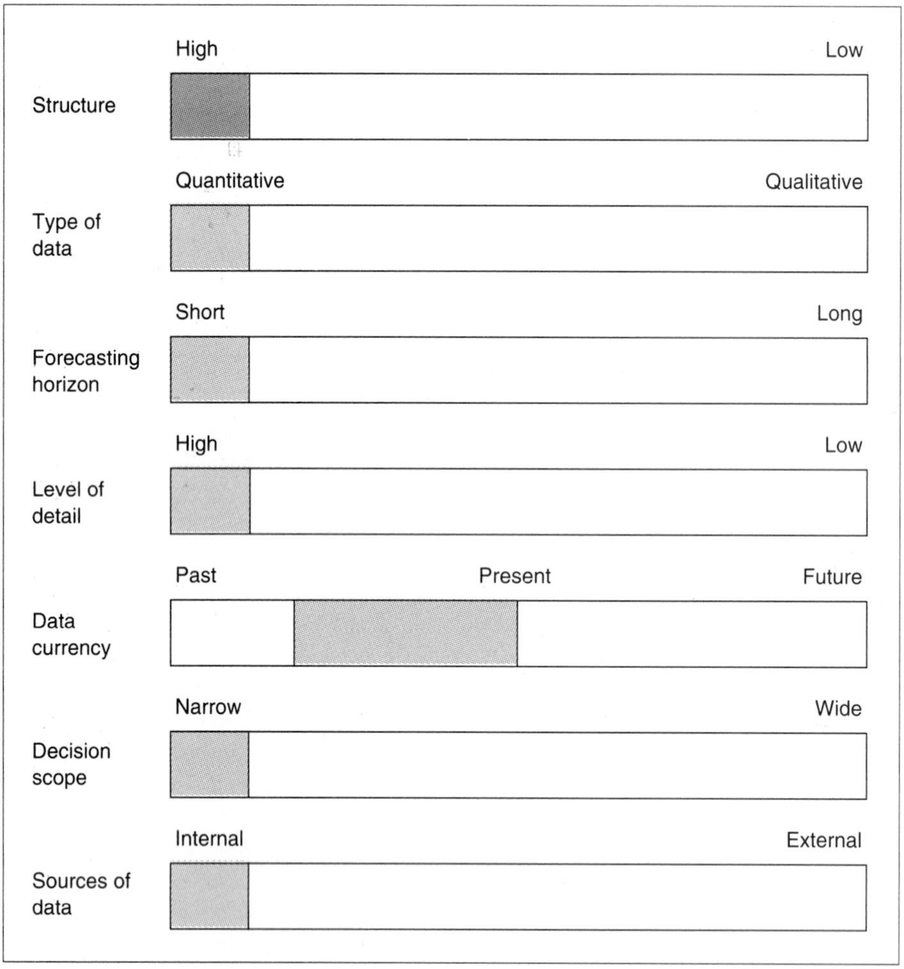

FIGURE 8.4   (a) Operational management information requirements

(continued)

business, as well as data on available revenues to support the firm's expansion and forecasted growth in the market.

Information Systems for Managers

A close study of information requirements at different managerial levels suggests that the information systems for each level have different characteristics. For example, the need of the lowest managerial level is for direct information on transactions within the organization, with a minimum of analysis required. The two types of MIS at this managerial level consist of *information reporting systems (IRSs)* and *structured decision*

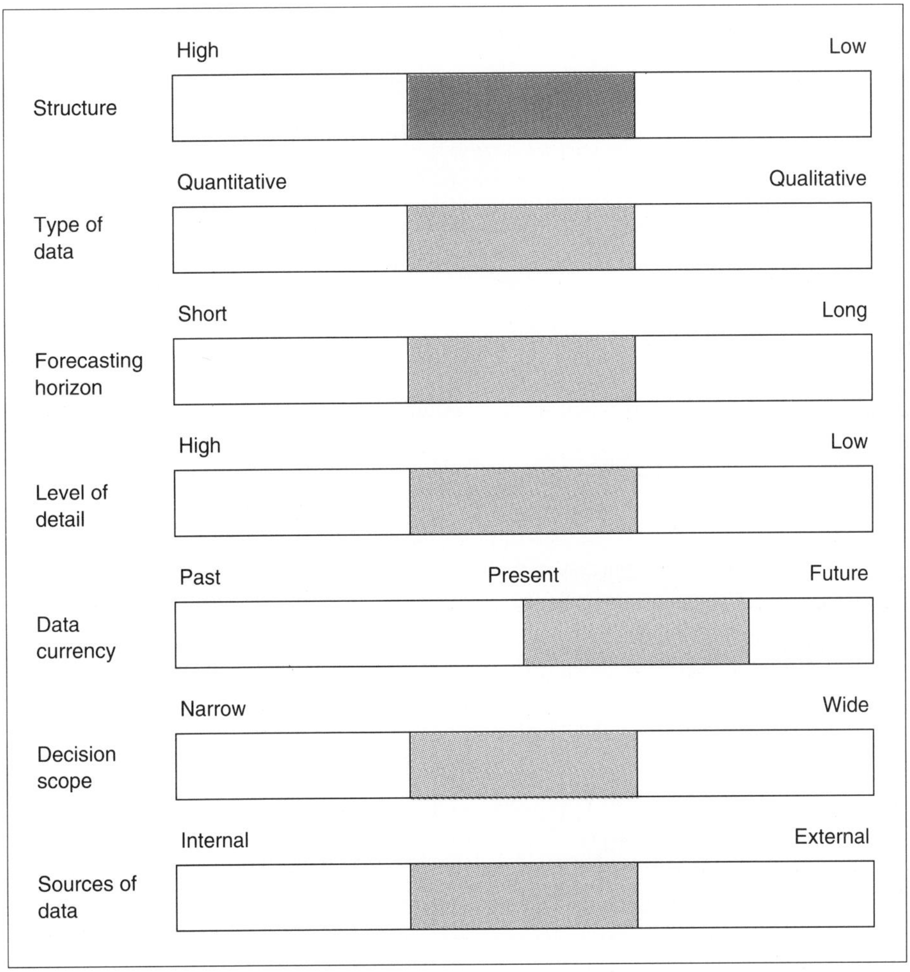

FIGURE 8.4 *(continued)*   (b) Tactical planning information requirements

(continued)

systems (SDSs). The IRS is closely coupled with the TPS, and in fact may be an added reporting function within it. Three types of reports are produced by the IRS:

- ■ *Periodic reports.* These might include a list of auto parts sold for the preceding week, or a weekly breakdown of sales achieved by each salesperson. These reports are automatically produced at identical intervals by the MIS, daily, weekly, or monthly.

- ■ *Ad hoc reports.* These reports are also known as demand reports, as they are not produced periodically but only on demand. For example, prior to taking remedial action in the case of an underperforming salesperson, the manager might request a report showing the salesperson's monthly performance for the preceding six months.

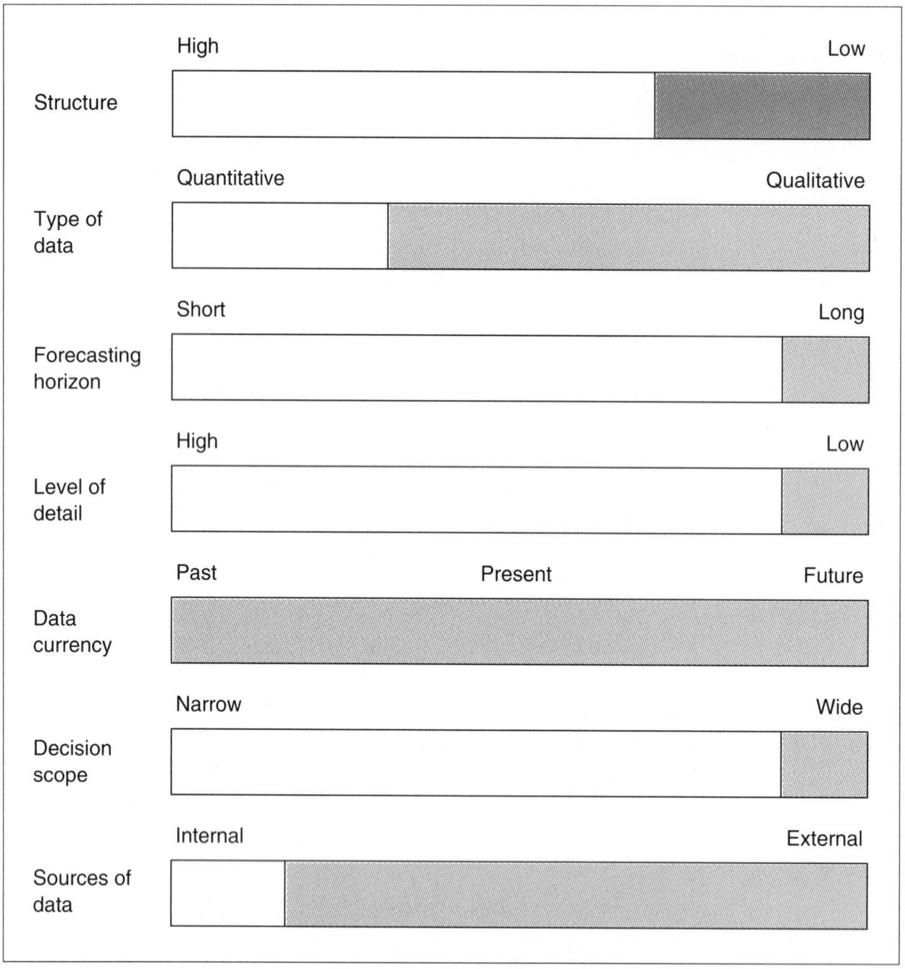

FIGURE 8.4 *(continued)*   (c) Strategic planning information requirements

This might help to indicate if current poor performance is temporary or likely to continue.

- ***Exception reports.*** TPS outputs can be overwhelming to the operational manager. Exception reports reduce the amount of information presented to the decision maker by documenting only instances where performance deviates markedly from what is expected. For example, only salespeople who excel or underperform would appear on the sales manager's exception report, reducing the report's size.

SDSs are another type of information system that help the operational manager to make structured decisions. For example, an inventory program might generate a list of auto parts to be reordered using a simple model. This list would serve as the basis of fresh orders initiated by the manager. Another SDS might help the user to determine a credit limit for new corporate customers by considering several factors, such as the customer's Dun and Bradstreet rating.

The analytic needs of middle-level managers making tactical, often ill-structured decisions are met by *decision support systems (DSSs). Executive information systems (EISs),* however, are designed to support the information requirements of top executives.

8.2 DECISION SUPPORT SYSTEMS AND _____ EXECUTIVE INFORMATION SYSTEMS _____

Decision support systems (DSS) and executive information systems (EIS) are two of the fastest-growing types of information systems. Many software packages with a wide range of capabilities are currently marketed as DSS or EIS, and they have made inroads into many industries as tools for supporting managerial decision making. Microcomputers have played a major role in the spread of both DSS and EIS by placing the computing resource within immediate reach of the manager and by providing improved user interfaces. It comes as no surprise then, that the majority of DSS and EIS products are either microcomputer-based or dual-platform (micro-mainframe) products.

Structured reporting systems (for example, the TPS) focus on *efficiency,* that is, transforming data into required information with the minimum use of computing resources. However, the emphasis for the DSS and EIS that support higher-level decision making is on *effectiveness,* or using information to produce improved decisions and thereby competitive advantage. This is evident as we examine the nature of such managerial decisions.

Managerial Decision Making

A major component of managerial responsibilities is decision making. Managers at all levels of the firm make numerous decisions during the allocation of resources in the production and marketing of their goods and services. The five decision stages are (1) information collection or intelligence, (2) design of alternatives, (3) choice of an alternative, (4) action taken, and (5) evaluation of the action taken.

Ill-Structured Decisions

In studying Figure 8.3, which illustrates the structuredness of decisions, two observations are relevant. The first is that structure is relative and not absolute. This means that the more resources available (for example, time, money, models, intellectual expertise) to support the decision, the more the decision may be further structured. Second, both highly structured and unstructured decisions do not require a great deal of decision support. Structured decisions can be automated through programming while highly unstructured decisions will benefit little from any formal analysis.

The boundary between structured and unstructured decisions is important in our discussion of DSS. This boundary is blurred, meaning that some organizational decisions possess both structured and unstructured features. For example, the firm's current position and available resources, dynamics of the environment, and possible outcomes may be known, but other facts may be less certain, such as the likelihood of outcomes, and such uncontrollables as competitor actions and consumer response. These types of decisions are referred to as semistructured or **ill-structured** decisions and are the focus of DSS.

A feature of ill-structured decisions is that they are rarely made in "one pass." Instead, they are complex, requiring reiteration, reanalysis, and (subjective) recalibration, a process that involves feedback and learning. Also, the decision maker often exhibits *satisficing* behavior, where optimal solutions are less important than "good enough" solutions.

Decision Support Systems (DSSs)

A DSS is a computerized model-based system that supports but does not replace ill-structured managerial decision making. Its model-based nature is in direct contrast to data-based reporting systems. A DSS allows the user to represent the environment, business phenomena, and decision dynamics within models and to test various assumptions with these models. The DSS may be rapidly recalibrated and run with different assumptions until the user is confident enough to make a decision based on DSS use.

The functions contained within a DSS permit flexibility and exploratory use by the decision maker.

- *Data collection and organization functions.* These acquire needed data for DSS models from internal and external sources. In particular, present-day DSS possess links to databases through staging software and LANs, enabling rapid creation of the DSS database.
- *"What-is?" or querying capabilities.* These obtain status information, either from the DSS or external databases
- *"What-if?" capabilities.* These allow the decision maker to test the effects of specific actions (through a model), to assess their likely consequences
- *Goal-seeking capabilities.* These suggest actions to be taken to achieve a goal specified by the decision maker
- *Presentation (for example, 2-D and 3-D graphs) and report generation capabilities.*

Table 8.1 highlights the fact that microcomputers are used in many contemporary DSS. With regard to software, 4GLs (discussed in Chapter 6) are preferred to 3GLs. Also, DSS developers are more likely to be managers or their specialist support staffs, with direct users being managers or their intermediaries.

Figure 8.5 illustrates the use of a marketing DSS by a product manager responding to reduced sales of the firm's major product. The manager's initial action was to collect data relating to the product's current marketing strategy and the competitors' products (for example, product features and price). Data on available marketing instruments such as advertising media costs and costs of new distribution channels were also collected. A marketing model was designed to test the effects of various marketing strategies, and then a strategy was chosen, which was implemented and evaluated to determine if its objectives, for example, improved market share, were met.

TABLE 8.1   Popular DSS products

Product Name	Interface Mode	Vendor	Mini/Mainframe Product Available
20/20	Command	Access Technology	—
Personal W	Menu	Comshare	System W
Expert Choice	Menu	Decision Support Software	—
IFPS Personal	Menu	Execucom Systems Corp	IFPS
Decision Aide II	Menu	Kepner Tregoe, Inc.	—
DSS Workbench	Menu	Lloyd Bush Software	—
MDS Outline	Menu	MDS Inc.	—
Smartforecast II	Menu	Smart Software, Inc.	—
EXEC**U**STAT	Menu	Exec**U**Stat, Inc.	—
EXPRESS/PC	Menu	Information Resources	EXPRESS
Focus/PC	Menu	Information Builders, Inc.	Focus
NOMAD 2	Menu	Must Software International	NOMAD 2
PARADOX	Query by example	Borland International	—
RAMIS/PC	Menu	On-Line	—
SAS/PC	Menu	SAS Institute, Inc.	SAS
SPSS/PC+	Menu	SPSS, Inc.	SPSS
Powerplay	Menu	Cognos, Inc.	—
Excel	Spreadsheet/menu	Microsoft, Inc.	—

Selecting DSS Development Tools

The traditional systems development cycle is unsuitable for developing DSS, due to the speed at which the DSS, particularly ad hoc DSS, are required to be operational. Traditional TPS development often takes between six and twelve months, with a backlog sometimes stretching back a year or more. If a DSS was developed in this way, the "window of opportunity" may be past, for example, a new product launch may have taken place.

3GLs are also not recommended for DSS development due to the length of time required for program design, coding, and testing and the difficulty of rapidly modifying written programs. Most DSS development takes place using 4GLs or specialized DSS-building tools, which enable DSS creation in a matter of days or weeks, instead of months or years.

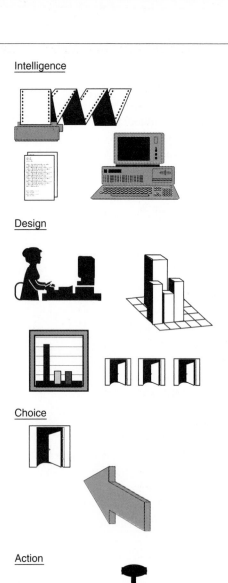

Intelligence

Data collection was performed from:
• Market surveys
• Trade publications
• Interviews with competitiors
• Competitors' filed financial records
• Internal sources

Design

A marketing DSS was created and calibrated with:
• Market $ shares of the products
• Unit sales
• Market segments
Market assumptions, scenarios, and actions were iteratively tested.

Choice

Based on DSS use, the following changes were proposed:
• Change advertising media.
• Increase advertising spending.
• Reduce price of the product

Action

The proposed recommendations were adopted and implemented.

Evaluation

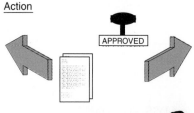

• Managerial satisfaction regarding DSS use was high.
• Increased product sales were noted after marketing actions were taken.

FIGURE 8.5   DSS product marketing example

Sprague and Carlson have proposed a taxonomy consisting of DSS tools, DSS shells, and specific DSS, to show how DSS are constructed (Figure 8.6). The top level represents *specific DSS* containing models (for example, market models) calibrated with relevant data (for example, product, competitor, and market data). They are built using *DSS generators*—software programs that are subdivided into two major types. The first comprises *general-purpose* DSS generators, such as Lotus 1-2-3, dBase (productivity packages), and application generators like TELON, FOCUS, and RAMIS II.*Special-purpose* DSS generators include IFPS, used to create financially oriented DSSs and SAS, commonly used to create statistically based DSSs. DSS tools are hardware and software components that may be used to develop DSS generators. An example is Visual C, used for rapid system development.

Table 8.1 is a list of popular DSS development generators. It lists the product's manufacturer and the mainframe version of the product, if one exists.

DSS are model-based systems and all DSS generators have modeling capabilities. Microsoft Excel, for example, uses a spreadsheet paradigm with a macro language. Other generators use high-level languages to create required models. Figure 8.7 illustrates the structure of a model-based DSS and highlights several important components. The first is the *user interface,* which allows the user access to DSS functionality. The *model base management system (MBMS)* manages the DSS models and enables them to be set up, calibrated, linked, and executed. The models used within DSSs fall under optimization, heuristic, or descriptive models. **Optimization models** provide an optimal solution (if one exists) and are available for many operations research problems (for example, transportation and facilities location). They have also appeared recently in spreadsheets such as Excel and Lotus 1-2-3 as "backsolving" capabilities. **Heuristic models** produce good but not necessarily optimal solutions and are used when it may be too expensive or time consuming to produce an optimal solution. **Descriptive models** include simulation models, which

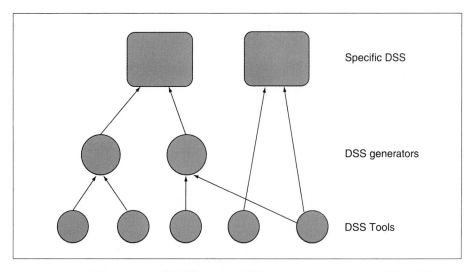

FIGURE 8.6   Hierarchy of DSS tools, DSS generators, and specific DSS

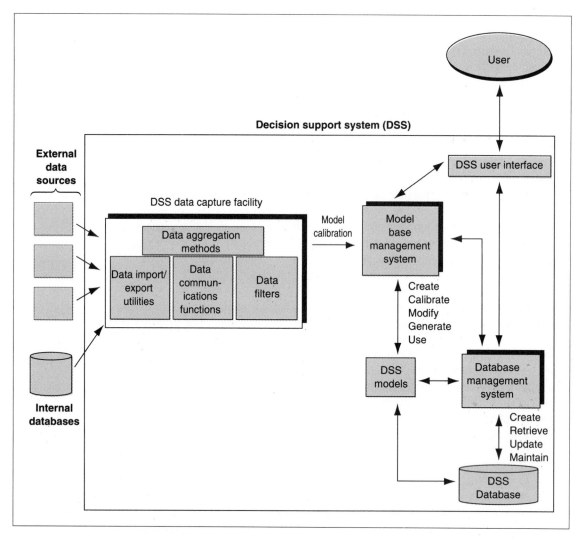

FIGURE 8.7   Structure of a DSS

attempt to describe a phenomenon as closely as possible to test the outcomes of various actions. This is also referred to as the "what-if?" modeling capability. The *DBMS* manages the DSS database, as described in Chapter 7, while a *staging mechanism* enables the collection and filtering of data from internal and external sources.

In selecting DSS-building tools or generators, the developer should note hardware and software constraints. In addition, either a normative or a descriptive approach may be taken to model selection, for example, using optimization models or simulation models (see Box 8.1). As usual, features will be selected to match desired DSS functionality and environmental factors.

BOX 8.1

Group Support Systems (GSS) involve the use of information technologies to support and improve typical meeting processes. These systems are designed to overcome the problems often found in conventional meetings, such as lack of a clear plan or structure for the meeting, dominance by strong personalities, pressures for conformity, lack of creativity, rushing to judgment, and other problems. Research to date seems to show that use of a GSS may result in more efficient meetings, the generation and consideration of more alternatives, improved structure in meetings, the ability to use more sophisticated decision making techniques, the involvement of more participants, and other benefits. A GSS can be useful for a wide variety of group-oriented business applications such as strategic planning, hiring decisions, corporate re-structuring, total quality management, focus groups, purchasing decisions, negotiations, and so on.

While we can conceive of meetings that differ in time and space (for example, where one or more members are in a remote location connected to the group through telecommunications links), so far most of the work in GSS has focused on same-time /same place situations. This is usually referred to as a ``decision room'' approach. With the rapid development of telecommunications and virtual reality technologies, future GSS R&D may focus more on meetings dispersed in time and space.

In a typical GSS decision room, several PCs are connected through a local area network (LAN) and placed on tables that face the front of the room, often in a U-shaped configuration. Normally, at least one PC is attached to a video projector or other device that can display a computer screen at the front of the room. Participants in a GSS meeting will sometimes be using their own PCs to type in ideas, comments, or ratings, and at other times they will be viewing and discussing displays shown at the front of the room.

MeetingWare for Windows (MW/W) is a GSS developed for the decision room ap-proach. MW/W includes a number of flexible tool modules that can be combined into a customized script, or agenda, for a specific meeting. In a general sense, it includes tools to support these generic meeting processes:

- Generating ideas (electronic brainstorming and commenting)
- Discussing, editing, and organizing ideas
- Sharing information (spreadsheets, databases, etc.)
- Evaluating ideas (voting, rating, selecting, etc.)

A common pattern would be to start by generating a list of ideas using electronic brain storming. For example, Figure 8.8 shows the display that would be projected on a screen at the front of the room after participants have started to enter ideas about how to improve parking on a university campus. Note that the anonymity of the author is protected.

Figure 8.9 shows a MW/W tool being used to help the group discuss and organize the ideas (this would be displayed on a large screen at the front of the room). The top of the screen presents the ideas from the brainstormed list one at a time, and they are then discussed, edited, and entered into a structured outline in the bottom window.

(continued)

BOX 8.1 *(continued)*

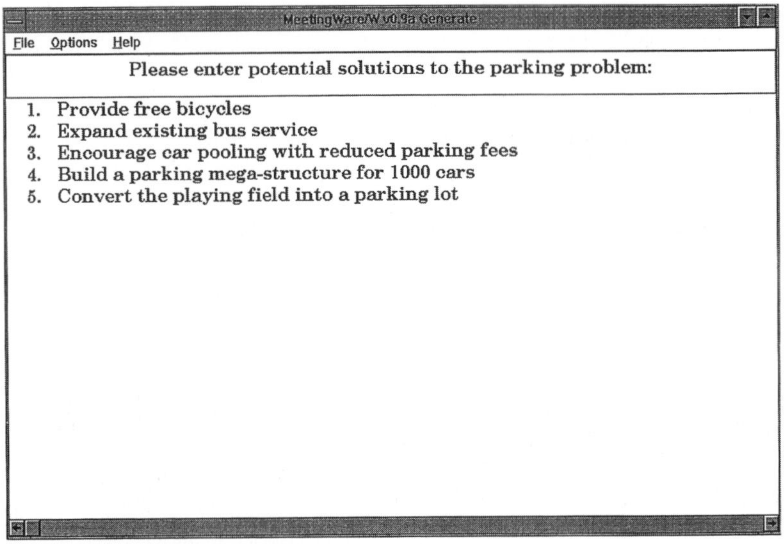

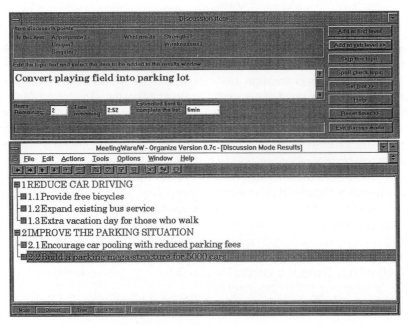

FIGURE 8.8   Parking problem screen

FIGURE 8.9   Convert playing field screen

BOX 8.1 *(continued)*

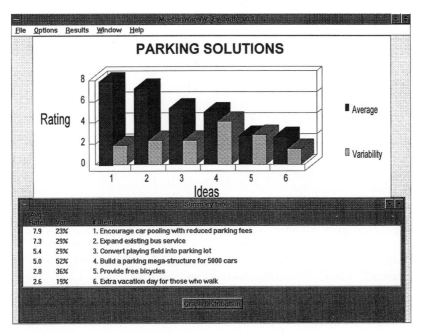

FIGURE 8.10   Parking solutions screen

Note the use of timers to help keep the group within schedule.

Figure 8.10 shows a summary table and graph that would be displayed at the front of the room after the group participants have each entered their ratings into their own PCs. The graph shows the average ratings for each item, as well as a measure of variability, or disagreement in the ratings. Notice that there is considerable disagreement about item #4. While the final results are public, individual ratings remain anonymous.

Over time, new GSS tools will be developed to support group work. Look for the integration of GSS products with other software for scheduling, communications, joint document development, and project management under the more general name of collaborative software or groupware.

Contributed by Dr. L. Floyd Lewis II of Western Washington University, Bellingham, WA.

Executive Information Systems (EISs)

The firm's top executives are the primary clientele of **executive information systems (EIS).** EIS are less flexible than DSS, but their strength is in presentation and reporting capabilities, to enhance the executive's understanding of historical and current performance and future trends in the firm, industry, country, and so on. These abilities support the managers in *tracking* and *controlling* the enterprise.

EIS have simple, mostly GUI-based user interfaces to encourage direct use by executives. They support executive decision making by providing data aggregation capabilities, but they also feature *drill-down* or disaggregation capabilities to view details behind subtotals and totals. For example, the executive might examine in more detail the sales data reported for a region to see if the cause of low sales is a few poorly performing stores or a slowdown in the whole region. *Exception reporting* is also featured in EISs, together with tracking of selected items.

The staging mechanism of the EIS enables information to be collected from both corporate and external databases. The major differences between EIS and MIS are the clientele (EIS are directed solely at top managers); user interfaces (which are simpler in EIS); and in features (for example, EIS' drill-down and disaggregation capabilities, which are absent in most MIS).

Examples of EIS are

- *Executive Edge:* from Execucom Systems Corp.
- *Commander:* from Comshare, Inc.
- *CEO:* from Data General Corp.

All three EIS products are mainframe-based products with a PC front-end, a typical EIS configuration. The mainframe performs the major data querying functions, while the PC handles the user interface requirements and some data filtering functions. Comshare's Commander edge user interface is shown in Figure 8.11.

Developing DSS and EIS

The traditional systems life cycle is unsuitable for DSS and EIS design as the formal justification usually required during the life cycle may be irrelevant. As an example, consider the portfolio manager using a DSS to support decisions on securities. The benefits of such a DSS are qualitative and indirect, resulting from improved decisions. While financial benefits will likely result from DSS use, they cannot be quantified with great precision. Thus, many DSS are justified by the expectation of their ultimate benefits and not by any rigorous cost-benefit analyses.

DSS may be either ad hoc or institutionalized. *Ad hoc DSS* support the single, often immediate (and urgent!) decision, such as deciding how best to resist or perform a hostile takeover. There is little continuing commitment, and the quality of the system is not an overriding objective. Likewise the user interface and documentation for this temporal system will not necessarily reflect a need for long-term use. Conversely, *institutionalized DSS* support recurrent decisions. For example, a product manager continually needs to take market actions concerning the firm's product(s). An institutionalized marketing DSS in this case would require commitment in the form of resources for the long term. Other requirements are high-quality user interfaces, documentation, and system integrity.

The DSS development cycle includes the stages listed below.

1. *Entry and problem definition.* The decisions, decision makers, and decision context are identified and described.
2. *Decision analysis and predesign.* Key decisions are analyzed for structuredness, managerial level, inputs and outputs, and other characteristics.

3. *Design of the DSS model base, database, and user interface.* These three DSS components are specified, creating a blueprint for the DSS. The DSS is then created, using either DSS tools or generators.

4. *Experimentation and initial use.* The DSS is iteratively used and refined until it satisfies its acceptance criteria.

These four stages characterize the ad hoc DSS's life cycle and are performed iteratively until the decision is made and the DSS discarded. For institutionalized DSS, however, two further stages are

5. *Training and implementation.* Users are trained to use and maintain the DSS. Facilities are also prepared, and the DSS is installed.

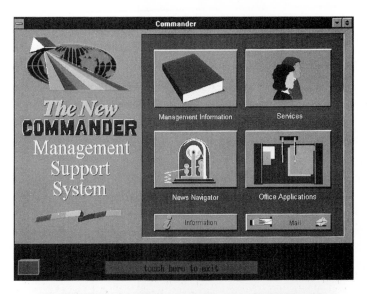

FIGURE 8.11   Opening screens for Comshare's Commander   *(continued)*

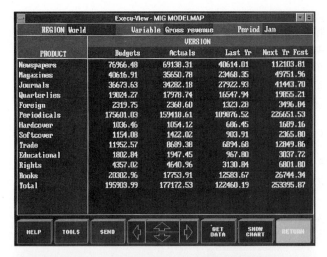

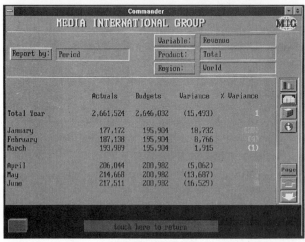

FIGURE 8.11 *(continued)* Two report screens generated by Commander

(continued)

6. *Maintenance and evolution.* After implementation, errors in the DSS are fixed and it is continually refined to adapt to changing user needs.

EIS development will generally follow this pattern, but it will benefit more from high-level, powerful development tools to create the easy-to-use interfaces and sophisticated querying capabilities.

8.3 ARTIFICIAL INTELLIGENCE SOFTWARE FOR MICROCOMPUTERS

For many years, scientists pursued the goal of replicating or mimicking human intelligence using computer hardware and software in a broad area of research known

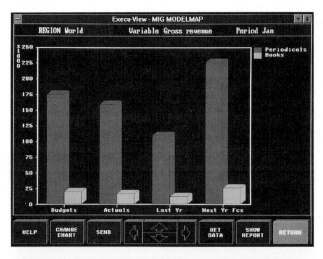

FIGURE 8.11 *(continued)*   Graphing *(top)* and querying functions
(bottom) of Commander

as **artificial intelligence**(AI). AI's major emphasis is to reproduce the functionality of
the human decision maker through software, but not necessarily by modeling the actual
structure of the human mind. Once esoteric subjects, AI and AI-based applications have
now become commonplace in many different locations.

AI is important to the manager because of the many tasks performed in business
settings that require expert skills. The costs of this intellectual expertise have in many
cases remained the same or even increased over time, in comparison to those of other
resources such as machinery and computers. The technology provided by AI enables the
support and/or replacement of these human decision makers with computer-based
systems.

The market for AI-based applications exceeded $600 million in 1992. Organizations
adopted them in a broad spectrum of tasks ranging from financial advising to robot
control in auto manufacturing. After many years of lofty claims regarding the potential

of AI, most commercial AI applications now appear in more modest bread-and-butter applications such as expert systems used in narrowly defined business and industrial applications.

AI-Based Applications

Seven major areas of AI are shown in Figure 8.12. They include machine vision; robotics; speech, handwriting, and natural language processing; game playing; and expert systems (ESs).

Machine vision applications use specialized hardware and software to capture images of different objects and correctly identify them. They attempt to mimic human vision in several steps.

1. First, the image is captured, using a video camera (or scanner, and so on).
2. An analog-to-digital converter converts the analog picture into a bitmap.
3. The AI program then identifies objects in the photograph using templates and specialized methods for distinguishing edges, foregrounds, and other features.

Machine vision is used for industrial quality control and in providing guidance for machine movement.

Robotics is also used in industrial contexts. Robots are programmable machine devices that perform physical tasks that can be performed by human workers. They are used in factories owned by Honda, GM, and other manufacturing firms. The Apple Powerbook line of notebook computers is also assembled by robots in an automated factory.

The fictional T2 robot in the movie *The Terminator* is a futuristic type of robot called a *cybernetic organism* or *Cyborg*—part-human, part-robot. *Androids,* lifelike robots (such as the T1000 in the same movie) are also popular subjects in science fiction and futuristic movies.

Today, robots are found in service environments like hospitals and offices. For example, Robby, Transition Research Corporation's *Helpmate* robot, is used in Abington Memorial Hospital in Pennsylvania to deliver patient meals to different areas of the hospital (see Figure 8.13). Using a stored map of the whole hospital, Robby avoids obstacles, gets on and off elevators, and politely asks people to step out of its way. The advantages of robots are increased productivity and reliability,

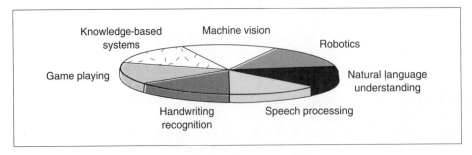

FIGURE 8.12   The different areas of artificial intelligence

lower cost than human workers, and use in hazardous tasks such as bomb disposal.

Speech processing was discussed in Chapter 4 and it covers both *speech recognition and speech synthesis.* The former captures the spoken word using a microphone and analog-to-digital conversion, similar to machine vision systems. The sounds are then matched against a template of stored words. Speech synthesis is the reverse process, with the computer generating spoken words and sentences for the human user. Common applications are computer-aided training, multimedia presentations, voice input to different programs, and voice mail.

Natural language understanding, discussed in Chapter 4, has proven to be one of the most difficult areas in applied AI. Problems of semantics, ambiguity, metaphors, and dialects give this area its complexity. One popular application is the use of near-natural language for interrogating databases, as provided by packages such as INTELLECT.

Finally, *game playing, theorem proving,* and *general-problem-solving* programs have proven to be mainly of academic interest so far, with the exception of the commercial KBS-based games like Chess and Go.

Expert Systems

Expert systems (ESs) are the AI area with the most applications, and thousands of expert systems are used in all types of organizations. An ES is a computer program that provides advice comparable to that of a human expert. ESs have been developed and used for applications as diverse as equipment configuration and troubleshooting, loan management, tax planning, medical diagnosis, and factory design.

An ES interacts with a human user by asking the user questions. By combining user responses and stored knowledge, it produces recommendations in a given area. Its

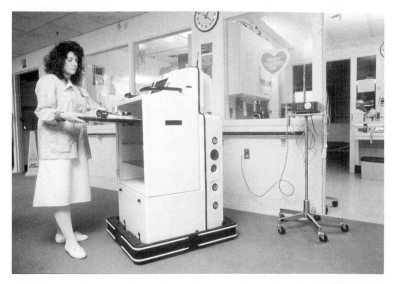

FIGURE 8.13   "Robbie"—TRC's Helpmate robot at work delivering meals

knowledge domain is typically narrow (for example, configuring a single brand of computers), with poor or meaningless results produced if the user decides to seek advice on another domain (for example, on tax planning, in the previous ES). The structure of an ES is shown in Figure 8.14. A *user interface* and *explanation facility* are used to capture user inputs and present the ES's recommendations and the reasons for those recommendations. An *inference engine* enables the ES to "reason with" or manipulate stored knowledge in the *knowledge base* and user-entered knowledge, to produce new facts, diagnoses, and recommendations.

Expert systems use symbolic representations—that is, symbols with intrinsic meaning to encode knowledge captured from domain experts. Often, this knowledge is captured in the form of facts and rules. For example, a credit manager might employ the following rule for approving a consumer loan.

IF Credit_Rating is Good

AND Loan_Request > 0.3 * Yearly_Net_Pay

AND Revised_Amt is accepted

THEN Decision is Approve_Loan

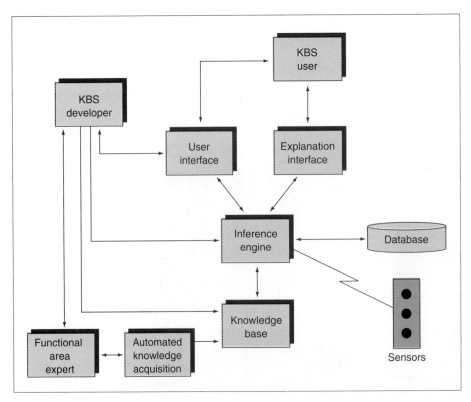

FIGURE 8.14   Structure of a knowledge-based system

This rule states that loan applicants with a good credit rating who place a loan request that is more than 30% of their yearly net pay but accept a smaller revised loan amount are approved for loans. This type of ES is called a rule-based system. It uses tens, hundreds, or even thousands of rules like the one above to make decisions. The ES operates by successively asking the user for responses to the premises of the rule (for example, "What are the applicant's current liabilities?"). User responses determine which rules succeed or fail and the system's recommendations. See Figure 8.15 for sample ES dialogue using 1st Class.

ESs can handle uncertainty (for example, "I'm 50 percent certain . . . ") and incomplete knowledge (for example, "I don't know") in much the same way as a human expert can and still provide diagnoses nonetheless. Their advantages include the permanence of their knowledge, as opposed to temporal human expertise. They are also consistent, are cheaper than human experts, can be widely disseminated, and may combine the knowledge of multiple human experts.

Table 8.2 provides a list of commercial expert systems used in a variety of areas and firms. They range from *XCON,* used for configuring minicomputers in Digital Equipment Corporation, to *ExperTax,* used to provide tax advice.

How are ESs developed? The two major approaches to ES development are using ES *languages* or *shells.* The former are specialized languages, such as Prolog (PROgramming in LOGic), LISt Processing language (LISP), and SMALLTALK, an object-oriented language (see Chapter 6). However, ES shells are powerful enough to satisfy most needs and are easy to use. They have a built-in user interface, knowledge base, and inference engine. This leaves only the task of entering knowledge (in the form of facts and rules, say) to the ES developer. This relieves the developer of the arduous task of hand-coding these KBS components, which are needed only for very specialized problems.

Examples of ES shells include programs like Paperback Software's *VP-Expert,* AI Corp.'s *1st Class,* and Exsys Inc.'s *EXSYS,* among many others. They allow the creation of ES with several hundred rules and make it easier to develop ES.

ESs have moved from research into commercial practice and are now embedded in many traditional programs, such as tax preparation packages and spreadsheets. If a knowledge domain is narrow, possesses clearly identifiable expertise that is scarce and/or costly, and involves an important, fairly structured decision, then an ES may be used as a decision-support or replacement tool, or even as a training tool for new personnel.

Artificial Neural Networks

Artificial neural networks (ANNs) are computer models predicated upon the physical characteristics of the human brain. They are used in such AI applications as handwriting, image, and speech recognition, and as expert systems. ANNs possess large numbers of interconnected cells, analogous to human neurons, which collect and propagate signals through the human sensory system, as shown in Figure 8.16. **Input cells** enable the input of the object's characteristics to the ANN. Intermediate cells, or "hidden units," receive inputs from preceding cells and pass on outputs to subsequent cell layers. Finally, **output cells** present the results or outputs of the network as a whole.

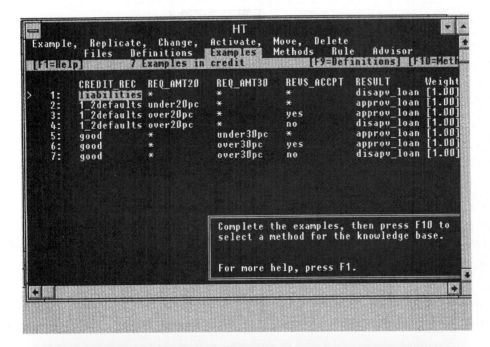

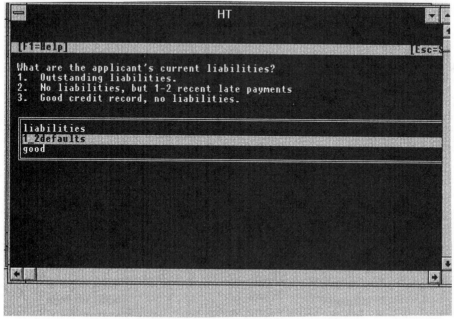

FIGURE 8.15   The 1st Class ES: A loan approval rule base (*top*) and dialogue (*bottom*).   (*continued*)

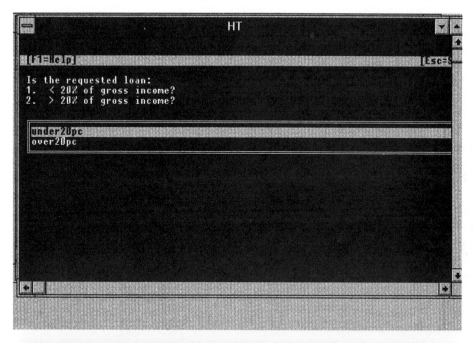

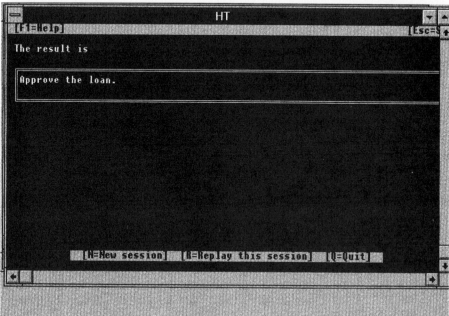

FIGURE 8.15 *(continued)*   The 1st Class ES: Continued ES/user dialogue
                            (top) and loan decision *(bottom)*

TABLE 8.2 An illustrative list of expert systems

Expert System	Description
ExMarine	Used for insurance underwriting at Coopers and Lybrand. Developed using the Goldworks KBS development shell, ExMarine suggests premiums for insurance applicants, using stored knowledge of insurance policies and entered applicant knowledge. ExMarine is a frame-based system and represents an operational use of KBSs.
CATS-1	Another operational KBS, used to diagnose and recommend solutions to problems in diesel-electric locomotives. Developed using the Forth language by GE, CATS-1 is a rule-based system, deployed in railroad minor repair shops repairing locomotives made by General Electric.
XCON	XCON is a well-known KBS developed and used by Digital Equipment Corporation for equipment configuration. It uses acquired knowledge of computer components, their interactions, and user-entered requirements in the form of expert heuristics, to configure DEC minicomputers for their customers.
CALLISTO	This is rule-based KBS used for project management, also used at Digital Equipment Corporation. It incorporates project managers' heuristics and knowledge of PERT/CPM techniques. It models the interactions between tasks, resources, and entities such as suppliers, to derive the consequences of changes within a project.
ISIS	A KBS developed at Carnegie-Mellon University for scheduling in large-scale job shops, ISIS possesses knowledge of the manufacturing environment (i.e., resources, activities, costs, and so on) and applies its encoded heuristics to develop schedules for manufacturing operations.
FMSCS	FMSCS uses production rules and incorporates the heuristics of an expert forecaster. It is used to select the best forecasting method in a specific context, from among time series, causal, and judgmental forecasting methods.
ExperTax	This KBS is located even higher in the hierarchy of management activity. It is a KBS designed to support corporate tax planning. Developed by Coopers and Lybrand, it is a frame-based system designed for use by accounting staff to analyze tax data and identify important issues for the tax planners.
FADES	FADES is used for facilities layout. It employs first-order predicate logic (via a Prolog interpreter) to represent knowledge of equipment, facilities, product characteristics, and algorithmic models. FADES selects the appropriate algorithmic facilities layout model in various contexts, using resident heuristics and supplied knowledge of the manufacturing setting.
Strategic Management of Technology	Developed by Arthur D. Little, Inc., this KBS is used at the level of strategic planning, to develop R&D investment plans for corporations.

When used as an ES, the ANN's outputs are the ES's recommendations, with different outputs selected for different user inputs.

Before an ANN can be used, it must be trained using many examples. In handwriting identification, for example, the features (or bitmaps) of all possible characters are entered into the system, together with the correct answer, that is the actual ASCII

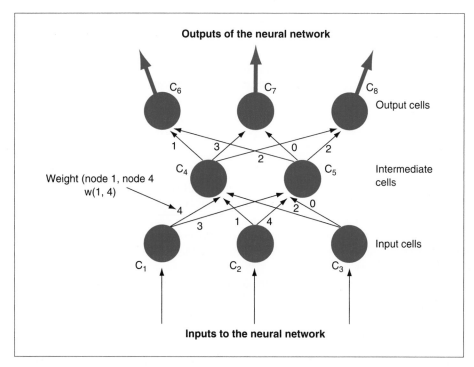

FIGURE 8.16   Structure of a neural network

characters. The network eventually learns to correctly approximate and identify the features of handwritten characters using a set of weights attached to cell interconnections. Further characters will then be correctly identified, as shown in Figure 8.16a, using the knowledge encoded in the weights.

8.4   MULTIMEDIA

Multimedia is an exciting new concept and set of technologies that are advancing in popularity and use on microcomputers. The term *multimedia* implies combining multiple media within the microcomputer for use in a variety of applications ranging from presentations to improved forms of computer-aided instruction. It offers new methods for information delivery, presentation methods, user interfaces, and reducing training costs.

What Is Multimedia?

To define what multimedia is, we must first understand what it is not. Multimedia is not a single technology or software application but instead a combination of hardware and software that incorporates multiple media within a single medium, the desktop computer. Computer/user interaction has traditionally used two media-text and graphics, with users creating text-based documents and spreadsheets, or graphs and drawings, using various software. Multimedia has integrated these two media with *video, animation,* and *sound.* For example, presentations can incorporate simple transition effects (for example, fades, wipes, and dissolves) between slides and more sophisticated animation sequences, and even sound. Also, many multimedia tutorials now include both sound effects and animation sequences to demonstrate various concepts and enliven training.

Hardware and Software Requirements for Multimedia

A multimedia system includes a microcomputer, special peripherals, and software, as shown in Figure 8.17. The multimedia PC (MPC) specification was created by the *Multimedia PC Marketing Council (MMC),* founded by Microsoft and other vendors of multimedia products. It comprises the necessary hardware and software components to run multimedia. Historically, multimedia was mostly performed on Macintosh and Amiga platforms, but the largest market segment is now IBM-compatibles.

Standard microcomputers cannot run multimedia applications without special peripherals. Some preconfigured microcomputers are sold as "multimedia machines," but standard PCs may also be upgraded by the user. Two essential upgrades to the basic microcomputer are

- **CD-ROM** *drive* (or **laser disk player**) with a supporting controller card, for displaying animated sequences. CD-ROMs, however, have a slower data transfer rate than laser and hard disks, limiting animation speed and sophistication.

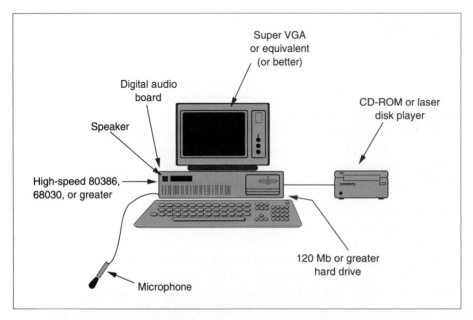

FIGURE 8.17   Hardware requirements for a multimedia system

- *Digital audio board* (8-bit or 16-bit), with stereo input and output, plus a microphone and/or speakers. This captures sounds digitally and replays them to the user. Sound boards "sample" sound at different frequencies (typically 22 Mhz and 44.1 Mhz), with higher frequencies requiring more data storage but providing better quality.

The underlying microcomputer must also be powerful enough to run the high-resolution video, animation sequences, and audio that are part of multimedia applications. For IBM-compatibles, the 80386DX running at 33 Mhz with SVGA is minimal (see Figure 8.18). Storing audio and bitmapped video requires a large capacity hard disk drive, 170 Mb and upward, although more powerful systems are preferable. To convey an idea of multimedia storage requirements, a single 8-bit color video screen requires 468 K of storage. Smooth animation requires 30 frames or screens per second, implying 14 Mb for a second's worth of animation or about 1.4 Mb, when compressed at a 10:1 ratio. Ten seconds would require 140 Mb uncompressed or 14 Mb compressed. If sound is included, these storage requirements would be higher still (up to 20 K per second of audio).

Software requirements for multimedia differ for creators and users. For each, an OS with multimedia hooks is desirable. System 7 for the Macintosh, for example, has audio capabilities; while Microsoft's Windows 3.1 contains extensions that allow Windows-based multimedia programs to communicate with peripherals. In addition, peripherals (for example, CD-ROM, laser disk, and even videotape players) are sold with software drivers that interface between the devices and the OS. See Figure 8.18 for a multimedia presentation.

Applications and Opportunities for Multimedia

In office buildings and supermarkets in Atlanta, automated kiosks offer customers a new and innovative way to get their photographs developed. Developed around IBM PS/2s and touch screens, these interactive kiosks allow customers to enter identification data, photographs to be developed, and payment by cash, check, or credit card to the kiosk through a machine-guided dialogue with a "video photo counselor" named Debbie. Film is periodically picked up by the photographic firm, developed, and returned to the kiosk, where, on a subsequent visit, the customer retrieves the developed film.

For managers considering the implications of multimedia and its potential impact, one feature stands out: the considerable cost of multimedia hardware and software. Making an existing microcomputer *multimedia-capable* can easily double its original cost. A minimal CD-ROM-audio card combination costs between $600 and $1,500, including software. Using a laser disk could easily add another $1,500 to the total. The costs of a new operating system software (for example, Windows) are additional if required, as are costs of upgrading the hardware and the multimedia software. As an example, each kiosk in the preceding case costs over $12,000.

Greater costs are incurred if an authoring capability is required to enable use of the multimedia PC to create multimedia software in-house. The cost of authoring software can easily reach $5,000 for the more sophisticated programs. Low-end authoring software includes packages like Claris's *HyperCard* (Macintosh) and Asymetrix's *Multimedia Make Your Point* (IBM) are sub-$100 packages that enable the

FIGURE 8.18 Macintosh (*top*) and PC (*bottom*) multimedia
systems   (*continued*)

FIGURE 8.18 *(continued)*   Multimedia presentation created using video
inputs

quick production of multimedia presentations. At the high end, Aimtech's *Iconauthor*
(IBM) and Authorware Professional's *Authorware* (Macintosh) cost $5,000 and $8,000
respectively. (Figure 8.19 shows some multimedia software.)

The cost of developing multimedia applications can also be considerable, depending
on the sophistication. For interactive instructional packages, many of which have
powerful scripting tools and icon and image libraries, this cost may easily exceed
$100,000. The in-house developer requires design experience to produce high-quality
multimedia programs.

The five major application areas for multimedia are:

1. *Interactive videodisk instruction (IVI).* Using multimedia for instruction involves
   the creation of training sequences on CD-ROM or laser disk. The latter provides
   smoother animation with faster access and data transfer times. A study of IVI in the
   U.S. Army reports significant reductions in training times and costs using IVI (up to
   30 percent less), with improved retention and self-paced learning as additional
   benefits.
2. *Presentations.* Multimedia can also improve the quality of presentations by
   incorporating sound, animation, and high-resolution graphics.
3. *Information kiosks.* The film-processing kiosks discussed earlier are examples of

FIGURE 8.19   A sampling of multimedia software products

automated multimedia presentations. Other examples are kiosks that allow customers to choose interior designs for houses by interactively selecting different designs and having them displayed by the multimedia system.

4. *New product announcements.* Organizations use multimedia tools to create new product announcements on disk and distribute them as a means of advertising. This is becoming popular with colleges and other service organizations.

5. *Entertainment.* Multimedia packages also enable the user to create entertainment materials. Programs such as Macromind's *Mediamaker* (Mac) can combine inputs from VCRs, video cameras, and graphics programs to produce "movies" on videotape. Even more sophisticated multimedia applications are used in the film industry, as seen in such films as *Terminator 2* and *Jurassic Park.*

Multimedia is clearly a technology of the present as well as the future and offers firms opportunities to reduce the costs of training while improving training effectiveness, create better presentations, provide new delivery methods for advertising, and support new entertainment approaches.

8.5   GROUPWARE/ELECTRONIC MAIL

Most decisions and major activities in any organization involve individuals working in teams or groups. For example, a manager preparing for a major product marketing drive collaborates closely with other marketing managers and with production and finance managers and salespeople. They communicate through formal and informal meetings, telephone conversations, memos, and formal documents such as market reviews and plans.

Much of the software and hardware we have discussed are oriented toward the single user. Even multiuser databases and operating systems are usually introduced to enable the processing of multiple users' tasks concurrently on a single machine. However, the product manager's decision problem requires more than just different individuals working in isolation on the same hardware or operating system. Group activities require communication between different managers to inform, instruct, jointly define objectives, define methods and criteria for solving problems, and select and refine solutions to problems. The various software that perform these functions are collectively called **groupware.**

One can define three basic ways in which people work in groups.

1. *Independently.* People work individually on subtasks that make up a whole, for example, salespeople may work relatively independently to fulfill their part of an overall sales goal.

2. *Interdependently.* Work is passed from one individual to another as part of a sequential work process. For example, a marketing plan might be sent to the finance manager for approval of requested expenditures.

3. *Interactively.* Several people engage in making decisions and/or working on the same activity (for example, document creation or decision modeling) at the same time.

These methods of group activities and interaction require more hardware and software support than is necessary for supporting single-user tasks.

Hardware and Software Requirements for Computer-Based Work Groups

The hardware that facilitates computer-based work groups includes user terminals and networking equipment, cabling, and network cards, for example. Networking equipment enables communication between different participants in the work or decision process and facilitates multiuser access to databases where group-related information is stored. Salespeople working independently require access to a centralized database of sales items. At the other end of the continuum, managers engaged in interactive DSS use or videoconferencing require sophisticated data communications equipment for data transmissions between the different participants and applications.

Software used for enabling computer-based work groups includes multiuser OSs and environments. These allow multiple tasks to run concurrently and enable data passing between applications, networking hardware and software, and groupware applications.

Groupware Applications

Many emerging groupware applications support the three work modes previously described. They include:

- *Electronic mail.* Otherwise known as E-mail, this software has been used for many years on mainframes. It enables users to compose and send text-based documents to other users or groups electronically. Once received in the user's electronic mailbox, messages may be viewed, printed, or forwarded to other users.
- *Voice mail.* More recent than E-mail, this involves digitizing voice messages, which may then be sent to other users. Voice mail can be used independently or as part of a multimedia document that includes text, voice, and/or animation.
- *Project scheduling.* This category of groupware is used to schedule projects with multiple participants. A central schedule is created from inputs (openings) supplied by the different participants and then disseminated electronically to the participants.
- *Meeting scheduling.* Related to project scheduling software, meeting scheduling or calendaring software prepares mutually convenient meeting schedules for multiple individuals. It uses the LAN to obtain availability information from involved individuals or computer-based files.
- *Teleconferencing/videoconferencing.* Teleconferencing uses data communications equipment to facilitate a group voice-only conference. Videoconferencing adds the extra element of video, enabling group members to view each other during the meeting.
- *Group decision support systems (GDSSs).* GDSSs have received much attention in recent years as specialized DSS software that enables a group of managers and/or staff specialists to communicate, create, and calibrate DSS models; test various scenarios and assumptions; and arrive at group decisions. In addition to microcomputer and networking hardware and software, special facilities (for example, special meeting rooms) are often required.

BOX 8.2

A GROUPWARE PROGRAM: LOTUS NOTES

Lotus Notes is a leader in the new and growing category of groupware. Developed by Lotus Development Corporation, it may be used on Intel-, Macintosh-, and UNIX-based microcomputers. Work groups using Lotus Notes use servers running OS/2, while clients can use Windows, OS/2, UNIX, and the Macintosh OS. It also operates over several NOSs, including Netware, LAN Manager, and Banyan Vines.

Lotus Notes features a free-form database in which text, sound, and graphics files can be stored. Overlayed on the database is a set of powerful groupware features. These include an E-mail facility that enables clients to communicate with one another. It includes standard mailing features such as reply, forward, use of mailing lists, and assigning priorities to messages. It also has a full-featured word processor on which messages and documents

which messages and documents can be composed. Such documents are not limited to text but may have sound or graphics objects embedded in them and transmitted with the document.

Lotus Notes supports translation into other E-mail software formats such as cc:Mail and VINES mail. Its capabilities may also be accessed from word processors and other programs. Furthermore, it supports group editing of documents and meeting scheduling. Price Waterhouse, a New York accounting firm, has up to 11,000 users of Notes world-wide. It is used for meeting scheduling as well as E-mail. Initially tested by a few users, it is now viewed as an indispensable tool by most of the 11,000 users for staying informed about the firm's activities and for planning and coordinating their work.

As a general category, groupware applications are rapidly growing. As companies attempt to make work groups more effective and efficient in the competitive 1990s, the importance of groupware for supporting the organization's activities will greatly increase in future years.

8.6   MICROCOMPUTER-BASED
OFFICE INFORMATION SYSTEMS

Discussing microcomputer hardware can create the misleading view that the workplace consists solely of microcomputers. However, they are used with **office information systems, (OISs),** technologies used in offices by secretaries, clerks, and other office workers to accomplish daily tasks. These include placing telephone calls, photocopying, and sending facsimiles. Many of the original office information technologies have already been incorporated within the microcomputer and related peripherals. For example, most workplace document preparation is now accomplished using word processors on microcomputers instead of the typewriter. The increasing functionality of the microcomputer will surely continue, especially with the advent of multimedia.

OIS Hardware

OISs are used alongside microcomputer technologies and include the following: (1) **photocopiers,** for producing multiple copies of documents of varying sizes and to a desired magnification. Microprocessors have made copiers smarter by encoding their functionality in silicon, enabling them to perform a wider range of copying tasks automatically, such as collating, stapling, and clearing jams. (2) **telephones,** which have also become smarter by using microprocessors to incorporate new features such as call waiting, digital signal transmission, conference calling, transfers, redialing, and connection with computers and private branch exchanges (see Chapters 9 and 10). (3) **facsimile machines,** which have supplanted telex machines for document transmission over telephone lines. They digitize and transmit documents over the phone lines much as a modem transmits data. The receiving fax then prints the transmitted message at its destination.

Integration with Microcomputer Systems

Software, copiers, telephones, and faxes are being incorporated into computer hardware and peripherals. Most microcomputers can be equipped with a *faxcard,* which fits into the microcomputer's expansion slot. Intel's *Satisfaxion* card, for example, provides both a modem and fax capability on the expansion card. It can display incoming fax messages on-screen and print them out on regular printers (for example, laser printers). Some laser printers also double as photocopiers, and document imaging systems will largely replace manual filing systems in the coming decade. Telephone-related capabilities are also featured in today's microcomputer through the use of modem cards, electronic and voice mail, and the use of computer-based private branch exchanges (PBXs) to route messages within the firm and to external destinations.

CHAPTER SUMMARY _____

Information is an organizational resource that is processed and disseminated in many forms by computer systems. One category of these systems is management information systems (MIS), which provide structured decision making and reporting capabilities to managers at operational, tactical, and strategic levels. They supply periodic or ad hoc reports, which may be either comprehensive, aggregated, or exception-based. In addition, they provide automatic decision-making capabilities for highly structured managerial decisions.

Decision support and executive information systems (DSS and EIS) differ from traditional MIS in their focus—namely, on the tactical and strategic decisions made by managers at higher levels in the organization. DSS are model-based systems that allow model building, linking, calibration, and execution to support ill-structured managerial decisions. Such decisions are characterized by risk, complexity, and the need for subjective judgments, reiteration, and reanalysis. Reporting, display, "what-if?", and goal-seeking capabilities are key functions supplied DSS-building tools. EIS are user-friendly tools that support users at the highest managerial level. They provide aggregation, summarization, and drill-down capabilities behind GUIs. Once solely mainframe based, many DSS and EIS are now common on the desktop.

Artificial intelligence (AI) has supplied a number of important advanced computer applications. The foremost of these are expert systems (ESs), programs that mimic the expert problem-solving skills of human expertise. Currently, ESs are used in areas as diverse as tax preparation, medical diagnosis, and equipment maintenance. Other AI applications include handwriting, speech recognition, and speech synthesis, which are already present in slate and desktop computers; and computer vision, robotics, and game playing.

An increasingly prominent part of the microcomputer revolution is multimedia, or the integration of text, graphics, video, animation, and audio on the desktop. Using authoring programs and appropriate hardware (for example, CD-ROMs, sound cards, and video players), multimedia applications may be created and used for training, presentations, and advertising.

Groupware comprises hardware and software elements that enable users to work together in computer-based work groups. Applications include E-mail, voice mail, meeting and project scheduling, tele- and videoconferencing, and group DSS. As organizational structures change in the 1990s and beyond, the need for and importance of these applications that create more effective work groups will grow.

Finally, office information systems coexist with microcomputers in the workplace to support the user's daily tasks. The major office automation technologies include photocopiers, facsimiles, and telephones. They are based increasingly on microprocessor technologies and may have all of their features integrated within the microcomputer in the near future, much in the same way as the typewriter and manual filing systems have.

REVIEW QUESTIONS

1. Describe the function of a firm's transaction processing system.
2. Is the warehouse manager making a decision regarding the use of new warehousing capacity engaged in operational, tactical, or strategic decision making?
3. Describe two types of internal and external information the above manager might require.
4. Define periodic, ad hoc, and exception reports.
5. Would you recommend the use of a DSS to support a bank's loan approval decision making for its individual customers? Why or why not?
6. Why are activities like formulating a marketing campaign nonprogrammable? What type of information system would you recommend for this activity?
7. Describe three important DSS capabilities and the model types that support each one.
8. Describe why an executive might want to utilize an EIS's drill-down feature.
9. What is an expert system (ES)? Describe a method used by ESs to represent knowledge.
10. What are the advantages ES shells have over ES languages in developing ESs?
11. What are the media incorporated on the desktop microcomputer by multimedia microcomputer systems?

12. Rate the suitability of a 286-based microcomputer for creating multimedia presentations and for running multimedia applications.
13. Describe three groupware applications. Describe how users performed these functions prior to using groupware.
14. What are office information systems (OISs)? Describe three OIS technologies.
15. How are OIS technologies currently being integrated in the microcomputer?

EXERCISES

1. Suppose a sales manager requires an information system to help track product sales, to ensure that sales targets for the different stores are being met. What type of information system is most suitable—MIS, DSS, or EIS? Is there a specific type of report that is suited to these requirements? What is it and what will it contain?
2. Following poor sales of supermarket-branded products, the sales manager in Question 1 seeks to make new product-pricing decisions. What type of information system is best—MIS, DSS, or EIS? What will the structure of the information system look like? Discuss how the new system will be used.
3. Are Lotus 1-2-3 and dBase examples of general-purpose or special-purpose DSS generators? How does each differ from the other category? Give two examples of the other category of generators. Which type of DSS generator would you use to support the analysis of sales data to determine important relationships between advertising outlets and specific market segments?
4. How would you define an expert? What are the dangers involved in incorporating the knowledge of multiple experts in an expert system? How can these be avoided or handled?
5. What demands does multimedia make on the microcomputer? How are these best handled?

SUGGESTED READINGS

Anthony, R. N. *Planning and Control Systems: A Framework for Analysis.* Cambridge, Mass.: Harvard University School of Business Administration, 1965.

Arinze, B., "Market Planning with Computer Models: A Case Study in the Software Industry", *Industrial Marketing Management, 19,* pp. 117–129, 1990.

Beer, J., and Freifel, K. "Multimedia Special Report: Super Tutorials." *PC World,* May 1991, pp. 192–194.

Donovan, J. J., and Madnick, S. E. "Institutional and Ad Hoc DSS and Their Effective Use." *Data Base,* Vol. 8, No. 3, Winter 1977, pp. 79–88.

Fox, J. "When Worlds Collide: Demystifying Multimedia." *PC Today,* June 1991, pp. 6–12.

Garnto, C., and Watson, H. J. "An Investigation of Database Requirements for Institutional and Ad-Hoc DSS." In R. H. Sprague, and H. J. Watson, (eds.), *Decision Support Systems: Putting Theory into Practice.* Englewood Cliffs, NJ: Prentice-Hall, 1986.

Ignizio, J. P. *Introduction to Expert Systems: The Development and Implementation of Expert Systems.* New York: McGraw-Hill, 1991.

Knight, K. K. "Connectionist Ideas and Algorithms." *Communications of the ACM,* Vol. 33, No. 11, 1990, pp. 59–74.

PC Week Special Report on Groupware. PC Week, October 26, 1992.

Sprague, R. H., and Carlson, E. D. *Building Effective Decision Support Systems.* Englewood
   Cliffs, NJ: Prentice-Hall, 1982.

Turban, E. *Decision Support and Expert Systems.* New York: Macmillan, 1990.

West, N. "Multimedia Design Tools." *MacWorld,* November 1991, pp. 194–201.

CHAPTER 9

INTRODUCTION TO LOCAL AREA NETWORKS

INTRODUCTION

Microcomputers were initially used by single users mostly in a stand-alone mode to process such applications as word processing, spreadsheet, and accounting programs. In the late 1980s, this was followed by the rapid growth of networks designed to interconnect these microcomputers. Such *local area networks (LANs)* were used to share programs, data, and hardware among several users. They also enabled designers of computer systems to spread processing loads among less expensive microprocessor-based systems. The media for creating LANs include the twisted-pair wires used in the public telephone system and the highly visible fiber-optic cable, among others. The communication control devices used to interface computers and communications media are also important in LAN development.

Several network topologies or architectures have been developed, and they use transmission methods called *protocols* to transmit data between nodes on a LAN. More than half of all microcomputers in corporate America are now networked, and this number is increasing. The number of LAN options and configurations is extensive, and an understanding of media, topology, device, user, and software characteristics is necessary for creating cost-effective, efficient, reliable networks. Here we examine the various pieces of the networking picture.

Learning Objectives

After reading this chapter, you will be able to:

- Identify the benefits of LAN implementation and use in a specified user environment
- Make informed selections of LAN media
- Select appropriate communication control devices for diverse LAN functions
- Describe the differences between the major LAN protocols and topologies
- Make the required decisions for setting up a functional LAN

CASE 9.1

USING A LAN FOR DISTRIBUTION MANAGEMENT AT MERRY-GO-ROUND ENTERPRISES INC.

Merry-Go-Round Enterprises, Inc. recently doubled its distribution capabilities to 830,000 square feet as part of a $25 million expansion. In planning for an increase in distribution, the $761 million company faced an "unbelievable tracking problem," as described by the IS project manager. The existing AS/400-based system was used to track the locations of different products. The fact that these problems did not materialize, the IS manager says, is due to the replacement of the AS/400 with an entirely new microcomputer-based LAN.

The new information system consists of four Ethernet LANs and one Token-Ring LAN, all of which are interconnected. The applications running on the LANs include programs for product location and process management. Others include programs supporting automatic routing and control of products, energy management, and advanced diagnostics. Workers also use hand-held radio terminals to read bar codes on every box, tote, and trolley at the distribution center. The terminals signal notification of job completion and conveyor belts automatically move products to the next destination.

Merry-Go-Round's LAN-based system now tracks 2 million articles of clothing stored in the distribution center and manages every distribution step, ranging from sorting to storing to shipping. Following the expansion and implementation of their LAN-based system, revenues at Merry-Go-Round have increased from $197 million to $230 over the most recent 3 quarters. Profits have also increased.

Adapted from J. McMullen, "No Longer Running in Circles," *Information Week*, November 23, 1992, pp. 40–44.

9.1   JUSTIFICATION FOR LOCAL AREA NETWORKS (LANs)

The 1960s and 1970s were characterized by mainframe and minicomputer use. In the 1980s, the stand-alone microcomputer received the most attention, quickly becoming the largest computing category in unit and dollar sales. In the 1990s, the **local area network (LAN),** composed of interconnected computers (primarily microcomputers), became the most important computing model for system development. The reason LANs became so important to the information systems infrastructure of so many firms lies in the limitations of dispersed, stand-alone microcomputers within the firm and the new opportunities presented for lower-cost distributed computing.

Isolated computing meant that communication between users was limited to hard copy or to the "sneakernet" method, whereby floppy disks would be manually transferred between machines. In addition, expensive devices such as plotters could not be shared by multiple users, nor could multiuser applications be used, as there were no communication links between users' machines. LANs provide a solution to these problems by supplying high-speed data communication links between users' micro-computers. With the spread of LANs, LAN implementation and management issues are currently in the forefront of IS strategies.

Definition of LANs

A LAN is a *privately owned* set of computers and communications control devices that are interconnected using high-speed data communication links. LANs reside in a restricted geographical area such as a building or set of buildings. Also, they do not use a common carrier's (for example, AT&T) transmission media for data transmission, in contrast to WANs. The two major features of LANs are *high-speed data transmission* and the *sharing of computing resources.* Other features include *access to external databases, groupware,* and use of less expensive hardware platforms for *distributed processing.*

High-Speed Data Transmission

The central feature of LANs is their ability to carry out high-speed data transmission between interconnected devices. Consider the hypothetical transfer of a 10 Mb file between two microcomputers. Prior to high-speed LANs, two ways to carry out this transfer were over the telephone lines using modems or physically carrying disks to the second minicomputer. Using a modem (a data communications device discussed in Section 9.4) operating at 4,800 bps (bits per second) and asynchronous transmission of 10 bits/character (see Section 9.3) the file transfer takes approximately

$$\frac{(10 * 1024 * 1024) \text{ bytes} * 10 \text{ bits per byte}}{4800 \text{ bps}} \text{ seconds} = 21,845 \text{ seconds}$$

or just over 6 hours! In contrast, LANs support data transfers ranging from 10 Mbps (megabits* per second) to 100 Mbps (million bits per second) and more. In the case of the 10 Mb file transfer, which is not an uncommon file size, data transfer time on a 16 Mbps LAN would be a more acceptable 3.93 seconds:

$$\frac{(10 * 1024 * 1024) \text{ bytes} * 6^{\dagger} \text{ bits per byte}}{(16 * 1000 * 1000) \text{ bps}} \text{ seconds} = 3.93 \text{ seconds}$$

Sharing the LAN with other user transmissions will also increase the 3.93-second transmission time.

Common data types transmitted between stations include documents, E-mail messages, and programs. Many new data types, such as bitmapped images, sound, and animation, are even more dependent than data files upon high-speed transmission capabilities. LANs provide the most practical means to effect these transfers.

---

* 1 megabit is equal to 1 million bits in the data communications context.

† LAN traffic takes the form of variable-length packets with leader and trailer information. With data compression, text data averages about 6 bits per character.

Sharing Hardware and Software Using LANs

In the early part of the microcomputer era, it was difficult to cost-justify the purchase of many peripherals. For example, laser printers or 40 Mb hard disks costing upward of $5,000 in the early 1980s were too expensive to consider for every worker in a department. Even if a laser printer was used by one user for only a small fraction of the day, it could be shared with other users only by exchanging positions at terminals. LANs enabled several users to share expensive devices such as hard disks, plotters, and laser printers efficiently. Users could send output to a printer or use a hard disk as though they were local devices, resulting in improved device utilization and cost savings (see Figure 9.1).

Today, the need to share expensive devices is just as important. Users frequently require access to data shared with other individuals. A LAN allows rapid access to these files without having to replicate them in different locations with the attendant risks and costs. *File servers* are powerful computers that store files that are accessible to all network users. The affordability of large-capacity storage devices has made them common LAN fixtures. Other servers allow collective use of I/O devices such as modems, communications control devices, and facsimile machines, resulting in savings similar to those provided by file servers.

The ability to share software is another major LAN feature. Placing a word-processing program such as WordPerfect on a file server allows it to be shared by network users, saving storage space on individual machines. It also allows for easier software updates at one central location and lower-cost site licenses, which are available for most major applications. A site license for, say, twenty WordPerfect users, could be dynamically enforced by the server, which would not permit more than twenty copies

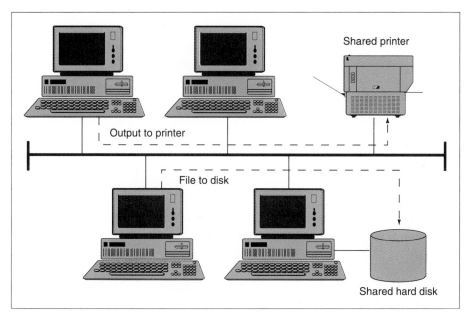

FIGURE 9.1   Sharing expensive devices using a LAN

of WordPerfect to be active at any one time. Usually, such site licenses cost less per machine than an equivalent number of individual licenses. Multiuser applications such as dBASE also benefit from LANs, which allow concurrent access to created databases.

Access to External Databases through LANs

The desire for corporate data stored on the firm's larger computers and external databases often cannot be satisfied solely by the file server. Much organizational computing requires data from other departments within the firm and from external organizations. For example, a small securities firm requires daily access to stock market data from the providers of such services. Using a modem, this data could be downloaded to microcomputers on the LAN. Other communication control devices, for example, gateways, facilitate data transfers to and from external computers and networks (see Figure 9.2).

Using appropriate communication control devices can provide a group of microcomputers with a common point of access to external databases. This enables information systems planners to distribute the cost of modems, gateways, and other devices among many network users. The result of this is improved cost-justification and simplified access to the network.

Working in Groups Using LANs

DBMSs are the key piece of software for creating multiuser databases, but LANs allow multiuser database access on the microcomputer platform. With *on-line transaction*

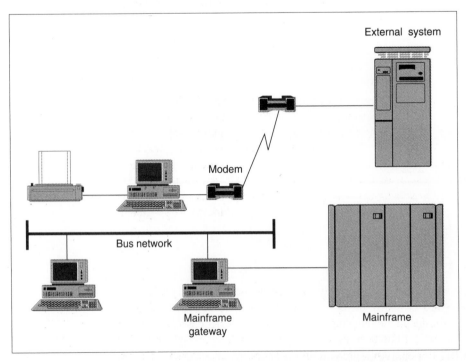

FIGURE 9.2   Use of modem and gateway to access external databases

processing (OLTP), multiple users need to access transaction files concurrently. LANs and network operating systems (NOSs) provide support for microcomputer-based OLTP. The high throughput of a LAN is more significant as transactions become more voluminous and use bit-encoded images and sounds, such as those in document imaging and multimedia applications.

Other applications used by computer-based work groups benefit from LANs, including group scheduling, project management, and DSS applications. As their use increases, so will the need for improved LAN throughput and reliability to support them.

Distributed Processing Using LANs

The early motivation for the development of LANs was to share hardware and software and to facilitate rapid file and document transfers. With newer microcomputers based on more powerful microprocessors (for example, the Pentium and the 68040) and workstations, the focus has turned to distributed processing using these machines. **Distributed processing** is the geographical dispersal of parts of the firm's computer system (hardware, software, and data), with interconnections accomplished through communications media. Figure 9.3 illustrates two distributed processing configurations. These are (1) distributed processors using a single database and (2) distributed processors with multiple databases. Strategies for distributed processing are further discussed in Chapter 10.

Chapter 1 discussed the greater cost effectiveness of microcomputers and work-stations in comparison with minicomputers and mainframes. Spreading processing and data storage over many smaller but corporately more powerful computers provides firms with the opportunity to significantly lower processing costs. *Client/server computing,* an important approach to distributed processing, is also discussed in Chapter 10.

9.2   MEDIA FOR NETWORKING _____

In configuring a LAN, it is necessary to select the **communications medium** over which data is transmitted. Several alternatives are available to the LAN planner. They vary in cost, capabilities, and ease of implementation and each supports various data transmission methods. They can be divided into two broad classes: *conducted media* and *broadcast media.* Conducted media are tangible, solid media. They are the most widely used and include twisted-pair, coaxial cable, and fiber-optic cable. Broadcast media on the other hand include infrared and radio transmission. Microwave is another broadcast medium used primarily for wide-area networks that interconnect locations in different cities, states, and countries.

Twisted-Pair Cable

The least expensive cable for a LAN is **twisted-pair cable,** that is, ordinary telephone copper wire. It comprises two thin strands of intertwined copper wire and is in large-scale production for the public telephone network. Twisted-pair costs between 5¢ and 25¢ per foot of cable and has been used for many years for voice-grade analog transmission, in public networks. Over these long distances, its data capacity reaches 14,400 bps in uncompressed form but exceeds 56 bps when compressed. These rates

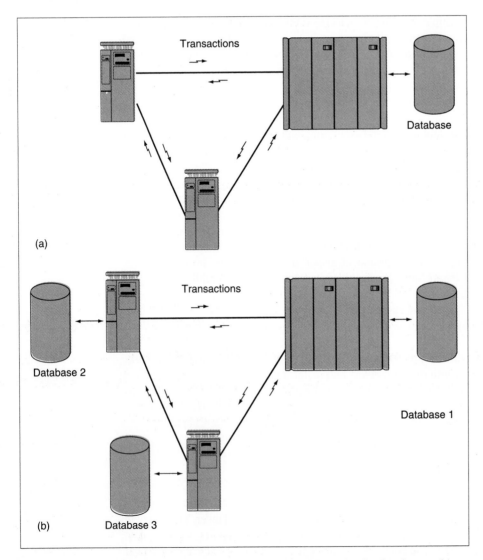

FIGURE 9.3 (a) Distributed processing system with a single database; (b) Distributed processing system with multiple fully or partially replicated databases.

are achieved using *modems* that transform digital computer signals into analog signals for transmission over telephone wires, and vice versa, at the message's destination.

A disadvantage of twisted-pair cable is its vulnerability to electrical interference, which may occur if electrical equipment is in close proximity to the cable or during electrical storms. In either form, signals transmitted along the cable can be corrupted. With voice (or analog) traffic, the effects are usually not noticeable and the caller's words remain identifiable. With data traffic, in the form of 0s and 1s, interference is much more destructive. Shielding the twisted-pair cable with a plastic coating is one method for reducing its vulnerability to interference. The two available alternatives are *unshielded twisted-pair (or UTP)* and *shielded twisted-pair (STP)*.

Another problem with twisted-pair cable is *attenuation,* or the weakening of the signal over long distances. Its use in networks is limited to several hundred feet, unless communication control devices called repeaters are used to strengthen and amplify the signal.

In LANs, transmission between interconnected devices occurs entirely in digital form. Twisted-pair is extremely popular for creating LANs, with transmission speeds now exceeding 100 Mbps. Also, most buildings contain networks of twisted-pair cable, preinstalled for telephones. In newer buildings, this built-in network may be used to carry voice and data traffic using *private branch exchanges or PBXs* (see Section 9.3). Twisted-pair is currently used for all major LAN architectures or topologies.

Coaxial Cable

Coaxial cable is a popular medium for LAN implementation. In its basic form, it comprises a central metal conductor surrounded successively by insulating material, a metal shielding, and a plastic outer covering (see Figure 9.4). The signal in the coaxial cable is carried by the central conductor. It is identical to the cable used in the home for cable television and it costs significantly more than twisted-pair, from 50¢ to several dollars per foot. Its theoretical data capacity is 400 Mbps, which is greater than that of twisted-pair.

Coaxial cable can be used over longer distances than twisted-pair with less attenuation. Being more resistant to electrical disruption of transmitted signals, it also features lower error rates. The two basic types of coaxial cable are *thick* and *thin* coaxial cable, the latter being also known as cheapernet (see Table 9.1). Thick coaxial cable can be used for longer distances (up to 500 meters) without the use of repeaters—devices that amplify and retransmit signals.

Fiber-Optic Cable

Fiber-optic cable is receiving the most attention in current network development due to its immense data transmission capabilities. Data is transmitted through a fiber-optic cable using light pulses, not electrically, as in twisted-pair and coaxial cable. It has a theoretical data transmission rate of over 2 Gbps, but one standard, *FDDI (fiber distributed data interface),* specifies a transmission rate of 100 Mbps over distances of up to 200 kilometers. Repeaters are not required for LANs based on fiber-optic cable. A fiber-optic cable consists of a thin strand of glass or plastic through which light pulses are transmitted. This strand is surrounded successively by opaque plastic **cladding,** to prevent light pulses from escaping, and by a second plastic covering (see Figure 9.5).

Fiber-optic cable is up to twenty times lighter than coaxial cable but is equally sturdy. Additionally, since it is composed of glass (or plastic), it does not corrode like copper-based twisted-pair and coaxial cable. Signals are transmitted in the form of light pulses, so they are not susceptible to the same electrical or magnetic interference as are other conducted media. Furthermore, fiber-optic cable offers more security since attempts to tap its signal are easily detected in the form of lost light, instead of just

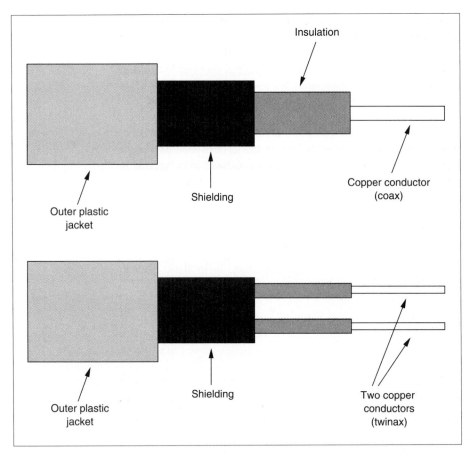

FIGURE 9.4   Coaxial cable and twinaxial cable

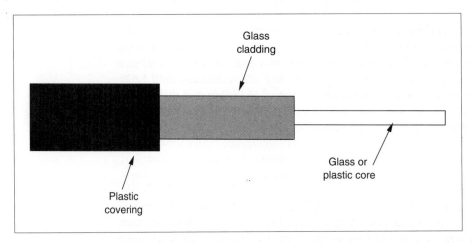

FIGURE 9.5   Fiber-optic cable

weakened signal strength. Its large capacity makes it the best choice for LAN "backbones," major highways for transmitted data.

Broadcast Media

Another category of media is broadcast media. **Broadcast media** are not tangible, but they enable data propagation through the air in the form of electromagnetically radiated waves. Examples of such generated waves are *X-rays* and *ultraviolet rays,* at the highest frequencies, and *AM radio waves* at lower frequencies. Several firms supply commercial networking hardware that transmit data using *infrared light.* The main advantage of LANs based on infrared transmission is that the installation costs associated with conducted media are greatly reduced.

Microwave and satellite transmission use very-high-frequency (VHF) radio waves to transmit data. *Microwave transmission* is land-based and capable of transmission speeds of over 45 Mbps. *Microwave Communications International (MCI)* is a U.S. telecommunications provider whose services are largely based on microwave transmission. *Satellite transmission* employs transmission devices called transponders on satellites that are in geosynchronous orbit (22,300 miles) around the earth. It allows data transfers between remote locations at speeds comparable to microwave (see Figure 9.6). Both radiated media are used mainly for interconnecting different LANs to create wide-area networks or WANs.

Media Characteristics

An important data transmission characteristic is the direction of the data flow on the medium, as governed by the communications devices. The three modes of data flow are simplex, half-duplex, and full-duplex data transmission. In *simplex transmission,* data flows in only one direction. Keyboards, most monitors, and some printers are examples of equipment that uses simplex data transmission. In *half-duplex transmission,* data may flow in both directions on the medium, but not simultaneously (for example, most CB radios). In comparison, *full-duplex transmission* involves simultaneous bidirectional data transfers. LANs use half- or full-duplex data transmission.

LAN media may also utilize broadband or baseband transmission. In *broadband transmission,* the medium's bandwidth is divided into several channels, each of which carries data (see Figure 9.7). Broadband is expensive to implement but provides high aggregate data-carrying capacity and is used mainly for LAN backbones. Most LANs use the less expensive *baseband transmission,* in which the medium uses only one channel. Data transfer is accomplished by voltage fluctuations, and high-speed data transfers are supported using baseband transmission.

9.3   LAN TYPES AND FEATURES _____

Investing in a LAN can be costly, requiring significant outlays for additional hardware and software. LAN decisions are also complex, with many alternative solutions often available. Even though the potential benefits are great, before developing a LAN it is necessary to consider whether it is really required. Alternatives to full-fledged LANs

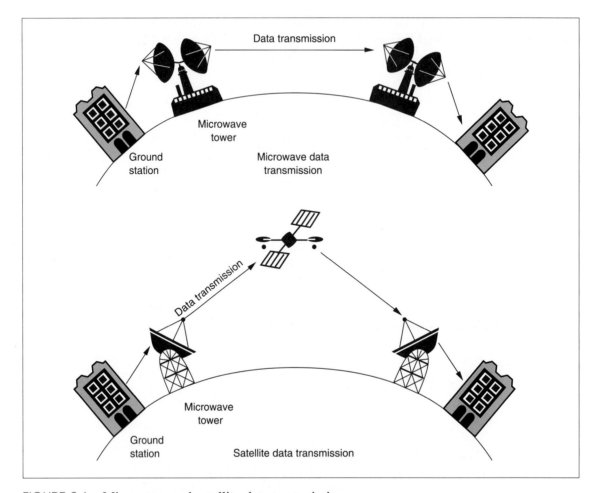

FIGURE 9.6   Microwave and satellite data transmission

exist, such as data switches, zero-slot LANs, and multiuser microcomputer systems. These are all less expensive options, but they provide fewer capabilities than LANs. Nevertheless, they have their place in situations where user requirements are not extensive.

Whether LANs or sub-LANs are selected, two major factors, LAN topologies and protocols, must be considered. *Topologies* are widely adopted physical layouts or architectures used to organize the hardware, that is, computers, communication control devices, and cabling. *Protocols* refer to the rules governing data transmission within these architectures.

Alternatives to LANs

In some situations where LANs are being discussed, what is really required is a device that permits device sharing (for example, printer sharing) or limited data transmission between user terminals. Several less costly alternatives to LANs provide these capabilities.

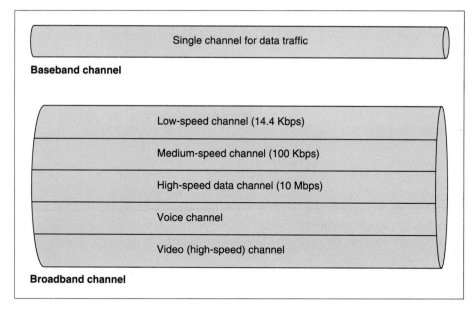

FIGURE 9.7   Baseband and broadband channels

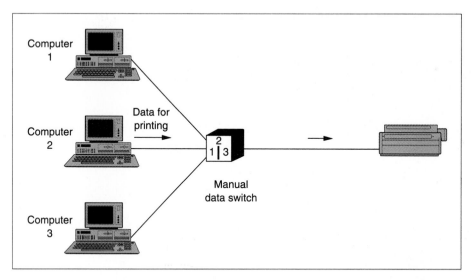

FIGURE 9.8   Use of a (manual) data switch for printer sharing

- **Data switches.** These allow users to manually or automatically establish connections between computing devices. As shown in Figure 9.8, one such switch permits several connections to be established between incoming devices (for example, microcomputers) and outgoing devices (for example, printers), but not simultaneously. Three users may share a single printer, by manually turning a switch that connects a user to the printer. Other data switches enable ad hoc circuits to be established between two computers as needed. The speed of data communication using a data switch is usually limited to the speed of the computers' serial or parallel ports (20 Kbps to above 100 Kbps).

More sophisticated data switches feature automatic *electronic switching* of circuits (without human intervention), *data buffering,* to allow data to be temporarily stored until the receiving device is available, and *data transmission* between microcomputers.

- ***Zero-slot LANs.*** These are limited forms of LANs that do not use a *network interface card* (or *NIC*) for connecting terminals. Instead, they involve running cables between microcomputers using their serial or parallel ports. Because no internal expansion slots are used, they are called *zero-slot Lans* (see Figure 9.9). These LANs enable automatic routing of data to the appropriate terminal or peripheral on the network under the control of a NOS. An example of a zero-slot LAN is *LocalTalk,* used by Apple Macintoshes, each of which comes equipped with a LocalTalk serial port that transmits data at 235 Kbps. Also, the networking software is contained in the Macintosh OS.

- ***Multiuser microcomputers.*** As we saw in Chapter 3, microcomputer capabilities have vastly increased over the past decade. Many high-end microcomputers now have the computing power to concurrently process applications for many users, who may be using either dumb terminals or microcomputers, similar to multiuser minicomputer and mainframe systems. Their key elements are a *host computer*

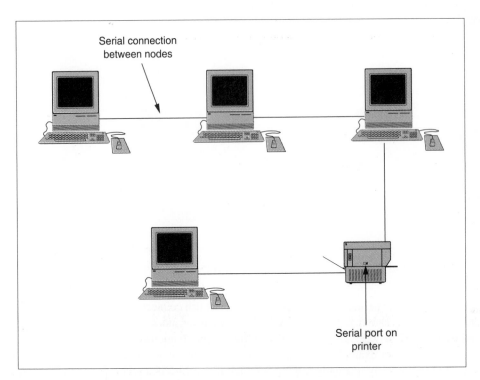

Serial connection between nodes

Serial port on printer

FIGURE 9.9   Zero slot LANs connected using a serial connection

and an appropriate *multiuser OS.* The host microcomputer requires a powerful processor, such as a fast 80386 or better, a 68040, or a RISC-based processor.

Common features include increased memory for the system's users, increased secondary storage capacity, and 32-bit data buses for handling the I/O traffic between the host and terminals. The **multiuser OS** assigns segments of processing timeslices to each terminal, manages the use of virtual memory, and handles contention for resources. Examples of such operating systems are *SCO Unix* and *VM 386,* for IBM-compatibles. See Figure 9.10.

Bus Networks—Ethernet

LANs based on the bus network were the earliest to be widely used. The predominant bus network is **ethernet,** initially developed by Robert Metcalf at Xerox Corporation in 1972. Ethernet's topology consists of a central "backbone" or highway to which all terminals and devices are attached (see Figure 9.11a). An extension to this basic topology comprises additional *spurs* (or branches) on the network, as shown in Figure 9.11b. Thick coaxial cable has historically been used as the backbone for the ethernet network, with thin coaxial cable used for the spurs. Currently, both shielded and unshielded twisted-pair may also be used to implement an ethernet LAN, as specified in the IEEE 802.3 standard.

The IEEE standards committee has defined standard media specifications for Ethernet (see Table 9.1). For example, the 10BaseT standard provides for 10 Mbps baseband (digital) data transmission using twisted-pair cable.

A major characteristic of a bus topology is the independent connection of devices to a common channel. If any device is disabled or not connected, the network remains

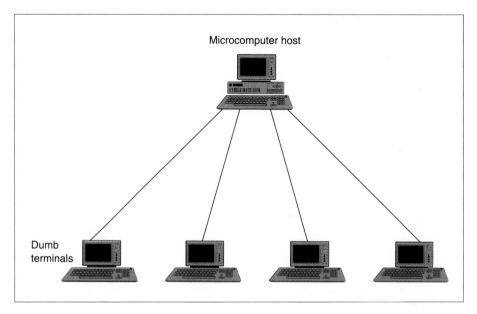

FIGURE 9.10 Multiuser microcomputer network

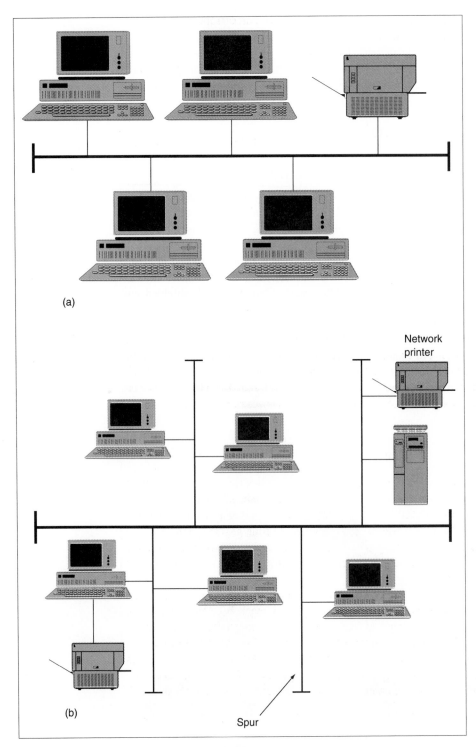

FIGURE 9.11 (a) Basic ethernet network; (b) ethernet backbone with spurs.

TABLE 9.1   IEEE 802.3 subcommittee standards for ethernet
LAN architectures

Standard	Medium*	Transmission	Speed	Segment Length
1Base5	thicknet coax	Baseband	1 Mbps	500 meters
10Base5	thicknet coax	Baseband	10 Mbps	500 meters
10Base2	thinnet coax	Baseband	10 Mbps	200 meters
10BaseT	twisted-pair	Baseband	10 Mbps	200 meters
10Broad36	thicknet coax	Broadband	10 Mbps	3,600 meters

*Both twisted-pair and fiber-optic cable are now viable substitutes for thicknet coax.

unaffected; the network is not disabled if a device is disabled. A bus network is a very effective means of interconnecting different types of devices, for example, printers and various microcomputers.

Data transmission on an ethernet LAN may reach a maximum of 10 Mbps and up to 1,024 stations may be interconnected. Setting up such LANs is also less expensive than token ring networks (see below), costing about $150 per NIC. The length of the network is limited by the cable type, at 500, 200, and 100 meters respectively for thick coaxial cable, thin coaxial cable, and twisted-pair. A new standard, **fast ethernet,** is now becoming available and features a transmission rate of 100 Mbps, representing a major upgrade for ethernet LANs.

Ring Networks—IBM's Token Ring

Ring networks are the second most popular LAN architecture. They have been popularized by IBM's implementation, the *IBM token ring network.* In ring networks, terminals are arranged in the shape of a ring, with each terminal attached to two others (Figure 9.12a), and data transmission proceeds around the ring, moving from sender to receiver. IBM's token ring network is actually a *star-wired ring,* in which one or more devices are attached to *multi–station access units* (or *MAUs*), which are in turn attached to the ring (see Figure 9.12b).

Fiber-optic cable and shielded and unshielded twisted-pair are used to create ring-based LANs. Data transmission on this topology may reach 16 Mbps, higher than ethernet's 10 Mbps. In a token ring LAN, up to 255 stations may be attached. If more are desired, multiple rings may be connected using a *bridge,* as discussed in the next section. Using fiber-optic cable, a ring can be extended to 4,000 meters, although rings using twisted-pair cabling without repeaters are limited to about 700 meters. Token ring LANs are more expensive than ethernet LANs to set up, costing up to $300 per NIC.

Star Networks

Another major LAN architecture is the **star-based LAN,** which organizes stations in a spoke layout around a central hub (see Figure 9.13). Data transfers between nodes must

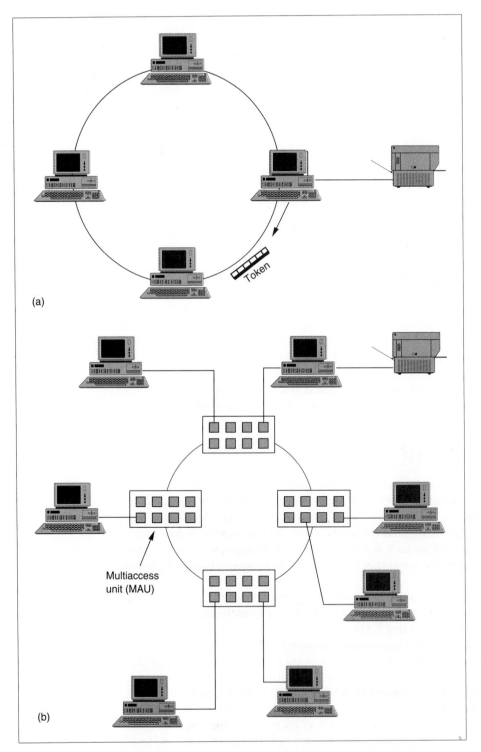

FIGURE 9.12 (a) Ring network; (b) token ring network with MAUs.

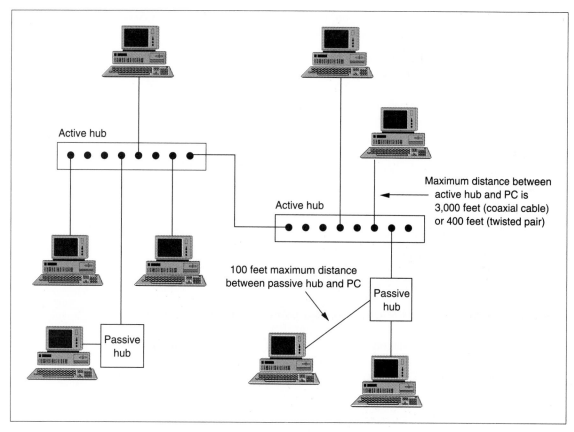

FIGURE 9.13 ARCnet configuration using active and passive hubs

therefore pass through the hub, which serves as a network traffic supervisor. The most widespread star-based LAN implementation is **ARCnet.** In this LAN, there are passive and active hubs: *Passive hubs* connect a cluster of four terminals (up to 400 feet away), while *active hubs* connect other hubs and terminals (up to 2,000 feet), and provide signal amplification. Terminals may be connected to both active and passive hubs, but passive hubs may not be connected to other passive hubs (see Figure 9.13).

The speed of data transfer on ARCnet LANs is 20 Mbps (previously 2.5 Mbps), and up to 255 users may be connected to the network. The media used on ARCnet LANs include UTP, STP, and fiber-optic cable.

LAN Protocols

The topologies above are an essential feature of LANs. Another equally important feature is the **LAN protocol,** a set of rules that govern how data is transmitted between LAN stations. An analogy to a protocol is the informal set of rules regulating the exchange of information in a classroom. First, the professor speaks, after which students raise their hands to ask questions or to respond to the lecture; they then speak in turn, when called upon by the professor. There are three major protocols used with LANs, each of which is generally associated with one topology.

- **Polling.** This protocol is used in multiuser systems, where each terminal is polled in turn, to see if it has any data to send. If it does, the data is transmitted to the server or hub and retransmitted to the receiving terminal. Each node is polled according to a scheduled interval determined by the host computer or network server.
- **Carrier sense multiple access/collision detection (CSMA/CD).** CSMA/CD is used in bus networks. First, a terminal monitors a line for data traffic to determine if data transmission is occurring. If not, it transmits data and listens to detect if a simultaneous transmission from another terminal has transpired. If this has happened, that is, a collision, the terminal waits a random amount of time to avoid another collision and then retransmits the data. Such networks may become saturated by the frequent transmission of large numbers of messages. It is also difficult to achieve successful transmission when the network is physically dispersed or supports a large number of users.
- **Token passing.** This protocol is used primarily in ring networks but is also possible with bus topologies. A *token* is a unique string of bits that moves from node to node around the LAN. A station cannot transmit a message without the token. When a station receives the token, it sends a message, receives an acknowledgment, and releases the token to the next station in line (Figure 9.12a). The use of token passing ensures equal access to all stations by not allowing any one user to dominate the network, because the token must pass through all other stations before any one station gets another opportunity to send data. Figure 9.14 shows the use of token passing on a bus network.

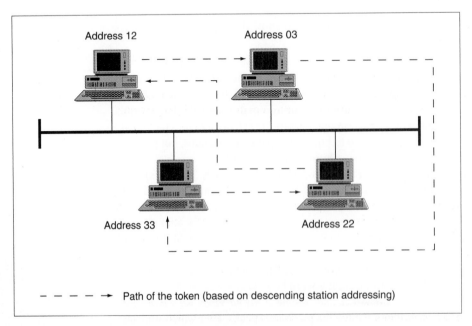

Address 12   Address 03

Address 33   Address 22

- - - - - → Path of the token (based on descending station addressing)

FIGURE 9.14   Token passing on a bus network

Two additional protocols, *asynchronous* and *synchronous* transmission, are not LAN protocols but are used in systems that frequently interact with LANs. **Asynchronous transmission (async)** involves the transmission of one character at a time along a transmission medium, usually from a dumb terminal to a host computer. A parity bit plus start and stop bits are added to the 7-bit ASCII character for a total of 10 bits. Transmission rates are usually low using async (about 9,600 bps). It supports low-speed devices, switched lines, irregular transmissions, and ASCII-based devices. In **synchronous transmission,** used mainly on WANs, data is sent in packets of many bytes in precisely timed (or synchronized) sequences. Its transmission rates (up to 56 Kbps) and error detection are superior. This form of data transmission is common between high-speed devices, mainframes, leased lines, fixed origins and destinations, and scheduled periodic transmissions. See Figure 9.15.

The Open Systems Interconnection (OSI) Model

LAN software and hardware encompass many techniques and architectures used for networking, which has introduced incompatibilities between LAN components provided by different suppliers. The International Standards Organization (ISO) has proposed the **open systems interconnection (OSI)** model in an effort to provide networking standards. The OSI model has seven layers (see Figure 9.16), with networking functions specified for each layer. This framework enables suppliers of networking hardware and software to develop compatible products based on the different OSI levels.

The data transmission methods and media we have discussed involve the three lowest OSI layers, the *physical, data link,* and *network* layers. They include physical and electrical transmission characteristics for the communications medium, error detection and correction of data signals, and the routing of messages between stations. The other levels (*transport* to *application*) feature application-related functions for checking transmitted data packets, establishing interapplication connections, encryption, data compression, and determining formats of application data.

Even though the motivation of the OSI model was to encourage standardization between different manufacturers' products, incompatibilities routinely exist, as support for different levels varies among products. Communication control devices (and software) enable applications, stations, and entire networks to communicate by performing the required transformation of different data formats.

9.4   Communication Control Devices

Terminals and transmission media are not the only hardware requirements for computer networks; **communication control devices** are also required. They transform data signals between diverse formats and increase the efficiency of data transmission within and between LANs.

Modems

Individuals travel to different cities for meetings, conferences, and expositions. They often take laptop or notebook computers to perform computer-related tasks, such as

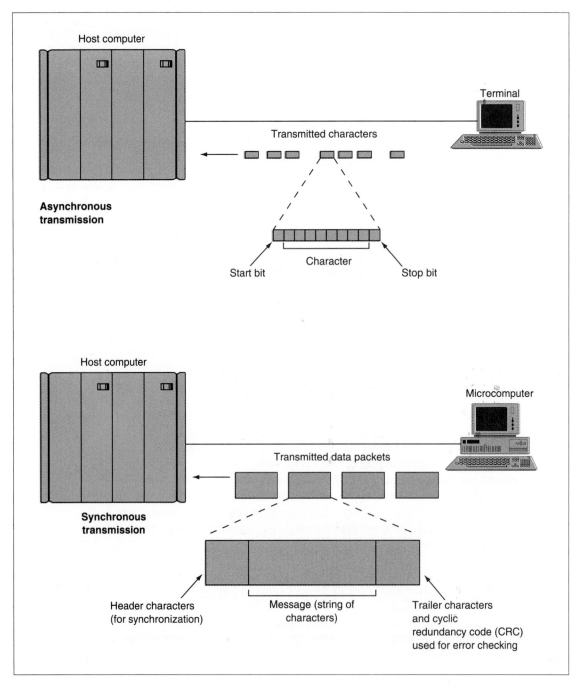

FIGURE 9.15   A comparison of asynchronous and synchronous transmission

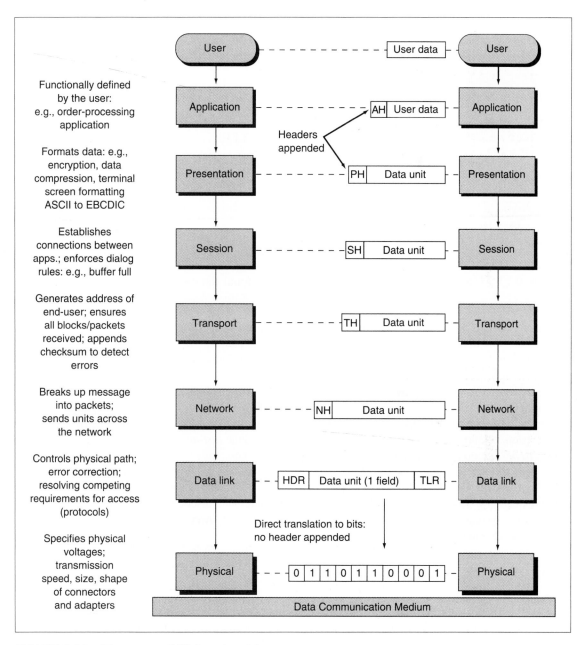

Functionally defined by the user: e.g., order-processing application

Formats data: e.g., encryption, data compression, terminal screen formatting ASCII to EBCDIC

Establishes connections between apps.; enforces dialog rules: e.g., buffer full

Generates address of end-user; ensures all blocks/packets received; appends checksum to detect errors

Breaks up message into packets; sends units across the network

Controls physical path; error correction; resolving competing requirements for access (protocols)

Specifies physical voltages; transmission speed, size, shape of connectors and adapters

FIGURE 9.16   The seven OSI functional layers

creating memos, letters, reports, spreadsheets, or transaction logs. Often they require data from corporate databases.

Modems (modulators-demodulators) are data communication devices used to establish communications links between remote computers, enabling the transmission of data between them over telephone lines. They transform a digital signal from a

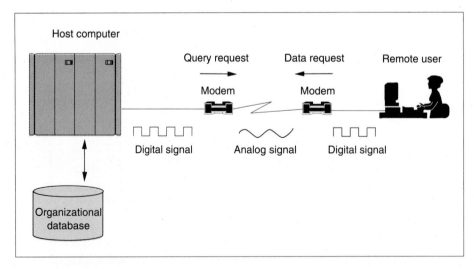

FIGURE 9.17   Use of a modem to access the organizational database

computer port into an analog signal (modulation) and transmit it over the telephone lines. Another modem on the receiving end demodulates the analog signal, returning it to digital form for the receiving terminal (Figure 9.17). Using a *dial-up facility* in this way, users may access their host computers from remote locations.

Modems range in price from $40 to over $400, depending on transmission speed and other functions. Common data transfer rates on modems are 4,800 bits per second (bps), 9,600 bps, 14,400 bps, and 19,200 bps, with higher rates usually achieved using data compression techniques (see Box 9.1). Common functions include *last-number redial, variable speed, auto-disconnect, speed-dialing,* and many others.

Modem software incorporates such error-checking methods as *cyclic redundancy checking (CRC)* to detect errors caused by line noise, spikes, and surges caused by a common carrier's (for example, AT&T) transmission equipment. Modems enable remote users to create ad hoc connections from far-flung locations at lower transmission rates than LAN rates.

Multiplexers and Concentrators

Modems are not integral parts of a LAN but enable its connectivity with remote computers. Two other devices that add similar functionality to a LAN are multiplexers and concentrators. In any networked computing environment, there is usually a mix of devices operating at various speeds. One possible arrangement for supporting many dumb terminals is to give each terminal its own direct point-to-point connection to the host computer, as shown in Figure 9.18a. A more efficient arrangement, however, is to use two multiplexers, as shown in Figure 9.18b. A **multiplexer** collects data transmissions from several low-speed devices and transmits them along a higher-speed line to a host computer (and vice versa) through another multiplexer. The multiplexer is a passive device without computing functions that simply

BOX 9.1

A PRIMER ON MODEM STANDARDS

LAN managers routinely provide access to computing resources to remote users, who may be employees either traveling or working from home. Access to servers and other hosts is supported by modems over the public telephone network. As with most hardware decisions, the available choices have mushroomed over the past few years. Few managers fully understand modem transmission standards, the role of data compression, and error checking protocols. The major standards, as defined by the Consultative Committee on International Telephony and Telegraphy (CCITT) are listed below.

V.17. This represents a facsimile transmission mode of 14.4 Kbps and is incorporated in newer modems. It is also known as Group 1 and is preferable to V.29 (see below).

V.29. These modems transmit data at 9.6 Kbps in full-duplex mode (4-wire) or simplex mode (2-wire). It is also used by Group 3 facsimile machines.

V.32. These are 2-wire, full-duplex modems which transmit data at 9.6 Kbps, but their speed can be doubled or quadrupled up to 38.4 Kbps using V.42bis data compression (see below).

V.32bis. These are 2-wire, full-duplex modems which transmit data at 14.4 Kbps and their speed can also be quadrupled up to 57.6 Kbps using V.42bis data compression.

V.32terbo. This is a proprietary 2-wire, full-duplex standard for modems transmitting data at 19.2 Kbps. It may be quadrupled to 76.8 Kbps using V.42bis. It is seen as a stopgap between V32bis and V.fast.

V.fast. This represents an emerging standard used by new 2- and 4-wire, full-duplex modems to transmit data at 28.8 Kbps. V42bis data compression is used to attain 115.2 Kbps transmission speed.

MNP 2–4 and V.42. These are standards for error control over synchronous and asynchronous links.

MNP 5. This is a data compression protocol that compresses data by a factor of 2:1 on modems.

V.42bis. This data compression protocol compresses data by a factor of up to 4:1, but in practice, rarely approaches the theoretical fourfold maximum.

Older V.32 modems costing $100–$200 have now been superseded by V.32bis modems costing only about $20–$100 more, with newer V.32terbo and V.fast modems (costing $300–$700) used at the high end. Most modems also support facsimile transmissions.

The top theoretical modem transmission rate is 115.2 Kbps, in modems that combine V.fast and V.42bis. Finally, modem purchasers should note that the rate data is accepted from the computer (known as the DTE rate) need only be four times the modem's basic transmission rate (the DCE rate); for example, 14.4 Kbps DCE and 57.6 Kbps DTE. Higher DTEs (for example, 115.2 Kbps on a V.32bis/V42bis modem) will provide only about 5–10% speed improvements, as the maximum data compression rate is 4:1.

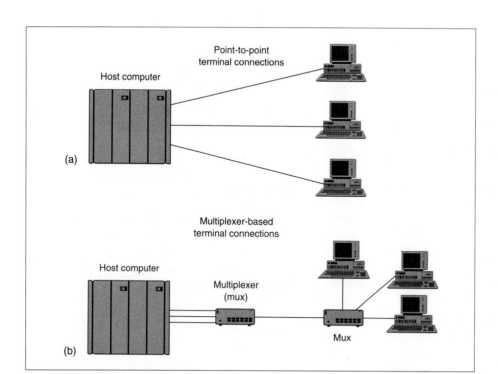

FIGURE 9.18   Use of point-to-point and multiplexer data connections

collects and forwards data in accordance with prescribed protocols. Its approaches to performing these functions are

- *Frequency division multiplexing:* allocating separate frequency bands to different terminals
- *Time division multiplexing (TDM):* allocating fixed time slots for data transmission to each terminal
- *Statistical time division multiplexing (STDM):* a variation on TDM, where no time slots are allocated to inactive devices

Concentrators work similarly to multiplexers by collecting signals from several devices for transmission. The objective is to lessen the use and cost of the transmission media in a network. The major difference is that concentrators are full-functioning computers and are used singly, not in pairs like multiplexers (see Figure 9.19). In addition, they provide buffering, data validation, data compression, and other intelligent functions and they can route data transmissions to more than one host.

Network Interface Cards (NICs)

In LANs, **network interface cards (NICs)** are used to connect terminals to the network. The NIC is an expansion card with logic circuits for electronically transmitting and receiving data on the transmission medium. They typically contain a memory buffer to

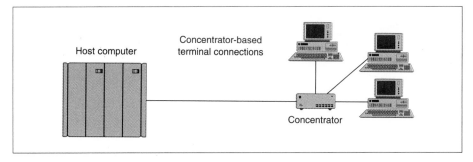

FIGURE 9.19   Use of a concentrator for mainframe terminal
                connections

hold transient data and are topology dependent, meaning that different types of NICs exist for ethernet, token ring, and ARCnet LANs. Many third-party manufacturers of NICs exist, enabling the use of off-the-shelf cards for different LAN types, for example, token ring LANs. *T connectors* are used to attach the NIC to coaxial cable, while *telephone cable connectors* (for example, *RJ-11 and RJ-45 jacks*) are used for attachment to twisted-pair cable (see Figures 9.20a and 9.20b).

Repeaters

Repeaters are used to extend the range of LANs. As discussed earlier, data transmissions are subject to attenuation, or the weakening of signal strength over distance. A repeater amplifies the signals it receives and transmits them to the next LAN segment, allowing the use of a longer length of cable. It is not possible to use an unlimited number of repeaters, as *propagation delays* (the time taken for a message to travel from sender to receiver) build up with each new repeater. Lengthy propagation delays ultimately reduce the efficiency of data transmission.

Bridges, Routers, Brouters, and Gateways

As a business expands, more terminals may be attached to the LAN for additional users. This may eventually result in degraded LAN performance or the exhaustion of logical LAN addresses. For example, as the number of terminals in a token ring network grows, the time taken by the token to return to every terminal increases. Similarly, using the CSMA/CD protocol in bus networks, the number of collisions (and network congestion) may become great when the number of terminals increases or when they are geographically dispersed.

The LAN manager faced with this situation may split the network into two parts with the aid of a *bridge* or *router.* Consider the example in Figure 9.21a, where a large number of users on a token ring network are split almost equally between two departments. If symptoms of network congestion are becoming acute, the manager may choose to split the network into two (Figure 9.21b) connected by a bridge, both of which must be of the same LAN topology and protocol.

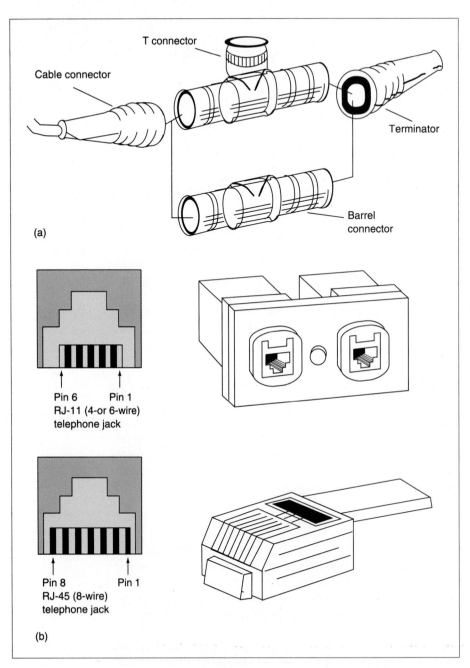

(a)

Cable connector

T connector

Terminator

Barrel connector

Pin 6　Pin 1
RJ-11 (4-or 6-wire)
telephone jack

Pin 8　Pin 1
RJ-45 (8-wire)
telephone jack

(b)

FIGURE 9.20　(a) Cable connectors and terminator; (b) telephone cable connectors.

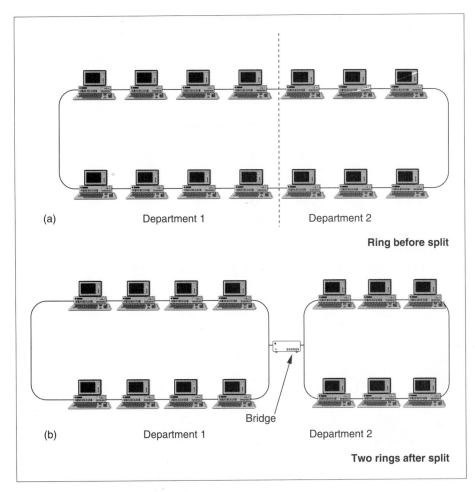

FIGURE 9.21   Use of a bridge to split a network

The bridge may be a dedicated device or a computer that performs the bridging function. On receipt of a data packet, the bridge examines it. If it is addressed to another network, it is passed to that network, otherwise it is passed to the next node (token ring) or dropped (Ethernet). The effect of using the bridge in the above example is to reduce overall LAN traffic, as most data transfers would take place within LAN segments.

Routers work in the same way as bridges but possess more intelligence. They are used to interconnect many similar LAN segments. A router calculates the most efficient path between multiple LAN segments for retransferring the data packet. **Brouters** are devices midway between bridges and routers, but they can handle only limited protocol conversion.

In situations with two dissimilar networks or in which a LAN is to be connected to a mainframe host, a **gateway** is required. A gateway is more complex than either a bridge or a router because it must convert not just LAN segment (or system) addresses but must repackage the data packets into an acceptable format for the destination system or LAN. Connecting a token ring LAN to an ethernet LAN or a mainframe host would be achieved using gateways, as shown in Figure 9.22.

Intelligent Hubs

Bridging and routing equipment has become more and more sophisticated to keep up with the demands of firms with hundreds of LAN users. The number of networked users has continued to increase together with their use of large data types, for example, bitmaps. **Intelligent hubs** provide the ability to create multiple LAN segments, each with the maximum throughput. See Figure 9.23a. For example, a 50-user ethernet LAN can be reconfigured within the hub through software to create two 25-user LANs. Each segment would have the full 10 Mbps bandwidth, improving overall performance. For example, Synoptics, *Lattisnet* hub supports up to five independent ethernet or token ring LAN segments in one unit. Also, the provision of a bridge/router per port allows a system such as Microcom's *Linkbuilder* to support up to eleven discrete LAN segments. See Figure 9.23b.

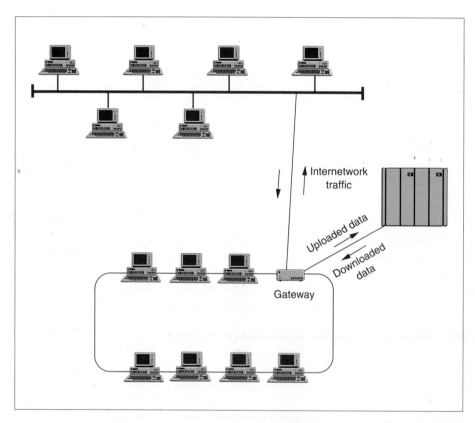

FIGURE 9.22   Use of a gateway to connect a token ring LAN with an Ethernet LAN and a mainframe host

Servers

LAN **servers** are computers that supply services to other terminals in the network, enabling sharing data, programs, and peripherals—LAN benefits discussed earlier. In medium- to large-sized LANs, the *file server* is a major part of the network. It is usually a minicomputer, a workstation, or a powerful microcomputer based on a Pentium or 68040 processor, with sizable RAM and hard disk capacities. User files and programs are stored on the server and retrieved over the network by terminals. More sophisticated file servers allow multiuser access to on-line databases and use *concurrency controls* such as file and record locking (see Chapter 10 for a fuller description). LANs that use a file server, such as Novell's Netware, are called

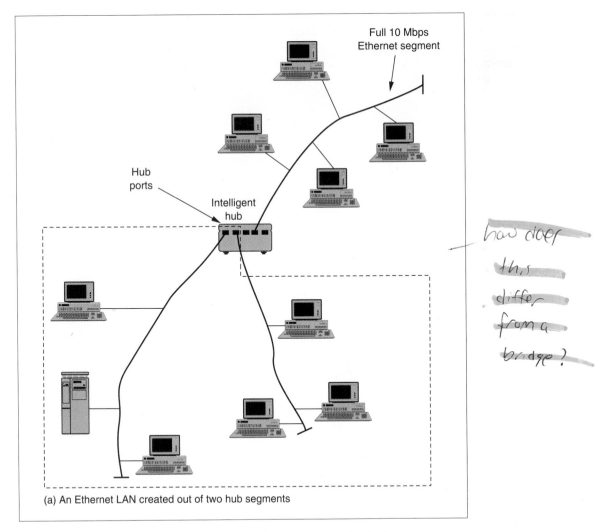

(a) An Ethernet LAN created out of two hub segments

FIGURE 9.23   (a) Use of an intelligent hub to create multiple LAN segments (*continued*)

FIGURE 9.23 *(continued)* (b) A bridging/routing hub for internetworking with WAN and LAN ports. The two cards shown allow four (three LAN/one WAN) and eight (four LAN/four WAN) connections, respectively.

centralized LANs. The server is usually *dedicated,* making it unusable as an individual terminal.

The *peer-to-peer LAN* (for example, Artisoft's *Lantastic*) is an architecture that does not use a central file server. Instead, the LAN OS is stored on every machine in the network and allows users to directly access files from other terminals. In a peer-to-peer LAN, the need for a dedicated server is eliminated, thereby reducing overall cost. This LAN type is mostly used for smaller networks.

Other types of LAN servers include

- *Printer servers.* These allow many users to share several printers connected to the server. Such servers require large RAM and hard disk capacities to act as buffers for printer output.
- *Facsimile and modem servers.* Facsimile machines and modems may also be connected to a central terminal in the network, for use by any other terminal in the network. Such attached modems also provide remote users with dial-in access to the network and act as communication management servers.
- *Computation servers.* This computing method enables cooperative processing of the client's tasks on both the client and the powerful server (see Chapter 10).

The Private Branch Exchange (PBX) and Digital Branch Exchange (DBX)

The cost of LAN cabling can be expensive for large networks, especially if the cables must be run through roofs, walls, and floors. Instead of installing new cable, managers can use the existing telephone wiring within their buildings to construct their LANs. Most buildings contain wiring for the telephone system and all but older buildings have adequate-quality twisted-pair to support LANs.

Private branch exchanges (or **PBXs**) were initially developed by the telephone companies to avoid the cost of supplying all workers in a firm with individual lines. As only 10 to 20 percent of telephones are in use at any one time, a local switching center (the PBX) could be installed to support 20 percent, say, of the potential load. These devices carry both voice and data traffic and can route calls within, as well as outside, the firm. Early PBXs supported data transmission rates of up to 56 Kbps within the firm using modems, but LAN rates of up to 10 Mbps are now available on newer **digital branch exchanges (DBXs).** Using DBXs, all data and voice communications are in digital form but must be converted to analog form for transmission over public telephone lines. Today's DBXs are viable options for LAN implementation.

Centrex

Centrex is a PBX variant that is operated by a telephone services provider but owned by the firm. Centrex equipment is located and maintained at the service provider's central office. It is therefore well maintained and reliable and relieves the using firm of the responsibility of maintaining the equipment. All the features of a PBX are contained in a Centrex, including routing of calls within the firm, call forwarding, and so on.

9.5 SETTING UP A LAN

Setting up a LAN is a multifaceted decision, involving consideration of user requirements and LAN characteristics. It requires a methodological approach and must be requirements led, not technology led. An important early decision is whether a LAN is required or whether a LAN alternative is appropriate. In creating a LAN, designers must plan for future as well as current requirements, to ensure that the LAN will satisfy changing needs. In addition to user requirements, LAN issues include media and topology, centralized versus peer-to-peer alternatives, LAN terminal and server characteristics, NOSs, and all costs.

Considering Requirements

Similar to decisions involving stand-alone systems, LAN decisions must be oriented to requirements and not to technological features. This also means that analysis of the LAN's *costs* and *benefits* is necessary.

Consider, for example, a legal services firm whose secretarial activities involve word processing on isolated microcomputers. While three of the five microcomputers in the firm are connected to dot matrix printers, only one is connected to the firm's laser printer. The office manager believes that productivity is wasted when the secretaries queue to use the computer with the attached laser printer. Based on further study, the manager has also found that only a small number of documents are shared among the secretaries. In this setting, an intelligent printer switching device with over five input and output ports would be sufficient for the firm's needs. Another possible alternative might be a zero-slot LAN, such as LocalTalk in a Macintosh environment, which could handle more demanding future requirements.

Seven years later, upon revisiting the legal services firm, we find the firm has grown and the number of microcomputers has expanded to fifteen. Its users now include some of the firm's lawyers, and new applications include maintaining the client database and accounting functions. The lawyers are also seeking access to external legal databases maintained by third parties. Now, the required high-speed data transmission, group access to external systems, and a multiuser database jointly call for a full-fledged LAN implementation. Other functions that would benefit from a LAN include (1) groupware; (2) document imaging; and (3) the potential for future expansion.

Making Topology and Media Decisions

Once it is determined that a LAN is required, two subsequent decisions must be made—the choices of LAN topology and media. The two major LAN topologies are *bus* and *ring-based* alternatives. Bus-based alternatives are usually ethernet LANs, which use CSMA/CD protocols. Some bus networks utilize token-passing protocols to avoid the penalties associated with contention. Ethernet LANs are currently the most popular network topology, due to the low cost per node (about $150) and comparatively early development. In situations with long and/or infrequent transmissions and fewer stations, collisions are less likely. Where there are many stations and frequent data transmissions, more collisions are likely using CSMA/CD and a token-passing bus might be preferable (see Table 9.2).

Peer-to-peer networks, for example, the Lantastic NOS, are the fastest-growing network topology in competition with ethernet-based LANs. They are less expensive, often costing less than $100 per NIC, and their data transfer rates now match Ethernet's 10 Mbps rate. Another advantage is more predictable LAN performance, since token passing prevents any one terminal from monopolizing the LAN's capacity.

The star topology using ARCnet is also inexpensive, costing about $150 per node. This LAN supports 20 Mbps (in practice, 16 Mbps) throughput and utilizes polling, thereby eliminating contention and collisions. There are fewer third-party NICs and software for building ARCnet LANs than the other two options, and up to 250 users can be supported on a single ARCnet LAN.

Once a configuration is chosen, networking media and devices must be selected. Multiple media can be used on the network, depending on function. For the main bus on an ethernet network, thick coaxial cable is often used, with thin coaxial used for spurs. More recent ethernet implementations use fiber-optic cable for the central bus. STP and UTP are attractive choices for spurs due to their lower cost and bulk compared to coaxial cable. The low cost of twisted-pair also makes it a popular choice for ring- and star-based networks, and many token ring and ARCnet LANs now use this

TABLE 9.2   Features of various LAN and sub-Lan architectures

	Cost	Speed	Topology	Protocols	Features	Uses
Hub-based ethernet	Cheap ($300/node)	10 Mbps along several channels	Hub-based bus	CSMA/CD token passing	High aggregate data traffic	Text, graphics, data files
Standard ethernet	Cheap ($150/node)	10 Mbps	Bus	CSMA/CD token passing	Many terminals and transmissions degrade LAN performance	Text, graphics, data files
Token ring	Cheap ($300/node)	16 Mbps	Star-wired' ring	Token passing	Gracefully degrades, fair access to terminals	Text, graphics, data files
Fast ethernet	Expensive ($800/node)	100 Mbps	Bus	CSMA/CD token passing	Very fast data channel	Full multimedia
FDDI	Expensive ($900/node)	100 Mbps	Ring	Token passing	Very fast data channel, fair access	Full multimedia
Arcnet	Cheap ($150/node)	16 Mbps	Star	Polling	Fast channel, no contention	Text, graphics, data files
SubLANs	Very cheap ($50–100/node)	20 Kbps– 2 Mbps	Varies	Usually polling	Slow data channels, no contention	Text, graphics, data files
ATM	Very expensive ($1,500/node)	52–155 Mbps	Hubs connected to WAN	Packet transmission and polling	Very fast data channel	Full multimedia
PBXs/ DBXs	Cheap ($100–300/ node)	56 Kbps– 10 Mbps	Star	Polling	Moderately fast channels, limited capacity	Text files (PBXs) Text, graphics, data files (DBXs)

medium. In an environment with several interconnected LANs, the favorite choice for LAN interconnection via a backbone is fiber-optic cable.

Comparing Centralized and Peer-to-Peer LAN Alternatives

A further choice faces the decision maker once LAN media and topologies are selected. This is the choice of a *centralized* or a *peer-to-peer* LAN configuration. **Centralized LANs** are the most widely used form of LAN organization. They use a dedicated server attached to all the shared peripherals. Dedicated servers cannot also be used by an individual but are suited to access by multiple users. Requests are made by the terminals to the server. Powerful server capabilities are necessary and supermicrocomputers are often designated to play this role. They provide greater security by storing and controlling all data in a central location and by preventing accidental rebooting or taking shared resources, for example, hard disks off-line.

Peer-to-peer LANs are more flexible than centralized LANs. Shared devices (for example, hard disks, facsimile cards, printers, and so on) can be located at the most suitable nodes and are not limited to the central server, which has the effect of distributing the processing load through the LAN. In addition, a computer does not have to be dedicated solely to server functions, making one more machine available to users. Added savings result from using less expensive peer-to-peer NOSs. The downside is that peer-to-peer LANs offer less functionality than centralized LANs. In addition, dispersed files are harder to back up, resource management is more complex, and there are greater security concerns. Newer peer-to-peer NOSs, such as Artisoft's Lantastic, are more fully featured, providing higher transmission rates and the ability to designate servers.

Selecting LAN Nodes and/or Server(s)

Nodes in a LAN may be user terminals, servers, communication control devices, and peripherals. **Terminals** can be classified as dumb and intelligent. A *dumb terminal* is essentially a combination of a keyboard and monitor, with a base unit for communications with its host computer. All user processing is performed on the host computer and displayed on the monitor. Microcomputer-based multiuser systems, with powerful microcomputer hosts, can reduce overall hardware costs. To connect dumb terminals to a host computer, a common option is to use a concentrator with multiple serial ports (for the terminals), and a high-speed serial or parallel connection to the host computer.

Examples of *intelligent terminals* are microcomputers with their own processing capabilities. To connect a microcomputer in a LAN, NICs must be acquired and inserted into internal expansion slots; standard card connections enable attachment directly to the network medium, or to devices such as MAUs. Microcomputers are often used as terminals, but they must have adequate RAM for the resident portion of the NOS.

Servers may be mainframe, minicomputer, or supermicrocomputer systems. The majority are supermicrocomputers, and as their capabilities increase, this trend will continue. A server has powerful processing and I/O capabilities for satisfying the demands made upon it by network terminals, for example, printing, filing, sending facsimiles, and database access. 80486s or 68040s are sensible minimum requirements, as are 32-bit data buses such as the EISA bus. The server's hard disk drives should be fast, with sub-12ms access time, and should incorporate disk caching (see Chapter 3). In addition, large amounts of fast RAM (8–32+Mb) are needed to buffer requests and files and to store multitasking programs and the NOS. Finally, a data backup subsystem and UPS are essential server components.

Communication control devices are used to configure, modify, and expand the network, including repeaters, bridges, MAUs, and modems. **Peripherals** such as printers, hard drives, and facsimile cards are also used as required. Generally, they are attached to terminals on the network, but newer peripherals, particularly network printers, may be attached directly to the network and appear as another terminal to which data (for printing) is transmitted.

Selecting a Network Operating System (NOS)

In a very real sense, the key part of the LAN is the NOS. In LANs, a portion of the NOS is loaded into computer memory when it is booted. It remains memory resident and controls the LAN's operation, protocols, and user requests. Requests for LAN services (for example, storage or printers external to the terminal) are intercepted by the *redirector* portion of the NOS and routed over the network. A fuller discussion of NOSs and their vendors takes place in Chapter 10.

LAN Installation

LAN development is no different from that of single-user systems, since both must proceed through a systems development life cycle. As described in Chapters 13 and 14, the systems life-cycle stages are also necessary for networked systems. LAN installation takes place during the implementation stage of the life cycle, and several guidelines regarding the developers and the process are useful.

First, LAN development can be carried out **in-house,** by **end users,** by the **information center (IC),** or by **systems professionals.** The ease of installation of printer switches, zero-slot LANs, and peer-to-peer LANs, suggests that they can be successfully installed by experienced users with minimal support from system professionals. These professionals are needed for larger, fully functional LANs and for internetworking, enterprise-wide networks, and client/server computing.

External networking consultants are used in situations similar to those requiring IC or MIS assistance. They are a substitute when there are no skilled networking professionals available within the organization. The current trend toward outsourcing both development and maintenance of LANs to external consultants is also seen as enabling firms to concentrate on their strategic missions.

Following the LAN planning process, network hardware is acquired. This includes terminals, cabling, peripherals, NICs, MAUs, bridges, routers, and other devices, which are then physically installed and connected in the chosen topology. Network installation is often carried out in a phased process, especially in end-user installation, with new terminals gradually added to the network. Most NOSs offer menu-driven installation on terminals and servers, in which passwords, user IDs, and access privileges are created, and station addresses and shared resources are designated. Testing of the network ensues, often aided by *network management software.* New stations and devices may then be added to the LAN and tested.

Finally, every LAN must have provisions for *backup, security,* and *reliability.* Backup is supported by backup programs that copy files to magnetic cartridges and disks, or optical disks. NOSs also allow the designation of a LAN administrator to monitor user access to LAN resources. Furthermore, such utilities as anti-virus programs are commonplace in LANs, as well as the RAID methods discussed in Chapter 5, for improved reliability and fault-tolerance.

SUMMARY

LANs are a rapidly growing area of computer technology, and many firms have implemented them to interconnect their dispersed microcomputers. The motivation for LAN adoption lies in many demonstrated benefits, such as high-speed data transmission between a firm's computing resources; sharing expensive hardware, programs, and data; access to external computer-based systems; and the ability to use groupware and to implement distributed processing.

Planning for LAN implementation must be *requirements driven,* not technology driven. The LAN must be cost-justified in the same way as other information systems, and it is important to evaluate whether a full-fledged LAN is required or if other alternatives might suffice. These alternatives include printer switches, zero-slot LANs, and less expensive peer-to-peer LANs. In some cases, a fully functional LAN may not be required, even when future requirements are considered.

In planning for a LAN's implementation, several factors must be considered. The first is the *networking media* to be used. Examples of conducted (physical) media are twisted-pair, coaxial cable, and fiber-optic cable, while the radiated media include infrared or radio wave transmission. The networking media are then arranged in a LAN structure, such as the bus, ring, or star topologies. **Ethernet** and **IBM's token ring,** the two leading LAN topologies, are bus- and ring-based architectures respectively. Token ring LANs are increasing in popularity due to their higher data transmission speeds and predictable behavior under heavy loads. The **OSI model,** proposed by the International Standards Organization (ISO), is a seven-layer model designed to promote product compatibility by vendors of data communications hardware and software.

Communication control devices are essential components of any LAN. They include intelligent hubs, bridges, and routers, all designed to facilitate communication across whole networks. Other devices are modems and gateways, which provide the ability to interconnect remote computers. Multiplexers and concentrators help to create more efficient networks while repeaters help extend the reach of the LAN. In recent times, private and digital branch exchanges (PBXs and DBXs) have enabled organizations to utilize the telephone wiring within their buildings to create LANs.

In developing a LAN, all of the preceding elements must be considered. LAN development and maintenance can be performed in-house—by users or systems professionals or by external networking consultants. The last two options are appropriate for very large and complex networks, while the first is suited to smaller sub-LANs or peer-to-peer systems. In any case, phased LAN implementation is often used to limit the risks involved in LAN deployment.

REVIEW QUESTIONS

1. Describe two limitations of stand-alone microcomputers in supporting office automation tasks.
2. List five benefits offered by LANs. Do these benefits relieve an organization of the need for a cost-benefit analysis?
3. What are two alternatives to a full-fledged LAN, and in what circumstances might they be selected?

4. List three devices that are commonly shared using LANs.
5. What transmission medium is already present in most modern office buildings?
6. What is the purpose of shielding twisted-pair cable?
7. How would you use thick and thin coaxial cable in implementing an ethernet LAN?
8. What are the main advantages of twisted-pair over coaxial cable?
9. How is data transmitted through fiber-optic cable?
10. What is a LAN backbone and what transmission medium would be most suited for use as a backbone?
11. What is a data switch? Distinguish between manual and automatic data switches.
12. What is the maximum data transmission rate on an ethernet LAN? Is it greater than that of a token ring LAN?
13. Describe the function of the token in a token-passing network. Can token passing be used on bus networks?
14. What communications device is used solely to extend the span of a LAN?
15. Describe the major difference between a PBX and a DBX.

EXERCISES

1. A graphic design studio employs several designers who collaborate on designs for customers' logos, newsletters, cards, and so on. Currently, eight stand-alone microcomputers are used in the firm. Collaboration involves several designers working on a hard copy of the design or sitting around a single workstation displaying the design. The manager feels that using a network to electronically transmit these files across the terminals will improve productivity. Most graphic files are 1–10 Mb in size, and many file transfers would occur each day in addition to other network traffic (for example, maintenance of a client database). What type of network would you recommend to the manager? Why?

2. A clothing retailer is in the process of installing a token ring network to interconnect 40 of its workstations. Applications to support include maintaining customer and supplier databases, processing sales transactions, and word processing. In studying their documentation, you observe that a regular 386SX with 4 Mb of memory and 100 Mb hard disk has been selected to serve as a file and printer server. Do you agree with this decision? If not, why, and what would you recommend in its place?

3. Describe and critically compare the token passing and CSMA/CD data transmission protocols. Which topology is each typically associated with?

4. Two departments in a New York college are currently using an ethernet LAN. Due to the building's architectural characteristics, each department occupies half of both the second and third floors. The LAN is used for groupware applications, such as E-mail, scheduling, and calendaring, as well as academic applications such as statistical packages. As the total number of users has increased to above a hundred, response time on the network has slowed appreciably. What data communications device(s) can the LAN administrator use to resolve the problem? How exactly would this work?

5. A dentist is seeking to implement a network to interconnect two microcomputers at her two clinics in different areas of the city. Is a LAN appropriate in this case? How would you suggest she resolve her problem?

Suggested Readings _____

Briene, D.,"Datacom Buyer's Guide: High Speed Modems," *Network World,* April 19, 1993, pp. 40–49.

Datapro Research Corp. *Datapro Reports on Computers,* Volume 3. New York: McGraw-Hill, April 1991.

Derfler, F. J. "Connectivity Simplified: LAN Fundamentals 1." *PC Magazine,* March 31, 1992.

Derfler, F. J. "Connectivity Simplified: LAN Fundamentals 2." *PC Magazine,* April 14, 1992.

Fitzgerald, J. *Business Data Communications: Basic Concepts, Security, and Design.* (4th ed.) New York: Wiley, 1993.

Fox, J. "Introduction to Local Area Networks." *PC Today,* August 1990, pp. 14–24.

Stamper, D. A. *Business Data Communications.* (3rd ed.) Redwood City, CA: Benjamin/ Cummings, 1992.

CHAPTER 10

ENTERPRISE COMPUTING

INTRODUCTION

In the minds of many, LANs represent the second phase of the microcomputer revolution, in which large numbers of microcomputers were interconnected. With current trends, more than 60 percent of corporate microcomputers will be interconnected in networks by 1995. As high-end microcomputers grow more powerful and networking software more sophisticated, LAN-based systems have appeared in on-line transaction processing (OLTP) roles. Using interconnected LANs in mission-critical applications signifies a maturing of the technology and a new, third phase of microcomputing. In the LAN's new role, reliability and security are important concerns, and to support these operational requirements, vendors of network software have created a new generation of improved NOSs and network management tools.

Some of the new software supports external data links, enabling remote LAN users to communicate using value-added networks (VANs), metropolitan area networks (MANs), and wide-area networks (WANs). New technologies such as integrated services data networks (ISDN), frame relay, and asynchronous transfer mode (ATM) have also contributed to improved performance of these new network types. The *enterprise network* describes the new organizational network comprising diverse computer types and interconnected LANs. It uses cooperative processing, mainly in the form of client/server computing, and incorporates features that make it an effective platform for the firm's OLTP.

Learning Objectives

After reading this chapter, you will be able to:

- Understand the major issues in LAN management
- Define any additional requirements to enable a LAN to support OLTP
- Make cost-effective decisions for tuning the performance of a LAN
- Outline the benefits offered by a WAN to a firm's LAN users
- Recommend new technologies for implementing enterprise computing

---

CASE 10.1

THE HIDDEN COSTS OF DOWNSIZING TO CLIENT/SERVER SYSTEMS

Client/Server systems is not always the panacea it is made out to be. Getting a ''right-sized'' system working properly can take several attempts and be full of surprises—both technical and organizational. In fact, it is really not accurate to call these new systems downsized in anything other than physical size. They often contain more computing power and handle more data than the mainframe systems they replace. Companies installing client/server systems are discovering that unanticipated issues are consuming resources that were never budgeted for. And that has caused the plug to be pulled on more than a few rightsizing efforts.

A major Southeastern manufacturing company found out the hard way that traditional processes and technologies won't work with client/server computing. After moving a customer database from a mainframe platform to a LAN-based system using an Oracle SQL server, system response time was unacceptable to users. The problem turned out to be the use of PC Cobol to construct SQL statements, despite IS attempts to blame poor performance on the server. After hiring an external consultant to rewrite programs in

C, processing time for jobs was greatly reduced.

Other firms report that downsizing often does not produce expected great savings. Although PCs and servers are much cheaper than mainframes, additional personnel and equipment infrastructure is needed to maintain system throughput, multiplying the cost of the system. Training costs and materials for system developers and consultants are two other costs involved in the transition to client/server. Yet other firms point to increased ''peer support'' or the time spent by coworkers helping each other. Some experts cite better applications as the main deliverable of client/server systems.

In order to be successful, a client/server solution must be implemented in an environment that can embrace the organizational changes the technology demands. Decades of traditional management and a mainframe-centric mentality can be tough to overcome.

Adapted from D. Van Kirk, ''The Hidden Costs of Downsizing to Client/Server,'' *InfoWorld*, January 11, 1993, p. 54.

10.1 MANAGING LAN-BASED TRANSACTION PROCESSING

The transition from mainframe-based information systems to systems built around networks of interconnected microcomputers (and other types of computers) is gaining ground as improved hardware and software become available. As a consequence, many MIS managers are faced with the task of moving mission-critical transaction processing to these new, downsized platforms. Interconnected networks of heterogeneous resources have proved to be more complex to control and manage effectively but are increasingly expected to provide levels of reliability and throughput identical to mainframes.

In networks with distributed and/or multiuser databases, these features are difficult to implement, with issues like concurrency control, database consistency, and heterogenous systems posing significant problems. We examine issues of network management for mission-critical networked systems together with system performance, network security, recovery from failures, and strategies for tuning LANs.

Transaction Processing on LANs

LAN-based **on-line transaction processing** (OLTP) is often derived using two approaches. The first involves building upward from stand-alone microcomputers. In many instances, these microcomputers are connected in networks, then internetworks, and linked to the firm's mainframe, or to other LANs. The second route involves the conscious decision to downsize or devolve from larger systems such as mainframes to a predominantly microcomputer- and LAN-based system. In both cases, the motivation is to obtain cost savings from

- Moving to less expensive microprocessor-based hardware platforms
- Requiring fewer resources to operate, maintain, and repair the new systems
- Reducing the personnel required to manage the downsized information system
- Using less expensive software developed for the microcomputer market

Furthermore, all the previously discussed benefits of LANs, such as device and data sharing, will also result from distributed processing systems based on LANs.

OLTP on LAN-based systems is somewhat similar to processing performed on large-scale computers, incorporating applications that use transaction databases, such as sales, inventory management, and A/R and A/P programs. It requires that these applications possess *multiuser capabilities,* to allow multiple users to perform transactions concurrently, requiring appropriate OSs such as Microsoft Windows NT, OS/2, and UNIX; and NOSs, such as Novell Netware and Banyan Vines (see Section 10.2). Mission-critical OLTP is also made possible, in part, by more powerful microcomputer hardware, such as 486-, Pentium- and 68040-based microcomputer servers. One further aspect of LAN-based OLTP is the set of personnel skills required to support such systems, discussed more fully in Section 10.5.

LAN Reliability and Throughput

For managers responsible for the firm's transaction processing, central concerns are *reliability* and *throughput.* Doubts were initially expressed whether LAN-based systems could demonstrate the same reliability and performance of mainframe systems. For early LANs, the answer was clearly no to all but the most undemanding of applications. To understand why expectations have changed, we must examine the reasons for the earlier negative responses and the changes since then.

1. Early microcomputers such as 286-, 386SX-, and 68020-based machines could not meet the processing demands of multiuser applications of the types described above. Their CPU and I/O capabilities were also not sufficient to enable them to serve as servers for tens or hundreds of users, and they lacked the reliability and fault tolerance found in larger systems.

2. Underlying **OSs,** such as early versions of 16-bit MS-DOS, had too many restrictions to effectively support large-scale transaction processing. These restrictions included limited memory access and little or no multitasking and multiuser capabilities. The same restrictions characterized early **NOSs.**
3. Microcomputer DBMSs could not fully support database requirements of mission-critical transaction processing, some of which included referential integrity, rolling back failed transactions, and managing distributed databases (see the next section). Also, most did not support **SQL,** the de facto relational language standard for internetwork and cross-platform data manipulation.
4. Earlier PC software did not provide transaction monitoring of the type prevalent in systems like *CICS (customer information control system),* used by IBM mainframes. Without such validation of transactions, there would be reduced confidence in the integrity of transactions in such applications as banking and airline reservations.

As more powerful hardware, operating systems, and applications software have become available, these managerial concerns have gradually lessened. Many examples of networks of primarily microcomputer-based LANs performing mission-critical OLTP now exist in a wide range of firms, and the number is rapidly increasing.

Keyport Life Insurance Company in Boston, for example, estimates that it reduced its IS budget by $3 million per year by downsizing from a mainframe to a fault-tolerant NetFrame server connected to some 150 microcomputers and 60 printers. This configuration is used to manage over 200,000 retirement investment accounts with the same reliability and security as was experienced with their old mainframe. Keyport is only one of the firms able to make the transition to client/server systems due to the heightened confidence in such systems.

LAN Multiuser and Distributed Databases

Mission-critical applications involve concurrent multiuser access to databases, and in some instances, the firm's database is also distributed across several departments. Both features are commonplace in mainframe environments but have only recently become available in LAN-based systems. In the case of multiuser database access, three key features must be provided by the DBMS:

- *File and record locking.* As we saw in Chapter 7, *record locking* is an important feature of multiuser DBMSs, which prevents simultaneous updates of database records by multiple users. Two methods of locking records are through **read locks** and **write locks.** A write lock is applied when a user updates the record and prevents other users from accessing the record until the lock is released. A read lock is issued when users seek only to read the record, for example, to retrieve the price of an item from the price file. Subsequent users may then place read locks on the record and read from but not write to the record. File locks apply to entire files and are less efficient (and popular) than record locks, which lock only the records that are needed.
- *Rolling back aborted transactions.* Multiuser databases must be able to recover from system failures, or risk inconsistent databases, as it is almost impossible to know which transactions in RAM were successfully completed and which were not. By keeping a log of transactions, DBMSs can roll back aborted transactions. Periodic *checkpoints* for a database are created (that is, completing all outstanding transactions

while preventing new ones), indicating stages it may be restored to. By holding a log of transactions following the checkpoint, consisting of images of the affected records before and after the transaction, a database may be restored to the last checkpoint if failure occurs, as shown in Figure 10.1.

- **Integrity constraints.** All databases require integrity constraints to govern the possible values of fields in files and their relationships with each other. For example, a person's age is not allowed to assume a negative value. **Referential integrity, a new feature on microcomputer DBMSs, ensures that changes that would leave a database in an inconsistent state are rejected.** For example, a foreign key's value could not be arbitrarily changed in a relation unless corresponding changes were made in the relation in which the field was a key. While common on mainframe relational databases, its incorporation on smaller-scale systems is both recent and necessary for mission-critical application support.

Distributed databases are physically spread out over two or more locations. A distributed database may be *nonreplicated, partially replicated, or fully replicated,* as shown in Figure 10.2. In the first case there is only one occurrence of any data item, and requests from remote locations will involve transmission of data over the data communications link. With partial replication, there is a greater probability that desired data is at a specific location, but any duplicated datasets must be simultaneously updated at every location in the system. Full replication guarantees the fastest access to data but increases storage costs, is complex to manage, and involves large data transfers for multiple database updates.

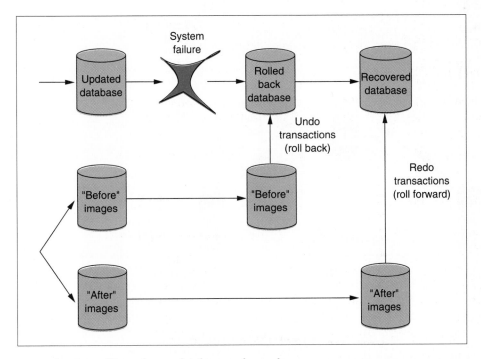

FIGURE 10.1   Restoring a database using a log

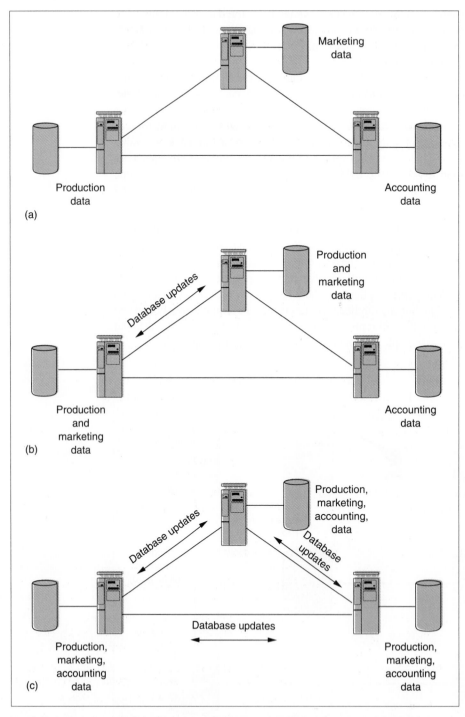

FIGURE 10.2 (a) Nonreplicated database; (b) partially replicated database; (c) fully replicated database.

Consider the distributed database configuration in Figure 10.2a, for example. It shows the firm's database split up between the marketing, production, and accounting departments. Benefits of this configuration include placing each part of the distributed database nearer the point of use, making for more efficient and rapid data access. In addition, user satisfaction is often higher from having files in-house, instead of at a remote data processing site. *Distributed database management systems (DDBMSs)* have until recently been the preserve of mainframes, but new microcomputer-based offerings by Oracle, Sybase, and Gupta now possess similar capabilities. Management of distributed database updates, use of sophisticated database operations such as JOINs on remote relations, and client/server capabilities are all critical in enabling LAN-based systems to support mission-critical OLTP.

Network Management

LANs in U.S. firms are increasing in size and complexity as growing numbers of workstations become connected in departmental and enterprisewide networks. Firms with 50-user LANs on a central server and 300+ users in internetworks with several servers, connected by bridges and routers, are now commonplace. These local area and enterprise networks are more complicated than ever before with (1) *heterogeneous devices* (2) *multiple protocols and topologies,* and (3) *diverse LAN media.* The new, mission-critical deployment of these systems makes the problem of network management even more crucial. Essential elements for network management on these new networks are described below.

A **network administrator**—an individual or group of individuals—is responsible for managing the firm's network. End users are occasionally responsible for managing departmental LANs, but the responsibility for internetworks, and in particular enterprisewide networks, usually falls on networking professionals. **Extensive documentation** of network components and their operation is indispensable for the personnel who support the LAN, and detailed repair and recovery procedures should be incorporated in the system's documentation.

Network management software has been developed to assist the network administrator in the task of network management. As shown in Table 10.1, several

TABLE 10.1   A sampling of LAN management software

Product	Company	OSs supported	Price	Description/Comments
Spectrum	Cabletron Systems Inc.	OS/2, UNIX versions	$18,000 and up	Supports SNMP, allows customized menus, works with a variety of hubs, routers, PCs etc.
HP Open View Network Node Manager	Hewlett Packard Co.	DOS/Windows, OS/2, Unix versions, Sun OS	$15,750	Supports SNMP and CMIP. Also supports TCP/IP and IPX/SPX and allows customized menus.
Netware Management System	Novell, Inc.	DOS/Windows	$4,995 and up	Works well with popular Novell LANs. Supports SNMP and TCP/IP.

vendors offer network management software for monitoring the status of networks, pinpointing faults in the network, and in some cases, taking corrective action to restore the network to normal operation. Most of these packages are based on a widely used network management standard, *simple network management protocol (SNMP)*. The SNMP protocol exists at the OSI application layer, which enables network activity to be collected in a uniform format across different networks.

The four components of SNMP and the newer SNMP-2 are as follows:

- The **SNMP protocol** or set of rules
- The **SMI (structure of management information),** defining how the network data is structured
- The **MIB (management information base),** describing how the status information on network devices is reported and stored
- The **NMS (network management system),** a console device that displays collected data from network devices. Currently, many vendors' SNMP products allow the display of network data on standard terminals.

Statistics collected by network management software include data from host computers, dumb and intelligent terminals, peripherals (for example, modems, printers, and hard disks), data communications equipment (for example, bridges, routers, and gateways), and communications media (for example, UTP, coax, and fiber). These statistics include:

- Performance statistics, such as processing rates and device utilization ratios
- Errors experienced by a device (for example, modem, bridge) or a transmission medium
- Normal and peak performance indicators for data communications and computing devices
- The current status of any attached device in the enterprise network

The role of network management software is increasing in importance as a way of managing complex network configurations. More recent software facilitates not only the monitoring of the network's status but also the control of network devices from the network administrator's terminal. Another protocol, called *communications management information protocol (CMIP),* was introduced by the International Standards Organization (ISO) to serve the same role as SNMP. However, the use of SNMP-based devices and software is more widespread, due in part to its simplicity and to its large installed base.

Network Security

The aim of **network security** in enterprisewide (and local area) networks is to prevent network access by nonusers of the information system and improper system use by authorized users. Network security strategies are not 100 percent foolproof but are intended to make unauthorized access unduly expensive and time consuming to intruders. Network administrators are responsible for network security and must balance the level of system security with the efficiency and performance of the system. Very complex and arcane security mechanisms may make the system all but unusable or cause it to perform inefficiently.

A basic security measure is *physical security* of the devices on the firm's network(s). Since physically walking off with a portable hard disk or laser disk is much easier than breaking an encryption code, vital network devices must be safeguarded with locks, guards, and electronic monitoring devices, to deter physical tampering or theft of devices. Another form of network security uses physical- or software-based *time and location restrictions* on the use of certain devices.

Password protection is also used to prevent unauthorized access to the system. Each user is assigned or chooses a unique secret password, which should not be the names of days, months, or the first and last names of the user, and so on. A multilevel method of passwords can also be used to assign multiple levels of data access and manipulation to users. *Encryption* involves the scrambling and descrambling of messages traveling between different stations on (or across) networks. A popular but controversial standard for encryption is the DES algorithm, which uses a 56-bit encryption key to produce 70 quadrillion possible outputs for a given piece of data. Without the key, a network intruder tapping the communications medium would find it very difficult to decipher the message within a reasonable time.

An *access log* is another valuable tool that alerts the network manager to attempts to access the network. This log indicates where these attempts were made from and when they were made. Finally, as indicated in Chapter 6, *anti-virus software* is an essential weapon in the arsenal of the network manager to prevent computer virus infections within and across LANs.

Network Failure and Recovery

Occasionally, information systems experience partial or complete failure. In enterprise networks, as in other types of information systems, the objective is to prevent failures, detect them when they occur, reduce their effects, and recover from them as quickly as possible. The effects of system failure on an enterprise network can be disastrous, ranging from the inability to access the firm's database to not being able to communicate with any other device on the network. The responsibility for network reliability and the maximization of network uptime rests with the network administrator. Possible types of failure are:

- *Hardware failure.* This includes failure of system units (for example, motherboards, power supplies) and peripherals (for example, printers).
- *Communication control device failure.* The failure of devices such as gateways, brouters, routers, and bridges falls under this category, as do breaks in cabling.
- *Software failure.* Software crashes caused by the OS, NOS, user applications, utilities, or the DBMS may also cause partial or total system failure.
- *People (and procedure) failure.* If procedures are incorrectly observed, this may result in system failure. This might be accidental or intentional (that is, sabotage).

Failure of mission-critical systems can be expensive, involving both the cost and effort of repairing the system and restoring it to normal operation. Repairing the system includes (1) time and materials required for hardware and software fixes and (2) lost productivity from deferred transaction processing. Suppose, for example, a software retailer has a 25-terminal LAN, with a central server holding the firm's customer and sales files. A failed server requires personnel time to isolate and repair the fault, new code to be written or purchased if required, and/or replacement hardware components. In the meantime, salespeople would be unable to access the data on the server or perform transactions for the duration of the system failure and recovery.

Constant *network monitoring* and *preventive maintenance* are necessary measures for preventing network failure. Lines may be physically checked for breaks or deterioration. Constant status data may also be collected from network devices and terminals using SNMP. Alerts that show degraded or erratic performance may result in remote component testing over the network or physical inspection and/or replacement of the component. These alerts and other status information aid in the detection and isolation of network errors and faults. Important tools in this area include the network management software discussed in the previous section and system performance management utilities.

Enterprise systems must be able to handle failures when they occur. The major approach used is to incorporate redundancy into the system to nullify the effects of such failure. Several such methods include

- Protecting the power supply, through the use of an **uninterruptible power supply (UPS).** The UPS prevents brownouts, "spikes", and power surges from affecting system devices and enables continued performance of the system for some time in the event of complete power failure.
- **Regular backing up** of the system's database. In enterprise networks, NOSs or backup software may be used to perform unattended backup of server databases and involuntary backup of individual users' files.
- Using **fault-tolerant systems.** Vendors such as Stratus and Tandem provide computers with redundant components that instantly come on-line in the event of system failure.
- Having **"hot" replacement** servers, terminals, or other devices as part of the network. These systems are actively involved in processing transactions and represent system overcapacity, which can be drawn upon in the event of failure of core system components.
- **Maintaining "cold" replacements** in storage. These systems and components (for example, expansion cards, power supplies, and printers) are kept in storage until a similar component fails. They are then quickly installed in the network.
- Using **data recovery techniques.** These include RAID and error checking and correcting (ECC) memory, used to rectify errors in secondary storage devices and RAM respectively. ECC is widely used in mainframe systems but is now available on high-end microcomputers such as Compaq's Proliant servers.
- Creating a **manual backup system** to process transactions while the computer system is down. Such a system provides degraded performance and requires data entry and processing when the system is restored.

Tuning Networks

As new resources and users are added to the network, it is likely that the initial network configuration may not support current requirements. Symptoms of inadequate performance include *performance degradation,* which may be manifested as slower inquiry response times or as missing or scrambled messages. This may require the network administrator to tune the network to obtain performance improvements. In addition, the availability of new technology alternatives (for example, new OSs or NICs) may provide opportunities for improving network performance. Tuning the network may involve

- *Upgrading the OS.* New OS versions often operate more efficiently than previous ones, thereby boosting overall performance. For example, performance gains result from upgrading OS/2 Version 1.3 on the network server to Version 2.0.
- *Upgrading the NOS.* This may also produce benefits similar to those resulting from an OS upgrade, from improved NOS performance.
- *Adding NICs to the server.* This approach is often used to decongest traffic across the server's NICs, a common bottleneck on networks, and is recommended to be tried prior to expensive server upgrades. Assuming bus mastering is being used (see Chapter 3), additional NICs can be very effective in improving network performance.
- *Upgrading the network server(s).* This can also improve the performance of the network. Approaches to upgrading the server include increasing server RAM; using a large, fast disk cache; attaching a faster hard disk with bus mastering and a local bus; moving devices such as hard disks from ISA to EISA controllers; and upgrading the processor (for instance, from a 486DX to a Pentium).
- *Upgrading/modifying communication control devices.* In some situations, networking devices can provide performance gains. For example, a repeater might solve the problem of missing data packets. Also, faster modems lower transmission time to remote users. A major upgrade route is incorporating faster NICs, such as 4/16 Mbps NICs and 32-bit and EISA-based NICs when upgrading a token ring network, which can improve network performance.
- *Using faster peripherals.* Moving from an 8ppm laser printer attached to a printer server to a 20ppm workgroup printer that is directly attached to the network and possesses a large RAM capacity, can reduce or eliminate printing-related bottlenecks.
- *Replacing faulty devices.* Poor connectors and badly shielded cables can also result in the deterioration of network performance. Their replacement or repair will produce significant performance improvements.

Network bottlenecks can be detected using a variety of software/hardware diagnostic tools available from many vendors. Even with diagnostic tools, it is best to experiment with various combinations of the above remedies before deciding on the appropriate tuning strategy for the network. As enterprise networks are more fine grained than centralized mainframe configurations (that is, with smaller components), there is usually more flexibility in the range of tuning options (shown in Figure 10.3) available to the LAN administrator.

10.2   LAN Vendors and Sources

LAN hardware and software can be purchased from a large number of firms. The key LAN component is the **network operating system (NOS).** The NOS manages data transmission between network nodes and provides the necessary command sets for users to perform file transfers, messaging, and other network-related functions. As indicated in the previous chapter, LANs may be installed and maintained by in-house personnel (end users or system personnel), value-added resellers of networking technology, or

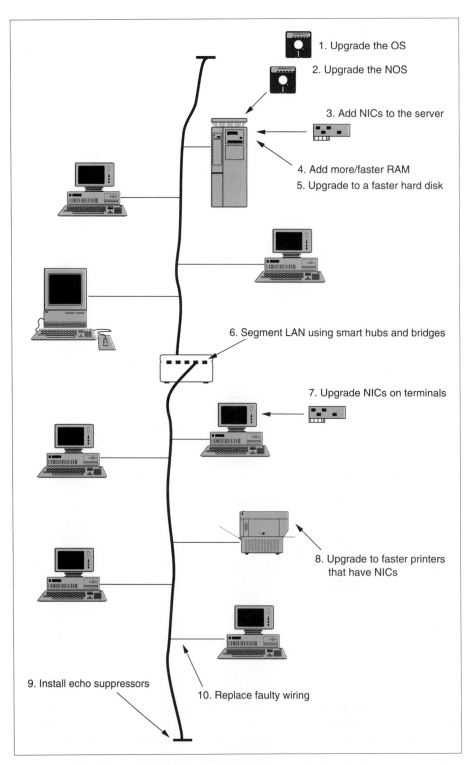

FIGURE 10.3 Network tuning options

third-party external consultants. Regarding the purchase of the NOS, there is a small number of major vendors in both the centralized and peer-to-peer categories, the most significant of which is Novell Inc. In this section, we examine the major networking firms and their products, the sources of LAN development, and *outsourcing*— an increasingly popular method for LAN maintenance.

LAN Vendor Overview

Many hardware and software vendors provide the technology required to create LANs. There are a large number of third-party vendors of equipment such as routers, bridges, and NICs. This section highlights NOS vendors, as the NOS is the key component of every LAN (see Table 10.2). While nearly every hardware component can be easily sourced from multiple vendors, company-specific NOSs manage all aspects of a network's operation.

The leading NOS vendor is *Novell Inc.,* with its **Netware** products representing over 60 percent of NOSs sold. Other major vendors are *Banyan Systems Inc.,* creditors of **Banyan VINES;** *Microsoft,* with **OS/2 LAN Manager;** and *Apple Computer,* who markets **AppleTalk.** A more recent alternative is Microsoft's Windows NT OS, with powerful networking features. These NOSs are all server based, in contrast to peer-to-peer alternatives, such as *Artisoft's* **Lantastic** and *Novell's* **Netware Lite.**

Novell, Inc. is the leader of the NOS vendors in market share and has the most applications written for its NOS products. Its five NOSs are *Netware Version 4, Netware Version 3.12, Netware SFT III, Netware Version 2.2,* and *Netware Lite.*

- *Netware Version 4.* Novell's top-of-the-line NOS is not primarily intended for departmental LANs, as are its other offerings, but for WANs. It has all the features of Version 3.12 (see below) but is designed to interconnect large networks and internetworks of over 1,024 users using a new network directing system.

TABLE 10.2   NOS vendors and systems

Vendor	System	Server Requires	Topology	Transmission Speed (Mbps)	Maximum Users
Novell	Netware Version 4.0	Centralized	Ring/bus	4/10/16/100	1,024/server
	Netware SFT	Centralized	Ring/bus	4/10/10/100	250/server
	Netware Version 3.12	Centralized	Ring/bus	4/10/16/100	250/server
	Netware Version 2.2	Centralized	Ring/bus	4/10/16/100	100/server
	Netware Lite	Peer to peer	Ring/bus	4/10/16/100	100/server
Banyan	Vines	Centralized	Ring/bus	4/10/16/100	Unlimited
Microsoft	OS/2 LAN Manager	Centralized	Ring/bus	4/10/16/100	992
AppleTalk	Local Talk	Peer to peer	Daisy-chain	230 Kbps	Up to 256
	Ether Talk	Centralized	Bus	10/100 Mbps	Up to 256
	Token Talk	Centralized	Ring	4/16 Mbps	More than 256
Artisoft	Lantastic	Peer to peer	Ring, bus, daisy-chain	2–10 Mbps	300/server

- *Netware Version 3.12.* This NOS is intended for use on servers that are minimally 386-based machines. It is centralized, requiring a *dedicated server,* and supports ring (token ring), bus (ethernet), and star (ARCNet) topologies. The server must run Netware 3.12, while clients may be DOS, Windows, UNIX, OS/2, or Macintosh machines. *Protocols* supported include TCP/IP, Novell's proprietary IPX/SPX, and Netbios. For network management, it supports SNMP and IBM's mainframe-based Netview network management protocols. It is intended for use in large networks of up to 250 users and allows print servers to be set up, as well as providing extensive network security features and chargeback facilities.
- *Netware SFT (system fault tolerance) III.* Netware SFT III is a variant of Netware v.3.12 designed specifically for mission-critical LAN applications. It supports such additional capabilities as redundant disk subsystems (disk mirroring and duplexing), handling disk defects transparently, and automatically reestablishing connections with nodes after a power failure at the server.
- *Netware Version 2.2.* This NOS supports 286-based servers. It requires a dedicated server and supports the same topologies as v.3.12—for example, ring (token ring), bus (ethernet), and star (ARCNet). The server runs the NOS, while clients may be DOS, Windows, or Mac OS machines. Protocols supported include TCP/IP, IPX/SPX, and Netbios. SNMP and Netview are also provided. Netware v.2.2 manages smaller networks—up to a maximum of 100 users—allows print server designation, and provides only marginally less network security than v.3.12.
- *Netware Lite.* Netware Lite is a very different product intended for use in small, peer-to-peer networks. Resources may be shared among all workstations, and both ring (token ring) and bus (ethernet) topologies are supported. Each workstation holds a portion of the NOS (37 Kb), which is much smaller than the memory required by the server version of 3.12 (over 4 Mb). Stations may be DOS, Windows, or Mac OS machines. Included protocols are IPX/SPX and Netbios. Netware Lite manages smaller networks than even v.2.2, and allows machines to be designated as servers. Security features exist, but they are less sophisticated than the other versions.

Microsoft's **LAN Manager** is another major LAN NOS (with 5 to 10 percent of market share) intended for use on 386 servers and above running OS/2. Servers are dedicated, and clients may be DOS-, Windows-, OS/2-, or Macintosh OS-based machines. LAN Manager supports Netbios, TCP/IP, AppleTalk, and (mainframe-based) LU 6.2 protocols, as well as SNMP and Netview. LAN Manager is a full-strength NOS intended for use in large networks and provides sophisticated network security features.

Banyan Vines *(Banyan Systems Inc.)* is a UNIX-based NOS primarily targeted at large corporations. It is used for both large LANs and WANs, with 486-based machines recommended as minimum servers. Banyan VINES supports both ring and bus network topologies, with its protocols including Netbios, TCP/IP, LU 6.2 (an IBM mainframe protocol), and AppleTalk. It is used for large networks and internetworks and supports sophisticated security and data encryption. Clients on Banyan VINES networks can be DOS, Windows, OS/2, and Mac OS machines.

AppleTalk is the NOS used on *Apple Inc.'s* microcomputers and supports three main topologies:

- *LocalTalk:* A peer-to-peer daisy-chained topology with a 230 Kbps transmission speed

- *EtherTalk:* A bus-based ethernet topology (10 Mbps)
- *TokenTalk:* A token ring topology (4/16 Mbps)

No additional hardware is required to use LocalTalk, as every Apple microcomputer comes equipped with a LocalTalk port. The LocalTalk peer-to-peer configuration is suitable for low-volume data transfers, but third-party cards are available for creating EtherTalk- and TokenTalk-based LANs for high-volume data transmission. The latter two use server-based topologies and can be interconnected with PC-based LANs and larger enterprise networks. Supported clients are Macintoshes running either Apple's OS or Apple's version of UNIX, A/UX.

Artisoft's **Lantastic** is the leader of peer-to-peer NOSs. It is used with PC-compatibles ranging from XTs to Pentiums and enables resources to be shared among DOS-based machines in a low-cost LAN configuration. Bus and star topologies are supported by Lantastic at different transmission rates, ranging from 2 Mbps to 10 Mbps. A zero-slot configuration offered by Lantastic also enables data transmission at serial and parallel port transfer rates. Servers may be dynamically designated on the network and extensive security features are provided.

Outsourcing LANs

Developing and maintaining a LAN or enterprise network can be a complex task requiring significant technical expertise. Developers require knowledge of the various topologies, protocols, and communications devices and must understand the capabilities of the diverse computers in the firm, as well as LAN–mainframe and LAN–WAN links. Many firms have outsourced some of the responsibilities for their networked systems as a more effective means of managing them. **Outsourcing** involves delegating some or all of the development and maintenance activities of the information system to an external firm for a fee. Between the two extremes of in-house support and outsourcing there are several intermediate levels. Activities that may be outsourced include

- *Systems analysis.* In this case, the external firm is responsible for investigating and determining information system requirements.
- *Evaluation.* The third-party firm might have the responsibility for evaluating alternative network solutions to satisfy determined requirements, which will include topologies, devices, protocols, procedures, systems, and so on.
- *System design.* The design of the computer network might again be the responsibility of the contracted firm.
- *Implementation.* This includes coding required for the network, user training, purchasing the required equipment, and equipment installation.
- *Maintenance.* This is the largest category of outsourced services. It includes preventive maintenance, network troubleshooting, repairing and restoring downed systems, and upgrading existing networked systems.

Firms that outsource any of these services expect certain benefits. A major motivation behind outsourcing is to relieve the firm from IS-related tasks in order to concentrate on their core businesses, such as retailing, farming, manufacturing, and so on. A related expectation is cost savings from the efficiencies of the service providers, who have greater technical expertise. Outsourcing might also result from a firm's constraints, such as the lack of capital for acquiring necessary personnel, building space, equipment, or other resources for operating a networked system.

Firms can outsource their IS requirements to hundreds of firms that offer a variety of outsourcing services. The firms fall into four general categories.

1. *Network vendors.* These are vendors of networking hardware and software, such as *IBM, Novell Inc.,* and *Banyan Systems Inc.*
2. *Value added resellers (VARs).* VARs do not manufacture networking equipment or software such as NOSs but sell systems and services to the consumer. Examples of such firms are *ComputerLand* and *Entre.*
3. *System integrators.* These include such systems firms as *Anderson Consulting, American Management Systems Inc., and Computer Science Corp.* System integrators typically offer a greater variety and depth of services than VARs.
4. *Maintenance providers.* This last category includes firms that focus almost exclusively on system maintenance and support services for microcomputer-based systems, firms such as *TRW,* who provide remote diagnosis and repair services, on-site visits by technicians, and rapid delivery of spare parts.

While outsourcing offers potential benefits, it involves transferring some control of the firm's IS resources to an external party. It must be carefully managed and coordinated with the firm's remaining IS personnel to avoid redundancy or conflict between them and external consultants. Service providers should also be carefully matched with the service being outsourced, experience- and technology-wise. One major feature of today's improved technology is the increasing ability to perform remote diagnosis and problem solving, enabling many problems to be handled by service providers over telephone lines or WANs.

Outsourcing should not mean a total withdrawal or disinterest in the IS function that has been outsourced. Instead, management participation, oversight, and involvement are essential to enable outsourcing to work most effectively. Many firms have senior personnel responsible for the outsourced functions who typically have a sound grasp of both the firm's business and networking technology.

Personnel Skills for In-House LAN Development

Firms that perform most or all of their network development and maintenance in-house require personnel with suitable skills. These skills overlap with those of VARs, system integrators, and maintenance providers, and to a lesser extent, hardware and software vendors. Even if these responsibilities are handled internally, most firms still take out insurance in the form of extended guarantees and service contracts for more intractable problems. In-house personnel require skills in (1) systems—mostly microcomputers and workstations; (2) communications devices, for example, hubs, bridges, routers, and so on; (3) software, including OSs, NOSs, network management software, and applications; and (4) systems development methodologies.

They also require experience of preventive maintenance, troubleshooting, and diagnosis and the replacement and repair of network components. Other important skills include knowledge of the firm's business—for example, retailing and manufacturing—

and interpersonal and communications skills. These personnel requirements are discussed in more detail in Chapter 14.

10.3   THE LAN ENVIRONMENT

As LANs become commonplace, there is increasing demand for data access to other computing resources within the firm. LAN users in a branch of a firm may require data from the firm's mainframe or another branch's LAN in a different city. In such cases, the use of a LAN to link both locations is impractical due to the distances involved and a **wide-area network** (WAN) must be used. A special type of WAN, called a packet distribution network or PDN, is widely used to connect remote computing systems. PDNs may be public, using the public switched network, or private, with fixed circuits leased or data capacity purchased from a value added retailer (VAR). For this reason, such networks are also referred to as value-added networks or VANs.

A characteristic of WANs is their relatively slow transmission speeds compared to LANs. However, in recent times, much attention has been paid to high-speed networks used in metropolitan areas, namely **metropolitan area networks (MANs)** and fast optical fiber-based technologies, such as synchronous optical networks.

The Need for External Data Links

Consider a rapidly growing clothing retailer with an increasing number of outlets being set up in a tristate area. Historically, the firm has utilized a dial-up capability (4,800 bps modems) to upload sales data and inventory reorders to the main office. As the number of stores and types of data have grown from sales data to personnel data (for example, payroll data), the dial-up method using modems now takes an inordinately long time, and connections are often noisy, requiring even more time to retransmit corrupted data. The systems manager considers the costs of excessive line times and delayed transactions (for example, inventory reorders) as significant problems with the present system. Following a cost/benefit analysis of wide-area networking alternatives (see Figure 10.4a), the systems manager finally decides to use **dedicated leased lines** (fixed connections from a VAR) to connect the stores that transmit the largest data amounts to the headquarters facility, primarily for their reliability. For the smaller stores, the manager decides to retain modems, while upgrading them to 14.4 Kbps data transmission rate (see Figure 10.4b). This saves the firm more than $700 a month in data transmission costs, and the upgrade is paid for in 7.1 months.

Dedicated leased lines are one wide-area networking option for firms seeking to interconnect dispersed facilities and computing resources. Most WANs are owned by companies such as *AT&T, Tymnet,* and *Northern Telecom* and leased to user firms. They support a wide range of data transmission rates and must be carefully selected to suit the firm's needs.

Value-Added Networks (VANs)

Value-added networks (VANs) are a major vehicle for implementing WANs. They are also called **packet distribution networks (PDNs)** or **X.25 networks.** VANs were

CURRENT TRANSMISSION COSTS

Number of superstores	4
Daily volume per store (Mb)	2
Number of regular stores	20
Daily volume per store (Mb)	0.3
Aggregate data transmissions (Mb)	14
Aggregate using async transmission (bits)	146,800,640
Current transmission rates (bps)	4,800
Daily transmission time (minutes)	510
Monthly (20 days) trans. time (mins.)	10,194
Cost per minute	$0.10
Total monthly costs	***$1,019***

PROPOSED SYSTEM COSTS

Number of superstores	4
Daily volume per store (Mb)	2
Leased Lines for four superstores	***$258***
(100 miles * $0.53/mile * 4 stores)	
Number of regular stores	20
Daily volume per store (Mb)	0.3
Aggregate data transmissions (Mb)	6
Aggregate using async transmission (bits)	62,914,560
Current transmission Rates (bps)	40,000
Daily transmission time (minutes)	26
Monthly (20 days) trans. time (mins.)	524
Cost per minute	$0.10
monthly costs for other stores	$52
Total monthly costs	***$310***
Total monthly savings ($1,019–$310)	***$709***
Modem upgrade costs	$200
Number of new modems	25
Total modem upgrade cost	$5,000
Payback period for new equipment (months)	***7.1***

FIGURE 10.4   (a) data communications cost/benefit analysis at the clothing retailer.

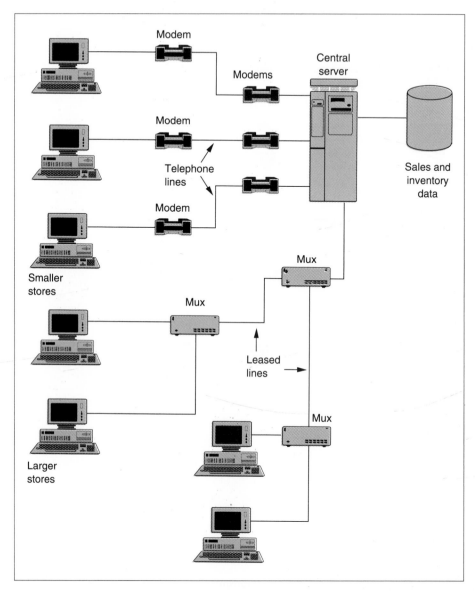

FIGURE 10.4   (b) New WAN configuration setup for the clothing retailer

developed by the Rand Corporation in 1964 and used to create the ARPANET network (now NSFNET) in 1967. They may be public, that is, offering capacity to the public by a VAN vendor (such as AT&T, ITT, MCI, and Western Union) or privately owned by a firm. VANs transmit messages in three ways: (1) as a switched line, where packets are transmitted over a fixed circuit for the duration of the exchange; (2) as a permanent leased line; and (3) using datagrams, where a message is broken up into equally sized data packets and each packet is independently transmitted over the network (see Figure

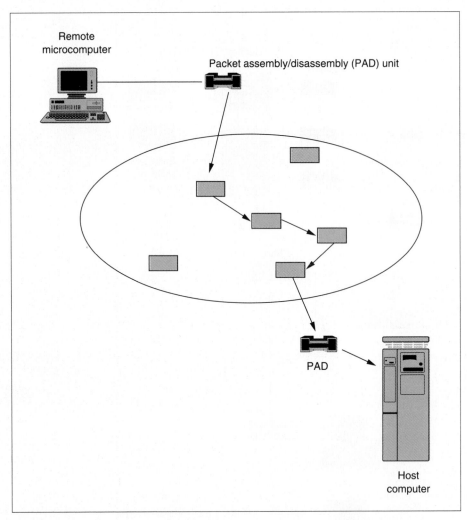

FIGURE 10.5   A packet distribution network (PDN)

10.5). Packets are checked at every node for errors before retransmission. Each packet may take an independent path to the ultimate destination, as shown in Figure 10.5, and at the destination, the packets are reassembled into the original message.

The service is termed *value-added* because the VAN vendor provides the packet transmission, routing, error checking, and other management functions. VAN users are usually billed according to the number of packets transmitted, making them more cost effective than dedicated leased lines, in many instances. A major problem with X.25 networks is their low data transmission rate (56 Kbps) in comparison to LAN speeds. X.25 networks are clearly superior to most modem transfer rates but can be a bottleneck when used to interconnect two distant LANs or in transmitting bitmaps or other bandwidth-intensive objects.

Other Wide-Area Networks

In the 1980s and 1990s, the number of WAN options has expanded rapidly, from modem-based and PDN options to faster data transmission alternatives. The major differences between WANs in general and LANs are:

- *The area covered.* This relates to local versus geographically remote connections (although some WAN connections may be used locally).
- *Transmission speed.* WAN transmission rates are a fraction of high-speed LAN data transfers, although this is changing (see Section 10.4).

The major WAN issue is providing faster speeds, which are necessary to cope with newer data types such as document bitmaps, graphics, digitized sounds, and high transaction volumes. Currently, firms involved in WAN selection have many technologies to choose from, including:

1. *High-speed modem connections.* Technology advances have increased modem data transmission rates to 115.2 Kbps on V.42bis modems. This involves using data compression over public switched circuits. This theoretical maximum is usually 30–60% less in practice.
2. *VANs (X.25 networks).* These were discussed in the previous section.
3. *Dedicated analog leased lines.* These are conditioned telephone-grade lines (often twisted-pair bundles) whose capacity is leased to businesses. The line's capacity is used exclusively by the firm, and various data capacities may be purchased. Examples are the T-1 to T-4 services offered by AT&T:
   - *T-1 lines.* These offer data transmission rates of 1.544 Mbps. **Fractional T-1** is a cheaper option for firms requiring smaller data transfers, and offers capacities in multiples of 64Kbps, up to T-1 capacity.
   - *T-2, T-3, and T-4 lines.* The three higher-capacity options offer data carrying rates of 6.3, 46, and 281 Mbps. They are expensive in comparison to leased analog and X.25 networks and are used only by the largest firms (T-2s are seldom used).
4. *Dedicated digital leased lines.* Digital services are offered by a number of vendors, including AT&T and Sprint, and will ultimately not require modems. While earlier data transmission rates were 64 Kbps, new digital technologies on optical fiber enable much higher transmission speeds (see ISDN and ATM in Section 10.4).
5. *Frame relay.* This is a fairly new *packet-switching* method that is significantly faster than X.25 data transmission, with speeds of up to 1 Mbps. It also uses digital rather than analog switches for data transmission (see Section 10.4 for more on frame relay).

Metropolitan Area Networks (MANs)

The IEEE 802.6 standards committee has been charged with developing standards for high-speed data networks for metropolitan areas. Emerging standards specify digital data transmissions of up to 155Mbps on optical fiber to transmit bitmapped images, voice, and full-motion video between multiple locations in a metropolitan area. These MANs will serve to interconnect a firm's geographically dispersed LANs using fiber-optic backbones.

A WAN Application: Electronic Data Interchange (EDI)

A new growing use for WANs is to implement **electronic data interchange (EDI)** between firms. EDI represents a means of rapid communication between trading firms, for example, organizations and their suppliers and commercial customers. Current methods of performing transactions such as reordering inventory items, making payments for goods supplied, and presenting purchase orders and invoices are made through the mail, by telephone, or by fax. EDI is increasingly being used to carry out these paper-based transactions electronically. Transaction data is generated by the firm's computer, and instead of being mailed is transmitted over a WAN to the trading partner's computers (see Figure 10.6).

The benefits of EDI include:

- Increased speed of transactions, such as inventory reorders and bill payment
- Improved accuracy of the transaction data, as data entry errors (for example, transcription and transposition errors) are reduced
- Cost reductions, as mail handling and postage costs are avoided
- A reduction in paperwork, printing, and stationery charges

The speed provided by EDI-based transactions is a powerful motivation for firms seeking to achieve trading efficiencies. One provider of EDI services, The Harper Group, uses EDI links to business customers and the U.S. Customs to carry out freight forwarding for these firms. In the case of one customer, Honda Motor Company, electronic data is transferred from Japan to Harper's computers using EDI, combined

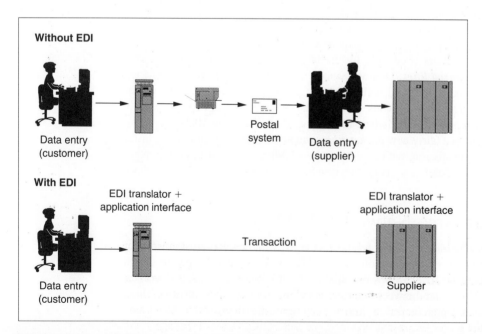

FIGURE 10.6   Linking customer to supplier using EDI

with the necessary importation data such as antidumping information, and transmitted electronically to U.S. Customs with the payment of import duties. Honda is then billed and makes payments electronically for Harper's services.

10.4 NEW WAN TECHNOLOGIES

The major objective of new WAN technologies is to achieve higher data transmission speeds between dispersed geographical locations, each possibly containing a local LAN. Such high-speed WANs close the gap between LAN transmission speeds and earlier WAN speeds and handle greater data volumes and objects. Two major trends are the adoption of fiber-optic cable as the medium for public switched networks by the providers of WAN services (for example, SPRINT and AT&T); and increased use of digital data transmission over these circuits, instead of analog transmission. The three major WAN technologies discussed here are *integrated services digital networks (ISDNs), frame relay,* and *asynchronous transfer mode (ATM).*

Integrated Services Digital Networks (ISDNs)

ISDN is a high-speed digital data communications service with an international flavor, as it is being implemented in Europe, Japan, and the U.S. ISDN is used to transmit multiple data types, such as data, voice, and graphics—all of which require considerable bandwidth. After a series of false starts, it is becoming more widespread, particularly in the United States, but some feel that it has already been superseded by the faster ATM. ISDN is protocol transparent, enabling it to be used to transfer data encoded using a variety of protocols (for example, IPX/SPX), and it provides data carrying capacity in multiples of 64 Kbps, up to 1.5 Mbps.

Moore Data's property imaging system illustrates one use of ISDN. Moore Data provides turnkey imaging systems for property sales to realtors and holds a central on-line database of photos and information about properties. Its customers access these photos and use them in selling the properties to private individuals. Prior to using ISDN, there were 2,400bps modem-based links between Moore Data and its customers, resulting in transfer times approaching 16 minutes for information that included color photos. Installing ISDN equipment at all its customer sites (and its own) enabled Moore Data to reduce transmission time to less than 3 minutes, saving time and money and improving its competitive advantage.

Frame Relay

Frame relay is a high-speed service provided by several communications vendors, such as AT&T and Cable and Wireless. It is similar to ISDN with regard to the intended data types. It is a packet-switched network, like X.25 WANs, but it offers superior performance to X.25 networks and is suitable for handling "bursty" data traffic common to LANs. It is becoming popular on leased lines, and vendors currently offer local frame relay circuits, called points of presence (POPs), for connecting various locations to the leased network.

Frame relay is faster than X.25 as it performs error checking only at sending and receiving nodes, not at intermediate nodes. This error checking is left to such network protocols as TCP/IP and not performed at lower layers, as in X.25 networks. On newer digital leased lines, error rates are much fewer, and corrupted packets are simply retransmitted. Data transfer rates on frame relay networks are in multiples of 64 Kbps, up to 2 Mbps. In fact, some organizations are using frame relay to replace their PBXs.

Asynchronous Transfer Mode (ATM) and Related Transmission Protocols

Most telephone providers have already replaced a significant portion of their circuits with optical fiber. Even as this happens, the need has grown for digital data transmission methods and protocols to handle high-bandwidth applications such as multimedia, distributed database replication, image scanning, and video conferencing. The most significant of the new protocols is known as **asynchronous transfer mode (ATM),** a network transport (layer) mechanism for use in both WANs and LANs. Most early deployment of ATM switches and controllers has initially occurred in LANs, although the reverse was expected.

ATM breaks up messages into 53-byte packets, (plus a 5-byte header), which are transmitted digitally on the communications medium (fiber or copper) over one or more routes, depending on whether the order of the packets is critical. It provides bandwidth in the range of 52 Mbps to 1.2 Gbps and beyond, offering LAN managers the opportunity to use common switches for high-speed LAN and WAN traffic. Many believe that ATM-based LANs will supersede FDDI and frame relay, which are now regarded only as interim solutions.

Synchronous optical networks (SONET) is a set of standards based on fixed point-to-point fiber connections between two locations. It provides an infrastructure for ATM-based services to operate on, with theoretical data transfer rates of up to 2.4 Gbps. One other standard being implemented by services providers is **switched multi-megabit digital services or SMDS.** This public service enables firms to have large switched (not point-to-point) volume data transfers without the use of multiple T-1s. For example, six regional stores might once have required six individual T-1 lines to the head office, but with SMDS only one each would be needed from the telephone provider to the main office and each regional store. Data traffic would be switched as required between locations. This service uses ATM as one vehicle for data delivery. See Figure 10.7 for ATM use for data transfers over a WAN.

10.5 ENTERPRISE COMPUTING: _____ THE ORGANIZATIONWIDE NETWORK _____

Enterprise computing marks a new phase in the transition from mainframe-based, centralized information systems to heterogeneous systems primarily based on

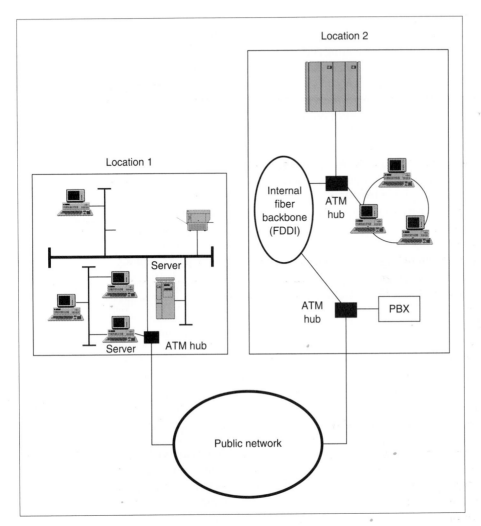

FIGURE 10.7   Use of **ATM** for **LAN** and **WAN** data traffic

microcomputers. Enterprise networks interconnect large and small computer platforms at all organizational levels and use distributed processing to take advantage of low-cost microcomputers. It is often associated with **downsizing** within the firms to obtain greater efficiencies in IS use and to improve managerial control.

An important concept in the enterprise computing framework is *client/server computing,* which utilizes distributed computing resources efficiently in satisfying processing requests at optimized server computers on the network. It represents a type of *cooperative processing,* where various computing roles and functions (for example, user interface, application front-end, and data manipulation) are shared across various computers. In this section, we examine the practice and benefits of IS downsizing, cooperative processing, and the client/server model.

Downsizing Organizations

One theme in the 1990s in many manufacturing and service sectors is to downsize firms in an effort to increase *efficiencies* and *competitiveness*. This has resulted in stripping away layers of management and increasing managerial spans of control. Enterprise computing helps to provide information required to support these managers' increased information needs. In the IS context specifically, downsizing has spearheaded a move to (largely) microcomputer-based networks.

The debate about whether mainframes will have a permanent place in the enterprise networks of the future (or even the present) continues, but as demonstrated in many instances, effective roles can still be found for mainframes in today's networks, as servers of vast repositories of information. Nevertheless, the price/performance exhibited by microprocessor-based systems allows the creation of enterprise systems that can handle the processing needs of large firms *without* a mainframe, and at greatly reduced costs. These costs cover support staffs, hardware, maintenance, and software—which, for mainframes, are very high. Consider the following examples:

- A manufacturer's system comprised a mainframe and several minicomputers in a distributed processing configuration. Faced with the vendor's intention to discontinue the minicomputer used by the firm, the decision was made to move to a Novell-based LAN system (with several interconnected LANs), while retaining the mainframe as a superserver.
- A large construction company with a mainframe, up to 25 minicomputers, and several hundred stand-alone microcomputers was similarly organized as a distributed system. In this case, the company decided to migrate entirely to multiple, interconnected LANs to support all of its processing activities. LAN interconnections were based on phone lines, linking far-flung parts of this decentralized organization.

In the first case, the mainframe computer was retained in the centralized firm due to concerns about the ability of microcomputers to support mission-critical applications. The firm used client/server software, which differs radically from terminal emulation software in functionality and independence of the user interface. In the second case, a distributed system matched the firm's structure and culture more closely but required rewriting applications previously located on the larger-scale systems. Both cases (and others in Chapter 11) illustrate alternative downsizing paths followed by organizations.

Cooperative Processing and the Client/Server Model

One of the key pieces of the enterprise network is cooperative processing, and its most prominent form is client/server computing. The Gartner Group defines **cooperative processing** as "two or more complementary programs interacting and executing concurrently on two or more machines as part of an overall business function, whereby each component exploits the operating characteristics of its respective platform." This form of processing is very different from *terminal emulation,* where powerful microcomputers utilize only a fraction of their processing power to emulate dumb mainframe terminals. In this case, intelligent terminals provide sophisticated user interfaces and perform some data manipulation in addition to interacting with server machines.

With traditional microcomputer file servers, data queries result in the transfer of the required files to the requesting terminal, where they are manipulated (for example, using PROJECT, JOIN, or other operators). This creates heavy network traffic, as whole files are transferred to the requester, and processing inefficiencies, since most requesting terminals do not have the processing power (CPU, disk speed, RAM) of larger servers. In client/server computing, clients' processing requests are performed by the server, which might be a mainframe, minicomputer, or microcomputer. Processing is carried out closest to the physical devices on which data is stored, and on machines optimized to perform high-speed database processing and computations. Such machines feature large disk caches, fast hard disks, RAID organization, and powerful processors. Only the results of processing are sent to the client by the server, which in the case of a database query, might mean 10 records versus 100,000 (see Figure 10.8).

Servers in a client/server configuration may provide *processing, printing, fax,* or *database (query) services,* although database querying is the most important and receives the most attention. The communication links discussed in Chapter 9 and in this chapter are in themselves insufficient for cooperative processing. Programs that enable interaction between clients and servers are the main challenge for software vendors and operate at the top layers of the OSI model to enable transparent calls for service from clients to servers. (See Box 10.1.)

A client/server configuration uses a front-end program on the client's workstation and a back-end program on the server. Messages are passed between these programs in the form of service requests and responses to these requests. SQL is the language of choice for database-oriented client/server applications, with SQL queries processed on the server.

Vendors of client/server products include Oracle, Gupta Technologies, and Sybase. Gupta's SQL Windows PC-based product enables developers to rapidly build graphical object-oriented client/server applications. Users may query the server's database and browse through (relational) tables on the server and obtain query responses much faster. In one firm, financial data is downloaded to the microcomputer server nightly, and users now receive responses from this server in a matter of minutes, instead of days, as it took on the mainframe. Microcomputer manufacturers also consciously market top-end systems as capable of fulfilling server roles for mission-critical applications.

SUMMARY _____

Enterprise computing is an important system development model for the 1990s. Its importance grows as LAN use reaches maturity and the need to interconnect computing resources in all parts and levels of the firm increases. LANs are now in daily use in many organizations for on-line transaction processing. Many of the requirements faced by developers of larger systems, such as reliability, throughput, transaction monitoring, and system recovery, are being addressed by both the vendors and users of these largely microcomputer-based systems.

Network software vendors such as Novell Inc., Microsoft, and Banyan Systems Inc. have produced increasingly sophisticated operating systems that incorporate features

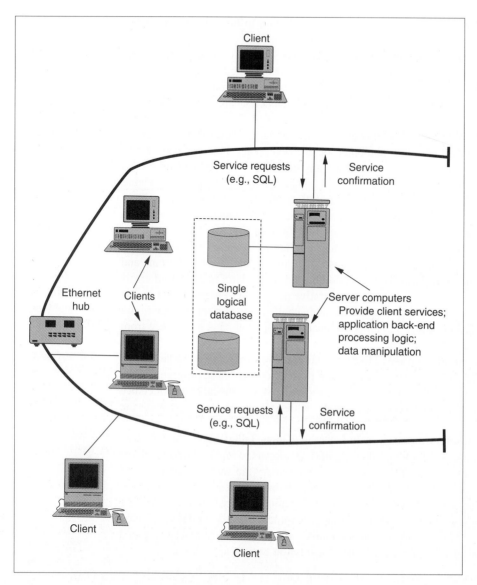

FIGURE 10.8 An advanced client/server configuration

once found only in mainframe OSs. Gupta, Oracle, and others have also incorporated features such as rollback of transactions and referential integrity into their DBMSs to enable transaction processing systems to competently handle mission-critical applications. A popular method of relieving the firm of the effort needed to handle increasingly complex enterprise networks is to *outsource* these networks to external firms, a process that must be carefully managed to be cost effective. Whether or not the organization outsources, new technical skills are required to manage enterprise networks.

GLUING TOGETHER HETEROGENOUS PLATFORMS WITH MIDDLEWARE

As client/server applications become widely deployed, a category of software called **middleware** is rapidly increasing in importance to system developers. Middleware comprises a software layer inserted between applications and the network to manage interactions between different applications on heterogeneous processing platforms. Middleware is crucial to relieve system developers from the need to write the code to enable disparate client/server systems to communicate. It is thus invaluable in downsizing and reengineering efforts. There are three broad classes of middleware marketed by several vendors.

Remote procedure calls (RPCs) are programs used to link closely interacting programs running on different platforms, such as workstations and PCs. They provide an appropriate avenue for running parts of a program on multiple processors, such as with a client using a computational or database server. Very fast network connections are necessary for RPCs to work, as they assume the called function is always available. While RPCs cut down development time, they can be complex to use, often requiring addressing and other data relating the called server. Hewlett Packard and Netwise are two vendors of RPC software running across PCs, Macintoshes and UNIX machines.

Message queuing software is a second type of middleware used to connect loosely-coupled applications on different platforms. They are simpler than RPCs, consisting of about four commands and several error conditions and using local or remote queues to store messages en route to destinations. Temporarily downed servers result in storing the message until it is restored. It is therefore best for such transaction processing as shipping and purchasing, where the transactions are not very time-critical. Vendors of message queuing software include Covia Technologies Inc., IBM, and PeerLogic Inc.

Lastly, **object request brokers (ORBs)** represent the most recent middleware type and are based on object-based programs running across a network. ORBs are invoked by object-oriented programs running on a client, which return objects from other networked computers (through their own ORBs). Using ORBs hides the complexity of accessing remote applications. Only the name of the object and several parameters are required to obtain the object from across the network. ORB vendors include DEC, Hewlett Packard, IBM, and Hyperdesk Corp.

The use of rapidly maturing middleware will enable easier and quicker system development as developers can be freed to focus on applications and not on their interaction. In fact, the market for middleware products is expected to grow from $50 million in 1993 to over $1.2 billion by the year 2000, reflecting its rapid adoption.

The need to interconnect LANs has led to the development of WANs, whose data transmission rates have usually been much slower than on privately owned and operated LANs. Older packet-switching X.25 networks and dedicated leased lines are now being replaced with new and faster digital transmission technologies such as the integrated services data network (ISDN), frame relay, and asynchronous transfer mode (ATM). While these WAN technologies are being implemented, it is envisaged that even higher multi-megabit WAN transmission will result from increased use of fiber-optic cable for WANs.

A recent occurrence is *downsizing* in organizations to reduce costs and increase efficiencies. The enterprise network has been used in a similar fashion to downsize the information processing resources in organizations, moving from mainframes to heterogeneous environments of mainly microcomputers and workstations. The *client/server computing model* is popular for implementing enterprise computing. In this model, *clients*—usually microcomputers—request services from servers (any computers) attached to the network. It provides a powerful model for *distributed, cooperative computing* in the firm that enables the use of less expensive microprocessor platforms. Client/server computing is now used for sophisticated mission-critical applications of large size.

REVIEW QUESTIONS

1. What is on-line transaction processing (OLTP)? Give two examples.
2. What are four potential benefits of moving from mainframe systems to LANs?
3. Discuss three concerns that IS managers have had in moving their OLTP to microcomputer-based LANs. Has anything happened to change these concerns?
4. Is it more efficient to lock records or files when using a multiuser database? Why?
5. What does it mean to roll back a transaction? Why are transactions rolled back?
6. What is the simple network management protocol and what is its importance to the network administrator?
7. Describe three types of network security measures. Which of these would be the most effective in preventing the tapping of the communications medium?
8. What is the importance of a user's network being Netware-compatible?
9. What is electronic data interchange? What are five of its potential benefits to organizations?
10. Discuss the potential benefits and risks of outsourcing network development and/or maintenance.
11. Compare the point-to-point leased line and X.25 packet-switching WAN implementations. In what situations would you recommend either?
12. Describe how client/server computing differs from traditional host-based processing and the use of file servers. What are its strengths in comparison with them?

EXERCISES

1. Explain to an information systems manager considering the purchase of a multiuser DBMS for the firm's microcomputer-based LAN why it is more appropriate, efficiency-wise, to purchase a DBMS that uses record locking instead of file locking.
2. A firm is making the transition from an older IBM 3081 mainframe to a LAN that uses several database servers. There will be about 90 networked users in the new system. Would you recommend using a more expensive DBMS with a rollback feature for mission-critical OLTP or simply use periodical tape backup? Why or why

not? How about if the applications supported were word processing, spreadsheets, and utilities?

3. What types of data are collected by SNMP-compliant devices on a LAN or internetwork? If the SNMP console indicates that a network is becoming saturated, in what ways can the problem be resolved?

4. Discuss the pros and cons of hot and cold replacement servers.

5. A LAN with a 33 Mhz 486 database server (4 Mb of RAM and 1 NIC) is suffering from degraded response time to requests from clients. The LAN currently uses Netware 2.11. Also, the applications are data intensive, using sales, customer, A/R, and A/P files. Discuss three tuning options you would use in increasing order of cost.

6. A company wishes to interconnect LANs in its two locations in different cities. The MIS manager does not want a dedicated leased line between the two locations but instead a high-speed switched WAN interconnection with data transmission rates of over 1 Mbps. What are the available options for the firm?

REFERENCES

Alter, S. *Information Systems: A Management Perspective.* Reading, MA: Addison-Wesley, 1992.

Datapro Reports on Computers, Volume 3. New York: McGraw-Hill, April 1991.

Datapro Workgroup Computing Series: Systems Software (OS/NOS/GUI), Volume 1, Number 1. New York: McGraw-Hill, July 1992.

Dix, J. "Users as Architects." *Network World Supplement,* January 27, 1992, pp. 7–8.

Eckerson, W. "Smack-Dab in the Middle," *Network World,* June 21, 1993, pp. 43–45.

Fox, J. "Introduction to Local Area Networks." *PC Today,* August 1990, pp. 14–24.

Fox, J. "Outsourcing Your Network." *PC Today,* March 1991, pp. 16–21.

Guglielmo, C. "Global Transport." *Corporate Computing,* June/July 1992, pp. 238–243.

ISDN: Digital Frontier. Corporate Computing, August, 1992, pp. 92–112.

Kerr, J. "One Last Chance for ISDN." *Datamation,* May 1, 1992, pp. 65–68.

Network World/Enterprise Technology Center Network Test Series. Network World, January 20, 1992, pp. 1, 43–45.

Ryan, B. "You've Been Framed." *Byte,* July 1991, p. 163.

Stamper, D.A. *Business Data Communications.* (3rd ed.) Redwood City, CA: Benjamin/Cummings, 1992.

Stang, D. "NOS' No-Fault Insurance Varies Widely." *Network World,* March 29, 1993, pp. 1, 48–51.

CHAPTER 11

NETWORK-BASED BUSINESS APPLICATIONS

INTRODUCTION

The cases discussed in Chapter 2 detailed the efforts of firms that deployed LANs to support the information requirements of small groups of users in mostly single locations. These applications are typical of the second phase of the microcomputer revolution. The four cases described in this chapter characterize the third phase of this revolution, in which groups of users in remote locations, each possibly with their own LANs or stand-alone machines, are interconnected in WANs using data communications hardware and software. In two cases in particular, the client/server model is used to distribute computer resources within the firm.

Case 11.1 discusses Rohm and Haas's transition from mainframe-based processing to the client/server computing model. The case offers some perspective on the personnel skills and managerial issues involved in making this transition. Case 11.2 takes a more detailed look at the technologies involved in client/server computing at UPS, where a large-scale IT effort has resulted in an effective enterprise network of heterogeneous computing resources. In Case 11.3, the Intermountain Health Care HMO case is outlined. At Intermountain, over 50 medical facilities have been internetworked using a combination of LAN and WAN technologies to lower long-distance communications costs, provide faster information to users, and reduce IS support costs. Finally, the Avon case (Case 11.4) describes the adoption of handheld terminals by the Avon sales force to directly enter orders for cosmetics. This form of portable computing, similar to UPS's use for parcel delivery, has helped Avon to improve the efficiency of the order-entry process and the productivity of its salesforce.

Learning Objectives

After reading this chapter, you will be able to:

- Understand practical issues involved in creating complex enterprise computing systems spanning remote locations.

- Identify how workflows and business activities can be made more efficient and effective using available computer and communications technologies.
- Express the importance and contribution of contemporary enterprise computing systems to a firm's competitive position.

CASE 11.1

ROHM AND HAAS: BUILDING SKILLS FOR THE NEW ERA OF CLIENT/SERVER COMPUTING

Chic Sailes is the manager of personal computing services at Rohm and Haas, the $3 billion company that makes Plexiglas and other chemical and related products. He describes his job as a "delicate balancing act." Rohm and Haas has over 1,000 personal computer users in its head office, equally divided between Apple Macintoshes and IBM-compatibles with MS-DOS and Windows. The growing availability of packaged software has made system development far easier, but the shifting of applications from mainframe computers to PCs is part of the company's adoption of a client/server architecture. "Moving to this new architecture will be a culture shock to both the technical staff and users. When you start changing the way of doing things that has been around for years, you can't just plug it in. You must demonstrate its worth and value to the organization."

The six-person help desk in Sailes's unit receives over 4,000 phone calls a month. To complement this overloaded service, Rohm and Haas buys products in bulk from a supplier that provides technical support and also draws on its own corporate computing group for evaluation of new products, including "connectivity products." The client/server architecture involves a joint project between his group and the mainframe development staff, a first for them both. Previously, Sailes's team was an autonomous service group with no systems development responsibility. It also did

not have to deal with issues other than local area networking.

Sailes joined Rohm and Haas as an accountant and was introduced to personal computers as a user. He moved to his new job in 1989 to challenge himself professionally. "The technology is changing so rapidly that it provides you with a tremendous opportunity to really make a difference in your organization." He feels his background is a major asset in his work. "I bring a slightly different perspective to the table, because I've been in the business community." He reads everything he can get his hands on in order to keep up to date about technology and products. At the same time, he sees it as essential to meet regularly with individuals and departments in his user community, to make sure he knows about their needs and concerns. "I'd rather be more involved with applying the technology to the business and handling analyses of how a business process can be improved through technology than in studying the nuts and bolts of the computer."

Sailes is representative of a new type of professional in the information services field. He did not rise through the ranks of either telecommunications or information systems personnel and lacks much of the technical background needed for meshing standard end-user computing on personal computers into a new companywide client/server platform. He has a level of knowledge

(continued)

CASE 11.1 *(continued)*

ROHM AND HAAS: BUILDING SKILLS FOR THE NEW ERA OF CLIENT/SERVER COMPUTING

that few people in either telecommunications or IS can easily build: business experience, hands-on experience as a user, and knowledge of a wide range of PC software, much of which has never existed in either of those communities. Examples are desktop publishing, multimedia, and software for graphics presen tations.

Client/server computing is a growing force in the information technology field.

Many companies report difficulties in finding good people, retraining technical staff, and even deciding exactly what skills and jobs are required to plan and implement it. Sailes represents part of the skill base.

Source: P. Keen and M. Cummins, *Networks in Action.* Belmont, CA: Wadsworth, 1994.

Questions for Discussion

1. What are your opinions regarding the advantages and disadvantages of giving nontechnical people responsibility for IS groups such as personal computing? What, in particular, are the strengths that Sailes brings to his management of personal computing at Rohm and Haas?
2. Why do you think Sailes describes his job as a "delicate balancing act"? Are the obstacles that he might have faced in moving to a LAN-based system purely technical?
3. Sailes describes his group as working with the mainframe group for the first time. How do you think responsibilities in this project should be divided between both groups?

CASE 11.2

UNITED PARCEL SERVICE: IMPROVING PARCEL DELIVERY USING CLIENT/SERVER TECHNOLOGY

In 1907, two Seattle teenagers, Jim Casey and Claude Ryan, hopped on their bicycles and began delivering telephone messages and small parcels for local department stores. From these humble beginnings, the company they founded, United Parcel Service of America, Inc., would pedal its way to the very top of the delivery business, offering service that was both relatively inexpensive and relatively quick. UPS was able to ride its formula to market success for more than 50 years. Then, in 1973, a new company called Federal Express Corp. arrived on the scene and rewrote the rules of the game. By offering air delivery that emphasized fast service rather than price, Memphis, Tennessee-based FedEx carved out a unique niche as the first overnight service in the small package business. For Atlanta-based UPS, competing on price would no longer do. Customers quickly came to demand reliable, overnight service.

"This business is based on time," says Richard Murray, a principal of Boston-based IS consultancy Nolan, Norton & Co. "Federal Express has been able to charge a premium because it guarantees next-day delivery by 10:30 A.M. Slower in delivery, privately held UPS was slow to respond to the business challenge. It didn't launch domestic overnight air service until 1982, nearly a decade after FedEx. And even though FedEx had introduced real-time tracking and tracing in 1980, UPS didn't even begin to automate until 1986. But what a difference a few years can make. Since 1986, UPS has built a leading-edge IS shop. To fully appreciate the change, consider that in 1984, UPS's total investment in computer technology was $42 million; between 1986 and 1991, UPS increased its information technology (IT)

spending nearly tenfold, buying hardware and software worth $1.5 billion, or an average of $300 million a year. In the five years ending in 1996, UPS expects it will spend another $3.2 billion on IT. "We set up a whole new architecture," recalls Rino Bergonzi, UPS's vice president of IS. "We had no infrastructure, so we were able to back away and start from scratch."

UPS's IS group, led by senior vice president of IS Frank Erbrick, is not just throwing money around for its own sake—it has greatly expanded the company's capacity. *In 1992*, UPS delivered 2.9 billion parcels and documents generating a net income of $700 million on $15 billion in revenue. The company delivers 11.5 million packages a day, of which 750,000 are shipped by air. It has accumulated a fleet of 122,000 trucks and 162 airplanes and expanded its delivery routes to more than 500 airports in 180 countries, largely with the help of IT-backed systems.

In fact, UPS now credits its ability to maintain its position as a worldwide market leader (though FedEx continues to dominate the U.S. overnight business) to its massive information system overhaul. Before doing anything else, UPS had to overcome a corporate culture skeptical of automation. Over the years UPS had developed a series of finely tuned standard operating procedures. To save its delivery truck drivers precious minutes, for example, the company welded ignition keys to pinky rings the drivers wear so they never lose their keys. UPS also instructed them to climb aboard their trucks left foot first to avoid wasted steps. The procedures were so fine-tuned, in fact, that UPS often considered it

(continued)

United Parcel Service: Improving Parcel Delivery Using Client/Server Technology

impossible to produce greater efficiency with automation. But once the decision was made to bring information management up to competitors' standards, UPS drove ahead with vigor.

In 1986, it made what was considered a radical decision at the time: It moved from a mainframe-based system to client/server technology. Indeed, in 1986, UPS had one IBM 3083 mainframe in Paramus, New Jersey, and about 100 IS employees. Today, UPS owns 6 mainframes, 96 minicomputers, 77,400 handheld computers, and 39,500 PCs, 18,000 of them networked on 600 LANs. It has nearly 3,000 IS employees and a brand new $100 million data center in Mahwah, New Jersey, in addition to the data center in Paramus. UPS's 4.1 terabytes of disk storage hold delivery information on some 1 billion packages.

Giant Steps

UPS's charge into IT investment is helping the company get a jump on its competitors. In the first six months of 1989, UPS turned a profit of $356 million after taxes, earning more than any of its top rivals. During the same period, FedEx reported a $2 million loss, and Airborne Freight Corp. showed profits of just $12 million.

In addition, UPS last year introduced several innovative products for large customers that are made possible by IT, including Maxitrac, which gives customers on-line access to UPS's delivery information, and Maxiship, which automates customers' shipping departments. UPS also plans to raise itself to technological parity with FedEx by finally launching a realtime tracking system. UPS also began an IT-supported logistics service that helps solve customer

shipping problems. For example, UPS picks up electronics components from customer plants and drops them off in a single, consolidated shipment at one delivery point. Customers have also asked for the flexibility to reroute packages already in transit, but ''we're not clear on how we're going to do that yet,'' says Erbrick.

''Customers are getting more sophisticated,'' notes Joseph Pyne, UPS vice president and ground marketing manager. ''In the past, they would pick the mode of transportation. Now, they don't care how a package gets there. They just want it there when they want it.'' UPS fully intends to take information-based shipping to the next level. ''By the turn of the century,'' explains Erbrick, ''transportation companies will really be logistics companies.''

UPS has made some strides in that direction. In 1991, it launched Inventory Express, which warehouses customers' products and then ships them overnight to any destination the customer requests. Customers using the service can transmit electronic shipping orders to UPS by 1 A.M. for delivery by 10.30 that same morning. UPS won't name names but it maintains that several dozen customers have signed up for Inventory Express, including a medical equipment manufacturer and a credit card company. The UPS Information Systems group is particularly proud of its new real-time tracking. When the system goes on-line early next year, customers will be able to access up-to-the-minute delivery and billing information.

Using handheld computers, drivers will instantly transmit pickup and delivery information, including customers' signatures, using a cellular network that connects to UPS's

(continued)

UNITED PARCEL SERVICE: IMPROVING PARCEL DELIVERY USING CLIENT/SERVER TECHNOLOGY

fiber-optic X.25 packet-switching network. The drivers' computers attach to a new combination cellular modem/telephone from Motorola Inc. that automatically dials the closest of some 44 cellular carriers nationwide. The high-speed X.25 network, called UPSNet, links 1,308 distribution sites worldwide through 40 switches. Nonetheless, UPS still has additional work to do. FedEx continues to dominate the $14.5 billion express package business in the United States with a 34 percent share of revenue. UPS ranks second with 22 percent of revenue. The next closest rival is Airborne, which has 8 percent of the market, according to the Colography Group, a research and consulting group in Marietta, Georgia. See Figure 11.1 for UPS's system.

UPS is also chasing FedEx in the area of logistics management. FedEx launched its logistics service in 1988 and boasts some high-profile clients. In a deal last spring, for instance, Federal Express Europe Inc. won a ten-year, $260 million outsourcing contract from London-based designer Laura Ashley Plc. for a merchandise and warehouse tracking system (*Information Week*, March 23, 1992, p. 12). The IS group at UPS has been intimately involved with the drive to forge a global logistics business. When UPS began overseas expansion in 1976, particularly in Europe and the Pacific Rim, so did IS.

To expedite import clearance of international shipments, UPS transmits documentation on each shipment over its X.25 network to the UPS facility at the destination before the packages actually arrive. The shipping information is forwarded to customs officials, who clear the shipment or flag it down for inspection. UPS sends electronic shipment information directly to customs officials in the United States and Canada.

Partly because of its advanced systems, UPS has been much more successful in Europe than FedEx, which scaled back its operations there recently, citing a $113 million loss for the prior fiscal year. FedEx now offers transcontinental service between the United States and Europe from its hub in Brussels. It also has an agreement with Australia-based TNT Ltd. to distribute packages on its behalf from Brussels to ten European countries. FedEx, which had hoped to expand its own service within Europe, tried to build an internal infrastructure from the ground up; UPS, however, chose to grow through acquisitions.

Since entering the European market via Germany in 1976, UPS has acquired fifteen European package-delivery companies, including, in 1990, Belgium-based Seabourne European Express Parcels—a strategic coup because it gave UPS the governmental licenses necessary to offer cross-border service in Europe. Indeed, UPS employs more than 25,000 people in Europe and carries about 600,000 packages daily, generating annual revenue of $1.2 billion.

In the Pacific Rim, UPS offers service only from the region to other points on the globe. "The Pacific Rim is primarily an exporting region," says Gary Adams, UPS's customer service systems manager.

Excess Baggage

With its worldwide infrastructure in place, UPS is ready to compete in the increasingly competitive air freight market. "There is tremendous price competition because
(continued)

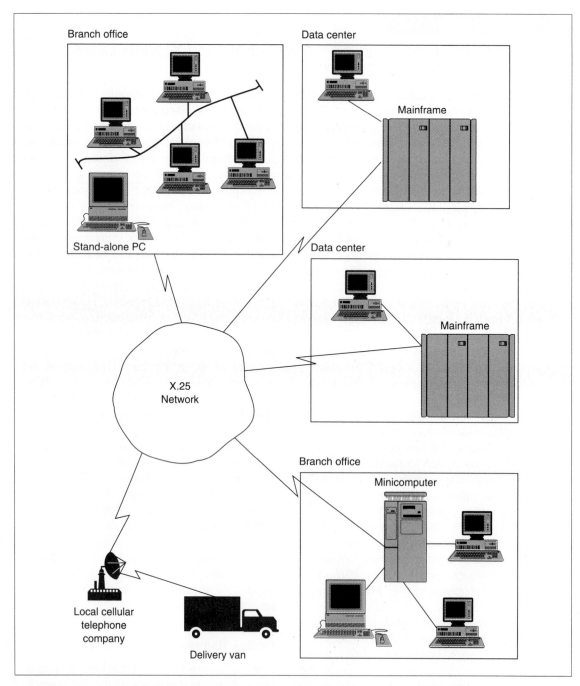

FIGURE 11.1 UPS's client/server computing configuration

CASE 11.2 *(continued)*

UNITED PARCEL SERVICE: IMPROVING PARCEL DELIVERY USING CLIENT/SERVER TECHNOLOGY

capacity is being added faster than the market can absorb it," says Theodore R. Scherck, president of the Colography Group. One new source of capacity is passenger airlines' updating their fleets with new, wide-body airplanes. These carriers are aggressively pursuing freight business: The cost of flying passenger planes is borne by travelers, so the airlines can charge less to fly packages than their cargo-carrying counterparts. Meanwhile, just as cargo ca pacity is increasing, shipment sizes are decreasing, primarily as a result of JIT (just-in-time) inventory methods, which depend on small, frequent shipments.

Where does that leave a shipper such as UPS? In the value-added logistics business. Manufacturers are now insisting on real-time tracking information and global coverage and "we're going beyond the shipping room," declares Erbrick.

"What any one of these companies is trying to do," explains Nolan Norton's Murray, "is to become a substitute for the internal logistics departments. They have to prove that they can do it faster and cheaper."

Source: Linda Wilson, "Stand and Deliver," *Information Week*, November 23, 1992, pp. 32–37.

Questions for Discussion

1. What are the major computing and data communications elements of UPS's WAN?
2. Why do you think UPS chose to create its own X.25 network instead of using dial-up transmission over the public network?
3. How has the client/server IS infrastructure UPS has invested in helped them to achieve competitive advantage in the parcel delivery business?
4. Discuss the significance of UPS's handheld computers. What abilities would they lose if these computers were not available?

CASE 11.3

INTERMOUNTAIN HEALTH CARE: USING A WAN AT A HEALTH CARE PROVIDER

With the cost of health care rising precipitously every year, health care providers have been casting around for ways to keep down costs without adversely affecting the quality of their services. Intermountain Health Care (IHC), an Atlanta-based nonprofit health care provider, managed to save more than a million dollars a year while improving service to its patients in Utah, Wyoming, and Idaho. Beginning in 1990, IHC has implemented wide- and local area network technologies to network almost 50 medical facilities.

IHC began designing an enterprisewide network in 1989, according to Blake Jensen, assistant vice president of information systems/telecommunications at IHC. "We were in the process of looking at how to make the health care environment within our service area more efficient," says Jensen. "With the cost of health care in the nation soaring, we were looking for ways to reduce costs and improve access." The company needed to integrate its hospitals more tightly as they were clustered in regional areas and tended to duplicate coverage. "The best possible way to facilitate the needs of the community is to not have those hospitals competing against each other," Jensen says. The company's solution was to assign specialties to specific facilities and keep them from overlapping. That created a need for enhanced communications among facilities. "Information flow becomes that much more critical," Jensen adds.

IHC's solution was to implement a T-1 backbone net to link all its major facilities. The company's T-1 backbone connects several hub facilities via AT&T Acculink T-1 nodes. The company uses the hub sites to reach smaller facilities, which can access the backbone

and other locations through their local hubs. The backbone supports LAN connectivity via bridges. The company has at least two host computers at each of the larger cities it serves, including the IBM Application System/400s and Tandem Computer, Inc., Data General Corp., and Prime Computer, Inc. systems. See Figure 11.2.

That setup saves the hospital system more than half a million dollars a year. "We're saving $600,000 in long-distance charges alone," Jensen says. "We've had to make long-distance calls between facilities as well as calls to communities outside those facilities. Those are all local calls now." Tying six platforms together without a consistent WAN was also costing the company about $600,000 a year, he adds.

In addition, the company needed to share information within each facility. A single LAN connects all of the equipment within a given site. The company has installed fiber-optic cable throughout its hospitals, although it is still using ethernet hubs. "We put the cable in with the idea of using FDDI in the future if we need to," Jensen explains. The central servers on the network—one per facility—are Intel Corp. 80486-based personal computers. The front-ends have no hard drives; they are attached instead to a large disk subsystem that can store 25G bytes of data.

By using servers attached to large disk subsystems, IHC has addressed one of the major bottlenecks in large LANs. "Speed has been a problem with the file server end," Jensen says. "You would submit a request and the disk drive simply wasn't fast enough to respond. The approach we took was *(continued)*

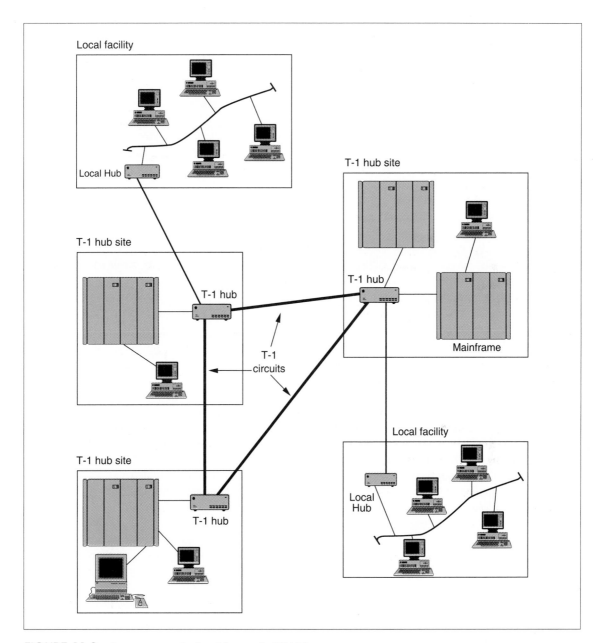

FIGURE 11.2   Intermountain health care's WAN

CASE 11.3 *(continued)*

INTERMOUNTAIN HEALTH CARE: USING A WAN AT A HEALTH CARE PROVIDER

reducing disk access as much as possible.'' Access on the LAN he says, ''is as good, if not better, than access to the C drive.'' This approach has helped. ''One of our hospitals has 600 attached PCs,'' Jensen says. ''Peak load is about 200 users, which is fortunate since that's about all the network can handle. We are starting to bump into barriers.''

Users usually get network access on a first-come, first-served basis, although the clinics are granted priority. IHC, nevertheless, prefers the single, large LAN rather than interconnected smaller ones. ''When you don't have to support a departmental LAN,

you don't have to interface to their LANs,'' Jensen says. ''In a lot of cases, that provided additional degradation of response.'' A single LAN also lowered overhead costs for the company. ''If you have multiple LANs in a hospital, you have multiple individuals doing support,'' he says. ''Our experience was there were some highly paid professionals or clinicians spending an inordinate amount of time doing backup and support. We drew that support back.''

Source: Jerry Lazar, ''Dialing for Health Care,'' *Network World*, November 23, 1992, p. 42.

Questions for Discussion

1. What factors at Intermountain Health Care (IHC) called for the internetworking of diverse computing resources?
2. Why do you think IHC chose the T-1 as the backbone between its different locations instead of ordinary leased lines or dial-up options?
3. At one of IHC's hospitals, the 600-user, single-server LAN is becoming saturated. Discuss the options available to the systems manager at IHC if more users must be added to the LAN.

CASE 11.4

AVON PRODUCTS: REMOTE ORDER ENTRY FOR COSMETIC SALES

The familiar doorbell-ringing Avon Products, Inc. representative is being brought into the 1990s. In addition to carrying sample cases of cosmetics, toiletries, and gift items, some sales representatives now carry handheld computer terminals. The portable order entry terminal (POET) eliminates virtually all paper from the ordering process. Sales representatives enter order data into the terminal and then use a standard RJ-11 telephone connection and AT&T's 800 services to dial into one of two AT&T conversant voice response units at Avon's Rye, New York, headquarters. For encouraging development of a system that combines both voice and data transmissions from remote users, as well as for placing state-of-the-art technology in the hands of a relatively low-technology workforce, Avon has been awarded honorable mention in Network World's User Excellence Awards. Sales representatives dialing into the company's network are greeted in voice mode by the conversant voice response units, which lead callers through several voice prompts and on-screen messages before cutting over to data mode and letting remote users upload orders. After the order data is sent, the system, in use since January 1992, switches back to voice mode to send error messages and to confirm the order. The voice response unit then uploads the data to Avon's host computer on-site.

Not all of Avon's 500,000 salespeople use POET. Its use has been limited to about 20,000—less than 5 percent of Avon's salespeople. The terminals, for which the reps pay a nominal monthly fee, are offered to top sellers, says Robert Hughes, manager of telecommunications at Avon. ''It's an incen-tive. They feel good about it because it represents a commitment. They feel more professional because it is a professional tool.'' See Figure 11.3 for Avon's system.

By giving the terminals only to the best salespeople, Avon is getting more productivity out of the top 4 percent of its sales force, an improvement that comes from the increased speed of order entry. Before POET, sales reps would prepare a paper-based purchase order on a booklet-length form, Hughes says. They would then mail the purchase order to their local Avon branch, where it would be scanned into the network and processed. POET eliminates the mailing entirely and allows sales representatives to sell for three to four days more in a two-week sales cycle, rather than stopping early to file the written orders. This translates into a 5 to 10 percent increase in sales, according to Hughes. Avon began developing the system's specifications in 1990, and they were provided to IBM and, later, AT&T. AT&T developed POET's telecommunications software within two to three months, says Steve Cafiero, AT&T's national account manager. ''Avon approached me, saying they had a project dubbed POET,'' he recalls. ''They needed a quick turnaround and an answer on what AT&T could provide.''

The hardware was not a problem, but it took some research and custom design to come up with software that would combine voice and data on the same call. The result was ''a real show piece,'' Cafiero says. POET was completed in November 1991 and put in to use two months later. Avon, however, owns owns the source code for the software,

(continued)

CASE 11.4 *(continued)*

Avon Products: Remote Order Entry for Cosmetic Sales

Cafiereo says somewhat regretfully. Avon is more than pleased with the results of the POET project, Hughes says. The system was designed modularly and can theoretically support any number of users. Avon intends to arm half of its sales force—250,000 users—

with the POET devices in the next two to three years.

Source: Jerry Lazar, ``Calling Avon,'' *Network World,* November 23, 1992, p. 44.

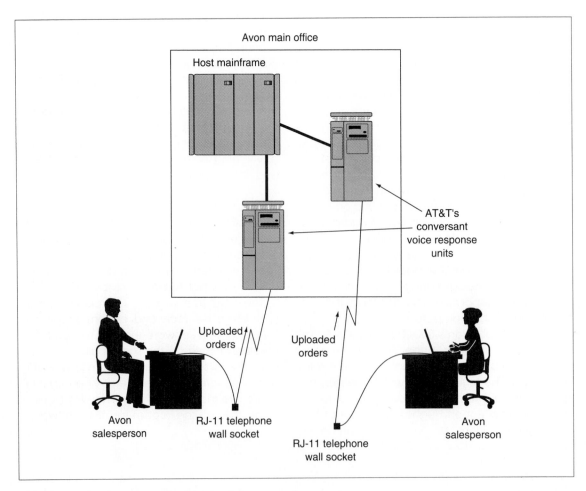

FIGURE 11.3   Remote order entry at Avon products

Questions for Discussion

1. The Avon case describes the use of handheld computers for remote order entry. What are the major components of Avon's computer and data communications systems?
2. Do you see any security risks associated with the Avon system? If so, how can they be minimized?
3. What are the advantages of cellular transmission over the dial-up option used by Avon's POET terminals?
4. How has the POET system improved productivity at Avon? Would you have begun system implementation with Avon's top salespeople (5 percent)? Why or why not?

ANALYSIS AND DESIGN OF MICROCOMPUTER SYSTEMS

INTRODUCTION

Similar to developing mainframe-based systems, developing microcomputer-based systems must be carefully planned and managed. It involves investigating system requirements and then developing, implementing, and maintaining a system over its life span. This process is called the *system development life cycle* (SDLC). Systems professionals use a variety of development methodologies and techniques to perform SDLC activities. *Structured methods,* in particular, are important in designing maintainable systems. *Phased development* is used to implement portions of a system over time, while *prototyping* is often used to obtain user feedback to a proposed information system. Also, project management techniques help monitor and manage the system's progress over time, with their emphasis on measurable system deliverables.

Following the initial request for an information system, systems developers investigate the request, examine the system's feasibility, and determine user information requirements. In the design stage, the system's developers specify how these requirements will be satisfied by a system comprising hardware, software, people, procedures, and data. User involvement throughout the SDLC is also necessary for creating successful and relevant system solutions.

Learning Objectives

After reading this chapter, you will be able to:

- Use the SDLC model as the basis for planning system development activities
- Apply user participation and prototyping techniques to improve understanding of user requirements

- Apply structured analysis and design methods to determine user information requirements and to specify appropriate information system design alternatives
- Understand the major differences of emphases between large-scale and microcomputer-based system development
- Make use of project management and estimation techniques to more effectively manage information system projects

12.1   THE SYSTEMS DEVELOPMENT LIFE CYCLE (SDLC)

The sequence of activities leading to the deployment of a computer-based information system is referred to as the **systems development life cycle** or **SDLC.** These activities have the objective of creating an information system (IS) to satisfy the information requirements of its users. Early IS development resembled a craft skill, with highly proficient individuals given a free rein and seemingly unlimited resources to develop and maintain systems, but the development process lacked methodological rigor and rarely incorporated project management techniques. Costly system failures eventually led to pressure for more effective project management.

In the 1970s, project management methods such as the Critical Path Method (CPM), project estimation techniques, and feasibility analyses became widely used. In the 1980s, *structured methods* made the greatest impact on system development approaches by adopting a top-down view of system development and a focus on progressively decomposing functions to lower levels of detail. They also emphasized system modularity and documentation. Systems developed using structured approaches were easier to develop and maintain. In the 1990s, computer-assisted systems engineering (CASE), joint application development (JAD), and rapid application development (RAD) are taking important roles in information system development. These methods are discussed here along with structured methods and project management techniques.

Features of an Information System

Information systems transform data into information to satisfy the user's information processing needs (see Figure 12.1). Example inputs to an IS include customer transactions and user queries, while outputs include reports, transaction logs, and error reports. The concept of a *system* is a central one: a set of interrelated components located within a given boundary that work together to achieve a specific purpose. *Computer-based information systems* have computers as central components that transform data inputs into information outputs. Examples include sales processing systems, marketing decision support systems, aircraft tracking systems, and expert systems for diagnosing equipment malfunctions.

Information systems have five components: *hardware, software, people, procedures,* and *data,* as shown in Figure 12.2. People perform procedures using data stored in the system and inputs from the system's environment. Outputs are also generated by these procedures alongside outputs of materials, products, and services. Software automates procedures and runs on computers to process data, as required by the user. Figure 12.2

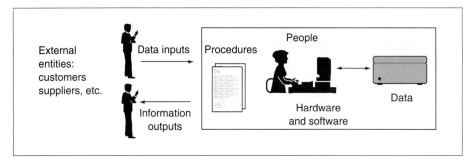

FIGURE 12.1   An information processing system

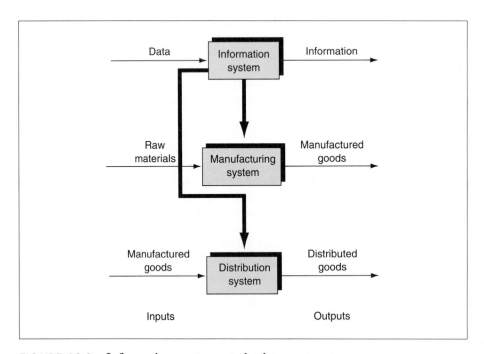

FIGURE 12.2   Information systems and other system types

illustrates that information systems are not the only systems in organizations but are intertwined with materials handling, manufacturing, distribution, and other organizational systems.

Information systems also comprise *formal* and *informal* components, and in designing effective systems, both of these components should be identified. For example, industrial slowdowns often involve workers working according to the "rulebook," which results in degraded performance as rules are followed down to the last detail. Interestingly enough, if the formal system was followed in normal times, the use of the rulebook would make no difference to productivity—the exact opposite of what happens during such slowdowns.

Four additional features of information and other systems are *boundaries, resources, constraints,* and *inertia.* **Boundaries** define the scope of the information system's components and are important in planning and managing the SDLC. In gradually phasing in a system, for example, all phases must be carefully defined and resources allocated to cover them. All five system components are **resources,** along with finances allocated to the project. **Constraints** on an information system are also important, and they include compatibility constraints (for example, operating system or hardware constraints), financial and skills constraints on system development and maintenance, and deadlines on system delivery. Finally, all systems possess **inertia,** or a built-in resistance to change. Anticipating and overcoming this inertia are important tasks for the system developer.

Defining the Systems Development Life Cycle (SDLC)

System development is initiated in one of two ways. Sadly, the most common motivation is often a *reactive motivation,* or developing a system to solve immediate, pressing problems. Consider a small mail order firm whose information system includes five networked 286-based machines (one acting as a file server) and that processes its sales, A/R, A/P, and inventory management transactions, plus managerial reports. As business expanded, response time by the firm's 386-based server slowed appreciably, all hard disk space was used up, and some serious bugs were found in the existing set of software programs. This resulted in expensive billing mistakes and lost business and customer goodwill. The firm's decision to begin work on another information system after a particularly poor sales period can be characterized as a reactive response to current problems.

Conversely, the *proactive motivation* involves system development based on future opportunities, for example, in the market, available technology, and legislation. For example, many firms began to downsize their mainframe- and minicomputer-based systems in advance of mature software tools needed to make client/server computing a reality. Initial small projects helped them to develop skills and the infrastructure needed to make use of cheaper computing platforms when improved tools were finally delivered.

However an information system is started, the SDLC is generally used as a road map of systems development activities by participants in the development process. Often, system development methodologies—specific implementations of the **systems development life cycle (SDLC)**—are used by systems analysts for guidance and to provide enterprisewide system development standards. Examples of these methodologies are the structured methodologies advanced by *Edward Yourdon and Tom De Marco* and *Chris Gane and Trish Sarson.*

The objectives of the SDLC are, first, to investigate and accurately capture user requirements. Thereafter models of the required IS are successively created using modeling tools, eventually resulting in an IS. Effective use of the modeling tools results in systems that satisfy both acceptance criteria and user requirements. The SDLC model and accompanying approaches are preferred alternatives to the ad hoc methods that preceded them. Using the SDLC model—the product of many years of collective systems development experience—makes better managed projects and higher-quality information systems more likely.

Stages of the SDLC

The SDLC begins and ends with the user in focus, and all the resources and technical sophistication of the system exist solely to meet the user's information processing needs. We can identify six stages of the SDLC.

- **System investigation.** This stage clarifies the request for an information system and involves an initial feasibility study for the proposed system.
- **Requirements determination.** If the initial proposed system is feasible, the full system requirements are determined through this process. A formal *steering committee* is set up to oversee the whole development process and a combination of methods is used to capture and document the system's requirements.
- **Evaluation of alternatives.** Every statement of requirements will have a set of broad alternative system solutions that represent appropriate solutions. Several of these alternatives are evaluated to select one for eventual development.
- **System design.** The design stage represents the transition from the user-focused front-end of the SDLC to the greater technical involvement required to create the system. System design results in a detailed specification of the computer-based elements (hardware, software, and database) of the system, together with accompanying user roles and procedures. See Figure 12.3.
- **System development.** Following the design stage, the system is built. A major part of this task is the design, coding, and testing of the system's software, and creation of the database structures and programs. In some instances, existing hardware is used while other situations require the purchase of new hardware.
- **System implementation.** The implementation process is important to the success of the information system and must be carefully planned. It involves facility preparation and installation of the new hardware and software in the workplace. Also included are the migration of files and databases to the new system and user training in new system procedures. Often a phased approach to implementation is used to reduce the risk associated with implementation.
- **System operation and maintenance.** Implemented systems are often used for years before the need to replace them with a new system arises. During this time, they must be maintained to fix flaws that were not detected in the development phase and to handle new user requirements. The effectiveness of the development stages directly determines how much maintenance effort will be required for any information system.

Additional aspects of the SDLC are its *iterative* and *overlapping* nature. Developers may return to prior stages of the life cycle if more details on some aspect of the system is needed or refinements are required for the current design. Generally, the later in the SDLC iteration occurs, the more expensive it is. This is a reason for the maxim: *Get It Right the First Time!*

As shown in Figure 12.4, the stages of the SDLC may overlap, especially in large projects characterized by large project teams. Parts of a system may be coded even while others are being designed, which often makes good scheduling sense and enables

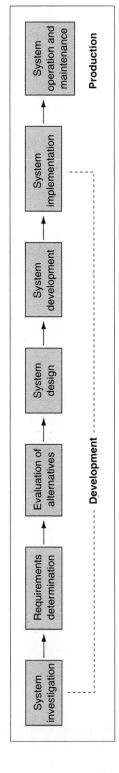

FIGURE 12.3 The systems development life cycle (SDLC)

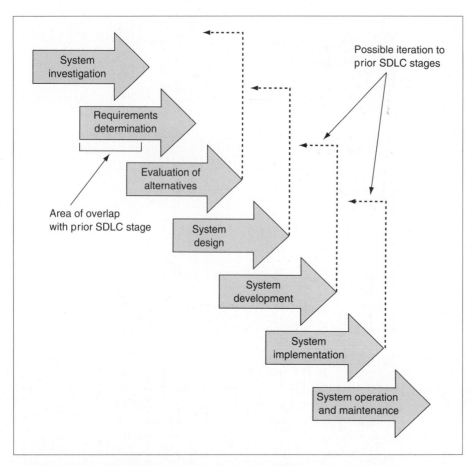

FIGURE 12.4 An overlapping and iterative SDLC

simultaneous use of different project participants, for example, end users, systems analysts, and programmers.

Variations on the SDLC—Phased Development and Prototyping

Two important variations on the SDLC are **phased development** and **prototyping.** Every information system has a limited amount of funds to devote to its development. Often the funds are not all available immediately but only over a period of time. In such cases, the system development must be divided into several sequentially implemented phases. For example, a firm might implement a new order processing system in multiple phases, beginning with order taking, inventory management, and accounts receivable modules. Later, accounts payable and purchase order modules may be implemented. Phased system development is also useful in demonstrating a project's feasibility and/or cost effectiveness at reduced risk to the organization.

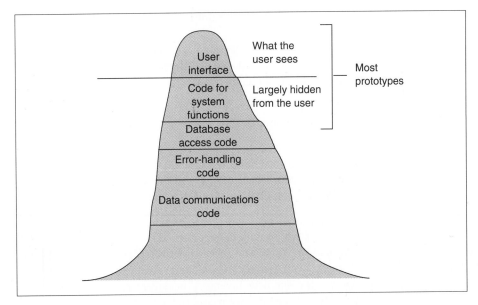

FIGURE 12.5   The iceberg model of an information system

Creating a system prototype may also help to reduce the risk and uncertainty surrounding an information system. A prototype is a working model of the proposed information system, which is developed to elicit user feedback and usually demonstrates some aspect of the system's use to its eventual users. The major objective of prototyping is to improve requirements determination and design through user reaction to the prototype. Prototyping efforts focus primarily on the user interface and not the underlying system functionality, as it is the main part of the system seen by users (Figure 12.5). Prototyping is frequently associated with *rapid application development (RAD) methods, CASE tools,* and the *joint application development (JAD) approach,* all of which aim for more accurate system specification and rapid system development. These are discussed in later sections.

Methods for Managing the Development Effort

Central to better-managed information systems development are methods for managing the SDLC. Project management tools such as the *critical path method* (CPM), *project evaluation and review technique (PERT),* and *Gantt charts* are routinely used, as well as estimation methods to gauge the effort required for system development.

The concepts of deliverables and milestones are fundamental to managing the SDLC. A **deliverable** is a tangible part of the information system that is the stated result of some system development activity. For example, an appropriate deliverable might be "Produce a fully coded and tested submodule for the accounts payable module." By keeping the focus of management on deliverables, managers avoid activities that have no outputs that contribute to the information system. The two allowable types of deliverables are:

- *System product deliverables.* These are operational parts of the information system, in particular, software programs and hardware components.
- *Process product deliverables.* These are important but nonoperational parts of the information system. Examples are system specifications produced at different stages of the SDLC, for example, the requirements determination and design specification reports.

Activities with no measurable outputs are discouraged in the planning process. Examples include

- "Work for twenty hours on the payments program module"
- "Interview prospective vendors of our new inventory management software"
- "Meet with the steering committee regarding the information system's design"

In the first case, working for twenty hours does not guarantee or even encourage meaningful progress. This could be recast as a system product deliverable: "Produce a fully coded and tested payments program module" (a system product deliverable). Likewise, the second instance might be restated: "Write up a comparative evaluation report for the products of prospective vendors for our new inventory management software" (a process product deliverable). Finally, the third statement could be reworded as: "Document the recommendations of the project's steering committee on the information system's design specifications" (a process product deliverable).

Milestones are dates on which deliverables will be delivered. Monitoring milestones is an effective way to determine actual progress of the SDLC and to determine whether the project is on schedule. Too few milestones make it difficult to accurately monitor the progress of the information system, while too many increase the administrative and management overhead required. A rule of thumb is about four milestones per individual every month. In Figure 12.6, we can contrast the use of several milestones versus a single milestone.

There are several reasons why multiple milestones are preferable to very few (or even one) milestones, as shown in Figure 12.6.

- Multiple milestones spread development effort over the duration of the SDLC and avoid a last-minute rush to complete the whole system shown in Figure 12.6b. This is usually characterized by work of a lower quality.
- As indicated earlier, it is easier to track system progress and stay informed of problems in the SDLC with more frequent milestones. As a result, corrective action may be taken earlier in the SDLC to bring the system development back on track.
- It is also easier to split up a project with many deliverables among a team consisting of several members. One large deliverable is harder to delegate, assign responsibility for, and manage.

Another important concept for the manager is the *noninterchangeability* of people and (development) months. An instinctive reaction to a late project is to delegate extra personnel to a task. As indicated by Frederick Brooks in his book, *The Mythical Man-Month,* this is often the worst course of action. Consider a four-person, four-month project (sixteen effort-months or EMs), which is one schedule-month late after two months of development. Even assuming the original estimate was correct, this leaves twelve EMs to be done in two months by four people.

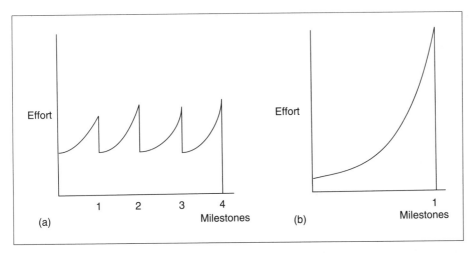

FIGURE 12.6   (a) An adequate number of milestones for an information
system project; (b) Too few milestones for an information
system project.

The decision to add two new team members may require two original members of
the team to train the new team members. This takes half a month, after which we
generously assume the new team members become fully productive. In the final month,
with six people, two members have worked for one month (two effort-months) and four
for one-half a month, resulting in a total of four EMs. In the final month, six people are
required to perform eight EMs (twelve minus four), still a difficult proposition.

To complicate matters further, there are productivity losses from *intercommunication*
and *management overhead,* which increases exponentially as team members increase.
There is also a practical limit at which subtasks may no longer be divided. In fact, as
shown in Figure 12.7, after a certain point, the addition of new team members only
increases the project completion time.

Managers utilize several methods for estimating time requirements for different
projects. None of these methods is perfect, leading some to the conclusion that no
estimates are preferable to inaccurate estimates. This is false. Though estimation
methods are imperfect, many are based on empirically derived formulas and experience
and can result in good estimates of project duration. Some approaches to estimating
project durations are:

- *The checklist approach.* This approach is appropriate for small projects. It involves
  adding the durations of all development activities, resulting in a total estimated
  duration. This estimation method benefits from prior experience of developing
  similar systems.
- *The three-times-programming rule.* The planner separates the program(s) into
  modules and then produces estimates for each module of the amount of time required
  to code them. If one assumes a 3GL is used, the total (coding) time for all the modules
  is multiplied by three to give an estimate of the time estimate for the SDLC (for
  example, a programming effort estimate of three months would translate into a

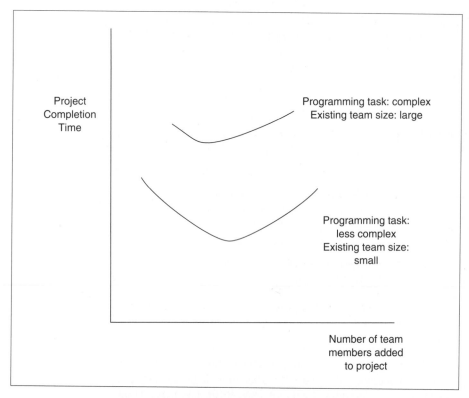

FIGURE 12.7   Programming tasks—project completion time increases as
team size increases

nine-month total development time). Using a 4GL would reduce only the
programming third of the estimate.

- **The lines of code model.** Several of these models were developed by Barry Boehm
  based on empirical studies of systems developed using 3GLs. One such model
  derives the number of effort-months required for system development using the
  formula

$$EM = 2.4 \ (KLC)^{1.05} \quad [KLC = \text{'000s of lines of tested code}]$$

For a project estimated to require 4,000 lines of tested code, the number of
effort-months required would be $2.4 \ (4)^{1.05}$, or 10.3 effort-months. Clearly, the major
requirement for using this lines of code model is programming experience, to
produce accurate estimates of the lines of code required for all modules of the
proposed system.

- **The function point model.** This model is more rigorous and sophisticated than the
  prior models and is especially useful in large projects. Generic input, output,
  interface functions, and so on are defined, with weights assigned to them based
  on their difficulty. For example, simple input and interface functions might rate
  three and five points each, while complex ones rate seven and ten points each,
  respectively.

Scoring every module based on its function and complexity produces a total function point (FP) score, which is used to derive the total effort-months required as follows:

$$EM = 0.036 * FP * PIF$$

PIF represents a composite project influencing factor score, a sum of scored factors associated with the total project, such as communications facilities, distributed processing requirements, and so on, which are individually scored between 0 and 5 (see Figure 12.8).

Step 1: Define the types of functions that will be created in the information system(s) being built. For each function, define its difficulty level (1–10) for simple to complex types.

	Weight				
Function	**Simple**	**Moderate**	**Average**	**Complex**	**Highly Complex**
Inputs	1	3	4	6	7
Outputs	2	4	5	6	8
Master Files	3	4	6	7	8
Inquiries	2	3	4	5	6
Interfaces	3	5	7	11	13

Step 2: Based on the number and type of functions to be coded, calculate the total number of function points contained in the system.

Function	**Difficulty**	**Level**	**Number**	**Complexity Weight**	**Function Points**
Inputs	Complex	1	1	6	6
Outputs	Moderate	3	3	4	12
Master Files	Moderate	4	10	4	40
Inquiries	Simple	2	3	2	6
Interfaces	Average	3	4	7	28
			Total Unadjusted Function Points (FP)		**92**

FIGURE 12.8   Using the function point model to estimate the required project effort (*continued*)

Step 3: Evaluate the number of project influencing factors (PIFs) involved in developing the system. This uses a scale ranging from 0 (little or no difficulty) to 5 (great difficulty).

Evaluation project influencing factors—PIFs (0 = little or no difficulty, 3 = average difficulty, 5 = great difficulty)

Communication facilities	0
Distributed processing	1
On-line processing	4
Data volumes and performance objectives	3
Complex processing logic	1
Multiple sites	4
Conversion difficulty	2
System flexibility	2
Total Project Influencing Factor Value (PIF)	**17**

Step 4: Calculate the total number of effort-months (EM) using the empirically derived formula **EM = 0.036 ∗ FP ∗ PIF.**

$$EM = 0.036 * 92 * 17 = 56.3 \text{ effort-months}$$

FIGURE 12.8 *(continued)*

After the tasks and subtasks constituting the SDLC have been defined and project estimates concluded, traditional project management models, such as CPM and Gantt charts, may be used to create a project schedule for the SDLC (see Figure 12.9).

12.2 SYSTEMS REQUIREMENTS DETERMINATION

The first set of activities in the SDLC are directed at improved understanding of the environment, participants, resources, and constraints associated with the needs the proposed information system will fulfill. Clarification of the problem and a feasibility assessment is followed by requirements determination. The evaluation of alternatives then ranks proposed solutions to the problem. The first two processes are discussed next, along with *joint application development* (JAD)—an approach for enhancing user participation in the SDLC stages.

The Initial Investigation

This is the first response to the request from end users or management for an information system. In this early stage, attempts are made to clarify the nature and scope of the requested system and to prioritize the requests received. The first ensures that the correct problem (or opportunity) is identified for development work. Prioritizing requests, on the other hand, reflects the limited resources available for system development. Participants in this stage include systems analysts, senior managers, and end users. One of their main concerns is that any proposed system advances the firm's strategic objectives and business plan.

A key part of the initial investigation is to conduct a series of **feasibility analyses** on the proposed system. These include *economic feasibility,* to determine whether the proposed system (only the broadest outline of which is currently known) will be both cost effective and affordable; *technical feasibility,* to ensure that the tools and technical expertise are obtainable or available within the organization to create the proposed information system; and *operational feasibility,* to determine whether the appropriate personnel skills are available to the firm for developing and supporting the system. The latter also focuses on whether the system can be developed within an appropriate time frame.

Determining Requirements

The determination of the systems requirements is possibly the most crucial stage in the SDLC, as subsequent system design and development will be based on the requirements specification. The requirements document is an output of this stage of the SDLC describing the *what* of the information system, that is, the functions it will be required to provide, as opposed to the *how,* or how these functions will be implemented in hardware, software, and so on. Three aspects of requirements determination are:

- Describing the form of the current system
- Defining problems with the current system
- Specifying the requirements of the proposed or new system

Not every problem requires an entirely new system. Some systems are evolutionary, requiring enhancements to the existing system while others represent a total replacement of the existing system's hardware and/or software. Whatever the degree of change, the intention of requirements determination is to obtain as accurate a picture of user requirements as possible.

Four major methods are used to obtain user requirements: *interviews, questionnaires, observation,* and *studying documentation.* They may be used singly or jointly in the traditional SDLC or together with the prototyping approach discussed earlier.

Activities	Duration (weeks)	Predecessor
1. Form project team	1	—
2. Perform initial investigation	1	(1)
3. Interview staff to determine requirements	2	(2)
4. Document requirements	2	(2)
5. Develop alternatives	1	(4)
6. Evaluate alternatives	1	(5)
7. Review selected alternatives	1	(6)
8. Specify screens and reports	2	(7)
9. Specify database models	4	(7)
10. Specify program structure	3	(9)
11. Design review	1	(10)
12. Complete system documentation	3	(10)
13. Code program modules	6	(11)
14. Build test files	2	(11)
15. Build procedure files	2	(11)
16. Test system	4	(13), (14), (15)
17. Test full procedure	6	(12), (16)
18. Management review	2	(17)

FIGURE 12.9   (a) Activities of a system development project (*continued*)

- *Interviews.* Interviews are nearly always employed, and they involve an interactive exchange between the system analyst and various users and managers involved with the information system. *End users, user managers, project sponsors, and members of related departments* are all potential interview candidates (see Figure 12.10).

    Interview questions must be carefully designed and may be either *qualitative,* that is, requiring opinions, or *quantitative,* requiring specifics of procedures, dates, numbers, and so on. In either case, their interactive nature allows immediate clarification of responses and allows them to be complemented by observation. Interviews may also occur in a group setting, but peer pressure and authority influences are potential hazards. As a requirements elicitation technique, interviews are relatively expensive to the firm—in lost productive time for interviewees—and for the analyst—in inter-

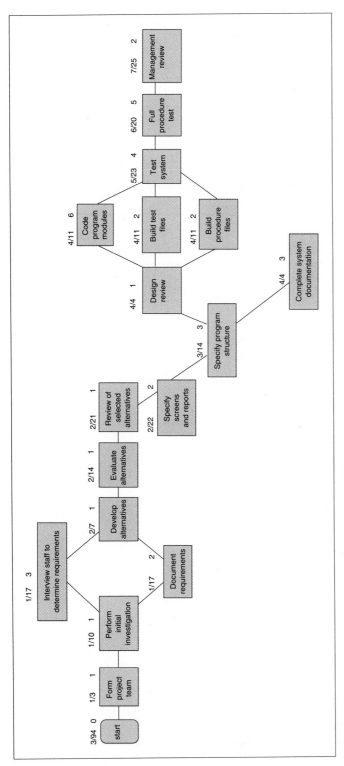

FIGURE 12.9 *(continued)*   (b) CPM network for loans management system project

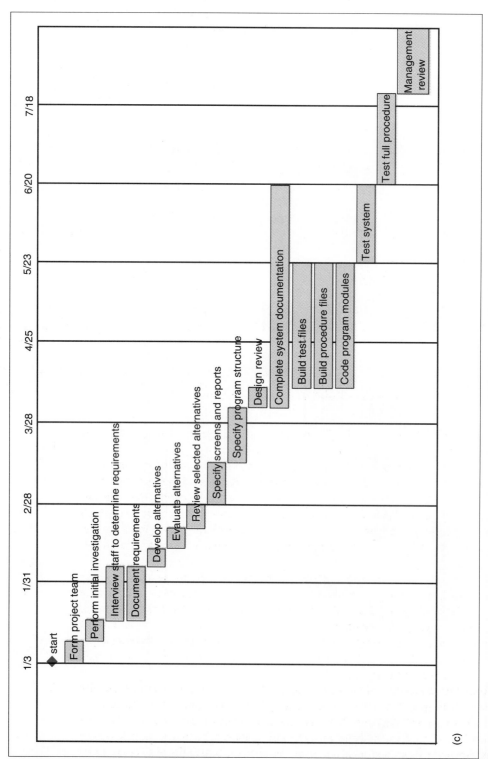

FIGURE 12.9 (*continued*) (c) Gantt chart for loans management system project

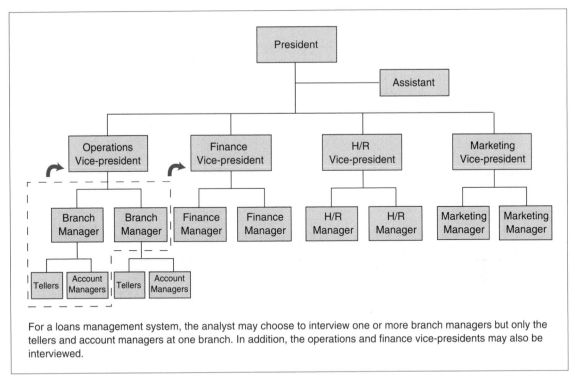

For a loans management system, the analyst may choose to interview one or more branch managers but only the tellers and account managers at one branch. In addition, the operations and finance vice-presidents may also be interviewed.

FIGURE 12.10   Potential interviewees on an organizational chart

view preparation and performance. Therefore, they are often supplemented by other methods.

- *Questionnaires.* Questionnaires are preferable to interviews if many responses must be collected and the cost of individual or group interviews is prohibitive. They require careful design and can be administered in a controlled setting, that is, under supervision at the workplace or by mail. The former method guarantees a very high response rate, while the latter generates response rates of 15–35 percent. Although it is inexpensive, questionnaire material cannot be clarified by either the questioner or respondent.

- *Observation.* In some instances, observation is desirable to develop a fuller understanding of a work flow or procedure. Observation requires investments of time and an understanding of the procedures and terminology studied and may also suffer from *poor sampling,* for example, a large variation from the norm on the day observation takes place. Possibly the greatest problem associated with observation is the Hawthorne effect, the phenomenon where workers alter their behavior if they know they are under observation.

- *Studying documentation.* Studying documentation is almost always used, especially in cases where specifications of the existing system's configuration, function, work flow, and so on are available. It is also the least expensive method of obtaining information, as the cost of collecting the information has already been borne by others. However, its second-hand nature leaves open the possibility of errors in initial data collection that may be difficult to correct.

Joint Application Development (JAD)

A major reason for system failures is lack of user participation in the SDLC. This often results in little or no *user internalization* of the system—it is perceived as "their" system, not "our" system—and may show up in active or passive user resistance to the new information system, an expensive and time-consuming condition to rectify. User participation is essential to obtaining the most accurate definition of the system's requirements. Users who work with the existing system have the greatest experience of it, which translates into the best understanding of its problems and requirements.

Joint application development (JAD) was developed by James Martin and Associates as a method for enhancing user involvement in system development. It uses as its enabling mechanism intensive **JAD sessions** in locations where outside distractions are eliminated. These meeting rooms do not have telephones, faxes, beepers, or any other links to the outside world. They are equipped with tools such as a *CASE station, white-boards, flip charts,* and an *overhead projector* to display various aspects of the system. Participants in JAD sessions include:

- **Users** from all the departments involved with the proposed system
- **Observers** from these departments
- **A facilitator,** who presides over the JAD session and mediates the interaction by its participants
- **A scribe,** who documents the proceedings of the JAD session

During JAD sessions, participants may not "pull rank" on subordinates. The sessions have an interactive nature as different users discuss problems and propose ideas. Models of the proposed information system in the form of *user interfaces, data flow diagrams (DFDs)* (see the next section), and *decision trees* are rapidly built using the **CASE station.** The facilitator must have excellent communication skills to elicit useful inputs from, mediate between, and facilitate interaction by JAD participants.

The aims of a JAD session vary, depending on the SDLC phase in which they are used. They may (1) define systems requirements, (2) select from among several system alternatives, or (3) sketch a broad conceptual design for the proposed system solution. Stated benefits of JAD are a reduction of the time required for the front-end activities of the SDLC and fewer communication problems between technical and nontechnical personnel.

12.3 STRUCTURED SYSTEMS ANALYSIS

Traditional system development methods used in the 1960s and 1970s resulted in a wide variety of information systems. Major managerial concerns arose regarding the number of system failures and systems delivered late. Often, delivered systems were poorly designed and hard to maintain. A backlog of applications often stretching back several years was one consequence of poorly designed systems. Another was the deployment of 60 to 80 percent of the average firm's IS resources on maintenance activities, with only 20 to 40 percent devoted to developing new systems. Of course, project planning methods helped to improve management of the SDLC. On the other hand, *structured methods* were directed at improving the developed system, resulting in easier-to-maintain delivered applications. They have been used with considerable success since the late 1970s and are now the predominant approach for system development.

What Are Structured Methods?

Structured methods are part of an approach within the SDLC for developing information systems that are well organized, better documented, and easy to develop. Such systems thus require less effort to maintain than those created using previous system development approaches. Central concepts to the structured approach are:

- *Top-down approach* to systems development
- *Functional decomposition* of higher-level system functions to lower-level ones
- *Stepwise refinement* of functions, that is, gradually increasing the precision and detail of decomposed functions
- Applying structured *tools and methods,* such as *data flow diagrams (DFDs), structure charts,* and structured database design and programming (Figure 12.11)
- Using small, relatively independent, and *loosely coupled modules* to construct systems
- An emphasis on *system documentation*
- Using *project management techniques,* with an emphasis on deliverables
- Applying the *SDLC model* to systems development

Modular systems developed using structured techniques consist of documented modules of limited size. Ten 50-line modules are significantly easier to code, understand, and maintain than a single 500-line program. Modules developed using the structured approach are also singular in purpose and very cohesive. Errors in a system can also be tracked down to single modules that can be more easily fixed. The ripple effect is familiar to experienced system developers in large nonmodular programs where a code fix causes other errors to ripple through the entire program. As part of an overall structured approach, structured methods produce savings in both the system development and maintenance phases of the SDLC. These methods are discussed next.

Data Flow Diagrams (DFDs)

As discussed earlier, the *requirements determination* stage of the SDLC employs such fact-finding techniques as interviewing and studying documentation relating to the current information system and user requirements. These fact-finding techniques are used to develop a model of information processing called a **data flow diagram (DFD),** a graphical model of the functioning of an information system. It employs a top-down approach to describe the data passing through a system, its sources and destinations, the processes that transform it, and places where the data are stored.

DFDs are created in the requirements determination stage following fact finding and serve as a reference point for subsequent programs, procedures, and data models created in the SDLC. A DFD uses just four symbols to create a map of an information system as it transforms the data flowing through it (see Figure 12.12).

- *External entities.* These are shown as squares, as in Figure 12.12a. An external entity is either a source of data that enters a process or a destination for a process's outputs.

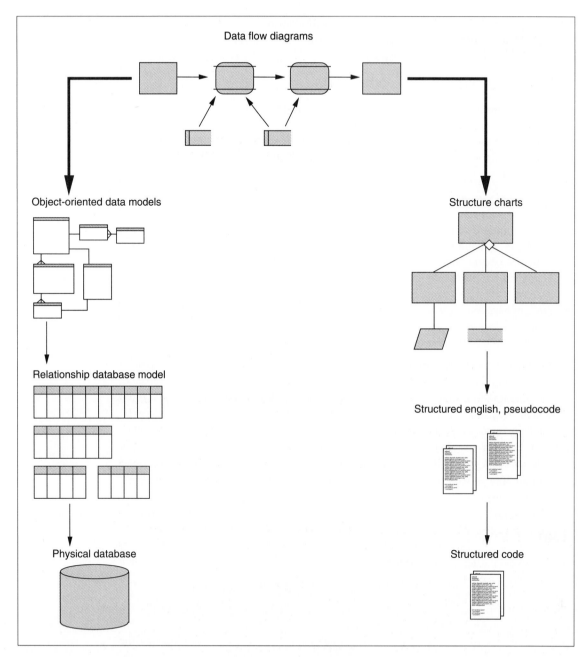

FIGURE 12.11   Some structured techniques used in the SDLC

Typical names for an external entity are CUSTOMER, SUPPLIER, CREDIT BUREAU, and MANAGEMENT.

- *Processes.* Processes are shown as rounded rectangles (see Figure 12.12b). They transform incoming data into outgoing information, and named by verbs. Examples

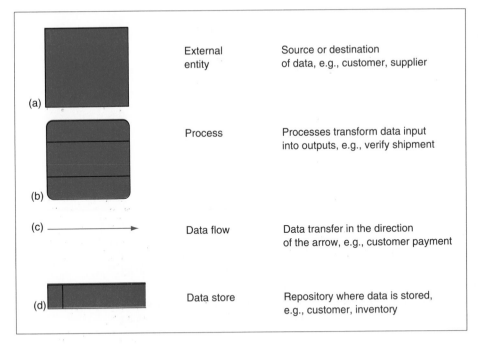

(a)	External entity	Source or destination of data, e.g., customer, supplier
(b)	Process	Processes transform data input into outputs, e.g., verify shipment
(c)	Data flow	Data transfer in the direction of the arrow, e.g., customer payment
(d)	Data store	Repository where data is stored, e.g., customer, inventory

FIGURE 12.12   Symbols for data flow diagram

are *Enter* application data, *Store* customer data, *Receive* product, *Apply* payment, and *Verify* shipment.

■ **Data flows.** Arrows are used to represent data flows, as shown in Figure 12.12c. They link processes, entities, and data stores, and labels indicate their content. For example, a customer might send a check (as payment) to our system, which would be labeled *customer check,* or simply *customer payment,* if other forms of payment were allowed.

■ **Data stores.** A data store is a repository where data is stored, and is illustrated as an open rectangle (for example, 12.12d). This data relates to a firm's processes and entities of interest; and examples are Customer, Inventory, Supplier, and Accounts Payable.

A key property of DFDs is that they are *nonimplementation specific.* In other words, they do not specify hardware, software, or even manual procedures (current or proposed) to perform or represent any of the processes, data flows, or data stores. This would prematurely lock the system design into the specific system components and leave no room for innovative designs that could improve the effectiveness and efficiency of work flows and information processing.

DFDs serve as a common reference point for both technical and nontechnical participants in the SDLC. They are relatively easy for the end user to understand yet provide a useful representation to base the system's design on. DFD construction begins from a top-level model through increasingly detailed models at lower levels.

Consider a firm that arranges loans to individuals if they meet predetermined criteria regarding their credit history, income, and existing debt obligations. Following a

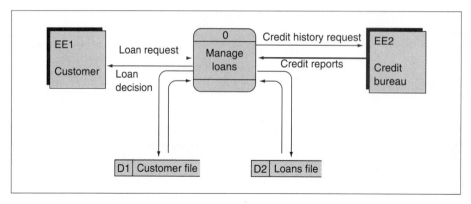

FIGURE 12.13   Context level DFD for loans management function

study of the firm's activities, the *context-level DFD* for the firm's activities is shown in Figure 12.13. A **context-level DFD** is a first-cut DFD that shows the highest-level processes that transform data. It shows a customer making requests to, and receiving loans or declinations from, the firm. A "manage loans" process uses stored information about loans and customers plus information from a credit bureau to determine the loan decision.

The context-level DFD shown in Figure 12.13 describes the overall loans management process. However, it is totally inadequate to describe the specific data flows and processes involved. In keeping with the top-down approach, the DFD is decomposed to a lower level of detail. Specifically, the process(es) are *exploded* to yield constituent subprocesses, as shown in Figure 12.14. This second-level DFD contains several processes that go further into the detail of the loans management process. The process of exploding the DFD often proceeds to the third or even fourth levels of resolution, until processes cannot be split any further.

In constructing the DFD, several rules govern the use of the symbols. These are summarized in Box 12.1, and their use results in well-constructed DFDs.

Decision Tables and Decision Trees

Often, the DFD does not provide sufficient information during analysis to explain the logic involved in certain processes. For example, the process, ASSESS LOAN does not supply the required logic to make the loan decision. Two methods for documenting the logic of such processes are decision tables and decision trees.

Decision trees are graphical, branching representations that illustrate conditions leading to decisions (see Figure 12.15a, p. 383). They clearly convey decision criteria, but not much else (for example, repetition). Also, they rapidly become unmanageable for many criteria.

Conversely, **decision tables** are more compact than decision trees and represent a series of decisions and criteria. They are a tabular form of representing decisions but do not appropriately handle iteration and other program structures. See Figure 12.15b.

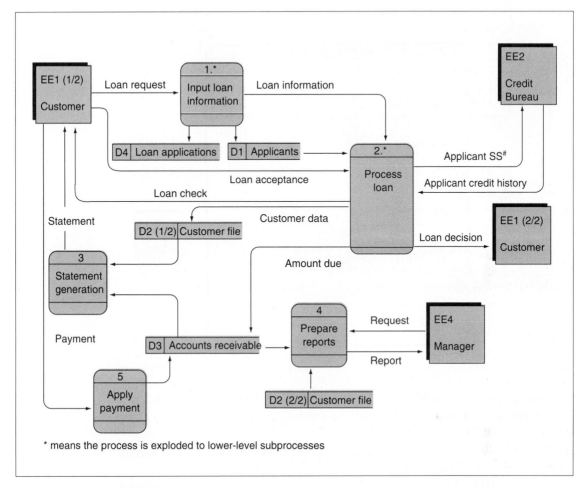

FIGURE 12.14   (a) First-level DFD for the loans management function *(continued)*

Evaluating System Alternatives

System evaluation is the appraisal of several broad system designs to select the best design alternative to proceed with. Evaluating system alternatives is a multicriteria decision process, and one major criterion is the cost effectiveness of each alternative design.

The DFD created in the requirements determination stage describes how information is currently processed. This DFD is often modified by adding or eliminating data flows, stores, entities, or processes, resulting in a new DFD that is the basis of the proposed system. For example, the first-level DFD shown in Figure 12.14a shows all payments being made by the customer, either personally or through the mail. In the proposed system, the intention is to include direct deposit of payments from the customer's bank as an alternative means of payment. This results in the modified DFD of Figure 12.16

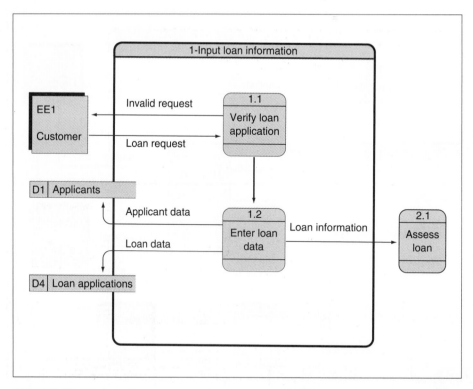

FIGURE 12.14 *(continued)*   (b) Second-level DFD: Exploding "Input loan information"

(p. 384) showing a new external entity, BANKS, and a new process to handle directly deposited payments from banks.

When the DFD is completed, it represents a means of communication between system users and designers as well as a canvas on which to create alternative designs. The first way in which alternative system designs may be proposed is through boundaries, which include the processes, data stores, and data flows to be automated. These boundaries often represent resource constraints on system development and equipment purchase. The second way of proposing alternative designs is through different combinations of system components (primarily hardware and software).

In evaluating system alternatives, the existing hardware/software system components and one or more new configurations are usually proposed as alternatives. The existing system typically involves fewer capital expenditures but may still be outscored when analyzing and evaluating alternatives on a whole range of factors other than short-term cost-benefit. Two frequently used sets of evaluation techniques are (1) cost-benefit analyses techniques such as *net present value* of system costs and benefits, which are used for short- to long-term forecasts; and (2) use of a multiple-criteria evaluation matrix for system evaluation. In the evaluation matrix, important system factors are weighted and scored for each system alternative presented. These factors or *evaluation criteria* fall into four general areas:

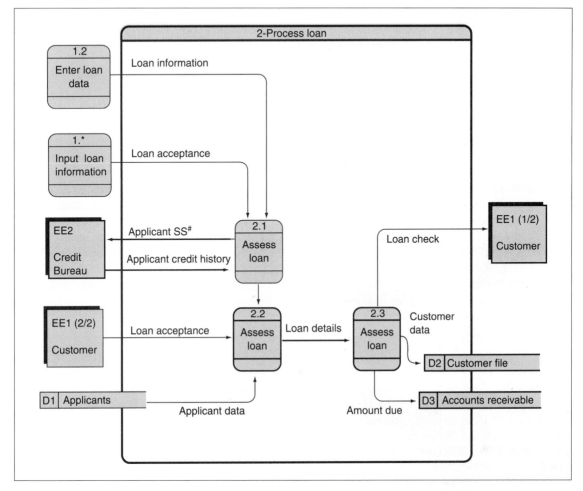

FIGURE 12.14 *(continued)*   (c) Second-level DFD: Exploding "Process loan"

- *Usage factors:* functionality, security, integrity, ease of use, maintenance agreements
- *Design factors:* modularity, flexibility, system quality, documentation
- *Development factors:* speed of design, available personnel, and software tools
- *Cost factors:* short-, medium-, and long-term costs and benefits

In the loans management example, two system alternatives can be derived from Figure 12.17. Automation boundaries are identical for both alternatives, except for the link between the firm and the credit bureaus. For the present, the decision is made to perform this function by fax to save costs. Subsequently, the alternatives differ not by boundaries but by combinations of hardware and software.

The first proposal specifies continued use of the firm's minicomputer. Its operation would be enhanced by reengineering existing programs and creating new ones, for example, the program for direct deposit of customer payments. The second option is favored strongly by the systems personnel and several end users and would replace this

---

RULES GOVERNING THE CONSTRUCTION OF DFDS

1. Processes contain imperative verbs, while nouns describe entities.
2. All but the most simple data flows must be labeled by a descriptor of the information passed.
3. Data flows do not carry materials (for example, books, machinery), only data (for example, orders, payments).
4. Data flows cannot pass directly from an external entity to a data store, which would imply direct access by a customer, say, to the firm's internal data files.
5. Only processes are exploded, not entities or data stores.
6. Data flows cannot pass between data stores—that is, files cannot automatically update other files—they must be updated by processes.
7. Data stores and external entities may be duplicated on the DFD (see Figure 12.14a), to allow for readability of the DFD.
8. DFDs must be kept nonimplementation specific, to prevent premature design.
9. If the output of a process or external entity drives another process, then data flows pass directly between them; otherwise a process that occurs independently may not have incoming data flows from either external entities or other processes (see ''produce management reports'' in Figure 12.14).

---

system with a microcomputer-based LAN. The evaluation of these two system alternatives is shown in Table 12.1. Also, **evaluation criteria** such as those in Table 12.1 and Figure 12.18 differ from **constraints.** While evaluation criteria are used to score and rank proposed system alternatives, constraints are used to eliminate certain alternatives from consideration, for example, not to consider any system priced over $100,000.

12.4   STRUCTURED SYSTEMS DESIGN _____

Following completion of the initial investigation, requirements determination, and evaluation, detailed design of the information system's components is carried out. Note that the outputs of systems analysis included the system's DFDs and outline design plus the evaluation report. In the **design stage** of the SDLC, the outline (or conceptual) design of the system is fully detailed. The specific means of implementing the DFD's functionality are defined with regard to the five system components: hardware, software, data, procedures, and people. The result of the design stage is a design specification, or blueprint, of the proposed information system.

Design of the System/User Interface

From the user's perspective, the most important system component is the *system/user interface.* While the functions of the system are important, the user interface is the part

Conditions	1	2	3	4	5	6	7
Credit record	Outstanding liabilites	1–2 recent defaults	1–2 recent defaults	1–2 recent defaults	Good	Good	Good
Requested amount	—	< 20%	> 20%	> 20%	< 30%	> 30%	>30%
Revised loan acceptable	—	—	Yes	No	—	Yes	No
Actions							
Approve loan application	—	X	X	—	X	X	—
Decline loan application	X	—	—	X	—	—	X

(a)

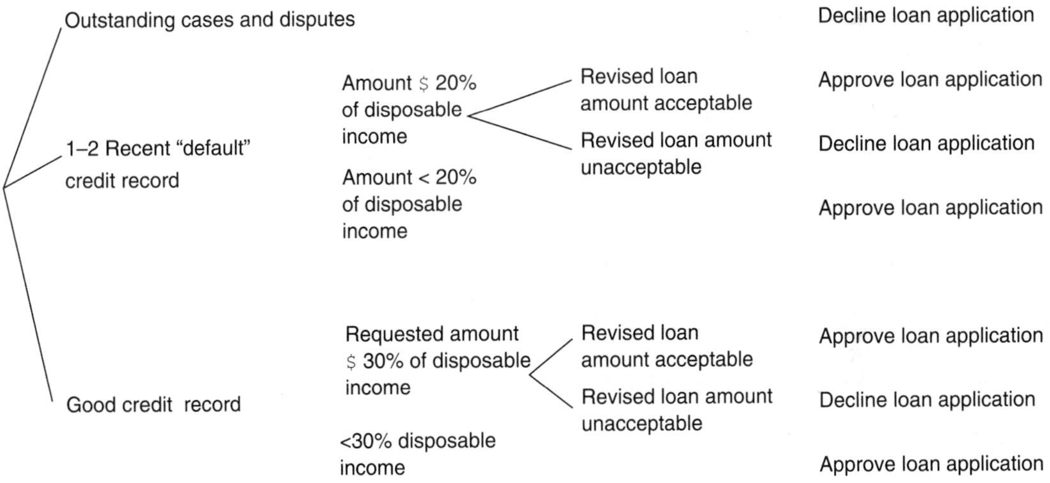

(b)

FIGURE 12.15   (a) Decision table for loan management evaluation process; (b) decision tree for loan management evaluation process.

of the system seen by the user and its design usually shapes the user's opinion of the system. This elevates the quality of the interface to central concern for system designers. The three parts of the user interface are **outputs, inputs,** and the form of **dialogue** chosen for the system. Important design principles for components of the user interface are:

- *Clarity.* This suggests that designs should be kept as simple as possible. If there is a choice between a simple and a complex interface with equal functionality, the simpler one should be chosen.

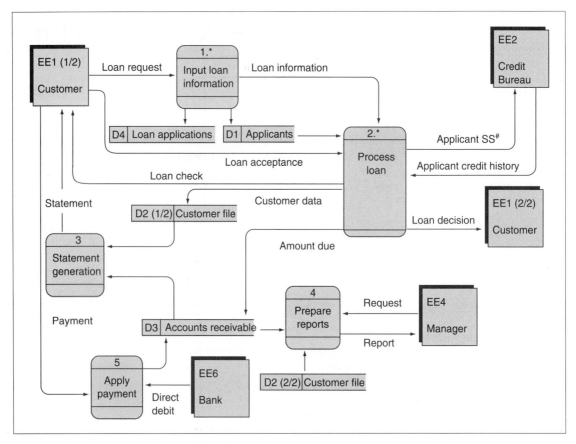

FIGURE 12.16 Modified second-level DFD for the loans management function

- *Conciseness.* This feature involves keeping the information preseented by a user interface to the bare minimum necessary for the user to understand and interact with the system.
- *Comprehensiveness.* The user should have all the information required to use the system. On a screen, for example, the user should be presented with a description of options available at that point, for example, application functions, ESCAPE, HELP, and EXIT.
- *Consistency.* Designers should make consistent use of keys on different screens. If the <F1> key represents the HELP function on one screen, it should not be changed to activate the EXIT function on another screen.
- *Coherence.* Screens, outputs, and inputs should be meaningfully designed for the user's benefit. Common conventions include a top-to-bottom, left-to-right approach for data in all interfaces. Additionally, interfaces may be tailored to specific applications and users through specialized icons, headers, and captions (see Figure 12.19, p. 389).

Two common types of printed **outputs** are internal and external documents. *Internal documents* are used within the firm for communicating transaction information and

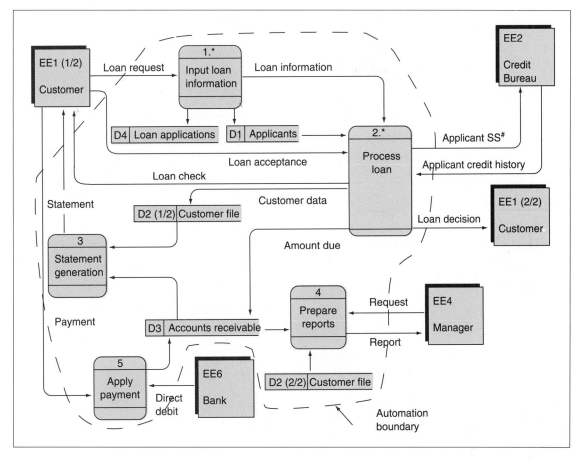

FIGURE 12.17   Second-level DFD for the loans management function

management reporting. Much closer attention must be paid to *external documents,* which include letters or newsletters to customers, stockholders, and suppliers; invoices, shipping notes, and receipts. These are critical revenue-obtaining outputs for the firm, and, as such, must be of high-quality appearance.

System **inputs** include *transaction data, letters,* and *turnaround documents.* The latter are sent out by the firm to a customer, who returns it to the firm for further processing. Examples are telephone bills that are outputs of telephone usage analysis. The bill is sent to the customer, who fills it out and returns it with a check for further processing (that is, payment processing).

Dialogue screens may be *menu driven, command driven, question/answer,* and *GUI based.* The first three screen types have been in use longer than GUIs, which are associated with newer microcomputer-based OSs, such as *Windows, OS/2,* and the *Macintosh OS.* Screens are characterized by a header, the main body of information, and Help, Escape, and Exit options. Command-driven dialogues are more suited to experts and regular system users, while menu-driven and GUI-based dialogues are easier for the nonexpert or occasional user.

TABLE 12.1   Evaluation of alternative loan management
system configurations (*continued*)

Evaluation Criteria	Weights (1–3)	System 1	System 2	System 1	System 2
		Score (1–10)		Weighted Score	
Ease of use	2.00	6.00	9.00	12.00	18.00
Functionality	2.50	8.00	9.00	20.00	22.50
Reliability	3.00	9.00	8.00	27.00	24.00
Ease of maintenance	1.50	7.00	8.00	10.50	12.00
Availability of applications	2.00	6.00	9.00	12.00	18.00
System flexibility	2.00	6.00	9.00	12.00	18.00
Expandability	2.50	5.00	9.00	12.50	22.50
Initial costs	1.00	9.00	4.00	9.00	4.00
Recurrent costs	2.00	6.00	8.00	12.00	16.00
Provision of decision support functions	2.00	5.00	9.00	10.00	18.00
		Total Score		**137.00**	**173.00**

Object-Oriented Database Modeling

Screen, output, and input design are important prerequisites for creating the proposed system's **database model.** The DFD's data stores are insufficient descriptions of the proposed system's database (see Chapter 7); thus a database model is required to fully describe the objects of interest to the firm, and their relationships, identifiers, and other characteristics lacking in the DFD.

Based on the database modeling techniques in Chapter 7, an object-oriented data model is created by the system designers and verified by users. For the loans management example, such a model is shown in Figure 12.20 (p. 390). It shows *applicants* placing *loan applications* for *loans*. Their *credit history* is obtained from *credit bureaus* and the loans are issued to *customers* (formerly applicants). Customers make *payments* on their loans or arrange to have them directly debited from their *banks.*

The object-oriented model is then transformed into a relational implementation model (in Figure 12.21, p. 391), using techniques described in Chapter 7. This model can be directly created using commercial RDBMS packages.

Structure Charts

The DFD is also an inadequate guide for the programmer to create code for the information system. It falls short of indicating the structure and relationship of the programs that constitute the system. Additionally, it does not reveal which files or

TABLE 12.1*(continued)*

Alternative 1		Alternative 2	
Current VAX minicomputer with 1 Gb hard drive, connected to five microcomputers (account managers) and to dumb terminal (tellers)	$0	1 Dell Pentium-based server running at 66 Mhz with mirrored 1 Gb hard disks	$10,000
		10 Dell 486-33 microcomputers to replace dumb terminals ($1,300)	$13,000
New program development on VAX	$4,000	Novell Netware v.4 (100 users)	$5,000
		Foxpro LAN and 10 ethernet NICs twisted-pair cabling for LAN ($250/node)	$4,000
		Program development	$7,000
		2 laser printers ($1,500) HP Laser Jet IV	$3,000
		4 impact printers ($350) Panasonic 2824	$1,400
		1 Hayes Modem (14.4 Kbps)	$400
		1 UPS unit	$500
		1 tape backup unit Colarado QFA 700 external	$1,000
		Supplies	$1,000
			$46,300
		Resale value of VAX minicomputer	$26,000
Total	**$4,000**	**Total**	**$22,300**

screens are used by each program module, and the specific data fields passed between modules. **Structure charts** are used for this purpose—to specify program modules and their interaction with other modules, screens, and files. The DFD provides overall guidance for the creation of the structure chart, with modules connected in a top-down hierarchy. Structure charts are constructed using five symbols (see Figure 12.22, p. 392):

- *Modules.* These are represented by a rectangle with the module name.
- *Connections.* Lines between higher-level and lower-level modules serve this function.

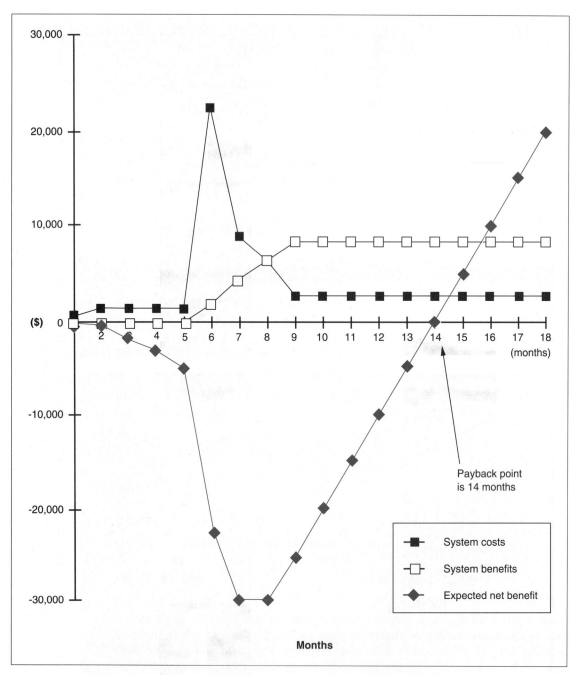

FIGURE 12.18   **Payback period for the loan management system**

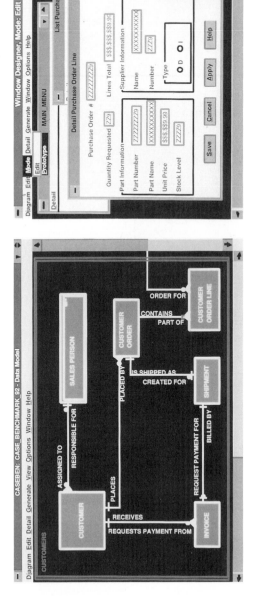

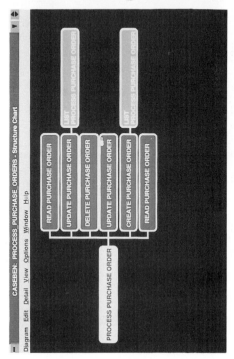

FIGURE 12.19   (*Top left*) Example data model created using the IEF CASE tool; (*top right*) designing a Windows-based user interface using IEF; (*bottom left*) structure chart created using IEF; (*bottom right*) code generation using IEF.

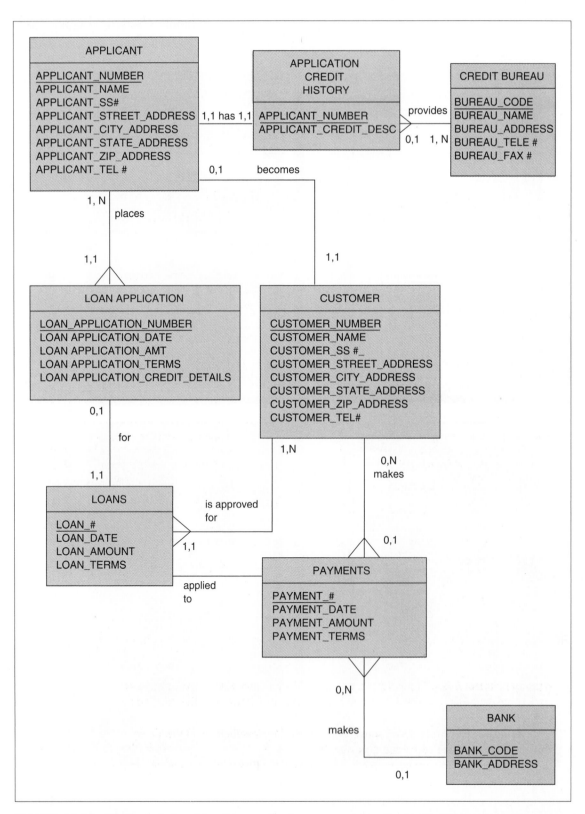

FIGURE 12.20 Entity-relationship diagram for loans management application

Applicant table

Applicant #	Applicant Name	Applicant SS #	Street Address	City Address	State Address	Zip Code	Telephone #

Customer table

Customer #	Customer Name	Customer SS #	Street Address	City Address	State Address	Zip Code	Telephone #

Loan application table

Loan Application #	Loan Application Date	Loan Application Amount	Loan Application Credit Details	Loan Application Terms	Applicant #

Loan table

Loan #	Loan Date	Loan Amount	Loan Terms	Loan Application #	Customer #

Bank table

Bank Code	Bank Address

Credit bureau table

Bureau Code	Bureau Name	Bureau Address	Telephone #	FAX #

Applicant credit history table

Applicant #	Applicant Credit Description	Bureau Code

Payments table

Payment #	Payment Date	Payment Amount	Payment Terms	Bank Code	Customer #	Loan #

FIGURE 12.21   Relational database model for the loans management example

- *Data and control flows.* These flows are illustrated by arrows with empty and shaded circles, respectively, attached to their bases, and are drawn parallel to module connections.
- *Screens.* The structure chart uses screens created during development of the dialogue components. They are represented as parallelograms.
- *Files.* Files are shown as two parallel lines and match the files (tables) in the system's database.

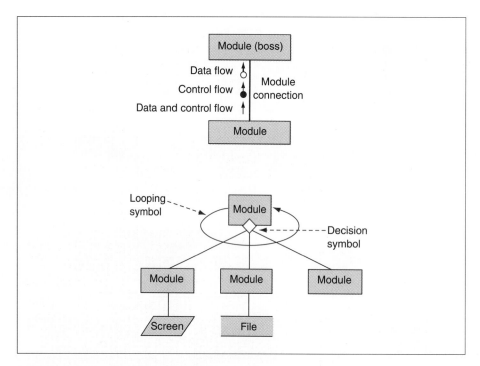

FIGURE 12.22   Symbols for structure charts

In designing structure charts, several pointers are relevant. First, the top module represents the overall program for the information system, while the lower-level modules are its subprograms. The modules defined by the system designer are always a *subset* of the DFD—the subset that is being automated. Key concepts relating to structure charts are:

1. ***Module size.*** Module size is determined by a combination of the language used and the module's cohesiveness. An ideal module performs a single, tightly defined function, for example, *"determine interest rate."* The cohesiveness of the module, that is, how well it performs a single function, is an important design criterion. Also, programs written in a 3GL result in larger modules than those written in a 4GL (for example, 50 lines versus 10 lines), owing to the greater functionality of higher-level languages.
2. ***Coupling.*** The degree of interdependence between modules is known as coupling. Ideal modules are as independent as possible, with a minimum of data and control flows passing between them. Programs consisting of loosely coupled modules are better for error detection, maintenance, and modifiability, as changes to modules do not ripple through to other modules. (See Figure 12.23.)
3. ***Fan-out and fan-in.*** Fan-out refers to the amount of control a module exercises, that is, how many modules it calls or supervises. This is usually kept under seven (7) to limit the complexity of the calling module. If exceeded, the calling module may become unduly large and more difficult to manage. *Fan-in,* on the other hand, describes how many modules call a single module. This number should be large, to

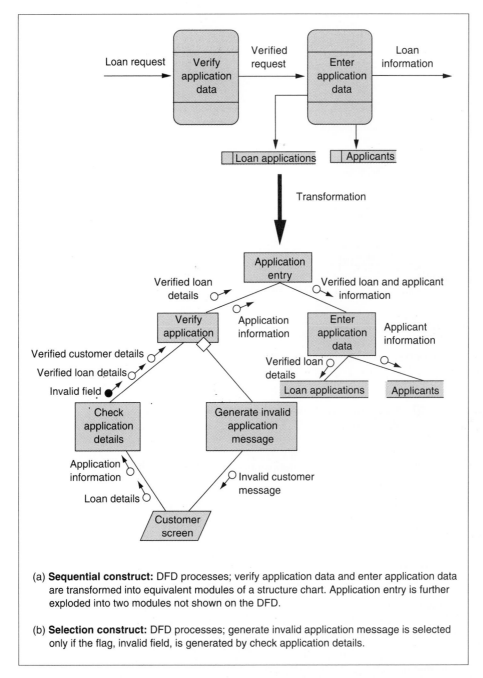

(a) **Sequential construct:** DFD processes; verify application data and enter application data are transformed into equivalent modules of a structure chart. Application entry is further exploded into two modules not shown on the DFD.

(b) **Selection construct:** DFD processes; generate invalid application message is selected only if the flag, invalid field, is generated by check application details.

FIGURE 12.23   Creating structure charts from data flow diagrams

(continued)

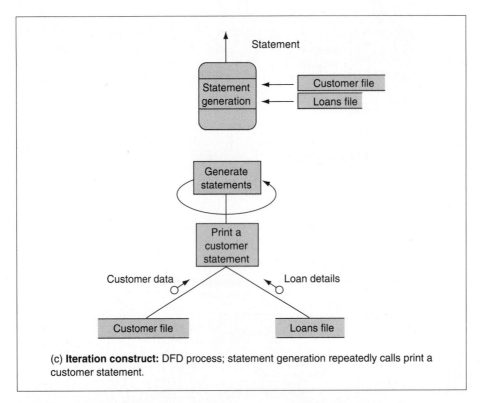

(c) **Iteration construct:** DFD process; statement generation repeatedly calls print a customer statement.

FIGURE 12.23 *(continued)*   Creating structure charts from data flow diagrams

promote reusability of code and also to prevent "reinventing the wheel"—that is, creating several modules with similar functions.

The structure chart for the loans management example is shown in Figure 12.24. It integrates the hierarchical program structure with the screens and files designed earlier.

System Documentation

Information systems are less tangible entities than artifacts like buildings and machines. Program functions, in particular, are not immediately apparent simply from observing pages of written code. **System documentation** thus has a greater role to play in the SDLC than in developing other types of systems. It must explain the functions of the system, clarify the design of its components, and enable analysts and designers to maintain the system. Information systems, often containing programs of hundreds of thousands of lines of code, are many times more complex than other types of designed systems. Each of the six stages of the life cycle described in the previous section has documentation deliverables associated with it, including

- A **system plan** for the initial investigation, documenting the initial system feasibility findings and clarifying the problem definition

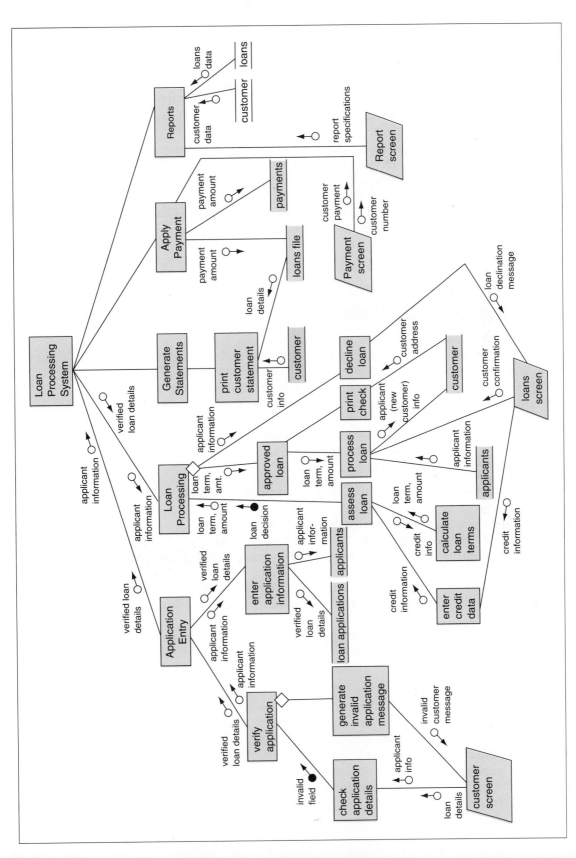

FIGURE 12.24   Structure chart for the loans management system

- A **requirements determination report** for the same stage in the SDLC, describing the results of systems analysis, and incorporating organizational charts, problem definition, and functional specifications—outlined primarily using the DFD
- An **evaluation report,** which evaluates broad design alternatives and their associated cost-benefit analyses
- **Design specifications,** documenting the detailed design of the five system components (hardware, software programs, people, procedures, and data)
- A **system development report,** comprising program documentation, facilities design, training procedures, and database conversion requirements
- An **implementation report,** providing blueprints of the system's actual hardware, software, and other components, that will be used in the maintenance phase of the SDLC

Computer-Aided Software Engineering (CASE) Tools

Creating various system models is time-consuming for system developers. For large information systems, designing and drawing large numbers of DFDs, ERDs, structure charts, and so on for many functional areas can lead to critical omissions and inconsistencies among diagrams. **Computer-aided software engineering (CASE)** tools have been developed and refined through the 1980s to increase the productivity of system developers. A CASE tool is a software program, usually running on a workstation or microcomputer that automates systems analysis, design, and/or software development. CASE methodologies make extensive use of structured methods, and enable the user to

- Use graphical tools to rapidly and easily create system models, for example, DFDs, ERDs, structure charts, and database definitions
- Create user interfaces in the form of screens and reports, by "painting" screens with the necessary captions and data fields
- Employ automatic code-generation features, based on module functional specifications
- Reengineer old systems by producing specifications for existing code, automatically documenting the code, highlighting coding inefficiencies, and restructuring the code more efficiently
- Promote consistency among all diagrams maintained by the software and ensure that structurally incorrect diagrams cannot be created (for example, DFDs that violate the rules described earlier); changes to a model are propagated across all others in the CASE repository

Several writers (for example, McClure) distinguish between *upper case* and *lower case* CASE tools. The former focus on the front-end of the SDLC and help the user to create DFDs, structure charts, E-R models, and relational schemas. They employ drawing tools that also ensure consistency between diagrams. Lower case tools, on the other hand, generate program code from entered design specifications. The most powerful tools, for example, Texas Instruments Information Engineering Facility (IEF), have both upper and lower case capabilities. See Figure 12.19.

To use CASE tools, developer training is required, but productivity gains of 100 to 800 percent have been reported. Examples of other CASE tools are **Excelerator, Information Engineering Workbench (IEW),** and **Teamwork.**

Rapid Application Development (RAD)

In Section 6.3, reference was made to the MIS backlog and to end-user development as one solution to it. A reason for the MIS backlog is that on average, 60 to 80 percent of all system development effort is used to maintain old systems, rather than develop new ones. Structured development approaches have been a central means to make systems easier to create and maintain. Another significant method in the early 1990s is **rapid application development (RAD).**

RAD is a system development approach popularized by James Martin. It features intensive effort by a small group of developers working closely with users to rapidly develop information systems. The system developers are specialists who are well versed in advanced tools, particularly CASE tools. Within a short but intensive time frame, they work with users to rapidly create a prototype of the proposed system with an emphasis on the core 20 percent of the system that supplies 80 percent of its functionality (the frequently quoted 80–20 rule). The remaining parts of the system are added following this main effort and this prototype is not discarded but transformed into the final production system.

With its user involvement, *joint application development (JAD)* is an important feature of RAD, along with *CASE tools,* knowledgeable *CASE specialists,* and *prototyping.* The end result is effective systems that are delivered faster than those created using 3GLs and traditional system development methods.

12.5   KEY ISSUES IN DEVELOPING_____
MICROCOMPUTER-BASED_____
INFORMATION SYSTEMS_____

Most experience in the systems development community has been in developing large-scale systems on mainframes and minicomputers. Much less cumulative experience exists for microcomputers and LANs, and even less on such architectures as client/server and enterprise computing systems. While developing all these systems involves the use of the SDLC model, differences in emphases exist between development on larger-scale systems and on microcomputer-based systems. Some of these distinct emphases are now discussed.

Developing Stand-Alone and LAN-Based Microcomputer Systems

Stand-alone microcomputer-based systems are conceptually simple to develop. They involve no major connectivity challenges (only to printers, and so on) and comprise the single PC and the end user's applications. Many user needs can be satisfied with off-the-shelf software, and the major OSs provide multitasking or task-switching. As data is accessed by only a single user, it is easy to manage, without the need for record locking. Similarly, user procedures are simple to define. See Table 12.2 for such development issues.

Networks are more challenging to the system development team. A LAN involves multiple users and often multiple departments, making the SDLC front-end (investigation, analysis, and evaluation) more complex and expensive. Often the hardware is from a single platform, although multiplatform LANs are becoming common. NOSs require more effort to set up, and any multiuser database applications require file and record locking for concurrency control. In implementation, bringing all the network components together calls for greater planning and troubleshooting than in the single-user case.

Developing Internetworks and Client/Server Systems

Building internetworks involves all the issues relating to LAN and stand-alone microcomputer-based systems development. Also, since multiple networks often cross departmental boundaries, the SDLC front-end activities involve more end users and objectives. A similar mixture of hardware is also more likely in an internetwork,

TABLE 12.2   Development issues for stand-alone systems and LAN

	Hardware	Software	People	Procedures	Data
Stand-alone systems	• No connectivity concerns • Single suppliers • Failure disables 100% of the system	• Stable software • No NOS, only OS • Applications tailored to the single user	• Single user or small number of users	• Simple operating procedures and error handling	• No file/record locking concerns • Single databases
LAN-based systems (additional features)	• Connectivity between different resources and possible platforms • Cabling and other setup complexity • Multiple suppliers and maintenance agreements • Failure can disable some applications	• OS and NOS required • Support of multiple applications • Groupware applications • LAN management software required	• Multiple users at different levels of expertise • LAN administrator required	• Failure, recovery, and backup procedures are more complex • Security procedures required	• File and record locking are issues • Data is more vulnerable to improper access and misuse • Backup using RAID techniques is becoming common

requiring appropriate hardware and software for the purpose of establishing connectivity among resources. Devices such as smart hubs and bridges will be needed, along with software capable of supporting multiple internetworking protocols, for example, TCP/IP and Novell's IPX/SPX.

With internetworks, network management increases in importance. SNMP-compliant hardware and software help the network administrator to control the internetwork and are essential internetwork components. Internetwork procedures and software must be developed to conform to higher standards of *fault-tolerance, data integrity,* and *system security* than either individual LANs or stand-alone systems. See Table 12.3.

Client/server systems are more complex than simple internetworks. The people and procedures issues are largely similar but major differences exist in technical areas (hardware, software, and data). Enterprise computing, which incorporates client/server processing, is characterized by multiple platforms, including larger-scale computers in addition to microcomputers and workstations. This requires hardware (for example, gateways) and software programs to handle an even greater number of protocol conversions than in internetworks. For database applications, client/server versions of DBMSs must be purchased or developed for both the front-end clients and back-end servers.

Regarding data, centralized databases are simpler in design than distributed databases. New client/server DBMSs such as Supra v3.0 by Cincom Systems, Inc. and Oracle 7 by Oracle Corporation support multiple platforms. These platforms include OSs on IBM mainframes (for example, VMS and MVS) and UNIX, DOS, Windows, and OS/2 on microcomputers. Additionally, they support relational distributed databases, with distributed two-phase commits and rollback (see Chapter 7). These two

TABLE 12.3   Development issues for internetworks and client/server systems

	Hardware	Software	People	Procedures	Data
Internetworks (additional features)	• Multiple platform, heterogeneous hardware • Bridging and routing hardware required • Low-cost servers (e.g., workstations and microcomputers)	• Capable OSs and NOSs with internetworking capabilities • Software required to translate protocols	• Many users at different locations	• Complex failure, recovery, and backup procedures	• Multiple databases across entire system • Possible use of distributed DMBS (DDBMS)
Client/server systems (additional features)	• Heterogeneous hardware • Specialized servers, e.g., Sequent and Parallan servers	• Front-end and back-end software interface required			• Database servers support data access

DMBSs characterize the transition to enterprise networks that is now in full swing in corporate America.

CHAPTER SUMMARY

Information systems comprise five components: *hardware, software, people, procedures,* and *data.* Systems developers use the SDLC model as a guide to create information systems. Its stages form a prescriptive guide to aid developers in defining existing information requirements; creating and preparing detailed system designs; and coding, testing, and implementing designed systems. Phased development is a variation on the traditional SDLC, allowing system implementation in several stages owing to risk, cost, or other constraints. Another variation is prototyping, which is used to provide an iterative, user-led definition of system requirements.

Managing the development effort is essential for the systems manager to avoid costly cost overruns and late system delivery. *Project management tools,* such as the critical path method (CPM) and Gantt charts, are now routinely used for managing the SDLC. Equally important are *estimation methods* for estimating the effort required to develop systems. The concept of *deliverables* is also vital in focusing the manager's attention on tangible, relevant parts of the system during development.

The emphasis on user participation in the life cycle has motivated approaches such as joint application development (JAD), which brings together designers and users in a controlled environment for intensive and highly productive system development sessions. JAD is often used together with structured analysis and design methods. These stress a *top-down approach* to system development and include such formalisms as data flow diagrams (DFDs) and structure charts. Using these approaches, functions are successively decomposed into lower-level ones until the entire system's functions and programs are specified.

Rapid application development (RAD) is effected by methods such as JAD, computer-assisted systems development (CASE) tools, and prototyping. Specialists familiar with these tools can use them to respond quicker to information requirements.

System development emphases differ according to the type of information system under development. *Stand-alone systems* are the most straightforward, with *LANs* introducing issues of hardware and software connectivity to the SDLC. *Internetworks* and *client/server* systems are even more complicated to implement, as issues such as multiple computer types, protocols, topologies, WAN gateways, and so on must be handled in the SDLC along with user functional requirements. In addition, requirements analysis often takes place across departments, making it more extensive. Only recently has capable software appeared to deliver security, reliability, and data integrity to internetworks and client/server systems suitable for mission-critical OLTP.

REVIEW QUESTIONS

1. What are the five components of a computer-based information system?
2. Give two examples that illustrate the informal components of an information system.

3. Describe the differences between the proactive and reactive motivation to develop information systems.
4. List the six major stages of the systems development life cycle (SDLC). In which of these stages are the users most involved?
5. Why is it important to "Get It Right the First Time" in the SDLC?
6. Discuss three reasons why a firm may choose to use the phased development approach.

EXERCISES

1. A mail-order clothing retailer has just completed a systems analysis, resulting in the proposal to install a network of microcomputers to support the salespeople and managerial staff. The system with the highest ranking in the SDLC's evaluation stage costs $67,000, which is $25,000 more than allowable expenditures in the current year. A second system, which falls within the current year's budget, ranked lower than the first system in both cost effectiveness and suitability to user requirements. Because scaling down the system is not desirable, what is your recommendation to the firm regarding system selection and implementation?
2. Why is it significantly more expensive to modify errors in an information system in the implementation stage than in the analysis or design stages? What are the comparative costs of making changes to the system in the implementation and operational stages of the SDLC? What is involved in each case?
3. For the information system components listed below, estimate the time (not effort-months) required for system development, given three available system developers.

Type of Module	Number of Modules	Effort-Months per Module
A/R	3	4
A/P	2	3
Inventory File Management	5	3
Customer File Management	4	2

4. Create a context diagram and a second-level DFD for a wholesaler of mens' ties. Orders are received from retailers and filled from an in-house inventory. If the requested items are out of stock, new inventory is ordered from suppliers. Include payments in your DFD, but no report generation. (As a guideline, your DFD will have eight to twelve processes). Assuming only 40 percent of the processes may be automated, propose automation boundaries that focus on improving the company's cash flow.
5. Develop an entity-relationship model for the above example. Show entities, attributes, identifiers, relationships, and cardinalities.

SUGGESTED READINGS _____

Boehm, B. *Software Engineering Economics.* Englewood Cliffs, NJ: Prentice-Hall, 1981.

Brooks, F. P. *The Mythical Man-Month.* Reading, MA: Addison-Wesley, 1979.

Burch, J. G. *Systems Analysis, Design, and Implementation.* Boston: Boyd and Fraser, 1992.

De Marco, T. *Structured Analysis and System Specification.* New York: Yourdon Press, 1978.

Gane, C., and Sarson, T. *Structured Systems Analysis: Tools and Techniques.* Englewood Cliffs, NJ: Prentice-Hall, 1979.

McClure, C. *CASE Is Software Automation.* Englewood Cliffs, NJ: Prentice-Hall, 1989.

Ricciuti, M. "Mainframe DBMS Power Unleashed." *Datamation,* October 15, 1992.

Yourdon, E. *Modern Structured Analysis.* New York: Yourdon Press, 1989.

DEVELOPING AND IMPLEMENTING MICROCOMPUTER SYSTEMS

INTRODUCTION

The SDLC includes both front-end analysis and design activities and back-end *development, implementation,* and *maintenance* activities. In the back-end phase, the system's detailed design is used as a blueprint to create the actual information system. Hardware is acquired, software is either purchased or coded, and procedures are developed for the system's users. Systems are later tested to ensure that they fulfill the functional requirements of their users. Program testing is a time-consuming part of the SDLC. Several testing strategies are used to test both individual program modules and the entire system prior to its actual use.

The proposed system's hardware may already be in use in the firm. Alternatively, it may be purchased or leased by the firm, often after a *request for proposal (RFP)* is issued to hardware (or system) vendors. During system development, procedures for end users and systems personnel must be well defined and matched to the computer processes as part of redesigned work flows. In *system implementation,* the information system is installed in the work environment. This process employs different strategies in various contexts to ensure the system's success.

Learning Objectives

After reading this chapter, you will be able to:

- Make better informed decisions regarding the purchase or custom-coding of programs needed to satisfy functional requirements
- Organize and manage the personnel and procedures in the software development life cycle (SWDLC) more effectively

- Prepare a request for proposal (RFP) for the suppliers of a proposed system's hardware and software components
- Design appropriate procedures for operating and maintaining an information system
- Develop appropriate training plans and implementation strategies for the information system

13.1 PROGRAM DESIGN AND CODING _____

Program design is the most technically demanding part of the SDLC. It features greater involvement by such technical personnel as programmers and analysts, and reduced participation by the end user. The design specifications created in the SDLC's front-end stages are the basis for coding or purchasing the required computer programs. With custom-coding, managers' concerns include planning and managing the SWDLC. Programmers are organized into groups to code program modules, and appropriate methods are used to measure programmer productivity. If other information systems exist, then the new system's hardware and software compatibility are key issues, to ensure the interoperability of both systems.

Package Acquisition versus Program Development

A major decision at the end of the SDLC design stage is whether to custom-code the information system's programs or to purchase an off-the-shelf software package. Both options have different implications for the costs and remaining duration of the SDLC; thus, the choice must be carefully considered. There is a much greater variety of off-the-shelf software for microcomputers than for larger-scale machines (for example, well over 25,000 titles for MS-DOS machines), covering almost every type of application. In addition, microcomputer software is likely to be purchased for hundreds of dollars (typically), instead of leased for thousands of dollars yearly as with mainframes. Off-the-shelf software packages have several advantages over custom-coded software.

- *Variety.* The large variety of software choices include multiple operating systems, languages, and applications.
- *Speed.* Off-the-shelf software can be implemented and running much quicker than custom-written packages, allowing quicker delivery of systems.
- *Cost.* As these packages are written for the mass market, they are invariably much less expensive than custom-designed software, which is written for one user.
- *Quality.* More resources (funding, expertise, tools, and so on) are available to develop off-the-shelf packages, as costs are recovered from many users. Off-the-shelf packages are thus of much higher quality than the custom-developed variety.
- Other important benefits include *increased productivity* of programmers and *improved estimates* of development costs—a historical difficulty with custom-coding.

There are risks associated with off-the-shelf software. First, it may not exactly match functional or design requirements, which requires its customization if possible, or forcing the user to adapt to the package's procedures. The second option may result in inefficient work flows. Second, the user may grow unduly dependent on the software vendor. If the vendor goes bankrupt, leaves the business, or provides poor service, system maintenance is made more difficult. Finally, there is a temptation to skip the SDLC stages if off-the-shelf software is used, resulting in an inappropriate system.

Either system professionals or end users may code custom-coded software and, in the process, use either a 3GL or a 4GL. Custom-coding is generally:

- *More relevant* to the functional requirements, as it is built for specific applications
- *Better documented* than off-the-shelf software, for which no source code or documentation may be supplied at all

As indicated, custom-developed programs are more expensive, do not have as much invested in their quality, and are not available for immediate use. Skilled programmers can reduce the effects of some of these factors, as can 4GLs and CASE tools with automatic code-generation capabilities. Nevertheless, in situations where off-the-shelf software is available and appropriate, it represents a better choice.

The Software Development Life Cycle (SWDLC)

The SWDLC serves a similar purpose to the broader SDLC, namely, to guide software developers through essential steps for producing well-structured and documented software with few errors. The SWDLC is used to create custom-coded software, although it is also applicable to off-the-shelf software that must be custom-tailored to a specific environment. It comprises three stages: *design, coding,* and *testing,* with most effort focused on the first and last stages. The *40-20-40 rule* ideally has 40 percent of the SWDLC effort spent in design, 20 percent in coding, and 40 percent in testing. Effort spent in design simplifies coding and results in software with the fewest possible errors.

Software design was introduced in Chapter 12 in the form of structure charts. Program designers also use *structured flowcharts* to describe the program's structure in greater detail prior to coding. Flowcharts use specialized symbols for processes, decisions, and iteration—the three major programming constructs. *Structured English* is a direct alternative to flowcharts and uses English-like commands for creating pseudo-code, which may be easily translated into a 3GL or 4GL. Structured flowchart and structured English equivalents of a part of the loans management structure chart are shown in Figures 13.1 and 13.2.

If the decision is made to custom-code the software, the previous program design methods can be used. End-users and professional programmers can use one of many 3GLs and 4GLs, as described in Chapter 6. End users are more likely to use such 4GLs as spreadsheet macros and application generators, while 3GLs are the province of professional programmers. CASE tools are also powerful options for automatically generating code (discussed in Chapter 12) and can greatly reduce the coding and testing parts of the SWDLC.

Testing is the final part of the SWDLC. It involves running the software through tests to detect and correct errors in the code. Software is not 100 percent error free, owing to the many different paths an executing program might take and the difficulty of testing all these paths in a reasonable time frame. The intention of testing is to reduce the number of bugs—software errors that cause system failure—to the barest minimum.

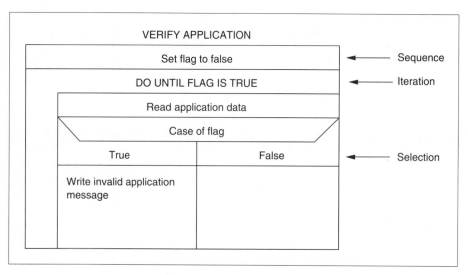

FIGURE 13.1   Structured flowchart for the "verify application" module

BEGIN Verify Application (; CUST_NAME, CUST_ADDR, LOAN_AMT, INCOME, DEBT)
        SET   ERR TO FALSE
        ┌─── REPEAT UNTIL ERR IS FALSE
        │   CALL Enter Application Date (; ERR, CUST_NAME, CUST_ADDR, LOAN_AMT,
        │   INCOME, DEBT)
        │
        │   IF ERR is true
        │   THEN
        │
        │
        │   Call Invalid Application Message (LOAN_AMT, INCOME, DEBT)
        │
        │
        │   ENDIF
        └─── ENDREPEAT

FIGURE 13.2   Structured English for the "verify application" module

Organizing for the SWDLC

The *project manager* is responsible for organizing the programming team for the SWDLC. There are different forms of organization with individual strengths and weaknesses. The most conventional is the **program development team**—a line organizational structure in which designers, coders, and testers are organized in groups that report to a manager (Figure 13.3). Each aspect of the SWDLC is handled by a group of programmers, with more experienced programmers assigned to the most important SWDLC phases: design and testing.

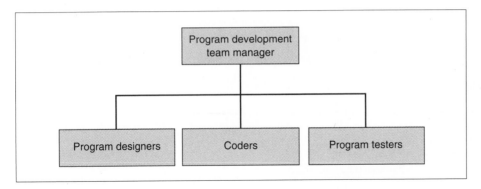

FIGURE 13.3   Structure of the program development team

The concept of the **chief programmer team** was popularized by IBM and by Frederick Brooks in his book *The Mythical Man-Month* as a means of relieving the best programmers of administrative responsibilities and of providing clear leadership and direction in the SWDLC. The *chief programmer* takes the lead in programming, aided by an *assistant,* who is a capable programmer and who can take over the chief programmer's role if needed. The chief programmer is unencumbered by reporting, documentation, budgeting, personnel allocation, and other administrative matters. These are handled by (1) a *librarian,* who maintains different program versions; (2) an *administrator,* who handles budgetary, personnel, and reporting tasks; (3) an *editor,* who documents programs; and (4) a *program clerk,* who performs secretarial duties. In large projects, *junior programmers* may code lower-level program modules. See Figure 13.4 for the team structure.

Egoless programmer teams comprise peer programmers who work in a network organizational structure, as shown in Figure 13.5. They review and critique the work of other programmers, and the absence of a leader is intended to remove the inhibitions and ego issues associated with rank and competition. This form of organization requires considerable communications overhead owing to the large number of links between all programmers. However, they have the potential to produce work of high quality owing to the increased involvement and responsibilities of the programmers. This form of organization closely resembles the total quality work team concept currently pursued by manufacturing firms.

Measuring Software Productivity

In Chapter 12, the emphasis on deliverables in the SDLC was highlighted. The same emphasis holds for the SWDLC, that is, a focus on measurable programs and documentation. In this regard, "work for ten hours on the credit processing module" is not an acceptable deliverable for the SWDLC, nor a desirable means of measuring software productivity. As suggested by Frederick Brooks, the mere allocation of person-months is not sufficient for success. Additionally, people and months are not interchangeable.

Two major means of measuring software productivity (also called software metrics) are the **L**ines **of** documented, **E**xecutable source **C**ode (or **LOEC**) model and the

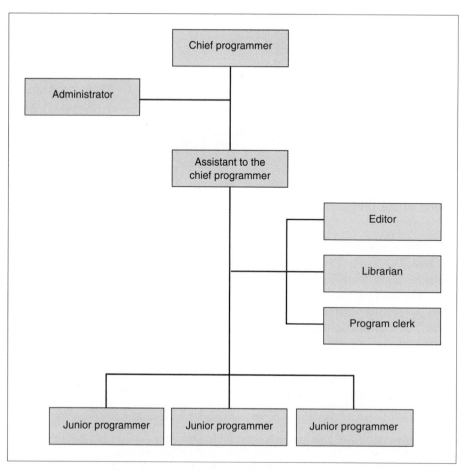

FIGURE 13.4   Structure of the chief programmer team

function point model discussed in Chapter 12. The LOEC model measures documented, working lines of code produced by programmers and is easy to use for managerial purposes. It must be adjusted to take into account the language used for software development. For example, 100 lines of 4GL code may translate into 400 lines of 3GL code, which in turn may be equivalent to 2,000 lines of assembly language code (see Figure 13.6). The productivity of programmers using different languages must be measured differently. An additional caveat with the LOEC model is that delivered code may vary wildly in quality, meaning that a slow programmer may actually be more productive than a fast programmer who creates error-ridden programs.

The function point model is a more objective method of measuring software productivity, which prevents programmers from writing verbose code to inflate their LOECs. It also takes into account the difficulty of the functions being coded, as writing networking code, say, is more difficult than creating screen interfaces and entering user input. As with the LOEC model, advanced tools (for example, CASE tools) can

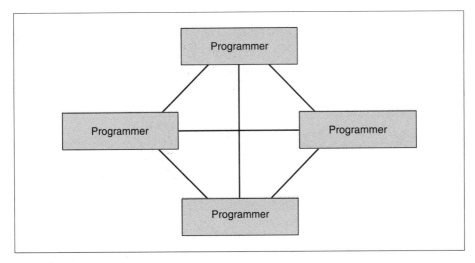

FIGURE 13.5   Structure of the egoless programmer team

increase productivity expectations, for example, function points/month for each programmer.

Program Documentation

Program documentation is important written and graphical material that accompanies software. It explains the functions of the developed software and helps future software maintenance. Programmers often have the urge to "develop now, document later," a practice that should be discouraged. The fallacy lies in the thought that avoiding documentation enables the program to be completed sooner, but the reverse is actually true for large programs: The absence of documentation only delays the delivery date of the programs being coded. Managers must ensure that delivered source code is comprehensively documented.

Clear documentation is also essential to ensure that the maintenance following the system's implementation is programmer independent, so that new programmers can understand the purpose and structure of code. Two types of software documentation are internal and external. *Internal documentation* is interspersed with the code and either heads a program module or describes the functions of specific lines of code (see Figure 13.7). *External documentation* accompanies the program and contains such features as its name, description, design and testing history, current version, resources used, and other pertinent information. Both types contribute to easier system maintenance.

Software Compatibility and Portability

Software development does not take place in a vacuum. Programs under development will coexist with older programs, and new hardware often runs alongside older

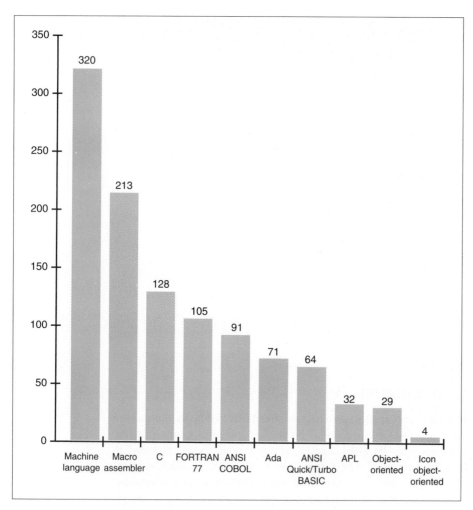

FIGURE 13.6   Number of lines of code per function point

hardware. **Software compatibility** is the ability of software to work together with other software, and/or hardware. It enables the successful exchange of data with other software programs in mutually understandable formats. There are four levels of compatibility of interest to developers.

1. *Operating system compatibility.* Running the software on, or exchanging data with another OS. For example, an accounting suite of programs is MS-DOS/Windows-compatible if it runs correctly with that combination of operating software.

2. *Application compatibility.* Exchanging messages with another application on the same or different hardware. If the accounting software above can export data in dBase or Lotus 1-2-3 formats, then it has some application compatibility with those programs.

Turbo C++ - [c:\tcwin\bin\interest.cpp]

File Edit Search Run Compile Project Browse Options Window Help

```
/*
 * An interest computing program with error checking
*/
 # include <stdio.h>

 main ()
 {
    double interest_rate;                        /* interest rate */
    double balance;                              /* balance at end of the year*/
    int year;                                    /* year of period */
    int period;                                  /* length of period */
    int flag;                                    /* indicates whether the program fail

    printf ("Enter interest rate, principal, and period: ");
    if (scanf ("%lf, %lf, %i", &interest_rate, &balance, &period) != 3)
    {
        printf("Error: Three numeric values were expected.\n");
        flag = 1;                                /* program has failed */
    }
    else
    {
        printf("Interest Rate:     %7.2f%%\n", interest_rate * 100);
        printf("Starting Balance:  %7.2f$\n\n", balance);
        printf("Year      Balance\n");
        for (year = 1; year<=period; year = year+1)
        {  balance = balance + balance * interest_rate;
           printf("%4i    $ %7.2f\n", year, balance);
        }
        flag = 0;                                /* program is successful */
    }
    return flag;                                 /* return success indicator */
    }
```

Program Name:	interest.cpp
Program Version:	v. 2.0
Program Size (text):	1,020 bytes
(object):	1,293 bytes
(linked):	24,304 bytes
Creator:	Sam McDonald
Date Created:	11-20-93
Last Modified:	3-15-94
Libraries Used:	<stdio.h>

FIGURE 13.7 (*Top*) A program for computing interest amounts written in Borland's Turbo C; (*bottom*) external documentation for the interest rate program written in C.

3. ***Database compatibility.*** The use of data structures and instructions that are understood by another DBMS. As an example, most relational microcomputer DBMSs use SQL (see Chapter 7) as a common DML.
4. ***Network compatibility.*** Applications using protocols based on the OSI seven-layer model can send messages across networks to other applications running on different operating systems or hardware.

There are several levels of compatibility that exist between different applications. Greater compatibility eases the maintenance burden and improves system functionality but can be expensive to incorporate in heterogeneous environments.

Project managers looking even further ahead are concerned with system **portability,** or in creating software that is easy to transfer or *port* to new hardware. Software may be ported as part of *software reengineering* in instances when new hardware is purchased to replace existing hardware. For example, a general ledger program written in RPG on the mainframe would be relatively easy to port to a microcomputer environment because microcomputer versions now exist.

Problems of compatibility are reduced by some software applications developed for multiple platforms. Products like *Oracle Corporation's* **Oracle** and *Computer Associates'* **Realia COBOL** work on both mainframes and microcomputers, and code taken from one environment will work with little modification on other platforms. On

---

MANAGING END USER SYSTEMS DEVELOPMENT

The preceding description of information systems development is more readily associated with the creation of larger information systems by systems professionals. End user development (EUD), however, is the rapidly expanding phenomenon of the 1980s and 1990s. EUD is the development of information systems by the system's end users, with only a limited role played by IS personnel. One estimate is that more than 70% of all corporate processor cycles are currently devoted to processing end user-developed applications.

Explaining the rise of EUD in firms is hardly a complex process. The large backlogs of applications in many organizations (the ``MIS backlog'') and subsequent appearance of high-level productivity tools such as spreadsheets, DBMSs, and 4GLs on affordable microcomputers have created the climate for the rapid growth of end user-developed applications. These increasingly powerful computers are used as effective vehicles for rapidly creating individual or departmental applications, many at the managerial level—for example, DSS, ES, and EIS. The development of middleware (see Box 10.1) has also aided the efforts of end-users working on heterogeneous systems.

While EUD offers the promise of faster applications developed and running on lower-cost platforms, managers must clearly understand relevant issues and risks. Some of these are described next.

- There is no substitute for cost/benefit analysis of EUD projects, regardless of how little the developed system will cost. Often the major cost of some systems is the cost of IS support in later years.
- The necessity of professional IS staff via an information Center is critical to EUD success.
- The quality of programs developed by users should be upheld through program documentation and discouragement of poor programming practices.
- The question of how many platforms and software will be supported by the organization is central. Standards are vital to avoid future system incompatibilities and the difficulty and cost of supporting myriad tools in different departments.

(continued)

the database front, SQL is similar in its use by DBMSs on different platforms. Also, languages like C and CASE tools run interchangeably on mainframes, minicomputers, and microcomputers. Generally, the more portability engendered by the choice of development tools, the more platforms the developed software can be moved to in future. (See Box 13.1.)

13.2   PROGRAM TESTING

No information system is ever totally defect free. All system components undergo testing during development to increase confidence in the system's performance. As software is the most complex component of information systems, programs are extensively tested in the final software development phase. Several testing strategies and

---

BOX 13.1 *(continued)*

MANAGING END USER SYSTEMS DEVELOPMENT

- Security is critical in firms supporting EUD. Data becomes more vulnerable to corruption, viruses, and intentional fraud by user programs if proper safeguards are not taken. Outputs and transactions for example, should be time- and date-stamped, whenever possible.

Regarding the data dimension, much damage can be done to corporate databases by allowing their unrestricted access by end-users. Some risks include violation of data integrity and the use of resource-hungry queries on central hosts by unknowing users. For example, a user might issue queries involving the JOINing (merging) of multiple, huge relations. An important decision, then, is how access to data is provided for EUD. Many MIS managers are settling for periodic (for example, daily) ''dumping'' of data extracts from central servers onto departmental servers for EUD querying, instead of allowing unrestricted access to corporate databases, thus enabling searches on lower-cost platforms. Managers are also aided by new tools that allow involuntary backup of individual

workstations, allowing efficient backup of local databases and applications created on end user microcomputers.

Usually, the size of the intended project is a major determinant of the feasibility of EUD. As users develop programs using Lotus 1-2-3, Excel, dBase, Focus etc., or write queries for data extraction in SQL, formulas must be validated, input checked, and security measures enforced. This is usually done with assistance from the Information Center (IC), whose role can best be defined as helping the end users to help themselves. The first IC was established by IBM Canada in 1976 primarily to train users and was successful in reducing IS maintenance from 70% to 33% of the total IS effort. Other than training, the IC assists with hardware and software, offers troubleshooting, and helps with larger, more complex projects. They also maintain software libraries and circulate newsletters that publicize services and software updates etc. Their enabling role has been shown to reduce total IS costs.

methods are used to improve the quality of designed software and decrease the occurrence of system failures after implementation.

The Need for Testing

In a program developed for a typical organizational application, there are a large number of potential paths through the program. In the case of a twenty-loop iteration, for example, there are 2^{20} or 1,048,576 possible paths. Exhaustive testing would involve executing the program through each individual path, and checking for errors.

Program testing is crucial in the SDLC due to the potential that software errors have for causing disruptions in the firm's transaction processing operations. Software errors or bugs range in their effects from the minor to the fatal. Minor errors include the wrong display of a screen's borders and wrong pagination in reports; more serious errors include incorrect calculations; fatal errors involve the system freezing or crashing, with all current transactions or processes lost.

The consequences of a prolonged systems failure include:

- The cost of detecting and correcting the software flaw
- The cost of restoring the system to its normal state after the error is corrected
- Lost organizational productivity while the software is being repaired

The importance of program testing is not to eliminate all software errors, which is virtually impossible, but to reduce them to a minimum to avoid failures. Software testers must thereby see their objective as trying to prove the program does not work and to find errors, not to prove the opposite. For this reason, it is not desirable for coders to test their programs as they are less likely to aggressively test their quality.

Testing Methods and Strategies

Program testing must proceed in a systematic way using a mix of two major testing strategies: black box and white box testing (see Figure 13.8).

Black box testing tests the program's modules as a "black box," or without concern for the specifics of its internal code. It is based on the system's functional requirements and expected outputs given specific inputs. It is used by software designers and end users to see if the program runs according to their expectations.

White box testing is the exact opposite of black box testing, with the tester stepping through the code to ensure it runs correctly. Programs are checked to see if correct paths are taken and storage locations have the proper values. White box testing is used primarily by programmers, and not end users, to test the structural integrity of the programs. Comprehensive testing uses both white box and black box testing for best results.

Software testers utilize two coding methods to test structured modules: unit tests and system tests. **Unit tests** are performed on individual modules of the program, while system tests are applied to all the modules of a program working together. Two unit-testing methods are top-down and bottom-up testing. *Top-down integration testing* begins by testing the topmost modules in the structure chart and working downward to lower-level modules (Figure 13.9a). In testing higher-level modules, lower-level ones are replaced by **stubs**—empty modules that return control (and data) to the upper-level

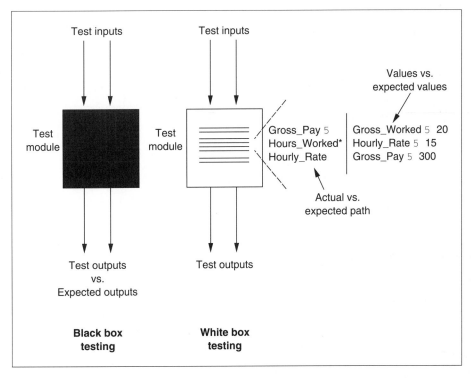

Test inputs   Test inputs

Values vs.
expected values

Test
module

Test
module

Gross_Pay 5   Gross_Worked 5 20
Hours_Worked*   Hourly_Rate 5 15
Hourly_Rate   Gross_Pay 5 300

Actual vs.
expected path

Test outputs   Test outputs
vs.
Expected outputs

Black box   **White box**
testing   **testing**

FIGURE 13.8   Black box and white box testing

module to ensure the independence of the test. Successive modules are tested from the top downward, as shown in Figure 13.9b. *Bottom-up integration testing* begins with the lowest-level modules and substitutes higher-level ones with **drivers,** empty modules that call the lower-level ones.

Top-down coding and testing enable a working prototype to be created earlier than in the bottom-up approach. This enables major conceptual errors to be detected earlier. In addition, difficulties in the topmost modules during bottom-up design may call for widespread changes in already written lower-level modules. Bottom-up testing (and coding) is only effective when lower-level modules are more complex and important than higher-level ones. Often, programmers combine both approaches in the "sandwich" approach to obtain the benefits of both.

Tests performed include checking for upper and lower limits of numeric inputs, ensuring that alphabetic input is not accepted by numeric fields and vice versa, trapping divisions by zero, and so on. Others include the handling of deadlock by multiuser DBMS programs and checking record updates and calculation results.

Performance tests and **peak tests** ensure that the system can handle normal and peak numbers of transactions with acceptable response times. **Volume tests,** however, ensure that the data storage requirements can be satisfied by the storage devices and software.

Alpha tests are performed on the first release of the software to the user, for testing in a real environment. This is a controlled test, which is performed under the supervision of systems personnel. **Beta tests** follow, after the errors detected in the alpha test have

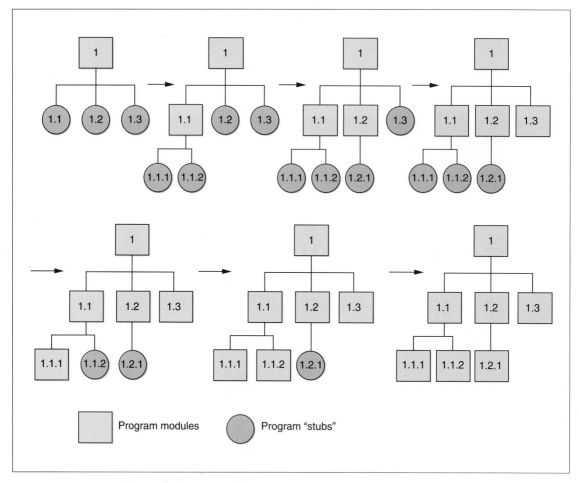

FIGURE 13.9 (a) Sequence of top-down testing (*continued*)

been corrected. Beta tests are the most advanced stage of the software before it goes into production (actual use), and the emphasis of testing is not only on software errors but also on usability factors, such as *ease of use, understandability,* and *the degree of fit to user requirements.*

Using Live and Artificial Test Data

When testing developed software, and especially during black box testing, several transactions are selected as experimental inputs to programs. This test data is either live or artificial. In alpha and beta tests, for example, **live test data,** that is, actual transactions, are passed through the system and the program's outputs are checked to determine whether the program is working correctly. Conversely, **artificial test data** may be developed by programmers, or automatically by special software programs as test inputs to the programs.

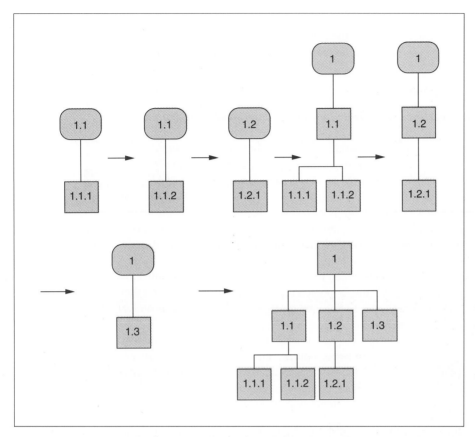

FIGURE 13.9 *(continued)*   (b) sequence of bottom-up testing.

Both live and artificial test data have their strengths and weaknesses. Live test data is actual transaction data that tests the software's ability to handle daily transactions. Its downside is that this data may be normal, clean data, which does not stretch the system's error-handling capabilities. Such data may not contain illegal or over-the-limit values; it may lack omissions, duplicated keys, and other features that would test the software's ability to handle abnormal conditions. Artificial test data probes these conditions thoroughly, examining beginning and end-of-range values, null values, and so on. However, the outputs of artificial test transactions can be verified only mechanically by the end user or tester only, and not in the context of actual transactions.

13.3   HARDWARE ACQUISITION

The information system's hardware is acquired in the latter part of the SDLC's design stage. To satisfy the proposed design, developers have many hardware vendors to choose from. These vendors offer a vast array of system configurations to address different user needs, but a systematic approach can make hardware selection and acquisition easier. For hardware and software, the development team often creates a **request for proposal**

(RFP) stating the requirements of the proposed hardware and software. Vendors then respond, describing the capabilities of their products and their fit to the stated requirements. Selected systems may then be leased or purchased, as described below.

Hardware Sources

Purchased hardware includes microcomputer (and other platform) systems, peripherals, power equipment, and specialized networking equipment. Sources for hardware acquisition depend on the resources available to research and evaluate systems.

Microcomputer hardware and software vendors advertise products in the trade literature—in computer magazines such as *Byte Magazine, Computer Shopper, InfoWorld, PC Magazine, MacUser, MacWorld,* and others. Networking hardware and software are advertised in *Communications Week* and *Network World. Information Week* and *Datamation* also display advertisements of vendors involved in enterprise-wide connectivity. Many of the advertisers in these trade magazines are **mail-order vendors.**

For the microcomputer buyer, mail-order purchases offer the quickest and most cost-effective purchasing method. Another approach is to purchase from a local retailer, which has the advantages of the user seeing and working with the system and of immediate delivery of stocked items.

Methods used to evaluate hardware (and systems) include: (1) **documented evaluations** in trade magazines; (2) limited or comprehensive **in-house testing;** and (3) through an **RFP** issued to system vendors. One evaluation from *Infoworld* magazine is shown in Figure 13.10. The systems group must examine such evaluations in the light of their own needs, scoring the items with weights that reflect their own priorities.

Studying documented evaluations is the least expensive method of evaluating hardware and software. In-house testing and evaluation are more expensive, if agreed to by hardware vendors. In smaller firms, limited evaluation is often performed by an ad hoc group, while larger firms may have system professionals specifically for that purpose. Hardware is evaluated most often by running the intended applications. Important considerations for the buyer are:

- **Hardware and software capabilities,** for example, speed, reliability, security, and ergonomics
- A **30-day money-back guarantee**
- **Warranties** and **extended warranties** on hardware, ranging from one to five years
- Responsive **on-site service**
- Availability of **value-added services,** such as network installation
- **Cost** of the hardware
- The quality of **vendor service**
- Availability of a **technical** (and, hopefully, toll-free) **hot-line**
- The **vendor's financial profile,** to avoid being left without support

Many firms utilize the 30-day money-back guarantee as an informal method of testing the capabilities of systems before purchase. In addition, the financial stability of the vendor is increasingly important as shakeouts of the market in recent years have left many users with worthless warranties following their vendors' bankruptcy.

The third method of system evaluation—the RFP—is used most often for large networked systems costing tens of thousands of dollars or more. These large systems are seldom mail-order purchases but are purchased instead from

- **Value added retailers (VARs),** such as *Entre, Computerland,* and *Nynex,* who sell hardware and software but focus on added services, for example, installation and maintenance
- **System consultants,** who range in size from small, one-office firms to large operations like *American Management Systems (AMS),* who deal mostly with large-scale projects
- **System integrators,** such as *Anderson Consulting,* who handle all aspects of large-scale projects, including reengineering and downsizing.

The Request For Proposal (RFP)

In large-scale projects, the development team often creates an RFP, which is made available to any of the preceding types of vendors. The RFP describes hardware and/or software requirements in enough detail to enable the vendors to provide proposals to satisfy them. The components of an RFP comprise:

- *Background information.* This describes the firm, its current objectives, and its environment.
- *Functional specifications and system design.* This resembles a checklist of features the system must possess and functions it must perform.
- *Benchmark test.* Benchmark tests for competitive systems are often included in the RFP to indicate how performance comparisons will be performed. Benchmarks for systems include running the intended application and simulating future applications. These tests may be performed on- or off-site.
- *Price and payment conditions.* The maximum cost of the system is also described in the RFP, along with payment details. These include the terms of the contract, payment schedule, delivery dates, warranties, and support arrangements.
- *Performance criteria and evaluation.* The RFP also contains an outline of the method by which competitive proposals will be evaluated. Criteria for comparison (for example, *performance, compatibility, reliability, user-friendliness*) and their importance are included. An *RFP table of contents* is shown in Figure 13.11.

Following the response of vendors to the RFP, benchmarking may be performed on the vendor's hardware at off-site locations, or in-house with vendor cooperation. This is followed by the evaluation of proposals meeting minimum requirements. Scoring models of the type shown in Figure 13.12, with attached weights, are the major means of evaluating submitted proposals. The top-scoring one or two systems are then examined more closely with regard to their substantive differences and how they would solve the firm's problems. One of these is then selected. Frequently, but not always, this is the highest-scoring system.

	Thomas-Conrad TC4045 16/4 Mbps Adapter/AT	3Com TokenLink III 16/4 ISA
Speed	284.9 minutes; 7 percent slower than Olicom. **279 of 300**	273.1 minutes; 3 percent slower than Olicom. **291 of 300**
Compatability	We found no compatibility problems. **Excellent** (25 of 25)	We found no compatibility problems. **Excellent** (25 of 25)
Flexibility	Supports I/O addresses 1A20, 2A20, 3A20, 3AA40, 3A60, 3A80, 3AA0, 4AE0; supports interrupts 2(9), 3, 5, 6, 7, 10, 11, and 12. **Excellent** (50 of 50)	Supports I/O addresses 0x20-23, 0x24-27; supports interrupts 2(9), 3, 6, 7. **Excellent** (50 of 50)
Documentation	Concise installation guide; detailed diagrams; table of contents but no index, glossary, or troubleshooting guides; an adhesive label lists configuration settings, and a pocket guide has diagrams of switch-block and jumper settings. **Very Good** (56.25 of 75)	Detailed diagrams; table of contents and index; no glossary or troubleshooting section; an appendix explains error messages and switch settings; a pull-out card contains pertinent phone numbers. **Very Good** (56.25 of 75)
Setup	Offers choice of jumper/switchblock or software-selectable configuration; WSGEN created the IPX.COM file using Thomas-Conrad drivers. **Good** (93.75 of 150)	Configurable via switch blocks; WSGEN uses generic Token Ring option to generate IPX.COM; built-in RPL (boot Programmable ROM) allows remote boot of workstations. **Satisfactory** (75 of 150)
Board design	Midlength card; mostly surface-mount technology; conveniently located jumpers and switches; no wire patches. **Excellent** (50 of 50)	Slot-length card; some surface-mount technology; switch blocks are accessible; one trace wire. **Very Good** (37.50 of 50)
Support policies	Five-year warranty; toll-free support 24 hours a day, seven days a week; BBS support. **Excellent** (50 of 50)	Lifetime warranty; toll-free support seven days a week, 24 hours a day; BBS support. **Excellent** (50 of 50)
Technical support	Friendly and knowledgeable; although staff did not offer to walk us through our problem, they offered helpful tips. **Very Good** (75 of 100)	Answered all our questions correctly; walked us through problems when asked. **Very Good** (75 of 100)
Price	**$495** for bus-mastering card with 128KB of on-board RAM; sold through dealers. **161.21 of 200**	**$695** for bus-mastering card with 64KB of on-board RAM; sold through dealers. **114.82 of 200**
	8.4	**7.7**

FIGURE 13.10   Token ring cards: Evaluation of network interface cards from *Infoworld* magazine   (*continued*)

Racal-InterLan TR16/4 ISA	SMC TokenCard Elite
267.6 minutes; 1 percent slower than Olicom. **297 of 300**	273.9 minutes; 3 percent slower than Olicom. **290 of 300**
We found no compatibility problems. **Excellent** (25 of 25)	We found no compatibility problems. **Excellent** (25 of 25)
I/O Addresses Supported: A00, A20, A40, A80; supports interrupts 3, 9, 10, 11. **Very Good** (37.50 of 50)	Supports I/O addresses 200, 220, 240, 260, 280, 2A0, 2E0, 300, 320, 340, 360, 380, 3A0, 3C0, and 3E0; supports interrupts 2, 3, 4, 5, 7, 10, 11, and 15. **Excellent** (50 of 50)
Concise and accurate; some technical illustrations; describes error messages and support services; table of contents and glossary. **Satisfactory** (37.50 of 75)	Provides full installation details; includes chapters on PCAgent and SNMP, LSP and LAPS, network planning, and source routing; also has troubleshooting section, specifications, table of contents, index. **Excellent** (75 of 75)
Easily configured using two switch blocks or with the MKFLASH utility, we used mostly default settings; WSGEN uses Racal drivers to generate IPX.COM. **Good** (93.75 of 150)	Possible through either easy-to-use software or conveniently located jumpers; pregenerated IPX drivers. **Very Good** (112.50 of 150)
Slot-length card; mostly surface mount technology; switch blocks are conveniently located; no trace wires. **Excellent** (50 of 50)	Full-length card; mostly surface-mount technology; no patches or jumper wires. **Very Good** (37.50 of 50)
Lifetime warranty period; toll-free support 8 a.m. to 6 p.m. Eastern time; BBS support. **Excellent** (50 of 50)	Five-year warranty; toll-free support from 8:30 a.m. to 6 p.m. Eastern time; BBS support. **Excellent** (50 of 50)
Never put on hold; calls returned promptly; courteous; questions answered accurately and promptly. **Very Good** (75 of 100)	Our questions were answered correctly; support staff was friendly, helpful, and knowledgeable, but they only walked us through problems when asked. **Very Good** (75 of 100)
$649 for bus-mastering card with 512KB on-board RAM; sold through dealers. **122.96 of 200**	**$399** for a non-bus-mastering card with 64KB of on-board RAM; sold through dealers. **200 of 200**
7.8	**9.1**

FIGURE 13.10 (*continued*)

1. INTRODUCTION
    i Structure and scope of the RFP
    ii Objective of the RFP
    iii Organizational background and philosophy
    iv Existing hardware/software environment
    v Existing business environment

2. GUIDELINES FOR VENDOR RESPONSE
    i Specifications for vendor response
    ii Vendor responses
    iii Evaluation schedule
    iv Evaluation criteria and process

3. REQUIREMENTS
    i Vendor data
    ii Vendor support and training
    iii Documentation
    iv Hardware and software details
    v Database model
    vi Tuning and measurement
    vii Functional requirements

4. COSTS
    i Summary of costs
    ii Sunk costs
    iii Recurring costs
    iv Price guarantee
    v Maintenance agreement
    vi New releases

5. SIGNATURE PAGE

FIGURE 13.11 Table of contents for loans management RFP

Purchasing and Leasing Options

Following hardware selection, it is then **purchased** or **leased.** Purchasing the system has several advantages, namely:

1. *Total cost.* The total amount paid is usually less than that paid under a lease, net present value of money notwithstanding, because most leases are characterized by high interest rates. Many *closed-end leases* also require a significant payment at the beginning and end of the lease period. For cash-rich firms, purchase is an especially attractive option.

2. *Control of the system.* The system or components purchased are under full control of the user, in contrast to the usage limitations often placed on leased systems. This provides greater flexibility for the client firm in deploying the information system.

3. *Long-term use.* If equipment is required for periods of three years or greater, the purchase option is usually preferable. Additionally, tax benefits can accrue

Evaluation Criterion	Weights (1–3)	Vendor 1	Vendor 2	Vendor 1	Vendor 2
		Score (1–10)		Weighted Score	
Degree of fit to requirements	3.00	7.00	8.00	21.00	24.00
Maintenance agreement	2.00	6.00	8.00	12.00	16.00
System flexibility	1.50	5.00	7.00	7.50	10.50
Expandability	2.50	6.00	8.00	15.00	20.00
Vendor training	1.00	9.00	8.00	9.00	8.00
Vendor financial strengths/ reputation	2.50	9.00	8.00	22.50	20.00
System cost	2.50	9.00	7.00	22.50	17.50
		Total score		**109.50**	**116.00**

FIGURE 13.12   Scoring model for loan management system proposal

from depreciation of purchased equipment, while for leased equipment they do not.

The major downside to purchasing hardware is the risk introduced by rapidly changing technologies. Life cycles for microprocessor platforms are currently about two years, and purchasing a system might result in the firm owning obsolete equipment. Some of the risk can be reduced by the purchase of modular systems (see Chapter 3), which allow them to be upgraded as improved system components are developed.

Firms that lease hardware can obtain new technologies almost as soon as they become available. Second, leasing gives firms access to systems they cannot purchase outright, a factor that may even decide a cash-strapped firm's existence. The counterweight to these benefits are the comparatively high costs of the leased system and possible constraints on the system's use. It is rarely worthwhile to lease microcomputers as yearly lease costs can often exceed purchase prices. Increasingly, only expensive WAN connection equipment such as ATM and ISDN hubs are leased (from telecommunications vendors).

13.4   DEVELOPING PROCEDURES

Information systems also feature procedures performed by people. We noted earlier that many operations and maintenance procedures are now carried out by software. In discussing procedures, we refer only to those associated with using the computer system and not the operational business tasks programmed into software. We further classify procedures into *operational procedures, failure/recovery procedures,* and *backup procedures.* Also, we can distinguish between those performed by users and by systems personnel.

Operational Procedures

Operational procedures are performed in operational use of the IS and include entering data, loading programs, and printing invoices and reports. They are user-initiated, but completed by the computer. For systems personnel, normal procedures include monitoring and evaluating computer performance, planning for hardware and software upgrades, and performing scheduled system maintenance. Regular backups of the system's data and programs and development and installation of new programs are also operational procedures. Similarly, these procedures are complemented by computer programs.

Failure and Recovery Procedures

Failure procedures are performed after system failures, which may mean resorting to a manual system or to an alternative computer-based backup system. In one hospital admissions department, a system failure initiates the registering of new admissions on paper until the system is restored. Well-designed information systems have as an integral component procedures performed during complete or partial failures. The analyst is usually responsible for developing these procedures, which include shutting down malfunctioning hardware, manually clearing paper jams, and aborting failed programs.

Recovery procedures restore the system to normal operation following a system failure. For the user, they range from rebooting (restarting) the computer, to rekeying transactions from the period of system failure. Information systems personnel should possess clear, documented procedures to initiate the system's recovery, including procedures to restore databases to a consistent state, apply accumulated transactions, and repair or replace defective hardware and software. The scope and cost of recovery procedures include those caused by disruption to the firm's operational activity and the cost of repairing the system. Repair and component replacement are less expensive for microcomputer-based information systems than for larger systems, and the maintenance costs for microcomputer installation reflect this.

Backup Procedures

Just after their lunch break, employees in your firm are busy taking customer orders, while it rains heavily outside. A sudden flash of lightning arcs across the sky, striking a nearby power pole and making some workers instinctively duck. Your file server and workstations lose power, along with the overhead lighting. When power is restored, the hard disk on the server is found to have crashed, with large amounts of data on it lost.

The preceding scenario dramatizes the importance of performing regular data backups on an information system. Without backup copies of the database, the above firm would have great difficulty restoring the database and suffer significant losses. Such data-related disasters range in seriousness from a user mistakenly overwriting a file, to the above situation. In fact, in some mission-critical applications, the loss of a firm's database may mean the firm's demise. Users and/or network personnel perform **backup procedures,** using backup software and hardware. Their purpose is to ensure speedy recovery from data-related disasters. Backup procedures, hardware, and software vary, depending on

- The type of application for which backup is being performed and the cost of data loss
- The size of the data files being backed up
- The available resources for the backup activity

The devices typically used for data backup are (1) floppy disks, (2) hard disks, (3) magnetic tape, and (4) optical disks. Magnetic tape is currently the most widely used device for tape backup but is not an automatic choice for all backup applications.

For the single microcomputer user, floppy disks and tape are common backup media. Microcomputer OSs, such as MS-DOS and the Macintosh OS, now incorporate backup utilities. Two common backup methods are *full backups* and *incremental backups:* The former back up the entire contents of the hard disk while the latter only store files that have been changed after the last full backup (see Figure 13.13). Typically, a full backup might be performed once a week, with daily incremental backups in the intervening period.

Backup utilities are also available off the shelf. Examples include **Central Point Backup,** from *Central Point Software* and **Norton Backup** from *Symantec.* These utilities offer more capabilities than microcomputer OSs, such as *unattended backup* and *data compression.*

For network file servers, where the consequences of data loss are potentially more serious, magnetic tape, optical disks, and hard disks are preferred backup methods. Their benefits are convenience, cost savings, and the ability to perform unattended backups (see Chapter 5). With the capacities of magnetic cartridges reaching 5 Gb or more in cartridge jukeboxes, more sophisticated backup software is required. Software utilities like **ARCserve v.4.0** from *Cheyenne Software* may be used to back up both the

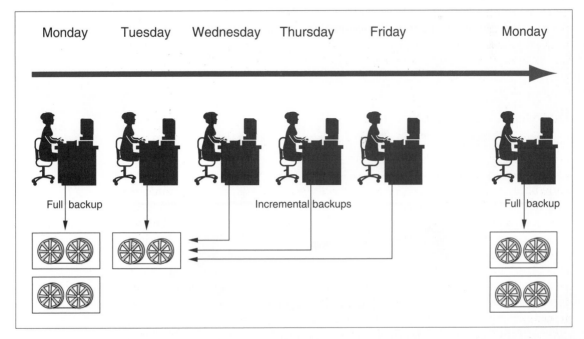

FIGURE 13.13   Creating full and incremental backups

fileserver database and files on individual workstations to tape, removable hard drives, or optical disks. See Figure 13.14.

For sequential files on SASDs, the primary method for backup is the *grandparent-parent-child* method, based on creating a new master file from the old by applying batched transactions (see also Chapter 7). Two prior generations of full backups (called the grandparent and parent) are preserved in off-site locations, as shown in Figure 13.15. The child, or most current master file, is kept on-site. If damaged, it can be recreated from the parent and the previous transaction file; likewise, the parent can be recreated from the grandparent and past transaction records.

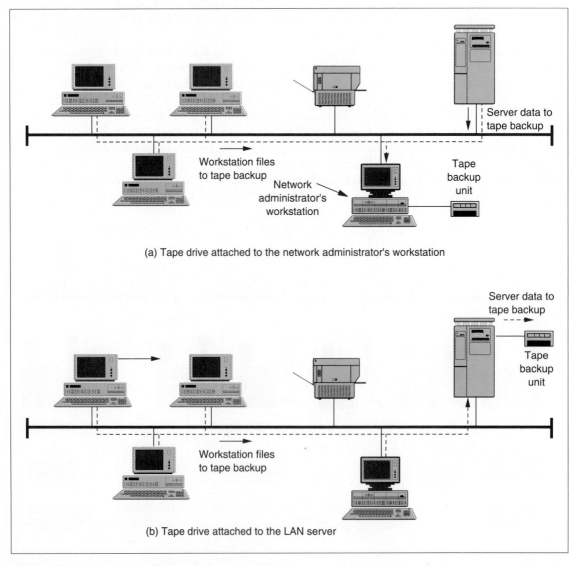

FIGURE 13.14   Two strategies for tape backup

In contrast to sequential files, master files on DASDs (using direct access methods) are updated in place, meaning that a single copy of the file is used during updating. *RAID (redundant arrays of inexpensive disks)* methods are becoming commonplace as a means of providing hot backups on primarily microcomputer-based platforms (see Chapter 5). RAID Level 2 provides disk mirroring, while Level 5 provides data redundancy through

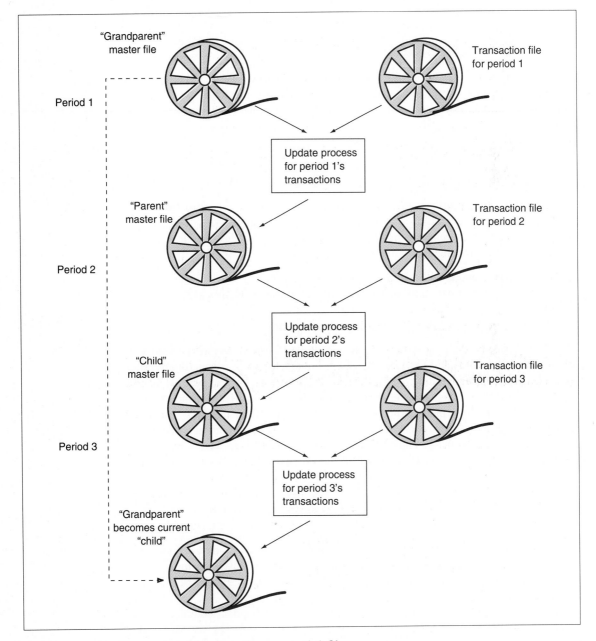

FIGURE 13.15 Generational backup for sequential files

parity blocks. Level 2 may be used as a complete means of data backup, while Level 5 may be combined with tape backup for increased protection.

Finally, some users prefer *rewritable optical disks,* with their huge data storage capabilities and direct access, to magnetic tape. In cases where selective restoration of files is required, they are clearly superior to sequential-access magnetic tapes. Most commercially available software now supports backups on rewritable optical disks.

13.5 MANAGERIAL ISSUES

Project managers constantly seek to make information systems secure, to prevent their unauthorized access, theft, and misuse. They also require mechanisms to prevent deterioration of data and program integrity. Another managerial concern relates to the challenges and risks of end-user development and effective methods to ensure its success.

System Security

Information system security is the vulnerability of the system to unauthorized access, data manipulation, and removal or tampering with physical devices. Surprisingly, perhaps, security violations are mostly perpetrated by workers in the firm, not by outsiders. Examples include

- Gaining illegal and unauthorized access to a system
- Entering fraudulent data into, or initiating illegal transactions on a system
- Theft of a firm's hardware and/or software
- Entry of computer viruses into the information system

In distributed systems spread out across multiple locations, system security is more difficult to provide. Devices are more vulnerable than in mainframe sites and data communications links are more exposed. Providing perfect security is cost prohibitive for most firms, and the manager must balance security measures against the cost of providing them. Another trade-off results from the way in which complicated system security measures rapidly make the information system less usable. For example, using eight layers of system passwords would be intolerable to users, so system designers must also continually balance usability against security.

To system developers concerned about security, several measures may be incorporated into the design of all five system components to make the entire system more secure.

- ***Physical security measures.*** Providing locks for rooms where vital data or equipment (for example, servers) are stored is a typical measure. Additionally, systems units and peripherals may be secured using steel cables and anchor plates. Hard disks may also be protected with locks to prevent unauthorized access.
- ***Encryption.*** Various encryption methods are often used for data communications across public or private networks, or even for storage of data on hard disks.

Additionally, "dongles" or coded keys are used by some software manufacturers to prevent the use of software packages by unauthorized personnel.

- *User identification and passwords.* These are commonplace software-based mechanisms used to limit access privileges in a system to authorized system users. *Call-back systems* also decrease the system's vulnerability to remote access by verifying a remote user's passwords and user ID and calling the user back on a number listed in the system's internal directory.
- *Validating data inputs.* Software checks can verify data inputs from data entry personnel and operational users to ensure they fall within predefined constraints. Fields with improper values automatically void the transaction and are logged on an error report.
- *Disaster planning.* Even with the security measures above, systems still face the risk of improper access. A disaster plan must be in place to recover from the effects of any such breaches of security and to log all attempted violations.

Ensuring Data Integrity

Data integrity is an important developer concern. Its loss may result from improper database access and manipulation, or from disk crashes. Such events may leave the database in an inconsistent state, which can bring about disputes with clients, lost business, uncollected bills and so on. For mission-critical information systems, such features as *two-phase locking, two-phase commit, snapshots,* and *rollback* (see Chapters 7 and 10) are required to ensure **atomic transactions**—transactions that are either fully completed or fully aborted.

Newer commercial microcomputer DBMSs (for example, *Sybase, Oracle, Ingres, Foxpro,* and *Supra*) incorporate these features, enabling them to be used for mission-critical client/server applications. Combined with well-designed backup procedures, anti-virus software, and the disaster and recovery planning methods previously discussed, database integrity can be protected.

Managing End-User Development

Software is developed by system professionals and/or end users. System professionals are formally organized in groups, as discussed earlier, and they follow the SDLC stages more rigorously and use formal productivity measures. Microcomputer-based systems often feature system development by the end user, a process called *end-user development* or *EUD. Managing EUD* is an added responsibility of today's MIS managers. It is not direct management, as with their own staffs, but instead, consists of setting policies and standards, providing training, and creating the appropriate technological infrastructure.

Standards are vital for both end users and MIS personnel. For example, in consultation with the users, the MIS department might provide support for only two spreadsheet packages, for example, Lotus 1-2-3 and Quattro Pro. This approach reduces the costs of supporting users across the firm and standardizes applications and compatibility by limiting software choices. Purchasing is also simplified for the MIS department, as site licenses can be purchased at reduced cost and easily used in a LAN.

Creating hardware and networking standards and software policies (for example, documentation methods for all developed software) are other specific management concerns for EUD.

The MIS group is also responsible for **providing access to data** on remote servers, enabling end users to *download* information from mainframes or other servers on the firm's network. The appropriate combination of hardware (for example, gateways) and software (NOSs) must be supported by the MIS department. This provides easy access to corporate and other databases and provides appropriate restrictions on data access to various users.

Technical support in developing applications is a key managerial concern. The MIS department must be prepared to deploy sufficient personnel and tools to assist end users in troubleshooting their applications during and after development. Many MIS departments provide *help lines* to aid users in this way, as well as on-site technical support. Some even provide *information centers* for end-user support, with tutorials, training, and a facility with microcomputers and end-user software for instructional purposes.

13.6 THE IMPLEMENTATION PROCESS

A characteristic of successful information systems development is the view of implementation as a distinct process and not an afterthought. Developed systems must be formally evaluated and accepted by the users before implementing the new system. To aid acceptance, user training takes place to acquaint users with the functions and procedures of the new system. The conversion process that follows introduces the system directly or gradually into operational use, depending on the risks involved in the transition and available funds. Following this transition, a postimplementation review examines any deviation between the system's performance and the original objectives.

Acceptance Testing

A formal process of **acceptance testing** precedes the introduction of the developed information system into the work environment. A **structured walkthrough** is an important part of this process, in which the system developers take the user through the components of the system, that is, input screens, output reports, demonstrated performance on realistic datasets, and so on. From the user group's perspective, the objective is to verify the match between the system's features and their functional requirements. The results of an acceptance test are

- The signed acceptance of the information system by the user group
- Revision of parts of the system that do not match user requirements
- In rare cases, the rejection of the entire system as unsatisfactory

The uncertainty surrounding the acceptance test can be reduced by using such techniques as prototyping and JAD, which involve the user on a continuing basis during the SDLC.

Installing Hardware and Software

New systems may require the installation of software on existing hardware or the installation of both hardware and software. In Chapter 3, we saw that facility requirements of microcomputer-based systems are not as rigorous as those of mainframes. Nevertheless, site preparation is required when any new hardware is introduced into the workplace. Relevant considerations are

- *Space.* This includes desk space for workstations and peripherals, and locations for servers and other critical system components such as mass storage and communications control devices (for example, hubs and routers).
- *Furniture.* Appropriate desks, chairs, shelves, and other furniture must be acquired and in place for the incoming hardware. Also included are *security devices,* for example, steel cabling and attachment bolts for computers and peripherals.
- *Network cabling.* For LANs and internetworks, cables must be carefully laid out, with a blueprint or schematic of the buildings used for planning.
- *Power protection.* Surge protection devices and uninterruptible power supplies (UPSs) are essential components of mission-critical systems and are important in site preparation.

File Conversion and Data Entry

Following site preparation, the hardware is brought into the workplace and the software is loaded. Cabling connections are made for LAN-based systems and a **burn-in test**—where the system is run continuously for 48–72 hours—is performed. Burn-in tests resulted from studies showing that most hardware failures occur within a short time after initial use. The test helps to identify and replace those components prior to actual system use.

Files in the old system are migrated to the new one through **file conversion.** The existing files may be in document or computer-readable form. Conversion of paper-based files is difficult and costly, with the two options being *manual data entry* and *scanning using OCR.* For large volumes, scanning and recognizing handwritten documents is now practical. For document imaging, however, scanning bitmaps without OCR is appropriate for file conversion. For typewritten documents, scanning is also practical, even for database applications, but requires human assistance to handle recognition errors. Scanning and subsequent processing of the text file into database fields is usually better than manual data entry using data operators, but both options should undergo a cost-benefit analysis.

If the existing information system is computer based, a program may be written to carry out the conversion between the current data formats and the new. Differences between the old and new files lie in

- *Media.* For example, conversion from magnetic tape to optical disk for backup purposes
- *Format.* For example, translation of dBase file formats to Oracle file formats
- *Data models.* For example, conversion from a hierarchical data model to a relational one
- *Content.* For example, new fields may be added to the records of certain files

Files that are subject to file conversion include (1) *master files,* (2) *transaction files,* (3) *index and table (reference) files,* (4) *backup files,* and (5) *graphics and sound files.* Many microcomputer-based software packages possess import and export features that simplify the process of file conversion and remove the need for special conversion programs.

User Training

User training is essential in implementing new information systems. The more the old and new systems differ, the more training is required for users. Decisions regarding user training cover the training medium, methods, content, and location, and have different cost-effectiveness implications depending on the context.

External vendors or in-house trainers may train the users of the new system. **External vendors** provide high-quality training for industry-standard packages (for example, dBase, Excel, and Windows). They are less useful, however, when the application has been developed in-house using a 3GL. **In-house trainers** are usually MIS professionals, but in organizations where large numbers must be trained, selected users can be initially trained and asked to train other users. Help desks and/or information centers may then be used to provide user support.

Common training methods are

1. **On-the-job training,** using system manuals that describe the system's functions. Using these normally presents a steep learning curve for users and one that may not be overcome by all users.
2. **Human instructors,** who are either in-house or external. Feedback, interaction, and personalized instruction are possible with this training method, and its effectiveness surpasses the on-the-job approach. The disadvantage of human instructors is their high cost.
3. **Computer-aided instruction (CAI),** which is widely used and costs considerably less than human instructors, but it is relatively impersonal and offers less flexibility and effectiveness.
4. **Learning through videos,** which involves the added expense of video players and requires the user to manipulate both the video player and computer simultaneously.
5. **Interactive video instruction (IVI),** a form of instruction that was discussed in Chapter 8. Using training programs stored on optical disks, the user may be trained through multiple media, that is, sound, text, graphics, and animation sequences. IVI is more interactive than the older CAI and is more effective. It costs more than CAI but is less expensive and more available than human instructors.

The *location* chosen for training is an important determinant of its effectiveness. Workplace training is subject to interruptions from colleagues and customers and other distractions. Conversely, off-site training is more secure from interruptions and distractions; however, it is more expensive and the system used may not reflect the actual information system. A compromise measure is to train users in special on-site locations, saving costs but ensuring relative seclusion.

System Conversion Strategies

System conversion is the culmination of the SDLC's implementation phase and involves the replacement of the old information system with the new. The conversion period is a critical time in the SDLC, but confidence in the system's performance is higher if system prototyping and extensive testing precede it. Conversion may be immediate or gradual, depending on the information system's characteristics and other factors, such as available resources. Generally four strategies are used by developers. See Figure 13.16 for a look at these methods.

1. *The direct cutover method.* This is also called the *cold turkey* method, where the existing system is wholly and immediately replaced with the new. This method has the most risk associated with it, as a failure of the new system will leave the firm without any primary method of processing transactions. For example, transaction processing may be switched from a minicomputer-and-terminal-based system to a networked system of microcomputers over a weekend. All the files would be migrated to the new system, and access to the minicomputer would no longer be available on the next workday.

   The direct cutover method, while risky, may be the only option available to a cash-poor firm without the resources for other forms of system conversion. A further reason for using this method is if the new system differs greatly from the old, and no meaningful comparison can be made between the two if they are run together. Additionally, the direct cutover method is suitable for small systems where the cost of failure is low.

2. *Parallel conversion.* This conversion method involves running existing and new systems together while comparing their outputs and performance. If the new system's performance is deficient, then it can be modified without any adverse impact on the firm's transaction processing. The price paid for this risk reduction is an increase in the firm's transaction processing costs, which are three to five times normal costs. In general, only mission-critical applications, where the old and new systems are largely identical, are appropriate candidates for the parallel conversion method.

3. *Phased conversion.* Large information systems are often implemented in phases owing to their size or to financial constraints; in each phase, selected functions of the system are implemented, until the entire system is in place. In phased conversion, more important phases are usually implemented first. For example, in the loans management case, the accounts payable module might be implemented first (increasing cash flow), with the input and processing of customer loan applications automated in a second phase.

   Phased conversion also reduces the risk associated with the conversion process and demonstrates the usability of the information system. A disadvantage is the risk of the phased-in component being incompatible with the remaining part of the existing system.

4. *Pilot project.* Another approach to implementing large projects is through the use of a pilot project, a fully featured information system implemented in one part of the firm. Success of the pilot project leads to system implementation in all other areas. The system is tested before its full adoption under conditions of reduced risk,

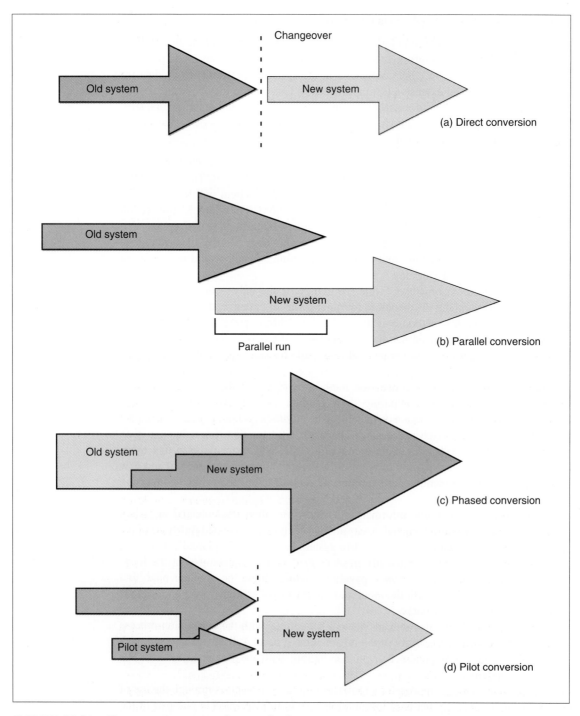

FIGURE 13.16   **Four system conversion methods**

similar to the phased implementation and the parallel run. However, it avoids the considerable costs of the parallel run and tests all the system's features, not only those of selected phases.

Postimplementation Review

A postimplementation review sets out to determine whether the original objectives of the system were achieved. This study takes place shortly after implementation and the system's performance, costs, and benefits are tracked and matched with prior expectations. In Figure 13.17, for example, tracking the new loans management system shows that both performance and costs were initially underestimated, while monetary benefits of the new system were slightly below initial profit estimates. This postimplementation review or audit is an avenue for the firm to evaluate how good their development methods and evaluation techniques were and indicate desirable future modifications to the information system.

CHAPTER SUMMARY _____

Following systems analysis and design activities, the design specifications are used to develop the new information system. For microcomputer-centered systems, many high-quality off-the-shelf packages are available to satisfy a wide variety of user requirements. In other cases, software is developed by end users or system professionals using a software development life cycle (SWDLC). Using carefully selected tools and organizational methods (for example, chief programmer teams and software metrics), software is developed to operate at a maximum level of reliability. To ensure reliability, software is tested using various techniques with both artificial and test data.

The next systems development stage is purchasing hardware. For enterprise systems, hardware sources include *mail-order operations, value added retailers,* and *local hardware and software vendors.* Often a request for proposal (RFP) is created and used to acquire data on proposed system solutions from various vendors and to evaluate submitted proposals.

Procedures are also developed for running the new system and for handling system failures. These procedures, together with system security and data integrity measures, are intended to maximize the system's reliability while keeping it secure from unauthorized users.

Poorly conceived implementation plans cause some system failures. All of its facets—user acceptance testing, hardware and software installation, file conversion, and user training—should be extensively planned with end-user representatives. Systems may be converted using direct, phased, pilot, or parallel conversion methods, depending on available resources and the importance of the new system. Following conversion, the system normally undergoes a postimplementation review to determine how much the original goals have been achieved.

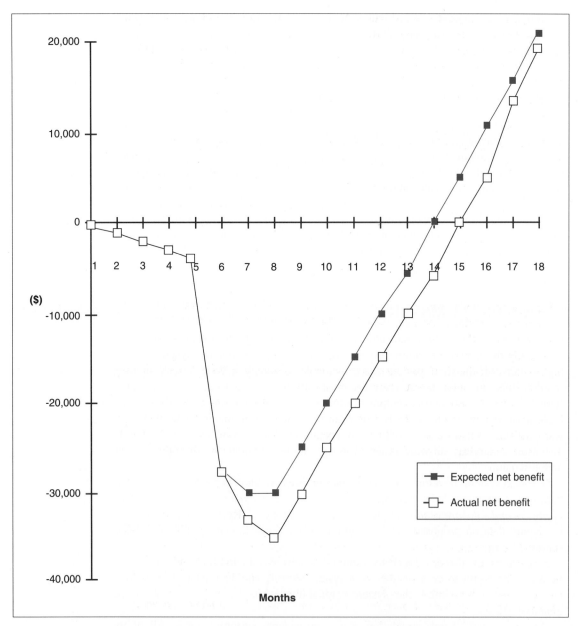

FIGURE 13.17   Postimplementation review of the loan management system

REVIEW QUESTIONS

1. Describe the three stages of the software development life cycle. Why should more effort be spent designing code rather than actually coding?
2. Describe three methods of organizing larger software development teams.

3. Why are programs developed with CASE tools more likely to contain fewer bugs than programs created using 3GLs?
4. What is the objective of a program tester? What are your suggestions to the project manager regarding the composition of the software testing team?
5. What modifications to the LOEC model are required to make it a better software productivity metric?
6. Describe the differences between black box and white box testing. Which of these is the user most interested in, and why?
7. What are the benefits of purchasing over leasing computer equipment?
8. List and describe two major features you would look for in a data backup utility.
9. What are three possible measures you could take to prevent theft of your firm's microcomputer hardware?
10. How can a software package with extensive data import/export capabilities save a firm time and money in implementing a new information system?

EXERCISES

1. Critically compare program development teams, chief programmer teams, and egoless programmer teams. Which form of organization is best suited to
   a. Small but critical projects, for example, a communications interface between a LAN and a minicomputer
   b. A large inventory control program, comprising over 300,000 lines of code
   c. A DSS for supporting a single marketing manager
   d. A large, complex program to support a space agency's rocket simulations
2. Examine product evaluations in a computer magazine, such as *Byte, InfoWorld,* or *PC World.* What, if any, are the weaknesses of these evaluations? How might potential hardware or software purchasers customize these evaluations to fit their individual needs?

SUGGESTED READINGS

Brooks, F. P. *The Mythical Man-Month.* Reading, MA: Addison-Wesley, 1979.

Boehm, B. *Software Engineering Economics.* Englewood Cliffs, NJ: Prentice-Hall, 1981.

Burch, J. G. *Systems Analysis, Design, and Implementation.* Boston: Boyd and Fraser, 1992.

Byte Lab Staff. "New LAN Backup Tools." *Byte Magazine,* April 1992, pp. 192–208.

Corporate Computing Staff. "Request for Proposal: The Challenge." *Corporate Computing,* Vol. 1, No. 4, October, 1992, pp. 130–131.

De Marco, T. *Structured Analysis and System Specification.* New York, NY: Yourdon Press, 1978.

Gane, C., and Sarson, T. *Structured Systems Analysis: Tools and Techniques.* Englewood Cliffs, NJ: Prentice-Hall, 1979.

LaPlante, A. "Checking Under the Hood." *Infoworld,* April 15, 1991, pp. 47–49.

McClure, C. *CASE Is Software Automation.* Englewood Cliffs, NJ: Prentice-Hall, 1989.

Mendelson, E. "Premium Insurance: Backup Software Gets Better." *PC Magazine,* June 11, 1992, pp. 103–136.

Ricciuti, M. "Mainframe DBMS Power Unleashed." *Datamation,* October 15, 1992.

CHAPTER 14

THE NEW FIRM—PEOPLE

INTRODUCTION

Enterprise computing, with multiple platforms and new technologies, is creating a demand for IS professionals with new skills. The **skill profiles** and opportunities in the middle to late 1990s include *data communications* and *advanced development tools* such as CASE, to complement interpersonal skills and 3GL expertise. This chapter opens by discussing the required skills and new opportunities available to the information systems graduate.

Legal and ethical issues are important societal concerns for workers using enterprise networks. In such systems, data is accessible much faster and in greater quantities than ever before. Much of this data is personal or copyrighted, raising questions of privacy and control in managing information systems. Also, as more workers use microcomputers in daily activity, **ergonomics** has become an additional concern in firms where they are prevalent. Furniture design, controlling CRT emissions, improving lighting, and preventing injuries related to computer use are essential parts of IS design. They all have a significant impact on both individual and group productivity.

Learning Objectives

After reading this chapter, you will be able to:

- Make selections from an information systems curriculum in preparation for emerging information system opportunities
- Propose safeguards for information systems to ensure that they operate within legal and ethical boundaries
- Incorporate ergonomic features into information systems to protect worker health and improve individual and group productivity

14.1   SKILL PROFILES FOR ENTERPRISE _____ COMPUTING SYSTEMS _____

As computer technologies are transformed by the growth of LANs, WANs, and enterprise systems, the skill profiles for information system professionals required to create and maintain these systems are also changing. Gradually, mainframe- and minicomputer-related skills are giving ground to expertise in networking and in specialist tools such as CASE. Crucially, *Fortune* magazine predicts impressive rates of growth for information systems professionals. These rates are 56% for programmers and 79% for systems analysts between 1993 and 2005. The skills required by these new professionals will be reflected in the areas of system development, specialized skills, and general business skills.

System Development Skills and Opportunities

The system development skills accorded the most importance in the past decade include structured development methodologies and third-generation languages, such as COBOL. Fully 80 percent of existing applications are written in COBOL, and it also accounts for nearly half of all current development work. In fact, several structured COBOL products (for example, *Micro Focus* **COBOL**) and object-oriented versions (*Accucobol's* **Accucobol-85**) now exist. Many surveys, however, indicate a definite trend toward other toolsets, such as:

1. *CASE tools.* With over 850 CASE products in the marketplace, their use as a means of improving productivity in systems development is growing. Skills in such CASE tools as *Information Engineering Facility (IEF), Information Engineering Workbench (IEW),* and *Excelerator* are now regularly advertised for by employers. Their use by developers is projected to increase dramatically over the next ten years.
2. *Structured analysis and design approaches.* Structured techniques are a central feature of CASE tools as well as 3GLs (for example, C, Pascal, and recently, COBOL). Current and future system developers require extensive experience in structured approaches for effective systems development.
3. *Fourth-generation languages (4GLs).* These include database-related languages (for example, SQL and xBase), application and report generators (for example, NATURAL, FOCUS, TELON), and spreadsheet macros. Increasingly, knowledge of these tools is required by end users and the systems personnel who support them.

The positions filled by individuals with these skills range from **business system analysts** to **programmers. End-user support specialists** are found in information centers and in other support roles. **Database designers** and **data communications specialists** (see below) will also have central roles in developing today's information systems.

Specialist Skills and Opportunities

Different specialists are important in developing enterprisewide systems. They include:

- *Data communications specialists.* These are individuals experienced in data communications hardware, software, and planning.

- *Multimedia specialists.* Specialists of this kind are familiar with multimedia applications and their development methods.
- *Document imaging specialists.* These specialists perform work flow redesign associated with document imaging and develop the hardware and software infrastructure to support it.
- *Artificial intelligence (AI) specialists.* AI specialists apply expert system and other AI techniques to developing AI-based system solutions to business and industrial problems.

Communication and Business Skills

Communication skills and an understanding of business remain highly rated expertise areas for new IS workers. **Communication skills** include the ability to interact with end users during requirements analysis and to make effective presentations to other technical personnel or to users. Surveys rank the ability to work effectively in teams highly, as evidenced in widespread use of such team-centered approaches as joint application development (JAD), rapid application development (RAD), and programming teams.

Business skills include an understanding of basic business functions, such as accounting, marketing, and production. Business and communication skills are particularly important in the front-end phase of the SDLC (analysis, evaluation, and design stages), where interaction with users is greatest.

End-User Development in the New Firm

A major trend in the 1990s is the flattening of organizations, as layers of middle management are stripped away to reduce organizational costs. A direct consequence of this is wider spans of control for managers remaining in the firm.

Enterprise networks are helping managers to handle this increased workload, and both managers and end users need new skills to work effectively in enterprise systems. Some of these include computer usage skills over and above basic computer literacy, to enable effective participation in JAD and other forms of collaborative systems development. Familiarity with GUIs, 4GLs, and SQL query formulation are examples of skills required by users.

14.2   LEGAL AND ETHICAL ISSUES _____

The view of information as an organizational resource has introduced questions relating to its use and possible abuse in information systems. For the firm's clients, the issue is who has access to their customer records and why. Employees, too, have undeniable privacy rights, and through a number of well-publicized court cases are testing the extent of these rights in the court systems. Software copyright is important to software developers in an age where programs are easily duplicated and transferred over both LANs and WANs to other users. Other legal and ethical issues are the often covert computer-aided supervision of workers and computer crime.

Access Rights and Consumer Privacy

In the middle of a particularly bitter election battle between two mayoral aspirants of a small town in Colorado, a newspaper thought to favor one of the candidates suddenly published a story disparaging the other candidate's creditworthiness. It gave details of the applicant's credit history over the preceding five years, showing how she had defaulted on three major credit card balances and two local furniture store payment plans.

The fictional account above illustrates issues surrounding the privacy rights of information that is stored in numerous consumer databases countrywide. Some might argue that revelation of the credit history of a candidate for public office is proper use of the information. Others, though, insist that such information is personal and unrelated to the election campaign. Few would disagree with the use of these personal credit records by a mortgage company deliberating on making a loan to the mayoral candidate, but almost everyone would agree that if the candidate was not running for public office, her neighbor should not have access to the same credit records. The question of access rights to consumer information contains many difficulties, some of which are being addressed by both state and federal legislation.

The three large credit rating companies, *TRW, Trans Union,* and *Equifax,* maintain credit information on over 160 million citizens. This information is accessible in a matter of seconds by merchants, clerks, and in essence, just about anyone, as demonstrated by a group of newspaper journalists who recently acquired and published the credit rating of a U.S. vice president. In addition to credit ratings, a large amount of information on practically all individuals in the United States—ranging from medical histories and insurance information to buying habits—is stored in computer-readable form and widely disseminated among credit bureaus, resellers of data purchased from bureaus, and many businesses.

The government itself remains involved in the issue of privacy of the individual's records. Using a process called matching, different agencies check for overlaps in program recipients, in cases where such overlaps are disallowed. For example, under the *Computer Matching and Privacy Act of 1988,* the Welfare Department and Department of Employment frequently match records to detect "double dippers"—people who are working and collecting welfare benefits. Protections for consumers are written into this law, such as notification to the individual under suspicion and their right to respond before any action is taken.

The ability to abuse consumer records is enhanced by computer and data communications technologies and individuals may seek access to these records for dubious, unethical, or even criminal purposes. Adequate provisions that guarantee reasonable individual protections and fair use will ultimately result from a mix of consumer pressure, business use, and legislative measures. An example of the effects of consumer action was the withdrawal by Lotus Development Corporation of a CD-ROM containing the buying habits of millions of U.S. households after privacy concerns were expressed by individuals and consumer groups.

The Ethics of Worker Privacy and Managerial Supervision

The rights of individuals in the workplace have received considerable publicity with the development of new technologies that enable greater managerial intrusion into workers' activities and communications. A suit was brought against *Epson America, Inc.* in California by several employees and ex-employees after it was disclosed that managers frequently read its employees' E-mail messages. Another firm, *Nissan USA,* successfully defended a similar court action by its employees, arguing that communications on company owned and operated equipment were not private.

A third case was pursued by *Borland, Inc.* against a former employee suspected of leaking confidential information to a competitor at which the employee later took up employment. Using records of the ex-employee's E-mail contents, Borland charged that unlawful disclosure of confidential company information had taken place. While most people would decry the leaking of a firm's confidential information, others disagree with unauthorized access to a worker's personal files. This is further complicated by the possibility of benign intrusions. For example, the journalist who is suddenly taken sick and whose notes are accessed from electronic files by his editor for an important breaking story would not greatly object to such an action.

Current federal law protects the confidentiality of data transmissions on public data transmission facilities but does not extend the same protection to communications on a firm's E-mail. Some state laws, such as California's (as in the above case), require the consent of both parties for access to E-mail contents. The outcomes of these and other cases will help in determining the legality of such intrusions. Currently, legal experts advise firms to simply state a formal policy on E-mail, that is, whether it allows such intrusion or not.

Another issue of worker privacy is the **computer-assisted managerial supervision** of workers. For example, telephone operators at several of the regional Bell telephone companies have their consumer dialogues and work rates monitored using computer technology. In addition, software packages such as Microcom's *Carbon Copy* (Figure 14.1) can display the worker's screen on that of the supervisor without the knowledge of the worker. The question arises as to whether this represents managerial prerogative or an unwarranted intrusion into worker privacy. As technologies become more advanced, managers will have even more sophisticated tools to monitor workers' activities. The dividing line between managerial and worker rights is far from clear at present. It is important for firms to have and to articulate a clear policy and to be aware of legal issues and emerging rulings surrounding such monitoring.

Software Copyright Issues

Software copy protection is a controversial issue. Its advocates say that copy protection is necessary to protect software developers from exploitation of their products. Detractors point instead to the inability to make backup copies of protected software and the inconvenience of hardware keys that are attached to serial or parallel ports to enable the software to work. Most software products are unprotected, with mostly higher-cost software utilizing copy protection.

Violation of software copyright is a problem as old as the computer itself. In the first place, most software is not bought, only leased to the specific individual, as reading of any software agreement will show. (Incidentally, these leases invariably contain disclaimers, relieving the software firm of any liability resulting from using software, whether bug free or not.) For sites with multiple users, software firms offer

- **Site licensing,** in which payment of a single, negotiated price enables the purchasing firm to use the software on all its computers.

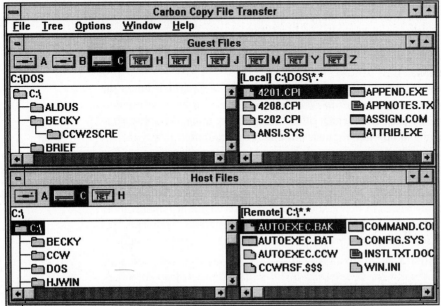

FIGURE 14.1   (*Top*) Major functions of the Carbon Copy data communications software package; (*bottom*) Carbon Copy's file transfer screen

(continued)

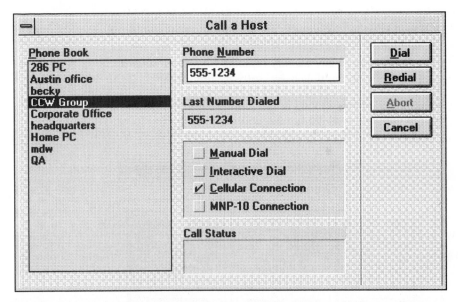

FIGURE 14.1 *(continued)*   Dialing a host computer using Carbon Copy.

- **Licensing utilities** for server-based software. For example, Lotus Development Corporation offers a licensing utility that counts the number of active copies of a program and refuses requests for additional copies until a current user quits the program.

Software piracy is illegal, and surveys show that a surprising number of people have no qualms, ethical or otherwise, about copying software. Besides copy protecting software, other options often used by software developers are to

- Price their software at low enough levels to discourage copying of software (and photocopying of manuals)
- Make use of laws such as the *Software Copyright Act of 1980,* which limits the making of copies for sale or as a gift to other individuals
- Offer software amnesty programs, which allow illegal users of copied software to turn in such software and buy the original, often at a reduced price
- Require user identification information (for example, the package registration number) before any kind of technical support is provided to the user

As most software is unprotected and software copyright is difficult to enforce, it is up to individuals and businesses to honor software copyright. While it remains more honored in the breach than in the observance by many corporations, countries, and individuals, the prices for software will remain higher than they otherwise would.

Fighting Computer Crime

Late one night, a hacker breaks into the information system of a car manufacturer and modifies the stress levels of an important auto component. The modification is not detected, and shortly after the car's launch, a disproportionate number of accidents plague the car. A rash of lawsuits contending manufacturer liability for a defective product is undertaken by some of the car's buyers.

Does the preceding example seem far fetched? Not with today's technology, which gives **"hackers"** the ability to challenge even the most sophisticated security barriers to information systems. Hackers are individuals who illegally break into and access information system functions and/or data. With many firms providing the capability of remote access by its users (for example, salespeople or conference attendees), firms face greater risks of unauthorized access.

Other computer crimes are committed by employees within the firm. The "salami" technique, for example, involves creating a software program that periodically transfers small amounts of money from many customer bank accounts into an account controlled by the employee. The amounts are not large enough to be noticed by the majority of the bank's customers.

The response of some firms that uncover such illegal activity and its perpetrators might be surprising to some. Often, these employees are dismissed quietly and without any legal action to avoid publicizing the vulnerability of the firm's information systems to computer-related fraud.

Ethics in Public Information System Forums

Electronic bulletin boards have become popular in recent years. Ethical and legal issues surrounding their use have being raised as the numbers of subscribers to these public information forums has increased in the last few years. These issues have involved the largest two services, **Prodigy**—a joint venture by *IBM* and *Sears*—and **CompuServe**—owned by *H&R Block*. These cases arose from the controversial and allegedly libelous nature of messages posted on these boards.

Prodigy stirred up controversy by its attempts to control the contents of messages posted on bulletin boards. The subscriber contract, in fact, gives the right to censor and exclude any posted messages that violate its standards. Prodigy implements this using a twofold combination of software that searches for offensive keywords in all messages and employees who read a much smaller number of messages. With over 11,000 messages daily from its estimated 1.5 million subscribers, the computer matching process was seen as the only viable method for filtering messages.

Compuserve has taken an opposite, hands-off approach to the contents of messages posted in it. It was sued by a newsletter *Skuttlebut,* who claimed libelous messages against it were published on Compuserve by a rival newsletter, *Rumorville.* Compuserve's claim of ignorance of the message's contents and of its own nonliability were apparently sufficient to have the case against it dismissed. Charges against *Rumorville,* however, remain pending.

Ultimately, the legal system will determine whether bulletin boards have the responsibility for their contents, similar to newspapers, or whether they do not, just as telephone carriers do not have liability for the contents of messages communicated over their networks.

14.3   ERGONOMICS

Ergonomics relates to the interaction of humans with the machines they use. In this context, it focuses on how the design of computer-related equipment and furniture affects user health and productivity. As computer usage has now reached 80 percent of all white-collar workers, the incidence of ailments directly and indirectly linked to computer use has greatly increased. These include **cumulative trauma disorders,** the most widely known of which is *carpal tunnel syndrome.* This particular ailment is characterized by pain and loss of feeling and control in the hands, and results mainly from repetitive motion (primarily typing) in positions that lack adequate wrist support. Other problems include headaches, blurred vision, and back pain. In competitive business environments, proactive ergonomic policies may be viewed as unnecessary expenses, but considering the cost of work-related ailments, which can exceed $30,000 from cases of carpal tunnel syndrome requiring surgery, ergonomically designed workplaces are a relative bargain.

Designing Furniture

Much of the furniture used in the corporate environment is either not specifically designed for computer use or has been retrofitted to incorporate good ergonomic design. Even ergonomic furniture may be used improperly, resulting a wide range of health problems. The consequences of these ailments include (1) increased sick time and larger medical bills, (2) lower worker productivity, and (3) higher worker compensation benefits.

Figure 14.2 illustrates an ergonomically well-designed workplace with the following major characteristics:

- The user sits upright at 90°, with feet flat on the floor (using a raised footrest if necessary), elbows at a right angle, and wrists resting on a padded surface.
- The user looks down at the screen at a slight angle (up to 4°).
- There is indirect lighting to reduce screen glare, and table lighting for documents.
- The chairs and other devices (for example, tables, monitor stands) are adjustable, for flexibility.

As is evident in Figure 14.2, ergonomics involves the combined design of several workplace components, not just one. While furniture is important, so is equipment. Anti-glare screens, higher scan (or refresh) rates, a smaller dot pitch, higher screen resolution, and noninterlaced screens are generally better for the eyes. 24-pin output from a dot matrix printer is also an improvement over 9-pin, but both are inferior to laser quality output.

Monitor Emissions

All operating electrical devices produce radioactive emissions, with monitors being no exception. The CRTs in monitors produce a variety of emissions, including X-rays, microwaves, heat, and ultraviolet light, among others. Many workers work for extended periods daily in front of monitors, and health concerns have arisen over such prolonged exposure to radiation.

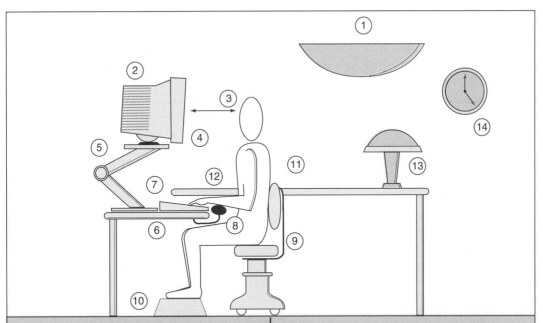

1. **Indirect Lighting** — Fixtures that bounce light off ceilings or walls provide a soft light that is less likely than harsh light to reflect off monitor screens and create glare.

2. **Monitor Height** — The top of the monitor should be no higher than eye level.

3. **Monitor Distance** — 16 to 22 inches is recommended for visual acuity; 24 inches or more is recommended if there are emission concerns.

4. **Monitor Display** — High-resolution, non-interlaced screen with dark letters on a light background, with an antiglare screen coating or antiglare filter.

5. **Adjustable Monitor Support** — The monitor should move up and down, forward and back, and tilt on its axis.

6. **Keyboard Support** — Adjustable from 23 and 28 inches in height. Operator's arm should hang straight down from the shoulder and bend 90 degrees at the elbow and enable the operator to type without flexing or hyperextending the wrist.

7. **Keyboard** — Adjustable tilt to enable the typist to keep hands in a straight line with the wrists and forearms.

8. **Wrist Rest** — Rounded, padded adjustable support for the heel of the hand or forearm, without constricting the wrist.

9. **Seat Height** — Adjustable from 16 to19 inches. Users should be able to bend their hips and knees at 90 degrees and sit with their feet flat on the floor.

10. **Foot Rest** — Enables typists with shorter legs to rest feet flat while working.

11. **Back Support** — Backrest should adjust up, down, forward, and backward to support the lumbar portion of the spine in the small of the back.

12. **Work Surface Height** — A comfortable height for reading, writing, drawing, and other non keyboard work.

13. **Reading Light** — An independent light source for reading letters, reports, books, etc.

14. **Clock** — Schedule regular breaks, preferably five minutes per hour.

FIGURE 14.2   Ergonomic office

A 1988 U.S. study found a higher rate of miscarriages among women who used monitors for twenty hours or more every week. While the study received much attention, many considered it flawed due to its statistically nonsignificant sample size. A second study carried out by the National Institute for Occupational Safety and Health in 1991 produced conflicting results, citing no heightened risks of miscarriages from extended periods of CRT use. Some observers equate current studies of the effects of monitor emissions to early studies of cigarette smoking, which often showed inconclusive results. Their conclusion is to regard emissions as nonbeneficial to the user and to seek reduced emissions from computer equipment.

Sweden is a world leader in setting emission standards that are much more stringent than those elsewhere. Their **MPR II** standard restricts the levels of electrical and magnetic radiation allowable from monitors and is now adhered to by many monitor vendors. A comprehensive list of measures that can be taken in the workplace includes

- Using reduced emission monitors that adhere to the MPR II standard
- Sitting as far back from the monitor as practical, as emissions drop off very rapidly with distance
- Using monitor radiation shields. Examples are the Norad shield and Norad Pro Tech. The former is a wire mesh that reduces emissions from the monitor's screen, while the latter reduces emissions from the sides of the monitor, where they are even higher.
- Using high-resolution, noninterlaced monitors with dot pitches of 0.28 mm or less and scanning rates of 72 Hz or greater
- Switching to LCDs whenever possible, as they produce much lower emissions
- Turning off the monitor when it is not in use

CHAPTER SUMMARY

Information systems development in the immediate future will reflect the almost wholesale transition to microcomputer-based systems by the late 1990s. The required skills for the new information systems professional differ greatly from those of even the recent past. Mainframe applications, operating systems, and languages (for example, COBOL) are being superseded in importance by CASE tools, structured methods, and 4GLs. Other important areas are data communications, multimedia, document imaging, and artificial intelligence. Additionally, business and interpersonal skills remain necessary, especially as JAD and similar approaches become widely used.

Increased connectivity and access to data by both individuals and firms have raised important privacy concerns. Current technology provides greater opportunities for the misuse of information held on individuals. Apart from consumer privacy, the privacy of worker communications and computer-based files on company-owned equipment has aroused much controversy. The issues include the ethics of covert, computer-aided managerial supervision and access to the above data. Trial cases are expected to affect management guidelines for such managerial supervision and the control of public bulletin boards.

Software copyright is a sensitive issue to both vendors and consumers. Software piracy robs software firms of billions of dollars of revenue yearly and some firms have turned to copy protection to reduce such losses. Other approaches, such as selling software at lower prices, site licensing, and prosecuting offenders, have also been applied with varying degrees of success. Other forms of computer crime are seen in the use of computers to perpetrate fraud and the intentional introduction of computer viruses into systems.

Finally, ergonomics has increased in importance in recent years, as the number of reported computer-related ailments has increased. These affect worker morale and productivity and increase health costs for the concerned firms. Redesigning furniture and work practices and reducing monitor emissions are all measures that support more ergonomic systems, which reduce the occurrence of computer-related ailments.

REVIEW QUESTIONS

1. List three important and relatively new information system skill areas in the 1990s. Explain why they are important to system development and maintenance.
2. Describe two older information-system-related skills that are still required for system development. How much longer do you think they will be critical for information systems personnel and why?
3. What is your view on copy-protected software? What are three steps software firms can take to reduce software piracy, apart from copy protection?
4. Describe three common computer-related ailments, and describe present-day solutions to prevent these ailments.
5. What are the major characteristics of an ergonomic workplace? Why is it viewed as a relative bargain to make the initial outlays for ergonomic furniture and practices?

EXERCISES

1. What do you think are the ethical issues surrounding managerial access to employee files stored in E-mail accounts. Do you think managerial access to these files is warranted in any circumstances? Why or why not?
2. As a network manager of a 60-user LAN, an audit of files on the servers and some individual machines has revealed that pirated software is widely used. Some of the packages display registration information for persons outside the organization. In addition, more copies than are authorized for two packages with a site license are in use. What measures can the network manager take to reduce the piracy problem?
3. Should electronic bulletin boards be held liable for their contents, as posted by subscribers? How can computer technology be applied to help prevent libelous or otherwise offensive messages being posted on bulletin boards?
4. As a systems manager involved in creating a RFP for microcomputer systems, one suggestion from the user group is that the new monitors should, at a minimum, meet the Swedish MPR II standard. Are there any other monitor characteristics you would add to the RFP? What are these and why are they important?

SUGGESTED READINGS

Huttig, J. W., Jr. "On-line Ethics." *PC Today,* January 1992, pp. 42–43.

Huttig, J. W., Jr. "Painless Computing." *PC Today,* April 1992, pp. 18–23.

Hsu, J. "Deadly Monitors? VDTs, Radiation, and You." *PC Today,* April 1992, pp. 24–26.

Leitheiser, R. L. "MIS Skills for the 1990s: A Survey of MIS Managers' Perceptions." *Journal of Management Systems,* Vol. 9, No. 1, Summer 1992, pp. 69–91.

Ricciuti, M. "Mainframe DBMS Power Unleashed." *Datamation,* October 15, 1992.

Richman, L. S. "Jobs That Are Growing and Slowing." *Fortune,* July 12, 1993, pp. 52–64.

Schwebach, L. "Reconciling Electronic Privacy Rights in the Workplace." *PC Today,* January 1992, pp. 38–39.

Snell, N. "Are You Ready for Cutting-Edge COBOL?" *Datamation,* October 15, 1992, pp. 77–82.

Speer, T. L. "Talking Tech with Your Lawyers." *Corporate Computing,* Vol. 1, No. 5, November 1992, pp. 21–22.

CHAPTER 15

FUTURE TRENDS FOR MICROCOMPUTER-BASED COMPUTING

INTRODUCTION

As we go through the 1990s, the transition to networked microcomputer platforms is well under way. Over 80 percent of Fortune 1000 firms are migrating their mainframe systems to internetworked enterprise systems, with many discarding their mainframes. New microprocessors now enable designers to pack mainframe-like power into smaller boxes at a mere fraction of the price. This trend also shows no signs of slowing down.

In this chapter, we examine these hardware trends that will define the form and performance of the microcomputer in the next decade. We discuss the software trends that will bring about new and innovative applications for both end users and system developers. Connectivity will continue in importance through 1990s as multimegabit pathways carrying voice, video, graphics, and text connect users at local, metropolitan, and remote locations. The information systems infrastructure required in the coming decade as a result of all these developments is examined, as are new working practices, such as EDI.

Learning Objectives

After reading this chapter, you will be able to:

- Assist in preparing an information systems strategic plan that takes account of new hardware platforms and technologies
- Prepare to adopt the new applications and user interfaces that will become widely used in the 1990s and beyond
- Make use of evolving connectivity tools to specify appropriate growth paths for enterprise systems
- Aid in the redesign of work practices and work flows to take advantage of advances in information technology

15.1 HARDWARE TRENDS _____

The driving force behind microcomputer hardware advances is "speed, speed, and more speed!" Since the original IBM XT was introduced in 1982, the processing power of IBM-compatibles has increased by a factor of over 300. Paradoxically, prices have fallen over this time period, and even more powerful processors are being developed to continue this trend. We examine the factors that contribute to faster microprocessor operation and what improved performance signifies for microcomputer applications. We also discuss trends in microcomputer peripherals.

Advances in Microchips

Microchips have relentlessly advanced in power and sophistication over the last decade. The *microprocessor* now processes data faster than many mainframes of the 1980s (and some in the 1990s). Intel's Pentium processor features more than 3 million individual transistors, runs at 66 Mhz, and produces about 112 MIPs. DEC's ALPHA chip is even more powerful, running at more than 150 Mhz and generating almost 200 MIPs. Four major areas of microprocessor development that contribute to greater microprocessor power are

1. *Increases in chip density.* The predecessor to the Pentium, Intel's 80486, had 1.2 million individual transistors on its surface, just over a third of the Pentium transistor count. Putting more transistors on the chip increases processing speed because of the additional functions now incorporated on a single chip and the shorter distances the signals have to travel.
2. *Adding features to the microprocessor.* These features include memory management functions, on-chip memory caches, and math coprocessors. These functions were performed by separate chips on 80386-based machines but integrated into the 80486 and Pentium processors, resulting in overall faster performance.
3. *Faster clock speeds.* Rising clock speeds are being used to produce more MIPs. From the early 4.77 Mhz of the IBM XT, clock speeds have risen to 100 Mhz on microcomputers based on the newest Pentiums.
4. *Multiple arithmetic units and pipelining.* Pipelining was introduced into the 80486 chip to enable instructions to be executed in an assembly line fashion, to raise instruction processing throughout. In the Pentium and ALPHA microprocessors, multiple processing units enable multiple instructions to be processed simultaneously, that is, parallel processing.

Unfortunately, packing circuits closer together and higher clock speeds has an unwelcome side-effect: increased heat generated by the processor. Pentium- and Alpha-based machines generate more heat than those powered by 386s and 486s. This heat can cause motherboard failures or even the melting of components. Many vendors who had advertised their 386 and 486-based machines as being 'Pentium-upgradeable' using Intel's "overdrive" kit now face such overheating problems.

While one long-term solution is Intel's imminent 3.3 volt version of the Pentium, shorter-term solutions include heat dissipating "fins" and sinks and small fans mounted on expansion cards, all of which are available from third-party vendors.

Future features of chips may include the use of materials other than silicon for chip fabrication. Microprocessors made of **gallium arsenide** generally run faster than silicon-based microprocessors but suffer from brittleness. Solving this problem may lead to more widespread use of this material. Finally, **power management functions,** while not contributing directly to overall processor performance, are now incorporated into such microprocessors as Intel's 386SL and 486SL to reduce microcomputer power consumption.

The vice president of Intel Corporation was quoted in MIS Week as saying:

> *By the end of this decade, Intel Corporation plans to produce a 250 Mhz micro-processor containing up to 100 million transistors, and performing 2 billion operations per second (2,000 MIPS). And if that is not enough, the chip will be 386-compatible.*
>
> *. . . By the end of the decade, mainframes are going to be slower than microcom-puters*

Others share this view of microprocessor power doubling every three years or so, as it has since the early 1980s. Whether or not microcomputers will be more powerful than the fastest mainframes is not important. What is more important is that they will provide unprecedented power to support *every type* of organizational application.

Memory chips have also benefited from the same advances that have created more powerful processors. Chip densities have increased rapidly from early 32- and 64-kilobit bit chips to current 8- and 16-megabit DRAMs. Access times of DRAM chips have also fallen from 180ns to below 70ns. Estimates of primary memory capacities for microcomputers in the year 2000 are in the gigabyte range, up from the current 4–64 Mb of today's microcomputers.

The managerial implications of these developments include the fact that powerful microcomputers have become much more affordable. This is important against a backdrop of increasing competitive, legal, and health influences within firms that constrain IS expenditures. Another consequence is that microcomputers are becoming even more of a commodity item, with fewer differences between the products of premier and clone vendors. Also, entry-level 386 and 486 machines, in contrast to earlier generations, are GUI ready and free from previous memory addressing limitations (see Chapter 3).

Intel 486 and Pentium-based microcomputers, Macintosh Quadras and Suns, and so on, at often startlingly low prices, are now used as file, data, and processor servers, sparing many firms from having to resort to mainframes based on large processing requirements. Finally, power management functions, now almost standard on note-books, will become widely used on desktop microcomputers, in power-conserving designs.

Advances in Peripherals

In the coming decade, advances in peripherals will mirror developments in micropro-cessors, although not at the same rate of speed. For example, the standard 10 Mb hard disk of 1982 was superseded by 100 Mb capacities ten years later. This is an increase by a factor of 10, not by the factor of 300 demonstrated by microprocessors.

Nevertheless, over the remaining part of the decade, peripherals will become smaller and more powerful for identical or lower prices. Specific categories of peripherals include:

1. *Monitors.* It is likely that in coming years, CRTs may be replaced by large active-matrix LCDs. The LCD's advantages are improved clarity, lower radioactive emissions, and smaller size. With color now widely used in LCDs, cost reductions and increases in size will make the LCD more prevalent on the desktop.

2. *Secondary storage.* Magnetic storage devices now support greater capacities by packing more bits in the same area while improving the precision of the read/write head assembly. These advances have seen *floppy disk capacities* rise to 20 Mb (*Insite's* **Floptical disk**) and 50 Mb (*Briar's* **Flextra disk**), using laser-guided read/write heads. By the end of the decade, 160 Mb floppies will be commonplace.

    Optical disks, which routinely store 2–5 Gb of data, will also have their capacities increase and access times decrease to become comparable with fixed (magnetic) disks. Typical fixed/optical systems will provide over 100 Gb of storage. Magnetic tape will also give ground to optical systems, even though capacities will be comparable.

    Flash RAM is another promising secondary storage medium that will be found in more systems, especially notebooks, in the next decade. Being much faster than optical or magnetic disks, only its high cost relative to magnetic and optical media prevents it from being a viable substitute today. Microchip miniaturization will raise chip densities, although multigigabyte chips for average systems may be too expensive for average users.

3. *Printers.* Advances in printers are also very much in evidence. Current trends call for faster printing speed, improved fonts, incorporation of color, and higher printer resolution. Laser printers have evolved from 300 dpi to 800 dpi resolutions at printing speeds of over twenty pages per minute. An important trend is direct printer connections to LANs through network interface cards.

To support faster peripherals, **faster data buses** will be used to move data between the peripherals and the processor. *EISA, MCA,* and more recently, the *local bus,* allow such data transfers at much higher speeds than previously. On a 66 Mhz Pentium-based machine, for example, the local bus enables data transfers at 66 Mhz, instead of the 8 Mhz rates of ISA buses. Also in evidence is the trend toward **bus mastering,** which allows devices to take control of the bus and transmit data on it without notifying the CPU.

Pen-Based and Portable Computing

Pen-based computing and **portable computing** are two important computing technologies, with private mail delivery companies such as Federal Express and UPS being major adopters. *Go System's* **Penpoint** and *Microsoft's* **Windows for Pen Computing** represent the predominant pen-based OSs for **slate computers.** Handwriting recognition is still below acceptable levels, but as hardware performance increases and handwriting recognition programs improve (using artificial neural network and other models), recognition rates will approach 100 percent—comparable to keyboard-based input.

Notebook computers now account for the majority of portable computer sales. Once regarded as distinctly inferior to desktop machines, technological advances have made them more comparable in features. These include smaller 2.5-inch fixed disks with capacities of up to 250 Mb; color screens with higher resolutions to 1024×768; and power-saving microprocessors (for example, the 80386SL and 80486SL). Future advances will include greater memory capacities and processing power, larger-capacity flash RAM modules, bigger and better color LCD displays, and environmentally friendly models, all at greater price/performance levels. (See Box 15.1.)

15.2 SOFTWARE TRENDS

Improvements in software will accompany those in hardware and peripherals. All varieties of software, including operating environments, productivity tools, languages, and applications, will become more powerful and sophisticated and take advantage of greater hardware capabilities. Some of the key trends in software include

- Increased ease of use of all software types
- Predominantly graphical user interfaces (GUIs)
- More functional software, with greater capabilities.

System/User Interfaces to the Year 2000

Of concern to system developers and users is the projected form of system/user interfaces in the coming years. Windows applications are now the most widely used on the desktop, underlining the fact that user interfaces are greatly influenced by the operating environments on which they are developed. One major characteristic of operating environments in the coming years is the unmistakable trend toward graphical user interfaces, or GUIs. GUIs will dominate the desktop in future years, taking the lead from character-based interfaces. In addition, operating environments will incorporate the handling of other media, for example, animation and voice, to support full multimedia interfaces. Major new operating environments, such as *OS/2, DOS 6.0, Windows NT,* and various UNIX versions (for example, *Mach* from NeXT computer, and *SCO Unix* from SCO) have all incorporated GUIs as the primary mode of system/user interaction.

Windows NT is a good example of the new operating environments designed to manage the increased resources available in the new computing configurations. It features *multitasking, multiprocessing, security features, fault-tolerant secondary storage,* and *networking support.* It requires 16 Mb of RAM to operate acceptably but offers performance at levels sought by MIS managers making the transition from mainframe systems to client/server computing. See Figure 15.2 for a Windows NT screen.

At the corporate level, operating environments will be required to support these features. Other features to be supported are *distributed processing, multiple hardware platforms* (Windows NT supports several RISC and CISC processors), and *application development tools* that ease system development. Windows NT, OS/2, and their future upgrades will continue the migration of mainframe OS features to the desktop. Significantly, many of the functions performed by utilities are now a part of feature-rich

BOX 15.1

THE COMING OF THE GREEN PC

Until recently, it was rare to think of the computer in environmental terms, but lately this has become commonplace. All aspects of the computer, ranging from its manufacturing to its maintenance, and its effects on users and the environment, have faced closer scrutiny as society and governments become more environmentally conscious. Some of the environmental issues surrounding the computer are:

- The release of chlorofluorocarbons (CFCs) into the atmosphere in the manufacture of computer circuit boards
- Large amounts of waste products generated by the computer industry and discarded by users; these include millions of toner cartridges, equipment packaging materials such as styrofoam, old diskettes and batteries, and obsolete computers
- Radioactive emissions from computer equipment, particularly CRTs
- Immense amounts of paper generated by computing-related equipment
- The large amounts of electrical power consumed by computers and peripherals

The responses to these issues by governments, the computer industry, and users are leading to the concept of the ``green'' PC in the mid-nineties. Apple computer for example, has developed a new manufacturing process for circuit boards that eliminates the use of CFC-based solvents. AT&T also reduced its CFC emissions by 86% between 1986 and 1993. Exhausted toner cartridges are now routinely refilled with ink by many companies that offer this service. Likewise environmentally-conscious firms have adopted policies that encourage recycling of other consumables like batteries and old diskettes; and donation, not disposal of old computer equipment.

The Swedish MPR II reduced-emissions standard is becoming more widespread on CRTs (see Chapter 14). Larger, desktop LCDs and wider use of MPR II-compliant CRTs will characterize the new green PC. Moving from softcopy to hardcopy, AT&T now recycles 60% of its office paper and uses double-sided copying. Such measures, taken together with the use of E-mail and document imaging is helping to cut down on the immense amounts of paper consumed in firms.

Power consumption is also an important area and one in which the government has led the push for more eco-friendly computers. New guidelines set by the Environmental Protection Agency (EPA) call for significantly reduced power consumption for microcomputer equipment purchased by its agencies. The *Energy Star* logo will appear on microcomputers, monitors, and printers that automatically power down after a period of disuse and consume 30 watts or less in standby mode.

These and other pressures have led manufacturers to introduce processors and systems with a host of power-saving measures. Intel's 386SL and 486SL; for example, were used in notebooks initially for their power-saving functions. These include a reduced power ``sleep'' mode when the computer is not in use, and computer designs that shut down the screen and hard disk, while saving the status of current programs. In the immediate future, most new desktop computers will have many of these power-saving features as just one more aspect of the ``green'' PC.

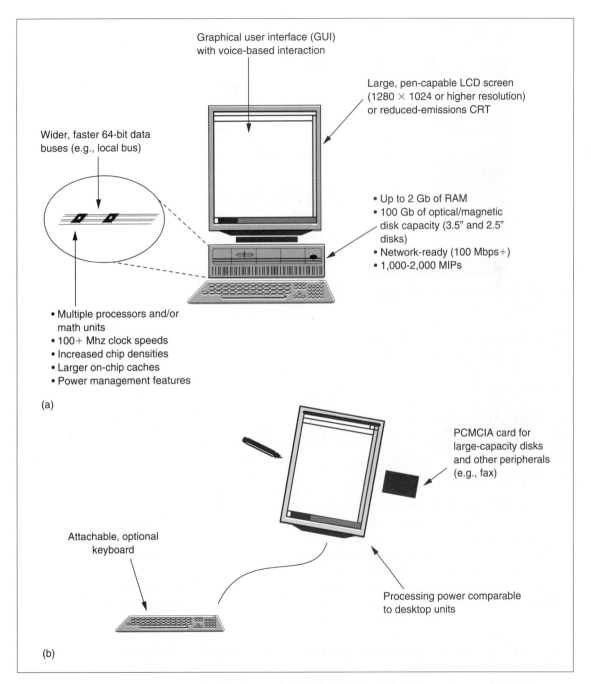

FIGURE 15.1   The microcomputer in the year 2000. (a) Future desktop microcomputer; (b) future pen-based notebook microcomputer.

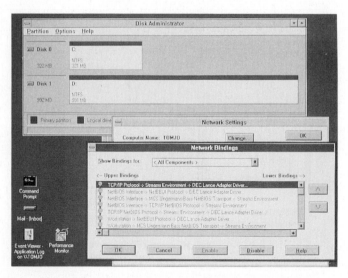

FIGURE 15.2   Windows NT operating system

operating systems. These include data compression and disk management functions, networking capabilities, and security features.

Trends in System Development Tools and Applications

System developers anticipate working with a wider variety of tools in coming years. These tools will have improved functionality and incorporate new programming paradigms and media. With over 800 products on the market, **CASE tools** will be important for system developers, particularly those tools that perform both upper case—the initial modeling stages of the SDLC—and lower case—the code-generation stages of the SDLC. This will help to move more of the burden of application development from the developer onto the computer itself.

The use of **object-oriented programming** has appeared in many programming languages, just as structured programming did in the 1980s. Third- and fourth-generation languages are incorporating objects to improve programmer productivity and promote code reusability. C++ compilers by Borland and Microsoft, and Pascal with Objects from Borland are examples of recent language compilers that utilize the object-oriented approach. They take advantage of larger storage capabilities to add features such as memory management, support for GUIs, an integrated coding and debugging environment, and libraries of predeveloped code. Microsoft's C++ for Windows, for example, requires over 25 Mb of hard disk capacity.

Productivity packages have been the mainstay of the end user and are expected to become even more feature laden in coming years. Spreadsheet packages like Microsoft's *Excel,* for example, incorporate statistical functions and extensive graphics and database features. They also incorporate optimization (or goal-seeking) models, multidimensional worksheets, and powerful macro languages for building sophisticated applications. The same trends are apparent with feature-rich word processing (for example, *Microsoft Word for Windows*) and DBMS packages (for example, Borland's *dBase IV*™).

Applications on microcomputers will also mirror advances in underlying hardware, operating systems, languages, and other development tools. They will utilize resources (for example, databases) from all over the organization and allow enterprise-wide communication through groupware and E-mail functions. They will also move toward more natural means of communication, such as voice-, pen-, and gesture-based input.

15.3 ADVANCES IN ORGANIZATIONAL CONNECTIVITY

There are specific trends in evidence for local and wide-area networks in organizations. The major one, of course, is *speed* to carry the increased data traffic resulting from new multimedia applications and increased organizational connectivity. Recent upgrades to ethernet and token ring networks transform them to 100 Mbps LANs from their current 10 Mbps and 16 Mbps rates, respectively. Transmission rates for wide-area communications are also set to increase, by almost an order of magnitude over current rates. ISDN and frame relay provide rates of up to 2 Mbps, but ATM over fiber-optic networks supports transmission rates of up to 155 Mbps on both LANs and WANs.

FDDI and CDDI

The **fiber distributed data interface (FDDI)** and the newer **copper distributed data interface (CDDI)** transmission protocol support 100 Mbps rates over fiber-optic cable and copper wire (for example, STP), up from current rates of 20 Mbps or less. NICs to support these new standards are now available off the shelf and will gradually become more widely used. The importance of these data rates is a renewed capacity to transmit document imaging data, real-time video, and sound, as well as improve the responsiveness of servers to attached clients.

Digital and Multimegabit Wide-Area Communications

Links between LANs at different sites are major bottlenecks in geographically dispersed organizations. Typically, bridges, routers, and gateways provide inter-LAN transmission rates substantially below those of the LANs themselves. The introduction of larger file types and transparent client/server access to distributed computers has brought about even greater traffic across remote LANs. **Frame relay** and **ISDN** are viewed as interim solutions to wide-area connectivity, providing transmission rates only up to 2 Mbps. With newer asynchronous transfer mode (ATM), current rates top 155 Mbps and will exceed 6 Gbps. *(See Figure 15.3.)*

Consider, for example, a user on a terminal on a future internetwork. While using a marketing DSS, the user requests information about the most profitable product line in a

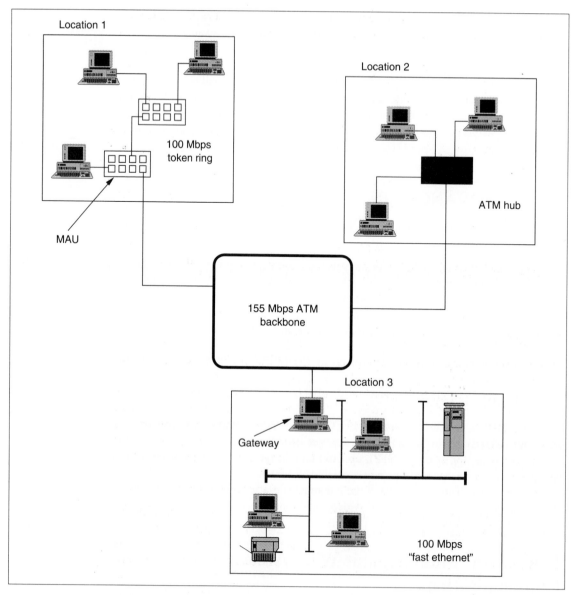

FIGURE 15.3 Future ATM-based network

sales region across the country. The user's query is routed to the local database server, which contains a part of a distributed DBMS. Using tables detailing the locations of the different data sets involved in the query and appropriate middleware (e.g., remote procedure calls), requests are made over high-speed (ATM) WAN connections to all the remote servers storing this data. The data is returned over the WAN to the local server, where it is assembled, transferred to the workstation, and presented to the user. Without high-speed wide-area links, such connectivity is very difficult to achieve. (See

Figure 15.4.) In the same way, document images, video clips, and other high-bandwidth items may be transmitted using public transmission facilities.

New Internetworking Software

Another vital key to future enterprise systems is the software required to support the various private and public data communications hardware. The major software types are the *network operating systems (NOSs)* and *distributed DBMSs.* **Novell Netware V.4.0** is a recent NOS designed with enterprisewide client/server applications in mind. It has an important feature called **netware directory services (NDS),** a distributed directory that allows databases on multiple servers to be viewed as a single logical database. Users may therefore request files in a location-transparent manner, with the location of files and maintenance and synchronization of file directories performed by Netware on the multiple servers. Use of NDS through *Netware* and the equivalent *Street Talk* mechanism in the Banyan Vines NOS permits more capable enterprisewide E-mail using packages like *Lotus Development Corporation's* **Notes.** They will also enable distributed DBMSs such as *Cincom's* **Supra** and *Sybase Inc.'s* **Sybase** to be used effectively.

Investment Implications for Firms

MIS managers are keenly aware of new pressures for higher productivity and closer scrutiny of capital and other expenses in almost every type of organization. At times of economic uncertainty and heightened competitiveness, the costs and benefits of making the transition to enterprise systems must be carefully studied. The major motivation of the transition, often called *downsizing* or *rightsizing,* is to produce **cost savings** and **improved productivity** through the use of lower-cost platforms. Benefits are also expected from reengineering current applications and from outsourcing various system development and maintenance activities to external firms.

The areas of investment for the firms choosing to make this transition include

1. *Computer hardware.* This comprises appropriate nodes and servers for the network. *Nodes* must be made network ready, and *servers* must have adequate performance, security, and fault-tolerant features. Also included are investments in *networking infrastructure,* for example, cabling and data communication devices (routers, gateways, and so on).
2. *Computer software.* Multiplatform *network operating systems (NOSs)* and *operating systems* that support distributed and client/server operations are essential for enterprise networks. Compared to mainframe operating systems, which are leased for tens or hundreds of thousands of dollars, the new OSs and NOSs range in price from $100 to $4,000. Also, *protocol converters* are required for these heterogeneous environments. New client/server software, such as *DDBMSs, E-Mail,* and *group- ware,* are also important applications for improving work flows.
3. *Training.* Training is required for system developers, who need different sets of skills than those traditionally used in mainframe environments. These new skills (for example, GUIs and networking) were discussed in Chapter 14. For end users also, training is required to make full use of new operating systems and applications with

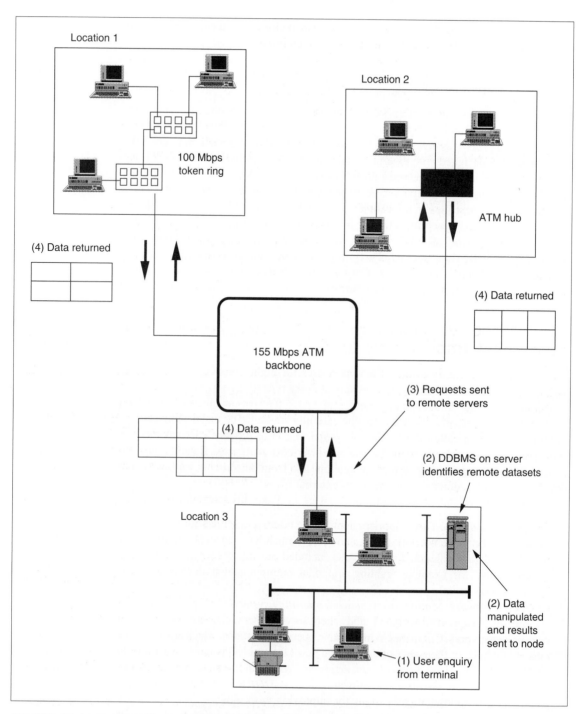

FIGURE 15.4   Data traffic on a future ATM-based network

more powerful capabilities, and to participate more effectively in end-user development using 4GLs and other tools.

4. ***People.*** MIS managers must make a sober assessment as to whether the skills for the enterprise networking reside within the firm. If this is not the case and outsourcing is not desired, then investments are necessary to attract and retain the appropriate personnel for developing such systems.

5. ***Data.*** In Chapter 10, enterprise systems were described as vulnerable to security breaches due to the distribution of enterprise data among the nodes on the network. DDBMSs should and do provide extensive security and data integrity features and are necessary purchases for an enterprisewide system. Prices for such systems are in the $1,500 to $5,000 range—large by xBase (for example, dBase and Foxpro) standards, but much less than mainframe products.

A careful cost-benefit analysis will help the manager determine the best way to move to distributed systems in an organized manner, without many of the surprises that have accompanied IS development in the past. See Table 15.1 for costs involved in such a transition.

TABLE 15.1   Costs involved in making the transition to enterprise systems

Classes	Types	Description/Comments
Hardware	Microcomputers	Must be made network-ready
	Servers	New multiprocessing servers from Trident, Sequent, Parallan, and Compaq are becoming common.
	Networking	Hardware includes NIC's Hubs, Routers, Cables, etc. Datamation quotes $1,270 as the average total cost per user when networking.
Software	Multi-platform NOS's	Examples are Windows NT, Netware, and Banyan Vines.
	Multi-platform operating systems	Windows NT, Unix
	Client/Server applications	Groupware, Transaction processing
	Client/Server Development tools	CASE tools, Object-oriented tools, multiplatform development languages, e.g., Micro Focus COBOL
Support staffs	LAN administrators	A commonly quoted ratio is one administrator to every 50 users.
Training	For users and support personnel	Training in the use of groupware and use of LAN features (users); training in LAN maintenance (support personnel)
Data	Distributed DBMSs with security and data integrity features	Includes data migration from larger platforms; applications may also be ported to workstations/microcomputer platforms.

15.4   GLOBALIZATION AND ENTERPRISE COMPUTING

New challenges have arisen for firms in the 1990s due to the globalization of industrial and commercial activity. Firms used to competing in local and regional markets must now adapt to competing at national and international levels. A firm's competitors are as likely to be in Taiwan or Japan as they are to be in New York. Global competition is enabled not only by faster materials handling but also by improved data communications on global communication systems. Aspects of global competition and of some of the data communications infrastructure that various firms have adopted are discussed here.

Increases in Global Competition

Data communications have helped to make the world a much smaller place, in the sense that communication links can be established between locations on different continents in a matter of seconds. With new approaches like just-in-time (or JIT) manufacturing, where inventories are minimized or eliminated, these communication links enable instantaneous transmission of various types of transactions. In the case of JIT, these might involve reorders of various components or raw materials from another country or continent. Another example is the airline industry, where data communications links enable passengers to make reservations on flights originating from other cities, states, or continents.

In markets with a free exchange of goods and information, data communications and wider use of microcomputers are helping to make information more important as a competitive resource. The U.S. firms who have moved manufacturing facilities offshore, for example, are able to do this only because of the ability to establish communication links between marketing, retailing, and product design divisions (usually left in the United States) and their manufacturing facilities overseas. A very different industry, the software industry, has also taken advantage of communications technology to gain competitive advantage. Microsoft, for example, has set up facilities in Dublin, Ireland, where local programmers are hired to work collaboratively on projects often supervised by personnel in the United States. Communications on program development are carried out using a WAN.

Data Communications Infrastructure for Operating Globally

Given the realities of global markets and competition, enterprise networks will become a widely used IS architecture in most large firms and will form essential parts of the data communications infrastructure needed to operate globally. Another significant trend for future data transmissions at both local and global levels is the move from analog to digital transmission on WANs. Transoceanic fiber-optic cable will increase the options for global business operations and the use of new trading methods, such as electronic data interchange (EDI). As illustrated in the Harper case in Chapter 10, EDI is now a competitive necessity for trading with several companies. Intercontinental high-speed communications will also lower the costs of such data exchanges.

Many of the newer NOSs reflect the need for increased connectivity at all levels of operations. They use protocols that fit well with wide-area communications technologies, such as frame relay, ISDN, and ATM. For example, the global messaging capabilities of Netware 4.0 and Banyan Vines allow location-independent access to data in global networks. In addition, they use new 2-byte coding systems for data transmission, to enable the transmission of Japanese Kanji characters and other international coding systems, which number over the 256 possible codes in ASCII.

CHAPTER SUMMARY

Recent microcomputers that are based on newer microprocessors have opened up new opportunities for firms to deploy effective information systems in organizations. IBM-compatibles already operate at processing rates of more than 100 MIPS, rates only formerly associated with mainframes. The future will usher in even more powerful microcomputers at identical or even lower prices, as miniaturization and techniques like parallel processing combine to improve price/performance ratios.

The microcomputer in the early twenty-first century will likely be a machine operating at more than two billion instructions per second. It will have up to 2 gigabytes of RAM and secondary storage capacity in the tens of gigabytes. It will likely host a user interface that enables the user to interact with the computer through the spoken word and handwriting in addition to the keyboard. OSs will be graphically oriented, with ever larger applications and languages displaying increasing functionality.

The enterprise network will substitute for the centralized mainframe, which was the prevailing computing model from the 1940s onward. This model will include LAN data transmission rates exceeding 100 Mbps and WAN rates of 1.5 Mbps (ISDN) as an interim stage. Subsequently, LAN and WAN rates will exceed 155 Mbps using ATM for both local and wide-area connections. New NICs and switching equipment for the initial higher transmission rates are already available from vendors and will enable the transmission of new data types such as sound, images, and video.

For firms making the transition to enterprise systems, new purchases will include development tools such as CASE, object-oriented languages, and NOSs, in addition to systems and data communications equipment. In this new era, information system managers must invest wisely in skilled personnel as well as hardware and software because of the greater pressures from global competition, legal and ergonomic issues, and their associated expenditures. Globalization also offers opportunities to adopt new technologies for competitive advantage. Videoconferencing and electronic data interchange (EDI) are good examples of future applications that will use increased connectivity to improve work flows and lower costs, helping to make firms more productive.

REVIEW QUESTIONS

1. List three major architectural approaches that will be used to give microprocessors increased performance in future years.
2. Explain why system buses such as the local bus will become even more important in future microcomputers.
3. Describe two major advantages that a desktop LCD has over a conventional CRT.
4. Discuss two trends in user interfaces on desktop microcomputers. How does current hardware constrain the use of such interfaces?
5. What is the importance of new LAN transmission speeds, such as fast ethernet's 100 Mbps, on the potential data types that may be transmitted on LANs?
6. What are some of the opportunities afforded by ATM to firms in the future? Aside from the hardware components, what new software will take advantage of the higher bandwidth of WANs?

EXERCISES

1. Describe the different areas of investment in computer and data communications technology that firms trading globally will have to be involved in. How do WAN links and applications increase competitive pressure on these firms?
2. Imagine setting up an insurance firm of 200 people in the year 2000. What types of computers do you expect to be using? For this type of company, do you expect to use a mainframe? What will be the technical specifications of the computers and data communications you will use?

SUGGESTED READINGS

Baran, N. "Rough Gems: First Pen Systems Show Promise, Lack Refinement." *Byte Magazine,* April 1992, pp. 212–222.

Burger, R. M. and Holton, W. C. "Reshaping the Microchip." *Byte Magazine,* February 1992, pp. 137–150.

Donovan, J. "Operating-System Trends." *Byte Magazine,* October 1992, pp. 159–166.

Holzberg, C. S. "Holographic Storage: The Future Is Now." *PC Today,* August 1991, pp. 19–22.

Lawton, G. "Here Comes Alpha." *PC Today,* May 1992, pp. 58–60.

McClure, C. *CASE Is Software Automation.* Englewood Cliffs, NJ: Prentice-Hall, 1989.

McCusker, T. "Novell Casts a Wider Net." *Datamation,* December 1, 1992, pp. 28–34.

Redfern, A. "Make the Right CPU Move." *Byte Magazine,* December 1992, pp. 114–128.

Ricciuti, M. "Mainframe DBMS Power Unleashed." *Datamation,* October 15, 1992.

Ryan, B. "Built for Speed." *Byte Magazine,* February 1992, pp. 123–135.

Udell, J. "Windows NT Up Close." *Byte Magazine,* October 1992, pp. 167–182.

COMPUTER GENERATIONS AND PROGRESSION

The origins of the modern computer can be traced back to the 1940s. The development of **ENIAC (Electronic Numerical Integrator and Calculator),** by Eckert and Mauchly in 1946, represented the first large-scale electronic computer. It utilized **electronic switching circuits** in the form of vacuum tubes as a means of amplifying or switching electrical signals. The term *electronic* meant that electrical signals could be switched and amplified without the use of moving parts, in order to perform required arithmetic and logic operations. Early computers were similar to ENIAC, often weighed several tons, generated a great deal of heat, required special environmental conditions (that is, humidity and temperature controls), and were prone to frequent failures.

EARLY COMPUTERS

Computers such as ENIAC were experimental or proof-of-concept in nature, often the results of collaborative efforts among universities, industry, and government agencies. Another early mainframe was **UNIVAC 1** (developed by the Universal Accounting Company), used in the U.S. census in 1950. Data entry for these early machines was primarily through punched cards or paper tape. Internal memory, however, consisted of thousands of vacuum tubes, and external storage was on magnetic tape.

TRANSISTORS AND THE SECOND GENERATION

In 1943, the founder and then-president of International Business Machines (IBM), Thomas J. Watson, Sr., remarked, "I think there is a world market for about five computers." Clearly this grand target has been exceeded by more than a few machines since then! A significant development in the computer chronology was the development of the **transistor,** a *solid-state circuit* with lower power requirements, higher reliability, and lower cost than vacuum tubes. This brought about smaller computers produced for a mass market. Magnetic core memory also gradually replaced vacuum tubes, and magnetic disks were introduced for mass storage purposes.

THE INTEGRATED CIRCUIT _____
AND THE THIRD GENERATION _____

The next major computer development was that of the **integrated circuit** or **IC.** The integrated circuit captured entire electronic circuits on silicon chips. The IBM 360 mainframe, one of the first to employ ICs, was manufactured in 1964. New minicomputers like the Digital PDP 11 and the VAX, which were physically smaller than mainframes, were also developed using ICs. One further feature of this computer generation was the development of **operating systems**—programs designed to manage the computer's hardware resources.

MICROPROCESSORS AND _____
THE FOURTH GENERATION _____

Computer scientists soon recognized the potential for incorporating even greater numbers of circuits on chips. The next generation of computers had much higher densities, as scientists managed to squeeze greater numbers and layers of circuits onto identical chip areas. The **microprocessor,** developed in this era, represented the important step of placing a computer's **central processing unit (CPU)** on one chip. The term **large-scale integration** (or **LSI**) was used to describe both the logic and memory chips resulting from this *scaling-up* of chip densities.

   Local area networks or **LANs** straddle the fourth and fifth computer generations. **LANs** enabled the interconnection of computers and related devices to achieve several goals, namely (1) sharing expensive devices such as laser printers and fax machines, (2) sharing information, and (3) enabling group access to other networks or larger computers. As powerful computers began, for the first time, to serve as file servers, or even processing hosts for networks, networking software also increased in sophistication to handle the necessary security, data integrity, and data routing capabilities.

ENTERING THE FIFTH GENERATION _____

Ideas differ as to the exact nature of fifth-generation systems. However, a common strand runs through existing suggestions: the provision of much greater computing power and sophisticated software, and an order of magnitude jump in price/performance over historical levels. Several major features of fifth-generation systems (all of which exist to some degree in today's systems) are

   Very large-scale integration. This is achieved by packing greater numbers of individual circuits per given chip surface area. Escalating chip densities will characterize fifth-generation computers in the coming years. Intel's latest microprocessor, the Pentium, for example, has over three million individual circuits (nearly three times as many as the 80486) and is capable of processing over 100 million instructions per second. Microprocessors using *gallium arsenide, superconductors,* and *optical processors* will provide significant gains over silicon technologies. Additionally, memory capacities for all computers will greatly increase in line with higher densities.

- *Parallel processing.* This is the use of multiple processors and will appear more often in microcomputer systems, providing immense gains in processing speed. The resolution of such issues as memory access by multiple processors and appropriate parallel processing languages is setting the stage for parallel processing on desktop machines with more power than current mainframes.
- *Increased storage capabilities.* With the advent of optical disks, the prospect of massive multigigabyte [1 gigabyte (Gb) = 1,048,576 kilobytes/chars] secondary storage on microcomputer-based systems is now a reality. Arrays of read/write optical disks (each with over 1 Gb capacity) supply storage capabilities previously associated with larger computers.
- *Multimedia.* This represents the convergence of data, graphics, and sound on the desktop microcomputer. Multimedia will be a major technological and marketing trend in the 1990s and beyond. New multimedia-ready microcomputers combine video and graphic sequences with voice and data for use in such applications as presentations, visual databases, and computer-aided instruction.
- *Increased connectivity.* This is an important feature of fifth-generation computer systems, to handle greater data communications volumes flowing within and between organizations. This is partly attributable to the opportunities offered by fiber optic and other technologies, and to the spread of distributed computing. Distributed processing options range from microcomputer-based LANs to enterprise computing networks combining a variety of computer types.

Fifth-generation system features are supplying new capabilities to all types of computers, which will enable users to interact with computers in many new ways, such as natural language and through pen-based interfaces. Furthermore, the availability of increased computing power will lead to more complex networked configurations.

LARGE AND MEDIUM-SIZED COMPUTERS

Larger-scale computers have the same basic architecture as microcomputers, that is, processor, memory, buses, and peripherals. Major differences between microcomputers and larger computers include greater input/output and storage capabilities and their concurrent services to many multiple users. Supercomputers, however, excel in raw mathematical processing power.

MAINFRAMES, MINICOMPUTERS, AND SUPERCOMPUTERS

Mainframes were the earliest computers to be developed for commercial use. Systems such as the IBM 950, used in the 1950s, and the IBM 360 were designed to be used **concurrently** by many users. The term *concurrent* is not the same as simultaneous. Concurrent processing involves the processing of several programs (or jobs) interchangeably, piece by piece by the computer. The high speed of processing makes the computer's response appear instantaneous to the individual user. The mainframe takes advantage of comparatively slower human and peripheral performance to quickly switch between tasks, while appearing to be dedicated to the single user or peripheral. This process, involving the allocation of timeslices between various users, is called *timesharing* (Figure A2.1).

The greater I/O capabilities of larger machines result from the need to communicate concurrently with multiple users. However, the differences in the processing speeds of processors and peripheral devices are considerable. For example, mainframes generally operate in the tens of MIPS, while memory accesses are much slower, that is, millions per second (hence the need for memory caches). The fastest data entry operator might enter data at 300 bytes per second, faster printers operate at 600 characters per second, and even top-of-the-line fixed disks produce about 100–200 disk accesses per second. The mismatch between processor/primary memory

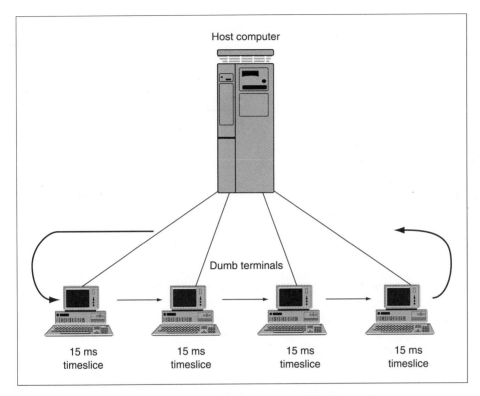

FIGURE A2.1   Timesharing and allocation of (15 ms) timeslices

subsystems and peripheral subsystems is obvious and acute, a mismatch that is generally handled using *preprocessors, buffers,* and *channels.*

Figure A2.2 also shows a mainframe serving several terminals. A preprocessor, called a *front-end processor* (or *FEP*), is used to handle the communication overhead associated with slow user terminals. It assembles incoming messages from many channels (lines) into temporary storage areas called **buffers** and sends them along a high-speed channel to the mainframe for processing. Likewise, it is responsible for addressing and transmitting mainframe outputs from the mainframe to individual users. Usually, the FEP is a minicomputer dedicated to this task of making more effective use of the mainframe's resources. Other types of buffering devices such as device controllers are discussed in Chapter 9.

Another feature of mainframes is **multiprocessing,** or the use of more than one processor. In mainframes like IBM's Model 3090 series (for example, the 3090-600J), multiple processors simultaneously handle several jobs. However, these earlier versions of parallel processing use independent processors, simultaneously working on different tasks to produce aggregate superior performance. For example, one processor might be running the payroll program, while another processes daily transactions. Variations of this architecture are now seen in advanced microcomputers.

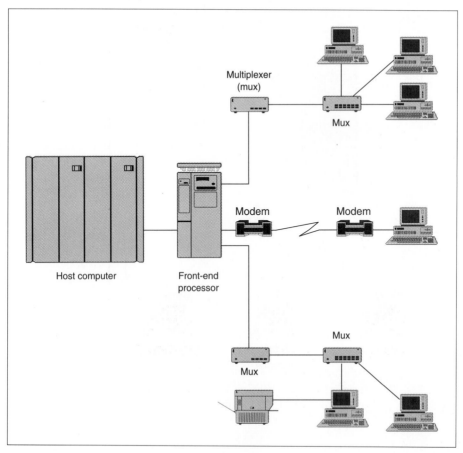

FIGURE A2.2   Use of a front-end processor

The term **batch processing** was initially associated with mainframes. Transactions are stored on media like magnetic tape or disks and periodically transmitted to the mainframe for processing in batches with the aim of making effective use of processing time. However, most mainframe computing today occurs in on-line or real-time modes. **On-line processing** indicates that the input terminal is connected directly to the mainframe (possibly through an FEP). In **real-time processing,** the terminals are on-line but processing results are instantly available, in time to influence future inputs. An example is airline reservations, where seat availability is checked before a seat is reserved (see Figure A2.3).

DMA (direct memory access) is used by minicomputers and mainframes, involving the use of a separate bus for independent memory access by faster peripherals. It improves efficiency by not having to go through the processor for access to memory. Another feature, discussed earlier, is *virtual memory,* long established in mainframe use.

Supercomputers excel in raw numerical processing. While their scaler or integer processing power is roughly equivalent to that of mainframes, they use powerful **vector processors** to process strings (or vectors) of numbers simultaneously. This increases

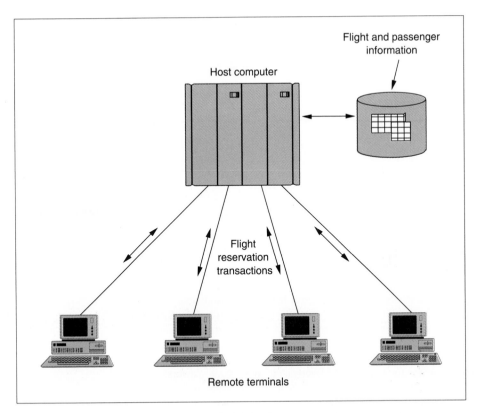

FIGURE A2.3   Flight reservations information system

their power considerably, to the extent that supercomputers are the most advanced computing resource currently available. Their processing power is not measured in MIPS, but in *MFLOPs* (megaflops), or millions of floating point operations per second. The Cray-3 supercomputer, for example, operates at about 16 GigaFLOPs. In comparison, the top-of-the-line 68040 microprocessor produces about 3.1 MFLOPs, 5,000 times less than the Cray-3's floating point benchmark. Supercomputers do not possess the I/O capabilities of mainframes and are not generally used for transaction processing. Their capabilities make them more suitable for scientific and engineering experiments, such as simulations that require immense processing power.

GLOSSARY

10BaseT Common ethernet LAN standard that specifies baseband transmission at 10 Mbps over twisted-pair cable.

arithmetic and logic unit Component of a microprocessor that performs its mathematical and computational operations under the direction of the microprocessor's control unit.

asynchronous transmission method Recent data transmission technology that breaks up messages into 53-byte packets for transmission over public and private networks (that is, WANs and LANs). Transmission rates range from 52 Mbps to 155 Mbps and beyond.

backward compatibility Ability of a processor to execute a prior processor's instruction set, in addition to other instructions. For example, Intel's 486 is backward-compatible with its 386 processor.

baseband transmission Transmission of a signal in digital, unmodulated form. It is typically in the form of direct electrical voltages and uses the entire data communications channel.

bridge Data communications device that connects two LAN segments with the same topology and protocols, for example, two 10 Mbps ethernet LAN segments.

broadband transmission Transmission of a signal in analog form over a channel. These transmissions are often divided into independent bands along which data transmission takes place.

brouter Data communications device that connects two LAN segments. It is midway between a bridge and a router and has some of the functions of each. *See bridge, router.*

byte Collection of 8 binary digits (bits), each of which may take a value of 0 or 1. A byte represents the contents of one memory address and many character codes, for example, ASCII and EBCDIC characters are 1 byte long.

C Third-generation programming language combining a high-level syntax and the ability to perform low-level hardware manipulation. It is closely associated with the UNIX operating system, which was itself written in C.

cache Buffer area between two computer devices that is used to compensate for speed differences between them. Data requests from the faster device result in more data than requested being fetched. Subsequent requests may be satisfied by the faster cache if the data is found there, saving processing time. *See disk cache and RAM cache.*

carrier sense multiple access/collision detection (CSMA/CD) LAN protocol or communication method used on bus networks. Stations transmit data if the LAN channel is clear. If simultaneous transmissions result in a collision of data packets, data is retransmitted from each node after a random waiting time.

centralized processing Form of processing where several terminals are connected to a powerful central computer that performs all the processing required by the terminal users.

centrex Privately owned telephone exchange operated by a telephone services provider. It has the same features of private and digital branch exchanges. *See private branch exchange (PBX)* and *digital branch exchange (DBX)*.

client/server computing Form of processing whereby client computers pass processing requests to interconnected server computers that satisfy these requests (for example, database queries). Results are returned to the client, which may further manipulate them and display them to the user.

clock Quartz crystal oscillator used as a timing device to synchronize the execution of instructions by a microcomputer. The frequency of emitted clock pulses is in megahertz or millions of cycles/second, with faster speeds producing faster instruction execution.

compact disk read-only memory (CD-ROM) Optical storage medium that uses the same technology as audio CDs. CD-ROMs require specialized equipment for initial mastering and in normal use, cannot be written to, only read. Their storage capacity is about 600 Mb.

compiler Computer program that translates programs written in a third-generation language such as COBOL into directly executable machine code. Compiled programs can subsequently be run independently of the compiler.

complex instruction set chip (CISC) Oldest processor architecture, which uses a wide variety of microcoded processor instructions (often up to 300). They generally demonstrate less powerful performance than RISC processors. *See RISC.*

computer Device comprising electronic and electromechanical components that performs logical and arithmetic processing of data using supplied instructions in computer programs.

computer-aided systems engineering (CASE) The use of special software (CASE tools) that automates parts of the SDLC, increasing overall efficiency of IS development.

control unit Processor component that supervises and synchronizes all the computer's processing operations.

CSMA/CD *See carrier sense multiple access/collision detection.*

data Raw collection of facts collected for processing by the computer. *See information.*

database Integrated collection of data stored in related files. In a database, redundancy is minimized and links between files are maintained by a DBMS. *See database management system (DBMS).*

database management system (DBMS) Software program that manages a computerized database or set of related files. It supports relationships between files and minimizes data redundancy. Also, the DBMS enables users to access and manipulate stored data, which the DBMS keeps secure through security and integrity mechanisms.

data bus Pathway of very thin wires on a microcomputer's motherboard used to carry signals representing data between the microcomputer's processor, RAM, and peripheral devices. *See system bus.*

data flow diagram (DFD) Graphical representation of an information system that shows data flows, sources, and destinations of data (external entities); data stores; and processes. DFDs are created in a top-down fashion, with high-level processes exploded to lower-level ones.

decentralized processing Form of processing now infrequently used, where stand-alone computers are used in different organizational units to support local information needs. Its major drawback is the difficulty of access to information and applications in other units. *See centralized processing* and *distributed processing*.

decision support system (DSS) Flexible, model-based information system that supports managers' decision-making. It contains graphics and reporting functions, plus goal-seeking, "what-if?," and other models to aid managerial analyses.

deliverable Tangible part of an information system or its documentation, whose development is assigned to system development personnel and is due by a specific date called a *milestone*. Milestones are used in system development planning and scheduling.

digital audio tape (DAT) Type of magnetic tape that measures 4 mm across and is capable of storing up to 2 GB compactly on a single cartridge.

digital branch exchange (DBX) Privately owned and operated telephone exchange that routes both voice and data transmissions using digital transmission between locations in the firm. Transmissions to external locations through public networks are translated into analog form. It is used to create low-cost LANs. *See private branch exchange (PBX).*

direct conversion System implementation method in which the old information system is discontinued and processing begins on the new system immediately after.

disk cache Cache used to compensate for speed imbalances between RAM and disk subsystems. Disk caches typically use specially designated RAM areas. *See cache, SRAM.*

disk duplexing Involves the use of multiple disk controllers to update multiple disks. Thus, if the primary controller card fails, control is transferred to the backup controller.

disk mirroring Also known as RAID level 1, in which two disks are simultaneously written to, resulting in their being in the same state. If the primary disk fails, data operations are immediately and transparently switched to the backup disk. *See RAID.*

distributed processing Form of processing whereby a firm's computer resources are dispersed within different organizational units but are interconnected through data communications channels. It allows local processing of applications, but these applications and their databases may be used from several organizational units. This processing model has the advantages of both centralized and decentralized processing. *See centralized processing* and *decentralized processing.*

document image processing (DIP) Storage and manipulation of documents electronically on computers and across networks. It involves capturing document bitmaps on computer storage media and providing their access to users via computer terminals.

downsizing Process of moving a firm's applications off large computers such as mainframes to smaller and lower-cost processing platforms, that is, networked microcomputers and workstations.

dual in-line package (DIP) Plastic or ceramic protective package that holds microchips and possesses extruding pins to carry signals between the microchip and the motherboard.

economies-of-scale Popular argument in the early computing era that held that larger computers and installations were more efficient costwise than smaller ones. It has since been refuted by the introduction of cheap microprocessors.

EISA bus 32-bit data bus developed by a consortium led by Compaq in competition with IBM's MCA bus. It permits faster data transfer rates than both ISA and MCA buses, at up to 33 Mbps.

end user Direct user of an organization's computer applications.

end-user computing (EUC) Development of computer-based information systems in which the role of the system developer is played by the end user. *See end user.*

end user development (EUD) Development of information systems by end users for individual and departmental applications. End users use such tools as networked microcomputers, spreadsheets, DBMSs, querying tools, and DSS.

enterprise network Network of interconnected computers ranging from mainframes to microcomputers. Interacting software applications distribute user processing tasks, for example, data manipulation and retrieval among larger computers or servers in the network.

EPROM (erasable programmable read-only memory)   Computer memory whose contents can be repeatedly erased (using ultraviolet light) and rewritten, after which it behaves like ROM, that is, retains its contents in the absence of electrical current. *See also memory, ROM*.

ergonomics   Science of adapting machines and working environments to workers.

ethernet   Local area network architecture in which various computing devices are connected to a central channel, which is a roadway for data transmissions between different devices. Ethernet uses twisted-pair, coaxial cable, and fiber-optic cable to transfer data at 10 million bits per second.

executive information systems (EIS)   Easy-to-use, GUI-based information systems created to serve the needs of top managers involved in strategic planning. EIS possess graphing, aggregation, and drill-down (disaggregation) functions.

expanded memory   Memory above MS-DOS's 1 Mb limit on IBM-compatibles. These memory contents are swapped into a 64 K page frame in the high memory of MS-DOS (between 640 K and 1 Mb) in 16 K chunks. An expanded memory manager program swaps required parts of programs in and other segments out as a program is processed (*see extended memory*).

expert system   Computer program that mimics the decision-making behavior of a human expert in making nontrivial decisions in a specific organizational role or function.

extended memory   On IBM-compatibles, memory above the 1 Mb addressed by MS-DOS that can be made accessible to programs using a program called an *extended memory manager*. *See expanded memory*.

fast ethernet   Evolving upgrade to the ethernet LAN topology that transmits data at 100 Mbps, in contrast to ethernet's 10 Mbps. *See ethernet.*

flash RAM   Recent RAM variant packaged in solid-state memory cards and used primarily on notebook microcomputers. It can be repeatedly overwritten but retains stored data in the absence of electrical current, making it comparable to EEPROM.

floppy disk   Circular plastic disk coated with magnetic oxide and used to store data in computer-readable form. Particles in the magnetic coating are magnetized in patterns to represent sequences of 0s and 1s that may be read or decoded later by a floppy disk drive.

floptical disk   Floppy disk that combines magnetic and optical technologies to store data. The drive's precision is greatly increased by the use of a laser-guided mechanism that enables very high storage densities to be attained. Storage capacities range from 20 Mb to 50 Mb.

fourth-generation language (4GL)   Nonprocedural, English-like programming language with looser coding conventions than such third-generation languages as Fortran and Pascal. This is high level in nature and includes such languages as spreadsheet macros and DBMS languages.

function point   This is a metric that represents the effort associated with coding functions of an information system, such as input, output, and inquiry functions. It is used in the function point model for estimating project effort.

gigabyte   Approximately one billion bytes of main memory or storage; or precisely, 1024 Mb (1,073,741,824 bytes).

hardware   *See computer.*

high-level language   Programming language nearer English in nature than the microprocessor's native binary code. Examples are third- and fourth-generation languages.

hub   *See intelligent hub.*

icon   Graphic symbol displayed on a screen that represents commands or files that the user can select.

IBM-compatible   Microcomputer that uses an Intel 80x86 (or compatible) microprocessor and can run programs written for Microsoft Corporation's MS-DOS operating system.

industry standard architecture (ISA) 16-bit system bus architecture, used from 286-based microcomputers onward, which transfers data at up to Mbps. It is being replaced in many instances by EISA, MCA, and local bus alternatives.

information Processed data for a specific purpose that has meaning to an individual(s).

information center (IC) Department staffed by information system professionals whose role is to assist users involved in end user computing (EUC) and end user development (EUD). IC activities include training, troubleshooting, and helping users develop systems.

input device Device used to input data to a computer in computer-readable form. Four major categories are keyboards, direct-entry devices (such as light pens), input-output devices (for example, facsimile machines), and secondary storage devices (for example, fixed disks).

instruction set Set of machine code instructions that can be executed by a processor and is determined by that processor's physical design. *See backward compatibility and machine code.*

integrated circuit A miniaturized transistor or electronic switching device whose components are formed on a single piece of semiconducting material, for example, silicon.

integrated services digital network (ISDN) International wide area network standard for transmitting voice, data, and images in a protocol-transparent manner. Users can obtain ISDN transmission capacities in 64 Kbps increments up to 1.5 Mbps.

intelligent hub Data communications device that manages several independent LAN segments, effectively providing greater aggregate LAN capacity than a single LAN. It also allows the merging of different LAN segments under the LAN adminstrator's control.

interface Hardware/software facility through which message exchanges between two devices, or between a user and a device, take place. One example is two modems transferring messages. Another is a user using a word processing program (for example, the VDU, software, and keyboard provide the interface).

International Business Machines (IBM) Largest computer company in the world in both hardware and software categories. IBM introduced the IBM-PC in 1981 and subsequently created the IBM-compatible microcomputer segment.

interoperability Ability of two devices or systems to work together so that one understands messages passed from the other. This capability may be provided through software or hardware.

joint application development (JAD) Highly interactive form of system development involving both users and systems personnel. It uses CASE and other tools to iteratively develop system components for discussion by participants during JAD sessions. Outside distractions are minimized during these meetings.

large-scale intergration (LSI) Practice of fitting between 1,000 and 10,000 integrated circuits on a single microchip. *See very large-scale integration.*

light pen Special pen-shaped input device that emits a narrow beam of light. When this beam is detected by special screen hardware, its X-Y coordinates are passed to the running program, and the action option pointed to is invoked.

local area network (LAN) Collection of computers and peripherals interconnected by a data transmission medium (for example, twisted-pair cable), which is usually privately owned and operated and which enables sharing of data and peripherals.

local bus Extension of the fast processor/memory bus to peripherals. It is a 32-bit data bus, two variants of which are VESA's VL-bus and Intel's PCI. A major competitor to EISA and MCA buses, local buses transfer data at the speed of the processor, at up to 120 Mbps.

local talk Networking capability built into Macintosh computers that allows data communications between interconnected Macintoshes at rates of up to 235 Kbps over a serial channel.

machine code/machine language   Instructions that can be directly executed by a processor without further translation. Each processor has its own unique set of machine code instructions based on its architecture. *See* **instruction set.**

mainframe   Large and powerful computer costing over $1 million, capable of supporting hundreds of users concurrently. It is typically housed in specially designed facilities and requires environmental regulation to cope with dust, temperature, and humidity.

memory   Comprises electronic devices (that is, with no moving parts) used to store programs and data being executed. On such memory microchips, data is stored in binary form on microscopic two-state memory devices and accessed rapidly through electronic switching of circuits connected to the memory chips.

memory-resident programs   *See* **terminate-and-stay-resident programs.**

message queuing software   Middleware programs that interconnect loosely coupled applications across networks. Requests may be queued until the server becomes accessible. *See* **middleware.**

micro channel architecture (MCA)   Proprietary 32-bit data bus developed by IBM that permits faster data transfer rates than the ISA bus, at up to 40 Mbps.

microchip   Device made from a semiconducting element such as silicon. It contains many miniaturized integrated circuits, resulting in low-cost and high-speed functions, for example, transmitting electronic signals and storing electrical charges.

microcomputer   Also called a *desktop computer, personal computer,* or *PC,* a computer that fits on or under a desktop, costing in the range of $800 to $5,000 and based on microprocessor technology. It is most often a single-user machine but can also serve multiple users concurrently.

microprocessor   Type of microchip that processes the user's programs and data electronically. It consists of a control unit, which directs the computer's operations; an arithmetic and logic unit that performs required calculations; and registers for temporarily storing data.

middleware   Software layer inserted between applications and networks to enable applications on different systems interact transparently over networks. *See* **remote procedure calls, message queuing,** and **object request brokers.**

millisecond   Thousandth of a second. Disk access times are typically in milliseconds (e.g., 11 ms for a fast hard disk).

minicomputer   Computer that falls in between mainframe computers and microcomputers in size and cost. It serves many users concurrently but does not have the same staffing and environmental requirements mainframes have.

MIPS   Millions of instructions per second, a common but imperfect benchmark used to gauge how many instructions are executed every second by a microprocessor. While higher numbers indicate better performance, this benchmark is usually supplemented by other measurements of the computer performing representative tasks.

modem   Data communications device that transforms digital signals to analog (modulation), transmits the analog signals over telephone lines, and carries out the reverse transformation (demodulation) at the destination, to enable remote computer communication. Modem transmission rates range from 9.6 Kbps to over 57.6 Kbps.

motherboard   Microcomputer's main circuit board on which are located the microprocessor, memory and other logic chips, buses for data transfer, and interfaces to input/output devices in the form of expansion slots and ports. It measures several inches across, is bolted to the side or bottom of the microcomputer, and is supplied electricity by a power supply.

mouse   Handheld input device used to move the cursor across the screen and to select on-screen options, such as menu options and icons. The movement of the mouse is captured by internal sensors and passed to computer programs through a computer port.

MPR II Swedish-developed reduced emissions standard for display monitors. It is being adopted and mandated by many display manufacturers and corporate users.

MS-DOS Most widely used microcomputer operating system, developed by Microsoft Corporation for use on IBM-compatible microcomputers. Originally based on a command-line interface, MS-DOS has evolved into a menu-driven operating system.

multimedia Combination of hardware and software that integrates text, graphics, sound, video, and animation on a desktop computer. Multimedia systems are commonly used for presentations, database applications, and computer-based training.

nanosecond Billionth of a second. DRAM access times are in nanoseconds (e.g., 60 ns).

network administration A set of individuals with responsibility for setting up, operating, and maintaining an organization's data communications network.

network interface card (NIC) Computer expansion card that allows the computer to be connected to a LAN. It is connected to the computer's system bus through an expansion slot and to the LAN using specialized connectors.

network operating system (NOS) Complex software program installed with or without an OS that manages data transfers between terminals and devices connected to a LAN.

notebook computer Microcomputer that is under 7 lbs in weight and measures less than 8″ by 11″ wide. It uses color or monochrome flat panel displays, 2.5″ hard disks, and PCMCIA peripheral cards to achieve its small size.

object Structure that encapsulates both data and methods for manipulating it. Objects can have descendent objects that inherit their properties and can contain arbitrary, user-defined data types. Objects are frequently reusable between applications, saving considerable development effort.

object-oriented programming Programming using objects, as provided by object-oriented tools such as C++ and others. *See objects.*

object request broker (ORB) Middleware program used by object-oriented programs to request objects over networks. *See middleware* and *object.*

operating system Software program that insulates the user from direct contact with computer hardware. It manages the operation of hardware and supervises the running of users' programs. It also provides an interface through which the user may perform file, disk, and other processing operations.

optical disk Refers to various disk technologies that store large amounts of data and are read and written to using low-intensity laser beams. *See CD-ROM, WORM,* and *rewritable optical disk.*

output devices Devices used to transmit processing results to the computer user. Usually, the output is in human-readable form, for example, using output devices such as printers and video display units. In some cases, however, it may be in computer-readable form, for example, on tape or disk, for subsequent input to another computer system.

outsourcing Practice of contracting out systems development and/or maintenance of a firm's information system(s) to another party.

parallel conversion Risk-reducing system conversion approach in which the old and new information systems are run together for a period of time. Their outputs are compared to ensure the new system works correctly and the old system is then discontinued.

parallel processing Use of more than one processor within a computer to process instructions from one program simultaneously. Each processor handles different parts of the program in a cooperative fashion.

PC-DOS Version of the MS-DOS operating system created specifically for IBM's microcomputers using Intel's 80x86 microprocessors. *See MS-DOS.*

Pentium Intel's successor to the 80486 microprocessor, the standard for over 80% of the microcomputer market. It produces 112 MIPs at 66 Mhz and has such features as multiple math units and on-chip caches for speedy processing.

peripherals   Devices connected to and controlled by the computer. They include keyboards, display units, and disk drives and are used to input, output, and store data.

phased conversion   Risk-reducing system conversion approach in which the new system is brought in function by function or stepwise over a period of time.

polling   LAN protocol in which a host computer repeatedly checks all attached nodes in a round-robin fashion to see if they have any data for transmission.

Power PC   Microprocessor created by the collaboration of IBM, Apple, and Motorola. Slightly smaller than the Pentium, it exhibits comparable performance and is intended to run the next generation of OSs, such as Windows NT, the Macintosh OS, and various versions of PC-based UNIX.

private branch exchange (PBX)   Telephone exchange owned and operated privately by a firm. It routes both voice and data transmissions within locations in the firm and to locations outside it. It is one option for creating LANs without significant outlays on new cabling, that is, it can use the existing telephone wiring. *See **digital branch exchange (DBX)**.*

productivity package   Term referring to a class of software that includes word processors, spreadsheets, and data management programs. They help to improve the efficiency of everyday tasks, such as letter writing, filing, and financial modeling.

PROM (programmable read-only memory)   Computer memory that can be written to once by the user but thereafter takes on the properties of ROM; that is, its contents are then permanent (*see also **memory, ROM***).

proprietary software   Software program that is written for a specific number of users and a restricted hardware platform.

prototyping   Prototype that is a model of an IS but that is not fully functional. It is intended as a means of obtaining user input to IS design. It comprises the user interface, a few functions, and test data but lacks system interfaces, error trapping, and a fully populated database. 4GLs and CASE tools are commonly used for rapidly developing prototypes.

RAM (random access memory)   Computer memory used to temporarily store programs and data being executed. RAM is volatile, meaning that it loses its contents in the absence of electrical current (*see also **memory***).

RAM cache   Used to compensate for speed imbalances between processor and memory subsystems. RAM caches typically use static RAM or SRAM. *See **cache, SRAM**.*

rapid application development (RAD)   Speed-intensive form of system development in which CASE tools are used to quickly develop core IS functions. The developed system is not thrown away but enhanced to become the final system.

reduced instruction set chip (RISC)   A recent processor architecture developed by IBM that uses a relatively small number of microcoded instructions (about 70–80) and other features, for example, caches and pipelining, to provide powerful processor performance (*see also **CISC***). RISC is commonly used on workstations.

redundant array of inexpensive disks (RAID)   Set of six approaches that use multiple disks to provide fault tolerance for disk subsystems. The approaches or RAID levels (0–5) provide affordable on-line data backup for microcomputer-based systems. *See **disk duplexing** and **disk mirroring**.*

reengineering   Analysis of an information system and its reconstitution in a new, more effective form. Information systems and workflows alike can be reengineered.

registers   Temporary storage locations within the microprocessor itself used to store data such as processing results and the address of the current instruction. Their size determines the amount of data that may be processed within the processor at one time, for example, 8-, 16-, and 32-bit microcomputers.

remote procedure call (RPC)   Type of middleware used to interconnect tightly coupled programs across fast, available network connections. *See **middleware**.*

request for proposal (RFP)   Document circulated among selected information technology vendors and suppliers describing a firm's information requirements and inviting them to submit proposals that satisfy them cost-effectively.

resolution   Detail or crispness of images displayed on a monitor's screen. It is directly related to the number of individual pixels or dots within a given screen area.

rewritable optical disk   Form of optical/magnetic storage that enables the reading and overwriting of large data amounts on disks. *See optical disks.*

rightsizing   Process whereby a firm moves its transaction processing from one platform to another that supports processing activities more efficiently. Most rightsizing is from mainframes to internetworks of less-expensive workstations and microcomputers.

ROM (read-only memory)   Computer memory that permanently stores programs and data for computer use. ROM is nonvolatile, retaining its contents even when electrical current is discontinued. Computer start-up routines are typically held in ROM (*see also memory*).

router   Data communications device that connects several LAN segments with the same protocols and topology. It has more intelligence than a bridge and calculates the most efficient route for the data packet. *See bridge.*

scanner   Input device that captures digitized images of objects or pictures by detecting the intensities of reflected light. Handheld scanners are moved over a page's surface to capture the image, while documents are placed in fixed positions on flat-bed scanners.

secondary storage   Set of computer peripherals that store data in nonvolatile form, that is, their contents are preserved when the computer is switched off. They include floppy, fixed, and optical disks; and magnetic cartridges.

SIMMs   *See single inline memory modules.*

single inline memory modules   Small logic cards containing a row(s) of memory chips used to increase a microcomputer's RAM capacity. SIMMs may be inserted by the user into special slots on most microcomputer motherboards.

site license   License purchased from a software vendor that allows a specified number of users in a location to use the software. The software may be installed on a set number of computers, on all the firm's computers, or its use may be controlled by a server.

smart hub   *See intelligent hub.*

software   Set of instructions written in a programming language that may be processed by computer hardware to perform desired information processing functions.

spreadsheet   Software package that uses the metaphor of ledgers, comprising a grid of cells in which numbers, names, or formulas can be entered. It can be used to perform many types of financial analyses and calculations and possess extensive graphing abilities.

static RAM (SRAM)   Type of RAM with very fast access times of 25 ns–35 ns, which is used mainly for memory caching. *See RAM cache.*

structure chart   Tool for specifying an information system's program modules. It includes formalisms for modules, their relationships, and data and control flows. It can also show files, screens, and iteration and selection programming constructs.

structured analysis and design   Top down approach to system development that iteratively breaks down functions to smaller functions. It use results in well-documented information systems comprising loosely connected hierarchical modules with single entry and exit points.

structured query language (SQL)   De facto query and data manipulation language standard developed by IBM. SQL is a feature of most major DBMS products.

stylus   Pointing device used on pen-based notebook computers. Gestures are detected by the screen and either activate commands or are translated into text and images.

supercomputer   Large computer whose cost ranges from $2 to 20 million, which processes data in arrays, greatly increasing its processing power. It is used for computationally intensive tasks, such as weather forecasting and movie special effects, is housed in specially designed facilities, and requires environmental regulation similar to mainframes.

system bus Group of very thin wires on the system's motherboard, which connects the CPU with RAM and I/O devices. The system bus carries data, addresses, and control signals between the CPU, RAM, and I/O devices in the form of electronic signals. *See data bus.*

systems development life cycle (SDLC) Prescriptive multi-stage model describing a sequence of information system stages that begin with its conception, through its development and operation, to its eventual discontinuation.

terabyte More than a trillion bytes; specifically 1,024 gigabytes. *See gigabyte.*

terminate-and-stay-resident programs Type of program that remains in RAM even after the user has exited, thus terminating it. It can subsequently be activated by using a hot-key combination, for example, CTRL-F2.

token Circling pattern of bits used to control data transmissions on a token ring LAN. LAN nodes can transmit data only if they possess the token, thus preventing collisions of data packets in LAN operation.

token passing LAN protocol used on ring networks. Stations transmit data if a token or pattern of bits circling around the LAN is in their possession. After transmission, the token is released to the next node. This prevents data packets from colliding with others.

token ring LAN LAN architecture developed by IBM that organizes LAN nodes into a star-wired ring. This consists of multiaccess units (MAUs) connected in a ring, with each one connected to one or more network nodes.

transistor Solid-state electronic device (with no moving parts) that preceded the integrated circuit. *See integrated circuit.*

TSRs *See terminate-and-stay-resident programs.*

UNIX Multiuser, multitasking operating system developed by AT&T and coded in the C language; it is popular on many workstation, mainframe, and increasingly, microcomputer platforms.

user interface Set of features presented by application software that enables interaction between the user and the computer.

utility programs Small programs that perform a wide variety of tasks, such as file and disk management, virus detection and protection, and system diagnostics.

value added resellers (VARs) Retailers who purchase computer equipment from equipment manufacturers and bundle the hardware together with other services, such as software and system development, that is, adding value to the basic hardware.

very large-scale integration (VLSI) Fabrication technique in which over 10,000 transistors are placed on a single microchip. Current microprocessor densities exceed three million integrated circuits (for example, Intel's Pentium microprocessor).

video RAM (VRAM) Type of RAM that allows simultaneous reading and writing operations, thus allowing fast access times of about 35 ns. It is used mainly on graphics controller cards to store displayed images. *See RAM cache.*

virtual memory Section of a secondary storage device used to store currently running programs and data as if it were RAM. By swapping program segments between RAM and virtual memory, the computer's primary memory appears larger than it actually is.

virtual storage *See virtual memory.*

virus Computer program written to damage or otherwise adversely affect a computer system and its operations. Viruses often propagate themselves on disks and LANs and are designed to be difficult to detect.

wide-area network (WAN) Network that connects computing devices in geographically distant locations, for example, across cities, countries, and continents. Transmissions over fiber-optic cables, microwave, and satellites are common in WANs.

window Form of graphical user interface with images and text presented in a subset of an overall area that the user can scroll and page through. Windows can also be resized and are frequently accompanied by user-selectable menu items.

Windows Operating environment developed by Microsoft Corporation for use on IBM-compatible microcomputers. It is designed to add extra capabilities to the MS-DOS operating system, such as multitasking, a GUI interface using icons, and so on, and memory/disk management. *See MS-DOS and Windows NT.*

Windows NT Operating system developed by Microsoft Corporation for microcomputers and workstations based on Intel's Pentium and such RISC chips as the Power PC and MIPS4000. NT is fully multitasking, supports multiprocessing, and runs MS-DOS and earlier Windows programs.

workstation Powerful desktop computer usually based on a RISC processor and possessing powerful graphics capabilities. Workstations are mostly used for CPU-intensive tasks such as CAD/CAM and as servers in client/server networks.

write once, read many (WORM) disk Optical disk that can be written to only once; thereafter it is read only. It is widely used for archival purposes. *See optical disk.*

INDEX

Photo/Art Credits

Figure 1.1a Motorola/Melgar Photography, Inc.; **1.1b** Intel; **1.4 (left)** courtesy of Borland International; **1.4 (right)** courtesy of NeXT Corp.; **1.5** courtesy of Compaq Corporation; **1.6** courtesy of Egghead Software; **1.13** courtesy of Compaq Corporation; **3.1** Intel; **3.2** courtesy of the Computer Museum; **3.3** courtesy of the Computer Museum; **3.10** courtesy of ALR; **3.11 (top)** courtesy of ALR; **3.11 (left)** courtesy of Compaq Corp.; **3.11 (right)** courtesy of Compaq Corp.; **3.12 (left)** courtesy of Compaq Corp.; **3.12 (right)** Micro Express/KPR, inc.; **3/14** courtesy of ALR; **3.15** courtesy of ALR; **3.17** Micro Express/KPR, Inc.; **3.18** (left) courtesy of Apple Computer; **3.18 (right)** courtesy of Compaq Corp.; **3.19** courtesy of Apple Computer; **3.20** courtesy of Apple Computer; **3.21** courtesy of NeXT, Inc.; **3.22** courtesy of Sun Microsystems, Inc.; **3.23** courtesy of Insignia Solutions; **4.21 (right)** Kinesis Corp.; **4.2** courtesy of Logitech; **4.3** courtesy of AST; **4.4** courtesy of Microtouch Systems, Inc.; **4.5** courtesy of Caere; **4.6** adapted from Patrick Marshall, *PC World*, April 1992, p. 191; **4.10** courtesy of Logitech, Inc.; **4.11** courtesy of Videx; **4.12** courtesy of Videx; **4.13 (left)** courtesy of Sony Corp.; **4.13 (right)** courtesy of Panasonic Co.; **4.14** courtesy of Dragon Systems, Inc.; **4.20** courtesy of Toshiba America Information Systems, Inc.; **4.22** courtesy of Epson America, Inc.; **4.23** Hewlett Packard; **4.24** Hewlett Packard; **4.25** Hewlett Packard; **4.26** Hewlett Packard; **5.2** courtesy of Apple Computer; **5.5** courtesy of Liberty Systems; **5.7** Sony Corp.; **5.10** courtesy of Insite Peripherals; **5.12 (left)** courtesy of Seagate; **5.12 (right)** Connor Peripherals; **5.13** Sony Corp.; **5.14** courtesy of Pinnacle Micro; **5.15** courtesy of Connor Peripherals; **5.19** courtesy of Stac Electronics; **6.6** courtesy of Microsoft Corp.; **6.7** courtesy of Microsoft Corp.; **6.8** courtesy of Sun Microsystems, Inc.; **6.14** courtesy of Central Point Software, Inc.; **6.17** courtesy of Borland International; **8.11** courtesy of Comshare; **8.13** courtesy of Transition Research, Inc.; **8.18 (top)** courtesy of Apple Computer; **8.18 (bottom)** courtesy of ALR; **8.18 (continued)** courtesy of Radius; **8.19** courtesy of Egghead Software; **9.23b** courtesy of Microcom; **14.2** adapted from *PCToday*, April 1992, p. 19; **15.2** courtesy of Microsoft Corp.